# GUINNESS WORLD RECORDS 2022

Welcome to *GWR 2022*! This year, we are shining a spotlight on one of the most important issues of our time: the environment. Records lend themselves to this topic as they can provide a snapshot of its many complex aspects – the good, the bad and the ugly.

We dive into this edition with British eco-artist Jason deCaires Taylor, who has created the **most underwater art installations** (see p.43). Pictured is his most recent work – a series of carved heads that form the Underwater Museum of Cannes off southern France, which opened in Feb 2021. As with all of Taylor's submerged sculptures, they are made from non-harmful materials and are designed to provide habitat for native flora and fauna. They are also a way of driving ecotourism to coastal communities, meaning locals have more of a vested interest in conserving their shores.

The giant heads are based on six local people, including an 80-year-old fisherman and a nine-year-old school pupil.

# Contents

Welcome to the 2022 edition of the world's best-selling annual book, updated with thousands of new records. We celebrate astonishing achievements in nine superlative-packed chapters – each featuring a new and inspirational Hall of Fame inductee – and between each section we whisk you away on a virtual tour of world-class attractions.

## Roxanne Downs

Australian schoolgirl Roxanne Downs is the **youngest magazine editor**, having taken up her position at *It Girl* in 2017 aged eight years old. The magazine had decided to connect with its tween readers by hiring someone who knew their interests and concerns firsthand. "Roxy has always performed well in school at reading and writing," her father, Michael, explained, "so she was the perfect candidate for editor." The first issue under Roxanne's tenure hit news stands in Australia and New Zealand on 6 Apr 2017. Now she juggles schoolwork and chores with glamorous interviews and editorial meetings – and has overseen a rise in *It Girl*'s circulation under her editorship.

**What first attracted you to the role of editor for *It Girl*?**
I wanted to be part of something that was big in my age group and among my friends. I'm a child myself and *It Girl* is a magazine written for children. I hang out with others my age all day and I know what they like and what information they want to know.

**What kind of tasks and responsibilities do you have?**
I do all the main celebrity interviews. I also plan the theme of each issue, choose the cover talent and select what gifts we have each month. Sometimes I even go to retail meetings with our publisher. Big supermarket chains are always shocked when I walk into the boardroom.

**How do you fit it in with school and homework?**
I get the week's homework out of the way quick smart on Monday night. Then I can spend most of my time doing what I love.

**Who's been the most famous person you've interviewed?**
Probably Justin Bieber or JoJo Siwa, but there have been so many more. Authors, TikTok stars, singers, actors... I've lost count now!

**What advice would you give to other young people?**
Do the small things right every day. Big opportunities present themselves to people who are easy to work with, polite, focused and hard-working.

**What would be your dream job when you're older?**
A TV host, presenter or actor. And still a magazine editor, of course!

The Pop Culture chapter – which takes its design inspiration from comic books and graphic novels – features a selection of the most successful media franchises of all time. We turn the spotlight on billion-dollar brands and superlative superstars, from the movies, TV shows, videogames and comic books that our readers just can't get enough of.

### Young Achievers

Whether it's editing their own magazine, mastering freestyle football or breaking records at the X Games, there are remarkable youngsters – aged 16 and under – who have already made a name for themselves in their specialist fields. In Young Achievers, we interview eight such talented teens and find out why age is no barrier to becoming a record breaker.

### Augmented-reality dinos

We've once again partnered up with award-winning educational technology studio Peapodicity to bring our pages to life using augmented reality (AR). Use the free *AugmentifyIt®* app to see record-breaking dinosaurs roar into life from the pages of the book. See pp.40–41.

## Virtual Visits

If you can't get out to see the world's most popular museums, attractions, parks and galleries, don't worry: we'll bring them to you! With our Virtual Visits, we lead you through nine cultural sites – such as the Smithsonian, the Louvre, Australia Zoo and Kew Gardens – and point out their superlative features.

**100%** How big? Discover the true scale of some of our biggest and smallest record holders wherever you see the 100% icon.

### National Air and Space Museum

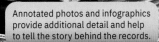

### Marawa The Amazing

Last year alone, GWR received and processed almost 42,000 record applications!

Annotated photos and infographics provide additional detail and help to tell the story behind the records.

**HALL OF FAME**

### Hall of Fame

Meet the latest inductees into the Guinness World Records Hall of Fame. Each candidate has been selected on the strength of their unique and significant contribution to record breaking. This year we include the likes of Sultan Kösen (**tallest person**), astronaut Peggy Whitson (**most spacewalks by a woman**) and Sir David Attenborough (**longest career as a TV presenter**).

### Continue the story online at guinnessworldrecords.com

Whenever you see this symbol, visit **guinnessworldrecords.com/2022** for bonus video content. Our video team has curated a selection of clips from the world's most awe-inspiring record holders, so don't miss the opportunity to see the records truly come to life.

# Editor's Letter

**T**he world has now experienced a full year of isolation and lockdowns thanks to COVID-19, but the record breaking hasn't stopped. A surge in online and socially distant attempts has kept our adjudicators busy...

Between 1 Apr 2020 and 31 Mar 2021, Guinness World Records received 41,959 claims from around the world – that's more than 800 applications a week. This figure might be down slightly on a normal year, but we've had anything but a "normal" year. Much of the planet has remained in lockdown throughout this period, and while some countries are starting to emerge from the coronavirus pandemic, others remain tightly in its grip.

In the UK, despite – or perhaps because of – COVID restrictions, a record was applied for every 2 hr 20 min during this period, and featured on these pages is a selection of some of the more high-profile success stories. As radio and TV shows slowly started inviting back guests and audiences, the appetite for record breaking returned, so a big thank you to the likes of *Blue Peter*, *Strictly*, *It's a Numbers Game* and *The Only Way is Essex* (see p.255) for asking us to adjudicate on air.

Of course, you don't need to be a TV, movie or sports star to qualify for a record: most of the applications received this year have come from the general public. These, and the records supplied by our growing team of consultants and researchers (see pp.250–51), have ensured that *GWR 2022* is as packed as ever with new and updated superlatives across the widest possible spectrum of record breaking.

Many of you went online to share your record attempts, and we were proud to partner with a number of institutions for their virtual campaigns. For Safer Internet Day on 9 Feb 2021, we worked with 2Simple and the UK Safer Internet Centre to ratify the **most pledges received for an internet-safety campaign in 24 hours**, logging 16,372 people who vowed to promote the #AnInternetWeTrust message.

We were also honoured to be part of World Book Day with author Jenny Pearson, as she and 62 of her pupils from St Margaret's Primary School in Durham marked the release of *The Incredible Record Smashers* by smashing their own record for **most people in an online reading video relay**.

Such projects show how record breaking can be used to make a difference in the world. Indeed, the theme of this year's edition reflects the biggest challenge faced by our planet: climate change. Across all

**Most fleckerls in 30 seconds**
GWR has been adjudicating records on the hit BBC TV show *Strictly Come Dancing* since 2011. On 20 Nov 2020, Nadiya Bychkova (UKR) performed 25 fleckerls in half a minute on the set of *Strictly: It Takes Two* (BBC) in Elstree. A fleckerl is a move in which a dancer rotates on the spot, and is most commonly associated with Viennese waltzes.

**Longest-serving TV actor in a single role**
Actor William Roache debuted as Ken Barlow in Episode 1 of *Coronation Street* (ITV, 9 Dec 1960–present). The Manchester-based show marked its 60th anniversary in 2020, making it the **longest-running soap opera**; more than 10,000 episodes have been broadcast to date. The record was accepted on behalf of the cast by Sally Dynevor (inset on the "Street"), who plays Sally Webster.

10 chapters, you'll see how this most important of issues affects every aspect of our lives. The first chapter is dedicated entirely to the matter (Environment, pp.14–31) and explores some of the superlative efforts being made to tackle the effects of climate change. We've also partnered with the charity Earthwatch, who share their tips on how your contribution, no matter how big or small, can make a difference; find out more at **kids.guinnessworldrecords.com**.

One group of people who are already making a difference are the record holders in our Young Achievers section (pp.176–83). These eight bright sparks are making scientific discoveries, tackling climate

**Most Beyoncé songs identified from their lyrics in one minute**
Clara Amfo named 12 tracks by "Queen Bey" in 60 sec in London on 11 Mar 2021. The DJ made her attempt live on BBC Radio 1, as part of a 24-hour fundraising effort to encourage people to donate to Comic Relief. "I was shaking the whole way through!" the Beyoncé superfan confessed afterwards.

**Most sound effects identified in one minute**
To mark her one-year anniversary as a presenter on *Capital Breakfast*, Siân Welby correctly named 38 sound effects in 60 sec on 26 Mar 2021, smashing the previous record of 23. The sharp-eared broadcaster has her own "Siân's Secret Sound" slot, where she asks listeners and her co-presenters to identify a mystery noise.

**Fastest time to wear 10 vests (blindfolded)**
On 13 May 2020, an unsighted Mwaka "Mwaksy" Mudenda donned 10 vests in 44.44 sec on the set of *Blue Peter* (BBC) in Salford. Her attempt was part of a tradition of staging GWR record attempts to introduce new presenters to the show, which was first broadcast in 1958 – making it the **longest-running children's magazine TV series**.

change head on, writing books, wowing TV audiences and winning pro sporting trophies, all before their 16th birthday! In a series of exclusive Q&As, we celebrate their incredible feats and discover that, thanks to such dedicated, hard-working youngsters, the future of the world is in good hands!

You'll find more inspiring individuals in the shape of this year's inductees to the GWR Hall of Fame. There are compelling environmental messages courtesy of veteran naturalist Sir David Attenborough and teenage campaigner Dr Mya-Rose Craig, and we take the opportunity to honour individuals who've made a difference to how women are perceived in otherwise male-dominated sectors, such as astronaut Peggy Whitson, mountaineer Viridiana Álvarez Chávez and human-rights activist Malala Yousafzai.

If you've been missing the chance to get outside and spend time in your favourite museums, galleries, parks and zoos, then you might appreciate our new between-chapter Virtual Visit features. Across the nine poster-like pages, you'll be whisked away for a whistlestop tour of sites such as the Smithsonian Air and Space Museum in Washington, DC, the Louvre in Paris, Australia Zoo in Queensland and Kew Gardens in London – locations that are either record holders in their own right, or contain record-breaking exhibits.

So, settle back and enjoy our round-up of record breaking from one of the strangest years in living memory. The very fact that records continue to be broken in these difficult times is testament to the indomitability of the human spirit!

*Craig Glenday*
Craig Glenday
Editor-in-Chief

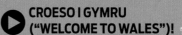

## CROESO I GYMRU ("WELCOME TO WALES")!

In 2021, GWR teamed up once again with Welsh-language broadcaster S4C to mark St David's Day on 1 Mar in superlative style. In all, 10 world records were broken across Wales, including…

**1.** Award-winning clog dancer Tudur Phillips performed the **most jumps over a handkerchief in 30 seconds** – 45 – in Bangor. (Did you know that clog dancing is an old Welsh tradition, involving both steps and tricks?)

**2.** Rodney the Dragon made the **most rugby-ball touches with the feet by a mascot in one minute** – 24 – at the Royal Welsh Showground in Builth Wells.

**3.** Elgan Pugh achieved the **fastest time to chop 10 logs in half with one hit** in 7.56 sec at the Royal Welsh Showground. In 2019, this ace woodcutter won the British Timbersports Championship for the fifth consecutive time.

**4.** Legendary rugby union player Shane Williams, who has scored an unmatched 58 tries for Wales, recorded the **most castles visited in one week by bicycle** – 50. Shane's 736-mi (1,184-km) tower tour lasted a week, starting on 22 Feb at Carreg Cennen and culminating at Dinefwr Castle on St David's Day.

### Most balls caught on a Velcro suit in one minute

Former England international rugby union player Ugo Monye caught 62 balls on his sticky suit, all thrown by host Andrew Mensah, on the set of *It's a Numbers Game* at BT Sport Studios in London on 28 Mar 2021. This record was the first of several scheduled to take place in the sports show's debut season.

**5.** COVID-19 restrictions may have outlawed face-to-face rehearsals, but Wales's proud choral heritage was well served by the **most people in an online singing video relay** – 55 – achieved by the Côr-ona Choir in Bangor. Each on-screen singer delivered a line from "Moliannwn", a much-loved Welsh celebration of spring's arrival.

**6.** Sam and Sue Franklin carried out the **fastest 20 m A320 aircraft pull by a team of two (female)** – 37.63 sec – in Barry. The pair, who are married and have a young son, both also qualified for the World's Strongest Woman 2021 contest, scheduled to be staged in Florida, USA.

### Most table-tennis balls bounced and caught in shaving foam on the head in 30 seconds

Adam Beales trapped 10 ping-pong balls on a foam-lathered helmet in half a minute on the set of *Blue Peter* on 17 Sep 2020. The 40th presenter in the history of the show, Adam let the plastic globes go to his head as part of the *Guinness World Records 2021* book launch.

### Most hamburgers assembled in one minute

Fun Kids Radio presenter George Butler prepped eight burgers in 60 sec in London on 29 Mar 2021. Each bun – which was uncut before the start, as per GWR rules – measured at least 4 in (10.16 cm) across, while the cooked hamburger patties each weighed 90.7 g (3.2 oz). A lettuce and tomato garnish completed the snack.

# Be an Activist

We've placed environmental issues at the heart of this year's *Guinness World Records* book. They're something we should all be concerned about – but they're also a challenge that we can rise up to meet together. You might even set a world record in the process...

Here, you'll find a selection of record holders who've tried to improve our planet by taking on environmental challenges. Some use their attempts to highlight issues that affect their world; others try to tackle them head-on. Whether it's recycling scrap materials to make giant artworks, helping to clean up your local area or simply by attending lessons, you too can use record-breaking to make a positive change.

There are all sorts of different ways to get active and get involved. You could go it alone – like the "Human Swan", conservationist Sacha Dench (opposite) – or enlist the help of your friends and classmates. By collecting and recycling everyday items of rubbish, the British International School of Jeddah (below right) were able to raise money for local disadvantaged children.

Even if you don't have a world record in mind, small acts such as litter-picking can still make a large impact on our world – and the more of us who do it, the better!

### Most plastic-bottle boats launched simultaneously
On 6 Oct 2017, pupils at St James' Church of England Primary Academy (UK) launched a flotilla of 330 plastic-bottle boats at a lake in Poole Park, Dorset, UK. The school attempted the record to highlight the issue of marine plastic pollution, and combined it with lessons on the environment. All the boats were recycled afterwards.

### Largest annual coastal clean-up project
The International Coastal Cleanup (ICC) has taken place every year since 1986, growing into one of the most extensive voluntary environmental initiatives in the world. At the 34th ICC in 2019, a total of 943,195 volunteers from 116 countries gathered 9,422,199 kg (20.7 million lb) of trash from 39,358 km (24,456 mi) of coastline. The project is overseen by Ocean Conservancy (USA).

### Longest underwater clean-up
Astro (MYS) organized a submarine clean-up operation lasting 168 hr 39 min at Tunku Abdul Rahman Marine Park in Sabah, Malaysia, on 13 Apr 2013. An international team of 139 volunteers performed 1,120 dives, recovering waste with a drained weight of 3,098.76 kg (6,831 lb).

## BREAKING RECORDS, MAKING A DIFFERENCE: ENVIRONMENTAL AWARENESS ON A GRAND SCALE

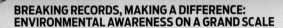

### Largest recycling lesson
On 30 Jan 2018, a total of 17,303 participants learned how to adopt a zero-waste lifestyle at an event staged by Virudhunagar Toastmasters Club (IND) in Tamil Nadu, India. The 40-min lesson was led by instructor T M Shyamraj. The attendance was an increase of more than 4,300 people on the previous record, which had also been set in Tamil Nadu in 2015.

### Longest chain of bottle caps
BISJ School (SAU) constructed a chain of bottle caps measuring 2,738.5 m (8,984 ft 6 in) on 4 Dec 2019 in Jeddah, Saudi Arabia. Participants collected a total of 323,103 used plastic lids, which were strung together using fishing line and thread. They were then taken to a recycling centre, generating funds that were used to buy specialist equipment for children with disabilities.

# Build a Bug Hotel with
# earthwatch
## EUROPE

**If you're inspired by De La Salle School's record-breaking insect hotel below, then why not make your own? Here, our friends at the charity Earthwatch Europe share their tips on making the perfect bug B&B.**

You might not be able to build a bigger bug hotel than the creepy-crawly condominium at De Le Salle School, but it's a fun project and you'll be helping your local insect wildlife. And by helping insects, you help the whole ecosystem! The kind of guests who will be attracted to your hotel will vary according to where you are in the world, but the aim is universal: creating an attractive new home for your tiny friends.

"Bugs are amazing!" says Earthwatch. "Over 75% of the world's food crops rely on pollinator species. If all the gardens in just the UK were turned into nature-friendly spaces, it would create a wildlife haven of over 430,000 hectares [1 million acres] in size. Imagine if we did that all over the world!"

The key is to pack your hotel with natural materials that dry out easily – mostly wood. Make sure you've got different-sized holes so different types of insect can make themselves at home – the holes should be smooth and free from splinters. This is where insects will shelter over winter and lay their eggs.

Finally, be sure to position the hotel in a safe and sunny place, fixed down so that it's not disturbed by the wind. Why not plant some native flowers nearby, too, to help your visitors find pollen?

*Wooden frame*
*Dry leaves*
*Drilled wood*
*Hollow stems*
*Bamboo*
*Twigs*

## Find out more

Earthwatch Europe is an environmental charity with science at its heart. They drive the change needed to live within our means and in balance with nature. They connect people with the natural world, monitor the health of our natural resources and inform the actions that will have the greatest positive impact. Earthwatch works to empower and inspire the next generation to take action for our planet by working with teachers and pupils. If you want to find out more and be part of their planet-saving science, visit **earthwatch.org.uk**.

## How to build a bug hotel

- A quick and simple option is to collect a bundle of twigs, sticks and hollow stems (such as bamboo). Tie them up together with string and then either hang the bunch in a sheltered place or wedge it into a hedge.
- You can also organize your sticks and stems in cardboard boxes – use dividers to make smaller compartments with different materials. This is what the previous record holders did (inset above and right).
- Alternatively, you can build a more complicated home. Use four small logs or pieces of *untreated* timber to build a frame – remember to only use recycled or reclaimed materials where possible. You can then stuff your frame with plant stalks and twigs.

## Largest insect hotel

Kieran Foster and De La Salle School (both UK) built an 81.26-m³ (2,869-cu-ft) minibeast mansion in St Helens, UK. It was completed on 20 May 2020, following nine months of planning and construction. The insect hotel has become home to a thriving community of wood-boring beetles, millipedes, centipedes, ants, bees and woodlice. De La Salle, which has been granted eco-school status, now plans on installing a large pond, reedbed and hedgerows.

*Rain-proof roof*

*Dead wood*

*Dry leaves*
*Wooden pallets*
*Hollow bricks*

For more information on insect hotels and other try-at-home projects, visit **kids.guinnessworldrecords.com**

## Largest mural from recycled material

A team of artists led by Moaffak Makhoul (SYR) spent six months creating a 720-m² (7,750-sq-ft) mural outside a primary school in the Al Mazzeh neighbourhood of Damascus, Syria. Completed on 27 Jan 2014, the piece contains scrap materials such as bicycle wheels, pipes and cooking utensils.

## Largest flag mosaic from recyclable material

Environmental activist Caroline Chaptini teamed up with the Green Community NGO (both LBN) to create a 302.5-m² (3,256-sq-ft) mosaic of the Lebanese flag, unveiled on 14 Dec 2020. It was made from collected reusable materials; the profits from their recycling were donated to charity.

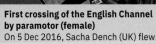

## First crossing of the English Channel by paramotor (female)

On 5 Dec 2016, Sacha Dench (UK) flew from France to the UK as part of a journey that saw her follow endangered Bewick's swans (*Cygnus columbianus*). Sacha's next goal is an around-Britain flight to raise awareness about environmental issues in the lead up to the UN Climate Change Conference, which is due to take place in Glasgow, UK, in Nov 2021.

# Virtual Visits

Global lockdowns to combat the COVID-19 pandemic deprived us of much-needed cultural enrichment and distraction. Theme parks, art galleries and museums that would usually teem with tourists saw their visitor numbers drop by more than 70% globally in 2020. But if you can't visit an attraction, then let us bring the attraction to you!

Between each chapter of this book, we'll whisk you away to nine superlative sites around the world for a "Virtual Visit". You'll unearth dinosaurs at Canada's Royal Tyrrell Museum, take in the sights at Yellowstone Park and meet aviation legends at the Smithsonian's Air and Space Museum. Stroll through the natural wonders in Kew Gardens, marvel at the jaw-dropping detail of Hamburg's Miniature Wonderland and enjoy the artistic riches of London's V&A and the Louvre in Paris. Animal lovers will relish the stop-off at Australia Zoo, while the Guangdong Science Center is pure sci-tech heaven.

You'll find your itinerary on this map, which is also dotted with iconic GWR title holders. Also pinpointed are the world's 20 most visited attractions. So, turn those pages and enjoy a cultural adventure from the comfort of your sofa.

## Key:

**VIRTUAL VISITS**

**Record-breaking places to visit**

**Most visited museums and attractions**

**ROYAL TYRRELL MUSEUM, ALBERTA (P.156)**

**YELLOWSTONE PARK, WYOMING (P.78)**

4, 9

13, 16

**SMITHSONIAN NATIONAL AIR AND SPACE MUSEUM, WASHINGTON, DC (P.12)**

**Great Pyramid of Cholula, Mexico:** Largest pyramid

**Amazon:** Largest rainforest

**Kerepakupai Merú (Angel Falls), Venezuela:** Tallest waterfall

**Easter Island, Chile:** Tallest moai

**Machu Picchu, Peru:** Most visited Inca site

**Rio Carnival, Brazil:** Largest carnival

## Most visited museums and attractions

Listed here are the world's top 20 most popular cultural destinations, as taken from the 2019 report published by AECOM and the Themed Entertainment Association. (F indicates that the museum or gallery allows free entry; P indicates paid entry.) The Louvre (see p.132) tops the listings, as it has for several years now. Altogether, these 20 locations welcomed nearly 105.5 million visitors through their doors in 2019. Each destination is numbered on the map above.

| | Museum | Highlights | Location | Visitors | Entry |
|---|---|---|---|---|---|
| 1 | Louvre (see p.132) | *Mona Lisa, Vénus de Milo, Liberty Leading the People* | Paris, France | 9,600,000 | P |
| 2 | National Museum of China | Stone Age ceramics, 3,000-year-old Houmuwu ding cauldron | Beijing, China | 7,390,000 | F |
| 3 | Vatican Museums | Sistine Chapel, Raphael Rooms, Gallery of Maps, Gregorian Egyptian Museum, Bramante staircases | Vatican, Vatican City | 6,883,000 | P |
| 4 | The Metropolitan Museum of Art | Temple of Dendur, Sphinx of Hatshepsut, *The Death of Socrates, Washington Crossing the Delaware* | New York City, USA | 6,770,000 | P |
| 5 | British Museum | Rosetta Stone, double-headed Aztec serpent, Sutton Hoo ship burial | London, UK | 6,208,000 | F |
| 6 | Tate Modern | *Marilyn Diptych, The Seagram Murals, The Uncertainty of the Poet* | London, UK | 6,098,000 | F |
| 7 | National Gallery | *Sunflowers, The Ambassadors, The Arnolfini Portrait, The Hay Wain* | London, UK | 6,011,000 | F |

| | Museum | Highlights | Location | Visitors | Entry |
|---|---|---|---|---|---|
| 8 | Natural History Museum | Pompeii casts, blue whale skeleton, earthquake simulator | London, UK | 5,424,000 | F |
| 9 | American Museum of Natural History | Ahnighito meteorite, Star of India sapphire, moai statue cast | New York City, USA | 5,000,000 | P |
| 10 | The State Hermitage Museum | Leonardo da Vinci Room, Malachite Room, Knights' Hall Kolyvan Vase, Peacock Clock | St Petersburg, Russia | 4,957,000 | P |
| 11 | Shanghai Science and Technology Museum | Exhibitions: *World of Robots, Light of Wisdom, Earth's Crust Exploration, Light of Exploration* | Shanghai, China | 4,824,000 | P |
| 12 | Reina Sofía | *Guernica, Man with a Pipe, The Musician's Table, Woman in Blue* | Madrid, Spain | 4,426,000 | F |
| 13 | National Museum of Natural History | Hope diamond, Butterfly Pavilion, Egyptian mummies | Washington, DC, USA | 4,200,000 | F |

**North-east Greenland:**
**Largest national park**

**KEW GARDENS (P.110)**
**AND V&A MUSEUM (P.214), LONDON**

5, 6, 7, 8, 17          10

1, 20

▶ **MINIATURE WONDERLAND,**
**HAMBURG (P.56)**

12          3

**LOUVRE,**
**PARIS (P.132)**

**Fogong Pagoda, China:**
**Tallest wooden pagoda**

**Great Wall of China:**
**Longest wall**

2, 18

14

11

**GUANGDONG SCIENCE CENTER,**
**GUANGZHOU (P.184)**

15

19

**Tokyo Skytree, Japan:**
**Tallest tower**

**Great Pyramid, Egypt:**
**Tallest pyramid**

▶ **Burj Khalifa, UAE:**
**Tallest building**

**Sahara, North Africa:**
**Largest hot desert**

**Statue of Unity, Gujarat,**
**India: Tallest statue**

The Grand Tsingy is a "forest" of sharp limestone pinnacles from the Jurassic period; some reach up to 90 m (295 ft) tall.

**Hang Son Đoòng, Vietnam:**
**Largest cave**

**Grand Tsingy, Madagascar:**
**Largest "stone forest"**

**Sudwala Caves, South Africa:**
**Oldest caves**

**Uluru, Australia:**
**Largest sandstone monolith**

**AUSTRALIA ZOO,**
**QUEENSLAND (P.32)**

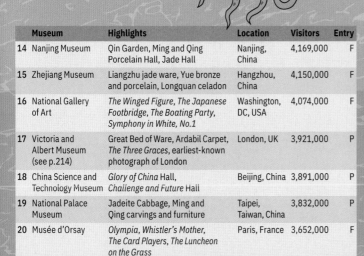

| | Museum | Highlights | Location | Visitors | Entry |
|---|---|---|---|---|---|
| 14 | Nanjing Museum | Qin Garden, Ming and Qing Porcelain Hall, Jade Hall | Nanjing, China | 4,169,000 | F |
| 15 | Zhejiang Museum | Liangzhu jade ware, Yue bronze and porcelain, Longquan celadon | Hangzhou, China | 4,150,000 | F |
| 16 | National Gallery of Art | *The Winged Figure*, *The Japanese Footbridge*, *The Boating Party*, *Symphony in White, No.1* | Washington, DC, USA | 4,074,000 | F |
| 17 | Victoria and Albert Museum (see p.214) | Great Bed of Ware, Ardabil Carpet, *The Three Graces*, earliest-known photograph of London | London, UK | 3,921,000 | P |
| 18 | China Science and Technology Museum | *Glory of China* Hall, *Challenge and Future* Hall | Beijing, China | 3,891,000 | P |
| 19 | National Palace Museum | Jadeite Cabbage, Ming and Qing carvings and furniture | Taipei, Taiwan, China | 3,832,000 | P |
| 20 | Musée d'Orsay | *Olympia*, *Whistler's Mother*, *The Card Players*, *The Luncheon on the Grass* | Paris, France | 3,652,000 | F |

1. Zaila Avant-garde

2. Chad McLean

3. André Ortolf

4. Ren Keyu

5. Andrea M

6. Andrey Maslov

7. Alexander Marchand

8. Thomas BVT

9. Cristian Sabba

10. Prabhakar Reddy P

11. R Sarangapani

12. Christian Rodríguez

13. David & Christian

14. Ashrita Furman

15. María & Christian

16. Silvio Sabba

17. KY Lim

18. Joel Strasser

19. M S Hasinie

20. R S Tharun

21. "Dragon" Taylor

22. S Kanishka

23. David Rush

24. Anthony Kelly

25. K Gokulnath

Each year, thousands of people around the world take on an array of challenges in celebration of Guinness World Records Day. For 2020 – a year like no other in our history – we turned to remote adjudications to assess as many records as possible in a 24-hr period. Here is a selection of the results from our "24 HOURS OF RECORD BREAKING".

* now Olivier Rioux (CAN), at 226.9 cm (see pp.66–67)

† now 215, by David Rush and Jonathan Hannon (both USA)

| | Title | Record | Holder |
|---|---|---|---|
| 1. | Most bounce juggles in 1 min (four basketballs) | 255 | Zaila Avant-garde (USA) |
| 2. | Most bowling balls held simultaneously | 16 | Chad McLean (USA) |
| 3. | Fastest time to drink one litre of lemon juice through a straw | 16 sec | André Ortolf (DEU) |
| 4. | Tallest teenager living* | 221.03 cm | Ren Keyu (CHN) |
| 5. | Most hula-hoop rotations around the bum in 3 min | 400 | Andrea M (UK, b. USA) |
| 6. | Fastest 100 m solving a rotating puzzle cube | 20.91 sec | Andrey Maslov (RUS) |
| 7. | Most full-twist back-somersault burpees in 1 min | 9 | Alexander Marchand (CAN) |
| 8. | Fastest 50-m rope climb | 3 min 19.68 sec | Thomas Butler Van Tonder (ZAF) |
| 9. | Most rope crossovers while skipping on one leg in 30 sec | 49 | Cristian Sabba (ITA) |
| 10. | Most bottle caps removed with the head in 1 min | 68 | Prabhakar Reddy P (IND) |
| 11. | Smallest pack of playing cards | 7 x 5 x 4.86 mm | Ramkumar Sarangapani (IND) |
| 12. | Fastest 100-m sack race | 25.96 sec | Christian López Rodríguez (ESP) |
| 13. | Most behind-the-back basketball passes in 1 min | 65 | David and Christian López Rodríguez (both ESP) |
| 14. | Most arrows broken with the neck in 1 min | 31 | Ashrita Furman (USA) |
| 15. | Most dice caught in 30 sec while blindfolded (team of two)† | 45 | María Rodríguez Cedillo and Christian López Rodríguez (both ESP) |
| 16. | Fastest time to build a 10-toilet-roll pyramid | 3.60 sec | Silvio Sabba (ITA) |
| 17. | Most disappearing cane illusions in 1 min | 26 | KY Lim (MYS) |
| 18. | Most clothes pegs (clothespins) on a beard | 359 | Joel Strasser (USA) |
| 19. | Most vehicle logos identified in 1 min | 99 | M S Hasinie (IND) |
| 20. | Longest duration on inline skates while spinning three hula hoops | 6 min 7 sec | R S Tharun (IND) |
| 21. | Highest throw and catch of a spinning basketball | 6.12 m | DeAndre "Dragon" Taylor (USA) |
| 22. | Most hula-hoop rotations around the foot while lying down in 30 sec | 136 | S Kanishka (IND) |
| 23. | Most juggling catches on a unicycle (blindfolded) | 463 | David Rush (USA) |
| 24. | Most targets hit with a blowgun blindfolded in 1 min | 11 | Anthony Kelly (AUS) |
| 25. | Most poi air wraps in 1 min | 77 | K Gokulnath (IND) |

GWR DAY
GUINNESS WORLD RECORDS

 26. Pavel Trusov
 27. K Nagaraj
 28. R Sarangapani
 29. Rishabh Jain
30. Rianna & friends

 31. Rocco Mercurio
 32. Dariusz Slowik
 33. AM Mendieta
 34. Dariusz Slowik
35. Shunichi Kanno

 36. Muhammad Rashid
 37. Omeir Saeed
 38. Mr Cherry
 39. Ryoji Watanabe
40. Martin Rees

 41. LA Beast
 42. James Rawlings
 43. Leah Shutkever
 44. Hijiki & Angora
45. Tinuke Oyediran

 46. Stefanie Millinger
 47. Deena Shipwright
48. "Wham" Middleton
49. Yu Te-Hsin
Adjudicator

| | Title | Record | Holder |
|---|---|---|---|
| 26. | Most full-extension punches in 3 min | 919 | Pavel Trusov (RUS) |
| 27. | Most spins of a 2-kg hula hoop in 1 min | 144 | K Nagaraj (IND) |
| 28. | Largest magnet sentence | 50,102 magnets | Ramkumar Sarangapani (IND) |
| 29. | Most table-tennis ball bounces on a racket blindfolded in 1 min | 146 | Rishabh Jain (IND) |
| 30. | Most spins of a hula hoop by a team of three in 1 min | 66 | S Rianna Andrea, Andriya Varghese and A S Ishwarya (all IND) |
| 31. | Most billiard balls held in one hand | 16 | Rocco Mercurio (ITA) |
| 32. | Heaviest weight lifted with the little fingers | 105.67 kg | Dariusz Slowik (CAN) |
| 33. | Longest table-tennis serve | 14.86 m | Alvaro Martin Mendieta (ESP) |
| 34. | Farthest horseshoe throw | 53.34 m | Dariusz Slowik (CAN) |
| 35. | Most drinks cans placed on the body using air suction | 20 | Shunichi Kanno (JPN) |
| 36. | Most martial arts kicks in 3 min wearing 5-kg ankle weights (one leg)‡ | 131 | Muhammad Rashid (PAK) |
| 37. | Farthest wakeboard ramp jump (male) | 21 m | Omeir Saeed Omeir Yousef Almheiri (UAE) |

| | Title | Record | Holder |
|---|---|---|---|
| 38. | Most nuts crushed by sitting down in 1 min | 122 | "Mr Cherry" Yoshitake (JPN) |
| 39. | Fastest vertical mile stair climbing | 1 hr 6 min 58 sec | Ryoji Watanabe (JPN) |
| 40. | Most magic tricks underwater in 3 min | 20 | Martin Rees (UK) |
| 41. | Farthest distance walking barefoot on LEGO® bricks§ | 3,886 m | Kevin "LA Beast" Strahle (USA) |
| 42. | Most toilet-paper rolls balanced on the head | 56 | James Rawlings (UK) |
| 43. | Fastest time to eat 15 Ferrero Rocher® | 2 min 1.7 sec | Leah Shutkever (UK) |
| 44. | Most alternate skips by a pair in 30 sec (single rope) | 71 | Hijiki Ikuyama and Angora Soncho (both JPN) |
| 45. | Most cartwheels on roller skates in 1 min | 30 | Tinuke Oyediran (UK) |
| 46. | Most consecutive L-sit straddle presses to handstands | 402 | Stefanie Millinger (AUT) |
| 47. | Most soccer penalties taken in 24 hr (individual) | 7,876 | Deena Shipwright (UK) |
| 48. | Farthest behind-the-back basketball shot | 13.86 m | Rochelle "Wham" Middleton (USA) |
| 49. | Oldest person to paraglide tandem | 105 years 58 days | Yu Te-Hsin (CHN) |

50

*Flags indicate the location of record attempts*

‡ now 143, by Ujjwal Sharma Thakuri (USA)

§ now 8,355 m, by John Wahl (USA)

● ● ●

GUINNESS WORLD RECORDS

# National Air and Space Museum

**S**pread across two vast locations in **Washington, DC, and Virginia, USA, the Smithsonian's glorious celebration of flight is the largest aviation and space museum in the world.** What makes this archive particularly special is that almost every artefact and vehicle – from balloons and biplanes to jet fighters and Moon landers – is either the real thing or the back-up. And, not surprisingly, there's no shortage of record-breaking exhibits to see.

The institution was founded in 1946 as the National Air Museum, with the purpose of recording the USA's central role in the history of flight. As the country's ambitions continued to expand, so too did the collection. In 1966, the name was changed to the National Air and Space Museum, and a decade later, under the directorship of the late Apollo 11

astronaut Michael Collins, the collection was relocated to a hangar-sized space on the National Mall. There, the enormous rockets and aircraft emerging from the Space Race could be displayed.

A second site – the Steven F Udvar-Hazy Center – was opened in 2003 to house even bigger items such as the Space Shuttle, and today, across the two locations, visitors can marvel at more than 68,000 exhibits.

So, join us now on a "flying" visit to some of the record-breaking sights on offer – a trip through time from the Wright brothers' first flight in 1903 to the final touchdown in 2011 of the Space Shuttle *Discovery*.

**Location:** National Mall, Washington, DC, USA (main site, pictured below); Chantilly, Virginia, USA (Steven F Udvar-Hazy Center)

**Established:** 1946

**Galleries:** 23

**Artefacts:** c. 68,378

**Total area (both sites):** 582,759 sq ft (54,140 m²)

**Annual visitors:** 4.5 million (2019)

One-piece cantilevered wing (41 ft; 12.49 m)

Streamlined wheel pants

Two-bladed, ground-adjustable propeller

**Lockheed Vega 5B**
On 20–21 May 1932, Amelia Earhart of Kansas, USA, became the **first woman to fly solo across the Atlantic**. She made the 14-hr 46-min flight from Newfoundland, Canada, to a farmer's field in Northern Ireland, UK, in her bright red, single-engine Lockheed Vega. Lightweight and streamlined, the Vega was a popular choice for adventurers in the 1920s and '30s.

Quartz windshields

Dark-blue paint

Titanium skin

**Lockheed SR-71 "Blackbird"**
With a top speed of Mach 3.3 (3,580 km/h; 2,220 mph), this sleek US Air Force spy plane is the **fastest crewed jet aircraft**. The two-seater "Blackbird" made its first flight on 22 Dec 1964, and would go on to fly top-secret missions for nearly 25 years. The aircraft was designed to operate at an altitude of 85,000 ft (25,908 m) – more than twice as high as a jet airliner.

Aluminium-infused rubber tyres

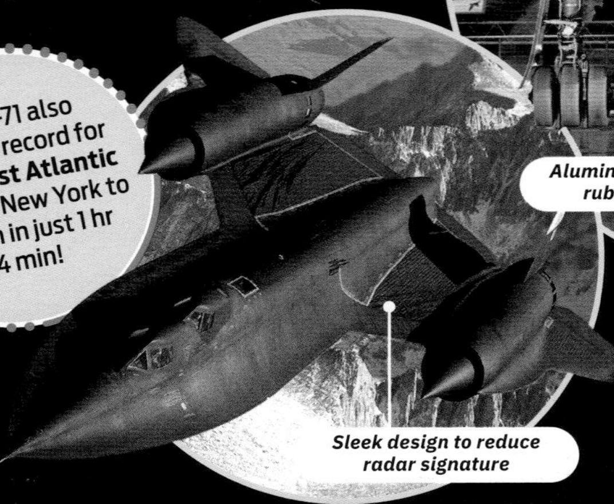

Sleek design to reduce radar signature

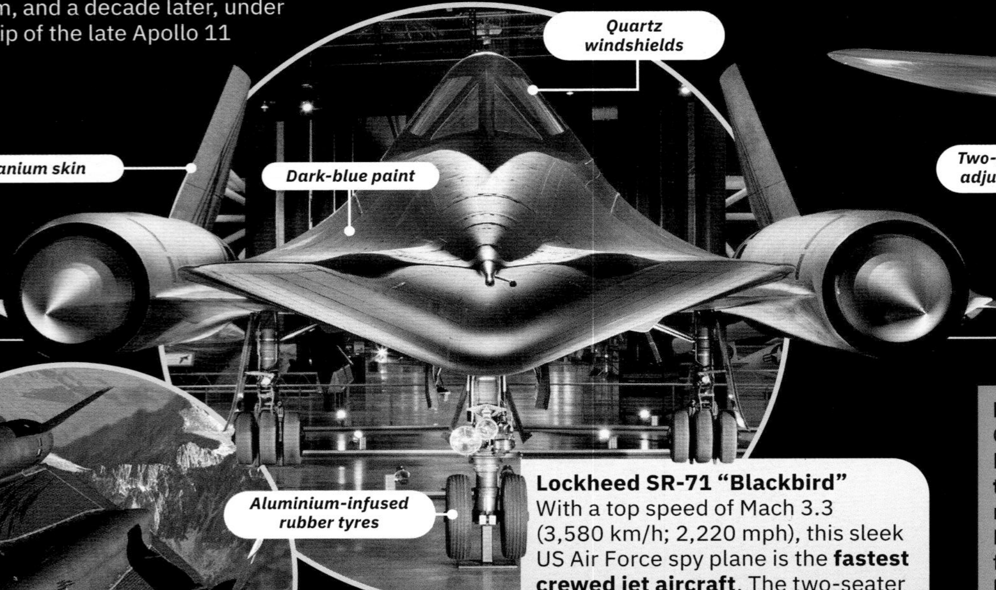

The SR-71 also holds the record for the **fastest Atlantic crossing:** New York to London in just 1 hr 54 min!

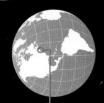

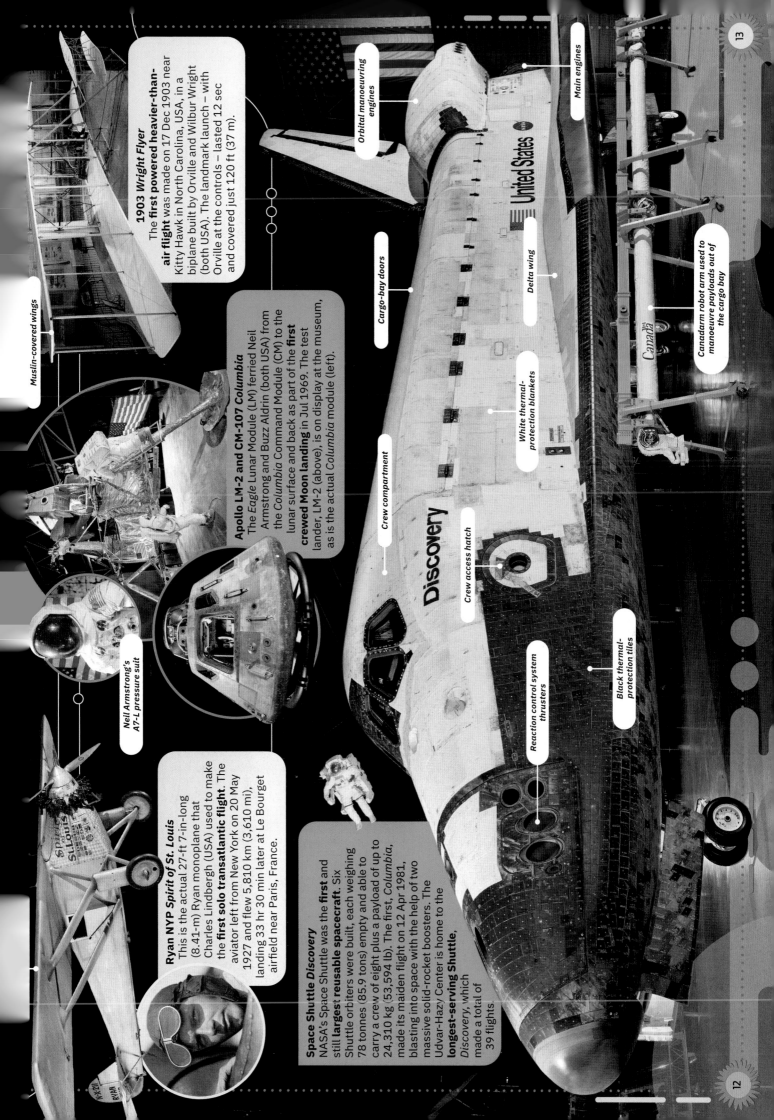

**1903 *Wright Flyer***
The **first powered heavier-than-air flight** was made on 17 Dec 1903 near Kitty Hawk in North Carolina, USA, in a biplane built by Orville and Wilbur Wright (both USA). The landmark launch – with Orville at the controls – lasted 12 sec and covered just 120 ft (37 m).

*Muslin-covered wings*

**Apollo LM-2 and CM-107 *Columbia***
The *Eagle* Lunar Module (LM) ferried Neil Armstrong and Buzz Aldrin (both USA) from the *Columbia* Command Module (CM) to the lunar surface and back as part of the **first crewed Moon landing** in Jul 1969. The test lander, LM-2 (above), is on display at the museum, as is the actual *Columbia* module (left).

*Neil Armstrong's A7-L pressure suit*

**Ryan NYP *Spirit of St. Louis***
This is the actual 27-ft 7-in-long (8.41-m) Ryan monoplane that Charles Lindbergh (USA) used to make the **first solo transatlantic flight**. The aviator left from New York on 20 May 1927 and flew 5,810 km (3,610 mi), landing 33 hr 30 min later at Le Bourget airfield near Paris, France.

**Space Shuttle *Discovery***
NASA's Space Shuttle was the **first** and still **largest reusable spacecraft**. Six Shuttle orbiters were built, each weighing 78 tonnes (85.9 tons) empty and able to carry a crew of eight plus a payload of up to 24,310 kg (53,594 lb). The first, *Columbia*, made its maiden flight on 12 Apr 1981, blasting into space with the help of two massive solid-rocket boosters. The Udvar-Hazy Center is home to the **longest-serving Shuttle**, *Discovery*, which made a total of 39 flights.

*Orbital manoeuvring engines*

*Main engines*

*Cargo-bay doors*

*Delta wing*

*Canadarm robot arm used to manoeuvre payloads out of the cargo bay*

*Crew compartment*

*White thermal-protection blankets*

*Crew access hatch*

*Reaction control system thrusters*

*Black thermal-protection tiles*

United States

Discovery

Canada

# Environment

Noor I and II use rows of 12-m-tall (39-ft) curved mirrors to heat a network of water-filled pipes up to 393°C (739°F).

## Largest solar thermal power station

The Noor Ouarzazate Solar Complex in Morocco harnesses the energy of the Sun to generate 510 megawatts (MW) of power using solar thermal technology. Solar thermal plants like this work differently to their more common photovoltaic (PV) counterparts (see p.25). While PV panels convert light directly into electricity, solar thermal facilities concentrate and store the heat from sunlight. That heat is then used to create steam that drives power-generating turbines.

Ouarzazate comprises three solar thermal facilities – Noor I, II and III – plus the smaller Noor IV that uses PV panels. Noor I and II utilize parabolic trough mirrors (see inset above), whereas Noor III (main picture) employs steerable mirrors called "heliostats" to focus light on to a central tower. The resulting energy is stored in reservoirs of molten salt, the heat from which is then drawn on to produce power during the night and on cloudy days.

The plant can output enough electricity to power a city twice the size of Marrakesh in Morocco, saving around 760,000 tonnes (837,750 tons) of carbon emissions.

The complex was built by a consortium including ACWA Power (SAU), SENER (ESP) and SEPCO (CHN).

Noor III

Noor II

Noor I

Noor IV

(see p.25)

**Mega-what?: getting a grip on power**
The megawatt (MW) – i.e., 1 million Watts – is the go-to unit used in the power industry to rate electricity production and demand. It's also a useful metric for records, as it enables us to compare the capacity of individual facilities as well as entire countries. Electrical output in the order of hundreds of megawatts is enough to power hundreds, or even thousands, of homes. For context, the average hourly power demand to keep the state of New York up and running is c. 18,400 MW.

# Climate Change

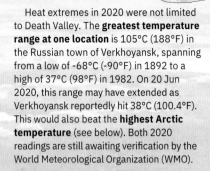

Almost all scientists now agree that human activity is causing global warming, which is driving increasingly extreme weather and environmental degradation. Recent decades have seen temperatures soar, allied to melting ice in polar regions. Rising sea levels have led to stronger storm surges, while hotter, drier summers have resulted in more savage wildfires. If left unchecked, both the human and ecological cost of these trends could prove devastating.

### Warmest average global ocean surface temperature
In 2019, the heat content for the upper 2,000 m (6,560 ft) of the world's oceans rose above the 1981–2010 average by 228 zettajoules – or 228 billion trillion Joules. This equates to a temperature rise of 0.075°C (0.135°F). That may sound like a tiny increase, but its effects on marine ecosystems are already taking their toll, particularly in coastal waters (see p.42).

### Highest temperature on Earth
On 10 Jul 1913, a reading of 56.7°C (134°F) was registered at Greenland Ranch in Death Valley, California, USA. There is some debate about the accuracy of such old data, though. On 16 Aug 2020, a temperature of 54.4°C (129.9°F) was *reliably* registered at Furnace Creek in Death Valley.

### First use of the term "climigration"
Human settlements have always been at the mercy of changing environmental factors, but the recognition that we could be partly driving these changes only really gained traction in the late 20th century. In 2009, lawyer Robin Bronen (USA) coined the term "climigration" to describe the forced movement of people as a result of climate change. She included it in a report on indigenous Alaskan villages (such as Shishmaref, above), whose residents had to relocate owing to vanishing sea-ice and thawing permafrost.

Heat extremes in 2020 were not limited to Death Valley. The **greatest temperature range at one location** is 105°C (188°F) in the Russian town of Verkhoyansk, spanning from a low of -68°C (-90°F) in 1892 to a high of 37°C (98°F) in 1982. On 20 Jun 2020, this range may have extended as Verkhoyansk reportedly hit 38°C (100.4°F). This would also beat the **highest Arctic temperature** (see below). Both 2020 readings are still awaiting verification by the World Meteorological Organization (WMO).

### Highest dewpoint temperature
The "dewpoint" marks the temperature to which air must be cooled to become saturated with water vapour, and is one method of determining humidity. At 3 p.m. on 8 Jul 2003, Dhahran in Saudi Arabia logged a dewpoint of 35°C (95°F) with an air temperature of 42°C (108°F). This resulted in an apparent temperature (i.e., "what it feels like") of 81.1°C (178°F).

### Highest "low" temperature in one day
Across a 24-hr period on 26 Jun 2018, the air temperature in the Omani coastal city of Quriyat did not drop below 42.6°C (108.7°F). The previous highest low was 41.7°C (107.1°F), recorded at Khasab Airport – also in Oman – on 27 Jun 2011, and equalled in Death Valley on 7 Jul 2012.

### Greatest ice-sheet melt in one day
Observations and modelling indicated that, on 31 Jul 2019, the Greenland Ice Sheet (GIS) generated 24 billion tonnes (26.5 billion tons) of meltwater in 24 hr – enough to fill 10 million Olympic-sized swimming pools. Some of this refroze on to the ice sheet, but more than half – 15.3 billion tonnes (16.9 billion tons) – is thought to have run into the ocean. As the GIS is the world's second-largest body of ice (after the Antarctic Ice Sheet), this has severe ramifications for global sea levels (see above).

### Highest sea-level rise
The year 2019 marked the greatest rise in sea levels since satellite altimetry observations began in 1993. The global average was 87.61 mm (3.4 in) above that of 1993, according to the National Oceanic and Atmospheric Administration (NOAA) – an increase of 6.1 mm (0.24 in) from 2018. Kiribati (pictured) is a low-lying atoll in the Pacific particularly at risk; rising oceans may soon force its 100,000-plus population to relocate.

Polar bears feed mostly on seals, but reduced sea-ice is driving their prey farther afield, jeopardizing the bears' future.

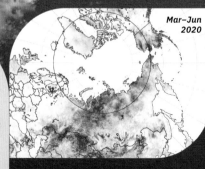

Mar–Jun 2020

### Lowest Arctic sea-ice extent
Each winter, the Arctic Ocean freezes and forms sea-ice that shrinks the following summer. Only 3.41 million km² (1.31 million sq mi) of ice remained at the end of the Arctic summer in 2012, as recorded on 16 Sep. The next-lowest levels – 3.74 million km² (1.44 million sq mi) – were seen in 2020, when it's likely the Arctic experienced its highest-ever temperatures (pending WMO ratification). The inset NASA heat map shows 2020's uncommonly hot spring season, particularly in northern Russia and Alaska, USA.

Algal bloom (in green)

## Largest dead zone

The Gulf of Oman – a 181,000-km² (70,000-sq-mi) stretch of sea between Oman and Iran – contains the largest oxygen minimum zone (OMZ, aka a "dead zone"). Oxygen concentrations often drop below 6 micromoles (μmol) per kg across the area, far under the 120 μmol/kg required to sustain many forms of life. There has always been an OMZ here, but since the 1990s it has grown and intensified, owing to warming seas. This has led to a huge decline in biodiversity, allowing vast algal blooms (above) to form.

## Largest iceberg

According to NOAA's National Ice Center, which monitors major icebergs using live satellite data, iceberg A23A was 40 nautical mi long and 34 nautical mi wide (74 x 63 km; 46 x 39 mi) as of 8 Jan 2021. Located in the Weddell Sea off Antarctica, it had an area of *c.* 4,000 km² (1,540 sq mi) – similar to the US state of Rhode Island. The previous record holder – A68A – broke into several fragments as it neared the island of South Georgia in late 2020.

## Largest ozone hole

The ozone layer is a thin section of Earth's atmosphere that absorbs most of the Sun's harmful UV radiation. Certain air pollutants deplete ozone molecules, causing thinning or even gaps in this natural shield. On 9 Sep 2000, a 29.9-million-km² (11.5-million-sq-mi) hole – about three times the size of the USA – appeared above Antarctica. Despite shrinking to less than half that size in Oct 2019, the following year it had grown back to 24.8 million km² (9.6 million sq mi).

## Most named tropical storms in one year

Storm events are grouped into categories based on their wind speed; they receive a name once they reach the status of "tropical storm", with sustained winds of 33 knots (61 km/h; 38 mph) or higher. The all-time record goes to 1964, when 38 named cyclones were logged in the West Pacific; of these, 26 escalated into typhoons.

The Atlantic witnessed its most intense storm season ever in 2020. In total, there were 30 named storms, 13 of which became hurricanes (as typhoons are called in the northern hemisphere). The season ended with Hurricane Iota (pictured is the Colombian isle of Providencia, post-Iota). It is only the second-known Category 5 hurricane to occur in November; the first was back in 1932.

## Largest climate-change protest

The Global Climate Strike in Sep 2019 was a week-long mobilization calling for more action on the climate crisis. It was spearheaded by Fridays For Future and School Strike 4 Climate – championed by Greta Thunberg – working with grass-roots activists, NGOs and charities. Across the two main strikes (20 Sep and 27 Sep), an estimated 7.22 million people in more than 160 countries took part (above is London, UK, on 20 Sep). There was even a rally in Antarctica, the **most southerly climate protest** (see p.28).

## Largest injection of smoke into the stratosphere by a wildfire event

Between Dec 2019 and Jan 2020, fierce bushfires burned some 5.8 million ha (14.3 million acres) of Australia – an area larger than Croatia. They also spawned a series of huge pyrocumulonimbus clouds. Around 400,000 tonnes (440,000 tons) of aerosol particles (a mix of carbon, smoke and condensed water) – similar in quantity to that produced by a moderate volcanic eruption – rose some 35 km (22 mi) into the sky. Millions of animals perished and air quality as far away as South America was affected. Global warming makes bushfires more frequent and more intense: less rainfall results in drier forest and grassland, far more susceptible to catching alight.

### Scorched Earth: 2020's fire outbreak

Australia was not the only place to see unprecedented wildfires in 2020. Drier and hotter climates are turning ever more terrain into a tinderbox.
• **California, USA** (below): 1.77 million ha (4.37 million acres) razed
• **Brazil:** *c.* 25% of the Pantanal (**largest wetland**) burned, along with nearly 2.2 million ha (5.4 million acres) of the Amazon (**largest rainforest**)
• **Siberia, Russia:** fires emitted around 250 megatonnes (275 million tons) of $CO_2$

# Rubbish & Recycling

### First shopping mall for recycled goods

ReTuna Återbruksgalleria in Eskilstuna, Sweden, opened on 28 Aug 2015 and is wholly dedicated to repaired, recycled and upcycled products. Residents deposit items (including furniture, computers, audio equipment and bikes) in workshops to be refurbished and resold. Run by the local municipality, the centre has created 50 repair and retail jobs, and houses start-ups and local artisans.

### First examples of recycling

Humans have repurposed objects for millennia, though whether this classifies as "recycling" depends on semantics. Our Stone Age ancestors in the Lower Paleolithic period (commencing 2.5 million years ago) likely reused parts of old axes to make new tools. Evidence for this comes from flint tools dating to 400,000–500,000 years ago found in the Tabun Cave, in what is now Israel. Other authorities regard the Bronze Age (3000–1200 BCE) as the dawn of modern recycling; as this alloy can be melted and recast, it can be completely recycled into the same or entirely different objects.

### First landfill sites

The city of Knossos on Crete (now in Greece) had landfill sites dating back to c. 3000 BCE. The ancient Minoan civilization of that era discarded solid garbage (including ceramic wine cups now thought to have been a single-use item) in large pits, which were then backfilled with soil over several levels.

### First book printed on recycled paper

Paper-maker Matthias Koops (UK) published *Historical Account of the Substances which Have Been Used to Describe Events, and to Convey Ideas from the Earliest Date to the Invention of Paper* in 1800. Its second edition in 1801 stated: "Printed on Paper Re-Made from Old Printed and Written Paper".

### Highest recycling rate

Liechtenstein recycles 64.6% of its waste – more than any other sovereign country – according to the 2018 *What a Waste 2.0* report by the World Bank and the International Bank for Reconstruction and Development. North Macedonia is the **country with the lowest rate of recycling** – 0.2%.

### Largest landfill site

Opened in 1993, the Apex Regional Landfill in the Nevada desert near Las Vegas, USA, occupies an area of 2,200 acres (890 ha) – about the same as 1,250 soccer pitches – according to D-Waste. At its peak in 2006, it was receiving 15,000 tons (13,600 tonnes) of municipal solid waste daily, though now around 9,000 tons (8,160 tonnes) is more typical. The facility is managed by Republic Services (USA).

### First recycled-cardboard book publisher

The publishing cooperative Eloísa Cartonera (ARG) was set up in early 2003 and is based in La Boca, Buenos Aires, Argentina. After the 2001 economic crisis, a group of writers, publishers and waste collectors known as *cartoneros* ("cardboarders") united to create affordable *libros cartoneros*, or books made from used cardboard. There are now some 250 *cartonera* publishers around the world.

Sail-fabric cover

Conveyor belt

Rotating forks

Water wheel

Solar panels

Containment boom

### Most floating debris removed by a trash interceptor

From May 2014 to Dec 2020, "Mr Trash Wheel" removed 1,408.07 tons (1,277.37 tonnes) of garbage from the mouth of the Jones Falls River in Baltimore, Maryland, USA. It is operated by the city's Waterfront Partnership. The total included more than 830,000 plastic bottles, 5,100 sports balls and enough cigarette butts to stretch for more than 150 mi (240 km). The inset shows the device collecting surface garbage, although a 2-ft (0.6-m) skirt on the booms also enables it to snag waste below the waterline.

## Largest human recycling logo

A group of 3,373 people formed the iconic three-arrow symbol at an event organized by India's Central Institute of Petrochemicals Engineering & Technology (CIPET). The attempt – which took place in Chennai, India, on 23 Jan 2019 – was arranged to raise awareness of biodegradable plastics and reusing plastic in general. It also marked CIPET's 50th anniversary.

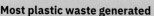

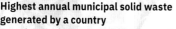

## Most glass bottles collected for recycling in one hour

Mayor Alberto Rojo Blas and the city council of Guadalajara in Spain oversaw the collection of 2,485 kg (5,478 lb) of glass bottles in 60 min on 16 Dec 2019. The event took place in Guadalajara's main square and was well attended by local school pupils. It was staged to promote recycling and to emphasize that we should all play our part in taking care of the planet.

## Most plastic waste generated

According to World Bank data, 242 million tonnes (267 million tons) of plastic garbage were produced in 2016. A 2020 study in *Science Advances* suggests that the USA may have contributed as much as 42 million tonnes (46.3 million tons) of this.

Micronesia (pictured) threw away the **most plastic per capita**: 308.25 kg (679 lb) per annum. Although this island nation has a very small population (it ranks 164th in plastic waste generated as a country), this is still concerning as inadequate waste management and a largely coastal populace risks more plastic ending up in the sea.

## Longest permanent bridge made from recycled materials

Completed in 2011, the Easter Dawyck Bridge over the River Tweed in Peeblesshire, UK, is 90 ft (27.4 m) long and made from more than 50 tonnes (55 tons) of waste plastic. It was built by Vertech Composites, aided by engineers from Cardiff University, UK. The bridge was created from a thermoplastic material dubbed "structural plastic lumber" (reconstituted plastic bottles and other household waste), and itself is 100% recyclable. With a load-bearing tolerance of up to 44 tonnes (48.5 tons), it can be used by pedestrians, cars and even heavy-goods vehicles.

## Highest annual municipal solid waste generated by a country

Based on the latest published data curated in 2018's *What a Waste 2.0* report, the USA produces *c.* 258 million tonnes (284.4 million tons) of municipal solid waste (MSW) – i.e., everyday household trash – each year. That equates to 1,260 times the weight of the Statue of Liberty.

The **lowest annual MSW** is 3,989 tonnes (4,397 tons), by Pacific island nation Tuvalu.

## Highest composting rate

*What a Waste 2.0* lists Austria as the top composting nation, converting 31.2% of its organic waste into natural fertilizer.

Antigua and Barbuda, North Macedonia, St Lucia, and St Vincent and the Grenadines share the **lowest composting rate**: 0.1%.

## Largest aluminium recycling plant (capacity)

The Nachterstedt recycling centre in Saxony-Anhalt, Germany – which is operated by Novelis (USA) – can process 400,000 tonnes (441,000 tons) of aluminium annually. That is the equivalent of 26.6 billion soda cans, though the plant handles 18 different types of scrap. Per day, the facility can forge 55 ingots from waste metal, each 12 m (39 ft) long and weighing 25 tonnes (27.5 tons).

- **Opened:** Oct 2014
- **Cost:** $258 m (£161.3 m; €205 m)
- **Area:** 60,000 m² (645,30 sq ft)
- **Employees:** *c.* 200
- **CO₂ emissions saved:** 3.7 million tonnes (4 million tons) per year

Across its entire global network, Novelis recycled more than 74 billion UBCs (used beverage cans) in 2020.

# Plastic

**100%**

**649.648 чm**

### First new species contaminated with plastic
*Eurythenes plasticus* is a deep-sea amphipod encountered for the first time in the Pacific Ocean in 2014. The shrimp-like crustacean was so named as one individual contained a 0.649-mm-long piece of microplastic (above) in its gut; the fibre was 83.74% similar to polyethylene terephthalate (PET). What makes this even more alarming is that *E. plasticus* lives in the hadal zone, at depths >6,000 m (>19,685 ft), indicating the extent of microplastic pollution. The novel amphipod was first described in *Zootaxa* on 5 Mar 2020.

### First plastic manufactured
The first engineered plastic was parkesine, patented by Alexander Parkes (UK) in 1856. Derived from plant cellulose, parkesine could be moulded when heated, but kept its shape once cooled. He unveiled his invention at the International Exhibition in London in 1862. The more famous Bakelite – invented by Belgian chemist Leo Baekeland in the USA in 1907 – was the **first fully synthetic plastic**.

### First one-piece plastic bag
Polythene (aka polyethylene) was discovered by accident in 1898 during experiments with hydrocarbons by German chemist Hans von Pechmann, but wasn't synthesized industrially until the mid-20th century. In 1959, this "wonder material" was used to make the very first single-piece plastic bag with incorporated handles, developed by engineer Sten Gustaf Thulin (SWE) as a means to reduce the deforestation caused by paper-bag production. The design was patented by packaging company Celloplast in 1965.

### First country to...
**Tax plastic bags**: In 1994, Denmark put a levy on bags for retailers, encouraging shops to advocate reusable bags. A ban on free plastic bags was announced by the Danish prime minister in 2019.
**Ban single-use plastic bags**: Bangladesh prohibited the use of thin polythene carrier bags in 2002. The landmark law sought to counter major issues with flooding that are exacerbated by such bags clogging up drains and waterways.

In 2018, some 6,000 students from 60 more UK schools were inspired to create their own bottle boats.

## KING OF THE (PLASTIC) CASTLE: ROBERT BEZEAU

In 2017, Robert Bezeau (CAN), aka The Plastic King, made a stately addition to his Plastic Bottle Village in Panama: a 14-m-tall (45-ft 11-in) fortress built out of 40,000 bottles – the largest plastic-bottle castle.

**What is your background?**
My background is in manufacturing electrical components. The passion for recycling started when I moved to Isla Colón in Bocas del Toro [in Panama], where single-use plastic was all over the island.

**What led you to create a village out of plastic bottles?**
I accumulated about a million PET bottles in a year and a half and was looking for what to do with them. I estimate that the village to date is built from around 200,000 bottles.

**Tell us more about the castle.**
The castle was built reusing 40,000 PET bottles. The challenge was that we had no plans – we improvised day by day. The core structure was made with steel and concrete, then all of the walls are cages filled with bottles. It rose one day at a time, one floor at a time, until we had reached four storeys!

**What sort of reaction have you had to your bottle buildings?**
At first, residents and officials of the island thought I was crazy – even my wife and son did! Then they were curious and let me continue to see what I was going to do next. As it grew, so did their intrigue. In 2017, I received an Energy Globe award – that made me feel incredible.

**Any advice for anyone looking to upcycle their own bottles?**
We need to convince our politicians to regulate packaging. How can it be right that we drink water from a PET bottle for eight minutes and discard it in nature for 800 years? If bottles are shaped so that they interlock together, it would allow us to reuse them and build all kind of structures, useful or decorative, such as benches, tables, fountains, storage boxes, dog houses... the possibilities are endless.

### Most plastic-bottle boats launched
A flotilla of 330 vessels made out of plastic bottles was launched on 6 Oct 2017 in a pond in Poole, Dorset, UK, by pupils from St James' Church of England Primary Academy (UK). All of the boats were collected afterwards and recycled, as the activity was designed to highlight plastic pollution and the importance of reusing materials.

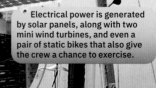
Electrical power is generated by solar panels, along with two mini wind turbines, and even a pair of static bikes that also give the crew a chance to exercise.

Designed to house a crew of six, the cabin is built from self-reinforcing plastic (a fabric made from PET fibres). It captures rainwater on its roof and has a composting toilet.

### ▶ Largest recycled-plastic sculpture (supported)

Monterey Bay Aquarium in San Francisco, California, USA, unveiled a life-size blue whale statue 25.9 m (84 ft 11 in) long and 4.2 m (13 ft 9 in) tall on 26 Nov 2018. The internal structure is steelwork, but its exterior panels are made from plastic debris such as detergent bottles and toys collected from in and around San Francisco Bay.

### Largest producer of plastic (industry)

Across all sectors, 407 million tonnes (449 million tons) of primary plastic (i.e., made from virgin material) was created worldwide in 2015. Of that, the packaging industry accounted for the biggest portion – 146 million tonnes (161 million tons) – as reported in *Science Advances* in Jul 2017.

### Deepest marine plastic found

A plastic bag was retrieved from a depth of 10,898 m (35,755 ft) in the Pacific Ocean's Mariana Trench. The discovery was made by the Global Oceanographic Data Center of the Japan Agency for Marine-Earth Science and Technology and discussed in *Marine Policy* in Oct 2018. This is extremely close to the ◗ **deepest point in the ocean**, with a series of submersible dives in this region in 2019–20 having established a new absolute bottom (see pp.128–29).

### Smallest marine microplastic

Microplastics are small plastic pieces less than 5 mm (0.2 in) in diameter that have become an increasing concern in recent years. Although it's widely accepted that this material likely breaks down into ever tinier pieces (i.e., nanoplastics), the smallest example found in the sea to date was 1.6 micrometres (µm) wide; a human hair is about 100 µm.

### Longest chain of bottle caps

A total of 323,103 plastic lids were strung into a 2,738.5-m (8,984-ft) chain by pupils at BISJ School in Jeddah, Saudi Arabia, as verified on 4 Dec 2019. The record aimed to shine a light on plastic pollution in the oceans.

### Most common consumer item

Estimates for the global manufacture of plastic bags number in the trillions, making them the most abundant consumer product in the world. In the USA alone, people throw away some 100 billion plastic bags every year; as they are manufactured from petroleum, this is equivalent to dumping nearly 12 million barrels of oil annually.

### Largest plastic catamaran

In 2009, David de Rothschild (UK) set sail on *Plastiki* (a nod to the iconic vessel *Kon-Tiki*) on a Pacific odyssey from California, USA, to Sydney, Australia. The 60-ft (18.3-m) twin-hulled boat was made from plastic bottles, reconstituted plastic and recycled waste products. The aim of the voyage was to show how waste can be utilized as a resource, and to draw attention to the "Great Pacific Garbage Patch" – a vast area of ocean blighted by an accumulation of marine debris (find out more on p.43).

*Plastiki*'s masts were formerly aluminium irrigation pipes, while the sails are made from reconstituted plastic bottles.

The hulls are lined with 12,000 plastic bottles, each filled with 12 g (0.4 oz) of dry ice and sealed. The solid dry ice converts to $CO_2$, providing buoyancy.

# Pollution

## Loudest industrial ocean noise pollution

Seismic airguns are used by the oil and gas industry to survey the seabed. The blast from an airgun array (which is typically towed behind a survey ship – see inset) can reach a sound pressure level of 260 decibels (dB) relative to the 1 microPascal (µPa) reference used in underwater measurements. Airgun blasts are audible for thousands of kilometres underwater and are known to cause hearing loss in some species.

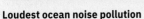

## Loudest ocean noise pollution

Although the frequent use of seismic airguns (see above) is the most ecologically damaging, it is not the loudest human-made sound to have been produced underwater. This record is held by the 1955 Operation Wigwam nuclear test, which saw the US Navy detonate a 30-kiloton nuclear warhead at a depth of 2,000 ft (610 m) off the coast of California. The volume of the explosion was calculated to have been 328 dB (re 1 µPa) at its point of origin and the sound reverberated around the Pacific Ocean for several hours. Eyewitnesses described the surface of the sea being littered with dead marine animals as far as the eye could see, killed either by the shockwave or by the burst of radiation.

## Worst radioactive waste accident

On 29 Sep 1957, the cooling systems failed in a nuclear waste container at the Mayak Production Association (see right), causing the slurry inside to explode with a force

equal to 100 tonnes of TNT. This blast sent a plume of irradiated dust downwind of the plant, spreading 740 petaBecquerels of radiation across the region. The reactor failures at Fukushima and Chernobyl have since led to larger radiation leaks, but this incident remains the biggest release of radiation from nuclear waste.

Today, the area downwind of the Mayak plant is closed to the public (warning sign pictured below) as the East Ural Nature Reserve. This was for many years the **largest radioactive exclusion zone**, though it was surpassed in 1986 by the Chernobyl Nuclear Power Plant Zone of Alienation, which covers an area of 2,600 km² (1,003 sq mi) in Kiev Oblast, Ukraine.

## Lowest Ocean Health Index score

In 2019, the Central American country of Nicaragua received an overall score of just 44 out of 100 in the annual Ocean Health Index rankings. This publication was put

## Most radioactive lake ever

Lake Karachay was located near the Mayak Production Association, a nuclear facility in Chelyabinsk Oblast, Russia. During the Soviet era, radioactive waste from the plant was routinely dumped into the lake. A study carried out in 1993 found that a person standing on the shore would receive a radiation dose of 5.6 Sieverts per hour. That's enough to be fatal in just 50 min. The lake was filled in with concrete during the 2000s using special lead-lined trucks.

## Largest freshwater blue-green algal bloom

In 2011, Lake Erie – one of North America's Great Lakes – was struck by a proliferation of algae. At its height in early October, the extent of the "bloom" (almost entirely *Microcystis*, a toxic cyanobacteria) covered more than 5,000 km² (1,930 sq mi) – about one-fifth of Erie's surface. Blooms like these are a result of agricultural run-off pollution, in which fertilizer is washed into waterways, creating conditions that enable algae to grow out of control.

together by Conservation International and the National Center for Ecological Analysis and Synthesis at the University of California, Santa Barbara, and considered a variety of factors including pollution, biodiversity and the strength of coastal economies. The country with the **highest score** in the 2019 rankings was Germany, with 86 out of 100, and the **highest clean waters score** (which looks at pollution levels only) was held by Canada with 94.

## Country with the worst air pollution

Bangladesh sits at the bottom of the table in the *IQAir 2020 World Air Quality Report*, with average PM$_{2.5}$ pollution levels (particulate matter with a diameter of less than 2.5 micrometres) of 77.1 micrograms per cubic metre (µg/m³). Bangladesh's poor air quality is caused by dense motor vehicle traffic, largely unregulated heavy

## Largest radio quiet zone

Non-ionizing radiation – created by, for example, radio broadcasts and mobile phones – is harmless to living creatures, but for astronomers it is a disruptive form of pollution. To prevent human noise drowning out signals from space, many radio telescopes operate within "radio quiet zones", where broadcasts are restricted by law. The largest of these is the Karoo Central Astronomy Advantage Area, which covers 106,306 km² (41,044 sq mi) of land – larger than Iceland – around the unfinished Square Kilometre Array in South Africa.

## Most light-polluted city

According to a 2018 report by the Center for Biological Diversity, St Petersburg in Russia is 8.1 times brighter at night than the global urban average. The nocturnal glow of modern cities – caused by industrial floodlights, street lights and other forms of artificial illumination – has been shown to negatively affect the health of both humans and animals.

Light pollution is so pervasive that some environmental groups have called for areas where artificial light is restricted by law. The **largest dark sky preserve** is Wood Buffalo National Park in Alberta, Canada, which covers 44,807 km² (17,300 sq mi).

industry and widespread use of polluting fuels for domestic heating and cooking. Significant progress has been made in recent years, however, with $PM_{2.5}$ levels having declined from 97.1 µg/m³ in 2018.

## Largest accidental oil spill

On 14 Mar 1910, workers digging a well in the Midway-Sunset Oil Field in California, USA, struck a pressurized underground deposit. The resulting oil eruption, known as the "Lakeview Gusher", broke the drilling equipment and formed a plume some 146 m (480 ft) high. Over the next 545 days, 1.37 million tonnes (1.51 million tons) of oil poured out of the ground, creating lakes and rivers of oil. The torrent eventually stopped on 10 Sep 1911, when the well collapsed in on itself.

## Largest fatberg

In Sep 2017, inspectors from Thames Water (UK) discovered a blockage in a sewer pipe under Whitechapel in east London. The obstruction turned out to be a mass of congealed cooking fat, wet wipes and other waste. This "fatberg" was 250 m (820 ft) long and weighed 130 tonnes (143 tons). Samples of the fatberg are now on display at the Museum of London.

## Largest urban noise monitoring system

Noise pollution is known to negatively affect both humans and animals, but scientists still have little data on the phenomenon. To remedy this, noise monitoring networks have been set up in cities around the world. The largest of these is operated by Bruitparif (FRA), which had 150 of its Méduse microphones installed in Paris as of Feb 2021. The maps below show sound levels (trending from quiet green to loud red) recorded by Bruitparif before and after the COVID-19 lockdown of spring 2020.

## Most polluted river

Analysis carried out in 2013 found that the Citarum River, which flows through the industrial districts to the east of Indonesia's capital, Jakarta, contains 1,000 times more lead than is considered safe, as well as sewage, domestic rubbish and toxic chemicals.

## Highest global CO₂ levels

According to figures published in Nov 2020 by the World Meteorological Organization, average levels of atmospheric carbon dioxide reached 410.5 ppm (parts per million) in 2019, a rise of 2.6 ppm on the previous year. Despite the worldwide industrial slowdown caused by the COVID-19 pandemic, early indications suggest that the rise in global $CO_2$ levels barely slowed in 2020.

## City with the worst air pollution

According to the *IQAir 2020 World Air Quality Report*, Hotan in Xinjiang, China, suffers the highest levels of particulate matter. The average level of $PM_{2.5}$ pollution was 110.2 µg/m³ in 2020, more than 10 times what is considered healthy, and double the level considered harmful. Hotan has the record in this year's rankings because the previous holder, Ghaziabad in India, has significantly improved.

Hotan's air pollution problems are exacerbated by frequent dust storms that blow in from the Taklamakan Desert.

# Renewable Energies

### First tidal power station

La Rance Tidal Power Station opened on 26 Nov 1966 in Brittany, France. It is still in operation today, more than 50 years later. The station has a 750-m-long (2,460-ft) tidal barrage and 24 turbines.

In 2011, La Rance was surpassed as the **most powerful tidal power station** by a facility at Sihwa Lake in South Korea. Its tidal barrage uses 10 submerged turbines that give the power station a total output capacity of 254 megawatts (MW).

### Most powerful hydroelectric power station

Completed on 4 Jul 2012, the Three Gorges Dam project in Yiling District, Hubei, China, has a total installed generation capacity of 22,500 MW. The turbines are driven by the waters of the Yangtze River (the sixth-largest river in the world by flow rate) and create enough electricity that they could, in theory, power the entire country of Belgium or the state of New Jersey in the US.

### Most powerful pumped storage station

The Bath County Pumped Storage Station in Virginia, USA, contains a pair of reservoirs separated in height by 380 m (1,246 ft). When demand on the electricity grid is low, excess power pumps water from the lower into the higher reservoir. When demand is high, water is released back into the lower reservoir via turbines. The station can generate 3,003 MW at maximum flow, which is 851 m³ (30,052 cu ft) per second.

### Most powerful wind farm

The Jiuquan Wind Power Base, aka the Gansu Wind Farm, is located on the edge of the Gobi Desert in Gansu, China. Fed by strong winds on a 1,650-m-high (5,400-ft) plateau, it has a capacity of 7,965 MW.

### Highest-altitude wind generator

The remote Peruvian community of Catac is served by a wind generator operating at an altitude of 16,000 ft (4,877 m) near the shrinking glacier of Pastoruri. It was installed by WindAid (PER) on 19 Jun 2013.

### First megawatt wind turbine

The 1.25-MW Smith-Putnam wind turbine was the first of its kind to generate more than 1 MW of electricity. Designed by engineer Palmer Cosslett Putnam, it was erected on a hill called Grandpa's Knob in Vermont, USA, and synchronized with the local power grid on 19 Oct 1941. The turbine operated intermittently until 26 Mar 1945, when a blade failed at a weak point that had not been addressed on account of wartime shortages.

### Most powerful geothermal power station

Situated in the Mayacamas Mountains of California, USA, the Geysers field consists of 22 geothermal power plants and has a total installed capacity of 1,517 MW. The site is spread over 117 km² (45 sq mi) and has more than 350 steam-production wells, which are drilled to tap the natural steam trapped below in a vast underground reservoir.

### Most solar-powered houses built in one calendar year

In 2019 (1 Jan to 31 Dec inclusive), Ichijo Co. (JPN) built 9,957 houses with large built-in solar arrays, as verified by independent research on 7 Dec 2020. Ichijo is also the **best-selling custom-home company (current)**, with sales of 13,896 custom-designed homes in the same period.

### Largest offshore wind farm

Hornsea One, a 1,218-MW development built by Ørsted (DNK), is located 120 km (75 mi) off the coast of Yorkshire, UK, in the North Sea. It is connected to the British national grid by an undersea cable. Each of the facility's 174 Siemens-Gamesa wind turbines measures 115 m (377 ft) to the rotor hub, making them 190 m (623 ft) tall including the length of the blades. A single rotation generates enough electricity to power a home for more than 24 hours.

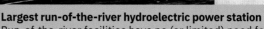

### Largest run-of-the-river hydroelectric power station

Run-of-the-river facilities have no (or limited) need for a reservoir, being powered by the natural flow of a river. The Chief Joseph Dam (opened 1979) on the Columbia River in Washington State, USA, is a concrete construction measuring 71 m high and 1,800 m in length (232 ft x 5,905 ft). Its 27 Francis turbines have a capacity of 2.62 gigawatts – enough to power the nearby city of Seattle.

## First house powered by hydroelectricity

Built in 1863, Cragside in Northumberland, UK, generated electricity using a turbine placed on a 103-m (337-ft) drop between two lakes on the estate. Owned by engineer and industrialist William Armstrong, Cragside was one of the first houses to boast hot and cold running water, central heating, telephones, fire alarms and a Turkish bath suite.

## Most northerly solar power plant

Batagay Solar Power Plant operates inside the Arctic Circle at 67.66°N in the Republic of Sakha (Yakutia), Russia. Developed by RAO Energy Systems of the East, it has 3,360 solar panels and a generating capacity of 1 MW.

## Most powerful solar chimney

A prototype solar chimney power station in Manzanares, Spain, produced 50 kW of electricity between 1982 and 1989. It was designed as a temporary structure, only to run for seven years before finally toppling over in a windstorm. The solar chimney was powered by a large area of greenhouses, inside which air was heated by the Sun before expanding upwards through a 200-m-tall (656-ft) updraught tower, powering turbines as it escaped.

## Highest power output from a tidal stream turbine

The SR2000 prototype generated 3,250 megawatt-hours between Aug 2017 and Sep 2018 at the European Marine Energy Centre's tidal test site in the Orkney Islands, UK. Built by Orbital Marine Power (UK), the SR2000 consists of a 64-m-long (210-ft) floating hull connected to a pair of 16-m-diameter (52-ft) rotors, which turn in the tidal current when the platform is anchored to the seabed.

## Most efficient hybrid biomass heating system (non-condensing)

Biomass boilers generate power by heating waste organic material. The Sommerauer ECOS 70–120 kW boiler has an efficiency of 98%, as verified on 3 Apr 2020.

## Largest producer of electricity from...

- **Geothermal power**: the USA, with 18,773 GWh (gigawatt-hours) generated from 2,540 MW of installed capacity.
- **Hydroelectric power**: China, with 1,199,200 GWh from 322,271 MW of installed capacity.
- **Marine power (wave and tidal energy)**: South Korea, with 485 GWh from 255 MW of installed capacity.
- **Offshore wind power**: the UK, with 26,687 GWh from 8,216 MW of installed capacity.
- **Photovoltaic (solar) power**: China, with 178,070 GWh from 175,286 MW of installed capacity.
- **Wind power**: China, with 366,452 GWh from 184,665 MW of installed capacity. (Figures for 2018, from the International Renewable Energy Agency.)

## Largest wind turbine

The General Electric Haliade-X measures 135 m (442 ft) to its hub, and has a rotor diameter of 220 m (721 ft), making the whole structure taller than the Washington Monument. The first prototype was built in Rotterdam, Netherlands, on 17 Oct 2019. With a generating capacity of 14 MW, the Haliade-X is also the **most powerful wind turbine**. A single rotation of the rotor generates enough electricity to power an average home for two days.

## Most powerful solar facility

Bhadla Solar Park in Rajasthan, India, possesses a total energy-generating capacity of 2,245 MW. It covers an area of 57 km² (22 sq mi) – almost as large as the country of San Marino. Construction began in Jul 2015 and the last phase of development was completed in Mar 2020. Solar parks are public-private projects, in which an area is zoned for photovoltaic power generation. This area is equipped with transmission cables and other infrastructure before being opened to private developers, who build and operate the power plants.

2018

2020

# Rebuilding Earth

Centuries' worth of industrialization, growing populations, global warming and related environmental damage have severely harmed our planet. Encouragingly, there is a growing ambition to try and rectify some of those mistakes, both for the health of the environment and for future generations. Here, we spotlight a range of alternative approaches and innovations that are seeking to lessen or reverse our impact on Earth, ranging from progressive laws and infrastructure to more eco-minded tech and engineering.

### First "circular economy" roadmap

The Ellen MacArthur Foundation defines a "circular economy" as consisting of a system based on minimal waste and pollution, maximizing the life of products and materials, and the regeneration of natural systems. In 2016, Finland became the first country to publish a national action plan towards achieving a circular economy, which set out how its society might move away from a linear economy by 2025.

### Highest public-transit mode share

Based on 2019 figures, approximately 81% of all journeys in Hong Kong, China, are made via public transport – a total of 12.4 million passenger boardings each day. It is one of the world's most densely populated cities: more than 7.5 million people live in a 1,110-km² (429-sq-mi) area, which is more than double the density of Manhattan in New York City, USA.

### Largest low-carbon city under construction

Masdar City in Abu Dhabi, UAE, will be a self-sufficient site causing minimal environmental impact – a sign of the country's commitment to greener projects. Work began in 2008 on an area of c. 560,000 m² (6 million sq ft). Progress has slowed, but it's intended that eventually 50,000 people will live and work here, in buildings that use low-carbon, locally sourced and recycled materials, and which are designed to lower both energy and water use by 40%.

### First modern arcology project

The idea of "arcology" (a portmanteau of "architecture" and "ecology") was conceived by Italian architect Paolo Soleri in the 1960s, as an alternative to modern urban sprawl. In 1970, work began on a prototype arcology town – Arcosanti – set in the Arizona desert, north of Phoenix. The construction and research work here explores the intensification of space and land use, self-containment of habitat and the conservation of energy and resources. The site's cafeteria (inset) is typical of Arcosanti's open-plan style.

### Largest afforestation project

Launched in 2007, the UN-backed "Great Green Wall" initiative is creating a 7,775-km-long (4,831-mi) belt of "regreened" land across sub-Saharan Africa from Senegal to Djibouti. It is a long-term programme, with some regions having seen more progress than others. But the end goals remain the same: to combat desert creep, make the land more cultivable and improve access to water.

### Most terrestrial protected land (country)

As of 2018, a total of 54.1% of Venezuela's total land area fell under some degree of legal protection, according to data collated by the United Nations Environment Programme's World Conservation Monitoring Centre. The South American country is home to the **tallest waterfall** – Salto Ángel (aka Angel Falls), with a total drop of 979 m (3,212 ft) – and Mount Roraima, the **highest mountain tabletop** at 2,810 m (9,219 ft). Both natural features are located in Canaima National Park, Venezuela's second-largest national park.

The French overseas territory of New Caledonia in the South Pacific had a slightly higher proportion of protected land – 54.4% – but is not a sovereign state.

### Largest vertical garden

Vegetation on the exterior of a building reduces its interior temperature and energy use, and also helps to combat urban air pollution. Cleanaway Company and Shine Green Energy Enterprise Co. (both CHN) planted a 2,593.77-m² (27,919-sq-ft) "green wall" in Kaohsiung, Taiwan, China, as verified on 29 Jun 2015.

In 2011, a series of green walls, up to 35 m (115 ft) high and totalling 5,324 m² (57,307 sq ft), were installed on several buildings belonging to Singapore's Institute of Technical Education. However, as this was across the façades of eight different blocks, it does not qualify for this record.

### Largest contiguous protected boreal forest

In May 2018, the government of Alberta, Canada, announced the creation of four new provincial parks – Kazan, Dillon River, Richardson and Birch Park – and the expansion of another, Birch Mountains Wildland. This gave protection to a stretch of boreal forest (aka taiga) spanning 67,700 km² (26,140 sq mi) – more than twice the size of Belgium. This cold-climate woodland is a haven for a range of wildlife.

### Whitest paint

Engineers at Purdue University in Indiana, USA, have developed an ultra-white paint with barium sulphate particles that is up to 98.1% reflective. Such sunlight-reflecting paints are a potential game-changer for cooling the planet and curtailing the use of energy-hungry air conditioners, particularly in cities. The scientists estimate that only 0.5–1% of Earth's surface (e.g., building roofs) would need to be coated in this paint to reverse global warming to date, as reported on 15 Apr 2021.

### First national park city

The UK's capital became the world's inaugural "National Park City" on 22 Jul 2019. This programme is a long-term vision that aims to make cities greener and healthier. London has a population of 9 million people and almost as many trees. Its varied habitats – ranging from parks, canals and woodlands to busy urban environments – provide a home to more than 15,000 species.

## Largest vertical farm

Opened in Nov 2016, a facility operated by AeroFarms (USA) in Newark, New Jersey, USA, can supply 2 million lb (907,000 kg) of greens to New Jersey and New York grocery stores each year. The farm grows 250 different types of vegetables and herbs, including kale (inset), rocket and mizuna, on trays stacked on 12-tier shelving units standing up to 30 ft (9.1 m) high. The site's aeroponic systems use 95% less water than field farming.

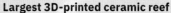

## First 3D-printed reef

In 2012, experts from Reef Arabia – a consortium comprising Sustainable Oceans International, DShape and 3D software specialist James Gardiner (AUS) – sank two 3D-printed reefs off the coast of Bahrain. Each weighs 1,100 lb (500 kg) and their non-toxic, sandstone-like material is designed to attract coral larvae and sea life. Pictured is one reef on its first day on the seafloor (left) and after several months (right).

## Largest 3D-printed ceramic reef

In Jul 2018, Alex Goad and Reef Design Lab (both AUS) installed an 8.7-m³ (307.2-cu-ft) reef on a coral nursery off Summer Island in the Maldives. It comprised a pyramidal lattice of 3D-printed units – designed by Goad – called MARS (Modular Artificial Reef Structures). The system was then seeded with coral fragments. While not a panacea to the problem of global reef degradation, such structures may help to replenish damaged coral and also offer shelter to other marine creatures (inset).

## Most environmentally friendly city

In the 2018 *Sustainable Cities Index* compiled by Arcadis, Stockholm was rated top in the "Planet" pillar, denoting environmental excellence. The Swedish capital was particularly praised for its "investment in sustainable infrastructure, low emissions and good air quality". Frankfurt, Germany, was in second place, followed by the Swiss city of Zurich, which had been No.1 in the previous survey.

## Largest landfill reclamation project

The former Fresh Kills Landfill was opened as a temporary waste site on Staten Island, New York City, in 1948. It was officially closed in 2001 when its trash mounds towered 70 m (230 ft) high in places – nearly twice the height of the Brooklyn Bridge! In 2008, work began on a 30-year project to transform the 890-ha (2,200-acre) dump into Freshkills Park. With sustainability front of mind, landscaping and replanting have already seen a resurgence of native flora and fauna.

When fully developed in the 2030s, Freshkills Park will be almost three times the size of New York's Central Park.

# Round-Up

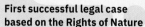

## Eco science at the top of the world

In 2019, a team of scientists and mountaineers scaled Everest (aka Sagarmāthā or Chomolungma) as part of the Perpetual Planet Expedition, funded by National Geographic and Rolex. It resulted in three records, comprising the **highest-altitude**…

**Weather station** (above): installed at "Balcony", a ridge situated 8,430 m (27,657 ft) above sea level (asl). It is the first-ever terrestrial weather station in the "death zone", which lies above 8,000 m (26,247 ft).

**Ice core** (below): 8,020 m (26,312 ft) asl, extracted from the South Col glacier. The complex operation involved a team of more than 30 scientists and Sherpas using a specially modified drill system.

**Microplastic on land**: several polymer fibres – most likely from clothing or tents – found at 8,440 m (27,690 ft) asl. The density was 12 fibres per litre of snow.

## First successful legal case based on the Rights of Nature

Activists representing the Vilcabamba River in Ecuador cited Article 71 of the country's constitution to raise a case against the Provincial Government of Loja and stop a road-building project. On 30 Mar 2011, the court ruled in favour of the river.

## Largest clean-up on Everest

Between 14 Apr and 29 May 2019, garbage weighing 10,386 kg (22,897 lb) – equivalent to about six mid-sized cars – was collected off the world's **highest mountain**. Organized by the Nepalese government, 12 Sherpas were engaged to gather the trash, which was mostly packaging, broken glass and thermal-insulation linings.

## Most participants in an underwater clean-up in 12 hours

On 15 Aug 2020, Discovery Taiwan (CHN) recruited 588 aquatic litter-pickers to collect marine waste in the waters off Keelung City, Taiwan, China.

## Smallest ecological footprint (per capita)

Environmental think-tank Global Footprint Network compares humanity's demand for our planet's natural resources with its capacity for regeneration. They estimate that current resource use is akin to 1.6 Earths. They can gauge a single country's impact via a metric known as "global hectares" – the area of biologically productive land needed to make what its population consumes and absorb the waste generated. Two countries share the smallest footprint: East Timor (aka Timor Leste) in south-east Asia and Eritrea in East Africa, each using 0.5 global hectares per citizen.

Qatar in the Middle East has the **largest ecological footprint per capita**, with each citizen utilizing 14.4 global hectares.

## Most pledges for an environmental sustainability campaign

Turkey's Ministry of Agriculture and Forestry inspired 789,522 people to commit to reduce food wastage, as verified on 11 Mar 2021.

### POLAR PROTEST: ON STRIKE IN ANTARCTICA

As part of the Global Climate Strike in Sep 2019 (see p.17), Germany's Benjamin Eberhardt (in pale green jacket above) and a few colleagues staged the most southerly climate protest at the South Pole (90°S).

**Why were you in Antarctica?**
As experiments operator, I was responsible for the continuous operation of the IceCube neutrino telescope from Oct 2018 to Nov 2019. As a "winterover", I was part of a crew of 42 who lived and worked at the South Pole in complete isolation during the long Antarctic winter.

**How did the strike come about?**
It was fascinating watching the development of protests worldwide from our remote outpost. One day, we heard that every continent was participating [in the Global Climate Strike] except Antarctica. People from multiple stations then got involved, so support was pretty international in the end.

## Highest EPI score (country)

The Environmental Performance Index (EPI) – produced by the USA's Yale and Columbia universities since 2002 – rates countries on issues such as air quality, sanitation, agriculture and biodiversity. In 2020, Denmark ranked top with an overall score of 82.5, putting it ahead of Luxembourg (82.3) and Switzerland (81.5).

The **lowest EPI score** in 2020's rankings was 22.6, for Liberia in West Africa.

## First zero-emission polar research station

Owned by the Belgian government and inaugurated on 15 Feb 2009, the Princess Elisabeth Base in Queen Maud Land, Antarctica, has all its energy needs met by renewable sources. This includes 380 m² (4,090 sq ft) of photovoltaic solar panels, 22 m² (237 sq ft) of thermal solar panels and nine wind turbines. It was built and is operated by the International Polar Foundation.

### What were conditions like?

It was about sunrise, which only happens once per year at the South Pole, and the weather was nice. So the temperatures outside were around -60°C (-76°F). This cold is somewhat challenging for photography – and it can be a bit painful when the wind blows – but we made it work.

### Do you think the world is starting to wake up to climate change?

Absolutely. It's great to hear so many calls to listen to the science. The fundamental mechanisms of anthropogenic climate change have been well understood for decades. So I think now it's all about awareness and convincing everyone that science enables us to tackle the crisis, while we still have a slight head start.

### ▶ Largest drinking-straw sculpture (supported)

Artist Von Wong (CAN) and his team created *The Parting of the Plastic Sea* to highlight the surge of single-use plastic in the oceans. The 3.3-m-tall (10-ft 9-in) piece was unveiled on 22 Jan 2019 in Ho Chi Minh City, Vietnam. Wong worked with Zero Waste Saigon (VNM), using 168,037 straws gathered by clean-up groups and Starbucks stores from across Vietnam.

### Youngest *TIME* magazine Person of the Year

Climate activist Greta Thunberg (SWE, b. 3 Jan 2003) was chosen as 2019's most influential person by *TIME*. She was 16 years 354 days old on the release of their year-end issue. That year, Thunberg was instrumental in rallying support for the Global Climate Strike (see p.17), which saw millions of people all over the planet (see Q&A left) demand more action on climate change.

### Most eWaste produced in one year

Electronic waste (eWaste) is unwanted electrical appliances with a battery or plug, e.g., computers, TVs and phones. Because such items are hard to recycle, they are a growing cause for concern. *Global E-waste Monitor 2020* estimated that 53.6 million tonnes (59 million tons) of eWaste were thrown away globally in 2019.

### Greatest distance sampled by a marine survey

The Continuous Plankton Recorder (CPR) Survey is one of the longest-running marine science projects. Established in 1931, it was originally intended to help assess herring numbers, but its scope today is far wider. Overseen by the Marine Biological Association based in Plymouth, Devon, UK, the CPR Survey uses towed marine samplers to collect plankton, providing valuable insights into issues such as climate change, marine litter (e.g., microplastic) and ocean acidification. By 31 Dec 2020, the project had studied 7,063,622 nautical mi (13 million km; 8.1 million mi) of ocean – equivalent to 326 circumnavigations of Earth – over its nine-decade history.

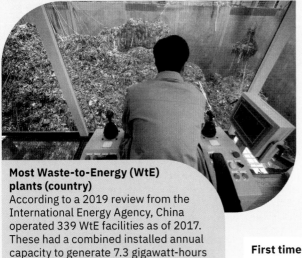

### Most Waste-to-Energy (WtE) plants (country)

According to a 2019 review from the International Energy Agency, China operated 339 WtE facilities as of 2017. These had a combined installed annual capacity to generate 7.3 gigawatt-hours of electricity by incinerating 100 million tonnes (110 million tons) of rubbish. China's WtE plant tally was set to increase to 400 by 2020.

### First time for human-made mass to exceed living biomass

Environmental scientists at the Weizmann Institute of Science (ISR) averred that the total weight of artificial materials such as concrete, asphalt and metal – dubbed "anthropogenic mass", meaning "born of man" or "human-made" – was set to outweigh living things (i.e., plants and animals). They estimated that artificial matter would surpass Earth's 1.1 trillion tonnes (1.2 trillion tons) of biomass by the end of 2020.

Pictured is Hong Kong in China, the city with the most skyscrapers: 2,580 buildings taller than 100 m (328 ft) as of 2019.

# Mya-Rose Craig

**VITAL STATISTICS**
**Name:** Mya-Rose Craig (Birdgirl)
**Born:** 7 May 2002
**Birthplace:** Bristol, UK
**Occupation:** Ornithologist, activist, speaker, blogger
**Honours & positions:** Honorary Doctorate of Science; founder & president of Black2Nature; patron of The Burns Price Foundation
**Bird species observed in wild:** 5,410 (as of 1 Apr 2021)

**B**irds have always been a passion for Dr Mya-Rose Craig (UK), aka Birdgirl. By 13, she had visited all seven continents in **her quest to see every single avian species; by 17, with over 5,000 species logged, she was halfway to realizing that goal.**

Her love of the outdoors and conviction that everyone should be able to enjoy its benefits have compelled Mya-Rose to take action. She was aged just 14 when she set up Black2Nature, a charity seeking greater equality in naturalism. She works closely with visible minority ethnic (VME) communities, who often have less access to the countryside. This involves hands-on initiatives such as organizing nature camps for city kids, but also providing a forum to address the root causes behind the lack of VME representation in this sector.

Passionate about preserving the planet for future generations, Mya-Rose has lent her voice to environmental causes too. This culminated on 20 Sep 2020 with a demonstration on a fragment of sea-ice (right). Working with Greenpeace, she voyaged deep into the Arctic to stage the **most northerly climate protest**, at 82.4°N. In a place so hard hit by climate change – 2020's sea-ice levels were the second-lowest on record (see p.16) – her message could not have been more stark.

**YOUTH STRIKE FOR CLIMATE**

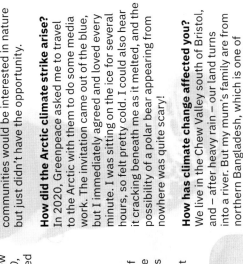

High on Mya-Rose's birdwatching wishlist is a trip to Papua New Guinea to see birds-of-paradise.

**1.** Mya-Rose has travelled extensively for birding. In fact, she is the **youngest person to birdwatch on every continent** – aged 13 years 234 days when she stepped on to Brown Bluff in Antarctica (her final continent) on 27 Dec 2015. On that trip, she saw snow petrels, Antarctic shags and emperor penguins (the **largest penguins**), to name a few species.

**2.** In recognition of her advocacy for greater equity and diversity in conservation, the University of Bristol awarded Mya-Rose an honorary Doctorate of Science in early 2020. Aged 17 at the time, she is thought to be the youngest person in the UK to receive this accolade. "Being awarded with an honorary doctorate was unbelievable. When I saw the email, I thought it was a hoax from my friends!" she confided to us.

**3.** In Feb 2015, Mya-Rose took part in a survey of the critically endangered spoon-billed sandpiper in Bangladesh. On the same trip, she delivered a talk about conservation in the capital, Dhaka.

**4.** Before embarking on her epic climate protest in the Arctic, Mya-Rose took part in a number of rallies closer to home. This included the Bristol Youth Strike 4 Climate march in Feb 2020 that was attended by Greta Thunberg (right); Mya-Rose was one of the speakers at the event.

### What drove you to start a blog?
When I was 11 years old, my parents started showing me a few blogs that had photos of birds. I had already spent quite a bit of time bird-watching abroad by then, so initially I wanted to just write about birds and birding. I had come up with the name "Birdgirl" when I was eight: I was going birding in Ecuador and needed an email address. It just stuck after that!

### Who inspired you growing up?
I think it's really important to have people who look like you to act as role models. My older sister, Ayesha, was a passionate birder and my first role model. I also grew up watching Steve Backshall's *Deadly 60*, which made me loving animals normal. I used to watch those TV shows on repeat and wanted to be Backshall! As a teenager, I was inspired by Liz Bonnin, who is a fantastic naturalist and TV presenter.

### Why did you set up Black2Nature?
When I was 13, I decided to arrange a weekend camp for young birders. Lots of people signed up, but they were all white boys – mostly from the countryside. This is when I had my lightbulb moment: there were almost no VME people out in nature. I worked hard to find five VME boys to come and got them all engaged, which made me realize that VME communities would be interested in nature but just didn't have the opportunity.

### How did the Arctic climate strike arise?
In 2020, Greenpeace asked me to travel to the Arctic with them to do some media work. The invitation came out of the blue, but I immediately agreed and loved every minute. I was sitting on the ice for several hours, so felt pretty cold. I could also hear it cracking beneath me as it melted, and the possibility of a polar bear appearing from nowhere was quite scary!

### How has climate change affected you?
We live in the Chew Valley south of Bristol, and – after heavy rain – our land turns into a river. But my mum's family are from northern Bangladesh, which is one of the countries most impacted by climate change. In 2018, there were unseasonal flash floods in my grandfather's village, which swept away the crops, leaving no rice to plant for the next harvest. There are already 4 million climate refugees in [the capital city] Dhaka.

Find out more about Mya-Rose in the Hall of Fame section at www. guinnessworldrecords.com/2022

# Australia Zoo

**Location:** Steve Irwin Way, Beerwah, Queensland, Australia

**Established:** 1970 (as Beerwah Reptile and Fauna Park)

**Key exhibits:** Mount Franklin Crocoseum, Tiger Temple, Elephantasia, Africa

**Area:** 750 acres (300 ha)

**Animals:** >1,200

**Staff:** >400

**Visitors:** 12 million (since 2001)

This wildlife wonderland is a lasting tribute to the vision of conservationist Steve Irwin and his wife, Terri. It's still a family affair today, despite Steve's tragic death in 2006, with Terri now ably assisted by their children, Robert and Bindi, and son-in-law Chandler (all pictured below left).

The story began in 1970, with Steve working for his parents at the 2-acre (0.8-ha) Beerwah Reptile and Fauna Park, where his passion for animal welfare began. The park has now blossomed into a 750-acre facility with hundreds of staff. It boasts seven habitat-specific wildlife exhibits, including the ever-popular Crocoseum (see below). "Our visitors often refer to Australia Zoo as a resort for wildlife," explains Terri. "We're also the most interactive zoo, giving our animals the enrichment of meeting our guests."

Steve made his name with the *Crocodile Hunter* TV series and crocs remain a focus for the zoo. "We encourage people to remember that conservation is not only about the cute and cuddly creatures, but also animals like crocodilians, snakes and sharks," cautions Bindi. Robert adds that Australia Zoo's crocodile research project "is making a huge difference in the protection of these beautiful modern-day dinosaurs".

The zoo's influence extends far beyond Beerwah. The fly-on-the-wall TV show *Crikey! It's the Irwins* offers a global audience a glimpse behind the scenes of life at the zoo. Moreover, they are committed to helping wild animals too. The family's Wildlife Warriors charity helps endangered species all over the planet, from black rhinos in East Africa to tigers in Sumatra, as well as multiple conservation projects closer to home. Here, we celebrate some of the record-breaking residents you can discover at Australia Zoo.

## Red kangaroo

Males of this iconic Aussie species – *Macropus (=Osphranter) rufus* – can stand as tall as a man, making it not only the country's largest mammal but also today's **largest marsupial**. Its muscular tail helps it to balance and propel itself as it hops. Kangaroos are one of just two known animals that can only move in a forward motion; the other is fellow native the emu (*Dromaius novaehollandiae*).

*Rudder-like tail*

*Huge feet for extra spring*

*Clawed paws*

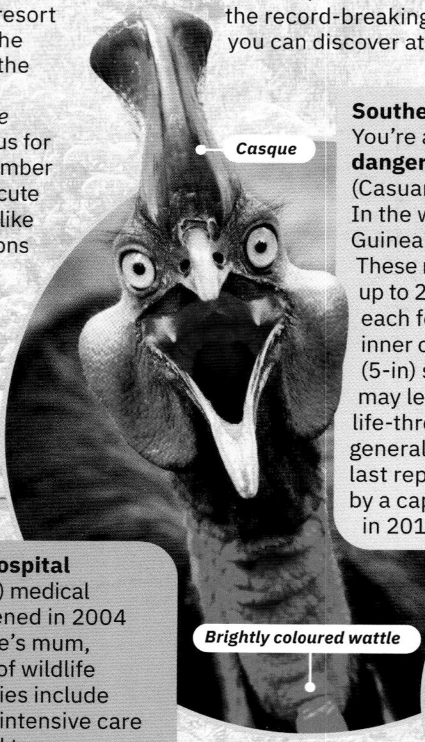

## Southern cassowary

You're able to safely see the **most dangerous birds** – cassowaries (Casuariidae) – at Australia Zoo. In the wild, they are native to New Guinea, Indonesia and Australia. These relatives of ostriches reach up to 2 m (6 ft 6 in) tall and on each foot have three toes, the inner one sporting a 12-cm-long (5-in) spike! If spooked, they may leap and kick, able to cause life-threatening injuries, but they generally try to avoid people. The last reported human fatality was by a captive bird in Florida in 2019.

*Casque*

*Toe spikes*

*Bristly feathers*

*Brightly coloured wattle*

## Australia Zoo Wildlife Hospital

A 1,300-m² (14,000-sq-ft) medical centre next to the zoo opened in 2004 and is dedicated to Steve's mum, Lyn, a fervent advocate of wildlife conservation. Its facilities include operating theatres and intensive care units. The hospital helped to save many animals, including koalas, during the bushfires of 2019–20, and has treated in excess of 100,000 patients.

## Forest

The zoo's African savannah exhibit is home to the **tallest giraffe in captivity**: Forest, who measured 5.7 m (18 ft 8 in) to the top of the ossicones (the bony stubs on top of his head) on 4 Dec 2019. In the wild, giraffes (*Giraffa camelopardalis*) are categorized as Vulnerable by the IUCN. Forest plays a key part in the zoo's breeding programme, fathering 13 calves since arriving here from New Zealand in 2009.

Grey-brown skin for camouflage

Large dewlap

Bony pseudohorn

## Rhino

The zoo is also home to the **oldest rhino iguana in captivity**. Rhino, as he's known, was born at Sydney's Taronga Zoo on 23 Feb 1980. He moved to Australia Zoo in 1993 and 2021 will see in his 41st birthday. Rhino iguanas (*Cyclura cornuta*) are named after the horn-like protrusion on their snout.

Want to hear more from the Irwins? Check out our exclusive Q&A at www.guinnessworldrecords.com/2022

Venom glands under lower teeth

Thick tail for storing fat

Five clawed toes

Bead-like scales

Bindi currently holds the record for the **most Instagram followers for a TV naturalist**: 4,217,080, as of 14 Jan 2021.

## Crocoseum

Here, Bindi is feeding a saltwater crocodile (*Crocodylus porosus*) in the zoo's Mount Franklin Crocoseum. This species is today's **largest crocodilian** and **heaviest reptile**: adult males average 4.9 m (16 ft) long, but can reach 7 m (22 ft 11 in) and weigh 1,200 kg (2,645 lb). Those formidable jaws inflict the **strongest crocodilian bite**: 11,216 N (2,521 lbf), similar to being crushed by a medium-sized car!

## Gila monster

Native to desert regions on the US-Mexico border, the Gila monster (*Heloderma suspectum*) is the **most venomous lizard**. Animal toxicity is measured using an $LD_{50}$ score (lethal dose, 50%), which is the amount of toxin required to be fatal in half of test subjects. For Gila monsters, as little as 0.4 mg/kg of venom can be lethal to mice, which means around 0.5 ml (less than one-tenth of a teaspoon) could kill a human. Luckily, these lizards are shy and unlikely to ever inject that much venom in one bite.

# Natural World

## Greatest deforestation by area

Global Forest Watch estimates that Brazil lost a cumulative area of around 24.5 million ha (60.5 million acres) of primary forest between 2002 and 2019. This represents 7.1% of the country's total in 2001. Recent years have seen an increase in logging and aggressive slash-and-burn policies, whereby farmers use fire to clear areas of rainforest for agricultural use (inset). This practice can often spark much larger wildfire outbreaks, such as those that ravaged Brazil in 2020.

One of the worst-hit regions is the Amazon – the **largest tropical rainforest** – around 60% of which falls within Brazil's borders. In total, the Amazon covers approximately 6.24 million km² (2.4 million sq mi) and hosts more than 10% of all global species of flora and fauna. The Amazon's trees absorb millions of tonnes of harmful greenhouse gases every year; however, these are released back into the atmosphere when burned. A decade-long study by Brazil's National Institute for Space Research, published in 2020, suggested that around one-fifth of the Amazon is now a "carbon source" rather than a "carbon sink".

Animals endangered by Amazonian deforestation include the giant otter and bald uakari monkey.

## CONTENTS

# Eco-Engineers

Clive Jones, John Lawton and Moshe Shachak coined the term "ecosystem engineer" to describe an organism that alters environments to create, modify or maintain habitats. There are two types. *Allogenic* engineers build physical structures, e.g., beaver dams, with found materials; *autogenic* engineers embody the habitat, e.g., coral reefs. Humans are prolific allogenic engineers, but here "animal" is taken to mean "non-human".

Surface

Horn

Head first

Exit tunnel

Bulb

### Loudest animal-made amplifier
Distributed throughout Eurasia, male European mole crickets (*Gryllotalpa vineae*) dig burrows with two horn-shaped openings that act like stereo speakers to attract mates. Once inside, the cricket rubs its forewings together to produce a sound; this is amplified up to 115 dB at the horns on the surface – a sound level equivalent to a lawnmower. Their chirrups can be heard as far away as 600 m (1,970 ft).

### Greatest organic wave protection
The physical structure of a coral reef is largely provided by stony corals – calcium carbonate skeletons made by colonies of animal polyps. Such reefs, which can take hundreds of years to form, attenuate about 97% of incoming wave energy, providing protection to some 100 million people living in coastal zones around the globe.

### Largest animal-made fishing nets
Certain pods of humpback whales (*Megaptera novaeangliae*) have developed an ingenious way to catch their food. Working in a group, they circle a school of fish or krill and blow bubbles to form a temporary "net", up to 30 m (100 ft) across. At a given signal, the whales break formation and swim into the corraled prey to gorge!

### Earliest planetary eco-engineering
The first cyanobacteria (photosynthetic microbes) that emitted oxygen as a waste product emerged *c.* 2.4 billion years ago. Eventually, by about 700 million years ago (MYA), this led to the oxygenation of Earth, allowing for other oxygen-producing species to evolve. This transformed all geochemical and atmospheric chemical processes on our planet. Microbes, along with primitive plants, were responsible for the **earliest terrestrial eco-engineering**, some 400–500 MYA. Plants continue to shape our planet to this day via processes such as soil stabilization and erosion.

### Most influential geomorphic agent
Humans (*Homo sapiens*) now shift around 10 times more rock/sediment on Earth's surface via construction and agriculture than *all* natural geological processes combined. This includes the impact of rivers, glaciers, slope erosion, wave action, wind and more. Over the past 0.5 billion years, natural physical and chemical processes are estimated to have lowered land surfaces by a few tens of metres per million years. In contrast, current human activity is shifting so much material – i.e., 40–45 gigatonnes per year – that it could bring down all ice-free continental land by 360 m (1,180 ft) in the same period.

### Largest animal bioturbator
Bioturbation is the reworking of sediment or soil by a life-form – an activity that provides food and shelter for countless species. By size, the biggest bioturbator is the grey whale (*Eschrichtius robustus*), measuring up to 15 m (49 ft) long and 41 tonnes (45 tons). Unlike other filter-feeding whales, which gulp their food in open water, greys favour bottom-dwelling shrimp. To capture this prey, they gouge out huge "feeding pits", up to 20 m (65 ft) long, in the seabed with their tongues. One study calculated that in a single summer (May–Oct), these cetaceans worked over 5.7% of the seafloor of the entire Bering Sea (*c.* 22,000 km²; 8,500 sq mi). It helps to explain their nickname: "benthic bulldozers"!

### Largest structures built by land animals
Arguably nature's most iconic eco-engineers are the beavers (*Castor*) of North America and Eurasia. Using mud, wood, vegetation and stones, they create dams to flood an area, then build lodges within the relative safety of the resulting ponds. The **longest beaver dam** – located in Wood Buffalo National Park in Alberta, Canada – is 850 m (2,788 ft), twice the length of the Hoover Dam.

**Busy beavers: key roles as wetland engineers**
• Mitigate against floods
• Recharge groundwater
• Improve water filtration
• Form drinking ponds for livestock and wildlife
• Create habitat for other species (e.g., up to 33% more plant diversity)

Beavers are also firefighters. Up to three times more vegetation is burnt by wildfires in wetlands without beaver dams.

## Most mud "air-freighted" by an animal

Cliff and cave swallows (*Petrochelidon pyrrhonota* and *P. fulva*) collect mud one beak-full at a time to make their communal abodes; one pair's nest requires ~1,000 round trips to build. A study in Texas, USA, estimated that swallows from 16 colonies transported 560 kg (1,235 lb) of sediment in a single summer season. Nesting sites grow over time; the biggest colony comprised 953.6 kg (2,102 lb) of dried mud.

**100%**

*Most worker termites are only 1 cm (0.4 in) long*

## Most soil/leaf litter raked by a land animal

According to a 2020 paper, the superb lyrebird (*Menura novaehollandiae*) radically reshapes forests in south-east Australia. Over a year, while hunting for food such as worms, the birds displace 155 tonnes (171 tons) of earth and leaf litter per hectare. With only one bird per 2.3 ha (5.7 acres), a single lyrebird might move 11 medium-size dumper trucks' worth of material per annum.

## Largest terrestrial eco-engineer

Weighing up to 7 tonnes (7.7 tons), African elephants (*Loxodonta africana*) are the **largest terrestrial animals** alive today. They are also the biggest "landscape gardeners". Their activities include knocking down trees (which prevents the savannah reverting to forest), digging up soil and silt (creating and maintaining waterholes), and forging kilometres of trails, which are then used by many species.

## Most rock eaten by a land animal

Two species of snail, *Euchondrus albulus* and *E. desertorum*, use a rasp-like tongue to crunch through limestone and reach lichen growing within. A study conducted in the Negev Desert in Israel, published in 1987, found that a single snail eats ~5 g (~0.17 oz) of rock per year. Collectively, they can excrete soil at an annual rate of 1.1 tonnes (1.2 tons) per hectare – comparable to the amount blown in as dust by the wind. Without these snails' contribution, the desert would be far less fertile.

## Tallest animal structures

Beyond humans, the loftiest abodes are built by termites (order Isoptera). Their mounds are made from soil, plant matter, saliva and faeces. Some of the tallest examples, reaching 8 m (26 ft), are those of cathedral termites (*Nasutitermes triodiae*) in Australia. Termites' architectural prowess does not only extend above the ground. The **largest underground animal city** was made by *Syntermes dirus* termites in Brazil, excavating 10 km³ (2.4 cu mi) of soil over ~4,000 years. In volume, that equates to around 4,000 Great Pyramids of Giza in Egypt.

*The internal design of termite mounds keeps them cool in the day and warm at night – the original air conditioning!*

## Most self-destructive eco-engineer

In 1890, some 250,000 pairs of Atlantic puffins (*Fratercula arctica*) bred on Grassholm, a 9-ha (22-acre) island off the coast of Wales, UK. By 1940, there were just 25 breeding pairs; today, few if any remain. Extensive burrowing to build their nests over 50 years stripped the grassy islet back to bare rock, ensuring their self-inflicted eviction.

*Spanning 230,000 km² (88,800 sq mi), the termite "megacity" in Brazil is larger than the island of Great Britain and visible from space!*

# Extremophiles

On these pages, we explore a range of remarkable life forms that can survive in the most inhospitable conditions. Some thrive in extremes of heat or cold that would destroy other organisms. Others live at dizzying, oxygen-depleted altitudes or in habitats – such as the ocean floor – that receive no sunlight and endure crushing pressure. Perhaps the ultimate extremophile is the tiny tardigrade, which can lay claim to many superpowers. Find out more below.

### First seeds to germinate on the Moon
On 3 Jan 2019, China's *Chang'e-4* lander made the **first landing on the far side of the Moon**. Its cargo included some cotton seeds (genus *Gossypium*), part of an on-board biosphere experiment to help prepare for eventual human lunar settlements. They sprouted four days later but died by 13 Jan, having succumbed to temperatures that plunged to -52°C (-61.6°F) during the lunar night-time.

### Least energy used by an organism
A paper published in *Science Advances* on 5 Aug 2020 revealed that certain microbes (particularly bacteria carrying out sulphate reduction and methane production) can survive in sediment beneath the seafloor on less than 1 zeptowatt of power, or $1 \times 10^{-21}$ watts. That's 50 billion billion

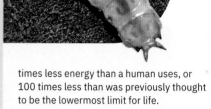

**100%**

### Most cold-tolerant insect
The red flat bark beetle (*Cucujus clavipes puniceus*, above) is native to Alaska, USA. In the wild, its larvae (pictured right, not to scale) have been seen to remain unfrozen at -80°C (-112°F), and under lab conditions withstood temperatures as low as -150°C (-238°F). To do so, they dehydrate, produce anti-freeze proteins and increase internal glycerol concentration so that their body fluids effectively turn into a viscous "glass".

times less energy than a human uses, or 100 times less than was previously thought to be the lowermost limit for life.

### Most heat-tolerant canid
Native to North Africa's Sahara Desert, the fennec fox (*Vulpes zerda*) can survive temperatures of over 38°C (100°F). In such conditions, it dissipates excess body heat by panting at up to 690 breaths per minute after chasing prey (as opposed to 23 breaths per minute at rest). The fennec is so acclimatized to high temperatures that it begins to shiver if the external temperature falls below 20°C (68°F). Its body temperature can rise to 40.9°C (105.6°F) before it begins to sweat, reducing water loss. At just 40 cm (1 ft 4 in) long, minus the tail, this species is also the **smallest fox**.

### Most salt-tolerant insect
The larvae of the brine fly (*Ephydrella marshalli*) inhabit saltwater lagoons. Under laboratory conditions they are capable of withstanding salinities of up to 5,848 mOsm (milliosmoles) per litre – that's almost five times saltier than typical sea water.

### Most methane-resistant animal
The methane ice worm (*Hesiocaeca methanicola*) is native to the Gulf of Mexico. It lives in huge numbers in mounds of methane clathrate – a crystalline hydrocarbon known as "methane ice" – some 700–800 m (2,300–2,600 ft) down on the seafloor. *H. methanicola* is the only animal known to survive in this methane-rich habitat, where it subsists on methanotrophic (methane-oxidizing) bacteria.

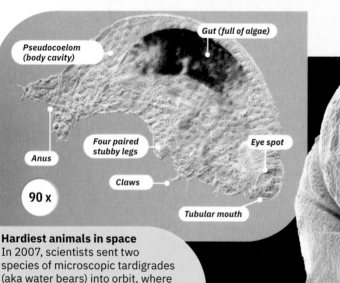

Pseudocoelom (body cavity)

Gut (full of algae)

Four paired stubby legs

Eye spot

Anus

Claws

Tubular mouth

**90 x**

### Hardiest animals in space
In 2007, scientists sent two species of microscopic tardigrades (aka water bears) into orbit, where they faced the airless vacuum of space and radiation levels that could prove fatal to a human. On their return to Earth, one-third were still alive.
The tardigrade is also the **most heat-tolerant animal**, enduring temperatures above 150°C (302°F). It can endure severe cold too: two specimens were revived after being frozen from Nov 1983 to Mar 2014 (the **longest time frozen in ice by a tardigrade**).

In Oct 2020, a new tardigrade was revealed. Its pigments allow it to endure levels of UV light that prove fatal even to other tardigrades.

## Most heat-tolerant bird

The gull-related African skimmer (*Rynchops flavirostris*) is indigenous to bodies of water and marshes in sub-Saharan Africa. On some breeding beaches, such as the shores of Lake Turkana in Kenya, the ground surface temperature can reach 60°C (140°F). To keep its eggs and chicks cool, when returning to the nest the skimmer swoops and lowers its feet to splash water on to its belly.

## Most cold-tolerant canid

Native to the Arctic regions of Europe, Asia and North America, the Arctic fox (*Vulpes lagopus*) can withstand environmental temperatures as low as -70°C (-94°F). It combats the cold by means of an extra-dense, multi-layered fur, and short limbs and muzzle to minimize body-heat loss; it can also reduce blood flow into its feet to prevent frostbite.

## Highest-migrating butterfly

A flock of small tortoiseshell butterflies (*Aglais urticae*) was observed flying over the saddle of the Zemu Glacier in Sikkim, an Indian state in the eastern Himalayas, at an altitude of 19,000 ft (5,800 m). The event was documented by the British entomologist C B Williams in a book published in 1958.

## Highest-living mammal

In Feb 2020, a yellow-rumped leaf-eared mouse (*Phyllotis xanthopygus rupestris*) was collected at 6,739 m (22,110 ft) above sea level on the summit of Volcán Llullaillaco on the Chile-Argentina border. The field study, detailed in a paper published on 16 Jul 2020, followed sightings of *Phyllotis* mice on the volcano seven years before, at a then-record altitude of 6,205 m (20,358 ft). Llullaillaco is the world's second-highest active volcano, after the 6,893-m (22,615-ft) Ojos del Salado in the same range.

## Longest duration without food for a fish

The West African lungfish (*Protopterus annectens*) can survive for four years (and possibly up to five) without food during periods of severe drought. To do so, it buries itself in the mud at the bottom of rivers or lakes, creating a mucous cocoon around itself, and entering a state of suspended animation called aestivation. It does not eat, drink or excrete until the rains come again, refilling the dried-out rivers and lakes, at which point it breaks out of its cocoon.

## Highest-living bird

The alpine chough (*Pyrrhocorax graculus*) is a species of crow native to lofty inland cliffs and mountain pastures in Spain and eastward as far as central Asia. It lives and breeds at altitudes of up to 6,500 m (21,325 ft). Some specimens have been seen scavenging as high as 8,235 m (27,018 ft).

## Deepest-living...

**Eel**: a specimen of *Ilyophis robinsae*, a type of cut-throat eel, was photographed 6,068 m (19,908 ft) down in the Kermadec Trench off New Zealand on 14 May 2014.
**Fish**: a Mariana snailfish (*Pseudoliparis swirei*) was collected at a depth of 7,966 m (26,135 ft) on 23 Nov 2014. It seems to be endemic to the Mariana Trench in the Pacific Ocean, the location of the Challenger Deep, Earth's **deepest point**. A fish from the same family (Liparidae) dubbed the "ethereal snailfish" was filmed at 8,143 m (26,716 ft), also in the Mariana Trench in 2014.

## HIGH LIFE vs LOW LIFE

**6,700 m (21,980 ft)**
Highest spider
Himalayan jumping spider (*Euophrys omnisuperstes*)

**5,800 m (19,030 ft)**
Highest mammalian predators
Snow leopard (*Panthera uncia*) and puma (*Puma concolor*)

**5,200 m (17,060 ft)**
Highest fish
Tibetan stone loach (*Triplophysa stolickai*)

**4,900 m (16,080 ft)**
Highest snake
Himalayan pit viper (*Gloydius himalayanus*)

**4,700 m (15,420 ft)**
Highest primate
Yunnan snub-nosed monkey (*Rhinopithecus bieti*)

**-6,957 m (-22,830 ft)**
Deepest octopus
Dumbo octopus (*Grimpoteuthis*)

**-7,584 m (-24,880 ft)**
Deepest starfish
*Porcellanaster ivanovi*

**-7,703 m (-25,270 ft)**
Deepest decapod
Benthesicymid prawn (*Benthesicymus crenatus*)

**-8,840 m (-29,000 ft)**
Deepest sponge
Cladorhizidae

**-9,066 m (-29,740 ft)**
Deepest hydrozoan
Rhopalonematid trachymedusa (*Crossota*)

Not to scale

# DINOSAURS

They may have gone extinct 66 million years ago (MYA), but dinos continue to capture our imagination. To celebrate these *roar*-some reptiles, we've teamed up with augmented-reality (AR) pros at Peapodicity to reanimate a few superlative species. Grab your phone/tablet and follow these steps:

- Download *AugmentifyIt®* for free from the App Store (iOS), Google Play (Android) or Amazon Appstore.

- Open the app, then hold the device's camera over an AR trigger like this >>>

- After a few seconds, you'll see the dinosaur stomp out of the page in all its 3D glory. Don't forget to turn on the sound too!

- For more information, check out **augmentifyit.com**, where you can also buy AR quiz cards featuring more prehistoric beasts (below).

## Spinosaurus
- **Lived: 95–70 MYA**

Aka "spine lizard" in reference to its prominent dorsal "sail". About 56 ft (17 m) long and weighed 7.5–10 tons (7–9 tonnes), making it the **largest carnivorous dinosaur** – some 14 ft (4 m) longer than the T. rex (see opposite)! Largest-ever land-based predator? Possibly. Most likely led a semi-aquatic lifestyle... Seems to be adept at catching fish and roamed rivers/shores of northern Africa, where the Sahara desert now lies.

## Triceratops
- **Lived: 68–66 MYA**

"Three-horned face" behemoth. **Longest dinosaur horns**, up to 4 ft (1.2 m) – shares record with Torosaurus and Coahuilaceratops. Still debate over horns' purpose. (Courtship? Combat?) All three part of Ceratopsia group. Triceratops horridus was the **heaviest ceratopsian**, at >15.4 tons (>14 tonnes) – 3x heavier than a bull African bush elephant!

Bony "frill" – to attract mates? Protect neck? Or for heat regulation?

## AUGMENTIFY IT®

### AUGMENTED REALITY BRINGS DINOSAURS BACK TO LIFE!

GWR asked Peapodicity co-founders Brett Haase and Ahrani Logan (below) about *AugmentifyIt®* and creating their own Jurassic pARk...

**So what exactly is *AugmentifyIt®*?**
It's about playing to learn: using augmented reality (AR) to make fun, memorable learning experiences by mixing the physical and digital worlds.

**How do you create an AR dinosaur?**
It requires a *lot* of research. And we don't really know their true colours or what sounds they made, so there has to be a lot of educated guesswork. The size of the dinosaurs for an AR experience also has to be factored in. They have to fit on the screen for the reader to view and not be so big that you lose sight of the AR target.

**Which was the most difficult dinosaur to "augmentify"?**
The *Diplodocus* was a bit tricky, because of the sheer length of it.

**Why do you think dinosaurs are timelessly popular?**
Because they're not like anything we know in the world right now. They're big, a bit scary, and they're the closest thing we have to dragons!

**What would you tip to be the "next big thing" in AR?**
It will most likely be AR glasses. We keep hearing about them, but we reckon there's a consumer-level product around the corner.

## Tyrannosaurus rex
• **Lived: 68–66 MYA**

Ferocious carnivorous dino. "King of the tyrant lizards" and **land animal with the strongest bite**. Maximum force generated (at back teeth) estimated to have reached 57,000 N (12,800 lbf) – three times more powerful than a lion's bite. Mouth lined with around 60 teeth, each c. 8 in (20 cm) long – many specialized for crunching through bone. First T. rex remains found in 1902 by fossil hunter Barnum Brown.

Around 39 ft (12 m) long

Top speed: 12 mph (19 km/h)?

## Ankylosaurus
• **Lived: 70–65 MYA**

Rugged herbivore. Dubbed "stiff lizard", as many of its bones were fused together. **Largest armoured dinosaur,** at up to 35 ft (10.7 m) long – 3x longer than a Ford Model T car. Very wide too – c. 8 ft (2.4 m). Thick, bony plates embedded in the skin, with double row of spikes along its back. Most distinguishing feature: bony clubbed tail. Evidence points to it being a self-defensive weapon, though unclear how it worked – possibly low sweeping motion into attacker's shins? Ouch!

Walnut-sized brain

## Stegosaurus
• **Lived: 155–145 MYA**

Plant-eater with formidable spiked tail. Known as "roof lizard", as palaeontologist who named it initially thought plates on its back lay flat, like roof tiles. Grew to 30 ft (9 m) long, but had only a 2.5-oz (70-g) brain – 0.002% of its average 3.6-ton (3.2-tonne) body weight – making it the **smallest-brained dinosaur.**

26-ft-long (8-m) neck

## Diplodocus
• **Lived: 155–145 MYA**

"Double-beamed" leviathan (a reference to paired chevron bones on underside of tail). Had **longest dinosaur tail,** at up to 43–45 ft (13–14 m) – around half the length of its entire body! Long neck gave it access to both high and low vegetation. Speculation that Diplodocus used its titanic tail as a whip-like weapon. Could it have moved fast enough to create a sonic boom?! Hmm, further research needed...

GUINNESS WORLD RECORDS®

# Ocean SOS

## Largest accidental marine oil spill

Around 779 million litres (205 million gal) of crude oil spilled into the Gulf of Mexico following an explosion onboard the *Deepwater Horizon* drilling rig on 20 Apr 2010. This is about four times the daily amount of oil used by the UK. NOAA analysis has concluded that thousands of marine mammals and turtles were killed by the spill, with a 50% decline in numbers of bottlenose dolphins in the area.

## First female NOAA chief scientist

Renowned oceanographer and marine biologist Sylvia Earle (USA) became the first woman to lead the science team at the National Oceanic and Atmospheric Administration (NOAA), in 1990. Earle is a pioneer of SCUBA and deep-sea submersible development. On 19 Sep 1979, she completed the **deepest untethered sea walk**, 381 m (1,250 ft) down on the seafloor off Hawaii, USA, in a diving suit called *JIM* (inset). Over a career spanning 50-plus years, Earle has become one of the leading advocates for protecting the oceans.

## Largest marine protected area

The criteria of a "marine protected area" (MPA) vary at a national level, but in general they seek to limit or ban activities such as commercial fishing and mining. Based on Marine Protection Atlas estimates, the largest MPA reported to the World Database on Protected Areas as "no take" (i.e., where no natural resources can be extracted) is 1,603,826 km² (619,240 sq mi) of zones within the Ross Sea region MPA in Antarctica. The largest MPA that is highly protected across its full extent – meeting the standards of the International Union for Conservation of Nature – is Papahānaumokuākea Marine National Monument in Hawaii, USA, at 1,508,847 km² (582,569 sq mi).

## Most acidic ocean waters (region)

The Bering Sea in the North Pacific Ocean can often reach pH levels as low as 7.7 in winter, when lower temperatures mean the water retains higher levels of carbon dioxide ($CO_2$). Although still alkaline, this is compared with an average pH level across the world's oceans of 8.1, so on that basis it is the "most acidic". The Bering Sea is susceptible to acidification on account of its cooler climate and limited water mixing.

The **most acidic ocean waters ever** are modelled to have been *c.* 6.6 pH during the Archaean eon, up to 4 billion years ago. In this period, atmospheric levels of $CO_2$ were significantly higher than they are today.

## Largest rhodolith bed

Rhodoliths are a form of coralline algae – a seaweed with a hard exterior. Like coral reefs, the habitat that they form on the seafloor is a haven for wildlife and plays a crucial role in marine ecology. The largest contiguous rhodolith bed covers 20,902 km² (8,070 sq mi), which is larger than Israel. It sits on the Abrolhos Shelf, off Brazil in the South Atlantic. This habitat is threatened by global warming and ocean acidification.

## Largest oceanic "garbage patch"

The North Pacific Central Gyre is a vast vortex of slowly revolving ocean water between North America and East Asia. Floating litter naturally concentrates at its centre – an area roughly the size of the US state of Texas. Known as the "Great Pacific Garbage Patch", it contains around 5.114 kg of plastic for every 1 km² (29 lb 3 oz per sq mi) of seawater. See Q&A opposite.

A major issue with marine litter is animals becoming caught up in it. The **earliest documented case of plastic entanglement** may date to 1947, when a herring gull was reported by Dr M A Jacobson as impeded by a piece of string. It's not known for certain if the string was made from natural or artificial fibres. The first unequivocal artificial marine entanglement was recorded as trawl twine in 1957 by scientists from the UK's Continuous Plankton Recorder (see p.29).

## Largest coral reef die-off

When water is too warm, corals expel the algae living in their tissues, turning them white and sometimes leading to their demise. As much as one-third of the world's coral may have perished during the 2014–17 Global Coral-Bleaching Event (GCBE), with up to 75% of global reefs experiencing bleaching-level heat stress to some degree. The 2014–17 GCBE was the third recorded since 1998 and lasted for an unprecedented 36 months. It was brought on by a run of hot years and a strong El Niño event in 2015–16.

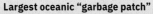

## Largest seagrass decline

Seagrasses are flowering marine plants that grow in shallow coastal waters. In 2010–11, an unprecedented marine heatwave off Western Australia led to a seasonal reduction of 1,310 km² (506 sq mi) of the seagrass meadows in Shark Bay – the largest of their kind in the world. The water temperature was 2–5°C (3.6–9°F) higher than average.

## TRASH TALK: LONGEST STAGE SWIM THROUGH THE GREAT PACIFIC GARBAGE PATCH

From 14 Jun to 31 Aug 2019, Ben Lecomte (FRA) swam 338 nautical mi (626 km; 389 mi), across 44 legs, through the largest agglomeration of marine debris in the world, known as the Great Pacific Garbage Patch (GPGP, see opposite).

### How did you first get into ocean swimming?
I never liked to swim in a pool. The feeling I get when I swim in the middle of the ocean has no match. It's a very pure activity, there is nothing between me and the environment. Also, I love adventures.

### What drove you to embark on the "Vortex Swim" project?
I had planned to swim across the northern part of the GPGP in 2018 [as part of an aborted cross-Pacific swim]. It was such an important location for communicating about ocean plastic pollution that we decided to make an expedition focused on the GPGP in 2019.

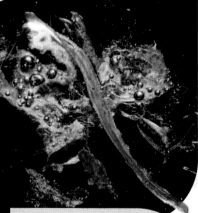

### Most common marine microplastic debris
Microplastics are less than 5 mm (0.2 in) in diameter; anything larger is known as macroplastic. The most ubiquitous microplastic in the ocean, comprising 35%, are textile microfibres (in white above), which largely come from laundering clothes. As well as being eaten by sealife, which can block the digestive tract, microplastic also raises the risk of chemical contamination.

### Why is waste so particularly bad in the North Pacific?
The GPGP is in the biggest ocean, with massive currents that bring all the debris into a vast area. I saw plastic every day from the first day to the last. After a while, I became numb to it because it was the norm.

### Do you think people realize just how polluted our oceans are?
I don't think people understand what it means to have 8 million tonnes [8.8 million tons] of plastic going into the ocean every year. Solutions have to be implemented at the source – because once the plastic is in the ocean, it's too late.

### Did you see anything positive?
I experienced amazing moments with wildlife. Every animal I encountered was curious and not at all afraid of me.

### Most public votes to name a research vessel
In Oct 2020, the RRS *Sir David Attenborough* embarked on sea trials before travelling to the Arctic and Antarctic to investigate the impact of climate change. The winner of a 2016 public poll to name the vessel was, in fact, *Boaty McBoatface*, with 124,109 votes. But it was eventually decided to name the ship after the iconic TV naturalist and environmentalist (see pp.54–55) instead.

### Most underwater art installations
Some conservationists are using art to raise awareness of the plight facing coral reefs – and to even help the reefs' recovery. Sculptor Jason deCaires Taylor (UK) has overseen 12 submerged art installations globally, comprising hundreds of individual sculptures. Completed in Apr 2020, *The Coral Greenhouse* (below) – off Queensland, Australia – is one of his latest projects. The main structure, standing 9.3 m (30 ft) tall, is fashioned from rust-resistant stainless steel, zinc and pH-neutral cement, and was seeded with some 2,000 live coral fragments. This artist also created the **tallest underwater figurative sculpture** – the 5-m (16-ft) *Ocean Atlas* (right) – in 2014, located off Nassau in The Bahamas. All of Taylor's aquatic artworks are designed to become part of the natural surroundings with time.

The Coral Greenhouse also includes sculptures of 17 children (based on real kids), flower pots, trees and workbenches.

# Trees

### Heaviest organism

"Pando" is a network of quaking aspen (*Populus tremuloides*) that weighs an estimated 6,000 tonnes (6,600 tons) and covers 43 ha (106 acres) of the Wasatch Mountains in Utah, USA. It shares a single root system and acts as one entity, with all the component trees changing colour or shedding leaves in unison. This clonal forest is comprised of around 47,000 individual stems.

### Largest canopy on a tree

Banyans spread by sending down cord-like appendages from horizontal branches that take root and become new trunks, so one tree can resemble an entire grove. Located in Anantapur, Andhra Pradesh, India, Thimmamma Marrimanu is an Indian banyan (*Ficus benghalensis*) whose multiple crowns merge to form a 2.19-ha (5.41-acre) canopy – equivalent to three soccer fields.

### Tallest palm tree

Palm trees grow upwards by adding leaves at the top of the trunk, without expanding their diameter. This means that only a handful of the *c.* 2,500 palm species can exceed 40 m (131 ft). The Quindío wax palm (*Ceroxylon quindiuense*) is a rare exception. One specimen in La Carbonera, Colombia, stood 59.2 m (194 ft 2 in) tall in 2017.

### Oldest trees

Based on core samples aged by dendrochronologists, the longest-lived species of tree is the bristlecone pine (*Pinus longaeva*) of California, USA. One unnamed living specimen was estimated to be 5,070 years old as of 2020. Among named examples, the most senior of these pines is Methuselah at 4,852 years old.

### Highest tree species

The Altiplano in the central Andes of South America is home to queñoa de altura (*Polylepis tomentella*), a small tree or shrub of the rose family (Rosaceae) that can grow up to 5,200 m (17,060 ft) above sea level.

### Remotest tree

A lone Sitka spruce (*Picea sitchensis*) grows on the subantarctic Campbell Island, 222 km (138 mi; 119.8 nautical mi) from any other tree. It is known as the Ranfurly tree, after the former Governor of New Zealand, who rumour has it planted it in 1901.

### Largest baobab tree

Baobabs (*Adansonia*) are famed for their broad trunks, which store vast amounts of water. Sagole Big Tree, a specimen of *A. digitata* in Masisi, Vhembe, South Africa, has a 60.6-m² (652-sq-ft) base and a height of 19.8 m (64 ft 11 in). Despite baobabs' bulk, their wood is very light; the Sagole Big Tree has an above-ground mass of "just" 54 tonnes (60 tons); two even larger baobabs in Africa have died in the last decade.

## TALL TALES: TREE HUNTER ROBERT VAN PELT

Dr Robert Van Pelt (aka "Big Tree Bob") is one of the world's foremost experts in giant trees and a celebrated tree illustrator. He is an affiliate professor at the University of Washington, USA.

**Have you always had a passion for big trees?**
I always had a passion for facts and figures – *Guinness World Records* was one of my favourite books. Big trees came later.

**What are the key skills required for tree hunting?**
Three reasons behind my own success: I know what the records are; I can judge size very well; and I know what I'm looking at. Identifying a species of tree from a long distance away has become second nature to me.

**What's the farthest you've travelled to measure a tree?**
My friend and I once spent four days trying to measure an alpine fir [*Abies lasiocarpa*] in Olympic National Park [in Washington State, USA]. We had to spend the night at the tree with

### Widest crown on a tree (single trunk)

Chamchuri is a rain tree (*Albizia saman*) with a crown diameter of 60.4 m (198 ft 1 in), located on the Thai Army cavalry grounds near Kanchanaburi, Thailand. As of 2018, its trunk girth was 9.15 m (30 ft) and the tree stood 17.6 m (57 ft 8 in) tall. Rain trees are native from Mexico to Peru, but are planted widely throughout the tropics and subtropics.

no sleeping bag or warm clothes and woke up to a thick fog. We had to climb a mountain peak to find our way back to base camp.

**Have you ever had any scary moments up a tree?**
Heaps! I've fallen while carrying equipment, got myriad cuts while scrambling to find a view of the treetop, and endured stings from hornets, nettles and blackberries.

**How easy is it to keep the location of big trees secret?**
Nearly impossible. But human trampling has led to the demise of many popular trees, especially in rainforests and on steep slopes, so protective steps must be taken.

**What can governments do?**
Trees are part of an ecosystem – they grow together and protect each other. We have to protect the environment they grow in, not just the individual tree.

## Giants of the forest

A coast redwood (*Sequoia sempervirens*) nicknamed Hyperion had grown to 116.07 m (380 ft 9 in) by 2019, making it currently the world's **tallest tree**. It was discovered on 25 Aug 2006 inside Redwood National Park in California, USA. Hyperion is shown below right in a set of illustrations created by Robert Van Pelt (see Q&A). To Hyperion's left is Centurion, the **tallest hardwood tree** at 99.82 m (327 ft 5 in); the mountain ash (*Eucalyptus regnans*) was measured in 2014 in Tasmania, Australia. Alongside Centurion is a giant sequoia (*Sequoiadendron giganteum*) named General Sherman, currently the **largest tree by volume** at 1,591 m³ (56,186 cu ft). It stands 83.6 m (274 ft) in Sequoia National Park, also in California.

### Tallest trees around the world

| Continent | Height | Species |
| --- | --- | --- |
| North America | 116.07 m | Coast redwood (*Sequoia sempervirens*) |
| Oceania | 99.82 m | Mountain ash (*Eucalyptus regnans*) |
| Asia | 98.53 m | Yellow meranti (*Shorea faguetiana*) |
| South America | 88.50 m | Red angelim (*Dinizia excelsa*) |
| Africa | 81.50 m | Muyovu (*Entandrophragma excelsum*) |
| Europe | 72.90 m | Karri (*Eucalyptus diversicolor*) |

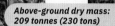
Foliage dry mass: 541 kg (1,193 lb)

Foliage: 1.68 tonnes (1.85 tons)

Above-ground dry mass: 209 tonnes (230 tons)

Age: 3,200 years

Age: 320 years (+/- 60 years)

Age: 1,260 years

Above-ground dry mass: 122 tonnes (134 tons)

Bark: 48 tonnes (52 tons)

Crown depth: 90.9 m (298 ft)

## Largest tree ever cut

The General Noble Tree – a giant sequoia (*S. giganteum*) from the Converse Basin Grove in California, USA – was felled in Aug 1892. It had an estimated volume of 1,250 m³ (44,140 cu ft) according to giant-tree hunter Wendell Flint, which would put it in the top 10 largest trees if still standing today. A section of the trunk was fashioned into a two-storey house to be exhibited at the 1893 Chicago World's Fair. For a time after, it was relocated to Washington, DC (inset).

# Carnivorous Plants

Some plants have evolved a startling strategy to secure nourishment: they catch live animals and then slowly digest them! Sundews catch insects in honey-sweet mucus; pitchers trap unsuspecting animals in vats of digestive fluid; other species use lightning-fast leaves. Their unusual diet means that meat-eating plants can often thrive in places that other plants would perish.

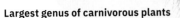

## Largest genus of carnivorous plants

As of Sep 2020, both the sundews (*Drosera*) and bladderworts (*Utricularia*) comprise around 248 species. The two also share the title of **most widely distributed carnivorous plants**, occurring on every continent bar Antarctica. Overall, there are around 860 known species of carnivorous plant, from *c.* 18 genera. Sundews use sticky mucilaginous (snot-like) secretions on their leaves to catch insects, while bladderworts employ vacuum-powered hollow sacs with touch-sensitive trapdoors (see above).

The record for **smallest carnivorous plant family** is shared by two families, each with a single species. Cephalotaceae is represented only by the Albany pitcher plant (*Cephalotus follicularis*) of Australia, while Drosophyllaceae's monotypic species is the dewy pine (*Drosophyllum lusitanicum*), native to the western Mediterranean.

## Fastest predatory plant

Aquatic bladderworts (*Utricularia*) use suction-based traps (i.e., bladders) with hair-triggered trapdoors to capture prey such as small crustaceans and insect larvae. The southern bladderwort (*U. australis*) has been recorded ensnaring victims in a mere 5.2 milliseconds, sucking in water at accelerations of up to 600 *g*! By comparison, the Venus flytrap (see opposite) takes around 20 times longer to catch its prey.

## Smallest genome for a flowering plant

No angiosperm has a smaller genome (total genetic make-up) than the *Genlisea tuberosa* corkscrew plant of Brazil. It has 61 million base pairs (the basic building blocks of DNA); by contrast, the human genome has *c.* 3 billion. Unusually, this meat-eating plant catches its prey underground, using root-like leaves. Tiny soil-dwelling organisms enter an opening in the leaf to seek food but the corkscrew shape, in tandem with backward-facing hairs, means that once inside they can't get back out!

## Oldest carnivorous plant fossil

As reported in 2015, carnivorous leaf fragments have been found dating to 35–47 million years ago (MYA) in the Eocene period. Fossilized in Baltic amber from the Yantarny mine near Kaliningrad in Russia, they have trapping organs akin to those of today's flycatcher bushes (*Roridula*) of South Africa. The leaves likely exuded a gluey excretion from the tips of tentacles (see arrows) to catch their prey. There have been claims of even earlier fossil evidence of carnivorous plants – perhaps as old as 125 MYA – but these are currently disputed by palaeobotanists.

## Largest carnivorous plants

There are various contenders for this title, depending on the criteria, but in terms of overall plant size they would all belong to the genus *Nepenthes*. These tropical pitcher plants are found mostly in parts of south-east Asia, notably Indonesia, Malaysia and the Philippines. Often seen as massive vining plants, some climb as high as 25 m (82 ft) into the rainforest canopy, forming huge, clumped growths.

Of all the carnivorous plants, those that digest the **largest prey** also belong to the Nepenthaceae family, of which *Nepenthes* is the sole genus (see below left).

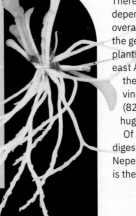

## What's in a name? Botanical nomenclature

- **Genus/species**: *Sarracenia flava* (or *S. flava*)
- **Hybrid**: a cross between two or more species, e.g., *Sarracenia leucophylla x flava*
- **Cultivar**: a formally described plant (can be a pure species or hybrid) to have been registered, e.g., *Sarracenia* 'Leah Wilkerson'
- **Unregistered selection**: an unassessed hybrid not yet recognized by the botanical community at large, e.g., *Nepenthes* "Leviathan"

## Highest carnivorous plant

The sticky-leaved *Pinguicula calyptrata*, a butterwort native to the Andes in South America, is found at elevations up to 4,200 m (13,780 ft). There is evidence that the alpine butterwort (*P. alpina*, right) reaches similar heights up to 4,100 m (13,450 ft) in the Himalayas. It's worth noting that *P. calyptrata* grows closer to the Equator, where high-elevation sites are not so frigid.

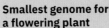

## Largest carnivorous plant traps (volume)

All pitcher plants use beaker-shaped leaves filled with digestive juices ("pitfall traps") to capture prey. The giant montane pitcher (*Nepenthes rajah*) of Malaysian Borneo can hold 3.5 litres (0.9 US gal) of water and stand up to 41 cm (1 ft 4 in) tall. *N. insignis*, *N. merrilliana* and some forms of *N. rafflesiana* grow traps of similar proportions. Frogs, small birds and even rodents number among their prey.

### First carnivorous plant hybrid

The pitcher plant *N. x dominii* was first exhibited in Jun 1862 at the Royal Horticultural Society show in South Kensington, London, UK, and is reportedly still in cultivation to this day. It was a cross between *N. rafflesiana* and (most likely) *N. gracilis,* developed by the British horticulturalist John Dominy in the late 1850s. Pitcher plants of the genus *Nepenthes* were widely hybridized during the great Victorian stovehouse era, which saw a rising enthusiasm for tropical plants grown in hothouses.

### First plant species discovered on Facebook

The magnificent sundew (*D. magnifica*) was identified by experts as a hitherto-unknown species in Jul 2015. Amateur researcher Reginaldo Vasconcelos had posted a photo of the plant that he had spotted three years earlier on a mountaintop in south-east Brazil. Leaves included, *D. magnifica* plants can grow to around 1.5 m (5 ft) long.

### Most expensive carnivorous plant

In Jul 2019, a male-flowering specimen of the "Leviathan" pitcher plant (a hybrid of *N. rajah x peltata*) sold for $4,500 (£3,540) to an anonymous buyer in the USA. "Leviathan" is one of several hybrids developed by American carnivorous plant hobbyist Jeremiah Harris (see below).

### Largest sundew

The largest discrete trapping leaves in the *Drosera* family are those of the king sundew (*D. regia,* above): each leaf grows up to 40 cm (1 ft 4 in) long and 1.2 cm (0.5 in) wide. It has a tiny range in South Africa. *Drosera erythrogyne,* a climbing species from Western Australia, produces a scrambling stem that can reach 3 m (9 ft 10 in) in total length.

### Tallest carnivorous plant traps

Predominantly found in wetland areas of North America, *Sarracenia* are distinguished by their slender, trumpet-shaped pitchers. Those of the yellow pitcher plant (*S. flava*) and crimson pitcher plant (*S. leucophylla*) reach 120 cm (3 ft 11 in). Occasionally, larger cultivars arise: a selection of *S. leucophylla* x *flava* (=*S. x moorei*) hybrid, named 'Leah Wilkerson', has recorded pitchers up to 130 cm (4 ft 3 in) from ground to lid tip.

### Fastest terrestrial predatory plant

The pimpernel sundew (*D. glanduligera*) of southern Australia has sensitive "snap tentacles", which rapidly curl inward when triggered. They can capture small insects, such as ants, within 75 milliseconds, catapulting the bug on to shorter tentacles covered in sundews' trademark natural "glue". These leaves move the victim towards the centre of the plant to be digested.

### Most southerly carnivorous plant

The sundew *D. uniflora* and the butterwort *P. antarctica* have both been found at 55.9°S in the Tierra del Fuego region (shared between Chile and Argentina) at the bottom of South America.

The **most northerly carnivorous plant** is the alpine butterwort (see opposite), which has been recorded at 79.3°N on the Norwegian archipelago of Svalbard, within the Arctic Circle. The only non-butterwort species that comes close to approaching this is the round-leafed sundew (*D. rotundifolia*).

### Largest trap on a Venus flytrap

Arguably the most famous carnivorous plant is the Venus flytrap (*Dionaea muscipula*). Measuring the longest dimension of the trapping leaf blade, excluding the marginal spines, the traps are typically 2–3 cm (0.7–1.2 in) long. The largest assessed *Dionaea* trap is a specimen (inset below) of the cultivar 'Alien', verified to be 5 cm (1.96 in) on 13 Sep 2020. It was grown in Colorado Springs, USA, by Jeremiah Harris (USA, right), who founded the Colorado Carnivorous Plant Society in 2003.

100%

Bugs beware: Jeremiah owns one of the largest private collections of carnivorous plants in the USA.

# Zoos & Aquaria

**Largest aviary**
South Africa's Birds of Eden encompasses a single enormous aviary occupying 2.3 ha (5.7 acres) – more than four soccer fields. It is covered by a wire mesh weighing 80 tonnes (88 tons). Opened on 15 Dec 2005, the park is home to some 3,500 birds representing around 220 species, including the scarlet ibis (right).

**First zoo**
Archaeological discoveries made in 2009 suggest the existence of a vast menagerie of animals at the ancient Egyptian settlement of Hierakonpolis dating back to 3500 BCE. The zoo contained more than 100 creatures, including elephants, wildcats, baboons, antelopes and hippos. The animals, who were likely to have been privately owned, were given special treatment in death; some were covered with linen and buried with pottery.

**First public aquarium**
On 18 Feb 1852, the Council of the Zoological Society of London (UK) commissioned the building of an Aquatic Vivarium at London Zoo. The exhibit opened in May 1853 and became known as the "Fish House". It was here that the term "aquarium" was coined in 1854 by naturalist Philip Henry Gosse.

**First nocturnal zoo**
Opened in May 1994, Singapore's Night Safari only welcomes visitors as the sun sets. It's home to some 900 creatures, including Asian elephants, Malayan tapirs (below), bats, pangolins and fishing cats. The animals are made visible thanks to artificial moonlight, which is dim enough to avoid disturbing them.

**Oldest zoo**
The Tiergarten Schönbrunn in Vienna, Austria, was created in 1752 by order of Holy Roman Emperor Francis I. Initially a royal menagerie, it has been open to the public since 1779 – more than 240 years! Located in the grounds of Schönbrunn Palace, the residence and its gardens (including the zoo) became a UNESCO World Heritage Site in 1996.

**Most visited zoo**
Based on the most recent figures available from the Themed Entertainment Association, Disney's Animal Kingdom in Lake Buena Vista, Florida, USA, received 13,888,000 visitors in 2019.

**Largest living coral reef exhibit**
Reef HQ Aquarium in Townsville, Queensland, Australia, features a marine "mesocosm" (an enclosure that emulates a real-world ecosystem) with an average volume of 2.8 million litres (740,000 gal) of seawater. The reef comprises more than 120 types of coral and contains 150 species of fish.

**Largest indoor desert in a zoo**
The Desert exhibit (below) at Royal Burgers' Zoo in Arnhem, Netherlands, spans 7,500 m² (80,700 sq ft). Emulating the Sonoran Desert on the US-Mexico border, the arid landscape accommodates more than 1,100 animals, including bobcats (inset), and 145 species of cactus.
Burgers also boasts the **largest indoor swamp in a zoo**. The Mangrove exhibit (right) spans 2,800 m² (30,140 sq ft) and contains around 1 million litres (264,000 gal) of water. The wetland is enclosed by a dome that stretches 17 m (56 ft) high and hosts a variety of mangrove-dwelling fauna, such as manatees (opposite).

**Most species in a zoo**
As of 1 Nov 2020, Moskovsky Zoopark in Russia's capital city played host to 1,226 different species of animal, ranging from large mammals, such as giant pandas, to tiny insects. As well as bespoke enclosures, the 21.4-ha (53-acre) site – established in 1864 – includes paddocks, an aquarium and an aviary.

## Largest indoor rainforest in a zoo

Opened in Mar 2016, the Rimbula exhibit at Wildlands Adventure Zoo in Emmen, Netherlands, has a total surface area of 16,764 m² (180,446 sq ft). Contained within a humidity-controlled greenhouse, the rainforest contains more than 16,000 tropical plants, 50 jungle animal species (such as Asian elephants) and even a river, upon which visitors can take a boat ride.

## Most zoos visited

On 6 Feb 2020, Jonas Livet (FRA) visited his 1,215th zoological institution – Natura Parc in Santa Eugenia in Mallorca, Spain. Jonas went to his first zoo in 1987 as a child, and was instantly hooked; today, he works as a zoo consultant.

## Largest collection of zoo/aquarium guidebooks

Leszek Solski (POL) had amassed 6,770 guides to zoos and aquaria as of 15 Oct 2020. Leszek, a zoo historian affiliated with Zoo Wrocław in Poland, started his collection in 1966 at the age of 13 with a guidebook from Calgary Zoo in Canada. His oldest example is from the long-gone Surrey Zoological Gardens in the UK and dates to May 1839.

## Oldest aquarium

SEA LIFE in Brighton, East Sussex, UK, dates back to 1872 (inset: colourized photo from the mid-1880s). It took three years to build at a cost of £133,000 – equivalent to around £5.5 m ($7.3 m) today. Beneath its Victorian brick archways, the present-day aquarium houses hi-tech exhibits and more than 150 species of aquatic animals, including rays, jellyfish, pipefish and terrapins (pictured).

## Most northerly zoo

The Polar Park Arctic Wildlife Centre in Troms, Norway, is located at a latitude of 68.69°N. Opened on 18 Jun 1994, the park is home to species native to the Arctic Circle, such as snow foxes and reindeer. For an immersive experience, visitors can spend the night with the zoo's wolf pack, thanks to a lodge within their naturalistic enclosure.

The **most southerly zoo** is Orana Wildlife Park, near Christchurch on New Zealand's South Island. Situated at 43.28°S, the park has been operating since 1976.

## Largest database of wild animals in human care

Since 1974, the Zoological Information Management System (ZIMS) has collated the inventories of hundreds of wildlife institutions around the world. As of 1 Oct 2020, the online database had listed 12,235,951 individual animals and 24,023 species since its inception. ZIMS is managed by Species360 in Minneapolis, Minnesota, USA.

## Largest gathering of zoo professionals

The US-based Association of Zoos and Aquariums regularly welcomes in excess of 2,500 delegates to its annual conference. The highest turnout was 2,785 in 2018 and took place at Seattle Aquarium.

## Most visited aquarium

Hengqin Ocean Kingdom (aka Chimelong Ocean Kingdom) in Guangdong, China, received 11,736,000 visitors in 2019, according to the Themed Entertainment Association. Its popularity is not surprising given it is the world's **largest aquarium**, with a total water volume of 48.75 million litres (12.87 million gal). It is also home to the **largest aquarium tank**, with 22.7 million litres (5.9 million gal) in the tank at any given time, where whale sharks – the **largest fish** (pictured) – are the star attraction.

# Conservation

### Conservation and COVID-19
GWR is proud to work with The Lion's Share (TLS), which seeks to give something back to the animals whose images are so often used by brands and the media. In response to COVID-19, TLS launched "Resilience in Wildlife Communities Grants" in Apr 2020. This initiative is to support those whose ecotourism-based livelihoods have been decimated by the pandemic, and in doing so help to protect endangered wildlife too. So far, nine areas have received bursaries. These include the Kunene region of Namibia – home to desert lions – where funding has gone towards setting up "virtual safaris". Other beneficiaries are the first marine turtle sanctuary in Sri Lanka and South Africa's Kruger National Park (above), which is patrolled by the Black Mambas, the first all-female anti-poaching unit.

### Most complete dodo
One species for which conservation infamously came too late is the dodo (*Raphus cucullatus*) – an extinct member of the pigeon family from Mauritius. This bird died out around the end of the 17th century, and its remains today are scarce. The most complete skeleton of a single dodo, with nearly all its original bones, is displayed at the Mauritius Institute in Port Louis (pictured). It was found in the early 20th century by amateur naturalist Louis Étienne Thirioux. Nearly all other dodo skeletons are composites of several birds' bones.

*Albeit far from complete, a specimen known as the "Oxford Dodo" in the UK does still have skin attached and one feather.*

### First beluga whale sanctuary
Marine wildlife charities Whale and Dolphin Conservation and the SEA LIFE Trust (both UK) have turned Klettsvik Bay at Heimaey Island, off south-west Iceland, into the world's first open-water reserve for beluga whales (*Delphinapterus leucas*). The natural inlet in which the Beluga Whale Sanctuary is based covers 32,000 m² (344,445 sq ft), with a depth of around 9.1 m (30 ft). Its first two residents – Little White and Little Grey – arrived there in Aug 2020 (inset) from an aquarium in China.

### Most abundant bird ever
Even the most prolific species aren't impervious to extinction. In the early 19th century, North America was home to some 10 billion passenger pigeons (*Ectopistes migratorius*). A single flock could contain more than 2 billion birds. But they were drastically over-hunted, notably for sale in city markets. In 1914, the last known specimen, an adult female called Martha, died in Cincinnati Zoo, Ohio, USA.

### Longest-running wild primate study
The Gombe Stream Chimpanzee Reserve study was initiated by primatologist Dr Jane Goodall (UK) on 14 Jul 1960, in what is now Tanzania's Gombe National Park. Since 1977, the research has continued under the auspices of the Jane Goodall Institute, and in 2020 the project celebrated its 60th anniversary. Located by Lake Tanganyika, Gombe is one of Tanzania's smallest national parks at just over 50 km² (19 sq mi), but provides a vital habitat to 100–150 chimpanzees (*Pan troglodytes*) as well as many other species.

### Most recent fish extinction
In Mar 2020, the International Union for Conservation of Nature (IUCN) declared that the smooth handfish (*Sympterichthys unipennis*) had died out. Only a single photograph of this species is known to exist, of a specimen previously collected *c.* 1802 in coastal waters off Australia by the French naturalist François Péron. It is the first marine bony fish to be declared extinct in modern times. Pollution, habitat loss and predation by invasive species have all played their part in its downfall.

Its official demise follows swiftly in the wake of the **most recent freshwater fish extinction**: the Chinese paddlefish (*Psephurus gladius*), announced extinct in Jan 2020. It had been categorized as Critically Endangered for some years and not seen since 2003 in either the Yangtze River basin or its East China Sea estuary – the species' last-known locations.

### Oldest koala sanctuary
The Lone Pine Koala Sanctuary was established by Claude Reid (AUS) in 1927 in Brisbane, Queensland, Australia, initially in response to the threat posed to the marsupials by the fur trade. Still operating today, it houses the most koalas in captivity, with more than 130 animals, alongside 70-plus other native species.

### First single of birdsong to chart in the UK
Released by the UK-based Royal Society for the Protection of Birds (RSPB), the single "Let Nature Sing" featured the calls of common garden birds such as the cuckoo (*Cuculus canorus*), blackbird (*Turdus merula*) and robin (*Erithacus rubecula*) alongside those of less familiar or endangered species. On 9 May 2019, it entered the Official Singles Chart at No.18

### First skydiving anti-poaching dog
On 17 Sep 2016, German shepherd Arrow and his handler, Henry Holsthyzen (ZAF), jumped from a helicopter 6,000 ft (1,828 m) above Air Force Base Waterkloof, near Pretoria, South Africa. The leap was part of an air show. While Arrow isn't the first dog to tandem skydive (inset), he is the first to do so as part of a pioneering programme to apprehend poachers from the sky.

# re:wild

"The Search for Lost Species" is an international campaign launched in Apr 2017 by nature charity Global Wildlife Conservation (now called Re:wild). Its mission is to compile a database of animals, plants and fungi that are lost to science (with no verified sightings in the wild for at least 10 years). Ultimately, it seeks to assist in their rediscovery and conservation should they still exist. As of 30 Nov 2020, the project had identified 2,127 entries for inclusion, the **most "lost species" sought by a conservation project**.

In all, 67 species were rediscovered in 2017–20 – six of which appeared on the charity's "25 Most Wanted" list. They included: (**1**) Jackson's climbing salamander (*Bolitoglossa jacksoni*, missing for 42 years); (**2**) Voeltzkow's chameleon (*Furcifer voeltzkowi*, unseen for 106 years); (**3**) the silver-backed chevrotain (*Tragulus versicolor*, missing for at least 29 years); and a record-breaking insect, the (**4**) **largest bee** (see below).

### Largest bee
Wallace's giant bee (*Megachile pluto*) can grow to 4.5 cm (1.7 in) long, with a wingspan of up to 6 cm (2.3 in). It is shown below alongside a honey bee (*Apis mellifera*). The species occurs only in the Moluccas Islands of Indonesia and was first described in 1858 by British naturalist Alfred Russel Wallace. It was lost to science for 38 years, but rediscovered in 2019.

**100%**

on the strength of 23,500 digital/CD sales. The RSPB's main goal was to highlight the crisis facing native birds, 40 million of which have vanished from the UK in the last 50 years, with 56% of species in decline.

### Most trafficked wild mammals
According to the IUCN, more than 1 million pangolins (family Manidae) were illegally traded between 2000 and 2013.

Pangolins have long been prized in some cultures for their meat and scales; the latter are used in traditional medicine. The World Wide Fund for Nature (WWF) and wildlife trade specialists TRAFFIC are working to reduce the demand for pangolins and to assist governments in cracking down on poaching. In 2017, commercial trade of all eight pangolin species was banned.

### Largest camera-trap wildlife survey
Every four years, India conducts a national census of its tigers (*Panthera tigris tigris*). For the fourth count, taking place in 2018–19, camera traps equipped with motion sensors were positioned in 26,838 locations across 141 sites, covering a total area of 121,337 km² (46,848 sq mi). In all, they captured 34,858,623 photos of wildlife, 76,651 of which were tigers. Based on these images, 2,461 individual tigers (excluding cubs) were identified. On a positive note, this was up one-third on 2014's census, but it may partly be down to improved surveying methods. The National Tiger Conservation Authority, the Wildlife Institute of India, state forestry departments and conservation NGOs all collaborated on the project.

### Greatest recovery by a bird species
Chatham Island robins (*Petroica traversi*, aka black robins) are endemic to New Zealand's Chatham Islands in the South Pacific, but as of 1980 only five remained in existence. Of these, just one was female. Local wildlife protection officers adopted an innovative conservation technique called "cross fostering", in which robins' eggs and hatchlings were given to similar birds to brood and raise. As a result, the species underwent a staggering comeback; as of the last count in Nov 2015, there were 289 adult birds.

### Greatest recovery by a bird of prey species
By 1974, there were just two Mauritius kestrels (*Falco punctatus*) in captivity and four in the wild, of which only one was a breeding female. As of 2013, their population stood at 350–500 birds (170–200 mature). Ring tagging (seen above), plus kestrel-friendly bird boxes and feeding stations have all contributed to this encouraging revival.

### Largest giant panda habitat
The Sichuan Giant Panda Sanctuaries in the Qionglai and Jiajin mountains of Sichuan, China, represent the largest contiguous habitat of the giant panda (*Ailuropoda melanoleuca*). More than 30% of the world's pandas live in this 9,245-km² (3,569-sq-mi) network of nature reserves and scenic parks, which became a UNESCO World Heritage Site in 2006.

The giant panda has been the iconic logo of the WWF since the charity was founded in 1961. With 5.4 million supporters as of 2017, it is the **largest environmental conservation organization**.

Panda protected areas also benefit other animals, including 70% of China's endemic forest mammals and birds.

# Round-Up

## Smallest reptile

Males of several species of dwarf chameleon (genus *Brookesia*) from Madagascar are small enough, when fully grown, to fit on a fingertip. The smallest is *B. nana*, as described in *Scientific Advances* on 28 Jan 2021. One adult male measured 13.5 mm (0.53 in) from snout to vent (anus) – or 21.9 mm (0.86 in) including the tail. Females are slightly longer, measuring 19.2 mm (0.76 in) from snout to vent and 28.9 mm (1.14 in) overall.

**100%**

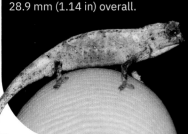

## Longest lightning flash

On 31 Oct 2018, a single "megaflash" of lightning spanned from north-east Argentina across Brazil to the Atlantic Ocean. It covered 709 km (440.6 mi) – greater than the distance between London and Edinburgh in the UK. The event was verified by the World Meteorological Organization (WMO) on 25 Jun 2020.

The WMO also ratified the **longest-lasting lightning flash** – 16.73 sec. This occurred on 4 Mar 2019 over northern Argentina. The average duration for a lightning bolt is just 0.2 sec.

## Most equable temperature (long period)

Since official temperature readings began there in 1960, Kwajalein in the Marshall Islands has neither dipped below 20°C (68°F) nor risen above 33.3°C (92°F) – a range of just 13.3°C (24°F).

In stark contrast, the town of Loma in Montana, USA, experienced a rise of 57.2°C (103°F) in just 24 hr on 14–15 Jan 1972. This is the **greatest temperature range in a day**.

## First amphibian with a venomous bite

The ringed caecilian (*Siphonops annulatus*) is a limbless, worm-like amphibian native to South America. It has glands in its jaws that secrete fluid containing enzymes frequently found in venom. Although many amphibians are infamous for their toxicity, such as poison-dart frogs, a 2020 study found this caecilian to be the first of its kind to deliver toxins by biting.

## Oldest DNA extracted

Mammoth teeth found preserved in permafrost near Krestovska in Siberian Russia have been dated to 1.1–1.65 million years old, as detailed in *Nature* in Feb 2021. It is the first time that genetic material exceeding 1 million years old has been sequenced. Although the teeth are similar to those of the steppe mammoth (*Mammuthus trogontherii*), it is believed they belonged to a more ancient type of mammoth that is yet to be classified.

## First dwarf giraffes

In Dec 2020, news emerged of two wild male giraffes (*Giraffa sp.*) showing signs of skeletal dysplasia, which can result in dwarfism. Gimli (pictured in 2017) from Uganda had an estimated height of 2.82 m (9 ft 3 in), though aged *c.* 14 months was sub-adult. By contrast, Nigel from Namibia was around four years old, making him almost fully grown. His height of 2.54 m (8 ft 4 in) is about half that of a typical adult for the **tallest animal**. In both cases, it is the proportions of body parts such as the legs, rather than stature, that indicate dwarfism.

## Smallest non-avian dinosaur egg

A fossilized egg from a theropod dinosaur – designated *Himeoolithus murakamii* – had dimensions of 45 x 20 mm (1.77 x 0.79 in), as described on 23 May 2020. Its estimated mass of 9.9 g (0.35 oz) makes it comparable in size to a quail's egg. The near-complete egg was discovered at the Kamitaki Egg Quarry near Tamba City in Hyōgo, Japan. It has an unusually elongated shape, with a length-width ratio of 2.25.

**100%**

## Largest tanzanite

One of the rarest gemstones on Earth, tanzanite is a blue-violet variety of the mineral zoisite and is found only in a small area in northern Tanzania. On 24 Jun 2020, news broke that mine owner Saniniu Laizer (above) had sold two of these valuable gems to the country's government for 7.7 bn Tanzanian shillings ($3.3 m; £2.6 m). The larger of the pair weighed 46,350 carats (9.27 kg; 20 lb 6 oz).

## Newest cetacean

On 10 Jan 2021, the discovery of a new marine mammal dubbed Rice's whale (*Balaenoptera ricei*) was announced following a study of baleen whales in the Gulf of Mexico. It had previously been identified as a form of Bryde's whale (*B. brydei*), but years of genetic analysis – and scrutiny of the skull of a deceased whale stranded in Jan 2019 – revealed it to be a separate species. It was named after the late American cetologist Dale Rice.

## Oldest rhesus monkey in captivity

A rhesus macaque (*Macaca mulatta*) named Isoko ("Shore" in Japanese) celebrated her 43rd birthday on 15 Apr 2021. Isoko was born at Kyoto City Zoo in Japan and has resided there her entire life. These Old World primates generally reach 25 to 30 years of age.

## Longest dive by a mammal

A Cuvier's beaked whale (*Ziphius cavirostris*) spent 3 hr 42 min submerged on a single dive. During a five-year study of 23 individuals in the waters off Cape Hatteras in North Carolina, USA, marine scientists used satellite tags to track a total of 3,860 dives. The longest of these descents extended the previous record – also set by a Cuvier's beaked whale – by 1 hr 25 min.

## Longest non-stop migration by a bird

On 27 Sep 2020, a male bar-tailed godwit (*Limosa lapponica baueri*) arrived at the Firth of Thames, near Auckland in New Zealand, having completed an epic 11-day, 12,200-km (7,580-mi) continuous flight from Alaska, USA. The satellite-tagged bird – nicknamed "4BBRW", after the blue, blue, red and white rings on its leg – reached a peak speed of 88.5 km/h (55 mph).

## Most four-leaf clovers collected in one hour (individual)

Gabriella Gerhardt (USA) gathered 451 of nature's lucky charms in 60 min on 21 Sep 2019 in Fitchburg, Wisconsin, USA. She has been collecting clover since 2010, and identified a patch of land rich with specimens for her record attempt.

## Coldest cloud tops

At 13:38 UTC on 29 Dec 2018, the *NOAA-20* meteorological satellite recorded an infrared temperature of 161.96 K (-111.19°C; -168.14°F) as part of a storm cluster in the West Pacific. Intense updraughts had pushed the high clouds – a phenomenon known as "overshooting tops" – to 20.5 km (12.7 mi) above sea level. The findings were reported on 22 Mar 2021.

## Most biodiverse island (flora)

The Pacific island of New Guinea is home to 13,634 species of vascular plant (i.e., those with internal vessels to transport water and nutrients), as revealed in *Nature* on 5 Aug 2020. The flora of the world's second-largest island (after Greenland) comprised 1,742 genera and 264 families, with 68% of species being endemic. Orchids (inset) account for one-fifth of all its plants.

## Largest oak leaf

An oak leaf found by Claire Larkin (USA) measured 42 cm long x 39.7 cm wide (1 ft 4.5 in x 1 ft 3.6 in) on 7 Mar 2020 in Livingston, Alabama, USA. Claire made the discovery while out for a walk in the woods on her family estate the day after Thanksgiving in 2019. It came from a cherrybark oak (*Quercus pagoda*), a tree native to North America whose leaves typically grow to 5–10 in (13–25 cm) long.

## Rarest hamster

In Jul 2020, the International Union for Conservation of Nature (IUCN) declared that the common hamster (*Cricetus cricetus*), despite its name, was now Critically Endangered. During the past century, its population has plummeted by over 90% in some regions, partly on account of trapping for the fur trade and extermination as a farmland pest. This species' lifespan and litter size have also dipped.

## Oldest penguin in captivity

A gentoo penguin (*Pygoscelis papua*) called Olde ("Great-granny" in Danish) was confirmed to be aged 41 years 331 days – more than double the typical lifespan of wild gentoos – on 12 Apr 2021. Olde has lived at Odense Zoo since 1 May 2003. She was hatched at Edinburgh Zoo in the UK in 1979, and lived in Montreal, Canada, for a spell before her move to Denmark.

# David Attenborough

HALL OF FAME

**VITAL STATISTICS**
Name: David Attenborough
Born: 8 May 1926
Birthplace: Isleworth, Middlesex, UK
TV debut: 2 Sep 1953 (*Animal Disguises*)
TV highlights: *The Life Collection* (1979–2020), *The Blue Planet I & II* (2001, 2017), *Planet Earth* (2006)
Documentaries hosted (series/one-offs): 100+
Knighted: 1985

The revered naturalist and campaigner Sir David Attenborough (UK) has become one of the most urgent voices on the need for environmental change. In his 90s, he is still exploring new ways to impart his message.

On 24 Sep 2020, Sir David achieved the fastest time to reach 1 million followers on Instagram, taking just 4 hr 44 min (a record that has since been surpassed, see pp.204–05). He opened his account with a video warning that "the world is in trouble"; six weeks later, he closed the account with the message that "What happens next is up to us."

The following month, Sir David was named a member of the Earthshot Prize Council, alongside Prince William. They are seeking to reward innovative ideas to repair environmental damage with five £1-m ($1.3-m) bursaries each year for a decade. If this ambition is realized, the Earthshot Prize will be the largest environmental award in history.

Even as he speaks out on green issues, Sir David has not slowed his broadcasting output. His most recent documentary series, *A Perfect Planet*, aired on the BBC in Jan 2021. This extended his record for longest career as a TV presenter to 67 years 151 days. Since his on-screen debut on 2 Sep 1953 – for BBC series *Animal Disguises* – Sir David has written and narrated a plethora of landmark TV productions such as *Life on Earth* (1979), *The Blue Planet* (2001) and, more recently, *Extinction: The Facts* (2020). He is the only person to have won BAFTA awards for series in black and white, colour, HD and 3D formats. In recognition of his work, he has received more than 30 honorary degrees and, in 1985, a knighthood.

Later in 2021 is set to see the release of *The Green Planet*, in which Sir David turns his gaze to plants and explores how they battle for survival. His near 70-year crusade to inform shows no sign of abating – if anything, the mounting environmental challenges facing Earth make the calls for change from this TV legend more pressing than ever.

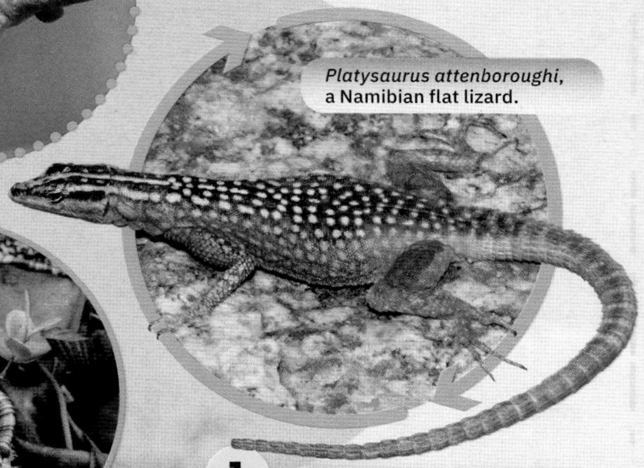

*Platysaurus attenboroughi,* a Namibian flat lizard.

*Attenborosaurus conybeari,* an Early Jurassic marine reptile found in Dorset, UK.

*Nepenthes attenboroughii,* a pitcher plant from the Philippines.

**1.** A variety of animals and plants have been named after Sir David. They include a rare echidna from New Guinea, an Ecuadorian tree and a Madagascan ghost shrimp, as well as those shown above.

**2.** One of his earliest series for the BBC was *Zoo Quest*, which ran from 1954 to 1963. Here he is seen with a young Prince Charles and Princess Anne, who paid a visit to the studio and met Cocky the cockatoo in 1958.

**3.** Sir David won his third Emmy on 19 Sep 2020 – "Outstanding Narrator" – for his work on *Seven Worlds, One Planet* (BBC America). He was presented the gong virtually by US comedian Rob Riggle (bottom left).

**4.** In Oct 2020, Sir David and Prince William launched the Earthshot Prize. It aims to find 50 solutions to the world's gravest environmental problems by 2030.

**5.** During his 1979 *Life on Earth* BBC series, Sir David captivated audiences with his encounter with the mountain gorillas of Rwanda. It has proved an all-too-rare success story. A 2016 census estimated the number of gorillas in the Virunga Mountains of East Africa at 604 – almost treble the population of 40 years earlier.

Pablo, otherwise known as "the gorilla that sat on David Attenborough", went on to lead a troop of 60-plus gorillas!

Find out more about Sir David in the Hall of Fame section at www.guinnessworldrecords.com/2022

# Miniature Wonderland

**A** warehouse in Hamburg provides a gateway to a fascinating Lilliputian world – and a record-breaking railway. In 2000, Frederik Braun came across a model railway shop in Zurich, Switzerland. It reminded him of a boyhood dream: to build the world's **largest model train set** (see below). Inspired by the idea, he swiftly won over his twin brother Gerrit and their business partner, Stephan Hertz (all DEU). Next, they recruited master model-maker Gerhard Dauscher and hired a team of artisans. By Aug 2001, they had built three mini-landscapes through which their railway could run. Representing Central Germany, Austria and the fictitious town of Knuffingen, they were dubbed "Theme Worlds".

Today, Miniature Wonderland's railway runs through nearly 1,500 m² (16,145 sq ft) of 1:87-scale landscape, including detailed facsimiles of landmark sites in Germany, Italy, the USA, Scandinavia and elsewhere. Fifty computers ensure the smooth running of the trains, flights to and from Knuffingen Airport and the journeys of model road vehicles.

Magnets inside each car's front axle react to wires in the streets. The software for Wonderland's "Carsystem" calculates the options for each car 20 times every second, providing autonomous movement and avoiding collisions. It's so lifelike that there are even police speed traps!

On 8 Nov 2015, Miniature Wonderland made it into *GWR* again – by upscaling! It organized the **largest human image of the Olympic rings**, consisting of 6,211 people, in Stadtpark, Hamburg. It's a safe bet that the Braun brothers' jaw-dropping mini-worlds will give rise to more surprises – and continue to break records – for many years to come.

### Location:
Kehrwieder 2/Block D, 20457 Hamburg, Germany

### Established: 2000

### Initial cost: €35 m
(£22.2 m; $34.6 m)

### Theme worlds: nine
(as of Feb 2021)

### Area: 7,000-m²
(75,340-sq-ft) venue; 1,499-m² (16,135-sq-ft) model layouts

### Annual visitors:
1.4 million (in 2019)

## Little wonder
Visitors are able to get very close to the exhibits, allowing them to fully appreciate their complexity and detail. The Italian Theme World covers 190 m² (2,045 sq ft) – about three times the size of a squash court – and took three-and-a-half years to build. It includes some 138 ships, 450 buildings, 10,000 trees and around 50,000 LEDs!

This colourful exhibit is modelled on Riomaggiore, a hillside village on the Ligurian coast of north-western Italy.

## Open-air concert
The main stage of this minuscule festival is given over to a set by a tiny facsimile of DJ BoBo. More than 20,000 music-fan figures fill the space, with their own campground, food and drink stands, and even portable loos (with lengthy queues, naturally). It took three months to construct.

*52 planes*

*479,000 LEDs (total)*

*269,000 figures (total)*

## Largest model airport
Knuffingen is a 150-m² (1,614-sq-ft) model airfield based on Hamburg Airport. It was nearly six years in the making and cost €4 m ($4.8 m; £3.6 m). The 52 aircraft are precise facsimiles of their real-life counterparts and move independently, taking off and landing via rigid wires. There are some 250 flights daily, while around 15,000 figures populate the site.

### Largest model train set

The Theme Worlds in Wonderland are linked by means of the model railway that first inspired the Braun brothers. It includes 15,715 m (51,558 ft) of track. In real-world terms, that converts to 1,367.2 km (849.5 mi) – the distance from Paris, France, to Warsaw in Poland – making it also the **largest model train set (scale length)**. Its 1,040 trains pull an estimated 10,000 wagons. Inside the control room (inset), monitors track the myriad journeys of Wonderland's trains and other vehicles.

### The Colosseum

A highlight of Wonderland's Italian Theme World, this likeness of Rome's Colosseum includes around 3,000 components and took nearly two years to make. Its real-life counterpart, completed in 80 CE, is the **largest amphitheatre**. Covering 2 ha (5 acres), it measures 187 m long and 157 m wide (613 × 515 ft) and could accommodate 87,000 spectators. (For another replica Colosseum, turn to p. 100.)

50 computers

947,500 working hours

*Frederik Braun*

*Gerrit Braun*

130,000 trees

4,340 buildings

15.71 km (9.76 mi) of track

1,040 trains

9,250 road vehicles

10,000-plus rail cars

On 17 Mar 2021, the longest melody by a model train was achieved by striking a line of 2,840 tuned water glasses.

1,380 signals

# Humans

## ▶ Largest afro (female)

Aevin Dugas (USA) is the proud owner of an eye-catching afro measuring 24 cm (9.4 in) high from the crown of her head, with a total circumference of 157 cm (5 ft 1 in). It was verified on 4 Feb 2021 in Gonzales, Louisiana, USA.

Social worker Aevin reclaimed the record from her compatriot Simone Williams, having previously held it for eight years. She has her hair cut regularly, to add layers and volume, and also styles it in a bun, braids or plaits. "When I first went natural, it was literally as if a weight lifted off my head," she told GWR. "As a woman you're told that straight hair is beautiful hair. This is crazy. The afro is my natural hairstyle and there can't be anything more beautiful than that."

Aevin can use up to five different conditioners at once when washing her record-breaking hair.

# Early Humans

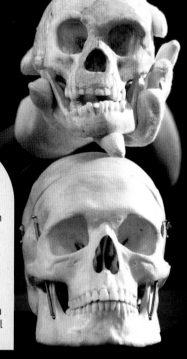

**H. floresiensis** **H. sapiens**

### Oldest hominin footprints
In 1978, tracks were found in Laetoli, north Tanzania, belonging to two or three hominins. They strode upright on the ashy plains there *c.* 3.6 million years ago (MYA). Some 70 footprints form two parallel trails about 30 m (100 ft) long.

**100%**

### Earliest stone tools
In 2015, compelling evidence was presented of stone tools dating to 3.3 MYA – *c.* 700,000 years earlier than previous examples from the so-called Oldowan era (2.6–1.7 MYA). The stone flakes, cores and anvils were unearthed at the Lomekwi 3 site near Lake Turkana in Kenya in 2011. This find predates the emergence of the *Homo* genus by several hundred-thousand years, suggesting that earlier hominins, such as *Australopithecus*, also made and used tools from their environment.

### Newest species of human
Described in 2019, *Homo luzonensis* has been dated to *c.* 67,000 to 50,000 years ago in the Late Pleistocene era. Its discovery was based on remains – including teeth and foot bones – excavated on the island of Luzon in the Philippines (see timeline below). The curved digital bones could imply tree-dwelling behaviour, a feature more often associated with the primitive hominin *Australopithecus*.

### Earliest hominin
In 2002, the discovery of a possible human ancestor some 6–7 million years old was announced. *Sahelanthropus tchadensis* was found in what is now a desert region of Chad. It was argued from the shape of the base of its skull that the hominin was able to walk bipedally. However, further evidence is required to place it more firmly on the human family tree.

### Shortest hominin
A female specimen of *H. floresiensis* was discovered in 2003 by Indonesian and Australian scientists in a cave on the island of Flores, Indonesia. Standing about 1 m (3 ft 3 in) tall, the species inhabited Flores until about 50,000 years ago. Dubbed the "Hobbit" by dig workers, this hominin lived at the same time as modern humans (*H. sapiens*), whom it may have encountered before becoming extinct. Pictured right, you can see the vast difference in skull size between the two.

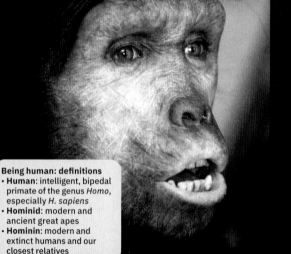

### First *Homo erectus* discovered
In 1891, the Dutch paleoanthropologist Eugene Dubois unearthed evidence of "upright humans" (*H. erectus*, see opposite) during a dig at Trinil in Java, Indonesia. Some of the fossils dated to *c.* 1.3 MYA, making *H. erectus* a probable direct ancestor of modern humans.

As a species, *H. erectus* is also the **longest-surviving hominin**. Fossil evidence indicates that in total it persisted for some 1.9 million years, from *c.* 2 MYA to *c.* 110,000 years ago. It lived about four times longer than our own species has to date, assuming that the earliest *H. sapiens* emerged around 500,000 years ago (see right). The oldest *H. erectus* remains were uncovered in Africa, where the species likely evolved before later migrating to Asia and Europe.

### Richest human fossil site
The greatest concentration of early human skeletons is from the Sima de los Huesos ("Pit of Bones") chamber, within a cave system in the Atapuerca Hills near Burgos, Spain (see also below). Since 1975, some 7,000 human bones and teeth have been excavated here, from about 28 skeletons.

### Oldest *Homo sapiens* bones
Genetic studies indicate that our species emerged at least 500,000 years ago. But in terms of the fossil record, the earliest *H. sapiens* bones date to *c.* 300,000 years, unearthed at Jebel Irhoud in western Morocco. As described in *Nature* in 2017, the people of Jebel Irhoud exhibited the facial traits of modern humans, but their skulls retained a more archaic elongated shape. Prior to this – and still the oldest *H. sapiens* bones with a more familiar globular braincase – are *c.* 195,000 years old, found at Omo Kibish in Ethiopia in 1967.

### First evidence of hominin cannibalism
In the Sierra de Atapuerca of northern Spain are prehistoric caves in which a possible human ancestor – *H. antecessor* – lived *c.* 850,000 years ago. Among the remains found here are skulls and other human bones displaying gouges and scars, suggesting that a tool had been used for skinning, scraping flesh and extracting marrow. The same markings are mirrored in animal bones found nearby.

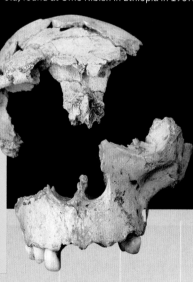

### Being human: definitions
- **Human:** intelligent, bipedal primate of the genus *Homo*, especially *H. sapiens*
- **Hominid:** modern and ancient great apes
- **Hominin:** modern and extinct humans and our closest relatives

## HUMAN EVOLUTION
### A snapshot of the *Homo* family tree

Pinpointing the origins (and demise) of early humans is notoriously tricky. Anthropologists have long relied on dating bones and rock to assess our ancestral lineage, but increasingly molecular studies of ancient DNA and genetic analysis of living human populations are expanding our knowledge. Here, the approximate spans of each *Homo* species (represented by blue bars) are based on current evidence in the fossil record.

Hominins possibly present in north-west China ∎

<< ∎ 2.8 MYA: LD 350-1 jawbone – the **earliest known *Homo* specimen** – found in Ethiopia

∎ *Australopithecus* becomes extinct

∎ More sophisticated Acheulean stone tools emerge, such as oval hand axes

● *Homo rudolfensis*

*Homo habilis*

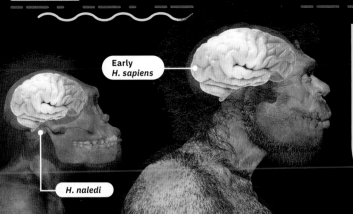

Early
H. sapiens

H. naledi

## First recognizable humans

If we define "human" as being a member of the genus *Homo*, then at least three early species are known from around 2 MYA: *H. habilis*, *H. rudolfensis* and *H. erectus* (right). Some experts assert that the first two of these species more closely resemble the hominin *Australopithecus*, in which case it is *H. erectus* that should be considered the earliest "true" human.

## Largest human brain

Modern humans have the largest brains in the *Homo* genus, varying from at least 1,000 to 2,000 cm³ (61–122 cu in); the latter exceeds that of any known early human. The largest estimate for a fossil is around 1,800 cm³ (110 cu in), for a *c.* 100,000-year-old skull from an unnamed species found near Xuchang, China. Above, the skull capacity of an early *H. sapiens* dated to *c.* 300,000 years old (see opposite) is compared with that of a contemporaneous hominin.

## Oldest human faecal matter

Fossilized human faeces from a Neanderthal campsite at El Salt near Alicante, Spain, has been dated to around 50,000 years ago. Analysis using gas chromatography at the Massachusetts Institute of Technology supports the view that Neanderthals (*H. neanderthalensis*) were omnivores, consuming both vegetable matter and meat.

## First human language

The ability to articulate is believed to have been dependent upon physical changes in the larynx (voice box), which was more ape-like prior to 2 MYA. The discovery of a human-like hyoid bone (which supports the tongue) at Spain's Sima de los Huesos site indicates that even early Neanderthals may have been capable of some form of speech as far back as 430,000 years ago. However, cognitive ability – also imperative for language development – is harder to ascertain.

*H. erectus* displays smaller back teeth, a less robust jaw and a more distinctively human skeleton than its two rivals.

## Oldest hominin infant

"Selam" ("Peace"), a possible human ancestor, died *c.* 3.3 MYA aged around three. Her remains were found on 10 Dec 2000 in Dikika, Ethiopia. Including a skull, torso, fingers and a foot, the fossils are the most complete specimen of *Australopithecus afarensis*. This is the same species as the more famous "Lucy", a 3.2-million-year-old adult female skeleton discovered nearby in 1974; Selam is sometimes referred to as "Lucy's baby".

100%

## Largest human teeth

Some early human and near-human relatives had much larger teeth than ours today. For example, *Paranthropus boisei* – which lived in East Africa about 2 MYA – had huge molars, with an average chewing surface of about 756 mm² (1.1 sq in) across three molar teeth. That is more than double the equivalent surface area of modern human molars.

---

• Possible first use of fire by humans

Hunting with spears may begin •

Age of *H. antecessor* fossils found in Western Europe •

Humans may start to wear clothing •

Homo sapiens
Denisovans
Homo luzonensis
Homo floresiensis
Homo neanderthalensis

Homo heidelbergensis

Homo naledi

• Last ice age begins

Homo erectus

• Use of ochre as a natural pigment
End of last ice age •

1,100,000 | 1,000,000 | 900,000 | 800,000 | 700,000 | 600,000 | 500,000 | 400,000 | 300,000 | 200,000 | 100,000 | Present

# Multiple Births

### Earliest evidence of twins
Two baby boys buried in the same grave – beneath the shoulder blade of a mammoth – were recovered during the excavation of an Upper Paleolithic site in Krems-Wachtberg, Austria, in 2005. In Nov 2020, DNA testing revealed that they were identical full-term twins who had died c. 31,000 years ago.

### Longest separated twins
Elizabeth Hamel (USA) and Ann Hunt (UK) were reunited on 1 May 2014 after 77 years 289 days apart. The twins were born Elizabeth and Patricia Lamb on 28 Feb 1936 in Hampshire, UK. They were separated shortly after birth when Ann was put up for adoption. Elizabeth, who knew of her twin, later moved to the USA with her birth mother, but Ann was unaware of her sister's existence until much later in life.

### Most premature twins
On 24 Nov 2018, Kambry and Keeley Ewoldt (USA) were born 125 days premature at the University of Iowa Hospitals & Clinics in the USA. The estimated date of delivery for the twins had been 29 Mar 2019; their gestational age was 22 weeks 1 day. At birth, Keeley weighed 490 g (1 lb 1.3 oz) and Kambry 449 g (15.8 oz). The twins were discharged from hospital in Apr 2019.

### Lightest twins at birth
On 19 Sep 2004, Mahajabeen Shaik (IND) gave birth to twins with a combined body weight of just 847 g (1 lb 13 oz). Hiba weighed 580 g (1 lb 4 oz) and Rumaisa 260 g (9.17 oz). They were delivered by Caesarean section at 25 weeks 6 days gestation in Maywood, Illinois, USA.

The **heaviest twins at birth** were born on 20 Feb 1924 to Mary Ann Haskin of Fort Smith, Arkansas, USA. They had an aggregate weight of 12.58 kg (27 lb 12 oz).

### Oldest conjoined twins
Lori Lynn and George Schappell (USA, b. 18 Sep 1961) were aged 59 years 186 days, as of 23 Mar 2021. The craniopagus twins have partially fused skulls but separate bodies, sharing bone, vital blood vessels and 30% of their brain. In 2007, they became the **first conjoined twins to identify as mixed gender** when George (b. Dori) declared he was transgender.

### Oldest male twins ever
On 23 Jan 2000, at the age of 104 years, Glen and Dale Moyer (USA, b. 20 Jun 1895, above right and left respectively) became the oldest living twins. Glen died on 16 Apr 2001, aged 105 years 300 days; Dale passed on 17 Jul 2004, aged 109 years 27 days.

The **female** record belongs to Kin Narita (right, top) and Gin Kanie (JPN, b. 1 Aug 1892). Kin died on 23 Jan 2000, aged 107 years 175 days; her sister passed away the following year, on 28 Feb.

### Oldest conjoined twins ever
GWR was sad to learn of the passing of Ronnie and Donnie Galyon (USA, b. 25 Oct 1951), who died on 4 Jul 2020 aged 68 years 253 days. They were born joined at the abdomen and spent more than 30 years travelling in circuses, sideshows and carnivals.

### Longest interval between triplets
The DeShane triplets of Norwood, Massachusetts, USA, were born 5 days 12 hr 34 min apart. Cian was born prematurely at just 22 weeks on 28 Dec 2019, while brother Declan and sister Rowan were born five days later on 2 Jan 2020. The triplets were born in separate decades!

### Oldest triplets (mixed)
Betty Woolf, Joseph Hocky and Minna Passman (USA, b. 27 Feb 1927) had their age verified as 93 years 174 days on 19 Aug 2020 in Carlsbad, California, USA. The triplets now live on different coasts but get together to celebrate their birthday.

### Rarest form of discordant twinning
Sienna "Sinny" Bernal (left) was born with a form of primordial dwarfism that is so uncommon, it has yet to be formally classified. But even rarer is the fact that she is the monozygotic twin of Sierra (both USA). The 22-year-old "discordant" sisters display the greatest height differential in identical twins: when last measured, Sinny stood 132 cm (4 ft 4 in) tall, while Sierra reached 170 cm (5 ft 7 in).

### Most twins in a school academic year
Visitors to New Trier High School in Winnetka, Illinois, USA, would be forgiven for thinking they were seeing double, as the 2016/17 freshman year contained 44 pairs of twins. Only three pairs (all female) were identical, while two sets were born on different days. The academic year had more than 1,000 pupils, meaning that the twinning rate at New Trier High was almost triple that of the US national average.

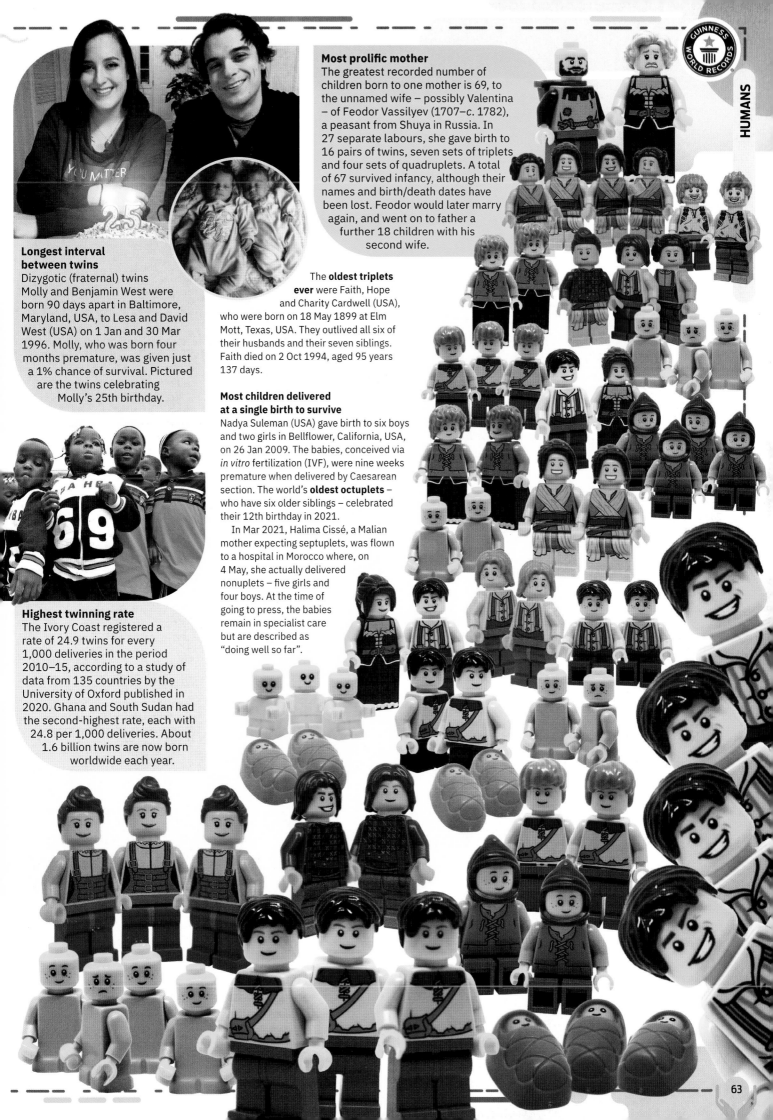

**Most prolific mother**
The greatest recorded number of children born to one mother is 69, to the unnamed wife – possibly Valentina – of Feodor Vassilyev (1707–c. 1782), a peasant from Shuya in Russia. In 27 separate labours, she gave birth to 16 pairs of twins, seven sets of triplets and four sets of quadruplets. A total of 67 survived infancy, although their names and birth/death dates have been lost. Feodor would later marry again, and went on to father a further 18 children with his second wife.

**Longest interval between twins**
Dizygotic (fraternal) twins Molly and Benjamin West were born 90 days apart in Baltimore, Maryland, USA, to Lesa and David West (USA) on 1 Jan and 30 Mar 1996. Molly, who was born four months premature, was given just a 1% chance of survival. Pictured are the twins celebrating Molly's 25th birthday.

The **oldest triplets ever** were Faith, Hope and Charity Cardwell (USA), who were born on 18 May 1899 at Elm Mott, Texas, USA. They outlived all six of their husbands and their seven siblings. Faith died on 2 Oct 1994, aged 95 years 137 days.

**Most children delivered at a single birth to survive**
Nadya Suleman (USA) gave birth to six boys and two girls in Bellflower, California, USA, on 26 Jan 2009. The babies, conceived via *in vitro* fertilization (IVF), were nine weeks premature when delivered by Caesarean section. The world's **oldest octuplets** – who have six older siblings – celebrated their 12th birthday in 2021.

In Mar 2021, Halima Cissé, a Malian mother expecting septuplets, was flown to a hospital in Morocco where, on 4 May, she actually delivered nonuplets – five girls and four boys. At the time of going to press, the babies remain in specialist care but are described as "doing well so far".

**Highest twinning rate**
The Ivory Coast registered a rate of 24.9 twins for every 1,000 deliveries in the period 2010–15, according to a study of data from 135 countries by the University of Oxford published in 2020. Ghana and South Sudan had the second-highest rate, each with 24.8 per 1,000 deliveries. About 1.6 billion twins are now born worldwide each year.

# Oldest...

### Vogue cover model
Dame Judi Dench (UK, b. 9 Dec 1934) featured on the cover of the Jun 2020 edition of British *Vogue* at the age of 85 years 150 days. One of the UK's most celebrated thespians, Dame Judi also holds the record for the **most Laurence Olivier awards won**, taking home eight trophies between 1977 and 2016.

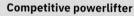

### Combined age of 16 siblings
As of 25 Feb 2021, the 16 Anderson siblings – born to Russell and Frances between 1930 and 1955 in Michigan, USA – had a combined age of 1,251 years 295 days. Arlene, Virginia, Joyce, Gordon, Marvin, Ronald, Wayne, Keith, Nancy, Carol, Gary, Susan, Sally, Kenneth, Bonnie and Dean have regular family gatherings and are pictured here in 1970 and 2019.

### Oldest person ever
The greatest authenticated human age is 122 years 164 days, by Jeanne Louise Calment (FRA, b. 21 Feb 1875). She died at a nursing home in Arles, France, on 4 Aug 1997, but not before becoming the **oldest actress** – in *Vincent and Me* (CAN, 1990) – and **surgery patient**, both at the age of 114. The latter record was broken in 2016 by one-time oldest living woman Chiyo Miyako (JPN, b. 2 May 1901), who survived the amputation of both legs aged 116 years old.

The **oldest man ever** was Jiroemon Kimura (JPN), who was born on 19 Apr 1897 and passed away on 12 Jun 2013, aged 116 years 54 days.

The **oldest man** record changed hands twice in the past year. Dumitru Comănescu (ROM, 21 Nov 1908–27 Jun 2020) passed away at the age of 111 years 249 days, just as work began on this edition. A new contender emerged from Puerto Rico: Emilio Flores Marquez was born on 8 Aug 1908 – the 8th day of the 8th month of the 8th year of the 20th century – and, as of 20 Apr 2021, was confirmed as being 112 years 255 days old.

### ▶ Woman
Kane Tanaka (JPN, b. 2 Jan 1903) was 118 years 108 days old as of 20 Apr 2021, making her the **oldest person**. The resilient Kane – the oldest Asian person ever – survived paratyphoid fever in her 30s, pancreatic cancer in her 40s and surgery for bowel cancer aged 103. She credits her long life to having a close family, eating well, sleeping well and keeping her mind sharp with mathematical puzzles.

### Competitive powerlifter
Edith Murway-Traina (USA, b. 8 Aug 1921) took up deadlifting and benching at 91 to indulge a friend who had "dragged [her] kicking and screaming" to the gym. The Floridian was soon hooked and began entering competitions. In her most recent event, on 10 Nov 2019, she placed second in her class with a 60-lb (27.2-kg) bench press aged 98 years 94 days!

Edith, a former line-dance instructor, hopes to compete in 2021 to celebrate her 100th birthday!

### COVID-19 survivor
Sister André (FRA, b. 11 Feb 1904 as Lucile Randon) – the world's second-oldest person (see below) – tested positive for COVID-19 on 16 Jan 2021. The Catholic nun, who has been blind for more than 75 years, was isolated in her retirement home in Toulon, France, but did not develop symptoms. She was given the all-clear in time for her 117th birthday.

### Competitive rope skipper
Annie Judis (USA, b. 23 Nov 1943) competed in the Southern California Open Jump Rope Championship on 29 Feb 2020 at the age of 76 years 98 days. The septuagenarian skipper, sporting a grey wig, shuffled slowly into position using a walking frame, then surprised the judges by throwing off her old-lady disguise and performing a 2-min 20-sec choreographed routine to the song "Sexy and I Know It".

| Top 10 oldest living people | | |
|---|---|---|
| **Name** | **Date of birth** | **Age** |
| 1 Kane Tanaka (JPN, left) | 2 Jan 1903 | 118 years 108 days |
| 2 Sister André (FRA, above) | 11 Feb 1904 | 117 years 68 days |
| 3 Francisca Celsa dos Santos (BRA) | 21 Oct 1904 | 116 years 181 days |
| 4 Jeanne Bot (FRA) | 14 Jan 1905 | 116 years 96 days |
| 5 Antônia da Santa Cruz (BRA) | 13 Jun 1905 | 115 years 311 days |
| 6 Tekla Juniewicz (UKR/POL) | 10 Jun 1906 | 114 years 314 days |
| 7 Thelma Sutcliffe (USA) | 1 Oct 1906 | 114 years 201 days |
| 8 Valentine Ligny (FRA) | 22 Oct 1906 | 114 years 180 days |
| 9 Anonymous (JPN) | 17 Dec 1906 | 114 years 124 days |
| 10 Hama Yasukawa (JPN) | 19 Jan 1907 | 114 years 91 days |

*Source: Gerontology Research Group; correct as of 20 Apr 2021*

### Soccer player
On 17 Oct 2020, Ezzeldin Bahader (EGY, b. 3 Nov 1945) played for the Egyptian third-division team 6th October at the age of 74 years 349 days. During the game – against El Ayat Sports – the retired civil engineer missed from the penalty spot. "Nothing is easy, but nothing is impossible," he said when handed his GWR certificate.

### Emmy Award winner
At the virtual Creative Arts Emmys on 15 Sep 2020, sitcom creator Norman Lear (USA, b. 27 Jul 1922) won the award for Outstanding Variety Special (Live), aged 98 years 50 days. His sixth Emmy, it recognized the second instalment of the two-part special *Live in Front of a Studio Audience: "All in the Family" and "Good Times"* (ABC, 2019).

### Competitive footbag player
Hacky-sacker Ken Moller (USA, b. 14 Jul 1947) entered the Intermediate Freestyle Routine event at the World Footbag Championships on 2 Jul 2020 aged 72 years 354 days. He performed to the Bee Gees' hit "Stayin' Alive".

### HGV licence holder
Trucker James Findlay Hamilton (b. 1 Jun 1936) of Airdrie in Scotland, UK, was still driving his heavy goods vehicle at the age of 84 years 245 days, as verified on 1 Feb 2021.

### Pilot
World War II "Flying Tiger" veteran Harry Moyer (USA, b. 30 Oct 1920) celebrated his 100th birthday in 2020 by circling his Mooney Mk 21 aircraft singlehandedly over San Luis Obispo in California, USA.

### Tandem skydiver
On 2 Jul 2020, at the age of 103 years 180 days, former aircraft builder Alfred "Al" Blaschke (USA, b. 4 Jan 1917) leapt from a plane over San Marcos in Texas, USA.

### Competitive tractor puller
The motorsport of tractor pulling requires the dragging of heavy weights along a 100-m (328-ft) track behind an antique or modified tractor. The oldest competitor in the field is Otto Graep (USA, b. 11 Nov 1919), who pulled at the Puget Sound Antique Tractor & Machinery Association show in Lynden, Washington, USA, on 1 Aug 2019, aged 99 years 263 days.

### Journalist
British-Israeli writer and broadcaster Walter Bingham (b. 5 Jan 1924 as Wolfgang Billig in the Weimar Republic) was 97 years 90 days old on 5 Apr 2021, as verified in Jerusalem. He contributes regularly to the *Jerusalem Post* newspaper, and hosts *The Walter Bingham File* on Israel News Talk Radio, making him also the **oldest radio talk-show host**.

### Office manager
As verified on 5 Nov 2020, Yasuko Tamaki (JPN, b. 15 May 1930) continues to work at the Sunco Industries Co. in Osaka, Japan, at the age of 90 years 174 days.

### Married couple
Ecuadorians Julio Cesar Mora Tapia (b. 10 Mar 1910) and Waldramina Maclovia Quinteros Reyes (b. 16 Oct 1915) were married on 7 Feb 1941 in secret because their families disapproved of the relationship. At the time of Sr Tapia's death on 22 Oct 2020, after 79 years of marriage, the couple had reached a combined age of 215 years 232 days.

### Captain Sir Tom Moore (1920–2021)
The passing of 100-year-old World War II veteran Captain Sir Tom Moore (UK, 30 Apr 1920–2 Feb 2021) was marked by a guard of honour at his funeral, a three-volley gun salute and a flypast from an RAF C-47 Dakota. By walking lengths of his garden, the inspirational pensioner raised £32.7 m ($44.5 m) for the UK's National Health Service during the COVID-19 pandemic – the **most money raised by a charity walk (individual)**. At the age of exactly 100 years, he also became the **oldest person to reach No.1 on the UK's Official Singles Chart** with the release of "You'll Never Walk Alone", featuring Michael Ball and The NHS Voices of Care Choir. His motto of "Tomorrow will be a good day" provided hope to many people during the lockdowns of 2020. He's pictured below being knighted by Queen Elizabeth II in Jul 2020.

Captain Sir Tom Moore
1920 - 2021
The Nation Salutes You

# Superlative Statures

**Junrey Balawing (1993–2020)**
Shortly after going to press with *GWR 2021*, we heard the sad news that Junrey Balawing had passed away. Junrey, the **shortest man (non-mobile)**, stood 59.93 cm (1 ft 11.5 in) tall when measured in Sindangan in the Philippines on 12 Jun 2011, on the occasion of his 18th birthday (pictured).

### 1. Shortest woman
▶ Jyoti Amge (IND) measured 62.8 cm (2 ft 0.7 in) in Nagpur, India, on 16 Dec 2011. Her vivacious charisma and determination to succeed has seen her become the **shortest actress**, playing Ma Petite in the critically acclaimed hit US TV show *American Horror Story*.

### 2. Shortest man
▶ When measured on 29 Feb 2020 in Bogotá, Colombia, Edward Niño Hernández (COL) stood 72.1 cm (2 ft 4.3 in) tall. It wasn't until Niño was aged 20 that the cause of his stature was diagnosed as severe hypothyroidism. "Size and height don't matter!" he insists. "I want people to meet who I truly am: small in size, big in heart!"

### 3. Shortest teenage twins (male)
On 7 Jan 2021, at the age of 17 years 100 days, Zachary and Tristan Lelièvre (both CAN) measured an average of 114.88 cm (3 ft 9 in). The identical twins, both born with achondroplasia – a bone-growth disorder – play elite badminton with the Montreal International Club and aspire to compete in the 2024 Paralympic Games in Paris. They are on course to secure the adult record for **shortest twins (male)** on 19 Sep 2021.

### 4. Shortest twins (female)
As verified on 25 Jan 2021, the shortest living female twins are Elisabeth and Katharina Lindinger (both DEU), with an average stature of 128 cm (4 ft 2 in).

### 5. Tallest twins (female)
Identical twins Ann and Claire Recht (both USA, b. 9 Feb 1988) were each found to have an average height of 201 cm (6 ft 7 in). The siblings signed up for the American University Eagles volleyball team in 2006, helping the side to secure three Patriot League tournament titles.

### 6. Tallest twins (male)
As of 1 Jan 2021, Robin and Brook Lopez (both USA) measured 213 cm (7 ft) apiece. Their outstanding height makes them a prime asset for the basketball court, and in 2008, they signed for the Phoenix Suns and New Jersey/Brooklyn Nets NBA teams respectively. Brook currently plays for the Milwaukee Bucks, while Robin turns out for the Washington Wizards.

### 7. Tallest firefighter
On 18 Aug 2020, the 211.2-cm-tall (6-ft 11-in) Brandon Berridge (USA, pictured inset) became the first person confirmed by GWR as the tallest living firefighter. He operates out of the Tullahoma Fire Department in Tennessee, USA. However, just as we were going to press with this edition, we received photographic evidence

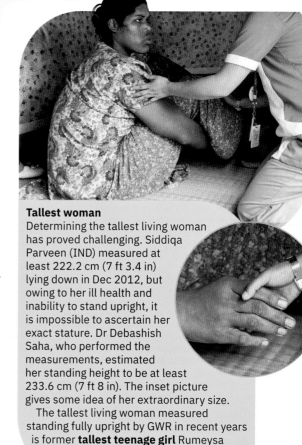

**Tallest woman**
Determining the tallest living woman has proved challenging. Siddiqa Parveen (IND) measured at least 222.2 cm (7 ft 3.4 in) lying down in Dec 2012, but owing to her ill health and inability to stand upright, it is impossible to ascertain her exact stature. Dr Debashish Saha, who performed the measurements, estimated her standing height to be at least 233.6 cm (7 ft 8 in). The inset picture gives some idea of her extraordinary size.

The tallest living woman measured standing fully upright by GWR in recent years is former **tallest teenage girl** Rumeysa Gelgi (TUR), who in 2014 stood 213.6 cm (7 ft 0.09 in) at the age of 17.

in support of a claim from Allan Mulkey (main image) of Harris County, Texas, USA. The images show him being measured at 221 cm (7 ft 3 in), although we await further video evidence before formally ratifying his stature.

**8. Tallest teenager**

Olivier Rioux of Beloeil in Quebec, Canada, stood 226.9 cm (7 ft 5.3 in) tall when measured on 19 Dec 2020 at the age of 14 years 321 days. As with the Lopez twins (see #6), his impressive stature soon attracted the attention of the basketball fraternity, and he signed for Real Madrid's team ("Los Blancos") in 2019, to play in the Castelldefels Under-13 International Tournament. To put Olivier's height into perspective, he's already taller than Tacko Fall (USA) of the Boston Celtics – currently the **tallest NBA player** at 226 cm (7 ft 5 in).

▶ **9. Tallest man**

Turn to our special Hall of Fame feature on pp.76–77 to learn all about the 251-cm-tall (8-ft 2.8-in) Sultan Kösen (TUR).

In 2011, Sultan Kösen became the first man taller than 8 ft (2.43 m) to be measured by GWR in more than 20 years.

# Body Art

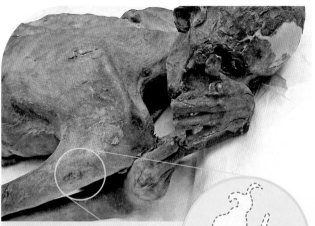

### Oldest figurative tattoos

Infrared technology has revealed inked designs on two mummies – found near the ancient Egyptian site of Gebelein – which date to 3351–3017 BCE. According to the British Museum, "Gebelein Man A" has tattoos of a Barbary sheep and a wild bull (inset, top and bottom respectively). "Gebelein Woman", the **oldest tattooed female**, has L- and S-shaped motifs upon her upper arm and shoulder. While not the oldest tattoos (see below), these are the earliest-known examples to represent identifiable figures, rather than just geometric shapes.

### Oldest tattoos

Discovered in 1991 in the Italian Alps, a mummified man dubbed "Ötzi" – thought to have been killed by an arrow strike around 5,300 years ago – has a total of 61 tattoos on his body. The simple geometric marks were created by slicing open the skin and rubbing in charcoal dust.

### ▶ Most tattooed man

Lucky Diamond Rich (AUS, b. Gregory McLaren, NZ) has spent more than 1,000 hr having his skin decorated by hundreds of tattoo artists. What started off as a full bodysuit of designs was later filled in completely with black ink – including the eyelids, the delicate skin between the toes and even his gums. Lucky, a sideshow artist and street performer, continues to tattoo white and coloured images over the black – a coverage estimated to now be over 200%.

### Most tattoos of...

**A single name**: 300, by Diedra Vigil (USA) as of 25 May 2020. The name? "Diedra".
**A cartoon character**: 52, of Rick from *Rick and Morty* (Adult Swim, USA), by Nikolay Belyanskiy (RUS) as of 31 Aug 2019.
**❍ Characters from an animated series**: 203, from *The Simpsons* (FOX, USA), by Michael Baxter (AUS) as of 3 Dec 2014.
**Skulls**: 376, by Charles "Chuck" Helmke (USA) as of 3 Dec 2016.
**Squares**: 848, by Matt Gone (USA) as of 7 Jul 2014.

### Most tattoos of a musician

Eminem super-fan Nikki Patterson (UK) sports 15 tattoos of the US rapper on her body, as verified on 31 Mar 2020 in Aberdeen, UK. Nikki was 19 when she commissioned her first Eminem tattoo. Her designs include artwork from the album covers *Recovery* and *The Marshall Mathers LP*, and also an image of the rapper with singer Skylar Grey.

### ▶ Most body modifications for a married couple

Victor Hugo Peralta (URY) and his wife Gabriela (ARG) have a combined total of 84 body modifications, as verified on 7 Jul 2014. These augmentations consist of 50 piercings, eight microdermals, 14 body implants, five dental implants, four ear expanders, two ear bolts and one forked tongue. Victor, who describes himself as a "beautiful monster", has a 95% tattoo coverage over his body.

### Longest-running tattooists

The Razzouk family of Jerusalem traces its ancestry back more than 700 years, when their forefathers in Egypt began tattooing Coptic Christians. The idea of marking a pilgrimage to the Holy Land with a tattoo continues to this day; the family's current store is operated by Wassim Razzouk, a 27th-generation tattooist who still uses centuries-old stencils such as the Jerusalem cross (inset).

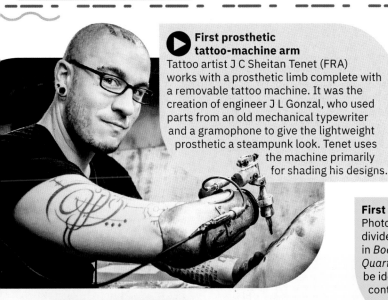

### First prosthetic tattoo-machine arm
Tattoo artist J C Sheitan Tenet (FRA) works with a prosthetic limb complete with a removable tattoo machine. It was the creation of engineer J L Gonzal, who used parts from an old mechanical typewriter and a gramophone to give the lightweight prosthetic a steampunk look. Tenet uses the machine primarily for shading his designs.

### First modern tongue bifurcation
Photographs of Dustin Allor (USA) with a divided tongue were first published in 1997 in *Body Play* (#16) and *Modern Primitives Quarterly* – making her the first person to be identified by name as having had this controversial body mod. Surgeons have warned of serious risks surrounding the splitting of the tongue.

### Most flesh tunnels in the face
James Goss (UK) has modified his features with the addition of 14 hollow, tube-like pieces of jewellery, as verified on 5 Dec 2020 in Bedford, UK. James improved upon the previous record, which had been held by Germany's Joel Miggler since 2014, by three.

### Most piercings (female)
Elaine Davidson (BRA/UK) received 4,225 piercings between Jan 1997 and 8 Jun 2006. At any one time, she is adorned with up to 460, and as of 2021 she claims to have had more than 11,000 in her lifetime. On 16 Sep 2012, Elaine achieved the **heaviest weight pulled by the tongue (female)**, using a meat hook to drag a volunteer and trolley weighing 113 kg (249 lb) at the South Bank in London, UK.

### Most piercings in the tongue
Francesco Vacca (USA) brought his number of tongue piercings up to 20 on 5 Jan 2017 at the Invisibleself piercing studio in Lyndhurst, New Jersey, USA.

### Most valuable dermal piercing
In Feb 2021, rapper Lil Uzi Vert (b. Symere Bysil Woods, USA) had a pink diamond worth $24 m (£17.3 m) secured on to his forehead by dermal piercing. He shared images on Instagram with the caption "Beauty is pain".

### Most body modifications (male)
IT consultant Rolf Buchholz (DEU) had 516 body mods during the last official count on 16 Dec 2012. His physical adornments included 481 piercings, two subdermal horn implants and magnetic implants in the fingertips of his right hand.

The **female** record is held by Maria José Cristerna (MEX), who has a total of 49 body modifications. These include significant tattoo coverage, multiple piercings and a range of transdermal implants on her forehead, chest and arms.

### Narrowest waist
Cathie Jung (USA) has a corseted waist with a circumference of 15 in (38.1 cm). Un-corseted, it is 21 in (53.3 cm). Inspired by her love for Victoriana, at the age of 38 Cathie began wearing a 6-in-wide (15.2-cm) training belt to gradually reduce her then 26-in (66-cm) waist. She has never defined her waist through surgical means.

### Largest lip plate
Women of the Surma people in Ethiopia prepare for marriage by inserting discs of increasing size into their lip to stretch it. These plates are made by the women themselves from clay, coloured with ochre and charcoal, and then fire-baked. In Oct 2014, the lip plate belonging to Ataye Eligidagne (ETH) was measured at a width of 19.5 cm (7.7 in) and a circumference of 59.5 cm (1 ft 11.4 in). Below, Ataye shows her lip with the plate removed.

# Superhumans

The people listed here can be considered "superhumans" for their ability to survive the most testing of circumstances. Take, for example, William Pace of Texas, USA (above). In 1917, at the age of eight, he was accidentally shot in the head. The bullet was never removed, but despite (or because of) this, he lived a normal life, dying some 94 years 175 days later: the **longest time to live with a bullet in the head**.

### Lowest body temperature survived

On 30 Nov 2014, a 27-month-old toddler wandered barefoot outside his grandmother's home in Racławice, Poland, during the early hours of the morning, when temperatures dipped to -7°C (19.4°F). The child, identified only as Adam, collapsed by a creek and lay for at least three hours before being discovered by police. He was rushed to hospital in a heated ambulance and successfully resuscitated, despite having a rectal temperature of just 11.8°C (53.2°F). He was up and walking within two weeks. "He plays, frolics, runs... he can even be unruly," said Janusz Skalski, the heart surgeon who led Adam's recovery team.

The **lowest intentional body temperature** was achieved by doctors treating a case of ovarian cancer in a 51-year-old woman. On 28 Dec 1955, the patient's heart rate was slowly decreased until cardiac standstill was reached. During this time, her body was cooled to 9°C (48.2°F), and remained at this temperature – supported by an artificial respirator – for one hour. She was revived and suffered no ill effects from the experience.

### Highest dry-air temperature endured...

**Clothed**: During US Air Force (USAF) experiments held in 1960, heavily clothed men were subjected to air temperatures that increased until an unbearable 260°C (500°F). For comparison, saunas are typically no warmer than 90°C (194°F).

**Naked**: In the same set of tests with unclothed subjects, the air temperature could be endured only up to 205°C (400°F).

### Highest contamination with radioactive material survived

In 1976, Harold McCluskey (USA), a worker at a plutonium plant in Washington State, was exposed to 500 times the safe *lifetime* dose of radioactive material. He was extracting radioactive americium from plutonium when the sample exploded, tearing off his mask and peppering his face with radioactive glass and steel. For a time, McCluskey was so radioactive that he could set off a Geiger counter from 15 m (50 ft).

### Highest blood-sugar level survived

The glucose content of blood is measured in millimoles per litre (mmol/L) or, in the USA, milligrams per deciliter (mg/dL), and the normal amount is *c*. 4–6 mmol/L (70–110 mg/dL). When six-year-old Michael Patrick Buonocore (USA) was admitted to the ER in East Stroudsburg, Pennsylvania, on 23 Mar 2008, his blood-sugar level had reached 147.6 mmol/L (2,656 mg/dL) – nearly 30 times the average.

### Longest survival without food

Although not recommended, a well-nourished individual can survive without medical consequences on a diet of sugar and water for 30 days or more. The longest period for which anyone has gone without

### Heaviest weight sustained on the body

Spanish welder and Muay Thai champion Eduardo Armallo Lasaga endured 1,483 kg (3,269 lb) of concrete masonry placed on his supine body on the set of *Lo Show dei Record* in Rome, Italy, on 4 Mar 2010. The 70 blocks – equivalent to 23 fully grown adult men – were placed quickly by a team of assistants and then held in position for a minimum of five seconds.

### Strangest diet

In 1959, Monsieur Mangetout, aka Michel Lotito of France, discovered an aptitude for eating glass and metal. Gastroenterologists who X-rayed his stomach described his ability to consume *c*. 2 lb (900 g) of metal a day as unique. His outlandish diet included 18 bicycles, 15 supermarket trolleys, seven TV sets, six chandeliers, two beds, a pair of skis, a computer, a coffin and – over the course of two years – a Cessna light aircraft.

18 · 15 · 7 · 1

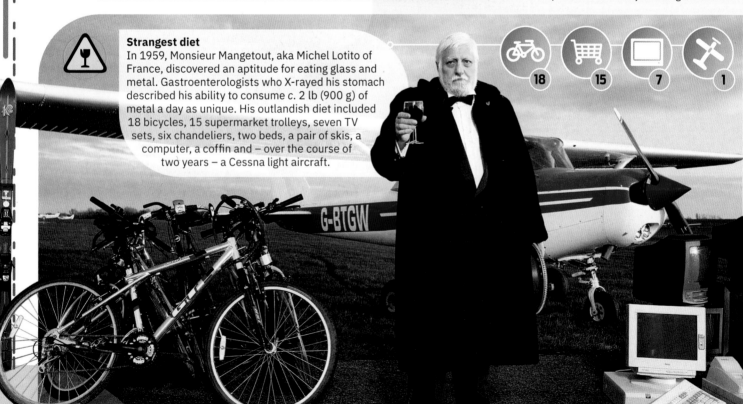

G-BTGW

solid food is 382 days, in the case of Angus Barbieri (UK), who lived on tea, coffee, water and vitamins in Maryfield Hospital, Dundee, from Jun 1965 to Jul 1966. His weight dropped from 214 kg (471 lb; 33 st 10 lb) to 80.74 kg (178 lb; 12 st 10 lb).

The **longest survival without food and water** is 18 days. Andreas Mihavecz (AUT) – an 18-year-old passenger in a road-traffic accident in Höchst, Austria – was mistakenly placed into a basement holding cell by police on 1 Apr 1979. He was then promptly forgotten about. On 18 Apr, he was discovered 18 kg (40 lb) lighter and close to death. The police officers involved were later jailed for 90 days themselves, although not without regular meals.

### Longest time holding the breath

**Male**: Budimir Šobat (HRV) held his breath voluntarily for 24 min 37.36 sec in Sisak, Croatia, on 27 Mar 2021.

### Longest full-body contact with ice

Romain Vandendorpe (FRA) spent 2 hr 35 min 33 sec up to his neck in ice cubes in Wattrelos, France, on 19 Dec 2020. The rules of this gruelling record dictate that the clock can only start once the box – with its footprint of 1 m² (10.7 sq ft) – is filled to the level of the participant's neck.

### Longest time spent in space

Cosmonaut Gennady Padalka (RUS) has spent more time off Earth than any other person. He broke fellow cosmonaut Sergey Krikalev's record of 803 days on 28 Jun 2015 – 92 days into his 168-day stay on the *International Space Station*. By the time he landed on 12 Sep, Padalka had spent a career total of 879 days – nearly 2.5 years – in space. One of the side-effects of long-term space travel is "spaceflight osteopenia" – a reduction in bone mass by more than 1% per month during weightlessness.

**Female**: Karoline Mariechen Meyer (BRA) held her breath for 18 min 32.59 sec at the Racer Academy swimming pool in Florianópolis, Brazil, on 10 Jul 2009.

### Longest submergence underwater

In 1986, two-year-old Michelle Funk of Salt Lake City, Utah, USA, made a full recovery – with an "intact neurological outcome" – after spending 66 min underwater, having fallen into a swollen creek.

### Highest g-force endured (non-voluntary)

IndyCar driver Kenny Bräck (SWE) suffered fractures of his right femur, sternum, a lumbar vertebra and ankles in a crash on lap 188 of the Chevy 500 at Texas Motor Speedway, USA, on 12 Oct 2003. Bräck's Dallara-Honda made wheel-to-wheel contact with another car, sending his vehicle high into the air and into a steel fence post. According to Bräck's "crash violence recording system", the 220-mph (354-km/h) collision resulted in a split-second deceleration of 214 g.

**The first person to conduct an untethered spacewalk** was Space Shuttle astronaut Bruce McCandless (USA) on 7 Feb 1984.

### Highest untethered human outside a vehicle

Our bodies are not designed for extremes of altitude, which is why we need protective suits and breathing apparatus. The highest altitude by a human outside a vehicle is 39,068.5 m (128,177 ft), by Felix Baumgartner (AUT) prior to his leap from a balloon over New Mexico, USA, on 14 Oct 2012. During descent, he went into a rapid spin but remained conscious and was able to re-stabilize. He also reached a peak speed of 1,357.6 km/h (843.6 mi/h; Mach 1.25), becoming the **first person in freefall to break the sound barrier**.

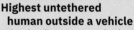

### Highest g-force endured (voluntary)

The "gravitational-force equivalent" – or "g-force" – is primarily a measure of acceleration or deceleration. To study the effects of such forces on the human body, USAF test subject Eli Beeding Jr was subjected to a deceleration of 82.6 g for 0.04 sec while travelling backwards on a rocket sled at Holloman Air Force Base in New Mexico, USA, on 16 May 1958.

# Whiskers

### Longest beard ever
Hans N Langseth (NOR) had facial growth measuring 5.33 m (17 ft 6 in) at the time of his burial at Kensett, Iowa, USA, in 1927. Natural beards rarely exceed 1–2 m (3–5 ft), so Langseth matted his dead whiskers into a coil, like a dreadlock. He requested that after his death, it should be cut off and kept for posterity, so his son donated the behemoth beard to the Smithsonian Institution in Washington, DC (below, from 1967).

### Heaviest weight lifted by beard
Antanas Kontrimas (LTU) lifted 63.8 kg (140 lb 10 oz) – in the form of TV presenter Gupse Özay – with his beard on the set of *Rekorlar Dünyası* in Istanbul, Turkey, on 26 Jun 2013. This marked the 10th occasion on which he bettered the record he first set in 2000, when he hoisted a 55.7-kg (122-lb 12-oz) volunteer.

### Longest beard ever (female)
In 1884, the whiskers of Madame Devere (aka Mary Ann or Jane Devere, USA) were measured at 36 cm (1 ft 2 in). She performed as a "bearded lady" at several circuses – often billed as the "Kentucky Wonder".

The **longest female beard** is currently that of Vivian Wheeler (USA). At its longest, it measured 25.5 cm (10.04 in) from the follicle to the tip of the hairs, as confirmed in Milan, Italy, on 8 Apr 2011.

### Youngest female with a full beard
Harnaam Kaur (UK, b. 29 Nov 1990) was aged 24 years 282 days when she was confirmed to have a full beard on 7 Sep 2015 in Slough, Berkshire, UK. At the age of 12, Kaur was diagnosed with polycystic ovary syndrome, which boosts the level of androgen (the "male" hormone) in women.

### Heaviest train pulled by beard
Ismael Rivas Falcon (ESP) tugged a 2,753.1-kg (6,069-lb) locomotive – heavier than two Mini cars – for 10 m (32 ft 9 in) using only his beard on 15 Nov 2001. The follicular feat was staged in Madrid, Spain.

### Longest moustache?
When last measured in 2010, the whiskers of Ram Singh Chauhan (IND) extended more than 2 m (6 ft 6 in) beyond his cheeks. What began as a humble moustache in 1970 now trails along the ground. Like the beard of Hans Langseth (above), it is matted – in this case, into two thick strands measuring 4.29 m (14 ft) from tip to tip. Chauhan still considers his growth to be a moustache, although in competitive facial-hair growing, a moustache is defined as whiskers growing only from the top lip (not cheeks).

The **heaviest road vehicle pulled by beard** is a car weighing 2,205 kg (4,861 lb). It was dragged across a distance of 40 m (131 ft) by Kapil Gehlot (IND) in Jodhpur, Rajasthan, India, on 21 Jun 2012. Gehlot – whose roster of party tricks also includes pulling cars with his beard while wearing roller skates – surpassed the record held by Lithuania's Antanas Kontrimas (above).

### Largest gathering of people with monkey-tail beards
This asymmetric facial hairstyle mimics the curving arc of a simian's tail, with one side of the wearer's face shaved clean. On 17 May 2013, Tom Shadmi (ISR) brought together a troop of 244 participants with monkey-tail beards in Tel Aviv, Israel.

### Largest gathering of people with moustaches
On 26 Nov 2010, a group of 1,131 moustachioed men assembled at the Xcel Energy Center in St Paul, Minnesota, USA. The event was organized by KARE 11 TV as part of "Movember", an annual fundraising project in support of men's health and prostate cancer.

The **largest gathering of people wearing false moustaches** comprised 6,471 participants and was achieved by the University of Colorado Health and the Denver Broncos (both USA). It took place at Sports Authority Field at Mile High in Denver, Colorado, USA, on 29 Nov 2015.

### Longest chain of artificial beards
Sharon Rose McKeever (IRL) linked up 508 fake beards in Baltimore, Cork, Ireland, on 3 Jul 2015. They stretched for 197.38 m (647 ft 6 in). All the beards were hand-knitted by McKeever herself in five days.

### Largest beard and moustache competition
A total of 738 pogonophiles came together for the World Beard and Moustache Championships (WBMC) on 1 Sep 2017. The event was hosted by Austin Facial Hair Club in Texas, USA. Inaugurated in 1990, the WBMC invites entrants to compete across more than 25 categories, including "Dali", "Musketeer" and "Fu Manchu".

The **most wins** at the WBMC is eight, by Germany's Karl-Heinz Hille, his most recent success coming in 2011. For the previous 12 years, Hille had competed in the "Imperial Partial Beard" category; this requires the cultivation of luscious sideburns (aka sideboards).

### Longest beard
Sarwan Singh's (CAN) facial hair combs out to a length of 2.49 m (8 ft 2 in), as confirmed in Surrey, British Columbia, Canada, on 8 Sep 2011. As a devout Sikh, Singh adheres to the articles of faith known as the "Five Ks", one of which ("Kesh") forbids the cutting of hair.

## Whisker world championships

In 2020, Guinness World Records' Editor-in-Chief Craig Glenday was invited to join the judging panel for the annual US National Beard and Moustache Championships. Owing to COVID-19 restrictions, the event was held online, allowing for 180 entrants from across the USA to show off their incredible facial hair in one of 20 categories.

**BEST IN SHOW ~ DREW MCNAUGHTON**
2020 NATIONAL BEARD AND MOUSTACHE CHAMPIONSHIPS

The overall winner was Drew McNaughton (above), who competed in the "Garibaldi" category, defined as a beard "wide and round at the bottom, and no more than 8 inches [20.3 cm] in length as measured from the bottom of the lower lip; while grooming aids are allowed, the more natural looking the better".

The competition was streamed on Twitch on 19 Dec 2020 and entry fees were donated to the charity Direct Relief. "It was an honour to be part of such a fantastic community," said Craig, who – despite 10 months of lockdown – was unable to grow a decent beard in time for the event!

### Thickest strand of hair

A hair's breadth varies depending on genetics and hair colour, ranging from 17 μm to 181 μm (micrometres, or millionths of a metre). A single strand plucked from the beard of Micah Dyer (USA) in 2013, however, was found to measure an unprecedented 477.52 μm.

### Most beards styled in one hour with an electric trimmer

Working against the clock, Dan Gregory (UK) neatened-up nine beards at the Allianz Arena in Munich, Germany, on 21 Sep 2019. The attempt was a collaboration with appliance manufacturer Braun (DEU).

### Most toothpicks in a beard (one minute)

Dean Carter (UK) filled his facial hair with 33 toothpicks in 60 sec as part of a record-breaking game show staged at the Haven Devon Cliffs Holiday Park in Exmouth, UK, on 11 May 2017. (See also right.)

### Longest chain of beards

On 2 Dec 2007, a total of 20 members of the Association of German Beard Clubs intertwined their whiskers to create a chain measuring 19.05 m (62 ft 6 in) long – twice the length of a London Routemaster bus.

### ▶ Most clothes pegs in a beard

For some people, it's what you put in your beard that counts. Joel Strasser (USA) accommodated 359 clothes pegs in his whiskers on 17 Nov 2020 in Yelm, Washington, USA. Strasser also holds the records for **pencils** (450, inset), **beard baubles** (542), **forks** (121), **golf tees** (607), **chopsticks** (520) and **toothpicks** (3,500)!

### Hairiest family

Victor "Larry" Gomez, Gabriel "Danny" Ramos Gomez, Luisa Lilia De Lira Aceves and Jesus Manuel Fajardo Aceves (all MEX) are four of a family of 19 that span five generations, all suffering from the rare condition called congenital generalized hypertrichosis (CGH), characterized by excessive facial and torso hair. The women are covered with a light-to-medium coat of hair, while the men of the family have thick hair on approximately 98% of their bodies, apart from their palms and soles. The family helped scientists with the analysis of the gene responsible for CGH; as a result, it was discovered that the condition is primarily associated with the X chromosome.

Geil shaved daily from her teens but, at the age of 39, she gave up the razors and treatments in order to cultivate a full beard.

### First female contestant in a "Full Beard" category at the WBMC

The wearing of artificial whiskers in the "Creative/Realistic" class allows those without facial hair – including women – to compete at the WBMC. In 2017, however, Rose Geil (USA) made history by competing in the natural "Full Beard" category. Impressively, she came in sixth place out of 107 competitors. The root cause of her hair growth is still to be confirmed.

# Round-Up

### First proven case of anthropodermic bibliopegy
There are currently c. 50 books supposedly bound in human skin, but tests to determine the exact origins of the bindings have only recently been developed. The first scientific confirmation of anthropodermic bibliopegy ("book-binding in human skin") came in 2014, when a team led by analytical chemist Dr Daniel P Kirby carried out tests on a copy of Arsène Houssaye's c. 1880 novel *Des destinées de l'ame* (*Destinies of the Soul*). The novel is housed in the Houghton Library at Harvard University (USA).

### Longest cardiac arrest
In 2017, a 31-year-old mountain climber identified only as "Roberto" spent 8 hr 42 min in cardiac arrest. He required medical assistance after losing consciousness during an attempt to climb the face of Marmolada in the Italian Dolomites on 26 Aug that year. At 7.48 p.m., medics at the scene recorded that he had no pulse. Revival efforts continued as he was transferred to hospital, where, at 4.30 a.m., with the aid of life-support procedures, his heart rhythm finally stabilized.

### Tallest actor
Former basketball player Paul "Tiny" Sturgess (UK) was the Harlem Globetrotters' tallest ever signing, standing 231.8 cm (7 ft 7.2 in) when measured in 2011. Now an actor, his credits include the movie *Fantastic Beasts: The Crimes of Grindelwald* (UK/USA, 2018) and the hit BBC TV sci-fi show *Doctor Who*.

### Shehata siblings
On 27 Apr 2021, GWR met Egyptian siblings Mohamed and Huda Shehata, who have a combined height of 414.4 cm (13 ft 7 in). Mohamed has the **widest arm span**, at 250.3 cm (8 ft 2.5 in), and **widest hand span** (31.1 cm; 12.3 in). Huda has both female records: an **arm span** of 236.3 cm (7 ft 9 in) and a **hand span** of 27 cm (10.6 in); her feet also broke a record (see right).

### Longest time touching the nose with the tongue
In an impressive show of lingual tenacity, Lukas Bikker (NLD) held the tip of his tongue to his nose for 14 min 1 sec in Gouda, Netherlands, on 13 Feb 2020. Breaking a record had long been on Lukas's bucket list.

The **longest tongue** is that of the USA's Nick Stoeberl, at 10.1 cm (3.9 in) from tip to middle of closed top lip.

Pratik's dream is to one day win a Mister World championship. "I want to live and breathe fitness," he says.

### Strength and stature
This line-up of muscled marvels begins on the far left with the **shortest competitive bodybuilder**, Pratik Mohite (IND), who is 102 cm (3 ft 4 in) tall, as verified on 8 Feb 2021. Pratik began working out aged 18 and won a medal at his first competitive bodybuilding event. He has since entered more than 40 contests.

The **tallest female professional bodybuilder** is Maria Wattel (NLD). A model and certified fitness trainer, Maria measured 182.7 cm (6 ft) as of 15 Jan 2021.

Also hailing from the Netherlands, Olivier Richters is the **tallest professional bodybuilder** at 218.3 cm (7 ft 1.9 in), as confirmed on 27 Apr 2021. Olivier's impressive stature has secured him several roles in big-budget Hollywood productions.

The record-breaking trio are pictured with fellow gym aficionado Tom Hänseler, who provides an all-important sense of scale.

## A NAIL TRIM AND A HAIRCUT – AND TWO GWR TITLES ARE UP FOR GRABS!

**A brace of GWR titles have become open to applicants again, after the holders opted to shear off their record-breaking assets.**

In Apr 2021, Ayanna Williams (USA) parted with the **longest fingernails on a pair of hands (female)**. Her 733.55-cm (24-ft 0.7-in) nails were cut off with an electric rotary tool (left) in Fort Worth, Texas. Ayanna certainly won't miss all the high maintenance, including manicures that took several days. What's more, she had to watch every movement she made, in case she damaged them – or hurt herself *with* them! And although they've been cut off, she'll still be able to see them – they're on display at the Ripley's Believe It or Not! museum in Orlando, Florida.

Nilanshi Patel (IND) parted with her own world-beating feature in Apr 2021. Having left it to grow for 12 years, her hair had reached 200 cm (6 ft 6.7 in) – the **longest hair on a teenager ever**. Of course, it took a lot of upkeep: her mother, Kaminiben (pictured below, who had her hair cut at the same time), had to help Nilanshi wash, dry and comb her luscious locks once a week. Once shorn, her hair was tied up into a bunch that weighed 266 g (9.4 oz). This former real-life Rapunzel now sports a stylish bob.

Got what it takes to claim one of these records? Then get in touch! Find out how to apply at **guinnessworldrecords. com/2022**.

### Lowest vocal note (female)
On 21 Feb 2021, professional singer Joy Chapman (CAN) hit $C\#_1$ (34.21 Hz) in Surrey, British Columbia, Canada. This is five notes from the bottom of an 88-note piano keyboard.

### Most babies born to a surrogate mother
As of Oct 2019, Carole Horlock (UK) had given birth to 13 babies – including a set of twins and a set of triplets – on behalf of eight different families. Carole also has two adult daughters of her own. "It doesn't worry me that my genetic offspring are being brought up by someone else," she maintains. "Biology is the easy bit; motherhood is the nurturing."

### Most family members born on the same date
The first of August is an important day in the Mangi family of Larkana, Pakistan. All nine members – father Ameer Ali, mother Khudija and their seven children – celebrate their birthday on that day.

### Most siblings to reach the age of 90
Ten brothers and sisters from the Clarke family of Loughrea, County Galway, Ireland, are aged 90 or more. They are Mary, John, Joe, Charles, Patrick, James, Hubert, Sarah, Margaret and Sheila, born to Charles and Margaret, as confirmed on 12 Apr 2021.

### Largest feet (female)
Huda Shehata's right foot measures 33.1 cm (1 ft 1.02 in) and her left is 33.06 cm (1 ft 1.03 in), as confirmed in Cairo, Egypt, on 27 Apr 2021. This equates to a man's US size 17 shoe (UK 16.5/European 53). (See also opposite.)

### Largest feet on a teenager (female)
Each of the feet belonging to Morgan Parsley (CAN, b. 6 Jan 2005) measures 30.9 cm (1 ft 0.16 in), as verified in Calgary, Alberta, Canada, on 16 Jul 2020. Although she was aged only 15 at the time, Morgan wore men's US size 14–15 basketball shoes (UK 13.5–14.5/ European 49–50).

### Most hair skips in 30 seconds
Laetitia Ky (CIV) jumped over a "rope" of her own hair 60 times in Abidjan, Ivory Coast, on 2 Mar 2021. For the attempt, Laetitia – an artist known for creating sculptures from her tresses – braided her natural hair before adding extensions and connecting the two together.

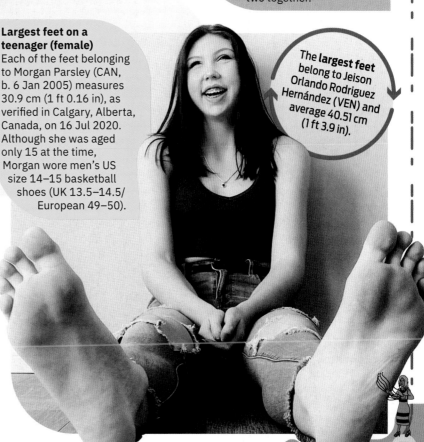

The **largest feet** belong to Jeison Orlando Rodriguez Hernández (VEN) and average 40.51 cm (1 ft 3.9 in).

# Sultan Kösen

**T**owering over the rest of the human race is Sultan Kösen of Turkey, who, at 251 cm (8 ft 2.8 in) tall, is a giant among men – literally!

The category of **◎ tallest living human** is a classic Guinness World Records title – arguably our most famous and iconic – but it's not one that changes (big) hands very often. For the past 12 years, the title has been held by Sultan, who was passed the baton in 2009 from the 236.1-cm-tall (7-ft 8.9-in) Bao Xi Shun of China. His incredible height confirmed Sultan as the first person measured in the 21st century to have exceeded 8 ft (243.8 cm), securing him membership of a rather exclusive club (see below).

Guinness World Records first met the 26-year-old Sultan on 11 Feb 2009, when his height was ratified at 246.5 cm (8 ft 1 in). But when he was re-assessed by our adjudicators just two years later, he had grown by 4.5 cm (1.7 in), proof that the tumour affecting his pituitary gland – the organ in the brain that regulates the production of growth hormone – was still present. Luckily, Sultan's new-found fame brought him to the attention of doctors at the University of Virginia Medical Center in the USA, who gifted him life-saving gamma-knife surgery and finally halted his growth.

Since then, Sultan has toured the world, astounding everyone with his stature. He is an unmissable ambassador for record-breaking, and a champion of those celebrating what it means to be unique. Thank you, Sultan!

**VITAL STATISTICS**
Name: Sultan Kösen
Born: 10 Dec 1982
Birthplace: Mardin, south-east Turkey
Height: 251 cm (8 ft 2.8 in)
Weight: 150 kg (330 lb 11 oz; 23 st 8 lb)
Hand span: 30.48 cm (12 in)
Feet: 36.5 cm (1 ft 2 in), left foot

1. Finding clothes and shoes that fit is a struggle, but Sultan has struck up a friendship with the German cordwainer George Wessels (top left), who specializes in making bespoke footwear for giants.

2. Basketball would be the obvious sport of choice for Sultan, and he did sign briefly as a centre with Turkish team Galatasaray in 2002... but he proved too tall and too heavy to play!

3. Sultan also has the **largest hands:** 28.5 cm (11.2 in) from wrist to middle finger tip. They measure 30.48 cm (12 in) across at full span.

4. The giant jet-setter – who can barely contort himself into a taxi – is pictured here during his travels to London and New York.

*Sultan has three brothers and a sister, all of whom are average sized. His rapid growth spurt didn't start until he was 10 years old.*

Find out more about Sultan in the Hall of Fame section at www.guinnessworldrecords.com/2022

Sultan is affected by both gigantism (extreme bone growth from early childhood) and acromegaly (continued excessive tissue growth in adulthood), both caused by the over-production of growth hormone. He's not unique in exceeding 8 ft (243.8 cm) but only 14 people – 13 men and one woman – have been ratified by Guinness World Records to have reliably exceeded this height. Meet the high-society members of the exclusive Eight-Foot Club!

### The Eight-Foot Club

| Name (Illustrated right to left) | Confirmed height |
| --- | --- |
| 1 Robert Wadlow (USA, 1918–40) | 272 cm (8 ft 11.1 in) |
| 2 John William Rogan (USA, c. 1868–1905) | 267 cm (8 ft 9 in) |
| 3 John F Carroll (USA, 1932–69) | 263.5 cm (8 ft 7.7 in) |
| 4 Väinö Myllyrinne (FIN, 1909–63) | 251.4 cm (8 ft 3 in) |
| 5 Sultan Kösen (TUR, 1982–) | 251 cm (8 ft 2.8 in) |
| =6 Don Koehler (USA, 1925–81) | 248.9 cm (8 ft 2 in) |
| =6 Bernard Coyne (USA, 1897–1921) | 248.9 cm (8 ft 2 in) |
| 8 Zeng Jinlian (CHN, 1964–82; tallest woman ever) | 247 cm (8 ft 1.75 in) |
| =9 Brahim Takioullah (MAR, 1982–) | 246.3 cm (8 ft 1 in) |
| =9 Patrick Cotter, aka O'Brien (IRL, 1760–1806) | 246.3 cm (8 ft 1 in) |
| 11 Morteza Mehrzadselakjani (IRN, 1987–) | 246 cm (8 ft 0.85 in) |
| 12 Constantin, aka Julius Koch (DEU, 1872–1902) | 245.8 cm (8 ft 0.8 in) |
| 13 Gabriel Estêvão Monjane (MOZ, 1944–90) | 245.7 cm (8 ft 0.75 in) |
| 14 Sulaimān 'Ali Nashnush (LIB, 1943–91) | 245 cm (8 ft 0.4 in) |

## VIRTUAL VISIT

# Yellowstone Park

O n 1 Mar 1872, US president Ulysses S Grant created a landmark in the history of conservation by inaugurating a "public park or pleasuring ground for the benefit and enjoyment of the people".

Yellowstone National Park is the world's **oldest national park**. It covers some 3,472 sq mi (8,992 km²), more than three times the size of Luxembourg, across three US states. The Roosevelt Arch (inset), at an entry point in Montana, bears a quote from Grant's founding legislation.

The park lies above an active supervolcano, and seismic activity is ongoing, with up to 3,000 earthquakes annually. Thousands of geysers exist here (see below) – hot springs of boiling water that burst into the air as underground steam expands up to 1,500 times its usual volume. Old Faithful, Yellowstone's most famous geyser, still erupts around 20 times a day. The park is home to a wealth of wildlife too, including 67 mammal species and 285 species of birds.

Yellowstone also serves as a barometer of climate change. Year-on-year temperature rises, and less precipitation, contributed to wildfires here in 1988. Dry conditions also encourage insect infestations, which damage forests, while warmer waters can harm fish. Only concerted efforts to address global warming can overcome such challenges. Encouragingly, conservation efforts are already underway to ensure that the park will be enjoyed by future generations.

**Location:** Wyoming (96%), Montana (3%) and Idaho (1%), USA

**Established:** 1872

**Area:** 3,472 sq mi (8,992 km²)

**Staff:** 386 (permanent)

**Archaeological sites:** more than 1,800

**Annual visitors:** 3,806,305 (2020 figures)

*Travertine*

### Tallest geyser eruption

The jets of Steamboat Geyser can reach in excess of 300 ft (90 m), though more minor eruptions of around 10–40 ft (3–12 m) are far more common. Between 1985 and 2017, there were just 15 eruptions, but recently this has accelerated to a rate of 128 major events from Mar 2018 to the end of 2020.

### Mammoth Hot Springs and Grand Prismatic

Mammoth Hot Springs is a series of rocky terraces (above) formed over thousands of years. The colourful bands comprise layers of a mineral called travertine, which is white when fresh and grey when weathered. At Grand Prismatic (below), heat-loving bacteria form coloured bands around a broad, 121-ft-deep (36-m) hot spring.

*370-ft (112-m) diameter*

### Highest concentration of geysers

Yellowstone National Park contains more than 10,000 hydrothermal features – at least half of the world's known examples. The extensive, intact ecosystem hosts thousands of hot springs, mudpots and fumaroles. It boasts in excess of 1,000 geysers – two-thirds of the planet's total.

## Spot record-breaking mammals

- **Largest canid:** The grey or timber wolf (*Canis lupus*) can reach a shoulder height of 2 ft 7 in (78 cm), with a head-body length of 5 ft 2 in (1.6 m).
- **Fastest land animal over long distances:** The North American pronghorn (*Antilocapra americana*) has been observed to run continuously at a speed of 35 mph (56 km/h) for up to 4.1 mi (6.6 km).
- **Largest deer:** The moose (*Alces alces*) is the mightiest member of the deer family. While the heaviest subspecies is the Alaskan moose (*A. a. gigas*) at up to 1,800 lb (816 kg), Yellowstone is home to North America's smallest (*A. a. shirasi*), with adult males averaging closer to 1,000 lb (450 kg).

Yellowstone's Junior Ranger programme teaches visiting children about the park and the vital importance of preservation.

### Largest hydrothermal explosion crater

When underground water is subjected to very high temperatures and pressures by interaction with volcanic heat, it causes hydrothermal explosions. As this superheated water nears Earth's surface, a sudden drop in pressure can cause a violent expansion of the water into steam. A series of such eruptions c. 14,000 years ago created the Mary Bay explosion crater in what is now Yellowstone Lake. The blasts left an enormous basin stretching 1.2 mi (2 km) wide.

*c. 1,000 mi (1,600 km) of trails*

Stone tools and projectiles found within Yellowstone suggest that humans were active here c. 11,000 years ago.

*Yellowstone River*

*Coniferous forests*

**Yellowstone by numbers**
- Highest point: Eagle Peak (11,358 ft; 3,462 m)
- Lowest point: Reese Creek (5,282 ft; 1,610 m)
- Forest: 80%
- Grassland: 15%
- Water: 5%

# Recordology

### JASON LIVERSIDGE – FASTEST ELECTRIC MOBILITY VEHICLE (PROTOTYPE)

Jason has motor neurone disease (MND), which has inspired in him a zest for new challenges. He's ascended the 1,085-m (3,560-ft) Mount Snowdon (pictured above with wife Liz) and descended 33.5 m (110 ft) into a pothole in the Yorkshire Dales (inset right with Liz and children Lilly and Poppy). Here – painstakingly "typed" out by Jason on a communications device – he describes driving the speediest mobility vehicle (see p.93).

**How does MND affect you?**
Since the first symptoms in 2008, I have slowly succumbed to the disease and now have about 5% movement. [My] lower limbs move a millimetre or so. My arms move enough to operate a joystick or mouse.

**What inspired you to try this record?**
I put my passion for speed and my disability together and came up with the fastest wheelchair... I know it is quite common to see a mobility scooter with a petrol engine on. I did a bit of research and found no record for [an] electric wheelchair.

**Tell us about your vehicle.**
We have Peugeot scooter wheels and 100-mph-rated tyres, which have been highly balanced. The front axle is custom-made with an adapted rack and pinion steering, with a high torque motor to turn it. The custom-built lithium-ion battery has a total voltage of 60 volts, and the rear axle is custom-made, with direct chain-drive by one motor.

**What was the most complicated step?**
By far the steering. While it is easy to make the wheels turn with a joystick, it is highly dangerous as steering is normally controlled by a wheel or handlebars, which give feedback. Not only does it need to [be] highly accurate, but it [only needs] minimal input from the driver.

**What does it mean to you to have a Guinness World Records title?**
My challenge was to achieve the record for my daughters and to leave the achievement behind... But the event has opened many new doors, including raising awareness and funds for the Motor Neurone Disease Association. Through the efforts of a few, many [people will] hopefully learn about this devastating illness, even in times of suffering with COVID. Having a life-limiting illness isn't a reason to stop living.

## CONTENTS

Jason has also abseiled off the Humber Bridge and lapped the Silverstone circuit in a Formula One-style racing car!

# Football Freestylers

Ash's other "in a minute" records include **most volleys** – 33 – and **most neck-catch passes** – 42 – both with Stephen Gray (UK).

## 1. Most hotstepper tricks in one minute

Areej Al Hammadi (UAE) performed 86 of these nimble-footed manoeuvres in 60 sec in Dubai, UAE, on 10 Jul 2020. One hotstepper involves bouncing the football with the sole of one foot so that it touches the ground and bounces up to the other foot. The trick is complete when the ball has touched the soles of both feet.

## 2. Youngest female competitor in a World Freestyle Football Championship

Alicia Bettahar-Sartori (FRA, b. 6 Jul 2007) was aged just 12 years 45 days when she appeared at the Super Ball in Prague, Czech Republic, on 20 Aug 2019. During the same year, Alicia reached the semi-finals of the French Championships.

## 3. Most backwards stepovers in one minute

Ash Randall (UK) racked up 99 reverse stepovers at Cardiff University Sports Training Village in Cardiff, UK, on 31 Oct 2013. The ball is rolled towards the participant, who must pass alternating legs over the ball without touching it.

## 4. Most rope skips while keeping a football in the air with the head in one minute

Kwok-Fai Law (CHN) skipped rope 138 times while heading a ball in the air in Hong Kong, China, on 2 May 2020. Law has been a freestyler and performer for more than 10 years.

## 5. Most seated revolve tricks in one minute

On 18 Mar 2018, high-school student Kouta Mochizuki (JPN) performed 134 revolve tricks sitting down in 60 sec in Fuji, Shizuoka, Japan. In this category, the attemptee flicks the ball into the air; while it's in mid-air, the other foot must circle once around the ball, which then returns to the kicking foot.

## 6. Most knee catches in 30 seconds

Ben Nuttall (UK) flicked a ball up with his foot and caught it between his knees 31 times in Birmingham, West Midlands, UK, on 20 Jun 2020. Ben improved on Ash Randall's previous record by eight catches.

## 7. Farthest distance juggling a football on ice in one hour

On 6 Mar 2020, John Farnworth (UK) juggled a ball 4.75 km (2.95 mi) in 60 min on the frozen Lake Baikal, Russia, in temperatures as low as -20°C (-4°F). The attempt raised money for Cancer Research UK.

On 12 Mar 2019, John took to the Sahara desert in Morocco for the ◗ **farthest distance juggling a football in one hour** – 5.82 km (3.61 mi). This time, he endured 40°C (104°F) heat to achieve his feat.

## 8. Most clipper tricks performed in one minute

On 20 Sep 2018, Marcel Gurk (DEU) performed 60 clipper tricks in 60 sec in Palmar, Mauritius. One foot travels behind the standing leg; the ball is then controlled using the inside (or instep) of the raised foot to kick it back into the air.

The **female** record – 33 – was achieved by Laura Biondo (VEN) in San Francisco, California, USA, on 19 Jan 2017. See below for more of Laura's achievements.

## ▶ 9. Most "around the world" tricks in one minute (female)

On 30 Oct 2017, freestyle champion and 11-time Guinness World Records title holder Laura Biondo completed 63 revolutions of her foot around a controlled ball in Miami, Florida, USA. The former Cirque du Soleil artist also holds women's one-minute records for the **most touches with the shin** (105), **with the head** (206) and, most recently, on 19 Jun 2020, **with the feet on a treadmill** (170, inset).

# WFFA
## WORLD FREESTYLE FOOTBALL ASSOCIATION

The World Freestyle Football Association (WFFA) is the governing body for this rapidly growing sport. Spanning 114 countries, the WFFA strives to inspire healthy, active lifestyles among participants of all ages.

The first iteration of the WFFA – Freestyle Football Federation, or F3 for short – was created in 2011 and the World Rankings System was introduced two years later. In 2017, this evolved into the WFFA, who are headquartered in Mississauga, Ontario, Canada. Live events (online and offline) consist primarily of one-against-one "Battles", with events taking place at National, Continental and World Open status levels. The winners of National Qualifiers annually land a place in the World Championships. As well as organizing contests, the WFFA also draws up rules and regulations.

Today, there are an estimated 10,000 football freestylers worldwide. WFFA competitions offer them plenty of scope to get creative with their skills and really push their boundaries. And the organization helps put individuals on the route to professional status too. Freestyling also helps to hone myriad personal attributes including balance, coordination skills and body confidence.

### WFFA world-beaters

So, who are the names to watch out for? The world No.1 is currently Erlend Fagerli (NOR, pictured), who is the first person ever to achieve the football freestyle "holy triple" – winning the National, Continental and World Open Championships in one year. Hot on his heels is Felipe Poblete (CHL), Latin American Football Freestyle champion in 2019. Ibuki Yoshida (JPN), currently ranked world No.3, is renowned as an "air technician" – one of the most demanding freestyle disciplines. Inspired? Discover more at **thewffa.org**.

| WFFA... | | |
|---|---|---|
| **Highest-ranked competitor*** | Erlend Fagerli (NOR) | World No.1 |
| **Most titles won** | Erlend Fagerli (NOR) | 11 |
| **Most titles won (female)** | Melody Donchet (FRA) | 5 |
| **Oldest competitor** | Vincent Grady (USA, b. 14 May 1976) | 43 years 98 days |
| **Oldest competitor (female)** | Minna Marlo (FIN, b. 23 Apr 1981) | 39 years 25 days |
| **Youngest competitor** | Fuuma Seino (JPN, b. 23 Nov 2011) | 9 years 59 days |
| **Youngest competitor (female)** | Alicia Bettahar-Sartori (FRA, b. 6 Jul 2007) | 12 years 45 days (see #2, opposite) |
| **First event** | World Tour, Kuala Lumpur, Malaysia | 18 Sep 2011 |
| **Largest event** | Super Ball 2019, Prague, Czech Republic | 434 participants (below) |

*At present, there are not enough female players at National level for women's rankings to be drawn up.*

**6**

**7**

**8**

**9**

*Super Ball 2019 in Prague, Czech Republic*

# Strength & Fitness

## Most wins of the Empire State Building Run-Up

Every year, athletes race up 1,576 steps to the 86th floor of the iconic New York skyscraper – a gain of 320 m (1,050 ft). Suzy Walsham (AUS) has won the women's event 10 times, in 2007–09 and 2013–19. She competed for Australia at the 2006 Commonwealth Games over 800 m and 1,500 m before switching to tower running.

The **men's** record is seven, by Thomas Dold (DEU), consecutively in 2006–12.

The **fastest Run-Up** is 9 min 33 sec, by Paul Crake (AUS) in 2003. Andrea Mayr (AUT) secured the **women's** record of 11 min 23 sec in 2006.

## Greatest vertical height stair-climbing in one hour

On 18 Nov 2020, tower runner Ryoji Watanabe (JPN) made repeated ascents of the staircase inside the Tokyo Skytree – which at 634 m (2,080 ft) is the world's **tallest tower** – logging a total climb of 1,425 m (4,675 ft).

## Fastest 2,000 m on the Concept2 indoor rower (female)

Brooke Mooney (USA) rowed 2,000 m (6,561 ft) in 6 min 21.1 sec on a rowing exercise machine on 24 Mar 2021. She broke the women's record during testing for the US National Rowing Team.

## Most consecutive back handsprings (one hand)

On 27 Mar 2021, Zama Mofokeng (ZAF) completed 36 one-handed backsprings in a row in Thembisa, South Africa. He extended his own record by two. On the same day, Zama also set the back-handspring records with **alternating hands** (31) and **interlocked hands** (36). He has been practising gymnastics since the age of 10.

## Heaviest sleigh pulled

Lutheran pastor Kevin Fast (CAN) donned a Santa Claus suit to haul a flat-bed truck and sleigh loaded with Christmas presents – a combined weight of 16.5 tonnes (18.1 tons) – along a 5-m (16-ft) course in his home town of Cobourg in Ontario, Canada, on 23 Nov 2020.

## Heaviest sumo deadlift in one minute (female)

On 1 Oct 2020, Linh Nguyen (USA) completed 49 repetitions in Aurora, Colorado, USA, lifting a total of 4 tonnes (4.4 tons). With a sumo deadlift, the lifter's hands are inside their legs when they grip the bar.

## Fastest 20 m walking on hands

On 15 Feb 2021, Zion Clark (USA) covered 20 m (65 ft) on his hands in 4.78 sec in Massillon, Ohio, USA, clocking a speed of 15 km/h (9.3 mph). Zion was born without legs as a result of a rare genetic disorder called caudal regression syndrome. He has wrestled for Kent State University and also competes in wheelchair callisthenics.

## Farthest distance on monkey bars in one minute

On 8 Jan 2021, Olivia Vivian (AUS) swung across monkey bars for a total distance of 54.50 m (178 ft 9 in) in 60 sec in Perth, Australia. Gymnast Olivia represented Australia at the 2008 Olympics before finding fame on *Australian Ninja Warrior*; in 2019, she won gold at the Ninja World Championships in Moscow, Russia.

## Longest Dinnie Stones hold

The Dinnies are a pair of lifting stones with a total weight of 733 lb (332.49 kg), named after the legendary Scottish strongman Donald Dinnie. Mark Haydock (UK) held them off the ground for 46.3 sec on 18 May 2019 in Potarch, Aberdeenshire, UK.

## Longest time to hold the yoga tree pose

The *vrikshasana* or tree pose is a standing yoga *asana* where one foot is held against the inner thigh of the other leg. On 25 Jan 2020, Bulut Quinlan Calis (TUR) balanced for 1 hr 14 min 43 sec in St Charles, Illinois, USA. It was the third time the record had been broken in 18 months.

The **longest time to hold the yoga downward dog pose** is 1 hr 18 sec, by performance coach and yoga teacher Kiki Flynn (USA) on 16 Aug 2020 in New York City, USA.

## Heaviest locomotive pulled

Strongman Jordan Steffens (AUS) hauled a 520-class locomotive and tender weighing 184.97 tonnes (203.9 tons) across 5 m (16 ft) on 30 Jan 2021 in Mount Barker, South Australia.

On 6 Mar 2021, Jordan teamed up with circus stars André Augustus and Emily Gare (both AUS, inset) to perform the **fastest 20 m by a three-person tower** – 16.23 sec.

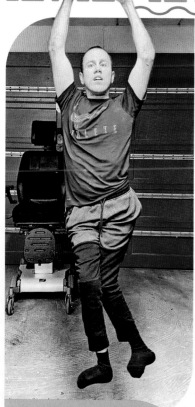

### Hand-release push-ups in one minute (male)

On 18 Dec 2020, George Kotsimpos (GRC) executed 64 push-ups where both his hands completely left the floor between repetitions. George – who broke the record in Heraklion, Greece, by six push-ups – was inspired to attempt this record after suffering a serious injury to his arm the previous year.

### Star jumps carrying an 80-lb pack in one minute

Fitness fanatic Irfan Mehsood (PAK) executed 36 jumps with an 80-lb (36-kg) backpack in Dera Ismail Khan, Pakistan, on 14 Dec 2020. He also holds the **60-lb** record of 27.

### Longest duration in the dead-hang position

Harald Riise (NOR) hung by his hands for 16 min 3 sec on 7 Nov 2020 in Bærum, Viken, Norway. He beat the previous record by more than two minutes. Harald, who has cerebral palsy, uses a wheelchair and cannot fully extend his arms. He spends 10 hr a week working out, focusing exclusively on the upper body.

### Most...
#### Jumping jacks in 30 seconds
Sixteen-year-old Harley Billingham (UK) completed 72 star jumps in half a minute on 18 Oct 2020 in Ascot, Berkshire, UK.

#### Archer push-ups in one minute
On 11 Mar 2020, Mohammad Feido (SYR) executed 93 archer push-ups – where the body is alternately lowered towards each hand, until a 90° angle is attained at the elbow of that arm – in 60 sec in Latakia, Syria.

#### Burpees on roller skates in one minute
On 17 Mar 2021, professional skater Tinuke Oyediran (UK, b. NGA) performed 33 roller burpees in 60 sec in London, UK. This was Tinuke's third GWR title, having claimed two on GWR Day (see pp.10–11).

#### Chest-to-ground burpees in one hour
Personal trainer Nick Anapolsky (CAN) completed 879 chest-to-ground burpees in 60 min in Kitchener, Ontario, Canada, on 6 Mar 2021.
Fellow Canadian Alison Brown set the **female** record of 730 in Listowel, Ontario, on 12 Jul 2020.

### Most back-somersault burpees in 30 seconds (female)

On 8 Mar 2021, Beth Lodge (UK) completed five burpees preceded by a backwards flip in Berinsfield, Oxfordshire, UK. She also achieved the **fastest 100 m by forward rolls** – 42.64 sec – on the same day. Scientist Beth is the first woman to reach the Eliminator stage on ITV's *Ninja Warrior UK*.

### Heaviest log lift (female)

On 4 Jul 2020, Andrea Thompson (UK) completed a log lift weighing 135 kg (297 lb) in Suffolk, UK. The four-time Britain's Strongest Woman set the record during a YouTube livestream as part of the World's Ultimate Strongman *Feats of Strength* series. She opened with a lift of 110 kg (242 lb) and went on to smash the previous best of 129 kg (284 lb).

### Farthest lache (bar-to-bar swing)

On 10 Nov 2020, real-life Spider-Man Najee Richardson (USA) flung himself 5.56 m (18 ft 3 in) – almost the entire length of a bowling lane – from one bar to another in Hainesport, New Jersey, USA. The ex-gymnast has featured on NBC's *American Ninja Warrior*, where his high-flying skills earned him the nickname "The Philly Phoenix".

### Chin-ups in 24 hours
Idai Makaya (UK) achieved 5,340 chin-ups on 25–26 Sep 2020 in Milton Keynes, Buckinghamshire, UK. His attempt was part of a drive to establish a charitable foundation in memory of his late brother, Garai.

### Pull-ups in 24 hours
On 26–27 Oct 2019, Brandon Tucker (USA) completed 7,715 pull-ups in 24 hr in Columbus, Georgia, USA.

### Squats in 24 hours
Joe Reverdes (USA) squatted 25,000 times in 24 hr on 4–5 Sep 2020, a pace of more than 17 every minute. The 53-year-old's record attempt took place in Johnston, Rhode Island, USA.

Andrea won Britain's Strongest Woman after just two weeks' training, having been talent-spotted in the gym.

# Mind Games

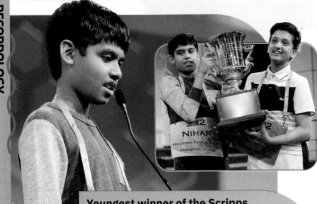

### Youngest winner of the Scripps National Spelling Bee (SNSB)

On 26 May 2016, Nihar "The Machine" Janga (USA, b. 18 Nov 2004) became joint champion – aged 11 years 190 days – with 13-year-old Jairam Hathwar (inset). The SNSB (USA) is the **longest-running spelling competition**, held annually since 1925 bar rare exceptions, including 2020, owing to the pandemic. The finale of the latest contest, staged on 28–30 May 2019, saw 1,399 words pronounced by 565 contestants – the **most words spelled at the SNSB finals**.

### First use of the term "spelling bee"

The word "bee" – used to describe a group of people assembled for a set task – is believed to have originated in the USA. Although spelling contests are thought to date back at least to the early 19th century, the first recorded use of "spelling bee" was in the Apr 1850 edition of the *Knickerbocker* literary magazine.

### Most words spelled backwards in one minute

Pam Onnen (USA) correctly spelled 56 random words in reverse in Hastings, Minnesota, USA, on 14 Jul 2020.

### Fastest Flash Anzan™ mental arithmetic

Developed in Japan by abacus teacher Yoji Miyamoto, this demanding test challenges "mathletes" to calculate the total sum from a series of three-digit numbers flashed consecutively on a screen, against the clock.
- **15 numbers**: 1.64 sec, by Hyuga Kinekawa (JPN) in Sakyō, Kyoto, Japan, on 8 Aug 2019.
- **30 numbers**: 3.33 sec, by Yuichiro Takakura (JPN) in Nagareyama, Chiba, on 20 Sep 2020.

### ▶ Highest score on *Times Tables Rock Stars* in one minute

On 4 Jun 2020, Nadub Gill (PAK) solved 196 division and multiplication problems in 60 sec in Long Eaton, Derbyshire, UK. This means that, on average, the 10-year-old was inputting three correct answers per second! On 7 Mar 2021, he bettered his own top score on this maths practice app, solving 202 sums. "It is like a dream!" Nadub said after first setting the record.

## FATHER OF THE CUBE: ERNŐ RUBIK

Hungary's Ernő Rubik invented and lent his name to the cube that has captured the imagination of puzzle fans and record-breakers alike for almost 50 years.

**What inspired you to design the original Rubik's Cube?**
In 1974, I was a young adjunct professor of design in Budapest. I was trying to explain descriptive geometry, focusing on the movements of 3D objects. That's hard to do just verbally, so I thought about how best to illustrate those concepts using actual objects.

**Was the solution algorithm there when the Cube was designed?**
It wasn't. It took me a month or so to find a solution to the puzzle I created – and I hadn't been certain that it was a task that could be accomplished by any human intelligence, let alone my own!

**What's the most complicated puzzle that you've designed to date?**
I don't think being complicated is something to aspire to, per se. The Cube's beauty is that it's very simple and insanely complex at the same time. It has 43 quintillion possible combinations and only one "solved" state.

However, there's no combination that would be more than 20 moves from the solution.

**What inspired your book *Cubed*?**
Honestly, I hate to write! I could not imagine how I could capture in words all my experiences, my time with the Cube and my life story. At the same time, I'm a big believer in "learning by doing", and writing a book offered a new perspective, a new way to understand the lasting impact of the Cube on the world and on my life. Finally, I decided to approach the task of writing as if it were a puzzle.

*Cubed: The Puzzle of Us All by Ernő Rubik was published by W&N Hardback on 15 Sep 2020*

### Fastest time to solve a 4x5 Klotski puzzle with one hand

On 18 Apr 2020, Ye Jiaxi (CHN) completed this sliding-block puzzle in just 12.389 sec in Xiamen, Fujian, China. The digitally dextrous competitor has also achieved the **fastest time** outright to solve the puzzle – 6.798 sec – and the **fastest time blindfolded** – 8.647 sec. The name of the game derives from *klocki*, a Polish term for wooden blocks.

Klotski puzzles are thought to date to the early 20th century. The aim is to slide the blocks so the largest one ends up in a specific slot on the board.

## Most binary digits memorized in 30 minutes

Memory athlete Ryu Song I from North Korea recalled 7,485 binary numbers at the 2019 World Memory Championships in Wuhan City, China. She was 2019's overall champion and is seen above (far left) with other medal-winning teammates. Emma Alam of Pakistan took the top spot at 2020's contest on 18–20 Dec, which took place online for the first time owing to COVID-19.

## Highest score in a Scrabble tournament

Toh Weibin (SGP) earned 850 points at the Northern Ireland Scrabble Championship held in Belfast, UK, on 21 Jan 2012.

The **highest score in a Scrabble game** is 1,049, by Phil Appleby (UK) in a match played in Wormley, Hertfordshire, UK, on 25 Jun 1989. It's worth noting that Appleby was playing under different circumstances to Weibin; as not a tournament, his opponent was less likely to block high potential scores.

Jesse Inman (USA) recorded the **highest opening score in a Scrabble tournament** – 126, for the word "MuZJIKS" (with a blank for the U). The record opening gambit was laid at the National Championship in Orlando, Florida, USA, on 26 Jul 2008.

## First crossword puzzle

On 21 Dec 1913, the Sunday "Fun" section of US newspaper *The New York World* included a crossword by Arthur Wynne (UK). It featured a diamond grid, simple (non-cryptic) clues and no black squares.

The **first cryptic crossword** appeared in 1925 in *The Saturday Westminster Gazette*. Although crosswords had previously included cryptic elements, its compiler – Edward Powys Mathers (UK) – used exclusively cryptic clues.

## Most wins of *The Times* National Crossword Championship

Mark Goodliffe (UK), who himself is a crossword setter, has been crowned *The Times*' crossword king 12 times (in 1999, 2008–17 and 2019). His 10-victory streak also stands as the **most consecutive wins**.

## Most rotating puzzle cubes solved while hula hooping

Noah Brauner (USA) called on both his mental and physical abilities to complete 200 standard Rubik's Cube puzzles while simultaneously keeping a hula hoop aloft. A random computer algorithm was employed to scramble the cubes in preparation for each new attempt. Noah's feat of dual agility was achieved in Newton, Massachusetts, USA, on 14 Mar 2020.

### World Memory Sports Council

Since 1991, the WMSC has overseen the competitive World Memory Championships. Participants are tested on their ability to memorize various categories of information within a limited time frame.

| | | |
|---|---|---|
| Most spoken numbers memorized at a rate of one per second | 547 | Ryu Song I (PRK) Year set: 2019 |
| Most decimal digits memorized in five minutes | 616 | Wei Qinru (CHN) Year set: 2019 |
| Most decimal digits memorized in one hour | 4,620 | Ryu Song I (PRK) Year set: 2019 |
| Most playing cards memorized in 30 minutes | 1,100 | Wei Qinru (CHN) Year set: 2019 |
| Most playing cards memorized in one hour | 2,530 | Kim Surim (PRK) Year set: 2019 |
| Fastest time to memorize and recall a deck of playing cards | 13.96 sec | Zou Lujian (CHN) Year set: 2017 |
| Most historical/future dates recalled in five minutes | 241 | Syeda Kisa Zehra (PAK) Year set: 2020 |
| Most names and faces memorized in 15 minutes | 218 | Emma Alam (PAK) Year set: 2020 |
| Most abstract images memorized in 15 minutes | 804 | Hu Jiabao (CHN) Year set: 2018 |
| Most random words memorized in sequence in 15 minutes | 410 | Emma Alam (PAK) Year set: 2020 |

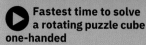

## ▶ Fastest time to solve a rotating puzzle cube one-handed

Max Park (USA) took just 6.82 sec to complete a 3x3x3 puzzle cube with his left hand on 12 Oct 2019. The speedy solution took place at the Bay Area Speedcubin' 20 event held in Fremont, California, USA. Max is a multi-record-breaking speedcuber; diagnosed at an early age with autism, he took up cubing as part of his therapy.

> Noah learned hula hooping from his mum, while his dad taught him how to solve a Rubik's Cube.

## Youngest winner of the World Quizzing Championships

Olav Bjortomt (UK, b. 13 Dec 1978) was 24 years 205 days old when he won the inaugural World Quizzing Championships on 5 Jul 2003. He has since claimed the title in 2015, 2018 and 2019.

## Fastest six-level Tower of Hanoi

This logic game comprises three pegs and a stack of six graduated discs that must be placed on another peg; discs are moved one at a time and must always conform to size order. Xia Yan (CHN) solved this puzzle in 31.81 sec in Xi'an, Shaanxi, China, on 8 Jan 2021.

## Most wins of the American Crossword Puzzle Tournament

Dan Feyer (USA) is an eight-time winner of this competition, his last victory coming on 24 Mar 2019. He has also recorded the **most consecutive wins** – six – beginning in 2010 and ending with the 2015 contest. In 2019, he saw off 740 other solvers, which was a record attendance for the event.

# Collections

### Most valuable insect collection

Entomologists Charlie and Lois O'Brien (both USA) gave their insect collection – worth some $10 m (£8 m) – to Arizona State University, USA, in Mar 2017. It has more than 1.25 million artefacts, valued at between $5 and $300 (£4–£240) each. (The inset shows a few of the million or so weevils.) They met at the university in the late 1950s and began collecting on their honeymoon. Charlie passed away in 2019, but the record remains a tribute to the years of dedicated collecting to which he and Lois devoted themselves.

### Washing machines

As of 5 Aug 2019, retired engineer Lee Maxwell (USA) was the owner of 1,350 unique washing machines, ranging from hand-cranked wooden contraptions to sleek white modern appliances. The collection is stored in a pair of converted barns at his home in Eaton, Colorado, USA.

### *Happy Days* memorabilia

Giuseppe Ganelli (ITA) owns 1,439 articles related to this popular 1950s-themed TV series, as confirmed in Codogno, Italy, on 18 Feb 2018. His favourite pieces are the original pinball machine used on the set in Arnold's Drive-In and a shirt worn by Ron Howard (who played Richie Cunningham) in one episode.

### *Ghostbusters* memorabilia

Robert O'Connor (USA) owns 1,221 *Ghostbusters*-themed items, as verified on 20 Jun 2020 in Elyria, Ohio, USA. He became hooked after a cinema trip to see *Ghostbusters II* (USA, 1989). Robert's favourites include a Kenner Stay-Puft Marshmallow Man plush (which was a gift from his grandparents) and a *Ghostbusters II* LP soundtrack signed by two of the series' stars, Dan Aykroyd and Ernie Hudson.

### Dinosaur-related items

As confirmed on 11 Mar 2020, Cesar Augusto Canales Cueva (PER) has accumulated 1,226 unique pieces for his dino depository, which he stores in Arequipa, Peru. The tally includes magazines, toys, cards, books, watches, posters, board games, buildable skeletons and keychains. As per the standard GWR guidelines for collection records, all these objects are commercially available.

### *Cars* memorabilia

Jorge Arias Garcia (MEX) owns 1,200 unique items related to Pixar's franchise *Cars*, as confirmed in Cuajimalpa de Morelos, Mexico City, on 18 Jul 2019. The first movie in the series was released in 2006; within a year, Jorge had accumulated the first 100 pieces for his collection.

### Dog-related items

Mary Elias (SYR) owns 1,496 canine objects, as verified in Dubai, UAE, on 2 Apr 2019. They include a huge variety of toys, mugs, kits, statues and napkins.

Carmen de Aldana (GTM) had the **largest collection of cat-related items** – 21,321, when last counted. It began when she purchased three small ceramic kittens in 1954, aged 13. Sadly, Carmen passed away in 2017.

### Lip balms

Chelsea Jerabek (USA) has 1,622 unique lip balms in her collection, which she began when she was aged 13. They were counted on 16 Feb 2020 in Lubbock, Texas, USA.

More than 1,000 Shopkins have appeared since 2014. The rarest is Cupcake Queen from Season 1; only 100 units were issued.

### Beaver-related items
As of 8 Mar 2020, Lori Gongaware (USA) had 1,456 items lodged at her home in North Chesterfield, Virginia, USA. Lori began collecting back in 2006; at first, the novelty of the idea amused her, but over time she discovered more about beavers and now considers them to be her "remarkable" spirit animal. Find out more about these rodents on p.36.

### Miniature tools
In 1974, German Lorenzo Juarez Calderon (MEX) began saving tiny tool replicas. By 14 Feb 2020, he had 2,512 mini utensils.

### Flamingo-related items
Deborah Buscher Leck (USA) had amassed 2,595 objects inspired by her favourite pink bird, as verified on 8 Nov 2019.

### LEGO® Minifigures
Konrad Pawlus (POL) – the founder of Minifigs.blog – was the proud owner of 5,544 Minifigures as of 13 Mar 2021.

### Ladybird-related items
As of 21 Nov 2019, Nadiia Komarova (UKR) had collected 5,555 items styled after the black-spotted beetles in Dnipro, Ukraine.

They include a vacuum cleaner and a cat house, although Nadiia is particularly fond of her ladybird-shaped mobile phone.

### Smurf memorabilia
Gerda Scheuers (USA) owned 11,455 unique Smurf items at the most recent inventory.

### Wine and champagne labels
Sophia Vaharis-Tsouvelekakis of Athens, Greece, began saving wine labels in 1986 on a holiday to Portugal. As of 9 Jul 2019, she had 17,758 unique items.

### Business cards
As of 26 Apr 2020, twin sisters Sri Navya and Sri Harsha Nune of Ahmedabad, Gujarat, India, had assembled 55,200 business cards.

### Shopkins memorabilia
Rhianna Connors (UK) owns 2,271 items related to these popular tradeable toys, as verified on 24 Sep 2019 in Swansea, West Glamorgan, UK. Eleven-year-old Rhianna is the sister of Lily (UK inset), who owns the **largest collection of Doctor Who memorabilia** (6,641 pieces), and Thomas, holder of two one-minute records for backwards basketball-throwing: the **most free throws** (13) and **half-court shots** (6).

### Lilo & Stitch memorabilia
Suzy Fisher (UK) has collected 1,907 items relating to this Disney sci-fi franchise, as verified in Birmingham, UK, on 11 Nov 2019. She is a mega-fan of the film and its theme of "Ohana" (Hawaiian for "family"). Suzy's collection began with a Stitch plush toy that her mum bought for her after they first saw the movie, and she applied for the record in honour of her mum. Other than this, her favourite item is a music-playing snow globe depicting a scene from the film.

# WWE

World Wrestling Entertainment (WWE) has gone by many names since its inception as Capitol Wrestling Corporation in 1953; it became WWE in 2002. But name aside, the ethos behind the promotion has always held true: epic clashes between big characters, both in and out of the ring.

Wrestling was in the blood for Bevis as her parents and two older brothers are all professional wrestlers too!

### Longest career
Up until late 2020, the most seasoned active wrestler on the WWE circuit was The Undertaker, aka Mark Calaway (USA). His tenure began on 22 Nov 1990, and despite "retiring" in 2017 he made several comebacks. Most recently, he fought (and beat) A J Styles (aka Allen Jones) at WrestleMania 36 on 4 Apr 2020. He once more announced his retirement at Survivor Series on 22 Nov 2020, exactly 30 years after his debut, parting with: "My time has come to let The Undertaker rest... in... peace."

### Most matches
**Male**: Kane, aka Glenn Jacobs (USA, b. ESP), had put in 1,665 appearances for the promotion as of 13 Oct 2020. **Female**: Natalya, aka Natalie Neidhart (CAN), is the most match-experienced woman, with 974 bouts to date.

### Longest-reigning champion
Debuting in 1949, The Fabulous Moolah, aka Mary Lillian Ellison (1923–2007; also see opposite) of South Carolina, USA, is the undisputed holder of the longest unbroken stint as world No.1. What *is* disputed is the length of her reign, based on the semantics of name changes and ownership of wrestling tournaments. WWE officially credits her reign as 10,170 days (almost 28 years), from 18 Sep 1956 to 23 Jul 1984. Other wrestling aficionados favour a shorter period of 3,651 days, cited by the National Wrestling Alliance. In either case, the "Moolah" comes out on top.

The **male** record is 2,803 days, set by Bruno Sammartino (ITA, 1935–2018), nicknamed "The Italian Strongman", between 17 May 1963 and 18 Jan 1971.

### Shortest-reigning champion
On 5 Feb 1988, André the Giant, aka André René Roussimoff (FRA, 1946–93), took down then-champion Hulk Hogan during a televised match. Controversially, just 1 min 48 sec after receiving his prize belt, he gave it away to Ted "The Million Dollar Man" DiBiase for an undisclosed fee. WWF's president Jack Tunney promptly nullified the transaction and the title was vacated.

### Longest WrestleMania winning streak
As well as being WWE's most enduring wrestler until late 2020, The Undertaker (above) enjoyed an uninterrupted run of 21 victories at the promotion's biggest event between WrestleMania VII (1991) and WrestleMania 29 (2013). He missed the 1994 and 2000 editions due to injury. What has come to be called "The Streak" in the wrestling annals was unceremoniously ended at WrestleMania XXX in 2014 after a 25-min bout with Brock Lesnar (USA), during which he was at the receiving end of three "F-5"s ("facebusters").

It's not the first time that Lesnar (b. 12 Jul 1977) had made a name for himself in the WWE community. He became the **youngest champion** after taking out The Rock (see below) at SummerSlam on 25 Aug 2002, claiming the world championship aged 25 years 44 days.

**FIGHTING** WITH MY **FAMILY**

IN CINEMAS MARCH 1

### Youngest Divas champion
Paige, aka Saraya-Jade Bevis (UK, b. 17 Aug 1992), triumphed over A J Lee (aka April Jeanette Mendez) at her debut Raw event on 7 Apr 2014. She was aged just 21 years 233 days when she lifted the Divas belt, going on to win it for a second time later that year on 17 Aug. Paige officially retired from WWE in Apr 2018, but her story was recently brought to life in the 2019 comedy-sports film *Fighting with My Family* (inset), featuring Florence Pugh as Paige and former WWE star Dwayne "The Rock" Johnson.

Kofi claimed the all-time tag-team-champion duration record in 2018, after surpassing the 934 days logged by Billy Gunn.

## Longest MITB briefcase ownership

"Money in the Bank" (MITB) is a "ladder match" in which the goal is to reach a briefcase (placed atop a ladder) containing an open contract for a championship bout. Carmella, aka Leah Van Dale (USA), won the inaugural women's ladder match on 18 Jun 2017, then – following a controversial disqualification – had to reclaim it nine days later. She waited 287 days before "cashing in" her prize. Her patience paid off, though, as it led to her first SmackDown Women's Championship title on 10 Apr 2018.

That age record was smashed, though, at WrestleMania 34, held in New Orleans, Louisiana, USA, on 8 Apr 2018, when Braun Strowman (aka Adam Scherr) "randomly" chose a 10-year-old boy from the audience to be his tag-team partner. Although the youngster – Nicholas Cone (USA), son of WWE referee John Cone – did not have to lift a finger, he technically still shared the title when Strowman singlehandedly routed the opposition.

## Most losses at WrestleMania

Of the 23 matches he has appeared in at "The Grandest Stage of Them All", Triple H, aka Paul Levesque (USA), has lost 13 of them. By contrast, The Undertaker has

## Most WWE Championship wins

John Cena (USA, left, with The Rock) enjoyed 13 reigns between 2005 and 2017. He also won three World Heavyweight Championships in that time, meaning he has the **most WWE world titles** (16), tied with Ric Flair, aka Richard Fliehr (USA).

The **female** record is even more complex (see **longest-reigning champion**, left). Many cite The Fabulous Moolah with eight titles between 1956 and 1999. But with an alternative view on tournament history, WWE recognizes Trish Stratus, aka Patricia Stratigeas (CAN, right), with seven wins.

participated in 27 matches at WrestleMania (1991–2020), winning 25 of them (see left).

## Highest attendance at a live event

WrestleMania 32, which took place at the AT&T Stadium in Arlington, Texas, USA, on 3 Apr 2016, attracted 101,763 fans. With total takings of $17.3 m (£12.1 m), it was also the **highest-grossing live event** in WWE history to date.

## Most WrestleMania events attended

Few WWE fans are as passionate as Charlie Adorno (USA), who in true wrestling style has his own nickname: "Ringside Charlie". He had been present at all 35 of the annual extravaganzas up to 2019, since the event began on 31 Mar 1985 in New York City (his hometown). Sadly, his unbroken run came to an end for WrestleMania 36 on 4–5 Apr 2020, because the latest edition took place behind closed doors with no audience owing to COVID-19 restrictions.

## Longest cumulative time as a tag-team champion

From his debut in 2008 up to Oct 2020, Kofi Kingston, aka Kofi Sarkodie-Mensah (USA, b. GHA), has earned 12 tag-team titles, totalling 1,191 days holding a belt. He won nine of those championships with the "New Day" stable, alongside Big E and Xavier Woods (aka Ettore Ewen and Austin Watson, both USA). This formidable trio has logged the **longest single reign as tag-team champions**: 483 days straight in 2015–16.

# Straightliners

All records set at Elvington airfield in North Yorkshire, UK

It is an ancient truth that the quickest path between two points is a straight line. Our land-vehicle speed consultants at the UK & International Timing Adjudication (UK&ITA) use the term "straightliners" for the top-speed events at tracks such as Elvington airfield in North Yorkshire and Pendine Sands in South Wales, UK. Whether it's a turbo-charged toilet or a motorbike powered by a helicopter turbine, the UK&ITA's Trevor Duckworth and Malcolm Pittwood (above, right to left) aim to ensure that contenders for world and national land-speed records can compete under all governances.

## Fastest bicycle in a slipstream (male)

On 18 Aug 2019, Neil Campbell rode at 280.571 km/h (174.339 mph) on a bicycle motor-paced behind a Porsche Cayenne driven by Adrian Dent (both UK). The previous men's record had stood for almost 25 years. The outright **fastest bicycle speed in a slipstream** is 296.009 km/h (183.931 mph), set by Denise Mueller-Korenek (USA) in Utah, USA, on 16 Sep 2018.

## Fastest motorcycle handlebar wheelie

On 15 Aug 2020, Jonny Davies (UK) performed a wheelie while sitting on his handlebars at 175.785 km/h (109.228 mph). He had to keep his balance in the face of a strong headwind while changing gears with his thumb. Jonny is an electrical engineer by trade who competes in UK and European freestyle stunt-riding competitions in his spare time.

## Fastest motorcycle wheelie over one kilometre

Ted Brady (IRL) reached a speed of 350.595 km/h (217.850 mph) while riding 1 km (0.6 mi) on his back wheel at the Motorcycle Wheelie World Championship on 19 Aug 2017. He was riding a c. 540-brake-horsepower turbo-charged Suzuki Hayabusa. Ted took advantage of strong tailwinds to record a clean run that outpaced the previous record by around 7 km/h (4 mph).

## Fastest toilet

The *HAWC* (*Highly Advanced Water Closet*) *Mk1* reached 113.531 km/h (70.545 mph) over a two-way 100-m (328-ft) straight on 15 Sep 2018. The lightning-quick loo was built by Robert English, Thomas Ellis, Joe Summers and William Beaty (all UK). The team of engineering enthusiasts from Harington School in Rutland, UK, built the vehicle as an extension project during their A-levels.

## Fastest headstand on a motorcycle

Marco George (UK) performed a headstand while riding at 122.59 km/h (76.17 mph) on 17 Aug 2019. Marco, a competition stunt rider, trained with his father for more than a year in preparation for the attempt. On the day itself, Marco overcame strong winds and equipment issues to more than double the speed of the previous record holder.

## Fastest wheelbarrow

On 16 May 2021, Kevin Nicks (UK) drove the *Barrow of Speed* at 74.335 km/h (46.190 mph). The three-wheel barrow is powered by a moped engine, and was built at no cost from scrap metal that contract gardener Kevin found lying around his workshop during the first UK COVID-19 lockdown. He is also the brains behind the **fastest shed** (see opposite).

**Fastest monowheel motorcycle**
This single-wheeled vehicle runs on a circular track, with the driver sitting inside the wheel; steering is achieved by shifting body weight, and braking done "very gently". Mark Foster (UK) rode *Trojan* at 117.346 km/h (72.915 mph) on 22 Sep 2019. It is the third machine designed by the UK Monowheel Team, who are aiming to hit 160 km/h (100 mph).

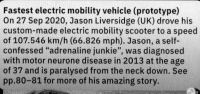

**Fastest electric mobility vehicle (prototype)**
On 27 Sep 2020, Jason Liversidge (UK) drove his custom-made electric mobility scooter to a speed of 107.546 km/h (66.826 mph). Jason, a self-confessed "adrenaline junkie", was diagnosed with motor neurone disease in 2013 at the age of 37 and is paralysed from the neck down. See pp.80–81 for more of his amazing story.

**Fastest shed**
On 27 Sep 2020, Kevin Nicks hit 170.788 km/h (106.123 mph) in his motorized garden shed. At the heart of the vehicle is a Volkswagen Passat with Quattro four-wheel drive, which Kevin refitted with a 450-horsepower V6 twin-turbo Audi RS4 engine. The shed was certified as roadworthy by the UK Driver and Vehicle Standards Agency.

**Fastest wheelie bin**
Engineer Andy Jennings (UK) reached a top speed of 72.568 km/h (45.092 mph) in his modified wheelie bin on 16 May 2021, battling rain and crosswinds that threatened to tip his vehicle over. Andy modified an upright green rubbish bin with a motorcycle engine, gearbox, ignition, bike seat and the steering from a mobility scooter.

Zef is the only person to have recorded 200-mph (322-km/h) runs on both four and two wheels at Pendine Sands.

**Fastest turbine-powered motorcycle**
On 17 May 2015, Zef Eisenberg (UK) rode a street-legal motorbike at a speed of 363.32 km/h (225.75 mph). Built by the MADMAX Race Team, the two-wheeler was powered by a modified upside down Rolls-Royce 250-C20B shaft turbine, taken from an Agusta 109A helicopter.
On 2 Oct 2020, Zef was killed following a crash at Elvington while attempting to break the British land-speed record. GWR was greatly saddened to hear of the passing of this indomitable record holder and racer, who loved to live life in the fast lane.

# Chillies

**Hot stuff!** This is the chemical that gives chilli peppers their burn: capsaicin. Chillies – or chilis, chiles – are fruits from the genus *Capsicum*, which has a number of varieties and cultivars. Capsaicin is a natural irritant, and its concentration in a pepper can be measured in Scoville Heat Units (SHU) – see chart far right.

### Earliest domestication of chilli peppers
Chilli crops (*Capsicum annuum*) were most likely planted for the first time around 6,000 years ago in north-east and east-central Mexico. This is according to archaeological, palaeoclimatic, linguistic and genetic evidence presented by Kraig H Kraft *et al* in the *Proceedings of the National Academy of Sciences* in Apr 2014.

### Largest producer of chillies
The country that grows the most chilli peppers is China, with 18,535,308 tonnes (20.43 million tons) of fresh and dried chillies produced annually as of 2018, according to the United Nation's Food and Agriculture Organization.

### Fastest time to eat 10 bhut jolokia chilli peppers
Amedonou Kankue (TOG) wolfed down 10 bhut jolokias (*C. chinense* × *C. frutescens*; 1 million SHU) in 30.70 sec on 19 Jun 2014. The record was contested between four fearless chilli eaters – including one-time record holder Jason McNabb – on the set of *Lo Show dei Record* in Milan, Italy. Amedonou celebrated his win with a well-deserved glass of ice-cold milk.

**100%**

### Heaviest chilli pepper
Green-fingered Dale Toten (UK) presented a prize-winning Poblano (*C. annuum*, 1,500 SHU) weighing 420 g (14.8 oz) at the 2018 CANNA UK National Giant Vegetables Championship held in Worcestershire, UK, on 29 Sep.

The following day, in Jona, Switzerland, the **longest chilli pepper** (inset) was measured at 505 mm (19.8 in). The Joe's Long Cayenne (*C. annuum*, 50,000 SHU) was submitted to the 2018 Great Pumpkin Commonwealth Swiss Championship by Jürg Wiesli (CHE) – a keen gardener and legal specialist in organic foods.

### Most Carolina reaper chilli peppers eaten in one minute
On 13 Nov 2016, Gregory Foster (USA) consumed 120 g (4.2 oz) of the world's **hottest chilli pepper** in 60 sec in Tempe, Arizona, USA. The fiery feat took place at an event organized by PuckerButt (see Q&A, right) at the Arizona Hot Sauce Expo.

The **fastest time to eat three Carolina reapers** is 9.72 sec, by Mike Jack (CAN) on 21 Nov 2020 in London, Ontario, Canada. See below right for more of Mike's crazy chilli-pepper conquests.

### Most chilli con carne eaten (Major League Eating)
Carmen Cincotti (USA) ate 2.438 gallons (9.22 litres) of "chilli with meat" in the six-minute timeframe allowed in Major League Eating (MLE) contests at the Orlando Chili Cook-off event in Florida, USA, on 17 Feb 2018. An accomplished pro eater, Carmen was, for a period in 2018, the second-highest-ranked eater in the MLE.

### Fastest time to eat 50 facing heaven chillies
On 8 Jul 2018, Tang Shuaihui (CHN) downed 50 facing heaven chillies (*C. annuum*, aka Chao Tian Jiao) in just 68 sec. This medium-hot variety is rated at 30,000–50,000 SHU, on a par with Tabasco chillies. The feat took place at the Feast of Fire and Ice Festival in Tanhe Ancient City, Ningxiang, China. Contestants competed in a 15-m-wide (49-ft) pool of water filled with 3 tonnes (6,600 lb) of less spicy locally grown chilli varieties.

### Q&A: SMOKIN' ED CURRIE, PUCKERBUTT PEPPER COMPANY

**Ed is a pepper breeder, founder of the PuckerButt Pepper Co. and creator of the Carolina reaper – officially the hottest chilli. Or is it?**

**Have you got even hotter chillies?**
Yes, we've got dozens that are hotter than the reaper.

**But you're keeping them under your wing for now?**
Yes, sir!

**What would you do if someone beat your reaper record?**
My team would want me to stomp on that right away! So, let someone have the record for a few months or a year... then I'd stomp in on it!

**Is chilli-growing a secretive or even cut-throat business?**
People think it's a cut-throat world, but it's really not. Most of us are

### Hottest chilli pepper
The most pungent pepper to have been assessed formally is the Carolina reaper (*C. chinense*), grown by Smokin' Ed Currie of the PuckerButt Pepper Company (both USA, see above). It rates at an average of 1,641,183 SHU, according to a series of tests conducted in 2017 by Winthrop University in South Carolina, USA.

family. There's a few nay-sayers, and there's always a little bit of drama on the fringes. But 99% of the people in the chilli world are friends or family. It's just that the "drama" people get most of the attention.

### How are you able to produce the hottest chillies?
We're the largest working organic hot-pepper farm in the USA so no one has the resources we have to grow and develop. And I'm only using 5% of the land available.

### Why do we love chillies?
They're a safe thrill-seeking thing: you can have a chilli experience and get over it – it's not going to kill you!

### ... although some of your peppers are so hot, they might!
No, there's no heat in a chilli. It's a chemical reaction that we *perceive* as heat. It *does* give you cramps – when you get into the super-hot chillies – but those are temporary.

### Largest...
**Chilli con carne**: A serving of beef chilli weighing 4,800 lb (2,177 kg) was dished up at the Spirit of Texas Festival in College Station, Texas, USA, on 4 Mar 2017. The dish – equal in weight to an adult black rhinoceros – was pepped up with 50 lb (22.6 kg) of chilli powder.

**Enchilada**: The municipality of Iztapalapa, Mexico, unveiled an enormous enchilada in the country's capital, Mexico City, on 20 Oct 2010. Weighing 1,416.14 kg (3,122 lb) – equivalent to two 11-a-side soccer teams – it was filled with chicken, courgette (zucchini), avocado, tomato, onion and chillies, all wrapped in a maize tortilla measuring 70 m (230 ft) in length. The dish's name derives from the Latin Spanish *enchilar*, meaning "seasoned with chillies".

**Burrito**: This spicy dish of tortilla-wrapped meat, beans and rice translates as "little donkey", although there was nothing little about the elephantine 5,799-kg (12,785-lb) burrito made by CANIRAC in La Paz, Mexico, on 3 Nov 2010.

### Most bhut jolokia chilli peppers eaten in two minutes
On 29 Feb 2020, Mike Jack (CAN) ate 246 g (8.67 oz) of bhut jolokias in 120 sec at the Heatwave Hot Sauce Expo in London, Ontario, Canada. Mike's bhut jolokia records include the **most eaten in one minute** – 97 g (3.42 oz), on 2 Mar 2019 – and the **fastest time to eat three** – 9.75 sec, on 26 Jan 2019. He's also set records eating the even more vicious Carolina reaper (see left).

## RED-HOT CHILLI PEPPERS: THE SCOVILLE SCALE

Wilbur Scoville (USA, 1865–1942) gave his name to the Scoville Organoleptic Test – the most famous measure of the hotness of a chilli pepper. While the rating was originally decided upon by a team of five expert tasters, today it's determined using less subjective laboratory tests. Scoville Heat Units (SHUs) go from under 100 for sweet peppers to over 2 million for the hottest cultivars.

The concentration of capsaicin changes throughout the fruit. The hottest part of the chilli is the placenta and the glands that extend from it.

1.6 m
**Carolina reaper**

1.3 m
**Naga viper**

1.2 m
**Trinidad scorpion**

1 m
**Bhut jolokia**

500,000
**Red savina**

100,000
**Habanero**

5,000
**Jalapeño**

<100
**Sweet pepper**

Scoville Heat Units are now determined using a process known as HPLC: high performance liquid chromatography.

Pedicel (stalk)

Calyx

Placenta

Ovules (seeds)

Edible pericarp

Capsaicin glands (or ribs/pith)

Locule (chamber)

Apex

The bhut jolokia – a former holder of the **hottest chilli** record – was cultivated in India and means "ghost chilli" in Assamese.

# Gastronauts

## Heaviest...

**Frybread**: The Leech Lake Band of Ojibwe (USA) cooked up a 68.12-kg (150-lb 3-oz) helping of this Native American deep-fried dough dish on 10 Aug 2019 in Cass Lake, Minnesota, USA.

**S'more**: At 155.58 kg (342 lb 15 oz), a s'more the weight of three adult women was made by Planetary Matters (USA) in Middlesex, Vermont, USA, on 28 Dec 2019. A mash-up of chocolate and marshmallow between Graham crackers, its name is a contraction of "some more".

**Rocky road**: On 25 May 2019, Matthew Williams and Mission Aviation Fellowship (both UK) presented a 334.1-kg (736-lb 9-oz) rocky road in Steyning, West Sussex, UK. Chocolate, nuts, marshmallows and biscuits come together in this toothsome indulgence.

**Bread pudding**: On 2 Aug 2019, a 1,424-kg (3,139-lb 6-oz) bread pudding – as heavy as a family car – was baked by a team headed up by Joseph Dias of Trinity Group (all IND).

**Mud pie**: A year prior to baking his prodigious pudding (above), Joseph Dias and his team dished up a mud pie weighing 1,345 kg (2,965 lb) – heavier than 20 average-sized adult men. A biscuit base was covered with a concoction of chocolate, cream and eggs, and served up in Panaji, Goa, India, on 3 Aug 2018.

## Largest...

**Wedding-cookie table**: On 11 Aug 2019, the Monongahela Area Historical Society (USA) laid a table with 88,425 cookies at the celebration of three marriages and three vow renewals. The ceremonies were held in Pennsylvania, USA, where there's a tradition of bedecking tables at weddings with cookies, sometimes in lieu of a formal cake.

**Donation of baked goods**: On 22 Oct 2020, Grupo Bimbo (MEX) presented 36,000 bread loaves – with a combined weight of 24,480 kg (53,969 lb) – to the food bank Alimento para Todos in Iztapalapa, Mexico City.

**Chocolate bar (area)**: Frits van Noppen, Jeroen Hollestein, Niek Verhoeven and Simon Koster (all NLD) created a 383.24-m² (4,125-sq-ft) chocolate bar – more than five times the size of a squash court – on 6 Feb 2020 in Rotterdam, Netherlands. White, dark and milk chocolate was used to render the image of a hospital ship on the bar, and proceeds from its sale were donated to the Mercy Ships charity.

### Most chicken nuggets eaten in one minute
The 60-second record for devouring battered or breaded boneless chicken pieces – based on the weight consumed – was broken twice in 2020. Nela Zisser (NZ, pictured) managed 298 g (10.51 oz) but within a month lost the title to Todd Fernley (USA), who chowed through 315 g (11.11 oz). The average fast-food-restaurant nugget weighs c. 16.5 g (0.5 oz).

**100%**

### Big fruit and veg

| HEAVIEST... | Weight | Name | Date |
|---|---|---|---|
| **Blueberry** (above) | 16.2 g (0.57 oz) | David and Leasa Mazzardis (both AUS) | 20 Sep 2020 |
| **Cherry** | 26.45 g (0.93 oz) | Silvia Salvi (ITA) | 26 Jun 2020 |
| **Red cabbage** (right) | 31.6 kg (69 lb 10 oz) | Neil Hands (UK) | 26 Sep 2020 |
| **Butternut squash** | 25.17 kg (55 lb 6 oz) | Christopher Brown (USA) | 26 Sep 2020 |
| **LONGEST...** | **Length** | **Name** | **Date** |
| **Leek** | 1.22 m (4 ft) | Peter Glazebrook (UK) | 26 Sep 2020 |
| **Snake melon** | 1.36 m (4 ft 5.5 in) | Kathy Ffoulkes (AUS) | 17 Feb 2020 |
| **Scallion** | 2.53 m (8 ft 3.6 in) | Zhangqiu District (CHN) | 15 Nov 2020 |
| **Salsify** | 5.57 m (18 ft 3.3 in) | Joe Atherton (UK) | 26 Sep 2020 |
| **Beetroot** | 8.56 m (28 ft) | Joe Atherton (UK) | 26 Sep 2020 |

*Sources: Great Pumpkin Commonwealth; CANNA/UK National Vegetable Society*

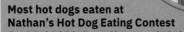

### Most hot dogs eaten at Nathan's Hot Dog Eating Contest
On 4 Jul 2020, Joey Chestnut (USA) chowed down on 75 hot dogs at the annual competition in Coney Island, New York City. At the same event, fellow American Miki Sudo (inset) secured the **female** record (48.5). The two also have the **most wins** and **most female wins** of the contest, respectively. Joey has had 13 victories from 2007 to 2020, while Miki has won every year since 2014, a total of seven wins.

**JOEY CHESTNUT**

### Major League Eating (MLE) records held
The world's premier overseer of competitive-eating contests stages some 70 events each year. Listed here are the all-time top 10 MLE contestants, ordered by the number of Major League records held as of 1 Jan 2021:

| Name | # | Recent records | Date |
|---|---|---|---|
| Joey Chestnut | 54 | Hot dogs: 75 in 10 min (see left) | 4/7/20 |
| Patrick Bertoletti | 32 | Pancakes (3.25 oz; 92 g): 50 in 10 min | 29/9/12 |
| Sonya Thomas | 21 | Oysters: 564 in 8 min | 3/6/12 |
| Geoffrey Esper | 10 | Bratwursts (4.5 oz; 127.5 g): 36 in 10 min | 24/8/19 |
| Bob Shoudt | 9 | French fries: 7 lb 14 oz (3.57 kg) in 10 min | 31/5/10 |
| Cookie Jarvis | 8 | Grapes: 8 lb 15 oz (4.05 kg) in 10 min | 1/11/05 |
| Eric Booker | 7 | Maui onions: 8.5 oz (241 g) in 1 min | 8/8/04 |
| Richard LeFevre | 5 | Huevos rancheros: 7 lb 12 oz (3.51 kg) in 10 min | 18/3/06 |
| Carmen Cincotti | 4 | Chilli: 2.438 gal (9.2 l) in 6 min (see p.94) | 17/2/18 |
| Gideon Oji | 4 | Beans: 10 lb (4.5 kg) in 1 min 45 sec | 21/4/20 |

*All nationalities USA; all records set under MLE guidelines*

▶ **Largest onion bhaji**
Oli Khan and a team from Surma Takeaway in Stevenage (both UK) cooked up a 175.48-kg (386-lb 13-oz) onion bhaji – made from 2,000 onions and 500 g (1 lb) of chillies – in London on 4 Feb 2020. The bumper-sized entrée, which had a diameter of 5 ft (1.52 m), was later shared out between the congregation of a local mosque and the homeless.

## Longest...
**Sheet of pasta rolled in one minute**: Samuel Tan (SGP) unfurled a 2.03-m (6-ft 7.9-in) pasta sheet in 60 sec in Singapore on 8 Oct 2020. The previous record had been held by TV chef Gordon Ramsay.
**Braided bread loaf**: JNF Australia and Grandma Moses (both AUS) baked a 10.087-m (33-ft 1-in) plaited loaf – the length of about 17 regular baguettes – in Sydney, Australia, on 14 Nov 2019.
**Nougat**: On 18 Sep 2019, Salvatore Bongiovanni and Bongiovanni SRL (both ITA) made a piece of nougat 1,004 m (3,293 ft) long – about 14 times that of a Boeing 747 airliner – in Mazzarino, Italy. Nougat is a chewy or brittle candy containing nuts and sometimes fruit; this one was made to promote local almonds and help keep alive ancient regional traditions.

**Most cookies baked in one hour**
Frank Squeo and Baking Memories 4 Kids (both USA) baked 6,018 cookies in 60 min in West Nyack, New York, USA, on 7 Dec 2019.

**Most dumplings made in one hour**
On 15 Sep 2019, Beata Jasek (POL) produced 1,066 plum-filled "pierogis" in 60 min in Iwkowa, Poland.

**Most flavours of ice-cream commercially available**
As of 14 Nov 2019, La Casa Gelato (CAN) was offering 238 varieties of ice-cream in Vancouver, British Columbia, Canada.

**Most eaten in one minute**
**Jam doughnuts**: Australia's Jesse Freeman consumed six of these gooey-centred

**Most mashed potato eaten in one minute**
André Ortolf (DEU) downed 1.12 kg (2 lb 7 oz) of mashed potato – about six typical portions-worth – in Augsburg, Bavaria, Germany, on 30 Nov 2017. André has a bottomless appetite for food-related records: he also holds 60-sec titles for the **most Marmite eaten** (368 g; 13 oz), **most jelly eaten with chopsticks** (716 g; 1 lb 9 oz) and **most Christmas stollen eaten** (336 g; 11 oz).

confections on *The Morning Show* in Sydney, New South Wales, Australia, on 1 Jun 2018.
**Sausages**: Competitive-eating champion Leah Shutkever (UK) dispatched 10 canned hot dogs in Birmingham, West Midlands, UK, on 7 Jun 2020.
**Peas (with a cocktail stick)**: David Rush (USA) pinned and polished off 108 peas in Boise, Idaho, USA, on 4 Dec 2018.
**Peanut butter**: On 17 Nov 2017, André Ortolf (above) wolfed down 378 g (13.3 oz) of nut spread in Augsburg, Germany.
**Baby food**: On 19 Nov 2020, as part of GWR Day (see pp.10–11), Ortolf also gobbled up 1,609 g (3 lb 9 oz) of baby food – equivalent to 14 standard 125-g (4.4-oz) jars.

**Longest puffcorn**
On 27 Aug 2020, Wotsits Giants (part of Walkers Snack Foods, UK) presented a 10.66-m (34-ft 11-in) puffcorn in Leicester, UK. It took an eight-person team 2 hr 29 min to make the super-sized snack, which is longer than a London Routemaster bus and had to be hand-baked as it wouldn't fit inside Walkers' ovens! The mega-Wotsit was later mounted for display on the factory wall.

The snack is around 160 times longer than a standard Wotsit Giant, but (as per GWR guidelines) exactly the same width.

# Big Stuff

**Largest Monopoly token**
FM Projects Limited (CHN) unveiled a 2.96-m-long (9-ft 8-in) likeness of a Monopoly racing car token in Hong Kong, China, on 28 Nov 2019. In Monopoly mythology, the car is held to be the property of Milburn Pennybags, the game's moustachioed mascot. It may have been inspired by a 1940s Kurtis Kraft Midget car or vintage '30s racers, such as the Mercedes-Benz W25.

**Largest jute bag**
On 3 Jul 2019, Cotton Bag Co. (UK) presented a jute bag measuring 22.5 m (73 ft 9 in) tall and 14.6 m (47 ft 10 in) wide in Bradford-on-Avon, Wiltshire, UK. The attempt coincided with International Plastic Bag Free Day and Plastic Free July, and was arranged to encourage the wider adoption of reusable bags.

**Singing bowl**
These vessels emit a resonant tone when struck, or when a mallet is run along the rim. György Juhász (HUN) presented a bowl with a width of 2.33 m (7 ft 7 in) in Garáb, Hungary, on 28 Feb 2019.

**Scissors**
Tekbaş Şirketler Grubu (TUR) performed a ribbon-cutting ceremony at a new development in Adana, Turkey, on 12 Oct 2019 using a pair of 3.01-m-long (9-ft 10.5-in) scissors – more than 10 times the average size.

**Christmas snowflake ornament**
On 28 Oct 2019, Universal Studios in Osaka, Japan, topped their Christmas tree with a 3.19-m (10-ft 5-in) snowflake.

**Googly eyes**
Austin McChord, Ryan Sasloe and Ed Lundblad (all USA) unveiled two jiggly eyes with a 12-ft (3.66-m) diameter – larger than a MINI Cooper car – in Norwalk, Connecticut, USA, on 27 Aug 2019.

**Papier-mâché sculpture (supported)**
Carnival Magic Theme Park in Phuket, Thailand, created a 5.95-m-tall (19-ft 6-in) papier-mâché likeness of an elephant, dressed as a circus ringmaster and wearing a top hat. The 4.3-m-wide (14-ft) "chewed-up paper" pachyderm was verified on 8 Feb 2020.

On the same day, Carnival Magic Theme Park displayed the **largest outdoor chandelier** – 11.69 m from top to bottom and 9.47 m in diameter (38 ft 4 in x 31 ft).

**Model of a human organ**
VPS Lakeshore – a hospital in Kochi, India – created a model of a heart measuring 9.69 m (31 ft 9 in) tall, as verified on 5 Jan 2019. It's around 80 times larger than the real thing. The giant installation was part of a health campaign.

**Tallest sandcastle**
On 5 Jun 2019, Skulptura Projects (DEU) unveiled a bonanza-sized beach attraction measuring 17.65 m (57 ft 11 in) tall at the 10th Sandskulpturen Festival in Binz, Germany. An international team of 12 sculptors and eight technicians worked for three-and-a-half weeks to complete the sandcastle. Its circular base had a diameter of approximately 26 m (85 ft 3 in). No additives were used in the water to bind the sand, and there were no internal support structures.

The colossal castle is made from 11,000 tonnes (12,125 tons) of sand, mixed only with water.

17 m

26 m

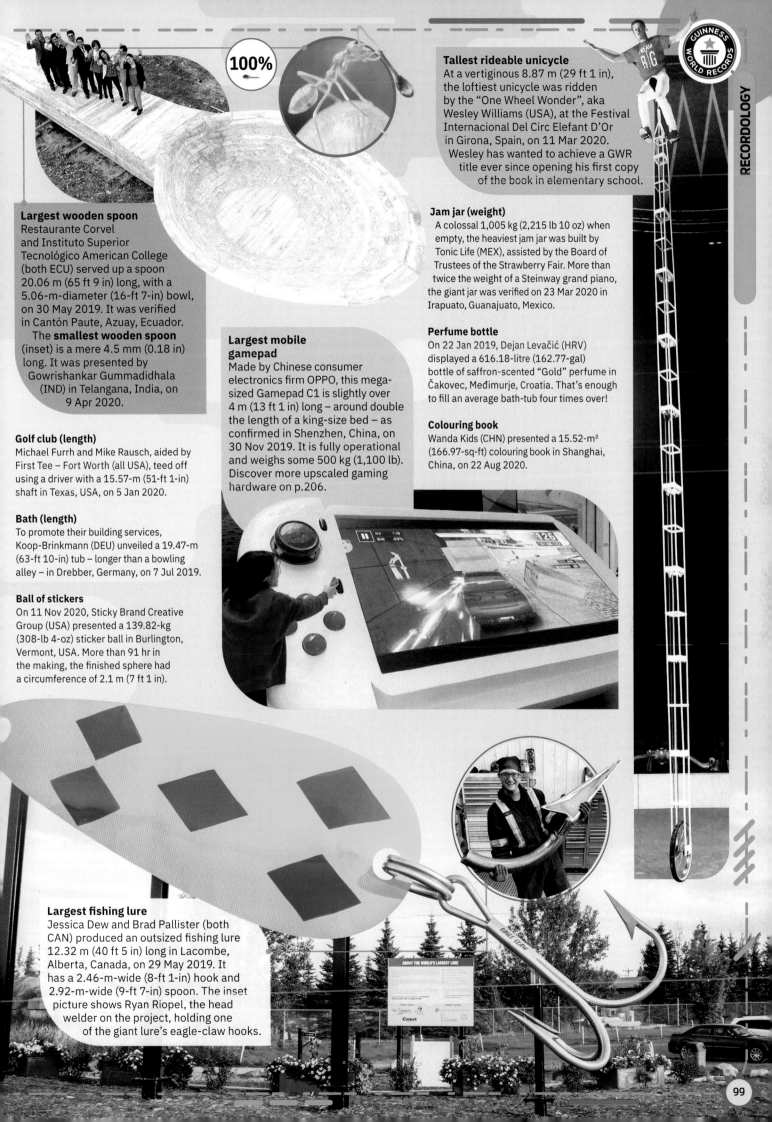

100%

## Largest wooden spoon
Restaurante Corvel and Instituto Superior Tecnológico American College (both ECU) served up a spoon 20.06 m (65 ft 9 in) long, with a 5.06-m-diameter (16-ft 7-in) bowl, on 30 May 2019. It was verified in Cantón Paute, Azuay, Ecuador.

The **smallest wooden spoon** (inset) is a mere 4.5 mm (0.18 in) long. It was presented by Gowrishankar Gummadidhala (IND) in Telangana, India, on 9 Apr 2020.

## Golf club (length)
Michael Furrh and Mike Rausch, aided by First Tee – Fort Worth (all USA), teed off using a driver with a 15.57-m (51-ft 1-in) shaft in Texas, USA, on 5 Jan 2020.

## Bath (length)
To promote their building services, Koop-Brinkmann (DEU) unveiled a 19.47-m (63-ft 10-in) tub – longer than a bowling alley – in Drebber, Germany, on 7 Jul 2019.

## Ball of stickers
On 11 Nov 2020, Sticky Brand Creative Group (USA) presented a 139.82-kg (308-lb 4-oz) sticker ball in Burlington, Vermont, USA. More than 91 hr in the making, the finished sphere had a circumference of 2.1 m (7 ft 1 in).

## Largest mobile gamepad
Made by Chinese consumer electronics firm OPPO, this mega-sized Gamepad C1 is slightly over 4 m (13 ft 1 in) long – around double the length of a king-size bed – as confirmed in Shenzhen, China, on 30 Nov 2019. It is fully operational and weighs some 500 kg (1,100 lb). Discover more upscaled gaming hardware on p.206.

## Tallest rideable unicycle
At a vertiginous 8.87 m (29 ft 1 in), the loftiest unicycle was ridden by the "One Wheel Wonder", aka Wesley Williams (USA), at the Festival Internacional Del Circ Elefant D'Or in Girona, Spain, on 11 Mar 2020. Wesley has wanted to achieve a GWR title ever since opening his first copy of the book in elementary school.

## Jam jar (weight)
A colossal 1,005 kg (2,215 lb 10 oz) when empty, the heaviest jam jar was built by Tonic Life (MEX), assisted by the Board of Trustees of the Strawberry Fair. More than twice the weight of a Steinway grand piano, the giant jar was verified on 23 Mar 2020 in Irapuato, Guanajuato, Mexico.

## Perfume bottle
On 22 Jan 2019, Dejan Levačić (HRV) displayed a 616.18-litre (162.77-gal) bottle of saffron-scented "Gold" perfume in Čakovec, Međimurje, Croatia. That's enough to fill an average bath-tub four times over!

## Colouring book
Wanda Kids (CHN) presented a 15.52-m² (166.97-sq-ft) colouring book in Shanghai, China, on 22 Aug 2020.

## Largest fishing lure
Jessica Dew and Brad Pallister (both CAN) produced an outsized fishing lure 12.32 m (40 ft 5 in) long in Lacombe, Alberta, Canada, on 29 May 2019. It has a 2.46-m-wide (8-ft 1-in) hook and 2.92-m-wide (9-ft 7-in) spoon. The inset picture shows Ryan Riopel, the head welder on the project, holding one of the giant lure's eagle-claw hooks.

# Master Builders

### Longest LEGO-brick bridge
The Institution of Civil Engineers (UK) pieced together a bridge spanning 16.92 m (55 ft 6 in) at the Ironbridge Gorge Museums in Shropshire, UK. Completed on 31 Aug 2019, it comprised 205,000 bricks.

### Largest LEGO-brick Notre Dame
On 9 Jan 2020, a 1:33-scale replica of the French cathedral was unveiled at the Wystawa Klocków ("Block Exhibition") in Warsaw, Poland. The sculpture was 2.72 m tall, 3.78 m long and 1.43 m wide (8 ft 11 in x 12 ft 4 in x 4 ft 8 in) and weighed around 250 kg (550 lb). Creator Ivan Angeli (SRB) spent 500 hr bringing Notre Dame to life, using more than 400,000 bricks. It was one of 120 famous buildings rendered in LEGO for the exhibition.

### Largest LEGO-brick stage set replica
To celebrate the 25th anniversary of the TV sitcom *Friends*, Warner Bros. Television commissioned Nathan "The Brick Artist" Sawaya (USA) to construct a life-size version of the Central Perk coffee house. The set was revealed in Las Vegas, Nevada, USA, on 19 Oct 2019. It used more than 973,000 bricks and covered 62.75 m² (675 sq ft). "We wanted to do this faithfully," Nathan explained, "so we spent a lot of time working on a lot of little elements."

### Fastest time to build the LEGO® *Star Wars Millennium Falcon* Microfighter
Twelve-year-old Haddon Haste (USA) assembled the *Star Wars* spaceship in 1 min 59.72 (par)sec on 12 Sep 2020 in Louisville, Kentucky, USA. Inspired by watching YouTube videos of fellow record holders Dude Perfect, Haddon spent the COVID lockdown preparing for his own attempt. He found a record that combined two of his biggest passions: LEGO and *Star Wars*.

### Largest LEGO-brick wind turbine
The LEGO Group (DNK) unveiled a 7.63-m-tall (25-ft) wind turbine on 15 May 2017 in Liverpool, UK. A team of experts spent 600 hr piecing together the giant generator, which was made from 146,251 individual bricks. The record attempt celebrated a new wind-farm investment that aimed to make LEGO a 100% renewable-energy company.

### Fastest time to build the LEGO *Star Wars Millennium Falcon*
On 18 Jul 2019, Johannes Roesch, Kathi Stutz, Ralf Johannes and Gabriel Cabrera Parra (all DEU) constructed the 7,541-piece Corellian YT-1300 light freighter in 2 hr 51 min 47 sec in Walldorf, Germany. The *Millennium Falcon* (kit #75192) was formerly the **largest LEGO set** on sale.

The **fastest time to build the LEGO Colosseum** – the new largest LEGO set as of Nov 2020 (see Q&A right) – is 13 hr 37 min 36 sec, by Paul Ufema (USA) in Forest, Virginia, USA, on 24 Feb 2021.

### Largest LEGO-brick ship
Dream Cruises Management Ltd (CHN) constructed an 8.44-m-long (27-ft 8.5-in) cruise liner, measured in Hong Kong, China, on 15 Nov 2017. Built from 2,518,266 bricks, it featured a swimming pool, basketball court and even a helicopter pad.

David's prosthetic arms are numbered MK I to MK IV (pictured), in the style of Iron Man's armoured suits.

### First functional LEGO prosthetic arm
Hand Solo, aka David Aguilar, from Andorra designed and built his own fully working arm using bricks from a LEGO Technic helicopter set (#9396). David, who was born without a right forearm, completed his first iteration in 2017. The purely mechanical prosthesis featured a moveable elbow joint and a grabber for picking things up, which he activated by bending his elbow. He has subsequently refined the design a number of times.

### BEE IS FOR BUILD: RUAIRI O' LEOCHAIN

Teacher Ruairi O' Leochain (IRL) is the brains behind the **largest plastic-brick beehive**. It measured 38 x 48 x 48 cm (1 ft 2 in x 1 ft 6 in x 1 ft 6 in) on 14 May 2020 in Athlone, Ireland.

**What gave you the idea to build a beehive out of LEGO bricks?**
A sense of wonder, I suppose! I love nature, I'm a beekeeper, and I thought that it would look cool if it worked. I knew that plastic would be safe for the bees, even if a layer of LEGO wouldn't provide as much insulation as a wooden or polystyrene hive.

**How long did the build take?**
About seven weeks or so, just an hour here and there when our first COVID lockdown hit. I had a "National" hive beside me for measurements, which are really important in beekeeping.

**How did your bee colony take to their new home?**
At first, they were confused by the fact that their entrances were at slightly different spots. But the colony did very well [and went on to produce honey]. I'm trained by Wildlife Rehabilitation Ireland, and any money I make from the honey goes towards vet bills, medication and housing for Irish wildlife. I've been contacted by beekeepers from Canada to Korea and Africa, wishing me well and asking about my future plans.

**So what *are* your future plans?**
I might try a LEGO birdhouse next year – they're a bit easier! Blue tits are common here in Ireland. I'd probably build a tiny attic space too, to hide a live-feed camera.

## COLOSSAL CREATIONS: ROK ŽGALIN KOBE

Launched on 28 Nov 2020, the 9,036-piece Colosseum (kit #10276) is now the ○ largest commercially available LEGO set. The model of the Roman amphitheatre measures 27 cm high, 52 cm wide and 59 cm deep (10 in x 1 ft 8 in x 1 ft 11 in). GWR spoke to its creator, designer Rok Žgalin Kobe.

**How did the Colosseum compare to other LEGO sets you have designed?**
I've been involved in nearly all of the LEGO Architecture sets since 2012 and have designed over 35 sets. But the Colosseum is still five times bigger than my previous largest. It had always been at the top of my to-do list – the hard part was doing the building justice. The design took half a year, from start to finish.

**What were the major challenges?**
Our model competency centre was worried that such a big model might not stay together if it was picked up and moved around. I offered a solution from architectural theory – the Colosseum would only be connected to its oval base at a few fixed points. It would be flexible enough to warp and bend when subjected to stress.

**Did you always intend for it to have so many pieces?**
We didn't set out to do the biggest LEGO model of all time; I set out to explore what would be the best execution of the Colosseum in LEGO bricks. But the more the model was being perfected, the more pieces went into capturing its details.

**How quickly can you build this set?**
I've built quite a few, but none in less than 30 hr. I wonder what the world record time could be? [See left for answer!]

**Largest collection of LEGO sets**
Frank Smoes (AUS) and his family owned a private collection of 3,837 LEGO kits, as verified on 9 May 2017 in Melbourne, Victoria, Australia. Frank was introduced to LEGO as a child in the 1950s, and began collecting in the late 1970s. He owns at least 1.2 million individual pieces. Frank's favourite set is #76052 – a Batman Classic TV Series Batcave – on account of its iconic characters and vehicles.

**Tallest LEGO-brick structure**
On 17–21 Jun 2015, LEGO Italia constructed a tower measuring 35.05 m (114 ft 11 in) – over half the height of the Leaning Tower of Pisa – in Milan, Italy.

The **longest LEGO-brick structure** was also built in Italy. On 13 Feb 2005, a 1,578.81-m (5,179-ft 10-in) millipede consisting of 2,901,760 bricks was unveiled in Turin. The build was organized by the shopkeepers' association at Shopville Le Gru.

**Largest LEGO-brick...**
**Batman symbol:** 2.042 m (6 ft 8 in) across, by Luo Wenqi, Ren Jie, Jiang Shuhe and Wang Haiqing (all CHN) in Nanchang, Jiangxi, China, on 11 Nov 2020.
○ **Ferris wheel:** 3.38 m (11 ft 1 in) in diameter, by Tomáš Kašpařík (CZE), verified in Utrecht, Netherlands, on 22 Oct 2017.
**Skeleton:** a 6-m-long (20-ft) actual-size skeleton of a *T. rex* dinosaur, built by Nathan Sawaya (USA, see left) in 2011.
**Cherry-blossom tree:** 4.38 m tall and 4.93 m wide (14 ft 4 in x 16 ft 2 in), made by LEGOLAND Japan in Nagoya, Aichi, Japan, as verified on 28 Mar 2018.

▶ **Largest diorama built from interlocking plastic bricks**
A *Lord of the Rings*-inspired scene conjured from 150 million toy bricks was unveiled on 10 Jan 2021 at Blocks Kingdom in the SMAERD Land children's museum in Shenzhen, Guangdong, China. It occupies a total area of 191.426 m² (2,060 sq ft) – about the same as 50 king-size beds. It took a team of 40 designers and builders more than three years to recreate Middle-earth in block form.

The Tolkien-themed diorama depicts epic battles such as Minas Tirith, Helm's Deep and Black Gate.

# Monster Trucks

Monster trucks have been wowing audiences around the world ever since Bob Chandler drove *Bigfoot*, the **first monster truck** (see right), over a line of junked old cars in Apr 1981. Today, dozens of over-sized trucks compete in Monster Jam – a scored competition that features racing and stunts.

### First monster truck
The monster truck phenomenon started in the late 1970s, when mechanic and off-road racer Bob Chandler (USA) began making modifications to his Ford F-250 pickup, which he called *Bigfoot*. In 1979, he added parts from a scrapped military vehicle that gave it the distinctive high ground clearance and massive wheels of the monster trucks we see today.

### First monster-truck backflip
On 27 Feb 2010, Cam McQueen (CAN) pulled off the first backflip in a monster truck, launching off a ramp at the Jacksonville Monster Jam in Florida, USA.

Just over two years later, on 23 Mar 2012, fellow Monster Jam driver George Balhan (USA) managed

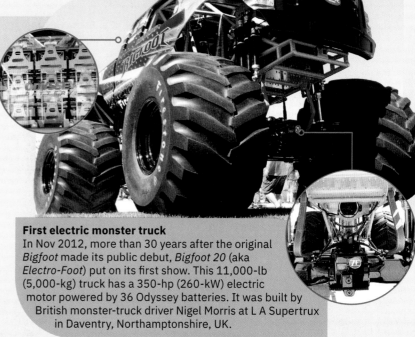

### First electric monster truck
In Nov 2012, more than 30 years after the original *Bigfoot* made its public debut, *Bigfoot 20* (aka *Electro-Foot*) put on its first show. This 11,000-lb (5,000-kg) truck has a 350-hp (260-kW) electric motor powered by 36 Odyssey batteries. It was built by British monster-truck driver Nigel Morris at L A Supertrux in Daventry, Northamptonshire, UK.

### Largest monster truck
Weighing in at 38,000 lb (17,236 kg), Bob Chandler's *Bigfoot 5*, now 35 years old, remains king of the monsters. It stands 15 ft 6 in (4.7 m) tall and uses the wheels from a 1950s all-terrain vehicle called the LeTourneau Sno-Train. Today, it is on display in St Louis, Missouri, USA.

two in a row without stopping, to set a new record for the **most consecutive monster-truck backflips**.

The quest for the **first monster-truck double backflip** is still ongoing, with several drivers having attempted it and wrecked their trucks in the process.

### Farthest monster-truck ramp jump
On 1 Sep 2013, Joe Sylvester (USA) reclaimed the flight-distance record by launching his truck *Bad Habit* 237 ft 7 in (72.42 m) in Columbus, Pennsylvania, USA. He had previously set the record at 208 ft 7 in (63.58 m) in 2010, only for Dan Runte to beat him by six feet in 2012.

The record for the **farthest monster-truck ramp jump in reverse** has remained with veteran driver and former champion

Michael Vaters (USA) since 2002, when he set the mark to beat at 70 ft (21.3 m) in Indianapolis, Indiana, USA.

### Most Monster Jam World Finals wins
Tom Meents (USA; see opposite) has won events at the Monster Jam World Finals 12 times since the event's first edition in 1999.

At the 2008 World Freestyle Championship in Las Vegas, Nevada, USA, Adam Anderson (USA, b. 5 Dec 1985) became the **youngest winner at the Monster Jam World Finals**. Adam won the freestyle event, driving *Taz* on 29 Mar, at the age of 22 years 115 days.

### First female Monster Jam driver
Former WCW/WWE wrestler Madusa (aka Debrah Miceli, USA) made her Monster Jam debut in 1999 driving a truck named after her alter ego. She would go on to become the **first female driver to win a Monster Jam Freestyle World Final**, in Mar 2004.

**12** **32** **7.5**

### ▶ Longest monster truck
*Sin City Hustler* is a 32-ft (9.75-m) monster-truck limousine built by Brad and Jen Campbell (both USA) of Big Toyz Racing. It stands about 12 ft (3.6 m) tall, weighs 7.5 tons (6.8 tonnes) and can hold up to 12 paying passengers for thrill rides around the desert in Nevada, USA.

## MONSTER JAM 2020

Between 22 and 25 Jun 2020, with their usual schedule of competition stops disrupted by the pandemic, the drivers on the Monster Jam tour assembled for a festival of record-breaking in Bradenton, Florida, USA. From dawn to dusk, this team of six drivers took the skills they use at Monster Jam tournaments – wheelies, stoppies, jumps and burnouts – and pushed them to record-breaking extremes. It was also a family affair, with siblings Adam, Krysten and Ryan Anderson each earning Guinness World Records titles.

**MONSTER JAM**

**Fastest speed**
Record: 100.3 mph (161.4 km/h)
Driver: Bryce Kenny (USA)
Truck: *Great Clips Mohawk Warrior*

**Farthest wheelie**
Record: 624 ft 10 in (190.46 m)
Driver: Adam Anderson (USA)
Truck: *Grave Digger*

**Farthest side-wheelie (bicycle)**
Record: 891 ft 10 in (271.83 m)
Driver: Ryan Anderson (USA)
Truck: *Son-uva Digger*

**Most donuts (spins) in one minute**
Record: 44
Driver: Bari Musawwir (USA)
Truck: *Zombie*
Bari also set the record for **most consecutive donuts (58).**

**Highest ramp jump**
Record: 33 ft 9 in (10.3 m)
Driver: Krysten Anderson (USA)
Truck: *Grave Digger*

**Farthest stoppie**
Record: 209 ft 2 in (63.77 m)
Driver: Tom Meents (USA)
Truck: *Max-D*

**Most monster trucks jumped by a monster truck**
Record: 8
Driver: Adam Anderson (USA)
Truck: *Megalodon*

# Odd Talents

### Longest time to swallow a sword

On 21 Jun 2020, Murray Molloy (IRL) held a sword in his throat for 13 min 12 sec in Murcia, Spain. An experienced performer, Murray first showed an interest in sideshow at a young age, when an "eccentric neighbour" taught him some magic tricks.

### Largest hole-digging championship

Narita Dream Farm (JPN) welcomed 1,452 people to the 20th All-National Hole Digging Competition in Chiba, Japan, on 2 Feb 2020. Teams compete for the Golden Shovel by digging the deepest hole in 30 min, although extra points are awarded for the "most creative hole".

### Longest bubble chain (hanging)

On 26 Oct 2020, Su Zhong Tai (CHN) linked up 61 bubbles in Taipei, Taiwan, China. It was around 145 cm (4 ft 9 in) long.

### Longest rubber-band chain (individual)

Sajankumar Arvindbhai Patel (IND) made a 6.5-km (4-mi) chain of bands, as verified in Anand, Gujarat, India, on 1 Jan 2020. Comprising 85,300 bands, it is longer than Paris's Champs-Élysées avenue and more than three times London's Oxford Street.

### Longest cornhole shot (blindfolded)

Cornhole is a game in which players throw bags of corn into a small hole at the end of a raised platform. Joshua Biggers (USA) landed a 32-ft (9.75-m) shot while wearing a blindfold in Clearwater, Florida, USA, on 19 Jul 2020. (See also p.233.)

### Heaviest weight lifted with little fingers

On 18 Nov 2020, Canada's Dariusz Slowik (b. POL) raised a 105.67-kg (232-lb 15-oz) weight – about the same as an adult giant panda – using only his *digiti minimus manus* (or pinkies) in Aarhus, Denmark. The feat took place on GWR Day that year. (See p.11.)

### Most BASE jumps in 12 hours by human-powered ascent

On 23 Oct 2020, Nicole Senecal (USA) made 37 BASE jumps in 12 hr from the Perrine Bridge in Twin Falls, Idaho, USA. She made each return trip on foot, hiking 148 m (486 ft) back up to the exit point on the bridge (inset). Nicole wanted to honour the women who had fought for the right to vote in the USA; the 19th Amendment to the US Constitution, which effected that result, had been ratified a century earlier.

121.8

52.5

Kurt Steiner (USA) achieved the **most consecutive skips of a stone on water** – 88 – near Kane, Pennsylvania, USA, in 2013.

### Farthest distance to skim a stone

Dougie Isaacs (UK) side-armed a stone 121.8 m (399 ft 7 in) across the surface of Abernant Lake in Llanwrtyd Wells, Powys, UK, on 28 May 2018. That's longer than an American football field. During the same event, Nina Luginbühl (CHE, above) broke the **women's** record with a skip of 52.5 m (172 ft 2 in).

Dougie has also achieved the **most wins of the World Stone Skimming Championships (men)** – eight. The **women's** record is held by the UK's Lucy Wood, with five victories, the last in 2018.

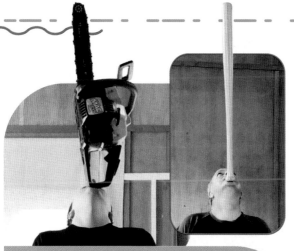

**Longest time to balance a chainsaw (chin)**
Circus artiste and accomplished balancer James "Jay" Rawlings (UK) kept a chainsaw upright on his chin for 13 min 5.38 sec on 23 May 2020. Jay broke seven records during lockdown. His father Steve (inset) also got in on the act, drawing on his 30-plus years of circus experience to record the **longest time to balance a baseball bat (chin)** – 2 hr 30 min 11 sec. All records were set in Chinnor, Oxfordshire, UK.

**Longest duration spinning 30 hoops simultaneously**
Mariam Olayiwola (UK) kept 30 hula hoops aloft for 35 sec in London, UK, on 22 Aug 2020. She is a member of the circus-arts troupe Marawa's Majorettes (see pp.108–09) and dedicated her record attempt to all the girls in her group. She hopes it will serve to demonstrate the strength and mental resilience required in the circus arts.

**Most consecutive stairs climbed while hula hooping**
Mr O!, aka ObaroEne Otitigbe (USA), hula-hooped his way up 734 stairs in Albany, New York, USA, on 25 May 2020.

**Most people standing on a bed of nails**
On 27 Oct 2020, a total of 151 firm-footed participants stood on nails in an event organized by GVOZDIMIRA 2020 and the Raivola hotel in St Petersburg, Russia.

**One-minute wonders: Most...**
**Basketball neck catches**: On 26 Oct 2020, Tarun Kumar Cheddy (MUS) threw a ball and caught it on his neck 48 times in Seizième Mille, Mauritius.
**Apples sliced while juggling knives (team of two)**: Blade-juggler David Rush bisected 40 apples thrown to him by his neighbour Jonathan Hannon (both USA) in Boise, Idaho, USA, on 7 Oct 2020.

**Most table-tennis balls hit with a nunchaku in one minute**
On 23 Dec 2020, inspired by martial-arts legend Bruce Lee, Xie Desheng (CHN) struck 35 ping-pong balls with a nunchaku, aka nunchucks. His sharp-eyed feat was live-streamed on *DouYu: The Challengers* in Beijing, China. Two months earlier, he had achieved the **most candles extinguished with a single martial-arts kick** – 28.

**Figures-of-eight with a sword**: Chirag Lukha (UK) performed 94 figures-of-eight in the air with a sword in Leicester, UK, on 18 Nov 2020.
**Skips on rollerskates**: On 10 Feb 2020, Zorawar Singh (IND) jumped a skipping rope 262 times in rollerskates in Delhi, India.
**Bullwhip cracks**: Jack Lepiarz (USA) cracked a whip 298 times in Somerville, Massachusetts, USA, on 6 Sep 2020.

*Record breakers have had to adapt to life in lockdown during the pandemic. For some, that meant going virtual in 2020:*
**Most people simultaneously...**
**Playing air guitar online**: 186 fans of the movie *Bill & Ted Face the Music* (USA, 2020), logged by Orion Pictures (USA) on 24 Aug.
**Toasting online**: 335 guests at the Amazon Web Services (USA) conference on 30 Nov.
**In a pizza party video hangout**: 907 patrons of Hormel Foods (USA) on 18 Sep.
**In a séance live stream on Facebook**: 9,317 viewers of TV show *UK Haunted* (Really, UK) on 1 Nov.

**Farthest distance to push a lawnmower in 24 hours**
On 22–23 Jun 2019, Andy Maxfield (UK) pushed a lawnmower for 92.80 km (57.66 mi) at Ewood Park in Blackburn, Lancashire, UK – the home ground of his favourite soccer team, Blackburn Rovers. His feat raised £4,500 ($5,730) for the Alzheimer's Society.
Previously, on 30 Jul 2017, Andy completed the **fastest journey from Land's End to John o' Groats on a ride-on mower** – 5 days 8 hr 36 min driving a John Deere X750.

**Most apples crushed in the hand in one minute**
Using only his right hand, Donnie Baxter (UK) scrunched 13 apples in 60 sec, breaking them into at least two pieces, at Acharacle in the Scottish Highlands, UK, on 11 Oct 2020. Later, the crushed fruit was baked in a pie. His feat fulfilled Donnie's childhood dream of achieving a GWR title.
The **most apples thrown and caught in the mouth in one minute** is 47, by Ashrita Furman and Bipin Larkin (both USA) in New York City, USA, on 27 Feb 2020.

# Round-Up

### Most ball-hockey-stick touches on a balance board in one minute
On 17 Oct 2020, 10-year-old Kaden Galatiuk (USA) hit a ball alternately with the inside and outside of his hockey stick 284 times while atop a "rola-bola" in San Antonio, Texas. Kaden dreams of one day playing in the National Hockey League.

### Largest drawing by an individual
On 3 Nov 2020, a 568.47-m² (6,118.96-sq-ft) artwork entitled *Doodle Project* was sketched by artist FRA!, aka Francesco Caporale, working with electronics company Xiaomi Italia (both ITA). More than twice the size of a tennis court, and packed with line drawings based on imagery that users had uploaded to DoodleDream.it, it was drawn in Altomonte, Italy.

### Largest banknote sentence
Ramkumar Sarangapani (IND) wrote "GWR Day 2020" with 5,005 one-rupee notes on 18 Nov 2020 in Dubai, UAE. The work measured 8 x 6.4 m (26 ft 2 in x 20 ft 11 in).

### Largest display of origami dogs
On 19 Dec 2020, Danilo Schwarz and Meire Matayoshi (both BRA) presented 1,010 paper pooches in São Paulo, Brazil.

### Longest conga line on rollerskates
On 1 Nov 2019, Shivganga Roller Skating Club (IND) assembled a skating conga line of 308 people in Belagavi, Karnataka, India.

### Farthest distance walking barefoot on LEGO® bricks
John Wahl (USA) took a "sole-destroying" 8.35-km (5.19-mi) stroll in Rogersville, Alabama, USA, on 28 Jun 2020.

The **farthest LEGO walk by a relay team in one hour** is 4.02 km (2.49 mi). Salacnib "Sonny" Molina, Kevin Strahle, Russel Cassevah, James Preseau Jr and Kirb Lim (all USA) crunched their way to glory in McHenry, Illinois, USA, on 27 Mar 2021.

### Tallest free-standing soap bubble
Marty McBubble, aka Graeme Denton (AUS), created a 10.75-m-tall (35-ft 3-in) bubble in Adelaide, Australia, on 30 Sep 2020.

### Tallest stack of bowling balls in three minutes (team of two)
Chad McLean and Steve Kloempken (both USA) balanced 11 bowling balls on top of each other in 180 sec in Brigham City, Utah, USA, on 3 Nov 2020.

### Largest collection of Converse shoes
Since 1992, Joshua Mueller (USA) has amassed 2,630 pairs of Converse sneakers – enough to wear a different pair every day for more than seven years! The count was verified in Lakewood, Washington, USA, on 30 Jul 2019. Joshua first claimed this record in 2012 and has steadily added to his hoard since. He hopes that his son will eventually take it over.

### Tallest popsicle-stick structure
Eric Klabel (USA) constructed a 20-ft 2.4-in (6.15-m) tower out of ice-lolly sticks, as confirmed in Naperville, Illinois, USA, on 14 Nov 2020. The rocket-shaped structure includes 1,775 individual sticks and is taller than an adult giraffe.

### Heaviest tomato
Dan Sutherland (USA) grew a tomato that weighed 10 lb 12.7 oz (4.896 kg) – about the same as an average domestic cat – when assessed in Walla Walla, Washington, USA, on 15 Jul 2020. The fantastic fruit – of the Domingo variety – was authenticated by the Great Pumpkin Commonwealth.

### Largest motorized K'NEX vehicle
On 19 Sep 2020, 15-year-old William Rose (UK) unveiled his re-creation of a World War I Mark I tank made from K'NEX pieces. Powered by more than 20 motors, the 3.9-m-long (12-ft 9-in) vehicle was driven at least 5 m (16 ft) up the street outside his home in Great Dunmow, Essex, UK.

### Largest collection of Coca-Cola memorabilia
Debbie Indicott (USA) has collected 2,028 items related to the iconic fizzy drink, as verified in Lenoir, North Carolina, USA, on 8 Oct 2020. Debbie began amassing Coca-Cola memorabilia after a trip to Las Vegas in 1990. Her favourite pieces are a set of 188 *National Geographic* adverts, as these were the trickiest items to get hold of. She hopes one day to buy a vintage Coke machine.

### Most trio waterskiers towed behind a single boat
"Trios" is a discipline in which two base waterskiers raise a third participant ("climber") clear of the water to perform lifts and manoeuvres. Fourteen trios from the Big Pull Team (USA) were towed behind a boat in Rock Island, Illinois, USA, on 15 Sep 2019. The base skiers wore a harness connecting them to the boat, which meant that their hands and arms were free for the exercises.

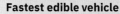

## Longest marathon hula-hooping
Jenny Doan (AUS) hula-hooped for 100 hr in Chicago, Illinois, USA, from 19 to 23 Nov 2019. Part of her motivation was to challenge herself physically and emotionally in an ultra-endurance event – one that earned her a big bruise (inset). Her feat raised funds for Mental Health America.

## Fastest 20-cone slalom dribbling a soccer ball
On 3 Jul 2020, Lucas Amar (USA) took just 17.05 sec to manoeuvre a ball between 20 cones, each spaced 50 cm (19.68 in) apart, in Rockville, Maryland, USA. Lucas demonstrated his fancy footwork in the parking lot of his elementary school.

## Most...
**Consecutive basketball free throws from a wheelchair**: On 29 Jul 2019, Kipp Watson (USA) completed 12 free throws in a row in Rio Rancho, New Mexico, USA. Kipp has been playing wheelchair basketball since the early 1970s, when he joined the Brooklyn Whirlaways.

**Hat flicks from foot to head on a unicycle in one minute**: Mushegh Khachatryan (ARM) flipped a hat from his foot to his head 16 times in 60 sec while keeping his balance on a unicycle in Yerevan, Armenia, on 28 Oct 2019.

## Farthest wakeboard ramp jump
On 22 Oct 2020, Omeir Saeed Omeir Yousef Almheiri (UAE) performed a 21-m (68-ft 10-in) ramp jump – more than the length of a bowling lane – on a wakeboard in Abu Dhabi, UAE. He beat the previous record, which had stood since 2004, by 6 m (19 ft 8 in).

**Soda-can tops torn off with the teeth in one minute**: Using his teeth, Charles Mady (CAN) bit the tops off 24 full and unopened aluminium drinks cans in 60 sec on 22 Jun 2020 in Windsor, Ontario, Canada.

**Foot taps by a team of two in 30 seconds (online)**: Father-and-son duo Silvio and Cristian Sabba (both ITA) performed 117 foot taps in Milan, Italy, on 24 Jun 2020. Their feat was equalled by Saar and Lior Kessel (both ISR) in Mishmar HaShiv'a, Israel, on 25 Jun 2020. Both records were lockdown #GWRChallenges.

**Poker chips balanced on one finger**: Rocco Mercurio (ITA) supported 200 chips on the index finger of his right hand in Villa San Giovanni, Reggio Calabria, Italy, on 10 Jul 2020. Silvio Sabba matched the feat in Milan, Italy, the following month.

## Fastest edible vehicle
On 18 Nov 2020, two 90%-edible cars were raced side-by-side at the ilani resort in Ridgefield, Washington, USA. The faster of the two was the white-fondant-covered car made from rice cakes and 139 vanilla sheet cakes with buttercream frosting. It was driven by former F1 and IndyCar racer Michael Andretti and reached 27.4 km/h (17 mph). The record, organized by Mike Elder (USA), also represents the **farthest distance by an edible vehicle** – 106.6 m (349 ft 9 in).

## Largest traditional dance costume
The Teivas Cultural, Recreational and Social Association unveiled an 8.01-m-tall (26-ft 3-in) outfit in Teivas, Portugal, on 20 Sep 2020. Draped over a metal frame was 166 m (544 ft 7 in) of fabric stitched with 4,000 red beads. It was modelled on a dress worn by traditional Morgadinha dancers.

## Largest popcorn machine
The recently opened Carnival Magic Theme Park in Phuket, Thailand, boasts a popcorn machine standing 7.89 m (25 ft 10 in) tall. It was measured on 26 Sep 2020. Also ratified on the same day at the theme park was the **tallest hanging lantern**; at 12.04 m (39 ft 6 in), it is longer than a standard telegraph pole.

# Marawa The Amazing

**P**erformer Marawa Ibrahim says that having a GWR title is like being a member of a "superpower club". But in her case, maybe that should be "hooper-power club"!

Born to a Somali father and Australian mother, Marawa spent much of her childhood travelling. A tour of Chinese circus schools convinced her to enrol at the National Institute of Circus Arts in Melbourne, Australia. She specialized in swinging trapeze, but it was the humble hula hoop — "super portable, super fun" — that Marawa knew held the key to her future.

She has gone on to teach and perform hooping around the world, from Nepal to North Korea. Along the way, she has featured on various Guinness World Records TV shows and broken a number of world records. Perhaps her most iconic feat is the ◉ **most hula hoops spun simultaneously** – 200 – which she achieved on 25 Nov 2015 in Los Angeles, California, USA. It was the fourth time she had broken the record. It's clear that Marawa is determined to fulfil her aim to "conquer the world with hoops!"

## VITAL STATISTICS
**Name:** Marawa Ibrahim
**Stage name:** Marawa The Amazing
**Birthplace:** Melbourne, Australia
**Inspirations:** Gymnast Olga Korbut, stage musical *Starlight Express*
**Qualification:** Bachelor of Circus Arts
**Current GWR titles:** 8
**Skills:** Hula hooping, high-heel roller skating, trapeze swinging
**Author:** *The Girl Guide*

Marawa's Majorettes have also achieved the most passes of a hula hoop by the feet in one minute by a team of eight – 26.

**Most hula hoops spun simultaneously on the waist (team)** Marawa has assembled her own crack troupe of super hoopers, the Majorettes. On 24 May 2017, they spun 299 hoops at the same time in London, UK. Inspired by the musical *Starlight Express* as a child, Marawa's always happy to strap on her skates. On 21 Aug 2013, she set the **fastest 100 m on high-heeled roller skates** – 26.10 sec (top).

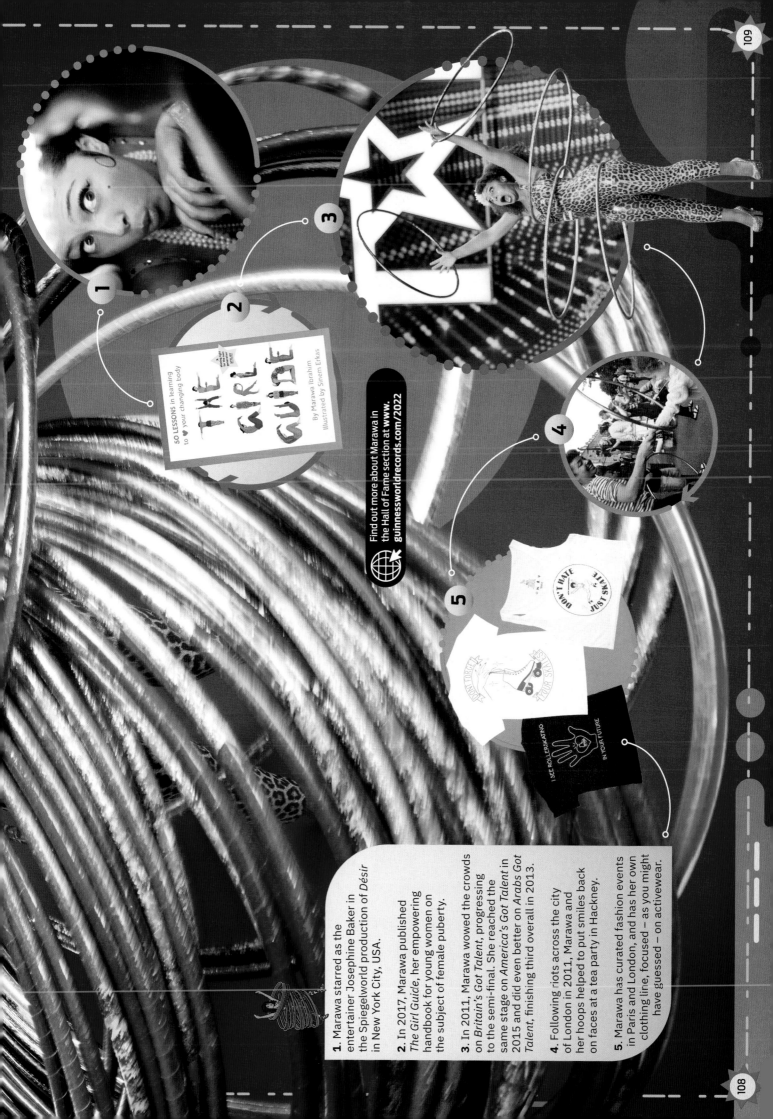

**1**

**3**

**2**

50 LESSONS in learning
to ♥ your changing body

THE GIRL GUIDE

By Marawa Ibrahim
Illustrated by Sinem Erkas

Find out more about Marawa in
the Hall of Fame section at www.
**guinnessworldrecords.com/2022**

**4**

**5**

DON'T HATE
JUST SKATE

IN YOUR FUTURE

**1.** Marawa starred as the
entertainer Josephine Baker in
the Spiegelworld production of *Désir*
in New York City, USA.

**2.** In 2017, Marawa published
*The Girl Guide*, her empowering
handbook for young women on
the subject of female puberty.

**3.** In 2011, Marawa wowed the crowds
on *Britain's Got Talent*, progressing
to the semi-final. She reached the
same stage on *America's Got Talent* in
2015 and did even better on *Arabs Got
Talent*, finishing third overall in 2013.

**4.** Following riots across the city
of London in 2011, Marawa and
her hoops helped to put smiles back
on faces at a tea party in Hackney.

**5.** Marawa has curated fashion events
in Paris and London, and has her own
clothing line, focused – as you might
have guessed – on activewear.

# Kew Gardens

**Location:** Richmond, London, UK

**Established:** 1759

**Area:** 330 acres (133.5 ha)

**Number of species:** 16,900 (as of 2019)

**Trees in arboretum:** 14,000 (2,000 species)

**Key features:** Great Pagoda, Treetop Walkway, Palm House, Temperate House

**Annual visitors:** c. 2.1 million

**R**oyal Botanic Gardens, Kew is a horticultural haven. Its unparalleled collection of flora makes it a must-see for pro and amateur botanists alike.

Founded as a modest garden in 1759 by Princess Augusta – wife of the then Prince of Wales – it grew with the merging of two royal estates in 1802 and passed from the Crown to the nation in 1840. Today, it houses the **largest collection of living plant species at a botanic garden (single site)**, with 16,900 species in cultivation in 2019; this is set to rise after an audit in 2021.

Kew boasts a variety of habitats across its 330 acres (133.5 ha). The humid Palm House (left) contains a wealth of tropical species, including the **oldest pot plant** (below right). The Princess of Wales Conservatory comprises 10 microclimate zones, each computer-controlled, while the grounds are home to 14,000-plus trees.

Over the course of its 250-year history, Kew has expanded its reach out beyond its south London origins. A satellite site at Wakehurst in West Sussex incorporates the Millennium Seed Bank, the world's **largest seed repository** with some 2.4 billion seeds from c. 40,000 species. Botanists from Kew travel the world, uncovering new superlative specimens of flora. These include the **most nocturnal orchid** (*Bulbophyllum nocturnum*) – its flowers open at night and wither come daylight – and the **largest banana tree** (*Musa ingens*), whose bunches can weigh up to 60 kg (132 lb)! Both are from the Pacific island of New Guinea, which is itself a record holder (see p.55).

From tiny seeds to giant trees, Royal Botanic Gardens, Kew is truly a window on to Earth's botanic bounty.

## Life in a glasshouse

Some of the most recognizable features at Kew are its Victorian glasshouses. Dating from 1844, the Palm House (left) contains its own mini jungle, including some species now extinct in the wild. Below is the Temperate House, built in 1899 and re-opened in 2018 after a five-year renovation; inset is a *Trachycarpus fortunei* palm from its early years. These collections offer rich possibilities for research into medicine and other fields for Kew's 350-plus scientists.

## Longest *Nepenthes* pitcher trap in cultivation

A pitcher on a carnivorous *Nepenthes truncata* at Kew measured 43 cm (1 ft 4.9 in) from base to tip of the lid on 15 Jul 2020. Like all pitcher plants, this species uses traps – actually modified leaves – to capture prey (see p.46). The slippery interior contains a pool of digestive juices.

## ▲ Tallest bloom

At 3 m (9 ft 10 in) tall, this titan arum flower (*Amorphophallus titanum*) – assessed by GWR at Kew in 2019 – was just shy of the record. That 3.1-m (10-ft 2-in) behemoth, measured on 18 Jun 2010, was grown by Louis Ricciardiello (USA) in Gilford, New Hampshire, USA. In bloom, *A. titanum* – aka the corpse flower – emits a foul stench, like rotten meat, to attract pollinating flies. Its whiff can be detected as far as 0.5 mi (0.8 km) away, also making it the ◐ **smelliest plant.**

Lid

Peristome (lip)

Tendril

Digestive zone

Spadix

Spathe

## Oldest pot plant

The Palm House is home to a prickly cycad (*Encephalartos altensteinii*) brought from South Africa to the UK in 1775. Often described as "living fossils", these tree-fern-like species are among the oldest surviving plants. Above, staff carefully re-pot Kew's long-lived cycad in 2009.

*50-m-tall (164-ft) octagonal folly*

**Largest waterlily**
The pads of the giant waterlily (*Victoria amazonica*) can reach 3 m (9 ft 10 in) wide, and are held in place by an underwater stalk some 7–8 m (23–26 ft) long. As illustrated by a Kew worker here, the undersurface of its leaves are supported by sturdy, rib-like crossridges to keep the pads flat and stop them collapsing. Their pattern is said to have inspired the network of metal girders around which the Crystal Palace was built for London's Great Exhibition in 1851.

*Crossridges*

*Constructed from 400 tonnes (441 tons) of weathered steel*

**A bird's-eye view**
Royal Botanic Gardens, Kew offers a spectacular mix of traditional and modern architecture. Built in 2008, the 18-m-tall (59-ft) Treetop Walkway allows visitors to stroll among the upper canopy and get up close with the flora and fauna amid the branches. Nearby, the 10-storey Great Pagoda was completed in 1762 as a gift to Kew's founder, Princess Augusta. Visitors with the stamina to take on its 253 steps are rewarded with stunning views across London.

*Can support a small child!*

**The "Old Lions"**
Pictured is a maidenhair tree (*Ginkgo biloba*), native to China, and one of the first of its species to be planted in the UK. It's one of Kew's "Old Lions" — trees that were moved here in 1762 from the Duke of Argyll's Twickenham estate, and the oldest trees on the site that can be accurately dated. But this specimen is still a youngster, relatively speaking: maidenhairs can live for some 3,500 years!

When it opened in 1852, Kew's Waterlily House was the world's widest single-span glasshouse.

**Smallest waterlily**
*Nymphaea thermarum*, aka the thermal lily, has floating leaves (pads) just 10–20 mm (0.3–0.7 in) across. It is extinct in the wild, but in 2009 horticulturists at Kew devised a method of propagating them. Today, the site has more than 50 specimens, some of which are in the Waterlily House.

*Penny-sized flowers*

**100%**

# Adventures

**Youngest person to row any ocean**
On 14 Jun 2020, Maxim Ivanov (BGR, b. 25 Aug 2003) set out to row the Atlantic aged 16 years 294 days. Teaming up with his father Stefan, an entrepreneur, he left Portimão in Portugal on an east-to-west heading on board *Neverest*. They rowed 4,444 nautical mi (8,230 km; 5,114 mi) to Barbados, arriving on 6 Oct 2020 after 114 days 9 hr 36 min at sea. This also makes Maxim the **youngest person to row any ocean in a pair**.

The Ivanovs had originally aimed to land in Brazil, but had to change plans on account of COVID-19 travel restrictions. It was the first recorded Atlantic crossing during hurricane season, and the pair spent days with their sea anchor deployed in the face of tropical storms and Hurricane Teddy.

Maxim and his father built their fibreglass boat *Neverest* in their own garage.

Growth happens outside your comfort zone

## CONTENTS

# Ultracycling

## Fastest time to cycle the length of Japan

Akihiro Takaoka (JPN) took just 6 days 13 hr 28 min to cycle his homeland, south to north, from Cape Sata to Cape Sōya. The journey lasted from 5 to 11 Aug 2020 and saw him break the existing record by more than 30 hours. Takaoka gave up his career as an investment banker to pursue his love of cycling and now owns a bike shop in Tokyo's Meguro district.

## Greatest distance in one year (WUCA)

Between 15 May 2016 and 14 May 2017, Amanda Coker (USA) rode 139,326.34 km (86,573.3 mi) – more than four times the equatorial circumference of Earth.

In the course of that trip, Coker broke two additional records. From 1 to 30 Apr 2017, she achieved WUCA's outright **greatest distance in one month** – 12,894.87 km (8,012.5 mi). And between 15 May 2016 and 11 Jul 2017, she registered the **fastest time to cycle 100,000 miles** – 423 days; her feat smashed – by 77 days – Tommy Godwin's 1939–40 record of riding this distance in exactly 500 days.

## Fastest circumnavigation by tandem bicycle

Rachael Marsden and Catherine Dixon (both UK) rounded the globe in 263 days 8 hr 7 min from 29 Jun 2019 to 18 Mar 2020. The weather and environmental conditions provided their biggest challenge: they faced a heatwave across Europe and monsoons in India and south-east Asia. Back in Europe, they had to race to reach home before the COVID-19 outbreak began closing national borders.

## Greatest distance in one week (unpaced)

From 28 Sep to 4 Oct 2020, Jack Thompson (AUS) rode 3,505 km (2,177 mi) in Seville, Spain. Thompson is a professional cyclist and achieving this GWR title had long been one of his goals. In order to remain safe in light of the coronavirus pandemic, he restricted his ride to within the borders of his country of residence.

## Fastest time to cycle across Ireland (male)

On 3–4 Jul 2020, Joe Barr (IRL) traversed Ireland north to south, from Malin Head to Mizen Head, in 21 hr 28 min, as ratified by WUCA. He clocked an average speed of 17.4 km/h (10.8 mph) over the 613-km (381-mi) ride. The 61-year-old cyclist achieved his feat as part of a north-south-north round trip, which he completed in 44 hr 15 min.

## Fastest time to cycle from Land's End to John o' Groats by handcycle

Mel Nicholls (UK) covered the length of the UK in 6 days 22 hr 17 min by handcycle, from 13 to 20 Jun 2019. This full-time athlete and British Paralympian has suffered multiple strokes, the latest in 2008. She competes as an endurance handcyclist and marathon wheelchair racer on the world circuit, and appeared at the London 2012 and Rio 2016 Paralympics.

## Fastest time to cycle the Manali–Leh Highway

Bharat Pannu (IND) took 35 hr 32 min 22 sec to traverse this high mountain road in northern India, finishing in Manali, Himachal Pradesh, on 11 Oct 2020. Overall, he covered a distance of 472 km (293 mi).

## Fastest time to cycle from Kashmir to Kanyakumari

In 8 days 7 hr 38 min, Om Hitendra Mahajan (IND) rode from Kashmir in the north of the Indian subcontinent to Kanyakumari in the south, which he reached on 21 Nov 2020.

## Greatest distance in six hours by a team of two on an outdoor track (WUCA)

Peter Horton and Mathew Hancox (both UK) rode 241.22 km (149.89 mi) in six hours at Quibell Park Stadium in Scunthorpe, UK, on 10 Oct 2020. Remarkably, Horton had been in a major accident just seven months earlier, resulting in a punctured lung and a broken pelvis, collarbone and hand.

## Farthest 24-hour road cycle (WUCA)

Slovenian long-distance cycling veteran Stanislav Verstovšek rode a distance of 914.020 km (567.946 mi) on 2–3 Jul 2020. He recorded an average speed of 38.08 km/h (23.66 mph) across the route in Prekmurje, Slovenia. During training, Verstovšek cycled more than 22,000 km (13,670 mi) – approximately double the full perimeter of Italy. (See table opposite for more.)

## Fastest circumnavigation by bicycle

Mark Beaumont (UK) cycled around the world in 78 days 14 hr 40 min, starting and finishing in Paris, France. He passed through 16 countries on his epic ride, which lasted from 2 Jul to 18 Sep 2017. Fellow Brit Jenny Graham holds the **female** record, circling the globe unsupported in 124 days 11 hr from 16 Jun to 18 Oct 2018. Her start and end point was Berlin, Germany.

GWR is proud to partner with the World Ultracycling Association (WUCA) to bring you many of the stellar endurance athletes on these pages. Founded in 1980, WUCA is the global authority on long-distance cycling. It maintains the largest database of cycling feats across a range of categories – managed by Larry Oslund – and certifies records for its members.

*WUCA monitors speed and distance records for three main ultracycling disciplines: indoor track, outdoor track and road. These are then subcategorized by type of bike, solo/team cycles, sex and age. Here, we showcase the overall speed-based individual record holders for the two non-indoor disciplines, which are correct as of 27 Apr 2021.*

### Outdoor track (female)

| Fastest... | Time | Name | Date |
|---|---|---|---|
| 100 km | 02:49.46 | Karen Taylor (UK) | 8 Aug 2018 |
| 200 km | 06:22.33 | Anna Mei (ITA, right) | 9 Oct 2020 |
| 300 km | 09:43.25 | Anna Mei (ITA) | 8 Oct 2020 |
| 500 km | 17:02.58 | Anna Mei (ITA) | 8 Oct 2020 |
| 100 mi | 03:10.27 | Barbara Buatois (FRA) | 13 Jul 2014 |
| 200 mi | 09:44.39 | Seana Hogan (USA) | 4 May 2012 |
| 300 mi | 16:25.21 | Anna Mei (ITA) | 8 Oct 2020 |

WORLD ULTRACYCLING ASSOCIATION
WUCA
ULTRACYCLING.COM

**Fastest outdoor track 500 km (female)**
On 8 Oct 2020, Anna Mei (ITA) cycled 500 km (310 mi) in 17 hr 2 min 58 sec at the velodrome in Bassano del Grappa, Vicenza, Italy. Mei achieved the record while trying for the **fastest 1,000 km**, but was forced to cut short the attempt owing to strain. Her ride also served as a fundraiser for the charity DEBRA, which supports children with rare skin disorders.

**Fastest road 500 km (female)**
Jen Orr (USA) cycled 500 km in 17 hr 33 min 7 sec on 7 Nov 2020 at Borrego Springs, California, USA. The experienced ultra-endurance cyclist faced winds of up to 80 km/h (50 mph) and outbreaks of rain, but fought through the conditions to achieve a string of records over a 24-hr period (see right).

### Road (female)

| Fastest... | Time | Name | Date |
|---|---|---|---|
| 100 km | 03:15.21 | Beatriz Baeza (ESP) | 2 Jun 2018 |
| 200 km | 06:35.40 | Jen Orr (USA, left) | 7 Nov 2020 |
| 300 km | 10:26.59 | Jen Orr (USA) | 7 Nov 2020 |
| 500 km | 17:33.07 | Jen Orr (USA) | 7 Nov 2020 |
| 100 mi | 05:15.06 | Pamela Atwood (USA) | 23 May 2006 |
| 200 mi | 11:14.44 | Jen Orr (USA) | 7 Nov 2020 |
| 300 mi | 16:56.02 | Jen Orr (USA) | 7 Nov 2020 |

### Road (male)

| Fastest... | Time | Name | Date |
|---|---|---|---|
| 100 km | 02:21.42 | Stanislav Verstovšek (SVN, left) | 2 Oct 2020 |
| 200 km | 04:44.09 | Stanislav Verstovšek (SVN) | 2 Oct 2020 |
| 300 km | 07:10.50 | Stanislav Verstovšek (SVN) | 2 Oct 2020 |
| 500 km | 12:18.42 | Stanislav Verstovšek (SVN) | 2 Oct 2020 |
| 1,000 km | 1:04:50.14 | Marko Baloh (SVN) | 25 Jul 2020 |
| 100 mi | 03:48.06 | Stanislav Verstovšek (SVN) | 2 Oct 2020 |
| 200 mi | 07:43.50 | Stanislav Verstovšek (SVN) | 2 Oct 2020 |
| 300 mi | 11:51.17 | Stanislav Verstovšek (SVN) | 2 Oct 2020 |
| 500 mi | 22:23.23 | Marko Baloh (SVN) | 25 Jul 2020 |

**Greatest distance in 24 hours on an outdoor track**
Ralph Diseviscourt (LUX) covered 915.395 km (568.8 mi) in Vianden, Luxembourg, on 11–12 Jul 2020. He also set a new **six-hour** total distance record – 251.343 km (156.2 mi) – as well as eight WUCA speed records on the day (see left). Like many of the riders on these pages, Diseviscourt – pictured above with his support crew – sought out new challenges during a year in which races were cancelled or abandoned because of the pandemic.

### Outdoor track (male)

| Fastest... | Time | Name | Date |
|---|---|---|---|
| 100 km | 02:19.13 | Ralph Diseviscourt (LUX, right) | 11 Jul 2020 |
| 200 km | 04:44.30 | Ralph Diseviscourt (LUX) | 11 Jul 2020 |
| 300 km | 07:12.42 | Ralph Diseviscourt (LUX) | 11 Jul 2020 |
| 500 km | 12:27.48 | Ralph Diseviscourt (LUX) | 12 Jul 2020 |
| 1,000 km | 1:07:23.01 | Francisco Vacas Rodriguez (ESP) | 6 Jun 2010 |
| 100 mi | 03:47.02 | Ralph Diseviscourt (LUX) | 11 Jul 2020 |
| 200 mi | 07:46.11 | Ralph Diseviscourt (LUX) | 11 Jul 2020 |
| 300 mi | 11:59.45 | Ralph Diseviscourt (LUX) | 12 Jul 2020 |
| 500 mi | 21:01.46 | Ralph Diseviscourt (LUX) | 12 Jul 2020 |

# At the Poles: The Arctic

The Polar Expeditions Classification Scheme (PECS) is a grading and labelling system for extended, unmotorized journeys in and around Earth's extreme points. It was established in 2020 and is managed by a committee of polar expedition specialists. Modes of travel, start and end points, routes, and forms of aid are defined under the initiative, which gives expeditioners guidance on how to classify, promote and immortalize their journeys. Over the next four pages, we present a series of significant polar firsts, as recognized by the experts at PECS.

### First solo ski expedition to the North Pole

Dr Jean-Louis Étienne (FRA) reached the North Pole on 14 May 1986, having skied alone and without dogs for 63 days. Dragging a sled behind him, he averaged 20 km (12.4 mi) – or 8 hr of skiing – per day. In 1989, Dr Étienne embarked on a 6,048-km (3,758-mi), seven-month-long overland crossing of Antarctica with Will Steger (see p.118).

### First surface crossing of the Arctic Ocean

The British Trans-Arctic Expedition – Wally Herbert (leader), Allan Gill, Major Ken Hedges and Dr Roy Koerner (pictured right to left flanking their base radio operator, Freddie Church, centre) – arrived at the Norwegian archipelago of Svalbard on 29 May 1969, after a 3,200-km (1,988-mi) journey from Alaska, USA, via the North Pole. Their epic 463-day trek included five months' overwintering on a drifting ice floe.

**1**

### First unsupported expedition to the North Pole

**5**

The Steger International Polar Expedition arrived at the North Pole on 1 May 1986, after a 56-day dogsled journey without resupplies that covered 790 km (490 mi). The eight-person team comprised Will Steger, Paul Schurke, Geoff Carroll, Ann Bancroft (all USA), Bob McKerrow (NZ), Richard Weber, Bob Mantell and Brent Boddy (all CAN). Bancroft was also the **first woman to reach the North Pole by surface travel**.

### First solo expedition to the North Pole

**2**

Naomi Uemura (JPN) made a 780-km (484-mi) journey across the Arctic sea-ice in a solo dogsled expedition that arrived at the North Pole on 29 Apr 1978. He had set out on 5 Mar from Cape Edward on Ellesmere Island, Canada. During his journey, he had to contend with a polar bear invading his camp and being stranded with his dogs on a section of ice floe.

### First ski crossing of the Arctic Ocean (vessel access and exit)

**18**

From 11 Sep to 7 Dec 2019, Børge Ousland (NOR) and Mike Horn (ZAF) skied 1,557 km (967 mi) across the Arctic ice cap. They disembarked from the sailboat *Pangaea* at 85.56°N and set off on a perilous 87-day journey, enduring -40°C (-40°F) temperatures, storms, 24-hr darkness and frostbite before they were picked up by the ex-polar research vessel *Lance* at 82.38°N.

Ousland and Horn used packrafts to negotiate their way across the "leads" – watery fissures in the polar ice.

Norway

Svalbard (NOR)

**Longyearbyen**

**Vesle Tavloya**

Lance

Kalaallit Nunaat
(Greenland)

Ward Hunt Island ④ ⑥ ⑦ ⑨ ⑩ ⑪ ⑫ ⑬ ⑯
Cape Edward ②
Drep Camp ⑤
Cape Discovery ⑭

Ellesmere Island (CAN)

North Pole

Canada

**Cape Arkticheskiy**
Severnaya Zemlya (RUS)

Russia

🔴 **Dogsled, foot**

⚪ **Ski haul**

🚢 **Vessel access/exit**

**Henrietta Island**
Sakha/Yakutia (RUS)

Pangaea

**Point Barrow**
Alaska (USA)

USA

## The Arctic Ocean: Remarkable unmotorized firsts on the frozen ocean

| | Record | Team | Km | Days | Mode |
|---|---|---|---|---|---|
| 1 | **First surface crossing of the Arctic Ocean (1968–69)** | The British Trans-Arctic Expedition (led by Wally Herbert, UK) | 3,200 | 463 | |
| 2 | **First solo expedition to the North Pole (1978)** | Naomi Uemura (JPN) | 780 | 55 | |
| 3 | **First ski expedition to the North Pole (1979)** | Dmitry Shparo, Vladimir Ledenev, Anatoly Melnikov, Yuri Khmelevski, Vasily Shishkarev, Vladimir Rakhmanov, Vladimir Davydov (all RUS) | 1,400 | 76 | |
| 4 | **First solo ski expedition to the North Pole (1986)** | Jean-Louis Étienne (FRA) | 780 | 63 | |
| 5 | **First unsupported expedition to the North Pole (1986)** | Steger International Polar Expedition (led by Will Steger, USA) | 790 | 56 | |
| 6 | **First ski crossing of the Arctic Ocean (1988)** | Soviet–Canadian Polar Bridge Expedition (led by Dmitry Shparo, RUS) | 1,725 | 90 | |
| 7 | **First unsupported ski expedition to the North Pole (1990)\*** | Børge Ousland, Erling Kagge (both NOR) | 780 | 58 | |
| 8 | **First solo unsupported North Pole ski expedition (1994)** | Børge Ousland (NOR) | 980 | 52 | |
| 9 | **First return ski expedition to the North Pole (1995)** | Richard Weber (CAN), Mikhail Malakhov (RUS) | 1,560 | 108 | |
| 10 | **First unsupported ski crossing of the Arctic Ocean (2000)** | Rune Gjeldnes, Torry Larsen (both NOR) | 1,700 | 109 | |
| 11 | **First solo crossing of the Arctic Ocean (2001)** | Børge Ousland (NOR) | 1,730 | 52 | |
| 12 | **First woman to ski unsupported to the North Pole (2002)** | Tina Sjögren (CZE/SWE/USA), with Tom Sjögren | 780 | 65 | |
| 13 | **First solo unsupported ski expedition to the North Pole from Canada (2003)** | Pen Hadow (UK) | 780 | 63 | |
| 14 | **First ski expedition to the North Pole to leave in winter (2006)** | Børge Ousland (NOR), Mike Horn (ZAF) | 950 | 61 | |
| 15 | **First crossing between Russia and Greenland (2007)** | Alain Hubert, Dixie Dansercoer (both BEL) | 1,650 | 106 | |
| 16 | **First expedition to the North Pole to arrive in winter (2007–08)** | Matvey Shparo, Boris Smolin (both RUS) | 780 | 84 | |
| 17 | **First unsupported ski expedition from the North Pole to Svalbard (2012)** | Timo Palo (EST), Audun Tholfsen (NOR) | 1,040 | 54 | |
| 18 | **First ski crossing of the Arctic Ocean (vessel access and exit) (2019)** | Børge Ousland (NOR), Mike Horn (ZAF) | 1,557 | 87 | |

*\*A third member was evacuated. PECS now classifies evacuation as a form of support but still acknowledges this expedition as a legacy unsupported record.*

⑤

# At the Poles: Antarctica

⑧ ⑬ ⑦

**First women to cross
the Antarctic landmass**
In Nov 2000, Liv Arnesen (NOR) and Ann Bancroft (USA) set off on a crossing of Antarctica from the "Blue One" runway in Queen Maud Land. They arrived at the South Pole on 16 Jan 2001 but were hampered by unusually calm winds, which meant they could not use their kite sails. With rations running low, their 94-day odyssey came to an end at the edge of the Ross Ice Shelf. The duo had pulled their 113-kg (250-lb) sleds across 2,747 km (1,707 mi) of icy terrain.
Six years earlier, Arnesen had become the **first woman to reach the South Pole on a solo expedition**, completing her 50-day journey from Hercules Inlet on Christmas Eve 1994.

**First solo crossing
of Antarctica**
On 18 Jan 1997, Børge Ousland (NOR) completed a 2,845-km (1,767-mi) kite-ski trek from Berkner Island in the Weddell Sea to McMurdo Sound. Ousland crossed both of the Ronne and Ross ice shelves, spending 64 days negotiating his 185-kg (408-lb) sled over glaciers and through sastrugi (ridges of hard snow). See pp.116–17 for Ousland's record-breaking exploits in the Arctic.

**First unmotorized crossing of Antarctica**
The 1990 International Trans-Antarctica Expedition travelled 6,048 km (3,758 mi) by dog sled from Seal Nunataks on the Larsen Ice Shelf to Mirny Station, via the South Pole. The 220-day trek (26 Jul 1989 to 3 Mar 1990) was intended to highlight the issue of climate change. The team was made up of Will Steger (USA), Jean-Louis Étienne (FRA), Geoff Somers (UK), Viktor Boyarsky (RUS), Qin Dahe (CHN) and Keizo Funatsu (JPN).

③

①

**First expedition to
reach the South Pole**
On 14 Dec 1911, Roald Amundsen (leader), Oscar Wisting (pictured), Helmer Hanssen, Olav Bjaaland and Sverre Hassel (all NOR) arrived at the South Pole following a 53-day march with dog sleds from the Bay of Whales. The party had pioneered a route up the previously unknown Axel Heiberg Glacier on to the Antarctic Plateau. They reached the Pole 34 days before the ill-fated expedition led by the UK's Robert Falcon Scott, in which all five men perished on their return journey.

**First East Antarctica ski expedition**
On 23 Nov 1999, Laurence de la Ferrière (FRA, b. MAR) departed the South Pole, on skis, for Dumont d'Urville on the coast, arriving on 6 Feb 2000. Along the route, she took core samples as part of a research project. This was not De la Ferrière's first time in Antarctica; three years earlier, she had made a 57-day solo trek from the Hercules Inlet to the Pole. She began her career as a mountaineer, and in 1992 climbed Everest without oxygen.

⑪

## Map Legend

- ◯ Station base
- ▢ Decommissioned station base
- Station base names in **bold**
- ● Coastal start/end
- ◉ Inner coastal start/end
- ◉ Inland start/end
- ▢ Ice shelf

- ● Dogs/ponies
- ● Ski
- ● Snowkite

## Map Labels

Seal Nunataks
Blue One (UK)
Novo (RUS)
Troll (NOR)
Roi Baudouin (BEL)
Filchner Ice Shelf
Berkner Island
Ronne Ice Shelf
Patriot Hills (USA)
Hercules Inlet
Pole of Inaccessibility (USSR)
Kunlun Station (CHN) Dome Argus
South Pole (USA)
Mirny (RUS)
Vostok (RUS)
Concordia (FRA/ITA) Dome C
Ross Ice Shelf
Framheim (NOR)
McMurdo (USA)
Scott Base (NZ)
Ross Island
Mario Zucchelli Station (ITA)
Dumont d'Urville Station (FRA)

## Antarctica: Remarkable unmotorized firsts on the frozen continent

| | Record | Team | Km | Days | Mode |
|---|---|---|---|---|---|
| 1 | First expedition to reach the South Pole (1911–12) | Norwegian South Pole Expedition (led by Roald Amundsen) | 2,700 | 53 | |
| 2 | First ski expedition to the South Pole (1985–86) | Robert Swan, Roger Mear (both UK), Gareth Wood (CAN) | 1,405 | 69 | |
| 3 | First unmotorized crossing of Antarctica (1989–90) | International Trans-Antarctica Expedition (led by Will Steger (USA) and Jean-Louis Étienne (FRA)) | 6,048 | 220 | |
| 4 | First snowkite crossing of the Antarctic landmass (1989–90) | Reinhold Messner (ITA), Arved Fuchs (DEU) | 2,390 | 92 | |
| 5 | First crossing of the classic route from Berkner Island to Ross Island (1990–91) | Sjur Mørdre, Simen Mørdre (both NOR) | 2,845 | 91 | |
| 6 | First solo expedition to the South Pole (1992–93) | Erling Kagge (NOR) | 1,375 | 50 | |
| 7 | First solo expedition to the South Pole (female) (1994) | Liv Arnesen (NOR) | 1,200 | 50 | |
| 8 | First solo crossing of Antarctica (1996–97) | Børge Ousland (NOR) | 2,845 | 64 | |
| 9 | First snowkite crossing of East and West Antarctica (1997–98) | Alain Hubert, Dixie Dansercoer (both BEL) | 3,924 | 99 | |
| 10 | First ascent (new route) of the Shackleton Glacier to the South Pole (1998–99) | Eric Philips, Jon Muir (both AUS), Peter Hillary (NZ) | 1,450 | 84 | |
| 11 | First East Antarctica ski expedition (1999–2000) | Laurence de la Ferrière (FRA, b. MAR) | 2,776 | 75 | |
| 12 | First unsupported snowkite crossing of East and West Antarctica (2000–01) | Rolf Bae, Eric Sønneland (both NOR) | 3,800 | 107 | |
| 13 | First women to cross the Antarctic landmass (2000–01) | Liv Arnesen (NOR), Ann Bancroft (USA) | 2,747 | 94 | |
| 14 | First solo crossing of East Antarctica (male) (2005–06) | Rune Gjeldnes (NOR) | 4,804 | 90 | |
| 15 | First unsupported expedition to the South Pole from Ross Island (2008–09) | Henry Worsley, Will Gow, Henry Adams (all UK) | 1,480 | 66 | |
| 16 | First unguided snowkite crossing from Novo to Hercules Inlet (2011–12) | Alberto Iñurrategi, Mikel Zabalza, Juan Vallejo (all ESP) | 3,270 | 55 | |
| 17 | First unsupported return South Pole expedition (2011–12) | Aleksander Gamme (NOR), James Castrission, Justin Jones (both AUS) | 2,260 | 87 | |
| 18 | First solo ski crossing of Antarctica (female) (2011–12) | Felicity Aston (UK) | 1,744 | 59 | |
| 19 | First full return South Pole ski expedition (2013–14) | Tarka L'Herpiniere, Ben Saunders (both UK) | 1,795 | 105 | |
| 20 | First solo snowkite expedition to the South Pole via the Pole of Inaccessibility (2014–15) | Frédéric Dion (CAN) | 4,171 | 55 | |
| 21 | First unmotorized journey to reach Dome Argus (2020–21) | Geoff Wilson (AUS, b. KEN) See also pp.128–29 | 5,179 | 58 | |

# Aquatic Odysseys

## Fastest time to sail around the British Isles (sub-40-ft vessel)

At 22:12 GMT on 9 Jul 2020, Ian Lipinski (FRA) crossed the virtual finish line at Cape Lizard in Cornwall, having sailed singlehanded around Great Britain and Ireland in 7 days 17 hr 50 min 47 sec. Lipinski had set off on board the offshore Class-40 yacht *Crédit Mutuel* on 2 Jul 2020. He broke the absolute around-Britain record set in 2018 by Phil Sharp and his crew by more than 10 hr, travelling at an average speed of 9.54 knots (17.66 km/h; 10.97 mph).

## Fastest open-water 10-km swim (one arm)

On 19 Dec 2019, Iranian swimmer Elham Sadat Asghari swam for 10 km (6.2 mi) using a single arm in 4 hr 58 min 32 sec in Chabahar Bay, Iran.

Asghari has also completed the **farthest swim while wearing handcuffs** (inset) – 5.488 km (3.41 mi) – in Iran's capital, Tehran, on 6 Feb 2019. This bettered her own record by more than 1 km (0.6 mi).

## First team to cross any ocean on board a kayak

Between 21 Oct 2015 and 30 Jan 2016, Levente Kovácsik and Norbert Ádám Szabó (both HUN) paddled the Atlantic east to west on board *Kele*. They set out from Huelva in Spain and landed on the Caribbean island of Antigua.

## STAND UP AND BE COUNTED: SHILPIKA GAUTAM

Between 2 Oct 2016 and 11 Jan 2017, adventurer-activist Shilpika Gautam (UK) travelled 2,641.3 km (1,641.2 mi) along the Ganges river in India, from source to sea. This represents the longest journey on a stand-up paddleboard (SUP).

### What made you decide to travel the Ganges on an SUP?

I wanted to find out why more people around the world don't have access to clean water. At the same time, I'd started to learn how to stand-up paddleboard on the canals of London. It seemed super-crazy to go from paddling 1 km to almost 3,000 km – especially as I'm not the best swimmer in the world – but that's kind of how my brain works!

### How did you prepare?

I practised for "Ganges SUP" by paddling the River Shannon in Ireland from source to sea.

## Fastest sailing circumnavigation

Francis Joyon (FRA) and a crew of five sailed around the world non-stop in 40 days 23 hr 30 min 30 sec on board the 120-ft trimaran *IDEC*. Their journey, from 16 Dec 2016 to 26 Jan 2017, covered 21,600 nautical mi (40,003 km; 24,856 mi) at an average speed of 21.96 knots (40.6 km/h; 25.2 mph). The voyage started and finished between the Le Créac'h Lighthouse off Brittany, France, and Lizard Point in Cornwall, UK, and was ratified by the World Sailing Speed Record Council.

## Fastest solo sailing circumnavigation (female)

Ellen MacArthur (UK) sailed around the world in 71 days 14 hr 18 min 33 sec from 28 Nov 2004 to 7 Feb 2005 in the trimaran *B&Q*. For three years, this was the overall **solo** record – which now stands at 42 days 16 hr 40 min 15 sec, by François Gabart (FRA), who circled the planet in his trimaran *MACIF* from 4 Nov to 17 Dec 2017.

## Greatest aggregate distance rowed on any ocean in a single expedition

Between 14 Jul 2018 and 29 Jun 2020, Karlis Bardelis (LVA) rowed solo across the Pacific from Callao in Peru to Malaysia's Pontian District – a journey of 11,393 nautical mi (21,010 km; 13,111 mi). His voyage took him 715 days 16 hr 5 min on board *Linda*. He rowed for 12–13 hr a day and stopped off at seven islands.

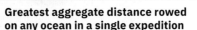

## Greatest distance by canoe/kayak on the ocean in 24 hours

On 13 Nov 2020, Quinton Rutherford (ZAF) paddled 122.7 nautical mi (227.2 km; 141.2 mi) off the coast of KwaZulu-Natal in South Africa. He set the record in a 6-m-long (19-ft) paddle-ski.

## Farthest swim with a monofin

To mark her 30th birthday on 17 Apr 2021, Estonian eco-athlete Merle Liivand completed a 30-km (18.6-mi) "mermaid swim" off Miami Beach, Florida, USA. As per the rules of the World Open Water Swimming Association, this discipline precludes use of the arms so relies entirely on movement of the core and lower body, propelled by a "tail". Liivand is a passionate advocate for cleaning up the oceans and with this swim particularly wanted to spotlight the "plastic pandemic" that has gone hand in hand with COVID-19, with a surge in single-use items such as masks.

## Youngest team to row around Great Britain

The "Exe Endurow" team (UK) had an average age of 22 years 206 days at the start of their row from and to Tower Bridge in London on 5 Jul 2020. Oliver Dawe-Lane (b. 17 Dec 1997), Arthur Chatto (b. 5 Feb 1999), Charles Bromhead (b. 1 Jan 1997) and Harry Lidgley (b. 21 Sep 1997) rowed 1,483 nautical mi (2,747 km; 1,707 mi) in 42 days, finishing on 16 Aug.

## What issues does the Ganges face?

We know that the Ganges has issues around pollution. In urban settings, you can smell it before you see it. But there are also barrages and artificial bridges being constructed across the river – and sand theft. The illegal mining of sand causes more floods every year.

## Were there any surprises on your journey?

I didn't expect to see as many dolphins as I did. I counted 867 doing an eco-conscious survey. It was a beacon of hope. I also loved the beautiful misty mornings, and watching the cows and buffalo swim.

## What did the journey teach you?

For women adventurers in particular: the world is kinder than we are told. Be smart, know your risk assessment, but go out there and challenge yourself.

## Longest open-saltwater SCUBA dive

On 5–11 Nov 2020, diving instructor Saddam Killany (EGY) spent 145 hr 25 min 25 sec on the floor of the Red Sea off Dahab, Egypt. He passed the six days exercising, praying and even painting, and strapped himself to a scaffold in order to sleep.

The **female** record is held by Cristi Quill (USA), who spent 51 hr 25 min submerged at La Jolla Shores in San Diego, California, USA, on 9–11 Jul 2015. She took on the record for the "Put Cancer Under Pressure" campaign.

## Longest distance swam underwater on one breath (open water, fins, male)

On 26 Nov 2020, Stig Severinsen (DNK) swam 202 m (662 ft 8 in) underwater on a single breath in La Paz, Baja California Sur, Mexico. Severinsen is a freediver and multiple world record holder whose lungs have a capacity of 14 litres (3.6 gal) – more than double the human average.

## Most northerly/southerly Ice Swims

Monitored by the International Ice Swimming Association, an Ice Swim is a minimum 1-km (0.6-mi) swim conducted in water that is under 5°C (41°F).
• **Male (N)**: 90°N at the geographic North Pole, by Lewis Pugh (UK) on 15 Jul 2007
• **Female (N)**: 78.3°N in Spitsbergen, Svalbard, Norway, by Kinga Korin (POL) on 27 Jun 2017
• **Male (S)**: 70.76°S in Long Lake, Queen Maud Land, Antarctica, by Ram Barkai (ZAF) on 7 Feb 2008
• **Female (S)**: 66.6°S in Hanusse Bay, off Graham Land, Antarctica, by Catherine Pendleton (UK) on 22 Feb 2020.

## Longest distance swam under ice on one breath (no fins, no diving suit, female)

Freediver Amber Fillary (ZAF) swam 70 m (229 ft) in the frozen-over Lake Oppsjø in Norway on 29 Feb 2020. She had been thwarted on a previous attempt in 2019 when she became entangled in ropes, but there were no problems this time. "I don't even feel the cold," Fillary said afterwards. "It just feels really good."

## Fastest solo monohull sailing circumnavigation (female)

Clarisse Crémer (FRA) completed the Vendée Globe round-the-world race in 87 days 2 hr 24 min 25 sec, arriving at Les Sables d'Olonne in France on 3 Feb 2021. She sailed in the *IMOCA 60 Banque Populaire X*. A relative newcomer to the sport, Crémer became only the seventh woman to rank as a Vendée Globe finisher since it began in 1989.

## Fastest one-way relay swim of the North Channel

On 2 Aug 2020, the "OA Giants" swam 18.6 nautical mi (34.4 km; 21.5 mi) between Northern Ireland and Scotland, UK, in 9 hr 2 min 41 sec. Keith Garry, Dominic Mudge, Bill Donnelly, Chris Judge, Colin Lindsay and John McElroy (all IRL) were piloted by Pádraig Mallon. Their feat was verified by the Irish Long Distance Swimming Association.

## Aleksander Doba (1946–2021)

GWR was saddened to hear of the passing of adventurer Aleksander Doba (POL, b. 9 Sep 1946) on 22 Feb 2021. Doba pushed the boundaries of open-water kayaking, completing the **most trans-oceanic kayak expeditions**: three, in 2011, 2014 and 2017. At the time of his third departure, he was the **oldest person to make a solo human-powered ocean crossing** (70 years 249 days), and he remains the **oldest person to kayak across an ocean**.

An explorer to the end, 74-year-old Doba died after summitting Mount Kilimanjaro – Africa's highest mountain.

# 8,000ers

### First married couple to climb the higher 8,000ers without bottled oxygen

Husband-and-wife team Romano Benet and Nives Meroi (both ITA) have ascended the world's five highest mountains without the use of supplementary oxygen. They scaled Lhotse on 16 May 2004, K2 on 26 Jul 2006, Everest on 17 May 2007, Kangchenjunga on 17 May 2014 and Makalu on 12 May 2016.

### First woman to climb the higher 8,000ers without bottled oxygen

Gerlinde Kaltenbrunner (AUT, right) reached the highest points of the top five mountains "alpine style" between 14 May 2001 and 24 May 2011.

The **youngest woman** to complete this challenge – and the **first** in an absolute sense – was Basque Spanish climber Edurne Pasaban (b. 1 Aug 1973, inset). She made her ascents between 23 May 2001 and 18 May 2009, but resorted to using bottled oxygen on Everest.

The "8,000ers" are the 14 mountains on Earth over 8,000 m (26,246 ft) high. There is a significant jump in height between the fifth and sixth peaks, and the five "higher 8,000ers", as they're dubbed, are the focus for records on these pages. Also, historical records regarding the climbing of some of the lower 8,000ers are currently under renewed scrutiny; the records listed here are considered undisputed, unless stated otherwise.

Nims was part of the Nepalese team that made the first ever ascent of the treacherous K2 in winter (see opposite).

### Fastest time to climb the higher 8,000ers with bottled oxygen

It took Nirmal "Nims" Purja Pun Magar (NPL) just 70 days to climb the higher 8,000ers in 2019. He topped Kangchenjunga on 15 May, Everest and Lhotse on 22 May, Makalu on 24 May and K2 on 24 Jul.

A former Gurkha soldier, Nims has also achieved the **fastest triple-header of the higher 8,000ers**. On 22 May 2019, he crossed from the top of Everest to Lhotse, then proceeded to the top of Makalu, arriving on 24 May – a total time of just 2 days 30 min.

### Highest mountain

In Dec 2020, surveyors from China and Nepal jointly announced the latest measurements for the ever-changing height of Everest (aka Sagarmāthā or Chomolungma) in the Himalayas. An increase of just 86 cm (33 in) on the long-accepted survey result of 1954 takes it to an elevation of 8,848.86 m (29,031 ft 7.6 in).

### First winter ascent of K2

On 16 Jan 2021, a group of 10 Nepalese climbers made the first winter summit of K2. They joined forces from competing teams to claim this mountaineering first.

### First undisputed ascent of Everest without bottled oxygen (female)

Alison Hargreaves (UK) reached the summit of Everest – without the aid of Sherpas or supplementary oxygen – on 13 May 1995. She went on to make the **first ascent of Everest and K2 without bottled oxygen (female)** when she climbed the second-highest mountain on 13 Aug 1995. Tragically, aged 33, she was killed while descending from the summit. Her climbing time of 92 days from peak to peak remains the **fastest ascent of Everest and K2 without bottled oxygen (female)**.

The first woman to declare the conquest of Everest without bottled oxygen was Lydia Bradey (NZ); her claim to have reached the very top of the mountain on 14 Oct 1988 remains disputed.

## FIRST ASCENTS

*first ascent made without O₂*

| | Everest 8,848 m (29,031 ft) | K2 8,611 m (28,251 ft) | Kangchenjunga 8,586 m (28,169 ft) | Lhotse 8,516 m (27,939 ft) | Makalu 8,485 m (27,837 ft) | Cho Oyu 8,188m (26,863 ft) | Dhaulagiri I 8,167 m (26,794 ft) |
|---|---|---|---|---|---|---|---|
| Male (with oxygen) | Edmund Hillary (NZ), Tenzing Norgay (IND/Tibet); 29 May 1953 | Achille Compagnoni, Lino Lacedelli (both ITA); 31 Jul 1954 | George Band, Joe Brown (both UK); 25 May 1955 | Fritz Luchsinger, Ernst Reiss (both CHE); 18 May 1956 | Jean Couzy, Lionel Terray (both FRA); 15 May 1955 | * | * |
| Female (with oxygen) | Junko Tabei (JPN); 16 May 1975 | * | * | * | * | Věra Komárková (CZE/USA), Margita Štěrbová (SVK/CZE); 13 May 1984 | * |
| Male (without oxygen) | Reinhold Messner (ITA), Peter Habeler (AUT); 8 May 1978 | Louis F Reichardt (USA); 6 Sep 1978 | Doug Scott, Peter Boardman, Joe Tasker (all UK); 16 May 1979 | Michel Dacher (DEU); 11 May 1977 | Marjan Manfreda (SVN); 6 Oct 1975 | Josef Jöchler, Herbert Tichy (both AUT), Pasang Dawa Lama (NPL); 19 Oct 1954 | Six-man Swiss expedition (Diemberger, Diener et al); 13 May 1960 |
| Female (without oxygen) | Alison Hargreaves (UK); 13 May 1995 (undisputed – see above right) | Liliane Barrard (FRA), Wanda Rutkiewicz (POL); 23 Jun 1986 | Ginette Lesley Harrison (UK); 18 May 1998 | Chantal Mauduit (FRA); 10 May 1996 | Catherine "Kitty" Calhoun (USA); 18 May 1990 | Véronique Périllat (FRA); 12 Sep 1988 | Lutgaarde Vivijs (BEL); 6 May 1982 |

## First joint ascent of the higher 8,000ers by siblings without bottled oxygen

Between 30 Sep 1991 and 6 May 1996, Basque Spanish brothers Alberto and Félix Iñurrategi climbed the top five mountains together without the use of supplementary oxygen. In doing so, they also broke the record for the **fastest ascent of the higher 8,000ers without bottled oxygen**, completing the challenge in just 4 years 219 days.

### First ascent of the higher 8,000ers

Jerzy Józef "Jurek" Kukuczka (POL) was the first climber to conquer all five higher 8,000ers, starting on 4 Oct 1979 and finishing by 8 Jul 1986. Four of the five climbs were made without bottled oxygen, but he resorted to it while climbing a new route up Everest's South Pillar in 1980. He died in Oct 1989 while ascending the South Face of Lhotse.

## First ascent of the higher 8,000ers without bottled oxygen

Between 8 May 1978 and 16 Oct 1986, Reinhold Messner (ITA) made alpine-style ascents of the top five mountains, completing the task in 8 years 161 days. As part of this, on 20 Aug 1980, he made the **first solo ascent of Everest without bottled oxygen**.

## Fastest ascent of Everest and K2 with bottled oxygen

Mingma Gyabu "David" Sherpa (NPL) topped Everest on 21 May 2018 and K2 on 21 Jul 2018 – a time of 61 days 55 min. The **female** record is 66 days by He Chang-Juan (CHN) in 2018, between 16 May (Everest) and 21 Jul (K2).

## First sea-to-summit ascent of Everest without bottled oxygen (non-motorized)

The first person to climb from sea level to the highest point on Earth entirely under his own steam was Tim Macartney-Snape (AUS). He departed Sagar Island in the Bay of Bengal, India, on 5 Feb 1990 and trekked to Everest, reaching the top 95 days later on 11 May 1990. He climbed without the assistance of Sherpas, fellow climbers or supplementary oxygen.

The **fastest** completion of this gruelling human-powered challenge is 67 days, by Kim Chang-ho (KOR). Kim began his "0 to 8,848 m" expedition on 14 Mar 2013 at Sagar Island and kayaked 156 km (97 mi) up the Ganges, cycled 893 km (555 mi) from northern India to Tumlingtar in Nepal, then walked 162 km (100 mi) to Everest base camp before summitting on 20 May.

The **longest-distance** version of this endeavour began on 16 Oct 1995, when Göran Kropp (SWE) departed Jönköping in Sweden and cycled c. 6,000 mi (9,656 km) to Everest. He made a push for the top on 3 May 1996 but turned back just 90 m (295 ft) from his goal owing to inclement weather. He tried again on 23 May, this time with success.

## Fastest sea-to-summit ascent of Kangchenjunga (non-motorized)

From Mar to May 2011, Christian Stangl (AUT) climbed from sea level to the top of Kangchenjunga, the world's third-highest mountain, under human power alone. He cycled from the Bay of Bengal in India to the Himalayas, walked for 11 days to Kangchenjunga base camp, then, without bottled oxygen, climbed to the top – an expedition of 76 days.

## Fastest triple-header of the higher 8,000ers with bottled oxygen (female)

On 29 Apr 2018, Nima Jangmu Sherpa (NPL) climbed Lhotse, the world's fourth-highest mountain. Just over a fortnight later, on 14 May, she successfully scaled Everest, and by 23 May had reached the top of Kangchenjunga, setting a new women's triple-header speed record of 23 days 18 hr 30 min.

| Manaslu 8,163 m (26,781 ft) | Nanga Parbat 8,125 m (26,656 ft) | Annapurna I 8,091 m (26,545 ft) | Gasherbrum I 8,080 m (26,509 ft) | Broad Peak 8,051 m (26,414 ft) | Gasherbrum II 8,034 m (26,358 ft) | Shisha Pangma 8,027 m (26,335 ft) |
|---|---|---|---|---|---|---|
| Toshio Imanishi (JPN), Gyalzen Norbu (IND); 9 May 1956 | * | * | Andrew J Kauffman, Peter K Schoening (both USA); 5 Jul 1958 | * | * | * |
| Mieko Mori, Naoko Nakaseko, Masako Uchida (all JPN); 4 May 1974 | * | Věra Komárková (CZE/USA), Irene Miller (USA); 15 Oct 1978 | * | * | * | Junko Tabei (JPN); 30 Apr 1981 |
| Reinhold Messner (ITA); 25 Apr 1972 | Hermann Buhl (AUT); 3 Jul 1953 | Maurice Herzog, Louis Lachenal (both FRA); 3 Jun 1950 | Peter Habeler (AUT), Reinhold Messner (ITA); 10 Aug 1975 | Four-man Austrian team (Buhl, Diemberger et al); 9 Jun 1957 | Josef Larch, Fritz Moravec, Johann Willenpart (all AUT); 7 Jul 1956 | 10-man Chinese team (Hsu, Chang, Wang et al); 2 May 1964 |
| Ursula Huber (CHE); 1 May 1988 | Liliane Barrard (FRA); 27 Jun 1984 | Wanda Rutkiewicz (POL); 22 Oct 1991 | Marie-Josée Vallençant (FRA); 27 Jul 1982 | Krystyna Palmowska (POL); 30 Jun 1983 | Halina Krüger-Syrokomska, Anna Okopińska (both POL); 12 Aug 1975 | Marianne Walter (DEU); 29 Apr 1983 |

# Ballooning

### First balloon flight
Father Bartolomeu de Gusmão (BRA) invented a model hot-air balloon that he flew indoors at the Casa da India in Lisbon, Portugal, on 8 Aug 1709. The Jesuit priest conceived several ideas for airships, including a flying vehicle shaped like a bird.

When the air inside a hot-air balloon is heated by a burner, it becomes lighter than the cold air on the outside, causing it to rise. Likewise, when the air temperature inside the "envelope" drops, so does the balloon. As wind direction varies at different altitudes, pilots can try to steer their balloon in the desired direction by hitching a ride on the right air stream.

### First crewed flight
On 15 Oct 1783, science teacher Jean-François Pilâtre de Rozier rose 26 m (85 ft) in a tethered hot-air balloon built by Joseph and Jacques Montgolfier (all FRA) in Paris, France. The flight lasted about 4 min.

On 21 Nov 1783, de Rozier was joined by François Laurent, the Marquis d'Arlandes (FRA), for the **first untethered crewed flight**. They took off from central Paris and landed 25 min later on the city outskirts. De Rozier died in a crash while trying to cross the English Channel in a balloon on 15 Jun 1785. He and co-pilot Pierre Romain (FRA) became the **first ballooning fatalities**.

## FLYING SOLO: FARTHEST SINGLE-HANDED BALLOON FLIGHT

On 12–23 Jul 2016, multidisciplinary adventurer Fedor Konyukhov (RUS) flew 33,521.4 km (20,829.2 mi) non-stop around the world in *Morton*. His solo journey, starting and ending in Western Australia, took 268 hr 20 min – the fastest circumnavigation by balloon. Both records were ratified by the FAI.

**Did you always have a hunger for adventure?**
Yes, since childhood. At the age of 15, I rowed across the Azov Sea in a traditional fishing boat.

**What challenges did you face while flying around the world?**
I was in a non-pressurized gondola, which meant I was breathing bottled oxygen for 11 days. If the supply system had failed, I would have died in seconds. I could only nap for 20–30 min at a time while the autopilot maintained altitude. After four days, the cabin heater broke down, dropping the gondola temperature to -40°C (-40°F). Every day, I was on a learning curve.

**How did you shave two days off the previous fastest circumnavigation?**
The first few days over Australia were quite slow, but when the balloon entered the jet stream, my speed rose to 200 km/h (124 mph). I stayed in a powerful jet stream for most of the flight. Our team performed well on the ground and I made no fatal mistakes in the air.

**Can you see a point when you will call time on adventuring?**
My records require piloting skills, concentration and knowledge – there is no age limit in such projects. I knew that I would walk to the North Pole, climb Everest, sail round the world and row the oceans. If I was 20 years younger, I would aim to be the first person to land on Mars.

### First circumnavigation by balloon
On 20 Mar 1999, Bertrand Piccard (CHE) and Brian Jones (UK) crossed the "finishing line" of 9.27°W over Mauritania in North Africa to complete the first-ever non-stop around-the-world balloon flight. They had taken off on 1 Mar 1999 in *Breitling Orbiter 3* from Château-d'Oex, Switzerland.

When Piccard and Jones landed on 21 Mar, they had covered 40,814 km (25,361 mi) – the **farthest balloon flight**. This was ratified by the Fédération Aéronautique Internationale (FAI).

### First solo circumnavigation by balloon
Steve Fossett (USA) flew alone around the world in *Bud Light Spirit of Freedom*, a 140-ft-tall (42.6-m) mixed-gas balloon. He took off from Western Australia on 19 Jun 2002 and landed on 2 Jul at Eromanga, Queensland. A day earlier, Fossett reached a top speed of 322.25 km/h (200.23 mph): the **fastest speed by a crewed balloon**. This latter category is not monitored by the FAI.

### Highest crewed balloon flight
On 24 Oct 2014, Google executive Alan Eustace (USA) reached 41,422 m (135,898 ft) above New Mexico, USA, ascending in a pressure suit tethered to a helium balloon. Using an explosive device to detach from the balloon, he performed the **highest freefall parachute jump**, hurtling 41 km (25.4 mi) back to Earth in about 15 min after a two-and-a-half-hour ascent. Find another stratospheric record leap on p.71.

### Fastest straitjacket escape while suspended from a hot-air balloon
On 22 Jul 2017, daredevil escapologist Super Ning (CHN) freed herself from a straitjacket in 53.70 sec while dangling 30 m (98 ft) above the ground in Weihai, Shandong, China. The **highest suspension straitjacket escape**, meanwhile, is 7,200 ft (2,194.5 m) over Knoxville, Tennessee, USA, by Scott Hammell (CAN) on 13 Aug 2003.

### Fastest time to fly a hot-air balloon in all 50 US states
Andrew Holly (UK) completed a ballooning tour of the USA in 43 days 3 hr 11 min, making a separate flight (including take-off and landing) in every state in a lightweight balloon named *G-UNKY*. He began in Louisiana and covered the contiguous 48 states in 33 days. He went on to Alaska and finished in Hawaii on 24 Mar 2016.

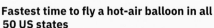

### Longest-duration flight in a hot-air balloon

On 9 Feb 2017, Fedor Konyukhov (see Q&A left) and Ivan Menyaylo (both RUS) flew non-stop for 55 hr 9 min 57 sec. They took off from Rybinsk, Russia, and flew south 1,029 km (639 mi) to Krasny Kut near the Kazakh border. Their long-haul ballooning record was ratified by the FAI.

### Highest flight in a hot-air balloon

Aged 67, Dr Vijaypat Singhania (IND) ascended to 21,027 m (68,986 ft) in a Cameron Z-1600 balloon over Mumbai, India, on 26 Nov 2005. That's twice the cruising altitude of a commercial airliner.

### Deepest underground balloon flight

On 18 Sep 2014, Ivan Trifonov (AUT) descended 206 m (675 ft) to the floor of Mamet Cave in Obrovac, Croatia. To allow entry through the narrow entrance, Trifonov used a smaller balloon and sat on a pair of gas cylinders rather than in a basket. The full descent and ascent took just 25 min. After the flight, he stated: "It was very hard. I don't think anyone else will repeat this venture."

### Highest flight in a hot-air balloon (female)

Austrian aeronaut Heidrun Prosch reached an altitude of 10,773 m (35,334 ft) on 19 Aug 2002. Accompanied by skydiver Paul Steiner, she took off from Ried im Innkreis and landed in Vöcklabruck, Austria. Prosch's love-affair with the skies began at an early age – her father took her on glider flights when she was just three!

### First Pacific crossing by hot-air balloon

On 15–17 Jan 1991, entrepreneur Richard Branson (UK, left) and Per Lindstrand (SWE) completed a 7,500-km (4,660-mi) voyage from Japan to Canada's Northwest Territories. Their balloon, the 73,600-m³ (2.6-million-cu-ft) *Virgin Otsuka Pacific Flyer*, was at the time the largest ever flown. The intrepid pair had already achieved the **first Atlantic crossing by hot-air balloon**, on 2–3 Jul 1987.

### Greatest mass hot-air balloon ascent

On 6 Oct 2019, a total of 524 hot-air balloons were launched during the morning mass ascension at the 48th Albuquerque International Balloon Fiesta in New Mexico, USA. The 2019 event, which ran from 5 to 13 Oct, drew 588 registrations from 17 different countries. Among the eye-catching entries were many eccentric creations technically known as "Special Shape" balloons (see inset).

More than 850,000 people attended the 2019 Albuquerque International Balloon Fiesta.

# Epic Journeys

## Youngest person to visit every country in Europe

Mauritian Gevish Kumar Kheddo (b. 30 Nov 2000) completed a pan-European trek on 25 Jan 2020 at the age of 19 years 56 days. His adventure – which he fitted in around his full-time university studies! – lasted nearly two years, concluding in Reykjavik, Iceland. He's shown here during stopovers in Prague (Czech Republic, main picture), Athens (Greece, top) and Copenhagen (Denmark, right).

## Fastest circumnavigation by single-seat, single-engine piston aircraft

Matt Jones, Steven Brooks and Ian Smith took turns piloting a World War II Supermarine Spitfire Mk IX around the world in 122 days, returning home on 5 Dec 2019. Gerallt Jones, Lachlan Monro and Ben Uttley (all UK) provided support. Owing to the aircraft's limited instruments, flights took place only during daytime and in clear weather.

## First circumnavigation by autogyro

On 22 Sep 2019, James Ketchell (UK) concluded a 175-day flight around the world, having travelled some 44,450 km (27,620 mi) in a Magni M16C autogyro. His open-cockpit aircraft has a top speed of 70 knots (129 km/h; 80 mph), around half that of the average helicopter. He broke his journey into 122 hops, as his autogyro has a limited range of c. 1,300 km (800 mi).

## Fastest time to...

**Cross the USA on foot (female)**: Sandra Villines (USA) walked across America in 55 days 16 hr 23 min from 11 Sep to 5 Nov 2017. She began in San Francisco, California, and ended in New York City.

**Visit all 48 contiguous US states by bicycle (female)**: Paola Gianotti (ITA) cycled through all adjoining US states in 43 days between 1 May and 12 Jun 2016.

**Travel to all Hong Kong MTR stations**: On 1 Feb 2020, Jonathan Wong (CHN) took precisely 7 hr 36 min 10 sec to journey between each Mass Transit Railway (MTR) station in Hong Kong, China.

### Longest journey by...

| Vehicle | Distance | Holder(s) | End date |
|---|---|---|---|
| Kite buggy | 1,015 km | Pete Ash, Kieron Bradley, Brian Cunningham (all UK) | 21 Sep 2004 |
| Milk float | 1,659 km | Paul Thompson (UK) | 20 Sep 2015 |
| Pocketbike (minimoto) | 2,504 km | S Ýr Unnarsdòttir (ISL), M Reid, C Fabre (both USA) | 17 Sep 2016 |
| Roller skis | 2,783 km | Gerard Proteau (FRA) | 28 Jun 2014 |
| Land windsurfer | 3,410 km | Robert Torline (USA) | 16 Jun 2001 |
| Stilts | 4,804 km | Joe Bowen (USA) | 26 Jul 1980 |
| Excavator | 5,649 km | Norman Bartie (AUS) | 20 Apr 2019 |
| Crutches | 6,006 km | Guy Amalfitano (FRA) | 6 Sep 2013 |
| Cycle rickshaw (pedicab) | 6,248 km | Len Collingwood (UK) | 17 Sep 2018 |
| Kick scooter | 7,100 km | Kosuke Takizawa, aka Rake (JPN) | 21 Apr 2020 |
| Electric mobility vehicle (team) | 8,609 km | J Duckworth, J Seamons, S Parrott, J Uren, G West (all UK) | 17 Oct 2007 |
| Skateboard | 12,159 km | Rob Thomson (NZ) | 28 Sep 2008 |
| Tractor | 25,378 km | Hubert Berger (DEU) | 23 Oct 2016 |
| Electric scooter | 25,547 km | Song Jian, Yadea Technology Group (both CHN) | 28 Dec 2020 |
| Wheelchair (motorized, mouth-controlled) | 28,000 km | Chang-Hyun Choi (KOR) | 6 Dec 2007 |
| Wheelchair (manual) | 40,075 km | Richard Marvin "Rick" Hansen (CAN) | 22 May 1987 |
| Fire engine | 50,957 km | Stephen Moore (UK) | 10 Apr 2011 |
| Quad bike/ATV | 56,239 km | Valerio de Simoni, Kristopher Davant, James Kenyon (all AUS) | 22 Oct 2011 |
| Taxi | 69,716 km | Leigh Purnell, Paul Archer, Johno Ellison (all UK) | 11 May 2012 |
| Bus | 87,367 km | Hughie Thompson, John Weston, Richard Steel (all UK) | 3 Dec 1989 |
| Bicycle | 646,960 km | Walter Stolle (UK) | 12 Dec 1976 |

## Fastest solo Munro-bagging

To "bag a Munro" involves ascending one of the 282 peaks over 3,000 ft (914 m) in Scotland. Solo Munroist Donnie Campbell (UK) bagged all 282 in just 31 days 23 hr 2 min, ending in the Highland county of Sutherland, UK, on 2 Sep 2020. He cycled 1,443 km (896 mi) between the Munros and ran a total distance of 1,422 km (883 mi), of which 126,143 m (413,854 ft) was ascent – the equivalent of climbing Everest from sea level more than 14 times!

## Fastest time to visit all Swiss cantons

On 22 May 2020, Gian-Luca Bähler (CHE) travelled between all 26 Swiss cantons (small territorial districts) in 15 hr 30 min, ending in Ticino. The idea arose over drinks with colleagues, when Bähler declared that he knew almost the entire public transport timetable of Switzerland by heart. He then decided to put his knowledge to the test.

### First helicopter circumnavigation passing through antipodal points

The antipodes are points on Earth that are diametrically opposite to each other. From 8 Apr to 7 Aug 2017, Peter Wilson and Matthew Gallagher (both UK) flew a Robinson R66 around the world from Marlow in Buckinghamshire, UK, via the antipodes Palembang in Indonesia and Neiva in Colombia.

### Longest journey by electric skateboard

On 6 Jan 2020, Germany's Stefanie Hasbauer arrived in Porto, Portugal, having completed a 1,210-km (751-mi) trip on her electric skateboard. Hasbauer had to overcome a number of challenges: her skateboard was stolen before she even set out, although she soon found it. She also had to deal with 10 flat tyres en route.

### Fastest circumnavigation by car

The record for the **first and fastest man and woman to have circumnavigated the Earth by car** covering six continents under the rules applicable in 1989 and 1991 embracing more than an equator's length of driving (24,901 road miles; 40,075 km), is held by Saloo Choudhury and his wife Neena Choudhury (both India). The journey took 69 days 19 hours 5 minutes from 9 September to 17 November 1989. The couple drove a 1989 Hindustan "Contessa Classic" starting and finishing in Delhi, India.

### Most countries visited by electric car on a single charge

On 8 Jul 2016, Frederik Van Overloop (BEL) travelled through seven countries in a Tesla Model S car without recharging.

The **greatest distance by electric scooter on a single charge** is 656.8 km (408.1 mi), by Liang Zhihao, Liang Zhiqi, Liu Haifan and Zhao Yangzi, in Luoyang, Henan, China, on 21 Oct 2020. The record was sponsored by the Dongguan Tailing Electric Vehicle Co., Ltd (all CHN).

### First woman to complete the Four Poles Challenge

Vanessa O'Brien (UK/USA) summitted Everest on 19 May 2012, skied the last degree to the South and North Poles on 15 Dec 2012 (above) and 16 Apr 2013 respectively, and dived to the Challenger Deep on 12 Jun 2020 (see p.129). She thus became the first woman to visit the planet's highest and lowest points plus the two geographic poles.

### Oldest person to visit both Poles

Dr Buzz Aldrin (b. 20 Jan 1930) reached the South Pole at the age of 86 years 314 days on 29 Nov 2016. He had earlier visited the North Pole on the Russian nuclear icebreaker *Sovetskiy Soyuz* in Jul 1998.

Dr Aldrin is best known for his participation in the **first crewed lunar landing**. He set foot on the Moon's surface at 3:11 GMT on 21 Jul 1969, preceded by Neil Armstrong (both USA).

### Greatest vertical distance on foot in 24 hours (uphill and downhill)

Ben Wernick (UK) made 101 round trips up a hill in Glynogwr, Mid Glamorgan, UK, on 26–27 Sep 2020, each time logging a change in elevation of 224.52 m (736 ft 7 in). After 23 hr 43 min, he had travelled up and down a total of 22,676.52 m (74,398 ft).

### Most extreme points visited on land

David Tait (UK) has visited two points on Earth separated by an elevation of 10,910 m (35,794 ft). He climbed Everest (8,848 m; 29,029 ft – see p.122) five times, most recently in 2013. Then, on 18 Mar 2019, he descended to 2,062 m (6,765 ft) below sea level in the Mponeng gold mine in Gauteng, South Africa.

Baikal's frozen surface posed a potential hazard to both record attempts. In some parts, it was only around 10 cm (4 in) thick.

### Longest motorcycle journey on ice (off-road)

Kevin Emans (UK) rode his KTM 500 EXC motorbike for 743.43 km (461.94 mi) over Lake Baikal in Siberia, Russia, ending on 22 Feb 2020. His vehicle had no modifications except for spiked tyres and protective adaptations for cold weather. Emans rode as part of the Baikal Project team – six motorcyclists who attempted to ride the entire length of this frozen body of water – the world's **deepest lake** (1,642 m; 5,387 ft).

As part of the same challenge, the project's leader, Gary O'Keeffe (IRL), also achieved the **greatest distance driven on ice in one week** (inset), covering 798.3 km (496 mi) from 16 Feb to 22 Feb 2020. He drove a 1976 four-wheel-drive Russian UAZ van, which incorporated a wood-burning stove.

# Round-Up

### Most 3,000-m mountains climbed in one week
On 2–9 Aug 2020, Emily Woodhouse (UK) ascended 13 mountains taller than 3,000 m (9,842 ft) in Andalucía, Spain.

### Highest tandem parachute jump
Jim Wigginton (USA) and Arkadiusz Majewski (POL) parachuted together from 11,405 m (37,417 ft) in Wyszków County, Poland, on 25 Oct 2019. Their paired plummet raised funds for the Punya Thyroid Cancer Research Foundation. (For more of Wigginton's exploits, see opposite.)

### Highest-altitude road marathon
Winter Sports Federation Pakistan, Pakistan Air Force, Serena Hotels and Z Adventures (all PAK) organized a marathon at 4,693 m (15,396 ft) on the Khunjerab Pass, in the Karakoram Mountains, on 21 Sep 2019.

### Deepest underground marathon distance run (team)
Six relay runners – including UK Army Cadet ambassadors Sally Orange and Jordan Wylie – covered a combined distance of 42.5 km (26.4 mi) at a depth of 1,041.1 m (3,416 ft) below ground at the ICL-Boulby mine in North Yorkshire, UK, on 10 Oct 2020. The "Beneath the Surface" event raised funds for mental health charities.

### First person to visit space and the deepest point on Earth
On 5 Oct 1984, Dr Kathryn Sullivan (USA) was part of the crew of the *Challenger* Space Shuttle mission STS-41-G. Subsequently, on 7 Jun 2020, she plunged to the bottom of the Challenger Deep – Earth's ◗ deepest point, at *c.* 11 km (6.8 mi) – in the deep-submergence vehicle

*Limiting Factor*, which was piloted by Victor Vescovo – the Challenger Deep's **most frequent visitor** (see opposite).

### Farthest Ice Swim
**Male**: 3.5 km (2.17 mi), by Paul Georgescu (ROM) at Lake Snagov, Romania, on 10 Feb 2021. The swim lasted 57 min 56 sec. **Female**: 3.3 km (2.05 mi), by Carmel Collins (IRL) at Wild Water in Armagh, UK, on 21 Feb 2016. Both records were ratified by the International Ice Swimming Association.

### Farthest free-distance hang gliding using three turn points
Glauco Pinto (BRA) flew 630.9 km (392 mi) in his Laminar 14 Icaro 2000 hang-glider in Tacima, Paraíba, Brazil, on 10 Oct 2019. The turns enable the pilot to return to the start point. This record was verified by the Fédération Aéronautique Internationale.

### First electric-powered wingsuit
Stuntman Peter Salzmann (AUT) made the first flight in an electric-powered wingsuit, as confirmed in Nov 2020. He was dropped by helicopter at *c.* 10,000 ft (3,050 m) over the Austrian Alps, and – thanks to two chest-mounted 20-horsepower "impellers" on his BMW Designworks suit – reached a speed of 300 km/h (186 mph). This would keep pace with the peregrine falcon (*Falco peregrinus*), which, in a dive, is the world's **fastest bird**.

### ▶ Longest Tyrolean traverse over a lava lake
Widely used in mountaineering and caving, a Tyrolean traverse involves propelling oneself over a chasm along a rope fixed between two points. On 3 Dec 2017, Brazilian "adventure-doctor" Karina Oliani made a 100.58-m (329-ft 11-in) crossing over Erta Ale – an active lava lake in Afar, Ethiopia. Some six months in preparation, the traverse itself took only around five minutes.

### Longest unsupported unmotorized polar journey (PECS)
Vet-turned-explorer Geoff Wilson (AUS, b. KEN) covered 5,179 km (3,218 mi) on a kite-powered sled between 9 Nov 2019 and 7 Jan 2020, travelling in a loop from Thor's Hammer to Novolazarevskaya Station in Antarctica. His 58-day journey took in the Pole of Relative Inaccessibility – the farthest point in all directions from the coast – and Dome Argus. The latter is the highest point on the Antarctic Ice Sheet, at 4,093 m (13,428 ft) above sea level. Wilson is also the **first person to climb Dome Argus unsupported** (see p.118).

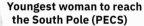

### Youngest woman to reach the South Pole (PECS)
Mollie Hughes (UK, b. 3 Jul 1990) was aged 29 years 191 days when she arrived at the South Pole on 10 Jan 2020 (inset), after a 58-day journey. She skied for 10–12 hours each day, pulling her supplies on a sledge, while enduring temperatures as low as -45°C (-49°F) and an eight-day blizzard that severely reduced visibility. Both Hughes' and Wilson's (left) records were ratified by experts from the Polar Expeditions Classification Scheme (PECS; see p.116).

## First blind person to lead a climb of the Old Man of Hoy

On 4 Jun 2019, blind climber Jesse Dufton (UK) led an ascent of the 137-m-tall (449-ft) Old Man of Hoy sea stack in the Orkney Islands, UK. His sighted partner, Molly Thompson, followed him up the east face. Dufton was born with just 20% of his central vision, with large blind spots; his limited sight continues to decline. On the ascent, he had only light perception to guide him.

### Fastest crossing of New Zealand on foot (female)

Menna Evans (UK) ran the length of New Zealand in 35 days 27 min between 1 Jan and 5 Feb 2020. Evans covered 34–40 mi (54.7–64.3 km) each day. She began each run at 6.30 a.m. to avoid the hottest part of the day, and experienced a vast range of weather conditions, from intense heat – which caused her to pass out at the end of her first day – to severe flooding on day 34.

### Fastest crossing of Lake Baikal on foot

Michael Stevenson (UK) traversed the frozen Lake Baikal in Siberia, Russia, in 11 days 14 hr 11 min. He set off on his 652.36-km (405.35-mi) solo expedition from Kultuk in the south at 7.19 a.m. on 25 Feb 2020. At 9.30 p.m. on 7 Mar 2020, he reached his destination: Nizhneangarsk in the north.

### Oldest person to cross the Grand Canyon rim to rim on foot

On 7 Nov 2019, John Jepkema (USA, b. 8 Jun 1928) traversed North America's most iconic gorge at the age of 91 years 152 days. He covered the distance via a series of trails, ending in Grand Canyon Village, Arizona. In all, Jepkema has hiked to the bottom of the Grand Canyon on six occasions – four times as part of a group and twice on his own.

### Fastest swim crossing of False Bay

Ryan Stramrood (ZAF) swam across this South African bay – a known breeding area for great white sharks – in 8 hr 39 min on 18 Mar 2021. Stramrood swam west to east from Miller's Point to Rooi-Els – the opposite direction to the five other solo swimmers to have finished the crossing.

The **female** record is 9 hr 56 min, by Annemie Landmeters (BEL) on 30 Jan 1989.

Barend Nortje, Anthony Pearse, Mark Chamberlin and Brad Gale (all ZAF) achieved the **relay** record – 7 hr 29 min – on 26 Mar 2021. All three of the above achievements were confirmed by the Cape Long Distance Swimming Association and the False Bay Swimming Association.

### Fastest crossing of Loch Ness by prone paddleboard

On 10 Aug 2020, James Fletcher (UK) paddled the length of the famous Scottish loch – c. 37 km (23 mi) from Fort Augustus in the south to Lochend in the north – in 4 hr 33 min 1 sec. Fletcher has a heart condition and used the attempt to raise awareness and funds for the charity Cardiac Risk in the Young.

### Longest continuous swim in a counter-current pool

Mayra Santos (BRA) swam for 31 hr 7 min in a counter-flow pool in Caniço, Madeira, Portugal, on 5–6 Nov 2020. These specially designed pools simulate the current in a river and have multiple uses, from physical therapy to helping professional swimmers train.

The **male** record is 25 hr, by Pablo Fernández Álvarez (ESP) in Madrid, Spain, on 6–7 May 2020. Both records were confirmed by the World Open Water Swimming Association (WOWSA).

## THE CHALLENGER DEEP: VOYAGE TO THE BOTTOM OF THE SEA

Sail c. 400 km (250 mi) south-west of Guam, plunge some 11 km beneath the surface of the Pacific Ocean and you'll find yourself in the Mariana Trench. At its south-west end lies the ◗ **deepest point in the sea** – the Challenger Deep, c. 10,934 m (35,872 ft) down. To date, just 17 people have visited this permanently dark netherworld, where the water pressure is more than 1,000 times that of atmospheric pressure at sea level – the equivalent of around 300 jumbo jets pressing down on a human!

On 7 Jun 2020, Dr Kathryn Sullivan (**1**) became the **first woman** (and the eighth person overall) to reach the Challenger Deep (see opposite). The former astronaut and NOAA administrator made her dive in the DSV *Limiting Factor*, piloted by explorer and retired US naval officer Victor Vescovo, who served as pilot on all of the following record dives. He has made the **most visits to the Challenger Deep** – 10, as of 11 Mar 2021 – logging some 30 hours on the seabed. In 2019, he became the **first person to reach the bottom of all Earth's oceans**.

On 26 Jun 2020, Vescovo took Jim Wigginton (b. 23 Feb 1949) on a 12-hour round trip to the ocean floor. Wigginton (**2**) is the **oldest person to reach the Challenger Deep**, at the age of 71 years 124 days.

The **first woman to reach Earth's highest and lowest points** is Vanessa O'Brien (UK/USA; **3**). She summitted Everest on 19 May 2012 and reached the Challenger Deep on 12 Jun 2020, five days after Dr Sullivan's descent (see also p.127).

On 5 Mar 2021, Hamish Harding (UK; **4**, on left with Vescovo) completed the **longest traverse of the Challenger Deep** – a 4.634-km (2.879-mi) odyssey that lasted for 4 hr 15 min. Harding's son Giles (**5**) was on board the support vessel DSSV *Pressure Drop*, and via social media documented his father's historic journey to a region that remains as mysterious to us, in its own way, as another world.

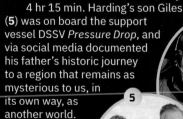

# Viridiana Álvarez Chávez

When Viridiana Álvarez Chávez took up serious exercise at the age of 28, she had no idea that it was the start of an exhilarating adventure that would lead her to the top of the world.

Growing up in the Mexican city of Aguascalientes, Viridiana had no experience of mountaineering. But having competed in a marathon and a triathlon, she sought a new challenge and began using internet videos to learn climbing techniques. Two years later, she scaled Mexico's highest mountain, Pico de Orizaba (5,636 m; 18,490 ft). The experience sealed a love affair with climbing that transformed her life. "I ended up giving up my office job to experience the magic of the mountains," she says.

Viridiana began a series of expeditions to the Himalayas, where she achieved the **fastest ascent of the top three highest mountains with supplementary oxygen (female)** – 1 year 364 days. Her first conquest, on 16 May 2017, was Everest, the **highest mountain**. Next came K2, where Viridiana became the first Latin American woman to reach the summit on 21 Jul 2018. On 15 May 2019, she completed her quest by topping Kangchenjunga.

Now Viridiana aims to conquer all of the 14 highest mountains on Earth – known as the 8,000ers. Given her unquenchable determination to succeed, no one at GWR would bet against her.

## VITAL STATISTICS
**Name:** Viridiana Álvarez Chávez
**Birthplace:** Aguascalientes, Mexico
**8,000-m mountains climbed:** 5
Everest (8,848 m; 29,029 ft)
K2 (8,611 m; 28,251 ft)
Kangchenjunga (8,586 m; 28,169 ft)
Lhotse (8,516 m; 27,939 ft)
Manaslu (8,163 m; 26,781 ft)
**Interests:** Marathons, triathlons, lecturing, wine-making

Extreme alpinism poses huge physical challenges. Oxygen levels above 8,000 m (26,246 ft) are only a third of that at sea level. This can result in nausea, dizziness and insomnia. Climbers are at risk of not only frostbite and hypothermia but also extreme sunburn. Viridiana's photo from Camp 4 on Everest (top), following a 19-hr return climb, testifies to the harsh conditions.

GUINNESS WORLD RECORDS
CERTIFICATE
The fastest ascent of the top three highest mountains with supplementary oxygen (female) is 1 year 364 days, and was achieved by Viridiana Álvarez Chávez (Mexico) from 16 May 2017 to 15 May 2019.

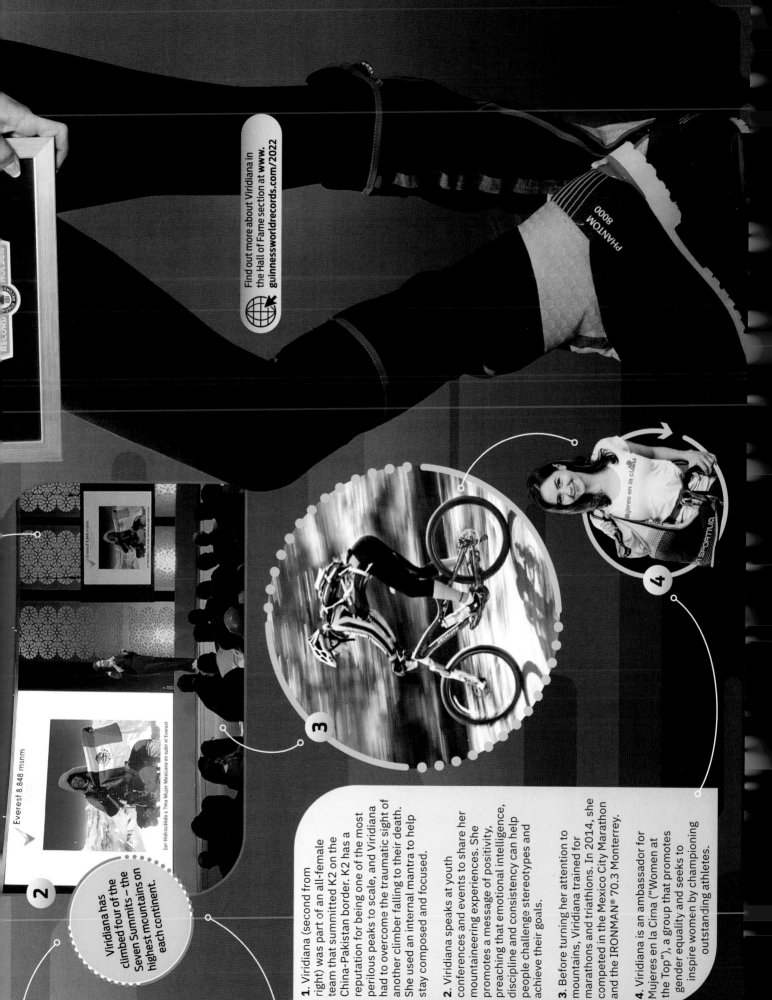

Find out more about Viridiana in the Hall of Fame section at www. guinnessworldrecords.com/2022

PHANTOM 8000

Everest 8,848 msnm

1er Hidrocálida y 7ma Mujer Mexicana en subir el Everest

Mujeres en la cIMa

LA SPORTIVA

**3**

**2**

Viridiana has climbed four of the Seven Summits – the highest mountains on each continent.

**4**

**1.** Viridiana (second from right) was part of an all-female team that summitted K2 on the China-Pakistan border. K2 has a reputation for being one of the most perilous peaks to scale, and Viridiana had to overcome the traumatic sight of another climber falling to their death. She used an internal mantra to help stay composed and focused.

**2.** Viridiana speaks at youth conferences and events to share her mountaineering experiences. She promotes a message of positivity, preaching that emotional intelligence, discipline and consistency can help people challenge stereotypes and achieve their goals.

**3.** Before turning her attention to mountains, Viridiana trained for marathons and triathlons. In 2014, she competed in the Mexico City Marathon and the IRONMAN® 70.3 Monterrey.

**4.** Viridiana is an ambassador for Mujeres en la Cima ("Women at the Top"), a group that promotes gender equality and seeks to inspire women by championing outstanding athletes.

# VIRTUAL VISIT

# Louvre Museum

**Location:**
75001 Paris, France
**Opened:** 10 Aug 1793

**Total area:**
244,000 m²
(2,626,394 sq ft)

**Gallery space:**
72,735 m²
(782,913 sq ft)

**Collection:** around
500,000 objects, with
35,000 on display

**Curatorial
departments:** 8

**Annual visitors:**
9.6 million (2019)

**S**itting proudly in the heart of Paris, the Louvre is a French national treasure, filled with a dazzling collection of artistic masterpieces.

The Louvre was originally built as a castle around the turn of the 13th century. In 1527, Francis I declared it to be his official residence, and work began to convert the fortress into a royal palace. In the wake of the French Revolution of 1789, it was decreed that the Louvre should open its doors to the people so that they could admire its artworks. Four years later, a total of 537 paintings were placed on show.

Today, the Louvre's viewable collection totals around 35,000 objects, ranging from the antiquities of Egypt and the Near East to world-famous paintings by masters such as da Vinci, Raphael and Michelangelo. Thousands of people flock

to the museum every day, walking through corridors and galleries that stretch for a total of 14.5 km (9 mi). Various extensions and additions means that the Louvre now covers 244,000 m² (2.6 million sq ft), making it the world's **largest art gallery**.

The Louvre will no doubt continue to change in the centuries to come. But for now, its status as the world's **most visited art gallery** remains unchallenged, with a record-setting peak of 10.2 million visitors in 2018. And with all the artistic delights on offer, is it any wonder?

### Christ and Abbot Mena
The **oldest Coptic icon** is found in the Louvre's Egyptian collection and dates to the 8th century CE. It depicts Jesus Christ (right, identifiable by the cross inside his halo) and an abbot from the monastery at Bawit in Egypt, where the icon was discovered in c. 1900. The Copts are an indigenous Christian community in Egypt.

### Urkesh Lion
In Room 302, visitors can find a small copper-alloy lion sitting atop a limestone tablet etched with the **oldest continuous Hurrian script**. (The Hurrians were a Bronze Age people who lived in Anatolia, Syria and Mesopotamia.) It dates to 2200–2100 BCE and is a "foundation peg": a talisman inscribed with a protective incantation and placed into the framework of a building – in this case, a temple dedicated to the Mesopotamian god Nergal.

### Mona Lisa
Leonardo da Vinci's portrait of the Italian noblewoman Lisa Gherardini is one of the most famous paintings in the world. It showcases da Vinci's *sfumato* technique, which uses glazes to create a "smoky" effect that softens the transitions between colours. The *Mona Lisa* was taken from the Louvre on 21 Aug 1911 – arguably, the **most valuable object stolen**. It was recovered two years later, and museum worker Vincenzo Peruggia convicted of its theft.

### Maerten Soolmans and Oopjen Coppit
On 1 Feb 2016, the Louvre and the Rijksmuseum in the Netherlands paid €160 m ($173 m; £121 m) for the joint acquisition of the **most expensive Rembrandt painting.** The life-sized pendant portraits of a newly wed couple, painted in 1634, are shared between the two museums but never separated.

**St Francis of Assisi Receiving the Stigmata**
A panel painting by Giotto depicting four scenes from the life of the Christian saint dates to c. 1300–1325 and is one of the oldest paintings in the Louvre. It is thought to have hung in the church of San Francesco in Pisa, Italy. The original frame bears the signature OPUS IOCTI FLORENTINI ("Work of Florentine Giotto").

3.13 × 1.63 m
(10 ft 3 in × 5 ft 3.6 in)

**Neolithic gypsum statue**
The oldest artwork in the Louvre dates to c. 7000 BCE. It was found at Ain Ghazal in Jordan and loaned to the museum in 1997.

Plaster shell with hollow interior

Richelieu wing

Napoleon courtyard

Entrants to the museum have to pass through the iconic Louvre Pyramid, a spectacular 21-m-tall (69-ft) glass structure in the courtyard that sits above the underground lobby. It was designed by the acclaimed architect I M Pei and completed in 1989.

**The Wedding Feast at Cana**
At 6.77 m tall and 9.94 m long (22 ft 2 in × 32 ft 7 in), this piece by Paolo Veronese is the largest painting in the Louvre. Completed in 1563, it sets the biblical tale of Jesus turning water into wine against the backdrop of a lavish Venetian wedding. No fewer than 130 characters are depicted.

The 67.3-m² (724.4-sq-ft) canvas took around 15 months to paint

In 1803, the Louvre was renamed the Musée Napoléon after the Emperor, who oversaw an expansion of its collection.

The western end of the Louvre courtyard was once fully enclosed, until the destruction of the Tuileries Palace in 1871

Tuileries Garden

Arc de Triomphe du Carrousel (1809)

Denon wing

# Science & Technology

**Largest solar furnace**
This nine-storey-high wall of mirrors is the heart of the Odeillo Solar Furnace, a scientific research facility near the town of Odeillo in south-west France. Light hits this 1,830-m² (19,700-sq-ft) parabolic reflector from an array of sun-tracking mirrors (called "heliostats") in the nearby fields. The reflector then focuses the light into a space about the size of a washing-machine drum in the laboratory tower, where temperatures of 3,000°C (5,432°F) can be reached within seconds on a clear day. The furnace began operation in Apr 1969.

## CONTENTS

Regular furnaces create combustion gases that can contaminate samples. Odeillo does not, making it ideal for scientific research.

HELIODYSSÉE

# Stargazing

### Planet with the shortest year
Exoplanet KOI 1843.03 is thought to complete an orbit of its parent star once every 4 hr 15 min. It was found by the Kepler Space Telescope and appears to be an iron-rich rocky planet around 10% smaller than Earth. Astronomers believe that the forces involved in the planet's extreme orbit have pulled it into a rugby-ball-like shape.

### Largest black hole collision
On 21 May 2019, two black holes – with estimated masses of 66 and 85 times the mass of the Sun respectively – met in what is known as the GW190521 collision. It was detected by two facilities designed to pick up cosmic gravitational waves: LIGO (USA) and the Virgo Interferometer (ITA).

The **lightest black hole** was discovered on 14 Aug 2019, when LIGO and Virgo observed gravitational waves from a black hole swallowing another object, in what has been dubbed event GW190814. The object being consumed had a mass only 2.6 times that of our Sun, while the main black hole was 26 times the mass of the Sun. As the smaller object's mass was measured with a high

### Most galaxies in a composite image
In May 2019, astronomers assembled nearly 7,500 exposures into one image of the distant universe. It contains 265,000 galaxies going back 13.3 billion years to just 500 million years after the Big Bang. Called the Hubble Legacy Field, it comprises images made by the Hubble Space Telescope over a period of 17 years.

degree of certainty as being too big for a neutron star, it must have been a black hole. It may have been formed by the merger of two neutron stars that had enough mass to collapse into a single small black hole.

### Longest supernova explosion
Typical supernovas explode with catastrophic fury and burn themselves out within months at most. However, SN 2016iet is an unusual supernova in that it was first detected brightening in 2016, with a 20-day rise in brightness to then a double peak in visible intensity, separated by around 100 days. It took a further 650 days to reduce in brightness to a point where the supernova explosion could be considered to have subsided – a total of 770 days. The supernova started life as a star with around 200 times the mass of the Sun. It was spotted by the European Space Agency's (ESA) Gaia satellite in Nov 2016. The longevity of this Type 1 supernova is unique in the history of supernova observations. A paper detailing the explosion was

published by astronomers at the Harvard-Smithsonian Center for Astrophysics (USA) in Aug 2019.

### Closest approach of an asteroid to Earth
On 16 Aug 2020 at 4:08 a.m., asteroid 2020 QC passed by Earth only 2,950 km (1,833 mi) above the southern Indian Ocean. Given its size (3–6 m, or 10–20 ft across) it would have been unlikely to pose any threat, but the light show as it hit our atmosphere would have been spectacular.

### First "Cotton Candy" class of exoplanet
In Dec 2019, NASA scientists using data from the Hubble Space Telescope announced they had identified three exoplanets (Kepler-51 b, c and d) that fall outside the normal classification of rocky Earth-like planets, ice giants like Neptune, and gas giants like Jupiter. They have extraordinarily low density, similar to cotton candy, or candyfloss, and are also known as "Super Puffs".

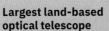

### Largest land-based optical telescope
Located 2,267 m (7,438 ft) above sea level on the island of La Palma in the Canary Islands, the Gran Telescopio Canarias (GTC) has a primary mirror with a 410-in (10.4-m) diameter. The mirror comprises 36 precision-ground hexagonal panels, all aligned to act like a large curved reflector. The telescope was inaugurated by Spain's King Juan Carlos on 24 Jul 2009.

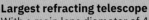

### Largest refracting telescope
With a main lens diameter of 40 in (1.02 m), the 124-year-old refracting telescope at Yerkes Observatory in Wisconsin, USA, is the world's largest. Instead of using a mirror to focus light, refracting telescopes do so with a lens at one end of a long tube, focusing the light on an eyepiece or similar instrument at the other end.

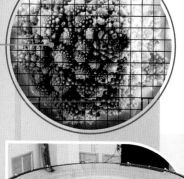

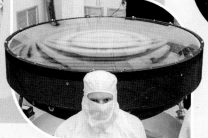

## Highest-resolution digital camera

The LSST Camera was designed for the Vera C Rubin Observatory (formerly known as the Large Synoptic Survey Telescope), which is under construction in Elqui Province, Chile. The camera uses an array of 189 CCD image sensors, giving a total resolution of 3.2 billion pixels. It also incorporates the world's **largest lens** (see right). The array was assembled at the SLAC National Accelerator Laboratory in California, USA, and first tested in Sep 2020. Pictured above right is a test image: a head of Romanesco broccoli, chosen for its intricate surface detail.

## Largest radio telescope dish

In Jul 2016, China completed the Five-hundred-meter Aperture Spherical Radio Telescope (FAST). It is located in the Dawodang depression – a natural basin in Guizhou, south-west China. The dish is made from 4,450 triangular aluminium panels. As its name suggests, FAST is 500 m (1,640 ft) in diameter, though only a 300-m-wide (984-ft) area is visible to the receiver at any one time.

## Largest lens

Completed in Sep 2019, the largest high-performance optical lens (above) is L-1, which was built for the Vera C Rubin Observatory's LSST Camera. At 1.57 m (5 ft 1 in), L-1 is the largest of the camera's three huge lenses, which focus light on to its 3.2-billion-pixel CCD sensor. The lens was made by Ball Aerospace and Arizona Optical Systems (both USA).

## First asymmetrical star oscillation

All stars wobble to a certain extent, but were thought to do so symmetrically about their axis of spin. In Mar 2020, however, scientists using data from NASA's Transiting Exoplanet Survey Satellite (TESS) found a teardrop-shaped star, HD74423, that oscillates only on one side. It is a binary star, accompanied by a smaller red dwarf star whose gravity creates its distinct oscillation and pulls at its surface, creating the teardrop shape. HD74423 is 1.7 times the mass of our Sun and 1,500 light years away from Earth.

## Closest exoplanet to Earth

In Apr 2020, a third exoplanet was discovered in orbit around the star Proxima Centauri – which at 4.2 light years (39.7 trillion km; 24.6 trillion mi) distant is the **nearest star** excluding the Sun. Named Proxima Centauri c, it has a more distant orbit than Proxima Centauri b (pictured), meaning that for some of its 1,928-day year it is Earth's nearest exoplanet neighbour.

The primary mirror comprises 18 ultra-light sections of beryllium. After launch, these will unfurl to take on their final shape.

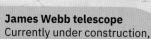

## Largest space telescope

The NASA Edwin P Hubble Space Telescope weighs 24,250 lb (11 tonnes), is 43 ft (13.1 m) in length and houses a 94.5-in-diameter (2.4-m) reflector. Named after the renowned US astronomer, it was launched into space at an altitude of 547 km (340 mi) by the US Space Shuttle *Discovery* on 24 Apr 1990.

## James Webb telescope

Currently under construction, and set to launch in Oct 2021 at time of press, this will succeed Hubble as the **largest space telescope**. A collaboration between NASA, ESA and the Canadian Space Agency (CSA), it will have a 256-in (6.5-m) primary mirror and will detect infrared light from distant objects. A five-layer sunshield, approximately the size of a tennis court, will protect it from any heat sources.

# Space Exploration

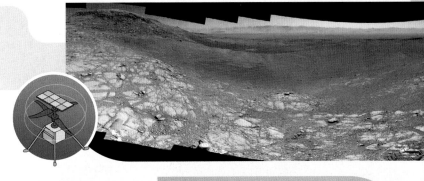

## Most visited space station

As of 5 Nov 2020, the *International Space Station* (*ISS*) had received 241 different visitors from 19 countries, ranging from South Africa to Kazakhstan. On 2 Nov 2020, the crew on the *ISS* celebrated the station's 20th anniversary – the **longest continuous human presence in space**.

The **fastest trip to the *ISS*** was made by the crewed *Soyuz MS-17* on 14 Oct 2020. The spacecraft launched from the Baikonur Cosmodrome in Kazakhstan at 5:45 a.m. UTC (Coordinated Universal Time) and docked with the *ISS*'s *Rassvet* module at 8:48 a.m. – a journey time of 3 hr 3 min.

## Closest orbit of a planetary body

On 6 Oct 2020, the NASA spacecraft *OSIRIS-REx* tightened its orbit around the asteroid 101955 Bennu, closing to an average altitude of 832 m (2,729 ft). This manoeuvre brought the spacecraft to within 374 m (1,227 ft) of the asteroid's surface at its closest point. On 20 Oct 2020, *OSIRIS-REx* descended from this transfer orbit to Bennu's surface and used an extendable arm to collect a sample.

## First commercial spacecraft to carry humans

On 30 May 2020, the SpaceX Crew Dragon Demo-2 mission blasted off from the Kennedy Space Center in Florida, USA. The private spacecraft transported NASA astronauts Doug Hurley and Bob Behnken on a 19-hr journey to the *ISS*, returning on 2 Aug 2020. The seven-person Crew Dragon capsule is based on a design that flew 19 missions to the *ISS* transporting cargo. The per-seat cost of a crewed flight on the Crew Dragon is around $55 m (£41.7 m).

**7    19    55**

## Largest planetary rover

On 18 Feb 2021, the *Perseverance* rover touched down in the Jezero Crater on Mars. Designed and built by NASA's Jet Propulsion Laboratory, *Perseverance* is a 1,026.4-kg (2,262-lb 12-oz), 3-m-long (10-ft) nuclear-powered rover, tasked with finding signs of past microbial life on the Red Planet. In addition to its scientific instruments, *Perseverance* also carries the experimental *Ingenuity* helicopter (see pp.146–47).

## First recorded marsquake

On 6 Apr 2019, NASA's *InSight* Mars lander detected the rumbling of a magnitude 2–2.5 quake. The Red Planet is only the third body in the Solar System, after Earth and the Moon, with measurable seismic activity. Unlike Earth, Mars possesses no tectonic plates – its quakes are thought to originate from contracting Martian crust as the planet cools over time.

## First historic oasis found on another planet

NASA's *Curiosity* Mars rover has been exploring the Gale Crater, a 100-mi-wide (160-km) ancient impact basin where it landed in 2012. Research published on 7 Oct 2019 in *Nature Geoscience* revealed that this shallow hollow held water around 3.5 billion years ago. The geological map formed by *Curiosity*'s work shows a landscape that would have once looked like the Quisquiro salt flat in South America's Altiplano – a less hostile environment than is observed today.

## First solar "campfires" observed

The European Space Agency's *Solar Orbiter* probe, launched on 10 Feb 2020, has confirmed the existence of solar flares that have been termed "campfires". Around the size of Germany, they are in fact much smaller versions of the sudden flashes of brightness on the Sun that can be observed from Earth.

## Closest approach to the Sun by a spacecraft

Launched in 2018, the uncrewed *Parker Solar Probe* has been studying the Sun's outer corona. It harnessed Venus's gravity to perform a series of increasingly close flybys that exposed it to temperatures of around 1,377°C (2,510°F). On 27 Sep 2020, the probe approached to a distance of 13.5 million km (8.4 million mi) from the Sun's surface. It was moving at a heliocentric speed (i.e., relative to the Sun) of 466,592 km/h (289,927 mph) – also making it the **fastest spacecraft**.

## Longest spaceflight by a woman

The debut mission of NASA astronaut Christina Koch (USA) ran for 328 days, from 14 Mar 2019 to 6 Feb 2020. Koch's stay on the *ISS* broke a record previously held by Peggy Whitson (see pp.154–55).

### Highest-resolution panorama of Mars

In Nov and Dec 2019, NASA's *Curiosity* rover took more than 1,000 images of the Martian landscape. On 4 Mar 2020, the images were stitched together into a single panorama, 1.8 billion pixels in size. The images were taken between noon and 2 p.m. over several days to ensure consistent lighting.

### Most distant solar-powered spacecraft

NASA's *Juno* probe has been orbiting Jupiter on an elliptical path since 5 Jul 2016. In Jan 2017, the solar-powered spacecraft reached apojove – its farthest point from Jupiter – when the gas giant was itself at its farthest point from the Sun, or aphelion. *Juno*'s distance from the Sun was calculated at 824 million km (512 million mi). It has three enormous solar panels with 18,000 individual cells.

In 2019, *Juno* provided the first view of Jupiter's north pole. Nine cyclones, each larger than North America, were observed slowly rotating around it. This is the **most storms photographed orbiting a planet's pole**. A similar set of cyclones were seen on Jupiter's south pole, but only seven existed as of Dec 2019.

### Most accurate clock in space

NASA's Deep Space Atomic Clock is designed to keep time to within one-ten-millionth of a second over the span of a year. It was launched into space on 25 Jun 2019 and activated on 23 Aug. The toaster-sized mercury-ion atomic clock (near right) is housed within the OTB-1 (Orbital Test Bed) satellite (far right). This technology will play a key role in NASA's plan to build a GPS-like system for space exploration.

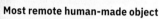

### Longest time between spacewalks

On 5 Mar 2021, JAXA astronaut Soichi Noguchi (JPN) completed the fourth spacewalk of his career 15 years 214 days after his third. He spent 6 hr 56 min outside the *ISS*, upgrading solar power systems alongside NASA astronaut Kate Rubins. Noguchi's three previous spacewalks took place during the STS-114 mission to the *ISS*, with the last on 3 Aug 2005.

### Most remote human-made object

Launched in 1977, *Voyager 1* and *Voyager 2* were sent to study the giant outer planets Jupiter, Saturn, Uranus and Neptune. Around 25 Aug 2012, *Voyager 1* became the **first probe to leave the Solar System** as it headed into interstellar space. As of 6 Nov 2020, *Voyager 1* was 22,684,987,276 km (14,095,797,590 mi) from Earth and still sending data to Mission Control in the USA.

### First observation of the Solar System's "Plasma Shield"

In Nov 2018, *Voyager 2* left our Solar System, crossing the boundary known as the heliopause. The probe collected data showing that the heliopause is marked with a layer of higher-density plasma with temperatures reaching 50,000°C (90,000°F). This plasma protects our Solar System from harmful levels of cosmic radiation. For more on *Voyager 2*, see p.148.

### Last crew on the Moon

The year 2022 will mark the 50th anniversary of the Apollo 17 mission, crewed by commander Gene Cernan (seated, below), geologist Harrison Schmitt (left) and pilot Ronald Evans (below right, all USA). On 11 Dec 1972, Cernan and Schmitt became only the 11th and 12th people to walk on the Moon. They spent 74 hr 59 min 40 sec on the surface, making Apollo 17 the **longest Moon mission**. On 14 Dec, they climbed back into the lunar lander and humans left the Moon for what was, so far, the last time.

A team of 18 astronauts has been selected for NASA's return to the Moon in 2024 as part of the Artemis programme.

# Architecture

### Most slender building

Located on "Billionaire's Row" in New York City, USA, 111 West 57th Street (near right) is 435.3 m (1,428 ft) tall but only 18 m (59 ft) wide at its base – a slenderness ratio of 1:24. Also known as the Steinway Tower, it was topped out on 20 Oct 2019. This style of building has emerged as a result of rocketing real-estate values, which make it commercially viable to build remarkably slim towers on small lots.

### Longest 3D-printed bridge

Professor Ma Guowei and a team from Hebei University of Technology (both CHN) built a 3D-printed concrete bridge with a 17.94-m (58-ft 10-in) arch span in Tianjin, China, as verified on 21 Jul 2020. Its design was based on a 1,400-year-old stone bridge. This technique, which adds cement matrix composites in layers, saves both on materials and labour costs.

### First underfloor heating

*Ondol* ("warm stone") thermal technology featured in traditional Korean architecture from no later than *c.* 1000 BCE. Hot air from a furnace was circulated under masonry floors via horizontal flues to a chimney on the other side of the building. Examples exist at Unggi in Hamgyeongbuk-do, North Korea.

### First commercial double-glazed windows

Refrigeration engineer Charles D Haven (USA) patented his "Thermopane" double-glazing system in 1934. It comprised a sealed sandwich of two panes of glass separated by dehydrated air. It first went on sale in 1938, with an improved version debuting in 1941.

### First passive building

Developed in Germany in the 1980s, the "passivhaus" standard emphasizes heavy-duty insulation and controlled ventilation. By reducing the exchange of air with the outside, passive buildings negate the need for conventional heating and cooling systems. The first buildings to meet the passivhaus standard were designed by architects Bott, Ridder and Westermeyer (DEU), and built in Darmstadt-Kranichstein, Germany, in 1990.

### Largest fountain

At 7,327 m² (78,867 sq ft), the Palm Fountain in Dubai, UAE, is 28 times the size of a tennis court! It was made by property developer Nakheel (UAE) and measured on 22 Oct 2020. The fountain puts on displays choreographed to music, and its tallest jet shoots up to 105 m (344 ft) in the air.

### Longest bridge

China's Danyang–Kunshan Grand Bridge on the Beijing–Shanghai High-Speed Railway is 164 km (102 mi) long. It crosses the 114-km (70.8-mi) Langfang–Qingxian viaduct, the second-longest bridge in the world.

### Most expensive plot of land

On 16 May 2017, the government of Hong Kong, China, sold a 31,000-sq-ft (2,880-m²) site for HK$23.28 bn (US$3 bn; £2.3 bn) to local firm Henderson Land Development. In Sep 2020, Zaha Hadid Architects revealed their design for a skyscraper on the site.

### Most powerful solar-powered stadium

The 9,600 solar panels on the roof of the Estádio Nacional Mané Garrincha in Brasília, Brazil, generate 2.5 megawatts (MW). The 72,800-capacity stadium was reconstructed in 2013 for the 2014 FIFA World Cup.

### Largest bicycle garage

There is space for 12,500 bikes at the Utrecht Stationstalling in the Netherlands. Set beneath the plaza outside the newly rebuilt Utrecht Centraal station, this storage facility was opened to the public in stages. An initial 5,000 spaces became available in Aug 2017 and the final section was opened on 19 Aug 2019. Its floors are colour-coded: grey for cyclists and red for pedestrians.

## Tallest residential building

The Central Park Tower (near left) is a 472.4-m (1,550-ft) skyscraper in New York City. It's home to 179 luxury apartments, a gym, private members club and rooftop pool. The cheapest units reportedly sold for more than $6 m (£4.4 m) each, while larger units on the upper floors are valued at $65 m (£47.8 m). The tower is owned by the Extell Development Company (USA) and was topped out on 16 Oct 2019.

## Most expensive stadium

Costs for the SoFi Stadium likely topped $5 bn (£3.8 bn). Located in the city of Inglewood in California, USA, the 70,240-capacity venue is shared by two NFL teams: the Los Angeles Rams and the Los Angeles Chargers. It hosted its first game on 13 Sep 2020 between the Rams and the Dallas Cowboys. Owing to COVID-19 restrictions, the arena was empty.

## Longest glass-bottomed bridge

On 10 Jul 2020, Lianzhou Qingtian Tourism Development Co. (CHN) opened a 526.14-m-long (1,726-ft) bridge with a glass walkway in Qingyuan, China. It's nearly five times longer than an American football field.

At 91.8 m (301 ft), the **longest cantilevered glass-bottomed skywalk** was built by Guizhou Shiqian Hot Spring Investment and Development Co. (CHN) in Tongren, China, as verified on 25 Sep 2019.

## Tallest...

• **House:** Antilia is the home of businessman Mukesh Ambani (IND). Completed in 2010, it stands 173 m (568 ft) high and has 27 floors, though their generous triple-height spacing means that it is as tall as a typical 60-storey office tower. It is located in Mumbai, India.

• **Cantilevered building:** The Central Park Tower (see top left) in New York City, USA, has a cantilevered section that extends 28 ft (8.5 m) from its eastern side, adding as much as 2,700 sq ft (250.8 m²) to each floor above 290 ft (88.4 m). This section reduces in size proportionally as the tower tapers towards the top.

• **Prefabricated building:** The residential tower 101 George Street in Croydon, London, UK, is 135 m (442 ft 10 in) tall. It was topped out on 1 Nov 2019, when the 1,526th module was set in place, just 35 weeks after the first modules arrived.

## Largest solar-powered building

Apple's headquarters in Cupertino, California, USA, is 260,000 m² (2,798,600 sq ft) in size. Designed by architects Foster + Partners, the gigantic ring-shaped building was opened in 2017. With an output of 17 MW, its rooftop panels (inset) also provide the **most powerful solar-power output from a single roof installation**. An additional 4 MW is generated by biogas fuel cells.

# e-Vehicles

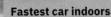

## Fastest 0–100 km/h by an electric car

Created by student team AMZ Racing (CHE), the Formula Student racing car *Grimsel* sped from 0 to 100 km/h (62 mph) in just 1.513 sec on 22 Jun 2016. The super-swift acceleration was helped by the car's carbon-fibre construction, reducing its weight to just 168 kg (370 lb). The attempt took place at Dübendorf Air Base in Switzerland.

## Highest electric vehicle market share

In Norway, electric vehicles make up most of the new car market. The number of such vehicles has been rising for several years, helped by generous tax incentives. According to the Norwegian Road Traffic Information Council, it hit a new high in Sep 2020, with 61.5% of all new cars being plug-in electric vehicles. Hybrids and plug-in hybrids accounted for another 20.1% and 7.3% respectively. Only 11.1% of new cars used internal combustion engines alone.

## Shortest charge time from John o' Groats to Land's End in an electric vehicle

Daniel North and Sean Miller (both UK) spent 1 hr 15 min 36 sec charging their 2019 Tesla Model 3 Performance while driving between Great Britain's geographical extremes. They reached Land's End in Cornwall on 19 Sep 2020, having made five stops to recharge.

## Most efficient electric vehicle on rails (prototype)

*Eximus IV* hit an average energy efficiency of 51.7 Watt-hours (Wh) per person/100 km in Delsbo, Sweden, on 17 Oct 2020. "Watt-hours" are a unit used to represent energy

## Fastest electric car (FIA-approved)

The *Venturi Buckeye Bullet 3* achieved an average speed of 549.211 km/h (341.264 mph) over a two-way flying mile at the Bonneville Salt Flats in Utah, USA, on 19 Sep 2016. Driven by Roger Schroer (USA), the car was designed and built by students at Ohio State University's Center for Automotive Research in partnership with French electric car designers Venturi. The record was ratified by the Fédération Internationale de l'Automobile in Nov 2017.

> The tiny motor nestles by the rear wheel. And the drinks bottle has been repurposed to house the batteries!

consumption over time (e.g., a 60-W light bulb left on for two hours will use 120 Wh of energy). *Eximus IV* is a tiny one-person locomotive, similar to the *Eta* car (opposite) but made to run on a train track. It was designed by students at Dalarna University (SWE).

## Highest altitude in an electric car

A Hyundai Kona Electric vehicle reached 5,771 m (18,933 ft) at Sawula Pass in Tibet Autonomous Region, China, on 8 Jan 2020, in an event staged by Hyundai Motor India.

The **highest altitude on an electric motorcycle** is 6,047 m (19,841 ft), by Francisco "Chaleco" López Contardo (CHL) riding a KTM bike on 22 Nov 2015. The Red Bull-sponsored ride took place on the Ojos del Salado – the **tallest active volcano**.

## Lightest electric bicycle (prototype)

Dennis Freiburg (DEU) hand-built a 6.872-kg (15-lb 2.4-oz) electric bicycle, as verified in Dortmund, Germany, on 3 Dec 2019. Freiburg wanted to build a super-light e-Bike that would enable him to commute to work, but would also be light enough to carry up flights of stairs. It can cover 40 km (25 mi) on one charge.

## Longest vehicle drift by an electric car

The term "drift" describes a technique in which a driver steers a vehicle in a controlled sideways skid. On 27 Aug 2020, Dennis Retera (NLD) put an electric car through a 42.171-km (26.203-mi) drift in the course of 210 laps at the Porsche Experience Center in Hockenheim, Germany. The feat was a collaboration with Porsche AG (DEU).

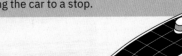

## Fastest car indoors

On 18 Nov 2020, racing driver Leh Keen (USA) reached a speed of 165.20 km/h (102.65 mph) in a Porsche Taycan electric sports car at the New Orleans Convention Center in Louisiana, USA. This record requires breakneck acceleration and hard braking – Keen had only 1,400 ft (426 m) of track in which to reach his record speed and then bring the car to a stop.

## Most efficient electric vehicle (prototype)

US undergraduate team Duke Electric Vehicles designed and built an electric car named *Eta* with an energy efficiency of 77.98 Wh/100 km. It was tested at GALOT Motorsports Park in Benson, North Carolina, USA, on 23 Jun 2019.

*Maxwell*, a combustion-engined car built by the Duke team, broke the record for the **most fuel-efficient vehicle (prototype)** on 21 Jul 2018. It achieved 0.0161 litres/100 km (14,573 mpg) at the same location.

## Greatest vertical distance by an electric forklift truck in one hour

On 9 Oct 2019, a battery-powered forklift truck climbed 623.73 m (2,046 ft 4 in) up a track leading to Velika Planina ("The Big Pasture Plateau") in Slovenia. The drive was coordinated by Jungheinrich AG (DEU).

## Greatest distance by an electric vehicle (non-solar)

Between 6 May and 12 Jun 2018, Stephen and David Ahart (both USA) drove 30,004 km (18,643 mi) in a Tesla Model 3, starting and finishing in Virginia, USA.

They set off on this road trip to mark David's retirement and they took the time to visit all 30 Major League Baseball stadiums over the course of the journey.

## Largest fleet of electric taxis

As of Jan 2021, the city of Shenzhen in Guangdong, China, had around 21,500 e6-model electric taxis, built by Chinese manufacturer BYD. Each cab is able to travel 300 km (186 mi) on one charge and they are expected to reduce carbon emissions by *c.* 771,000 tonnes (850,000 tons) per year. The smaller city of Taiyuan in northern China has had an all-electric taxi fleet since 2016.

## Largest parade of electric vehicles

Louis Palmer (CHE) brought together 576 e-Vehicles at Berlin Tempelhof Airport, Germany, on 23 May 2015. The event took place prior to the Formula E Berlin ePrix.

## Fastest electric ice-cream van

On 26 Oct 2020, Paddy McGuinness (UK) – co-presenter of BBC TV's *Top Gear* – hit a speed of 128.816 km/h (80.043 mph) driving *Mr Nippy* at Elvington airfield in Yorkshire, UK. A 1979 ice-cream van was modified with monster-truck tyres and converted to electric drive with Tesla and Mercedes batteries. Crucially, it could also dispense soft-serve ice-cream.

## Heaviest battery-powered vehicle

The eDumper, produced by Kuhn Schweiz AG (CHE), weighs 45 tonnes (49.6 tons), as confirmed in Apr 2019. When fully loaded, the battery-converted truck can transport a weight of up to 65 tonnes (71.6 tons). Every time the driver brakes, the eDumper's motor goes into reverse. This releases electricity, which can be stored and then sent back to the battery in a process known as "regenerative braking".

The heavier the eDumper's load, the more the driver has to brake to slow down. In turn, this regenerates more electricity.

# X-planes

The "X" classification is an official US designation, denoting "experimental". Many of the aircraft shown here were developed by the US Air Force specifically to trial cutting-edge technologies, or to test the latest ideas about aerodynamics. That said, not all X-planes are wholly new designs: they may be existing military or civilian aircraft under evaluation by the US Air Force. Here, though, we're also using "x" as shorthand for "extraordinary", to bring you an even broader spectrum of aeronautic absolutes that have pushed the envelope.

### First X-plane

Built from 1944 to 1945 and first flown on 19 Jan 1946, the Bell X-1 rocket aircraft represented the first time the US Air Force had commissioned the construction of a purely experimental aircraft.

On 14 Oct 1947, Captain Charles "Chuck" Elwood Yeager (USA) made the **first supersonic flight** in the X-1 over Lake Muroc, California, USA. Yeager reached Mach 1.06 (1,126 km/h; 700 mph) at an altitude of around 43,000 ft (13,100 m). The X-1 is now housed in the Smithsonian Institution (see p.12). Yeager passed away on 7 Dec 2020.

### First swing-wing aircraft

Variable-geometry wings allow a pilot to optimize a plane's layout for each stage of flight. At take-off, the Bell X-5's wings were swept back to 20°, but this could increase to 60° for better flight handling at higher transonic speeds (from around Mach 0.72 to Mach 1.0). It first flew on 20 Jun 1951.

### Fastest rocket-powered aircraft

The greatest speed ever reached by an air-launched crewed aircraft is Mach 6.7 (7,274 km/h; 4,520 mph), at an altitude of 31,120 m (102,100 ft). The feat was achieved by the experimental X-15A-2 aircraft, flown by USAF test pilot Major William "Pete" Knight over California, on 3 Oct 1967.

## TOP-FLIGHT ENGINEERING: CATHY BAHM

In 2004, NASA engineer Cathy Bahm was part of the team that produced the X-43A Hyper-X, a Mach-10-capable hypersonic drone – the fastest air-breathing aircraft (see below). She's currently helping to develop a new X-plane, due to fly in 2022.

**What are you working on now?**
I'm the deputy project manager for the X-59, a quiet supersonic demonstrator. It will be the quietest piloted aircraft in supersonic flight. In place of a loud, traditional sonic boom, the X-59 is designed to produce a quiet "thump" in flight.

**How can loud sonic booms be avoided?**
You have to design the aircraft so that the shock waves don't converge and combine into that traditional boom on the ground. For example, the X-59's really long nose is designed so that the shock wave coming off it doesn't combine with the shock wave coming off the wing.

**What is NASA hoping to learn from the X-59?**
Our mission is to figure out how people might react to the next generation of supersonic

aircraft. The X-59 will be flown over communities in the United States, and while the aircraft's design is state-of-the-art, we're less testing the vehicle than we are the response of communities on the ground to the vehicle and the noise it makes. What we want from the data we'll collect is for regulators to be able to say to commercial designers, "If your aircraft is below this noise level, then you can fly over land." That could open up supersonic travel everywhere.

**Is breaking Guinness World Records titles important to you?**
My GWR certificate is one of my prized possessions. Every time I do presentations in schools, I talk about all the things I've done, and I know that that's the thing they think I'm the coolest for. We don't have the plane, the X-43 itself. It's at the bottom of the ocean. So it's nice to have that kind of stuff to remember it by.

### First oblique-wing aircraft

The NASA AD-1 made its maiden flight on 21 Dec 1979, piloted by Thomas C McMurtry (USA). It had a single wing joined to the fuselage by a pivot in the centre. For take-off and landing, the wing would be at a 90° angle to the fuselage – like a conventional wing – but once in flight it could be tilted up to 60°, swept forward on one side of the plane and backward on the other.

### First airborne nuclear reactor

During the Cold War, the US Air Force researched aircraft that could stay aloft for months, driven by nuclear power. A converted B-36 bomber made 47 test flights between 1955 and 1957; an onboard nuclear reactor was operational for some tests but never powered the plane. The project was eventually cancelled.

### Fastest air-breathing aircraft

On 16 Nov 2004, NASA's unmanned Hyper-X (X-43A) scramjet aircraft reached

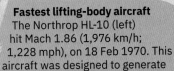

### Fastest lifting-body aircraft

The Northrop HL-10 (left) hit Mach 1.86 (1,976 km/h; 1,228 mph), on 18 Feb 1970. This aircraft was designed to generate lift using its teardrop-shaped body, allowing it to fly without wings.

The **most prolific mothership** is NASA's Boeing NB-52B (above, in flight), aka *Balls 8*. From 23 Jan 1960 to 26 Nov 1976, it carried out 233 mid-air deployments of crewed aircraft, alongside hundreds of missions involving uncrewed craft.

## Smallest crewed X-plane

The Bensen X-25B was a 3.45-m-long (11-ft 3-in), one-person autogyro. This tiny aircraft first flew at Edwards Air Force Base in California, on 5 Jun 1968. It was trialled as a possible escape vehicle: rather than use an ejector seat, the pilot would be launched clear of the plane in this tiny autogyro, which would then deploy its rotors, allowing its operator to fly clear.

## First circumnavigation in a solar-powered aeroplane

André Borschberg and Bertrand Piccard (both CHE) flew around the world in *Solar Impulse 2* from 9 Mar 2015 to 26 Jul 2016, powered entirely by energy from the Sun – as recorded by the Fédération Aéronautique Internationale (FAI). It took them 505 days 19 hr 53 min, although from Jul 2015 to Apr 2016, they were unavoidably delayed by extensive repairs to their aircraft in Hawaii, USA.

## Fastest electric aircraft over a 3-km course

During a flight on 23 Mar 2017 from the Dinslaken Schwarze Heide airfield in Germany, an Extra 330LE reached a top speed of 342.86 km/h (213.04 mph) – 18.84 km/h (11.71 mph) faster than the previous record holder. The pilot was Walter Kampsmann (DEU). The aircraft is a modification of the Extra 330 aerobatic plane produced by German manufacturer Extra Aircraft.

Mach 9.68 (c. 10,869 km/h; 6,754 mph), or almost 10 times the speed of sound. The autonomous drone was boosted to an altitude of 110,000 ft (33,528 m) by a Pegasus rocket launched from the Boeing NB-52B aircraft, then successfully burned its engine before plunging into the Pacific Ocean. Its deployment was the last operational mission for *Balls 8*, the **most prolific mothership** (see opposite).

## Fastest human-powered flight

Holger Rochelt (DEU) reached a speed of 44.26 km/h (27.5 mph) in *Musculair II* at Oberschleissheim, Germany, on 2 Oct 1985. The lightweight flying machine, constructed by the pilot's father, Gunther, weighed only 25 kg (55 lb) empty, despite its huge wingspan of 19.5 m (64 ft). It was powered by a pedal-driven propellor.

## Fastest flying boat

The Martin XP6M-1 SeaMaster, a US Navy four-jet-engined minelayer that flew in 1955–59, could reach 1,040 km/h (646 mph). Flying boats were once at the cutting edge of technology, but they were superseded by improvements in the range of land-based planes and the rise of aircraft carriers. Since World War II, they have had little military or commercial significance.

## Longest orbital flight by a reusable spacecraft

The Boeing X-37B autonomous spaceplane orbited Earth for 2 years 50 days from 2017 to 2019. It was launched atop a SpaceX *Falcon 9* rocket from Cape Canaveral Air Force Station in Florida, USA, on 7 Sep 2017 and returned on 27 Oct 2019. It landed on the old Space Shuttle landing runway at Florida's Kennedy Space Center.

## Largest aircraft by wingspan

The Scaled Composites Model 351 Stratolaunch, aka *Roc*, has a 385-ft (117.35-m) wingspan. It first flew on 13 Apr 2019, from the Mojave Air & Space Port in California. It was built by Scaled Composites and operated by Stratolaunch Systems (both USA).

The **smallest aircraft** to fly is the biplane *Bumble Bee II* (inset), designed and built by Robert H Starr (USA). Only 8 ft 10 in (2.69 m) long, it had a 5-ft 6-in (1.68-m) wingspan – less than that of a swan.

STRATOLAUNCH SYSTEMS

# Robotics

On board *Ingenuity* is a piece of wing fabric from the 1903 Wright Flyer – which made the first powered flight (see p.12).

### First controlled flight on Mars
On 19 Apr 2021, NASA's *Ingenuity* Mars Helicopter completed a 40-sec hop over the sands of the Jezero Crater. It was observed rising to an altitude of around 3 m (10 ft) by the nearby *Perseverance* rover (see p.138). This 1.8-kg (4-lb) craft is fully autonomous, with onboard computers that keep it within the narrow flight envelope required for the thin Martian atmosphere.

### Smallest liquid-fuelled robot
**100%** Developed by engineers at the University of Southern California, RoBeetle measures just over 1 cm (0.39 in) long and weighs a mere 88 mg (0.003 oz) – not including the weight of the fuel. The methanol in its fuel tank is released through a vent in the top, driving a shape-memory-alloy transmission connected to its legs. RoBeetle, which was revealed in *Science Robotics* on 19 Aug 2020, has a top speed of 0.76 mm/s (0.02 in/s), meaning it would take just under two minutes to walk the length of a credit card.

### Longest robot arm
In Apr 2021, the Canadarm2 – fitted to the *International Space Station* – celebrated its 20th "birthday". The 17.5-m-long (57-ft 4-in), seven-jointed arm was fitted to the station by Canadian astronaut Chris Hadfield on 22 Apr 2001. As it operates in a weightless environment, this long and spindly arm can be used to move almost anything around the station, from small experiments and astronauts to entire spacecraft.

The *ISS* is home to several robotic systems, including a flock of free-floating robot assistants. The **first autonomous camera drone on the *ISS*** was the Japanese Int-Ball, which arrived on 4 Jun 2017; it has since been joined by the European CIMON and NASA's three Astrobee robots.

### First tele-operated straight-razor shave
Researcher John Peter Whitney (USA) put himself on the cutting edge of robotics research in Jul 2020 by entrusting his personal grooming to a straight-razor-wielding robotic arm of his own design. The razor-robot was operated by barber Jesse Cabbage (USA), who carried out the motions that the arm then followed. Whitney emerged shaved and unscathed.

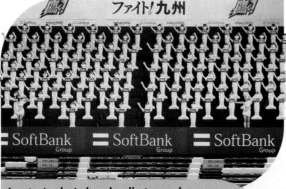

### Largest robot cheerleading squad
For their 26 Mar 2021 baseball game against the Chiba Lotte Marines, the Fukuoka SoftBank Hawks were cheered on by 100 SoftBank Robotics Pepper robots. A few of these 12-m-tall (3-ft 11-in) humanoid robots were hired by the Hawks in the summer of 2020, when COVID-19 restrictions left the team playing in an empty stadium, and the squad has kept growing since.

### ▶ Most UAVs airborne simultaneously
To celebrate the launch of Hyundai's luxury Genesis marque in China, Genesis Motor Sales staged a dramatic aerial display that used 3,281 uncrewed aerial vehicles (UAVs) fitted with coloured lights. Guided by a control computer on the ground, these drones arranged themselves into colossal 3D images and animations that hung in the air over the Huangpu River in central Shanghai.

The final count excludes 44 UAVs that did not make it back to the landing site at the end of the display.

### THE BEST OF BIONICS: CYBATHLON'S ROLAND SIGRIST

Since 2014, Swiss scientist Roland Sigrist has been working for Cybathlon, the **largest competition for people with disabilities and developers of technical-assistance systems**. Held every four years, the event has attracted more than 100 teams from all over the world.

**What is Cybathlon?**
The idea of Cybathlon is to promote the inclusion of people with disabilities and the development of assistive technologies that can support them in daily life. It's built around "races" in which each team's "pilot" (a person with a disability) has to complete the most everyday tasks in the fastest time possible.

The competition focuses the teams' efforts on user-centred design, meaning that people with disabilities and engineers have to work together.

**How do you plan the races?**
Our first question is always: "what are the needs of people with disabilities?" We then design

### Smallest walking robot
In Aug 2020, scientists at Cornell University (USA) built a quadruped robot that measured just 5 micrometres (µm) thick, 40 µm wide and 70 µm long. Its body has a series of photocells linked to each of its composite titanium and platinum legs. When a laser is directed at a photocell, it creates a current that moves the corresponding leg.

Slightly larger is the **smallest micro-electronic robot**, a more complex design developed earlier in 2020 by Vineeth Bandari (IND), Feng Zhu (CHN) and Oliver Schmidt (DEU). This 800-µm-long swimming robot has an antenna to receive power wirelessly, two independently controllable motors and an articulated arm that enables it to grasp microscopic objects. Devices such as this may one day help to perform microsurgery.

challenges around these needs. In the Powered Arm Prosthesis race, for example, we have tasks where pilots can use the prosthesis and the healthy arm together, and then other tasks where they can only use the prosthesis. One reason for this is because people may get into the habit of solving problems with the healthy limb only, which can lead to injuries from overuse.

### How does Cybathlon differ from the Paralympics?
We promote "techno-doping"! Robotic prostheses have the potential to allow more natural movements and don't just shift the effort to a person's remaining healthy muscles. We allow for any solution, provided it doesn't reduce the real-world practicality of a system.

### What's next for Cybathlon?
We saw big improvements between 2016 and 2020. We'll be making the tasks more challenging for the next event because we want to push the limits.

### First robot made from ice
IceBot is a 6.3-kg (13-lb 14-oz) wheeled robot composed of a set of sensors and actuators embedded into a body of frozen water. It was created in 2020 by a team from the University of Pennsylvania, USA, who wanted to make a robot that could modify or repair itself with materials from its environment. Such a design could be used for missions to Jupiter's icy moons.

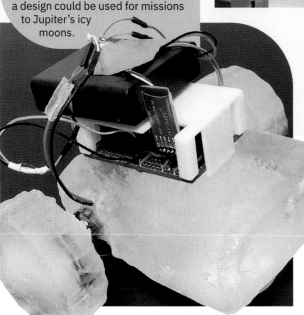

### Fastest 50 m swim by a robotic fish
Many roboticists today are interested in what is called biomimicry – imitating the forms and movements of living things. Since 2015, the BREED robotics team at Hong Kong University (CHN) have been studying fish to develop faster underwater vehicles. On 20 Oct 2020, their latest prototype swam the length of an Olympic pool in just 22.92 sec, putting the robot fish just a few seconds off human world record pace.

The **largest robotic fish** is the SHOAL, which was tested in Gijon, Spain, in May 2012. Each of the SHOAL robo-fish, which are designed to detect ocean pollutants, measures 1.5 m (4 ft 11 in) in length.

### Most UAVs launching fireworks simultaneously
On 30 Oct 2020, Korean car maker Kia added pyrotechnics to an already impressive display by 303 choreographed UAVs. The fireworks were released mid-flight over Incheon harbour in South Korea.

### First robot in a rap battle
Georgia Tech's musical robot, Shimon, first made a splash in 2017 as a jazz marimba player. Along with its creator, Gil Weinberg, Shimon has since gone in search of new musical horizons, releasing an album of original material and touring with its own band. In 2020, Shimon turned its talents to the world of battle rap, learning to improvise lyrics in response to its opponent's verses. In a video released on 24 Feb 2020, Shimon faced off against Atlanta-based rapper Dash Smith, coming up with creative, if sometimes baffling, responses to his rhymes.

### Highest jump by a quadruped robot
Cheetah 3, built by Sangbae Kim and his colleagues at the Massachusetts Institute of Technology, USA, can spring 78.74 cm (2 ft 7 in) off the ground. The 45-kg (99-lb) four-legged robot achieves this by pitching back on to its hind legs, then using them to push off vertically. Cheetah's smaller sibling, the Mini Cheetah, is even more agile and can do backflips!

Both have their feet planted firmly on the ground, however, when compared with the **most vertically agile robot** (a metric calculated by looking at the height and frequency of jumps). Salto-1P, developed at the University of California, Berkeley, in 2018, can cover 6 ft (1.83 m) of vertical travel every second. This one-legged robot uses fans and reaction wheels to orient itself in mid-air.

### Most push-ups by a humanoid robot
On 15 Oct 2016, Kengoro performed five consecutive push-ups. That's not a great feat for a person (the human record for **most push-ups in one minute** stands at 152), but it's an impressive achievement for this 167-cm-tall (5-ft 5-in) robot. Kengoro owes its strength to a lightweight 3D-printed skeleton and an evaporative cooling system that works like sweating.

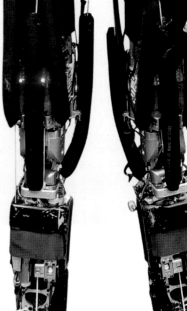

# History of Computers

### 1945: First programmable electronic computer
The Electronic Numerical Integrator and Computer (ENIAC) at the University of Pennsylvania, USA, carried out its first calculations on 10 Dec 1945. It consisted of many modules, each designed to perform specific mathematical operations or control tasks. The connections between the modules were designed so that ENIAC could be reconfigured for each set of tasks, or "program".

### 1947: First computer start-up
The Eckert–Mauchly Computer Corporation was founded by US researchers J Presper Eckert and John Mauchly on 8 Dec 1947. It was created to develop a commercial computer, the UNIVAC, based on work done by the pair on a successor to ENIAC (see above) at the University of Pennsylvania's Moore School of Electrical Engineering.

### 1948: Heaviest data reel
The paper tape reels fitted to the IBM Selective Sequence Electronic Calculator weighed 400 lb (181 kg). This electromechanical computer operated from Jan 1948 to Aug 1952. Only one was ever built, occupying a large room at IBM's headquarters in New York City, USA.

### 1954: Heaviest portable computer
The DYSEAC was a vacuum-tube computer built by the US government's National Bureau of Standards in Gaithersburg, Maryland. Made for the US Department of

### 1954: First electronic computer to ship 1,000 units
The first IBM 650 Magnetic Drum Data-Processing Machine was delivered on 8 Dec 1954 to the John Hancock Mutual Life Insurance Company in Boston, Massachusetts, USA. Almost 2,000 were made and the model stayed in production until 1962. The 650 was IBM's first computer targeted at medium-sized businesses.

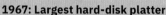

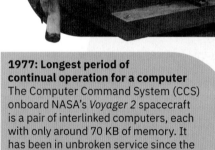

### 1967: Largest hard-disk platter
The Librascope Disk File drive took 48-in (121-cm) platters (disks). Only two of these hard drives were made. One was placed at the Stanford University AI Lab in 1967, the other at the Lawrence Radiation Laboratory (today the Lawrence Livermore National Laboratory). Each held six platters, weighed 5,200 lb (2,358 kg) and stored 48 MB of data.

Defense and completed in May 1954, it comprised two customized 40-ft (12.1-m) trailers: one for the DYSEAC computer, the other for its power supplies, cooling units and equipment space. The computer trailer weighed 24,000 lb (10,886 kg) and the support trailer weighed 16,000 lb (7,257 kg), giving a total mass of 40,000 lb (18,143 kg) – a "portable" computer heavier than three African elephants!

### 1962: First multi-platform videogame
In 1962, Steve Russell (USA) and a group of volunteer "hackers" coded *Spacewar* for a PDP-1 computer at the Massachusetts Institute of Technology. This fast-paced

### 1977: Longest period of continual operation for a computer
The Computer Command System (CCS) onboard NASA's *Voyager 2* spacecraft is a pair of interlinked computers, each with only around 70 KB of memory. It has been in unbroken service since the spacecraft's launch on 20 Aug 1977. As of 28 Jan 2021, the CCS – *Voyager 2*'s primary computer – had run for 43 years 161 days. Discover more about *Voyager 2* on p.139.

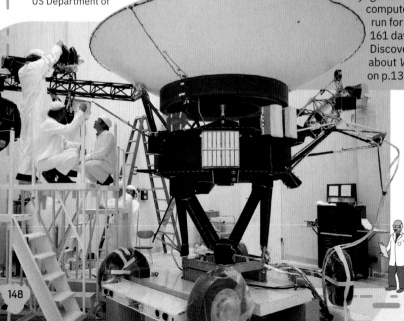

### 1982: Best-selling desktop computer
The Commodore 64 was made by Commodore International (USA) from Aug 1982 to Apr 1994. The exact number of C64s sold is unclear – the company's official figure was 17 million units, while a modern estimate puts it at around 12.5 million units. The **best-selling computer overall** is 2014's iPhone 6 (inset), with reported sales of *c.* 220 million units.

## 1991: First email sent from space

On 9 Aug 1991, the astronauts Shannon Lucid and James C Adamson sent an email back to Earth from the NASA Space Shuttle *Atlantis*. The message was sent over the AppleLink network to Marsha Ivins at the Johnson Space Center in Houston, USA. The full text read: "Hello Earth! Greetings from the STS-43 Crew. This is the first AppleLink from space. Having a GREAT time, wish you were here,... send cryo and RCS! Hasta la vista, baby,...we'll be back!"

multiplayer game spread to other institutions and, by 1972, had been ported to 14 different models of computer in locations as distant as Palo Alto, California, and Cambridge University in the UK.

## 1964: Oldest computer architecture

The IBM System/360 mainframe computer was launched on 7 Apr 1964. Its basic architecture – a term that includes how its memory is organized, how programs are controlled and the instruction set used by the processor – features in a line of IBM mainframes that are still sold today.

Such stability means that software written for this 58-year-old standard can still run on modern IBM machines, a feature that is reportedly crucial for two big IBM customers – the US Internal Revenue Service (IRS) and the Sabre Airline Reservation System. These organizations' systems are the strongest contenders for the title of **oldest software in**

**continuous use**. It has been claimed that the IRS Individual Master File contains code written as early as 1962.

## 1971: First microprocessor

Designed and built by Intel (USA), the first 4004 chip was completed in Jan 1971. The size of a thumbnail, this single-chip processor could perform 1,200 additions per second. Its successor, the 8008, which was released in 1972, could outperform room-sized 1950s computers.

## 2019: Most Loebner Prize wins

Founded in 1990 by US inventor Hugh Loebner, this annual contest awards prizes for AI programs that display human qualities. Stephen Worswick (UK) has won five times with his chatbot Mitsuku, most recently on 15 Sep 2019. Should an AI ever prove indistinguishable from a human, its designer receives $100,000 (£73,000) and the competition will close.

## 2020: Fastest computer

The supercomputer Fugaku is installed at RIKEN Center for Computational Science in Kobe, Japan. It has a High Performance Linpack (HPL) benchmark result of 415.5 petaflops (i.e., it can make 415.5 quadrillion computations per second). Fugaku's premier status was confirmed in the 55th edition of the *TOP500* list of the world's most powerful supercomputers, published in Jun 2020.

## 1993: Longest-running hacker convention

DEF CON began in 1993 as a party for members of "Platinum Net", a now-defunct Canada-based hacking network. Held in Las Vegas, USA, it attracts up to 30,000 people each year from both sides of the field of computer security. Tickets must be bought on site in cash, to avoid efforts by police to track attendees via their credit-card details.

## 2016: Largest microprocessor model

On 22 Jun 2016, James Newman (UK) completed his working replica of a microprocessor, housing 42,370 discrete transistors. His "Megaprocessor" displays the inner operations of the computers we use every day at a human scale and speed. More than 10,000 LEDs make it possible to see its logic circuits in action as data moves through the processor. The Megaprocessor is now on display at the Centre for Computing History in Cambridge, UK.

Fugaku's computational power is 2.8 times that of the previous record holder, Summit, which had held the top spot since Jun 2018.

# Cutting-Edge Science

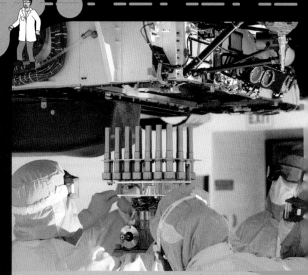

### Highest CASP score

The Critical Assessment of protein Structure Prediction (CASP) competition has run every two years since 1994. Entrants are tasked with identifying the 3D structure of various proteins from their amino acid sequences. The quality of each team's predictions are quantified using a 0–100 measure called Global Distance Test (GDT). At CASP14, AlphaFold – a system created by British AI lab DeepMind – earned a score of 92.4 GDT, as announced on 30 Nov 2020. Identifying the precise shape of proteins reveals their function, which is an essential step in the development of many medicines.

### First mRNA vaccine in clinical use

The Tozinameran COVID-19 vaccine was approved by the British Medicines and Healthcare Products Regulatory Agency on 2 Dec 2020. It was developed by BioNTech (DEU) with support from Pfizer (USA) and Fosun (CHN). This vaccine employs a kind of genetic code called "messenger RNA" (or mRNA) – a DNA-like set of instructions that stimulate a living cell to do something. The mRNA in Tozinameran makes cells produce a harmless fragment of the virus, which the immune system can then learn to recognize.

### First bacteria proven to survive in space

A study published in Aug 2020 revealed that dried pellets of *Deinococcus* bacteria affixed to the exterior of the *International Space Station* had survived for up to three years. The bacteria's longevity suggests that it might be able to survive the journey to Mars – and with it, the possibility of life having been carried between planets.

The **most radiation-resistant lifeform** is the related *D. radiodurans*. It can survive 15,000 Sieverts of gamma radiation, 3,000 times that required to kill a human.

### Largest merger of black holes detected by gravitational waves

On 21 May 2019, the Laser Interferometer Gravitational-wave Observatory and the Virgo detector identified a gravitational wave caused by the merger of two black holes some 17 billion light years from Earth. This event, subsequently named GW190521, appeared to have been marked by a bright flash of light. The black holes had a solar mass of 85 and 66 – i.e., had a mass 85 and 66 times that of the Sun. The findings were published on 2 Sep 2020.

### Cleanest manufactured objects

Sample return tubes loaded on to NASA's *Perseverance* Mars rover (see p.138) were put through a series of cleaning processes that reduced the quantity of organic compounds within them to no more than 150 nanograms per tube. By way of comparison, a single human thumbprint leaves 45,000 nanograms of organic material on a surface. With no contamination from Earth, scientists can be sure that any signs of life they detect really originated on Mars.

### First 3D-printed heart using human tissue

In Apr 2019, researchers at Tel Aviv University (ISR) created a miniature cellular heart from a patient's tissue. This tissue was processed into a "bio-ink" that was fed into a 3D printer and used to build an organ complete with blood vessels, ventricles and chambers – although it was not yet able to pump. The project leader, Professor Tal Dvir, believes that one day this technology could be used to produce a full-size functional human heart, with potentially life-changing consequences for patients awaiting heart transplants.

**100%**

### Finest woven fabric

Scientists at the University of Manchester (UK) produced a molecular woven fabric with 7.7 million strands per cm², as verified on 1 Jul 2020. The previous highest concentration of strands was thought to be finest Egyptian linen, with around 230 per cm². By using metal atoms and negatively charged ions, the team were able to weave together small molecular building blocks made of carbon, hydrogen, oxygen, nitrogen and sulphur atoms. Each layer of the molecular fabric is four nanometres thick – 10,000 times thinner than a human hair. These microscopic-scale fabrics are extremely strong and could be used as an ultra-fine filter or net.

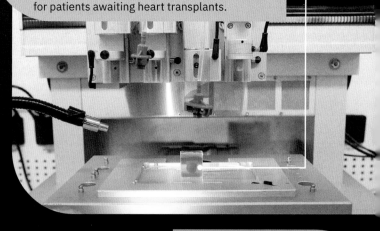

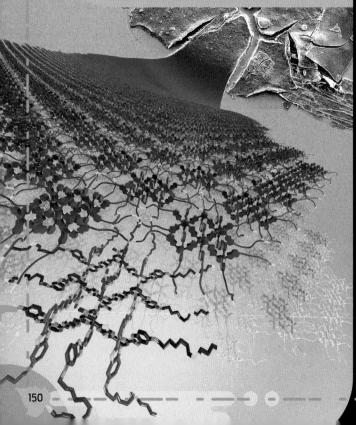

### First picture of photons in quantum entanglement (QE)

Described by Albert Einstein as "spooky", QE is a phenomenon in which two particles remain able to affect one another despite the physical distance between them. Although QE now forms the basis for quantum computing, it was not until Jul 2019 that scientists from the University of Glasgow (UK) were able to capture it using a super-sensitive photon camera. They illuminated a crystal with an ultraviolet laser, splitting photons of light and photographing their ensuing entanglement.

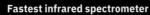

## First all-female Nobel Prize collaboration

Jennifer Doudna (USA, right) and Emmanuelle Charpentier (FRA, left) were awarded the 2020 Nobel Prize in Chemistry, as announced by The Royal Swedish Academy of Sciences on 7 Oct. The pair developed a technique known as CRISPR-Cas9 – often called "genetic scissors" – that can cut or overwrite sections of genetic code, making new medical treatments possible. To date, there have been 962 recipients of a Nobel Prize, but only 57 have been women.

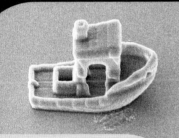

## Smallest boat

On 30 Oct 2020, a vessel measuring 11.5 micrometres (0.0004 in) – small enough to sail inside a human hair – set out on its maiden voyage. A reproduction of "Benchy the Tugboat", a model used to test 3D printers, it was made by a team at Leiden University (NLD) via a process called two-photon polymerization. The tiny ship propels itself with a platinum patch that reacts with a small quantity of hydrogen peroxide.

## Fastest infrared spectrometer

Infrared (IR) spectrometry is used for everything from analysing the gases that cause climate change to ensuring that food is safe to eat. It works by looking at the way wavelengths of IR light are affected by the medium they are measuring. Researchers at the Institute for Photon Science and Technology in Tokyo, Japan, have created an infrared spectrometer capable of sampling at 80 million spectra (light waves) per second. They used a quantum cascade detector to "slow down" laser pulses as they came from the sample material. Substances that would have once taken two years to analyse can now be processed in a single second.

## Smallest ultrasound detector

In Sep 2020, researchers at Helmholtz Zentrum München and the Technical University of Munich (both DEU) unveiled a blood-cell-sized device named the silicon waveguide-etalon detector (SWED). It uses miniaturized photonic circuits that sit on a silicon chip only 0.5 micrometers (0.000019 in) wide. Two-hundred of these chips in a row would still only span the thickness of a sheet of printer paper. Large arrays of these detectors could be used, for example, to make extremely detailed scans of internal organs before surgery.

## First battery-free handheld console

The Energy Aware Gaming Platform (ENGAGE) is powered by solar panels and the energy generated when users press buttons (piezoelectricity). It also makes use of a technique called intermittent computing to keep power usage low. ENGAGE was created by a team from Northwestern University (USA) and the Delft University of Technology (NLD). In future, these technologies could be used in situations where battery storage is impractical or power is very limited.

The Hero Arm has a selection of 3D-printed "skins", such as the official Frozen cover sported here by Evie Lambert.

## First medically certified 3D-printed bionic arm

The "Hero Arm", created by Open Bionics (UK) in 2018, is a lightweight prosthesis that can fit children as young as eight years old. Each arm is custom-built, using 3D-scanning and printing technology, and can reportedly lift up to 8 kg (17 lb). A motor that moves the fingers is controlled by muscles on the residual limb. Pictured is Cameron Millar, who was born without a right hand. He had his Hero Arm fitted with an official *Star Wars* cover. "I feel a lot like Luke Skywalker," Cameron said afterwards, "because he has a bionic hand too."

# Round-Up

### Highest-resolution satellite map of a planetary body
Published on 26 Feb 2020, the Bennu Global Mosaic shows the asteroid 101955 Bennu at a resolution of 5 cm (2 in) per pixel. This map was stitched together from 2,155 photos taken by the PolyCam instrument on NASA's *OSIRIS-REx* spacecraft between 7 Mar and 19 Apr 2019. This level of detail was achieved by keeping the spacecraft in an extremely low orbit.

### Largest map of the Milky Way
On 3 Dec 2020, the European Space Agency's Gaia Space Observatory published data of 1.811 billion mapped stars in our galaxy. Gaia's aim is to create a 3D map of the Milky Way, with the positional and radial velocities of the stars measured with unparalleled accuracy. Incredibly, 1 billion stars only accounts for *c.* 1% of those in the galaxy.

### Highest voltage from a potato battery
Universe Science Park (DNK) produced 1,950 volts from 300 kg (660 lb) of potatoes. The battery was wired together in Nordborg, Denmark, on 18 Oct 2020 to celebrate the 200-year anniversary of the discovery of electromagnetism by Danish scientist Hans Christian Ørsted. Potatoes contain phosphoric acid, which reacts when in contact with zinc to release electrons.

### Most missions flown by a rocket first stage
SpaceX Falcon 9 booster B1051 flew 10 missions between 2 Mar 2019 and 9 May 2021. In total, B1051 has launched around 130 tonnes (143 tons) of satellite equipment into Earth orbit, including a set of Canadian radar satellites, a Sirius XM broadcast satellite and 417 Starlink satellites. Just 56 days elapsed between its ninth and tenth missions.

On 24 Jan 2021, SpaceX's Transporter-1 mission lifted off from Cape Canaveral Space Force Station in Florida, USA. Its payload included the **most satellites launched on a single rocket** – 143. The flight is the first of many planned missions in SpaceX's Smallsat Rideshare Program, which is designed to offer a cheap ride to space for operators of small satellite payloads.

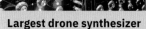

### Largest drone synthesizer
The KiloDrone consists of 1,000 analogue oscillators mixed together into a single output, tuned to play the same musical note. The mind-melting synth was built during the 2020 lockdown by LOOK MUM NO COMPUTER, aka Sam Battle (UK), in Ramsgate, Kent, UK, and verified on 25 Sep 2020.

### Longest fungal mycelium boat
Student Katy Ayers (USA) grew a 2.30-m (7-ft 6-in) canoe – christened *Myconoe* – from mycelium, the subterranean root-like part of a mushroom, as verified on 6 Sep 2019 in Grand Island, Nebraska, USA. The boat is still alive, and sprouts mushrooms every time it is taken out on the water. Ayers – who describes mushrooms as the "biggest ally for helping the environment" – was assisted by Ashley Gordon.

**100%**

### Largest soil sample returned from an asteroid
On 6 Dec 2020, personnel from the Japan Aerospace Exploration Agency (JAXA) travelled to Woomera in Australia to retreive a capsule that had been dropped from orbit by the *Hayabusa2* probe. Inside was a 5.4-g (0.19-oz) sample of asteroid 162173 Ryugu, then located *c.* 30 million km (18.6 million mi) from Earth. Having dropped off its cargo, *Hayabusa2* is now using its remaining propellant to conduct flybys of other asteroids.

### Largest projected videogame display
To celebrate the launch of *Destiny 2: Beyond Light*, Xbox Series X (USA) had the latest expansion to Bungie's long-running sci-fi shooter projected on to the side of Copper Mountain in Frisco, Colorado, USA. *Beyond Light* is set on Jupiter's ice moon Europa, so the snowy setting was appropriate. The projection covered an area of 1,773.6 m² (19,090 sq ft) and was played by snowboarder Grant Giller on 23 Nov 2020.

### First canine AR goggles
Military dogs can play a key role during conflict, using their enhanced sense of smell to detect explosives and other hazards. In Oct 2020, Command Sight (USA) unveiled a pair of dog-friendly augmented-reality goggles – nicknamed "Rex Specs" – that are enhanced with a remote camera and visual indicators that the dog can be trained to recognise. Instructors can now see what their dog sees, enabling them to direct their canine charges when they are out of sight.

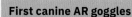

### ▶ Tallest building demolished in a controlled explosion

On 27 Nov 2020, Modon Properties (UAE) brought down Meena Plaza – four reinforced concrete buildings topping out at 165.03 m (541 ft 5 in) – in Abu Dhabi, UAE. The dramatic scene, lasting only 10 sec, was initiated by a detonating cord fitted with 3,000 delay detonators and 915 kg (2,017 lb) of explosives. This record was last broken more than 22 years ago.

### Longest digitally printed photograph

On 26 Sep 2020, a picture measuring 109.04 m (357 ft 8 in) was unfurled down the Schattenberg Ski Jump in Oberstdorf, Germany. It featured famous figures from the municipality and took 16 hr to print. It was the work of Canon Deutschland, Oberstdorf Tourismus, Oberstdorfer Fotogipfel and Ilford Imaging Europe (all DEU).

### Longest mobility scooter

Father and son Roy and Luke Finch (both UK) spent six weeks constructing a 3.10-m (10-ft 2-in) working mobility scooter, as verified on 26 Jul 2020 in London, UK. They used mostly free parts that other people had thrown away, so the project cost less than £100 ($127).

### First 3D-printed tortoise shell

In 2016, a Brazilian tortoise named Fred was found by the Animal Avengers volunteer group having lost about 85% of her shell following a forest fire. A replacement shell was designed using photos of healthy tortoises and printed out in four separate sections of corn-based plastic. An artist then painted the exterior of her shell so that it appeared more natural. The Animal Avengers have also 3D printed prosthetic beaks for injured birds such as toucans.

### ▶ First retractable proto-lightsaber

The Hacksmith, aka inventor James Hobson, and designer Bogdan Malynovskyy (both CAN) turned science fiction into science fact by creating the closest thing yet to the iconic *Star Wars* weapon on 8 Sep 2020 in Kitchener, Ontario, Canada. Hobson mixed compressed liquid propane gas with oxygen to create a brilliant jet of flame that burned at around 4,000°F (2,200°C) and was capable of cutting through titanium.

### Strongest supersonic parachute

The SR03 parachute, built by Airborne Systems (USA), withstood a peak load of 67,336 lbf (299.52 kN) at Mach 1.85 during atmospheric testing on 7 Sep 2018. Developed for NASA's Mars 2020 *Perseverance* rover (see p.138), it was made from materials such as nylon, Kevlar and Technora. On release, it expanded from a dense cylinder of folded fabric to a 21.5-m-wide (70-ft) canopy in just 0.4 sec.

### Highest launch from a Galilean cannon

The Italian astronomer Galileo proposed that dropping a stack of balls arranged in decreasing order of weight would see the topmost and lightest ball rebounding higher than the height from which it was dropped. A modern version of this "Galilean cannon" reached a height of 13.08 m (42 ft 10 in) on 6 Mar 2020 in Chapel Hill, North Carolina, USA. The "launch" was organized by the North Carolina Science Festival, UNC-Chapel Hill Department of Physics and Astronomy, and the University of North Carolina (all USA).

### Longest line of sight on Earth photographed

On 13 Jul 2016, Mark Bret Gumà (ESP) took a picture of Pic Gaspard, near the France–Italy border, from the summit of Pic de Finestrelles in the Pyrenees mountains, on the France–Spain border – 443 km (275 mi) away. The photo was taken using a Panasonic Lumix FZ72, following lengthy preparations to select the optimal date, time and location.

### Most overall wins of the Formula Student competition

Organized by the UK's Institution of Mechanical Engineers, Formula Student challenges university teams to design, build and run a single-seater race car. It held its first race in 1999. Rennteam Uni Stuttgart (DEU) has won the overall classification (which combines scores in both static and dynamic events) four times: in 2008, 2009, 2011 and 2016.

# Peggy Whitson

**D**uring a long and distinguished career at NASA, this experienced biochemist and astronaut racked up a string of GWR titles to go with her sterling scientific achievements.

Having grown up on a farm in Iowa, Peggy joined NASA's Johnson Space Center in Houston, Texas, USA, in 1986, going on to become project scientist for the Shuttle-*Mir* programme. Rising through NASA's ranks, by 2005 she was training as back-up commander for the *International Space Station (ISS)*, and four years later she'd become chief of the Astronaut Corps, organizing preparation and support for *ISS* crews. Peggy first flew to the *ISS* herself on 5 Jun 2002 with the Expedition 5 crew, becoming the space station's first NASA science officer. She conducted experiments into microgravity and human life sciences and made her first spacewalk, or extravehicular activity (EVA).

On 10 Oct 2007, with the lift-off of Expedition 16, she became the **first female commander of the *ISS*.** She held the post until 17 Apr 2008, resuming it on 9 Apr 2017 for Expedition 51, her last trip to the *ISS*. Six weeks later, on 23 May 2017, she made her tenth EVA, still the **most spacewalks by a female.**

Peggy retired from NASA in 2018. It's a mark of her stature that *TIME* magazine included this pioneering and inspirational figure in its annual list of the 100 most influential people.

**VITAL STATISTICS**
**Name:** Peggy Annette Whitson
**Born:** 9 Feb 1960
**Birthplace:** Mount Ayr, Iowa, USA
**Occupation:** Biochemist, astronaut, research scientist
**Joined NASA:** 1986
**Spacewalks completed:** 10 (60 hr 21 min)
**Total time in space:** 665 days 22 hr 22 min
**ISS command:** 19 Oct 2007–17 Apr 2008; 9 Apr–1 Jun 2017

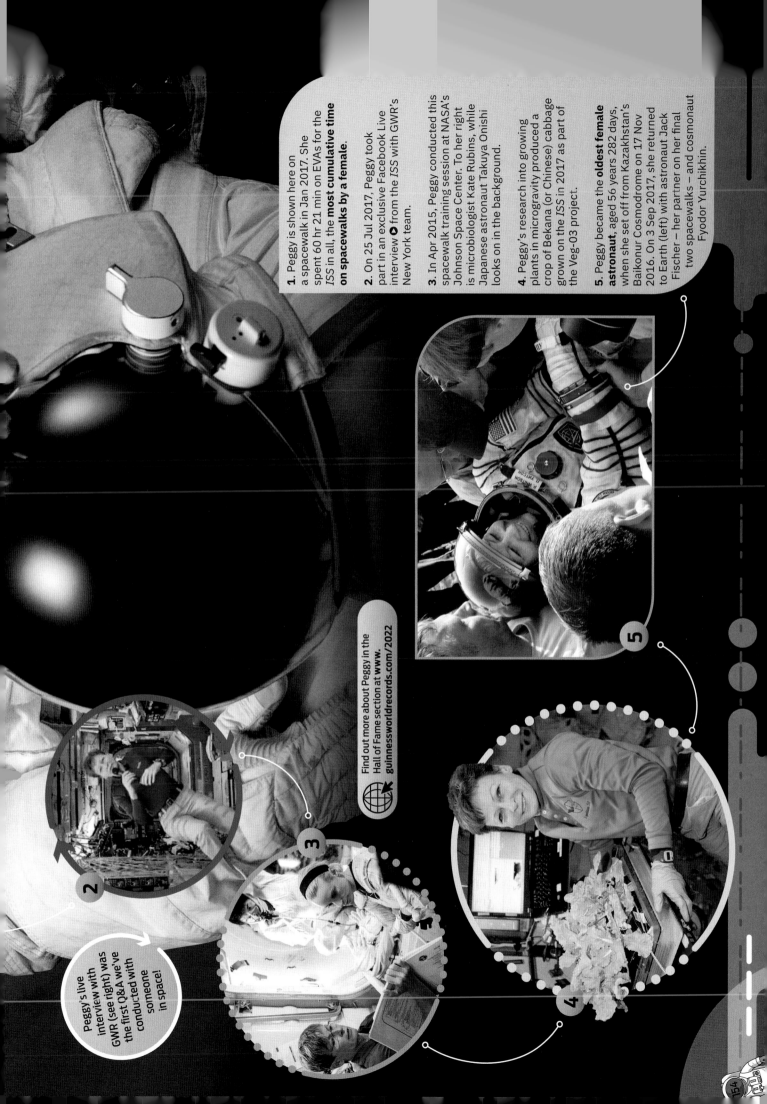

**1.** Peggy is shown here on a spacewalk in Jan 2017. She spent 60 hr 21 min on EVAs for the *ISS* in all, the **most cumulative time on spacewalks by a female.**

**2.** On 25 Jul 2017, Peggy took part in an exclusive Facebook Live interview ⊙ from the *ISS* with GWR's New York team.

**3.** In Apr 2015, Peggy conducted this spacewalk training session at NASA's Johnson Space Center. To her right is microbiologist Kate Rubins, while Japanese astronaut Takuya Onishi looks on in the background.

**4.** Peggy's research into growing plants in microgravity produced a crop of Bekana (or Chinese) cabbage grown on the *ISS* in 2017 as part of the Veg-03 project.

**5.** Peggy became the **oldest female astronaut,** aged 56 years 282 days, when she set off from Kazakhstan's Baikonur Cosmodrome on 17 Nov 2016. On 3 Sep 2017, she returned to Earth (left) with astronaut Jack Fischer – her partner on her final two spacewalks – and cosmonaut Fyodor Yurchikhin.

Find out more about Peggy in the Hall of Fame section at www.guinnessworldrecords.com/2022

Peggy's live interview with GWR (see right) was the first Q&A we've conducted with someone in space!

# Royal Tyrrell Museum

**S**ituated in the heart of the Canadian badlands – a natural treasure trove for dinosaur hunters – the Royal Tyrrell Museum of Palaeontology has amassed a world-renowned collection of fossils from all manner of ancient animals.

On 12 Aug 1884, a young geologist named Joseph Tyrrell stumbled across the skull of a carnivorous dinosaur in the rocky wilderness of southern Alberta. His 70-million-year-old find was the first recorded specimen of *Albertosaurus sarcophagus* ("flesh-eating lizard from Alberta"). A century later, in 1985, the Tyrrell Museum of Palaeontology opened its doors bearing Joseph's name. In 1990, Queen Elizabeth II bestowed the "royal" appellation on the institution.

The terrain surrounding the museum is dry and sparse, and extensively eroded; however, it is a hotbed for the remains of long-extinct species. Thousands of cubic metres of soil, gravel and bedrock are excavated in Alberta every year, and the museum works closely with industry to protect any palaeontological sites, as

well as conducting many of its own research digs, often leading to ground-breaking discoveries. One such find, unearthed in the 1990s, is a "mass-death assemblage" of between 12 and 24 tyrannosaurs in the nearby Dry Island Buffalo Jump Provincial Park – the **largest tyrannosaur bonebed.**

Today, the Royal Tyrrell Museum's comprehensive collection of fossils and geological specimens includes more than 350 holotypes, which define the name and characteristics of a species. Visitors can get up-close with the beasts of the prehistoric world, or at least as close as they dare...

**Location:** 1500 N Dinosaur Trail, Drumheller, Alberta, Canada

**Opened:** 25 Sep 1985

**Area:** c. 12,500 m² (135,000 sq ft)

**Catalogued fossils:** 170,000

**Permanently displayed fossils:** c. 800

**Annual visitors:** 430,000

*Semi-digested ferns found in stomach*

*Bony spines*

*Head*

**Best-preserved armoured dinosaur**
In 2011, a specimen of *Borealopelta markmitchelli* was uncovered in an oil sands mine still in its 3D form, with a covering of soft tissue comprising skin and keratinous scales. It's so well preserved that the remnants of its last meal remain in its stomach! Nodosaurs such as *Borealopelta* were closely related to the better-known *Ankylosaurus* (see p.41) – the **largest armoured dinosaur** (see p.41) – though they lacked the latter's famous clubbed tail.

*Body*

*Skull*

**Largest marine reptile ever**
The holotype specimen of *Shonisaurus sikanniensis* at the museum (right, with curator Dr Don Brinkman) is 21 m (69 ft) long – more than a bowling alley lane! *S. sikanniensis* belonged to the Shastasauridae family of Triassic marine reptiles called ichthyosaurs. In 2018, there were reports of a potentially even longer ichthyosaur – 26 m (85 ft) – but as this was based on a partial jaw bone, it remains a matter of debate.

**Most complete ornithomimid**
Ornithomimids are sometimes referred to as "ostrich dinosaurs", owing to their long necks, powerful legs and pointed beaks. This specimen of *Ornithomimus*, discovered on 12 Jul 1995, is nearly 100% complete, missing only some finger bones. Quill knobs on its arms suggest it had feathers. It was found in the classic theropod "death pose" – the head and tail thrown back over the body and limbs pulled in.

*Elongated neck*

*Quill knobs to which feathers attached*

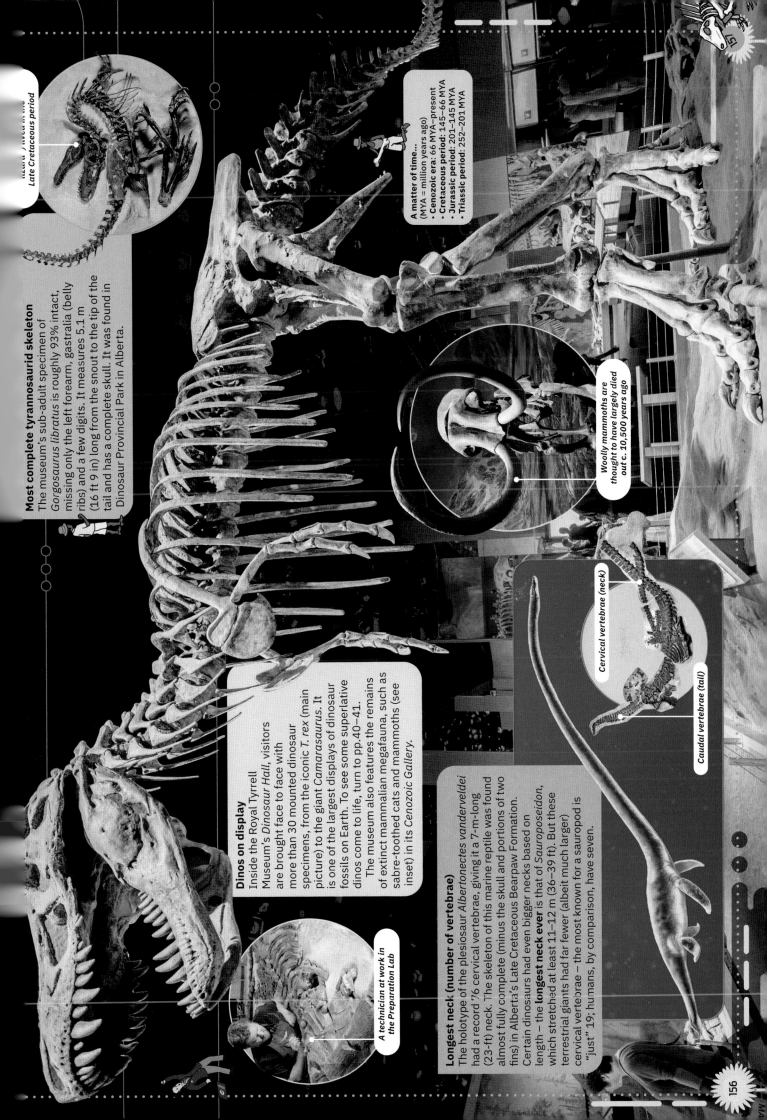

**Most complete tyrannosaurid skeleton**
The museum's sub-adult specimen of *Gorgosaurus libratus* is roughly 93% intact, missing only the left forearm, gastralia (belly ribs), and a few digits. It measures 5.1 m (16 ft 9 in) long from the snout to the tip of the tail and has a complete skull. It was found in Dinosaur Provincial Park in Alberta.

**A matter of time...**
(MYA = million years ago)
• **Cenozoic era:** 66 MYA–present
• **Cretaceous period:** 145–66 MYA
• **Jurassic period:** 201–145 MYA
• **Triassic period:** 252–201 MYA

*Woolly mammoths are thought to have largely died out c. 10,500 years ago*

*Cervical vertebrae (neck)*

*Caudal vertebrae (tail)*

**Dinos on display**
Inside the Royal Tyrrell Museum's *Dinosaur Hall*, visitors are brought face to face with more than 30 mounted dinosaur specimens, from the iconic *T. rex* (main picture) to the giant *Camarasaurus*. It is one of the largest displays of dinosaur fossils on Earth. To see some superlative dinos come to life, turn to pp.40–41.

The museum also features the remains of extinct mammalian megafauna, such as sabre-toothed cats and mammoths (see inset) in its *Cenozoic Gallery*.

**Longest neck: (number of vertebrae)**
The holotype of the plesiosaur *Albertonectes vanderveldei* had a record 76 cervical vertebrae, giving it a 7-m-long (23-ft) neck. The skeleton of this marine reptile was found almost fully complete (minus the skull and portions of two fins) in Alberta's Late Cretaceous Bearpaw Formation. Certain dinosaurs had even bigger necks based on length – the **longest neck ever** is that of *Sauroposeidon*, which stretched at least 11–12 m (36–39 ft). But these terrestrial giants had far fewer (albeit much larger) cervical vertebrae – the most known for a sauropod is "just" 19; humans, by comparison, have seven.

*A technician at work in the Preparation Lab*

# Society

**Most votes cast for a US presidential candidate**

Joseph Robinette Biden Jr (USA) received 81,281,502 votes in the 2020 US presidential election, according to the non-partisan *Cook Political Report*. This was 7 million votes more than his rival, Donald Trump. A bitter and divisive election drew a high turnout, with both candidates exceeding the previous high of 69 million votes, recorded by Barack Obama in 2008. Democrat Biden secured a decisive victory in the electoral college by 306 votes to 232.

Biden was joined on the ticket by trailblazing Californian senator Kamala Harris, who became the **first female**, **first Black** and **first South-Asian American US vice-president**.

OFFICE OF THE

PRESIDEN

## CONTENTS

Joe Biden (b. 20 Nov 1942) assumed office on 20 Jan 2021, aged 78 years 61 days. He is the **oldest US president.**

# Crime & Punishment

SOCIETY

### Greatest investment fraud

For at least two decades, US financier Bernie Madoff – the founder of an investment firm – took the principal invested by customers of his company's asset management division and deposited it in a personal bank account. By the time he was arrested on 11 Dec 2008, a total of $19 bn (£12.8 bn) had been paid in by 4,800 investors. The return on investment that his customers saw in their statements was entirely fabricated.

### First...

**Forensic autopsy:** In 1302, Italian physician Bartolomeo da Varignana performed a medico-legal autopsy following the suspected poisoning of nobleman Azzolino degli Onesti. Bartolomeo was later involved in several other autopsies.

**Country to abolish the death penalty:** Venezuela struck the death sentence from law in 1863, during the presidency of Juan Crisóstomo Falcón.

**Speeding fine:** On 28 Jan 1896, Walter Arnold (UK) drove his "horse-less carriage" through the village of Paddock Wood in Kent, UK, at 8 mph (13 km/h) – more than four times the speed limit. He was caught by a police officer on a bicycle and fined £4 and 7 shillings (about £260, or $350, today) on four separate counts; 10 shillings was for the speeding charge.

**Hijack of a commercial airliner:** On 25 Jul 1947, a group of disaffected army officers "skyjacked" a scheduled flight from Bucharest, Romania. When the flight engineer resisted, he was shot dead. The plane touched down in the city of Çanakkale in Turkey, where the hijackers were arrested. Their leader, Lieutenant Aurel Dobrea, was later tried and convicted of murder.

### Richest crime syndicate

The Solntsevskaya Bratva (aka the Russian Mafia) is an organized crime syndicate that began in the late 1980s in the Solntsevo district of Moscow. In 2014, *Fortune* magazine estimated that the Bratva had an annual revenue of $8.5 bn (£5.4 bn).

### Largest merchant ship to be hijacked

On 15 Nov 2008, pirates captured MV *Sirius Star* (UAE) off the coast of Somalia. The ship is around 330 m (1,100 ft) long with a gross tonnage of 162,252, and was carrying crude oil valued at $110 m (£74.2 m). It was released on 9 Jan 2009, reportedly for a ransom of $3 m (£1.98 m).

### Greatest banknote forgery

During WWII, the German officer Bernhard Krüger ran a forging operation, codenamed "Operation Bernhard", aimed at destabilizing the British economy. It involved more than 9 million fake British banknotes valued at £130 m ($520 m), in denominations of £5, £10, £20 and £50. They were produced by 140 Jewish prisoners at the Sachsenhausen concentration camp.

### Most frequently stolen painting

The *Ghent Altarpiece* – aka the *Adoration of the Mystic Lamb* – is a large early-15th-century Flemish painting completed by Hubert van Eyck and his younger brother, Jan. It has been stolen seven times, including thefts by invading French and German forces. In 1934, two of its 12 original panels were stolen; only one was ever traced.

### Longest criminal trial

The McMartin Preschool Trial was a case brought against the staff of a preschool in Manhattan Beach, California, USA, who were accused of running a satanic child sexual-abuse network. The trial ran for 919 days, from 14 Jul 1987 to 18 Jan 1990. The jury acquitted one defendant (Virginia McMartin) on all counts and deadlocked on the other (Ray Buckley), who was later also cleared. All charges were dropped.

### Largest art robbery

Thirteen objects worth some $500 m (£308 m) were stolen from the Isabella Stewart Gardner Museum in Boston, Massachusetts, USA, on 18 Mar 1990. They included Rembrandt's 1633 painting *The Storm on the Sea of Galilee* (above). Two men dressed as police officers (sketches inset) were buzzed into the guardroom during the night shift, then overpowered the guards. There have been no convictions and the works are still missing.

SEEKING INFORMATION

$5 Million Reward

## Oldest convicted bank robber

J L Hunter Rountree (USA, b. 16 Dec 1911) was sentenced to 151 months in prison on 23 Jan 2004 at the age of 92 years 38 days. He had stolen $1,999 (£1,243) from a bank in Texas, USA, on 12 Aug 2003. Rountree robbed his first bank some 12 years earlier. In an interview in 2001 he revealed, "A Corpus Christi [Texas] bank that I'd done business with had forced me into bankruptcy. I have never liked banks since." He added that the food in prison was better than in some nursing homes.

## Shortest jury deliberation

Nicholas Clive McAllister (NZ) was acquitted of cultivating cannabis plants at a hearing that lasted just one minute at Greymouth District Court in West Coast, New Zealand, on 22 Jul 2004.

## Largest mafia trial

A total of 474 people were formally charged in a trial of mafia suspects in Palermo, Sicily, Italy, beginning on 10 Feb 1986. In all, 426 of them were found guilty and 19 were sentenced to detention in perpetuity.

## Greatest jewel heist

On 28 Jul 2013, an armed man entered the Carlton International hotel in Cannes, France, and in 90 seconds stole diamond-encrusted rings, earrings and watches worth $137 m (£89 m). They were on show at the hotel. In 2019, royal jewellery thought to have an even higher value was taken from the Green Vault museum in Dresden, Germany, but its worth has never been officially confirmed.

## Greatest train robbery

Between 3:03 a.m. and 3:27 a.m. on 8 Aug 1963, a General Post Office mail train from Glasgow was ambushed at Sears Crossing and robbed at Bridego Bridge in Buckinghamshire, UK. A gang stole 120 mailbags containing £2,631,784 ($7,369,784) in banknotes en route to London to be destroyed. Just £343,448 ($961,978) was recovered. The haul would be worth more than £56.3 m ($77.2 m) today.

## Largest prison by population

The Silivri Penitentiaries Campus, or Silivri Prison, is in the north-west suburbs of Istanbul, Turkey. A Turkish parliamentary investigation in Nov 2019 found that the population had doubled to 22,781 – twice its intended capacity.

## Most life sentences

Terry Lynn Nichols (USA, inset) helped terrorist Timothy McVeigh plan the bombing of a federal building in Oklahoma, USA, on 19 Apr 1995. In all, 168 people were killed. Following two trials, McVeigh was sentenced to be executed by lethal injection and Nichols was convicted on 161 counts of first-degree murder and sentenced to 161 consecutive life terms without the possibility of parole.

## Greatest bank robbery

On 11 Jul 2007, the Dar es Salaam Investment Bank in Baghdad, Iraq, was robbed. The thieves made off with $282 m (£139.7 m) in US banknotes and 220 million Iraqi dinars (worth around $173,000, or £85,725, at the time). The theft was reportedly an inside job, with two or three (reports vary) of the bank's security staff involved. It is likely that the guards were either working for or with one of the sectarian militias active in Baghdad at the time. To date, no one has been charged.

## Largest prison farm

Covering 18,000 acres (7,300 ha), the Louisiana State Penitentiary is a working prison farm in the USA. It is surrounded on three sides by the Mississippi river. The farm has 2,000 head of cattle and produces around 4 million lb (1,814 tonnes) of vegetables every year. The facility is also the largest maximum-security prison in the country, with 5,489 inmates as of Jul 2020.

## First known use of a getaway car

On 14 Feb 1904, a group of robbers broke into the Collegiate Church of St Juliana in Santillana del Mar, Spain, and stole a huge haul of gold and silver church plate reportedly weighing 200 kg (440 lb). They made their escape in what was termed a "fast motor car"; the raid itself was described as "skilfully planned". Pictured right is an automobile of the period.

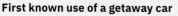

# Dogs

## Most tennis balls held in the mouth
Golden retriever Finley can carry six tennis balls in his mouth at once (one is obscured above), as verified on 23 Feb 2020 in Canandaigua, New York, USA. In an impressive act of oneup*dog*ship, this beat the mark of five balls set by a fellow retriever back in 2003. Finley is owned by Cheri and Rob Molloy (both USA), whose daughter, Erin, showcased his skill on Instagram.

## First domesticated animal
Fossil evidence suggests that Palaeolithic humans in east Asia had tamed dogs (*Canis lupus familiaris*) – by breeding aggression out of wolves (*C. lupus*) – at least 15,000 years ago. There is speculation it may have occurred earlier, though. In Jan 2021, a study in the journal *PNAS* postulated that Siberian hunters tamed wolves *c.* 23,000 years ago, while others still suggest as far back as 40,000 years.

## Most diverse mammal species
National canine associations worldwide acknowledge some 800 varieties of dogs, with The Kennel Club (UK) and the American Kennel Club recognizing 221 and 253 breeds, respectively. The smallest breed, Chihuahuas, usually stand 15–23 cm (6–9 in) to the shoulder; at the other end of the scale, Irish wolfhounds and great danes typically measure 90 cm (3 ft) tall.
The **tallest dog ever** was Zeus, a great dane that stood 111.8 cm (3 ft 8 in) to the shoulder on 4 Oct 2011. His owners were the Doorlag family of Michigan, USA.

## Oldest dog
As of 12 Nov 2020, miniature dachshund Funny (b. 27 May 1999) was the oldest living canine, aged 21 years 169 days. Her owner is Yoshiko Fujimura of Sakai, Osaka, Japan.
The **oldest dog ever** (to be reliably documented) was an Australian cattle-dog named Bluey, who lived for 29 years 5 months. Owned by Les Hall (AUS), the canine Methuselah was obtained as a puppy in 1910 and worked as a herder for nearly 20 years before he was put down in 1939.

## Crufts Dog Show
• **First Best in Show (BIS) winner**: The debut Crufts Dog Show – founded by British showman Charles Cruft – took place in 1891. However, the canine competition's coveted BIS title was not instigated until 1928. The inaugural BIS champion was Primley Sceptre, a fawn greyhound owned by Herbert Whitley (UK).
• **Most successful BIS breed**: English cocker spaniels have been BIS winners on seven occasions: in 1930–31, 1938–39, 1948, 1950 and 1996.

## Most tricks by two dogs in one minute
Border collies Wish and Halo performed 28 tricks in 60 sec with Emily Larlham (USA) in El Cajon, California, USA, on 22 Dec 2020. Emily is best known for her YouTube channel "Kikopup", where she posts videos on how to humanely train dogs without physical or psychological intimidation.
Earlier that month, Wish had also set the canine record for the **fastest 5 m crawl**: 2.175 sec.

## Fastest five wall runs
Daiquiri – an Australian shepherd – completed five wall runs in 9.24 sec under the stewardship of his owner, Jennifer Fraser (CAN), in Strathmore, Alberta, Canada, on 4 Oct 2020. This dynamic duo has notched up a rack of dog-gone amazing GWR titles (see below), all set in 2020.

| Daiquiri and Jennifer: roll of honour | |
| --- | --- |
| Fastest time to walk 30 m with a dog weaving through the legs | 13.55 sec |
| Fastest 30 m recall | 17.54 sec |
| Fastest time to walk 30 m with a dog's paws on the feet | 42.03 sec |
| Most toys retrieved in one minute | 15 |
| Most coins deposited into a piggy bank in one minute | 18 |
| Most weaves through the legs in 30 seconds | 37 |

• **Youngest BIS winner**: Owned by John T Barnard (UK), bulldog Noways Chuckles was aged 1 year 115 days when she took Crufts' top prize on 9 Feb 1952.
• **Oldest BIS winner**: A flat-coated retriever named Vbos the Kentuckian (aka Jet) was 9 years 195 days old when he triumphed on 13 Mar 2011. He was owned by Jim Irvine (UK).

## Most Instagram followers
Jiff the Pomeranian, aka Jiffpom, had 10,289,624 fans as of 22 Apr 2021. His feed features snapshots of him in various outfits, relaxing at home and attending red-carpet events such as movie premieres.

It may be in the genes... Lou (left and right) is distantly related to the previous record holder, a coonhound named Harbor.

## Longest ears on a dog
The ears of a black-and-tan coonhound named Lou, owned by Paige Olsen (USA), were each 34 cm (1 ft 1.3 in) long when measured on 30 Jul 2020 in Milwaukie, Oregon, USA. Her lengthy lobes are marginally shorter than the **longest ears on a dog ever**: a bloodhound named Tigger had a 34.9-cm (1-ft 1.7-in) right ear and a 34.2-cm (1-ft 1.5-in) left ear when checked on 29 Sep 2004. He was owned by Bryan and Christina Flessner of Illinois, USA.

## Farewell to Freddy
In Jan 2021, GWR bade a sad goodbye to Freddy, once the **tallest living dog**. Our condolences go to his owner, Claire Stoneman (UK). The giant great dane stood 103.5 cm (3 ft 4.75 in) to his withers (the ridge between the shoulder blades), as verified in Leigh-on-Sea, Essex, UK, on 13 Sep 2016. If you have a colossal canine who might be a contender, GWR is currently seeking a new holder.

## Most consecutive items caught
Sasha, an American Staffordshire terrier, deftly snaffled 10 snacks in a row, thrown from 3 m (9 ft 10 in) away by her owner Rocco Mercurio (ITA), in Villa San Giovanni, Italy, on 8 Jan 2021. A few weeks later, on 1 Feb, the dogged duo also registered the **fastest time to catch 10 items**: 9.69 sec.

## Fastest 5 m on a scooter by a dog and cat
Not *all* dogs and cats are adversaries, as proven on 19 Sep 2020 by Boston terrier Lollipop and his feline friend Sashimi, who scooted 5 m in 4.73 sec in Sparta, Ontario, Canada. Their owner is Melissa Millett (CAN; see below), who trains animals for film and TV.

The same day, Melissa's red heeler Jellybean (left) set the **fastest 5 m pushing a basketball** – 10.31 sec – and **most basketball bounces between a human and dog in 30 seconds** – 21.

*Melissa told us that deaf canine actors are at an advantage on set, as strange sounds or raised voices do not worry them.*

## Most expensive sheepdog
A one-year-old female red-and-white border collie called Kim commanded £28,455 ($38,893; including buyer's premium) at an online auction conducted by Farmers Marts in Dolgellau, Gwynedd, UK, on 3 Feb 2021. Kim was reared by Welsh farmer and sheepdog triallist Dewi Jenkins and purchased by Eamonn Vaughan (both UK).

## Fastest 5 m run backwards
Trained by Ana Odak (HRV), a border collie named Kota took just 2.42 sec to cover 5 m (16 ft 4 in) in reverse in Zagreb, Croatia, on 10 Jun 2020. Kota also works as a therapy dog, entertaining children and elderly people with her tricks.

## Most times to catch a flying disc over 5 m in three minutes
On 13 Jul 2013, border collie Rhino caught 24 flying discs thrown by his owner Tarkan Özvardar (TUR) – founder of the Ankara Canine College. The feat took place on the set of *Rekorlar Dünyası* in Istanbul, Turkey.

The **10 m** record is 20, by Oro and his owner Zachary Schultz (USA) in Minot, North Dakota, USA, on 8 Oct 2017.

### REIGNING CATS AND DOGS

Melissa Millett talks about her passion for training pets for acting roles, as well as the rewards and challenges of working with hard-of-hearing hounds.

**How difficult is it to train deaf dogs?**
Lollipop was really easy as a puppy, which inspired me to adopt another deaf dog. But Jellybean was high energy with some issues, such as obsessive shadow chasing and separation anxiety. The mental stimulation of work and learning tricks really helped him.

**How did you get your canine-feline scooter dream team to pair up?**
Lollipop and Sashimi love working together! They made up the scooter trick themselves when they were fighting for a turn! Often, the animals make up their own tricks.

**What was your most challenging showbiz job?**
Jellybean was in *Fractured* with Sam Worthington on Netflix. Mostly, I was behind or beside him. He was trained to react only to my body-language cues and was on a distracting set and outdoor location. But once cued to look at an actress, he didn't look back at me. We were so proud!

**How do you make work seem like play for your pets when training?**
Ensure that they have fun! Important factors include clear communication and working out which tricks match their personalities. Are they quiet thinkers? Athletes? Fearless on obstacles? And, of course, don't scrimp on the delicious treats – I pay well!

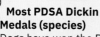

## Most PDSA Dickin Medals (species)
Dogs have won the People's Dispensary for Sick Animals' gallantry medal a record 35 times. The award has been bestowed 72 times in all (plus one honorary title) since its inception in 1943. Pictured is Kuno, the latest winner, on 24 Nov 2020. This brave Belgian Malinois sustained life-changing injuries in 2019, while serving with British forces, and now has two prosthetic paws.

# Royalty

### Oldest ruling house

The Yamato Dynasty – the Imperial House of Japan – has had a succession of 126 emperors who can trace their lineage back to the country's first head of state. Japan's current emperor, Naruhito, is a descendant of Jimmu Tenno, whose reign is traditionally dated 660–581 BCE, but was more probably c. 40–10 BCE.

### Youngest reigning monarch

King Oyo – aka Rukirabasaija Oyo Nyimba Kabamba Iguru Rukidi IV (b. 16 Apr 1992) – is the 28-year-old ruler of Toro, one of five Bantu kingdoms in Uganda, East Africa. He came to power at the age of three.

The **youngest reigning monarch of a sovereign country** is Sheikh Tamim bin Hamad al-Thani, Emir of Qatar (b. 3 Jun 1980). As of 29 Apr 2021, he is 40 years 330 days old. He became Qatar's ruler on 25 Jun 2013, aged 33 years 22 days, following the abdication of his father.

### Most valuable crown

The highlight of the British monarchy's crown jewels is St Edward's crown, made in 1661. Its solid 22-karat gold frame houses 444 precious or semi-precious stones, and it is considered priceless. In Oct 2019, however, research based on the International Gem Society's pricing guide valued each part and estimated its overall worth at $4,519,709 (£3.5 m).

### Most expensive royal wedding dress

On 22 May 2004, the future Queen Letizia of Spain wore a £6-m ($10.7-m) dress to marry the future King Felipe VI. It had a 4.5-m-long (14-ft 8-in) train and embroidery woven into the silk with gold thread.

### Most visited palace

The Forbidden City in Beijing, China, had more than 17 million visitors in 2018. Work on the site began in 1406, under Emperor Zhu Di, and lasted for 14 years, employing more than a million workers. Today, the Forbidden City covers 720,000 m² (180 acres) – larger than 100 soccer pitches – and includes 980 buildings.

### Longest reign in a sovereign state

Known as the "Sun King", Louis XIV of France enjoyed an uninterrupted rule of 72 years 110 days, from 14 May 1643 to 1 Sep 1715. His reign saw an era of unprecedented prosperity for his country. The **longest documented reign of any monarch** is that of Phiops II, a Sixth-Dynasty pharaoh of ancient Egypt. It began c. 2281 BCE, when he was six years of age, and is believed to have lasted for around 94 years.

### Tallest crown prince

Crown Prince Haakon of Norway stands 193 cm (6 ft 4 in) tall. He is the only child of King Harald V and Queen Sonja and became heir apparent when his father took the throne on 17 Jan 1991.

The previous holder of this title – 197-cm-tall (6-ft 5.5-in) Don Felipe de Borbón y Grecia – became the **tallest king** when he ascended the Spanish throne as Felipe VI on 19 Jun 2014.

### Most royals killed in a people's revolution

Between 1918 and 1919, a total of 15 members of the Russian Imperial Family were killed by the Bolsheviks during the Russian Revolution. They included Tsar Nicholas II, the Tsarina Alexandra and their five children, all of whom were assassinated at Yekaterinburg on 17 Jul 1918. Until Nicholas II's abdication in 1917, the House of Romanov had ruled Russia for 304 years.

The **most royals killed in an accident** is six. The wife, son, daughter-in-law and three grandchildren of Ernst Ludwig – brother of Tsarina Alexandra and the last

### Youngest queen consort

Born on 4 Jun 1990, Queen Jetsun Pema of Bhutan is the wife of the country's ruler, Jigme Khesar Namgyel Wangchuck and the youngest living queen consort. The couple married at Punakha Dzong on 13 Oct 2011, when she was aged 21 years 131 days. Polygamy is legal in Bhutan, but the king has vowed that he will never marry another woman.

### First Groom of the Stool

This official title evolved from that of Yoman (or Yeoman) of the Stool under England's Henry VI. Hugh Denys of Osterley (c. 1440–1511) was its earliest named holder, under Henry VII. Denys oversaw the king's toilet facilities and even monitored his bowel movements. However, the role later expanded, making him a close adviser to Henry, manager of the Privy Chamber and effectively the king's own treasurer. Shown is a "close stool" from c. 1650.

Hugh Denys (highlighted) appears in this scene of Henry VII on his deathbed in 1509. Denys's presence shows the Groom as a key player within the inner sanctum of the Tudor court.

Grand Duke of Hesse (reigned 1892–1918) – perished in a plane crash at Ostende, Belgium, on 16 Nov 1937. The Duke had died just a few weeks earlier from an illness.

### Longest-serving heir apparent
Britain's Prince Charles has been heir apparent for 69 years 82 days, as of 29 Apr 2021. He assumed the role on 6 Feb 1952, when his mother was crowned.

### Richest queen
In May 2020, the *Sunday Times* Rich List estimated the wealth of Queen Elizabeth II at £350 m ($430 m). Fine art, jewellery and property in England and Scotland account for just some of Her Majesty's personal wealth, which had actually diminished by £20 m ($24 m) since the previous year.

Elizabeth II owns more than a million works of art, the **largest private art collection**. Including some 7,000 paintings and *c.* 450,000 photographs, her collection is dispersed between 13 royal residences within the UK. Some items are owned by the Queen herself as an individual, while others are the property of the Crown.

### First monarch to catch COVID-19
On 19 Mar 2020, it was announced that Albert II, Prince of Monaco, had tested positive for COVID-19. While self-isolating, he continued to carry out his royal duties from within the confines of his private apartments in the palace. On 31 Mar, news broke of his full recovery, although he endured bouts of extreme fatigue for months afterwards.

### Richest monarch
King Maha Vajiralongkorn (aka Rama X) of Thailand enjoys an estimated personal wealth of at least $30 bn (£22.4 bn). The ruler's asset portfolio once belonged to the Thai crown – as an institution, rather than the sovereign. However, Vajiralongkorn was given control of the privy purse in 2018. He is also the owner of the 545.67-carat "Golden Jubilee Diamond", the **largest faceted diamond**.

### Longest-reigning monarch
Her Majesty Queen Elizabeth II – Queen of the UK and Head of the Commonwealth – succeeded to the throne upon the death of her father, King George VI, on 6 Feb 1952. As of 29 Apr 2021, she had reigned for 69 years 82 days. She is also the world's **oldest queen** and **monarch**, having celebrated her 95th birthday in 2021.

Elizabeth's husband, Prince Philip, the Duke of Edinburgh (UK, b. GRC, pictured below in 2017), was the **longest-serving consort of a monarch**. He sadly passed away on 9 Apr 2021 at the age of 99, after 69 years 62 days of service and more than 73 years of marriage.

### Most portrayed living monarch
Queen Elizabeth II has been depicted numerous times on stage and screen. Memorable portrayals among at least 60 TV shows, 63 movies and four plays include Helen Mirren's Oscar-winning turn in the movie *The Queen* (2006) – a role she reprised on stage in the Olivier-winning *The Audience* (2013) – and Olivia Colman in the TV drama *The Crown* (Netflix, 2016–present, above).

The Queen's image has appeared on the coinage of at least 33 nations, the **most currencies featuring the same individual**.

### Largest inhabited castle
The royal residence of Windsor Castle in Berkshire, UK, takes the form of a waisted parallelogram measuring 576 x 164 m (1,890 x 540 ft). Dating to the 11th century, the castle is sited on 13 acres (5 ha) of land.

The **largest inhabited-castle grounds** are at Balmoral in Royal Deeside, Aberdeenshire, UK. They include some 50,000 acres (20,230 ha) of land – an area larger than the countries of Liechtenstein and Monaco combined.

# Historical Gastronomy

The origins of many of our favourite foods are far from clear-cut. Archaeologists and historians continue to make fascinating – and sometimes contentious – discoveries about what our ancestors ate. Here, then, we present a smorgasbord of gastronomic relics (and firsts) for your delectation, based on the most recent research. Note: the sumptious buffet pictured does not illustrate the actual records; it's here merely to whet your appetite. *Bon appétit!*

## 1. Oldest cake

The Alimentarium Food Museum in Vevey, Switzerland, is home to a wheat cake dating from *c.* 2200 BCE. Found vacuum-sealed in a copper mould in the grave of Pepi'Onkh, who lived in ancient Egypt, its ingredients included sesame, honey and milk.

## 2. First commercial peanut butter

None of the origin stories for this spread are completely verifiable. The pre-Columbian peoples of Latin and South America, whose empires flourished between the 13th and 16th centuries, ground roasted peanuts into a basic paste. A patent for a commercial ground-peanut spread was filed in the USA by Canadian chemist Marcellus Gilmore Edson in 1884, although this, too, did not fully resemble the modern product. Cereal businessman John Harvey Kellogg (USA) also touted himself as its creator, filing two patents relating to the product and its manufacture on 4 Nov 1895.

## 3. Oldest bread

Archaeologists from the University of Copenhagen (DNK) found 14,400-year-old bread in Jordan's Black Desert. The recipe consists of flour made from wild wheat/barley and the dried pulp roots of aquatic plants. These were mixed with water to create a dough and then baked on hot stones. This discovery pushed back the earliest known bread by 5,000 years.

## 4. First "fair trade" coffee

In 1973, Fair Trade Original (NLD) imported the first fairly traded coffee from Guatemala, but the move to formally certify "fair trade" coffee began on 15 Nov 1988. On that date, Solidaridad – a Dutch Catholic aid organization working mainly in Latin America – created the Max Havelaar Foundation to benefit local farmers faced with plummeting world coffee prices.

## 5. First fermented food

Scientists long believed that fermentation as a means of preserving food originated in China, where rice, honey and fruit were fermented into alcohol (see #7). That theory was turned on its head by the discovery of a large deposit of fish bones in Blekinge, Sweden, in 2016. It provides evidence of food preservation by fermentation dating back to 7200 BCE, during the Mesolithic Stone Age.

## 6. First macaroni cheese

A recipe for pasta and cheese appeared in the *Liber de Coquina* ("The Book of Cookery"), an early 14th-century codex penned in Latin by an unknown scribe from the Neapolitan court. Fast-forward 400 years and a detailed recipe for macaroni and cheese featured in Elizabeth Raffald's 1769 cookbook, *The Experienced English Housekeeper*. In 1937, after the US food manufacturer Kraft debuted its still-popular Macaroni & Cheese Dinner, the dish became a kitchen-cupboard staple.

The **oldest solid cheese** residue dates from the 13th-century BCE tomb of Ptahmes, the mayor of the ancient Egyptian city of Memphis. Mass spectrometry was used to analyse a few milligrams of the sample, which revealed that it was a solid dairy product obtained by mixing the milk of cows with that of sheep or goats.

## 7. Oldest alcoholic beverage

Chemical evidence of an alcoholic drink dates back to *c.* 7,000 BCE, from pottery jars excavated at Jiahu, an early Neolithic village in the Yellow River Valley in Henan, China. The residues contained: tartaric acid (from grape and hawthorn fruit), beeswax compounds (from honey) and phytosterol ferulate esters (from rice). These telltale clues indicate the liquid in the vessels had been a cross between wine, mead and beer.

Over the following millennia, pottery vessels for storing alcohol were superseded by wooden barrels. The glass wine bottles with cork stoppers that we are more familiar with today didn't emerge until the 17th century. The **first documented corkscrew** is a French cage-style steel model from 1685. But long before then, corks were used to stopper bottles of cider and beer in England, and the earliest written reference to a corkscrew in English dates to 1681. Samuel Henshall, who was the rector at London's Bow Church, filed the first known patent for such a device in 1795 for the "Henshall button corkscrew".

## 8. First modern ice-cream maker

Historical gastronomy is not solely focused on recipes, but also culinary gadgets. Since ancient times, frozen ices and creams have been enjoyed by those wealthy enough to afford the laborious means of producing them. But in the mid-19th century, ice-cream finally became more affordable, thanks to a hand-cranked machine devised by Nancy Johnson (USA) in 1843. Unlike earlier models, her invention didn't have

to be constantly opened to be manually stirred; instead, an interior "dasher" churned the contents while a crank rotated the canister in a wooden tub, producing a uniformly smooth and creamy treat.

### 9. First hollow chocolate Easter eggs
In 1873, the first hollowed-out chocolate Easter eggs were produced by the British company Fry's, based in Bristol. The Easter treat really took off two years later, however, when rival firm Cadbury began filling their eggs with sugared almonds.

As for the **first chocolate**, since cacao featured prominently in the Olmec and Maya cultures of Mesoamerica, it has long been thought that its origins lie in Central America, *c.* 3,900 years ago. However, a 2018 study published in *Nature Ecology & Evolution* revealed evidence of early cacao processing from 5,300–5,450 years ago at the Amazonian site of Santa Ana-La Florida in Ecuador. This is the earliest known archaeological site belonging to the Mayo-Chinchipe Culture.

### 10. First modern waffle iron
While there's evidence from ancient Greece of metal tongs used to cook wafers over a fire, and long-handled Dutch examples dating to the 1300s, what we'd regard as a "waffle iron" today arrived in the mid-19th century. American inventor Cornelius Swartwout's patent (granted in 1869) transformed the centuries-old contraption used over an open flame into a compact, stove-top version. It was more practical and less likely to burn the waffles – or indeed the cook!

### 11. First popcorn
Evidence of popcorn has been radiocarbon-dated to some 6,700 years ago (*c.* 4700 BCE). Macrofossil corn cobs were unearthed between 2007 and 2011 at the Paredones and Huaca Prieta archaeological sites on Peru's northern coast. The dig's findings attest to the domestication of popcorn (*Zea mays everta*) by the 5th millennium BCE. Popped popcorn as a favourite snack really took off, however, when Charles Cretors introduced a mobile, steam-powered popping machine to the public at the 1893 World's Fair in Chicago, USA.

### 12. First cotton candy/candy floss
Ironically, this airy spun-sugar confection was invented by a dentist! In 1897, William Morrison collaborated with confectioner John C Wharton (both USA) in Nashville, Tennessee, on an "electric candy machine", in which sugar crystals were spun through a metal bowl with tiny holes. Their patent was granted in 1899. They introduced their invention as "fairy floss" at the 1904 St Louis World's Fair, priced at $0.25 a box. It was an instant hit, selling around 68,000 boxes.

### 13. First teabags
Several inventors could stake a claim to this record, all of them Americans. Legend holds that New York tea merchant Thomas Sullivan invented the teabag in 1908, but there were earlier prototypes. In 1836, the *Preston Temperance Advocate* referred to the use of a bag to make tea, and another precursor exists in Thomas Fitzgerald's 1880 patent for a long-handled muslin or cloth bag, secured to a float, to contain tea or coffee. Edward Dillingham's "Tea-Strainer" was patented in 1893, while Roberta C Lawson and Mary McLaren patented the "Tea Leaf Holder" in 1903.

# Pandemics

### Oldest contagious disease
Tuberculosis (TB) is a respiratory disease caused by *Mycobacterium tuberculosis*. The bacterium is thought to have existed in something similar to its modern form for more than 70,000 years, and may have been infecting humans since early prehistory.

### First recorded pandemic
The Plague of Athens spread throughout the Mediterranean in 430–426 BCE. Between 75,000 and 100,000 people died, the worst affected areas being in what is now Libya, Egypt and Greece.

### First quarantine
In 549 CE, the Eastern Roman emperor Justinian established the earliest legally enforced quarantine. During the pandemic known as the Plague of Justinian (which lasted from 541 to 549 CE), he passed a series of laws to bar plague-carrying "outsiders" of various kinds from the capital, Byzantium, and its environs.

### Longest incarceration for an asymptomatic carrier
Typhoid Mary, aka Mary Mallon (USA, b. IRL; below) was quarantined for 26 years on North Brother Island, New York City. Mary was a "healthy carrier" of typhoid who infected others while working as a cook. She was initially detained from 1907 to 1910, but was released after promising to leave domestic service. In 1915, another outbreak was traced to her, now working as a cook under a fake name. She was returned to North Brother Island and stayed there until her death in 1938.

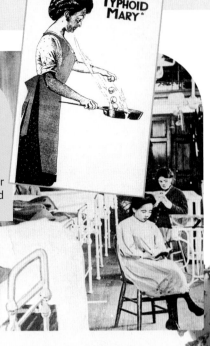

### First modern vaccination
British doctor Edward Jenner performed the earliest modern vaccinations (which expose patients to a weakened version of the target virus) in 1796. He had noticed that dairy workers were often resistant to the lethal smallpox disease, and proposed that this was because they had previously recovered from the less harmful cowpox.

In May 1796, he infected eight-year-old James Phipps with cowpox, and later with smallpox, which the boy did not develop. Jenner coined the word "vaccine" (from the Latin *vacca* for "cow") in a paper published in 1798, a nod to the role that cowpox had played in his success.

### Most infections traced to a single asymptomatic carrier
In Oct 1923, medical authorities in New Jersey, USA, reported that 107 people had been infected with typhoid by Tony La Bella, aka Frank Boni (USA, b. ITA). He had worked at several dairies in the greater New York metropolitan area. Unlike Mary Mallon (see above), Tony agreed to stop working in food preparation and escaped incarceration.

### Fastest vaccine development
The Pfizer-BioNTech "Tozinameran" COVID-19 vaccine was authorized by the British Medicines and Healthcare Products Regulatory Agency on 2 Dec 2020, just 337 days after the disease had been identified. Pfizer-BioNTech released the results of the crucial Phase III clinical trials in Nov 2020, ahead of all their rivals.

### Longest-lasting pandemic
The Seventh Cholera Pandemic began in 1961 in Indonesia and spread widely. As of 2021, some 60 years later, it is still ongoing and infects some 3–5 million people annually. Cholera is a bacterial infection passed on when people drink water contaminated with the bodily fluids of infected individuals. This can be hard to avoid in areas without clean water and reliable sewage systems.

### Deadliest pandemic
The Black Death was a pandemic that spread across Europe, Asia and North Africa from 1346 to 1353. It is blamed on a particularly deadly strain of plague (a disease caused by the bacteria *Yersinia pestis*). Estimates for the resulting death toll vary from 25 million to 200 million, with most falling in the 50- to 100-million range – as much as a quarter of the world's population at that time. Pictured below is a burial trench for plague victims in east London, UK.

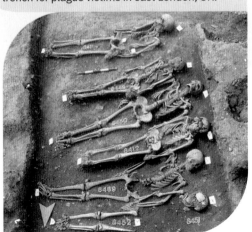

### Most successful immunization
On 9 Dec 1979, the Global Commission for the Certification of Smallpox Eradication declared that the world was free of this lethal disease. Formerly one of the world's deadliest plagues, smallpox was eradicated by the availability of one type of vaccine that proved effective against all forms of the disease. Its elimination involved following up all of the contacts of every affected individual and vaccinating them.

## Deadliest influenza pandemic

From 1918 to 1920, "Spanish flu" caused 50–100 million deaths worldwide. Its spread was aided by the movement of troop ships during the final year of World War I. Researchers are still unsure where the pandemic started. Its name derives from the fact that Spain provided extensive reporting on early cases, rather than it being the country of origin.

## Most common infectious disease

The common cold is endemic to every inhabited continent, and only the most profoundly isolated communities can escape frequent infection. It is caused by a range of different viruses, most commonly rhinoviruses, and the average adult suffers from two to three infections per year.

## Highest viral disease fatality rate

If not caught before symptoms appear, rabies has a fatality rate of effectively 100%, and kills around 17,000 people every year. There are only 14 known cases in which a patient has survived

## Most contagious disease

Measles is caused by the *Measles morbillivirus* virus. Its reproduction number ($R_0$) is between 12 and 18 – i.e., an infected person will pass it on to an average of 15 others in unvaccinated populations. Around 140,000 people die from the disease every year. Measles was effectively ended by vaccines in developed nations, but declining vaccination rates have seen its return. It remains a common childhood illness in less developed nations.

## Worst outbreak of dancing mania

Tarantism (aka choreomania, or dancing plague) was first described in the 11th century, but was particularly prevalent in southern Italy between the 15th and 17th centuries. Victims were seized by an uncontrollable urge to dance, and would writhe around for hours, or even days, before collapsing of exhaustion. The worst outbreak was recorded in Aachen, Germany, in 1374, which at its peak saw around 15 people a day dancing themselves to death in the summer heat. The cause of this disease is unknown, but the leading explanation is mass hysteria – it typically occurred at times of great stress and hardship.

symptomatic rabies, even with aggressive treatment. The disease can be treated, however, if an infected person receives a vaccine shot after exposure but before symptoms appear.

## Highest rate of HIV/AIDS infection

According to the most recent WHO figures (for 2019), the small African nation of Lesotho saw new HIV/AIDS infections in 6.43 out of every 1,000 citizens.

Lesotho is also the **country with the highest rate of tuberculosis infection**. Every year, 654 out of every 100,000 people there are diagnosed with the disease. The severity of the TB epidemic in Lesotho is a consequence of the AIDS epidemic, since AIDS weakens the immune system, leaving victims more susceptible to respiratory infections.

Coronaviruses are named for the crown (or "corona") of spike proteins that surround the spherical core of the virion (virus particle).

## First coronavirus pandemic

On 11 Mar 2020, the World Health Organization (WHO) declared COVID-19 a pandemic, meaning that there were significant outbreaks around the world. There have been coronavirus epidemics in the past, including SARS (2002) and MERS (2012), but these were contained before they spread globally. COVID-19 is also the **deadliest coronavirus outbreak**, with 2,490,776 deaths as of 25 Feb 2021. The response to COVID-19 has included the **fastest development of a vaccine** (see opposite), the first non-trial dose of which was given to the UK's Margaret Keenan (right) on 8 Dec 2020.

# Odd Jobs

### Coffin maker
Herbert Weber (AUT) built 707,335 coffins for woodwork suppliers Moser Holzindustrie between 5 Sep 1978 and 5 Sep 2008 in Salzburg, Austria. This is the **most coffins assembled in a lifetime**.

### Foley artist
In foley studios, live sound effects such as footsteps and banging doors are recorded and synchronized with the action on screen. The job is named after Jack Foley (USA), who performed this role at Universal Studios from the dawn of the "talkies". During his 40-year career, he is estimated to have walked 8,000 km (5,000 mi) recording the sound of footsteps for actors such as James Cagney, Marlon Brando and Kirk Douglas. This is the **longest distance walked on the spot in a career by a foley artist**.

### South Pole caretaker
Between 1997 and 2019, astrophysicist Robert "The Ice-Man" Schwarz (DEU/USA) spent the **most over-winters at the South Pole** – 15. He worked at Amundsen-Scott South Pole Station, maintaining science experiments and making telescopic observations. Sub-zero temperatures, isolation and six months of winter darkness were features of each "tour of duty".

### Elvis Presley tribute act
The King of Rock 'n' Roll has inspired a host of impersonators to take up his crown. The **longest career as an Elvis tribute act** lasted 48 years for Belgian hip-swinger Vick Beasley, who first strapped on his rhinestone belt in 1954 and performed his final professional show on 6 Jul 2002. Vick was made an Honorary Citizen of Tupelo, Mississippi, USA – Elvis's birthplace.

### Scale stunt double
For daredevils of the silver screen, size is not a factor. The **shortest stuntman** is Kiran Shah (UK), who stood 126.3 cm (4 ft 1.7 in) on 20 Oct 2003. Among his numerous credits since his screen debut in 1976 are *Superman* (1978), *The Lord of the Rings* (2001–03) and five *Star Wars* films (1983–2019).

### Alien actor
Bill Blair (USA) forged his thespian career playing monsters and otherworldly characters requiring special make-up or prosthetics. By 6 May 2011, he had achieved the **most special-effect make-up characters portrayed** – 202.

### Clock-tower guide
The Elizabeth Clock Tower at the Houses of Parliament in London, UK, is home to the "Big Ben" bell. As a tower guide, Brian Davis (UK) completed the **most steps climbed in a career** – 2,101,528. Brian recorded 6,292 ascents in the 13 years up to 1 Mar 1997. This is equivalent to more than 38 summits of Everest from sea level.

### Vegetable instrumentalist
The Vegetable Orchestra (AUT) are a 10-piece ensemble who play instruments such as the carrot marimba, the radish bass flute, the leek violin and the parsnip trumpet. Instruments are prepared fresh on the morning of a concert; afterwards, the edible pieces are served to the audience in a soup. As of Oct 2019, the ensemble had performed the **most concerts by a vegetable orchestra** – 331.

Mr Methane says he first got wind of his natural flatulist ability while adopting the "full lotus" yoga position.

### Flatulist
Mr Methane, aka Paul Oldfield (UK), entertains his audiences by passing gas at various pitches and in time with music. His first paid TV appearance as a "flatulist" (aka "fartist") came in Dec 1990, and in Oct 1991 he gave up his job as a train driver to register with Equity, making him the **longest-working flatulist**. He performs with Circus of Horrors and has appeared on numerous radio and TV shows.

### Human crash-test dummy
W R "Rusty" Haight (USA) has endured more than 1,000 automobile collisions in the course of his career as a "crash reconstructionist". Each time, Rusty and his vehicle are fitted with sensors to gather data on the impact. Despite driving at speeds of up to 86 km/h (53 mph), his worst injury to date is a small cut from an airbag.

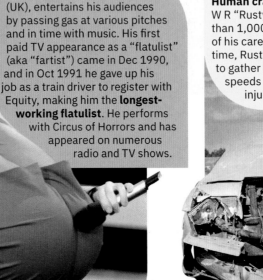

Modern-day Yeoman applicants have to be a warrant officer with 22 years' service in the British Army, Navy or Air Force.

## Sideshow artiste

In the course of her career, Daniella D'Ville (aka Danielle Martin, UK) has performed at the sharp end of dangerous implements such as swords, chainsaws and beds of nails. On 12 Oct 2013, she achieved the **fastest time to break 16 concrete blocks on the body (female)** – 30.40 sec – with the sledgehammer-wielding assistance of Johnny Strange (UK).

## Beefeater

Officially "Yeoman Warders", these ceremonial custodians of the UK's Tower of London have been tasked with guarding prisoners – and the British Crown Jewels – since the 15th century. While the roles were traditionally reserved for male candidates, in Jan 2007 Moira Cameron (UK) made history by becoming the **first female Beefeater**. The **first Black Beefeater** is British Army veteran Lawrence Watts (UK, inset), who was sworn into his "dream job" on 1 Mar 2016.

## Grave digger

The **longest career as a grave digger** was that of Johann Heinrich Karl Thieme, sexton of Aldenburg in Germany, who unearthed a recorded 23,311 graves during a 50-year career. After his own death in 1826, Johann's understudy dug his grave for him.

## Santa Claus

Obviously, the real Father Christmas is too busy delivering presents to make public appearances. In his stead, the **longest career as Santa Claus** is held by Dayton C Fouts (USA), who donned the red suit every year from 1937 until 14 Dec 1997. Dayton played the role for 55 years in Harvey, Illinois, USA, and for a further five in Tucson, Arizona.

## Forensic artist

The **most criminals positively identified from the composites of one artist** is 1,266, by Lois Gibson (USA) between 1982 and Feb 2021 in Texas, USA. She honed her skills sketching tourist portraits in San Antonio, Texas, before starting work for the Houston Police Department.

## Foot sniffer

As a deodorant tester for healthcare company Dr Scholl's in Cincinnati, Ohio, USA, Madeline Albrecht (USA) gained the unique distinction of the **most feet sniffed**: c. 5,600 over 15 years. She also smelled an indeterminate number of armpits.

## Coffee-bean taster

Gennaro Pelliccia's (UK) discerning taste buds have earned him the **highest-insured tongue** – £10 m ($14 m), as reported by Lloyd's on 9 Mar 2009. A Master of Coffee at Costa Coffee (UK), Gennaro tastes every single batch of beans made for stores.

The **highest-insured nose** belongs to vineyard owner Ilja Gort (NLD, inset) and is worth €5 m (£3.9 m; $7.8 m).

## TV gameshow clapper

At the last count on 9 Feb 2015, *Wheel of Fortune* hostess Vanna White (USA) had clapped her hands 3,721,446 times during the show's 32 seasons. Averaging 606 per episode, this makes Vanna the **most frequent clapper**.

## Train wrecker

Between 9 Sep 1896 and 27 Aug 1932, showman Joseph S Connolly (USA) staged 73 deliberate head-on collisions between locomotives for large crowds at state fairs across America. Railroad engineers built up the steam pressure on a pair of near-obsolete locomotives and set them in motion on a single length of track. "Head-on Joe" achieved the **most trains wrecked in a career** – 146.

THE MAN WHO
**Wrecked**
146 LOCOMOTIVES
THE STORY OF "HEAD-ON JOE" CONNOLLY
JAMES J. REISDORFF

# Round-Up

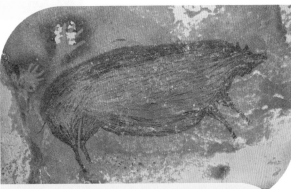

## Oldest painting (figurative art)

On 13 Jan 2021, the discovery of a piece of cave art at least 45,500 years old was reported in *Science Advances*. Found in the Leang Tedongnge limestone cave on the Indonesian island of Sulawesi in 2017, it shows a group of pig-like animals – likely the Sulawesi warty pig (*Sus celebensis*) – drawn in dark red and purple pigments, alongside hand stencils.

## Most expensive...

**Honey**: Ahmet Eren Çakır of Centauri Honey (both TUR) sold a sample of honey for €10,000/kg (£8,720/kg; $12,130/kg) in Istanbul, Turkey, on 16 Feb 2021. Only 10–15 kg (22–33 lb) of this bitter, dark honey is harvested per year.

**Leg of ham**: On 3 Feb 2020, Japanese luxury food importer Taishi Co. sold a leg of Iberian Bellota ham – from an acorn-fed, pure-breed pig – for ¥1,429,000 ($13,183; £9,983).

**Sheep**: On 27 Aug 2020, pedigree Texel ram lamb Sportsmans Double Diamond sold for £367,500 ($483,963) at auction in Lanarkshire, UK. His high rank in terms of breeding value justified the lofty price tag.

**Pigeon**: Two-year-old racing pigeon New Kim, bred and trained by Kurt Van de Wouwer (BEL), sold at auction for €1.6 m ($1.8 m; £1.4 m) on 15 Nov 2020.

## Largest litter of goats

On 16 Feb 2019, a Nigerian dwarf doe named Miller's Fairywood MP Angelica gave birth to seven kids at home in Gilbert, Arizona, USA. She is owned by Elizabeth Miller (USA).

## First lab-grown meat produced in space

Start-up food tech company Aleph Farms (ISR) used bovine cells to produce a sample of laboratory-grown meat on the *International Space Station* on 26 Sep 2019. The cells were grown into muscle tissue using a 3D printer, meaning that the meat was not only grown 399 km (248 mi) above Earth's surface, but was also slaughter free. (See also opposite.)

## Oldest continually operated signals intelligence facility

GCHQ Scarborough in Yorkshire, UK, was set up as a Royal Navy wireless telegraphy station in 1912 to monitor the Imperial German Navy's High Seas Fleet. It played the same role during World War II, and during the Cold War tracked Soviet military traffic. Today, as well as monitoring marine military communications, it acts as a general-purpose satellite office for GCHQ's main campus in Cheltenham, Gloucestershire, UK.

## Oldest pet cemetery

In 2011, Polish archaeologists working in Berenike – a ruined seaport on the Egyptian Red Sea coast – uncovered a pet cemetery dating from the 1st or 2nd century CE. It included the remains of 536 cats, 32 dogs, small monkeys and a juvenile baboon. Many showed evidence of domesticity, such as ornate cat collars (pictured).

> **Births** of more than three or four kids are rare. That they should all be healthy makes Angelica's feat even more remarkable.

## Largest net worth increase for an individual in 24 hours

On 20 Jul 2020, Amazon CEO and co-founder Jeff Bezos (USA) experienced an abrupt $13-bn (£10.3-bn) upswing in his wealth. Amazon.com shares rose by 7.9%, according to Bloomberg, taking Bezos's estimated net worth to $189.3 bn (£150.6 bn). The boost to share value was attributed to increasing optimism about online shopping trends.

## Oldest llama

As of 14 Nov 2020, Ramadan's Arapahoe Gold (aka Rapper, b. 2 Mar 1994) was aged 26 years 257 days. The retired show llama lives with his owners, Brian Kienenberger and Jodie McDonie of Olympia, Washington, USA.

## Most personal hygiene products donated in one hour

Indian philanthropist Lakshyaraj Singh Mewar organized the donation of 12,508 personal hygiene products to poor families in rural Rajasthan, India, on 25 Jan 2021. In Aug 2019, Mewar achieved the **largest donation of school supplies in 24 hours**, distributing 21 tonnes (23 tons) of textbooks and other items.

## ▶ Most tricks by a cat in one minute

Alexis and owner Anika Moritz (AUT) performed 26 tricks in 60 sec in Bruck an der Leitha, Niederösterreich, Austria, on 10 Jun 2020. Alexis's repertoire included high-fiving (above), head-shaking, crossing paws, spinning left and right, and opening a pot. She's had plenty of time to learn: Anika has been teaching her tricks since she was a kitten.

## First female to officiate the Super Bowl

Sarah Thomas (USA, right) was the down judge at Super Bowl LV in Tampa, Florida, USA, on 7 Feb 2021. She first officiated in 1999, at a varsity high-school game, going on to join the National Football League in 2015.

The **first female referee in a men's UEFA Champions League soccer match** is Stéphanie Frappart (FRA), for Juventus vs Dynamo Kiev in Turin, Italy, on 2 Dec 2020.

### First country to approve lab-grown meat

In Dec 2020, the Singaporean government granted tech start-up Eat Just (USA) approval to sell laboratory-grown chicken. The meat is created from chicken cells grown in a bioreactor and supplemented with plant-based ingredients. Currently around 14% of global greenhouse gas emissions are created by livestock farming.

### Oldest sweet shop

Ichimonjiya Wasuke (also known simply as Ichiwa) is a traditional confectionery store and café located in Kita-ku, Kyoto, Japan. It was founded in around 1000 CE, and as of Dec 2020 was run by Naomi Hasegawa, a 24th-generation descendant of the founding family. Its fare includes *aburi-mochi* (below): grilled rice-flour cakes coated with a sweet miso-paste sauce.

### Most civilian awards

On 11 Nov 2020, Japanese inventor and businessman Tsunejiro Koga received his 98th Medal of Honour with Dark Blue Ribbon – which is awarded to individuals for exceptional philanthropic donations. This is the 103rd civilian award he has received – a tally that includes the prestigious Order of the Rising Sun – since his first on 7 Nov 1982. Koga was a high-school dropout who spent his youth getting into trouble, and so he uses his philanthropic organization to help young people in similar situations.

### Most expensive sneakers (private sale)

On 26 Apr 2021 – a little less than a year after it hosted the auction record (see right) – Sotheby's announced that it had brokered the private sale of the only known pair of Nike Air Yeezy 1 Prototypes – the sneakers worn by Kanye West for his performances at the 2008 Grammy Awards. The black leather shoes – put on sale by noted collector Ryan Chang – were bought for a reported $1.8 m (£1.3 m) by RARES, a start-up focused on investments in collectible footwear.

It is the third-most expensive work by a living artist ever sold, only behind pieces by Jeff Koons and David Hockney.

### Most expensive digital artwork

*EVERYDAYS: THE FIRST 5000 DAYS* by Beeple (aka Mike Winkelmann, USA) was sold by Christie's for $69,346,250 (£53,339,800) on 11 Mar 2020. It collects the first 5,000 days of Beeple's one-a-day art project as a collage. It was sold using what is called a non-fungible token – essentially a digital certificate of authenticity whose identity and ownership is logged using a cryptocurrency-style blockchain. The same technology was used in the sale of the **most expensive tweet** (see p.205).

### Most expensive sneakers sold at auction

A pair of Nike Air Jordan 1s, game-worn by Michael Jordan in 1985, fetched $560,000 (£462,351) at an online auction held by Sotheby's on 17 May 2020. They had been expected to fetch up to $150,000 (£123,844), but the bidding increased by double this amount in the final 20 min of the sale. The shoes are mismatched in size (left: 13; right: 13.5) – as Jordan preferred when playing – and feature his signature on the right shoe.

# Malala Yousafzai

I t can take great courage to speak up for what we believe is right. In Malala's case, that bravery nearly cost her her life. Her "amazing feminist father" (Malala's words) – a teacher and school owner – believed that she should have the same opportunities as her brothers. After the Taliban seized her home city of Mingora in Pakistan in 2008, however, they banned many aspects of life, including female education.

In 2009, Malala's diary – in which she described life under the Taliban – became a blog for the BBC Urdu website. But as her fame grew, so did the danger. On 9 Oct 2012, a gunman boarded her school bus and shot the 15-year-old in the head. Thanks to life-saving surgery, Malala miraculously recovered. Along with her family, she moved to Birmingham, UK, for further treatment and then decided to stay; in 2021, Malala said she now considers the city "her second home". The attack only strengthened her resolve; she went on to set up the nonprofit Malala Fund, to invest in and advocate for girls' education.

In recognition of her efforts, on 10 Dec 2014 Malala jointly received the Nobel Peace Prize, making her – at 17 years 151 days – the **youngest Nobel laureate**. Her impassioned acceptance speech demanded education and basic rights for all children. Three years later, aged 19 years 272 days, she also became the **youngest UN Messenger of Peace**. Malala is living proof that we can all make a difference, no matter our age, gender or background.

**VITAL STATISTICS**
**Name:** Malala Yousafzai
**Born:** 12 Jul 1997
**Birthplace:** Mingora, Pakistan
**College education:** Oxford University (UK)
**Occupation:** Activist, speaker, writer
**Selected honours:** International Children's Peace Prize (2013); Nobel Peace Prize (2014); UN Messenger of Peace (2017)

**4**

**5**

**6**

In her 2014 Nobel lecture, Malala pleaded that her generation "be the last that sees empty classrooms, lost childhoods".

Find out more about Malala in the Hall of Fame section at www.guinnessworldrecords.com/2022

1. In 2013, on her 16th birthday, Malala made a powerful speech at the United Nations. She ended, "So let us wage a global struggle against illiteracy, poverty and terrorism and let us pick up our books and pens. They are our most powerful weapons."

2. Malala's acclaimed autobiography was published in 2013, with an abridged children's edition appearing the following year. It went on to sell more than 2 million copies worldwide.

3. Malala has inspired many other activists to stand up and be counted. These children appeared at an Indian protest rally in support of her in 2013. Their masks bear a slogan from a petition launched by former British Prime Minister Gordon Brown, who was then the UN's Special Envoy for Global Education.

4. In 2014, Malala became the **youngest Nobel Peace Prize winner**. She shared the award with children's rights activist Kailash Satyarthi. The citation acknowledged "their struggle against the suppression of children and young people and for the right of all children to education".

5. Malala is seen here in Lebanon in Jul 2015. She was inaugurating the Malala Yousafzai All-Girls School for more than 200 Syrian children living in refugee camps in the Bekaa Valley.

6. The documentary *He Named Me Malala* premiered in New York on 24 Sep 2015. Its director, Davis Guggenheim, stands at the rear left. Shazia Ramzan (far left) and Kainat Riaz (far right) were also injured in the bus attack on Malala in 2012.

# Roxanne Downs

**A**ustralian schoolgirl Roxanne Downs is the youngest magazine editor, having taken up her position at *It GiRL* in 2017 aged eight years old. The magazine had decided to connect with its tween readers by hiring someone who knew their interests and concerns firsthand. "Roxy has always performed well in school at reading and writing," her father, Michael, explained, "so she was the perfect candidate for editor." The first issue under Roxanne's tenure hit news stands in Australia and New Zealand on 6 Apr 2017. Now she juggles schoolwork and chores with glamorous interviews and editorial meetings – and has overseen a rise in *It GiRL*'s circulation under her editorship.

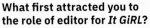

**What first attracted you to the role of editor for *It GiRL*?**
I wanted to be part of something that was big in my age group and among my friends. I'm a child myself and *It GiRL* is a magazine written for children. I hang out with others my age all day and I know what they like and what information they want to know.

**What kind of tasks and responsibilities do you have?**
I do all the main celebrity interviews. I also plan the theme of each issue, choose the cover talent and select what gifts we have each month. Sometimes I even go to retail meetings with our publisher. Big supermarket chains are always shocked when I walk into the boardroom!

**How do you fit it in with school and homework?**
I get the week's homework out of the way quick smart on Monday night. Then I can spend most of my time doing what I love.

**Who's been the most famous person you've interviewed?**
Probably Justin Bieber or JoJo Siwa, but there have been so many more. Authors, TikTok stars, singers, actors... I've lost count now!

**What advice would you give to other young people?**
Do the small things right every day. Big opportunities present themselves to people who are easy to work with, polite, focused and hard-working.

**What would be your dream job when you're older?**
A TV host, presenter or actor. And still a magazine editor, of course!

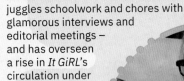

**1**. Roxanne met Australian actress and rapper Abbie Cornish (aka MC Dusk) at Sydney's Cafe Parterre for a journalistic grilling.

**2**. Someone who knows all about child prodigies is Iain Armitage, the star of CBS spin-off series *Young Sheldon*. He met Roxanne in 2019.

**3**. Roxanne has also interviewed dancer/singer/YouTuber JoJo Siwa, who made *TIME*'s list of the 100 most influential people in the world in 2020.

# Dara McAnulty

On 26 Oct 2019, Dara McAnulty (UK, b. 31 Mar 2004) became the youngest recipient of the RSPB Medal, the highest honour bestowed by the Royal Society for the Protection of Birds. Previous ornithologists to receive the accolade include Sir David Attenborough (see pp.54–55). Dara was aged just 15 years 209 days.

He began blogging and tweeting about nature at 12, inspired by the countryside of County Fermanagh in Northern Ireland. As someone who lives with autism, he found the calm focus required for wildlife watching therapeutic. But Dara also felt a need to speak out on environmental issues such as biodiversity loss and raptor persecution. He backed up his words with action, volunteering for beach cleaning and charity fund-raising. His increased media exposure has led to talks and TV appearances, while his debut book in 2020 was a hit with critics and readers alike (see right).

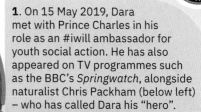

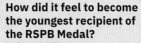

**1.** On 15 May 2019, Dara met with Prince Charles in his role as an #iwill ambassador for youth social action. He has also appeared on TV programmes such as the BBC's *Springwatch*, alongside naturalist Chris Packham (below left) – who has called Dara his "hero".

**2.** Dara has demonstrated at his local Fridays for Future climate strikes, the environmental movement initiated by Greta Thunberg (see p.29).

**3.** In May 2020, Dara published his first book, *Diary of a Young Naturalist*. It was awarded the prestigious Wainwright Prize for UK Nature Writing in Sep 2020.

**How did it feel to become the youngest recipient of the RSPB Medal?**
It felt really strange – previous recipients have dedicated their lives to conservation, so I wondered if it was premature! I have worked tirelessly, though, and campaigning for nature has taken over my life. To be rewarded for my efforts is a great honour and responsibility.

**What would you say to people who might claim "nature isn't for them"?**
I don't think it's that people don't care, but our fast-paced society has pushed nature to the fringes. We need everyone, especially educators and those in power, to get the message out there that we are dependent on nature.

**Do you think the world still underestimates the ideas and arguments of young people?**
I think young people do have refreshing ideas and energy that older generations could gain insight from. But we should all be working together. The changes we so desperately need for a healthy planet require everyone to understand what's at stake.

**What's your advice to people who want to get involved in environmental activism?**
I would start with your own garden, if you have one. Letting an area of your grass grow long or having pots of wildflowers can really help nature. To me, being an activist means caring for nature and sharing that passion with everyone you meet.

**What's the secret to a successful blog?**
Write about something you're really passionate about. Keep practising your writing and improving your style; make it unique to you.

**How does it feel to be part of the GWR family?**
So good! We have the *GWR* book in our Christmas pile every year and my dad has his old childhood copies. So, it's such a cool thing.

To discover more about record-breaking young achievers, visit kids.guinnessworldrecords.com

# Chinonso Eche

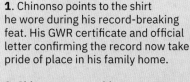

**W**hen this 11-year-old Nigerian soccer freestyler was gearing up to attempt a world record, he knew exactly what to do. Practise hard, believe in yourself and keep a level head at all times...

It worked out pretty well for him. Chinonso now holds the GWR title for the ❍ **most consecutive touches in one minute while balancing a soccer ball on the head**. He completed 111 touches in Warri, Nigeria, on 14 Nov 2019. You have to go the extra mile to earn the nickname "Amazing Kid Eche", but Chinonso more than earned the epithet. Watch the YouTube video of his feat and check out his phenomenal concentration and Zen-like calm. And he's not finished yet: find out about his plans for future records in his Q&A.

**Chinonso has a wealth of soccer ambitions. One of them is to play for Nigeria's national team, the Super Eagles.**

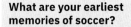

**1**. Chinonso points to the shirt he wore during his record-breaking feat. His GWR certificate and official letter confirming the record now take pride of place in his family home.

**2**. Chinonso counts his manager, Chukwuebuka Ezugha, among his freestyling idols, along with DJ Diveny, Séan Garnier and Erlend Fagerli.

**3**. A few shots of Chinonso in action during his record-breaking keepy-uppy performance at the Warri Township Stadium in 2019.

**What are your earliest memories of soccer?**
When I was around four years old, I used to love playing with every round object, even my father's cups! I started freestyle soccer at the age of eight.

**Who are your favourite freestylers?**
I'd have to include Lionel Messi and Ronaldinho, because they usually apply their freestyle skills while playing on the pitch and that's what I do too. I'm a midfielder and usually wear a number 8 or 10 shirt.

**Tell us about the training that went into your record.**
Once the date was fixed I stepped up my programme, increasing my juggling speed in order to beat the one-minute deadline.

**Was there any point at which you felt like giving up, or that the record was out of reach?**
No. I never felt discouraged because my team and family inspired me.

**How did it feel to receive your official GWR certificate?**
Really good! It's a dream come true to become the youngest Nigerian in the *Guinness World Records* book. My family was very proud of me.

**Any plans for more soccer freestyle records that you can tell us about?**
Plenty! Among other things, I want to run for the longest distance while balancing a ball on my head and juggle one ball for 2,000 touches while balancing another on my head.

**Can you suggest any easy tricks that beginners can try?**
First learn how to juggle a ball with both feet. Try using your knee too, then try balancing the ball on your back.

**What advice would you give to any other kids dreaming of GWR glory?**
Never give up! Always believe in yourself. And to the parents: learn to support and encourage your child's dream, as my family did.

# Gui Khury

**S**kateboarding is one discipline where youngsters can compete with – and often outperform – their elders. For proof, look no further than Gui Khury from Curitiba, Brazil.

On 8 May 2020, the 11-year-old pulled off the ❯ **first skateboard 1080 on a vertical ramp**. That's three complete 360° rotations in the air. Tom Schaar (USA) had achieved the **first skateboard 1080** back in 2012, but he'd used a "mega ramp", which enabled him to build up speed before the manoeuvre.

How did Gui hone his skills? During the COVID-19 lockdown, he patiently mastered the trick on a ramp in his grandmother's garden!

As if that weren't enough, the previous year Gui (b. 18 Dec 2008) had become the **youngest X Games athlete**. He was just 10 years 225 days old when he competed in the Skateboard Vert elimination round on 31 Jul 2019 in Minneapolis, Minnesota, USA.

**How does it feel to be the youngest X Games athlete of all time?**
It feels like a dream come true! I still can't quite believe that I even went to X Games.

**How did you celebrate after achieving your 1080?**
With a delicious home-made pizza and cake!

**What do your family and friends think about you becoming a record-breaker?**
Actually, my parents were filming the 1080, while two of my friends were watching. They were stoked!

**Are you now famous in your neighbourhood?**
Well... skateboarding is very popular in Brazil. I'm known in the skateboard community and this week a guy said to me, "Are you Gui Khury?" and we took a selfie.

**Who are your heroes – skateboarders or otherwise?**
Tony Hawk, Bob Burnquist and Danny Way.

**What other hobbies do you have outside skateboarding?**
I like to spend time surfing, snowboarding, wakeboarding and playing soccer.

**We hear you're now in training to take on the 1260 (three-and-a-half 360 spins). How's it going?**
It's actually going really well and I'm still training every day so one day I can land it.

**Finally: have you got any advice for other kids thinking of taking on a world record?**
Never give up and always be determined to do it.

**SKATEBOARD TRAINING FACILITY**

**1.** Gui is passionate about boarding of all kinds. He's also an avid surfer and snowboarder.

**2.** The skating sensation shows off his GWR certificates. Gui was performing on halfpipes at the age of just five. He was "the little one that drops in on the big ramps," says his father, Ricardo.

**3.** Gui is shown taking time out with world-famous US skaters Tony Hawk (left) and Kevin Staab. Tony – one of Gui's idols – pulled off the **first 900 on a skateboard** in 1999.

To discover more about record-breaking young achievers, visit **kids.guinnessworldrecords.com**

# Chloe Chambers

**T**he need for speed runs through the blood of Chloe Chambers (USA). Watching her father compete on the racetracks of New Jersey, she was determined to get behind the wheel. And now she has graduated from go-kart champion to world record holder.

On 21 Aug 2020, Chloe teamed up with Porsche Cars North America to attempt the **fastest vehicle slalom** in Readington Township, New Jersey, USA. Her task? To guide a Porsche 718 Spyder as quickly as possible around 50 cones each spaced 15 m (49 ft) apart. Chloe proved more than up to the challenge, taking half a second off the previous record as she slalomed through the course in just 47.45 sec. And all this at the age of 16, before she was even old enough to qualify for her full driver's licence!

**1**. Chloe showed a natural flair behind the wheel right from her very first go-kart practice, in 2011.

**2**. Chloe's family are her biggest supporters – both on and off the track.

**3**. The podium is becoming a familiar place for Chloe, who has won races at every level while progressing to "senior", the highest class in karting.

**4**. In Jan 2019, Chloe took the chequered flag at the opening leg of the ROK Cup USA Florida Winter Tour. She competed in the 100-cc Junior category.

**5**. For her GWR record attempt, Chloe swapped her usual go-kart for a Porsche 718 Spyder. "It was a great learning experience for me," she commented afterwards.

### When did you start go-karting?
I first got into karting when I was seven years old. I'd watch Formula One on TV with my dad and he used to do autocross and track days. One day, I asked my mom if I could drive too. I had my first go-karting lesson shortly afterwards. I started racing in the kid kart class, and won the championship in my first year.

### How did your record attempt come about?
The idea was Porsche's. I was contacted by a filming director on their behalf – after he asked me if I wanted to do it, he revealed that the company was Porsche.

### Were there any moments on the day when you feared you might not set the record?
When we first practised, I was quickly up to speed and close to the time required. However, the temperature made a big difference to the level of grip and the times possible. It wasn't easy but we worked great as a team and did it!

### How did it feel when you knew you'd broken the record?
I felt a great deal of relief and pride. Compared to other races I've won, this was more meaningful to me because this is a once-in-a-lifetime opportunity that most people don't get the chance to fulfil.

### You're also a black belt in taekwondo. Are there any similarities between racing and martial arts?
In both sports, you have to keep calm to perform at your best. They require focus, courage and good hand-eye coordination.

### Where would you like to be in 10 years' time?
I intend to be a Formula One world champion, and an Indy 500 and 24 Hours of Le Mans winner.

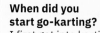

# Alexa Lauenburger

**G**rowing up in a house devoted to dogs, Alexa Lauenburger from Germany soon learnt how to take command. Now, she and her incredible pack of pooches are wowing the audiences of talent shows the world over.

Alexa's father, Wolfgang, comes from a circus background, so working with animals is a Lauenburger tradition. Alexa first stepped into the spotlight at the age of just nine, winning the German TV show *Das Supertalent*. Three years later, on 8 Dec 2019, she and Wolfgang put on a *paw*-fect performance for a team from GWR, setting five records in a day, including the **○ most dogs in a conga line** – eight – with Emma, Jennifer, Katy, Maya, Nala, Sabrina, Sally and Specki. As Alexa and her *wunder-hunds* find ever bigger and brighter stages, this talented trainer isn't done yet...

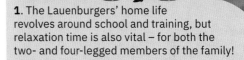

### How old were you when you started dog training?
I was five, although I started giving commands to the dogs when I was just one year old. I told them to get into a box and they did what I said!

### How many dogs do you have currently?
We have 13 in total, and my family are with them 24 hours a day. When I come home from school, I eat something quickly and then go to the dogs. Then I do my homework and go back to them.

### Are certain breeds of dog better at learning tricks?
It's all about the individual dog's character. Some are lazy, some are quirky; some really want to learn and others don't.

### What are the big challenges of performing with dogs in a studio in front of an audience?
Making sure that every trick really works and that I can entertain people. Usually I get really nervous, but when I do then the dogs do as well.

### How does it feel to have record-breaking dogs?
I'm really proud that they have so many [records]. When we got home, they all got a reward!

### What's your number-one tip for budding animal trainers?
It's really important when teaching a new trick that you match it to the dog's personality.

### What are your plans for the future?
My plan is to invent more tricks and teach them to my dogs. I really hope I get more shows because I love to perform and I know that my dogs do as well. Another thing I'm really clear on – when I'm older, I want to open a dog school.

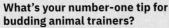

**1.** The Lauenburgers' home life revolves around school and training, but relaxation time is also vital – for both the two- and four-legged members of the family!

**2.** Alexa had earned three GWR certificates by the age of 12 – and she hasn't ruled out the possibility of trying for more...

**3.** In Oct 2019, Alexa and her conga-ing canines reached the Grand Final of *Britain's Got Talent: The Champions*.

**4.** On 8 Dec 2019, Alexa teamed up with Emma (pictured) to achieve the **fastest five hurdles cleared by a dog on hind legs** – 5.66 sec. The same day, she and Jennifer also set the **fastest 5 m backwards by a dog** (6.73 sec), but this has since been surpassed (see p.163).

**5.** Zoinks! Alexa reached the Finals of *America's Got Talent: The Champions* in Feb 2020, putting on a *Scooby-Doo*-themed routine.

To discover more about record-breaking young achievers, visit kids.guinnessworldrecords.com

# Gitanjali Rao

Curiosity and a relish for innovation have made Gitanjali (USA) an icon for young and old scientists alike. No surprise, then, when in 2020 she was named the first ever *TIME* magazine "Kid of the Year".

Aged 10, she was developing *Tethys*, a portable device that helps to identify high levels of lead in water; then came *Epione*, her early-warning tool for opioid addiction, and *Kindly*, AI-driven technology to detect cyberbullying. She's also given three TED talks and penned an inspiring STEM book (left).

But Gitanjali's impact goes far beyond her field. "From personal experience, it's not easy when you don't see anyone else like you," she told *TIME*. "So I really want to put out that message: if I can do it, you can do it, and anyone can do it."

**Who inspired in you the idea of making positive changes through technology?**
Scientists like Jonas Salk eradicating polio or Norman Borlaug [working to solve] world hunger are incredibly inspirational examples of how a single person's work has had an impact on the lives of billions. My hope is to make a small difference in my own way.

**Of all the projects you've initiated, which has been the most rewarding for you?**
The research on prescription opioid addiction using genetic engineering was personally rewarding, because I learned some complex concepts slowly over a span of two years.

**You don't seem like the typical teenager – or are you?**
I'm certainly like any other teenager! Like all my friends, I have my own challenges with doing my chores, managing time, prioritizing work and staying focused. [Gitanjali is also a pianist, fencer and aspiring pilot, making her first solo flight in Dec 2020 (above).] However, I do miss spending more time with friends.

**How important was it for you to be selected for the cover of *TIME*?**
The best part was that I got a platform to amplify my message that science can bring about significant social change and anybody can embrace scientific innovation to help solve our biggest problems.

**Where do you see yourself in 10 years' time?**
I have plans to expand innovation workshops that I conduct today globally, to grow beyond me with the help of other volunteers who can take it to other parts of the world.

**Do you have any advice for young people reading this?**
Take risks, find your own talent and use it to alleviate the problems in society. There's no limit to the amount of times we can fail, and we still have time to succeed in our endeavours.

**1.** Gitanjali is shown in the laboratory of associate professor Michael McMurray – her mentor – at the University of Colorado. At the time, she was working on methods to detect prescription opioid addiction.

**2.** She worked with Microsoft to develop *Kindly*, an app and Chrome extension to diagnose cyberbullying in real time. Her brother, Anu, is also pictured.

**3.** In 2017, Gitanjali presented *Tethys* at the STEM School Highlands Ranch in Colorado, USA, which she attends. Her invention won the Discovery Education 3M Young Scientist Challenge and a prize of $25,000 (£18,500).

**4.** Alongside other young inventors, she joined *Tonight Show* host Jimmy Fallon in 2018 to demonstrate how *Tethys* works.

# Zaila Avant-garde

Some young achievers aren't satisfied sticking to one discipline. Take Zaila, who's as comfortable on a basketball court as she is at a spelling bee.

She's shown below racking up the **most bounce juggles in one minute (four basketballs)** – 255 – in her home state of Louisiana, USA, on 2 Nov 2020. She's also set the **most bounces in 30 seconds (four basketballs)** – 307 – and **most basketballs dribbled at once** (six), tied with Joseph Odhiambo (USA). Not surprisingly, one of her aspirations is to one day play in the WNBA, although she's also considering a career in archaeology...

Zaila's heroes are equally eclectic and include LeBron James, Albert Einstein, Serena Williams and Malala Yousafzai (see p.174). She's a voracious reader, too, which helped towards another success: she won the inaugural Kaplan-Hexco Online Spelling Bee in 2020. Zaila was up against 88 competitors, but after six days competing she took the top spot by flawlessly spelling the word "Qashqai" – the name of a group of Iranian nomads.

1. The multi-talented Zaila is also an avid gymnast. "I've always just had too much energy," she admits.

2. As well as mastering freestyle basketball tricks in her spare time, Zaila plays for her school team, the Lady Eagles.

3. Her victory at the Kaplan-Hexco 2020 spelling bee won Zaila an impressive trophy – and a cheque for $10,000 (£7,600).

4. Zaila's basketball skills caught the eye of the legendary Harlem Globetrotters, whom she counts among her icons, and resulted in her performing with them. "It was a bit scary at first, but I don't get stage fright when doing things I'm really good at," she revealed later.

> "It's empowering to know that you've accomplished something that nobody else in the world has ever done before."

## Why were you particularly drawn towards basketball?
I had briefly tried other things like track and drumming, but I really liked the camaraderie that comes along with playing a team sport such as basketball. I began playing when I was five years old.

## Is it difficult fitting in training for a record with school and other hobbies?
It's very difficult sometimes. I've had to learn to manage my time really well. I do a lot of multi-tasking. I oftentimes work on my freestyle dribbling while practising my spelling. And sometimes I'll practise my spelling during breaks at basketball practice.

## In Aug 2020, you won a virtual spelling bee. Was there a moment where you thought "I could win this"?
After it was over, LOL. I was shocked when I won. But now that I know that I can compete with – and even win against – the other top spellers in the country, my confidence going into bees is much higher.

## Are there similarities between competitive basketball and spelling?
Definitely. They both involve a *ton* of practice, persistence and hard work. And they both help to teach important life lessons – such as how to study, how to work towards a goal and how to be a good teammate.

## How did it feel when you achieved your first world record?
It felt awesome. The previous record holder had set a really high bar, so getting there was literally years in the making. I was really happy to have achieved such a major milestone.

## Where do you keep your GWR certificates at home?
On the wall by my desk in my study area. I like to keep mementos from my most important accomplishments there for motivational purposes.

To discover more about record-breaking young achievers, visit kids.guinnessworldrecords.com

# Guangdong Science Center

**S**pace travel. The intricacies of the human body. Robots and virtual reality (VR). The history of transport. Eco-minded innovation. All this and much more comes together to form an attraction in China that itself is a record holder.

Topping 126,500 m² (1.36 million sq ft), the Guangdong Science Center is the world's **largest science museum**. Its status was formally reconfirmed in Dec 2020 when GWR adjudicator Angela Wu presented museum staff, including several public-engagement performers, with a certificate (right).

The hands-on museum is set on Xiaoguwei Island, within the Guangzhou University City campus. Think of it as an island of discovery to both educate and inspire. The wonder starts outside with its striking architecture: a five-pronged structure that resembles a kapok flower (left) – a symbol of Guangzhou. Themed aquatic displays take place on an 80,000-m² (861,000-sq-ft) artificial lake, while the grounds are filled with native flora and paths to wander. The vast plaza known as Science Square is used for temporary outdoor exhibitions.

Inside, you'll find 12 permanent exhibitions (a selection of which we

profile below) and a range of cutting-edge theatres, including one IMAX 3D facility and another devoted to 4D experiences. There are interactive simulators mimicking the effects of extreme weather and even a satellite launch. The *History of Science & Technology in Lingnan* pavilion outlines 6,000 years of technological development in this region. The question is: what will you discover first?

**Location:** Xiaoguwei Island, Guangzhou, Guangdong, China

**Established:** 2008

**Floor area:**
126,513.6 m²
(1,361,780 sq ft)

**Permanent exhibitions:** 12

**Construction cost:**
c. 1.9 bn yuan
($277 m; £151 m)

**Annual visitors:**
c. 2.2 million

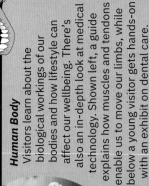

### Human Body
Visitors learn about the biological workings of our bodies and how lifestyle can affect our wellbeing. There's also an in-depth look at medical technology. Shown left, a guide explains how muscles and tendons enable us to move our limbs, while below a young visitor gets hands-on with an exhibit on dental care.

### Space Dreams
This exhibition traces the history of our fascination with flight, from hot-air balloons and hang gliders to spacecraft. As well as exploring the evolution of space technology, guests have the chance to experience the rotational forces that astronauts endure in space on a roller (left) that slowly tumbles its occupant through 360°.

### Transportation World
Take a whistlestop tour through different modes of transport, including cars, railways and ships, while also exploring what forms travel might take in the future. One of the most popular exhibits in this hall is the "pedal engine". The game transforms foot movements into kinetic energy, imitating the role of pistons in an engine. The more you pedal, the faster your car will go in a virtual head-to-head race!

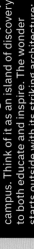

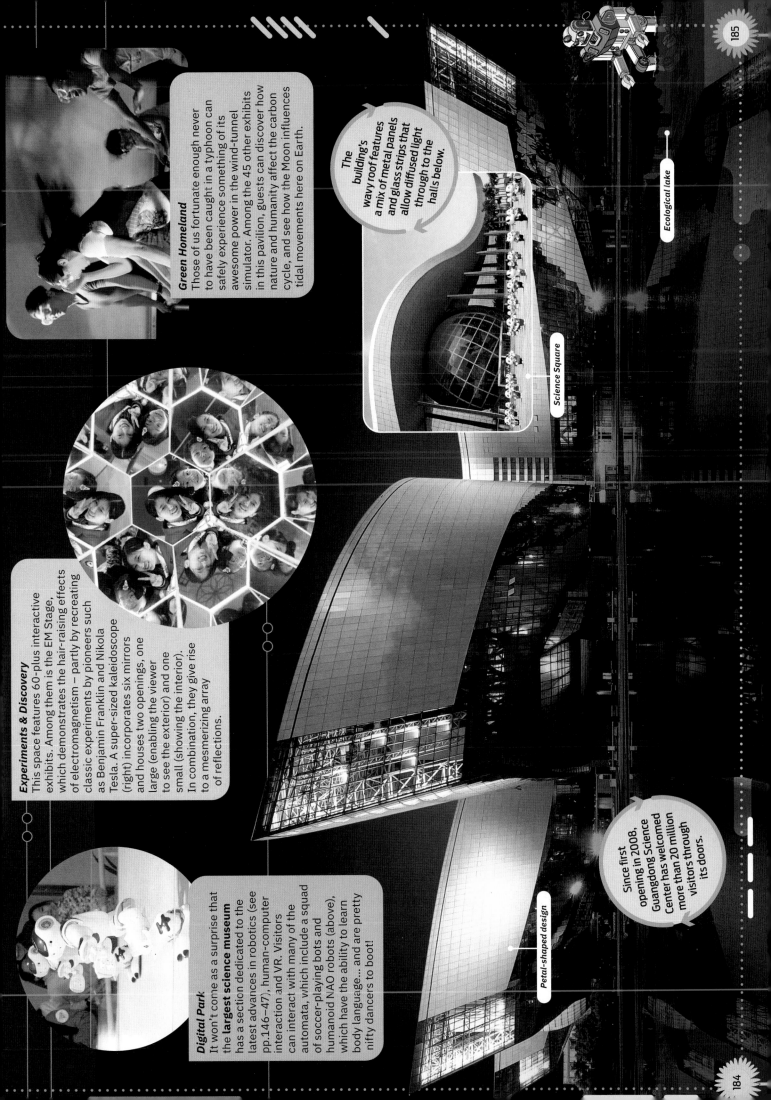

The building's wavy roof features a mix of metal panels and glass strips that allow diffused light through to the halls below.

Science Square

Ecological lake

### Green Homeland

Those of us fortunate enough never to have been caught in a typhoon can safely experience something of its awesome power in the wind-tunnel simulator. Among the 45 other exhibits in this pavilion, guests can discover how nature and humanity affect the carbon cycle, and see how the Moon influences tidal movements here on Earth.

### Experiments & Discovery

This space features 60-plus interactive exhibits. Among them is the EM Stage, which demonstrates the hair-raising effects of electromagnetism — partly by recreating classic experiments by pioneers such as Benjamin Franklin and Nikola Tesla. A super-sized kaleidoscope (right) incorporates six mirrors and houses two openings, one large (enabling the viewer to see the exterior) and one small (showing the interior). In combination, they give rise to a mesmerizing array of reflections.

### Digital Park

It won't come as a surprise that the **largest science museum** has a section dedicated to the latest advances in robotics (see pp.146–47), human-computer interaction and VR. Visitors can interact with many of the automata, which include a squad of soccer-playing bots and humanoid NAO robots (above), which have the ability to learn body language... and are pretty nifty dancers to boot!

Petal-shaped design

Since first opening in 2008, Guangdong Science Center has welcomed more than 20 million visitors through its doors.

# Pop Culture

**Largest multiplayer videogame battle**

Developed by Iceland's CCP Games, *EVE Online* is a futuristic massively multiplayer online role-playing game (MMORPG) set in space. On 6 Oct 2020, a total of 8,825 participants came together for a massive PvP (player-versus-player) spaceship battle dubbed "Fury at FWST-8" (pictured). Altogether, 11,258 characters from 114 different alliances took part in the epic engagement, which lasted for 14 hr.

At one particularly intense stage, 6,557 players were engaged at the same time – the **most concurrent participants in a PvP battle**.

Another monumental battle – dubbed "Massacre at M2-XFE" – took place on 30–31 Dec 2020. This 14-hr clash between two of *EVE Online*'s largest player-run coalitions resulted in losses of assets worth around 23 trillion ISK (Interstellar Kredits, the in-game currency); this equates to a real-world value of $378,012 (£278,375; €307,728), making it the **most costly videogame battle**.

The 2020 New Year's Eve "Massacre at M2-XFE" also broke the record for **most Titans lost in a battle**: 257.

## HELLO KITTY

### Largest collection of *Hello Kitty* memorabilia

Masao Gunji of Chiba, Japan, has amassed 5,169 unique *Hello Kitty* items at his (rather cramped) home in the city of Yotsukaidō – a collection that has taken him over 35 years to acquire.

*Hello Kitty* was created by the designer Yuko Shimizu in 1974 as part of her day job at the Japanese brand agency Sanrio, which specializes in *kawaii* ("cute") culture; because she was an employee, Yuko did not become wealthy from her creation, despite the brand having grossed an estimated $86 bn (£66 bn) to date.

Kitty might look like a cat but she is, in fact, a British schoolgirl called Kitty White who lives "just outside London". Kitty does, though, own a cat called Charmmy.

## MICKEY MOUSE

### Largest collection of Mickey Mouse memorabilia

At her home in Katy, Texas, USA, Janet Esteves proudly displays 10,210 Mickey Mouse collectables. Among the items logged during the last official count on 29 Apr 2016 were nine teapots, 23 golf balls, 54 puzzles, 145 car-antenna toppers and 422 keychains.

Walt Disney's mischievous rodent made his debut on 15 May 1928 in a silent, animated test movie called *Plane Crazy*, and later that year, on 18 Nov, thrilled audiences with his first public appearance in *Steamboat Willie*. In 1978, Mickey became the **first fictional character honoured on the Hollywood Walk of Fame**.

The **most expensive Mickey Mouse toy sold at auction** is a rare clockwork motorcycle made in Germany *c.* 1939 for the British market. In Oct 2000, it sold – in its original box – for $110,000 (£76,066) to the American collector Donald Kaufman.

## WINNIE-THE-POOH

### Largest collection of Winnie-the-Pooh memorabilia

There can be no more passionate a fan of A A Milne's honey-loving bear than Deb Hoffmann of Wisconsin, USA. At the last count on 20 Dec 2020, her collection of memorabilia relating to Pooh – aka Edward Bear – and his friends from Hundred Acre Wood numbered 20,000 unique items.

Pooh's very first appearance in print was in Milne's 1924 poem "Teddy Bear" in *Punch* magazine. Best-selling books followed – *Winnie-the-Pooh* (1926) and *The House at Pooh Corner* (1928) – and Disney acquired the movie and merchandising rights in 1961.

British author Alan Alexander Milne named his famous creation after a black bear from Canada called Winnie (short for Winnipeg), who lived at London Zoo from 1915 until her death in 1934.

# POKÉMON

**First Pokémon...** Rhydon was the first creature drawn by co-creator Ken Sugimori for *Red/Blue* (1996, see below right).

**Tallest...** At 20 m (65 ft 7 in), the gigantic, energy-absorbing Eternatus is the loftiest in the Pokédex.

**Shortest...** Sharing this record at a mere 10 cm (4 in) tall are the mini monsters Flabébé (left), Joltik (right), Cutiefly, Comfey, Cosmoem and Sinistea.

**Slowest...** Three Pokémon are the most lethargic: Pyukumuku (above), Shuckle (below left) and Munchlax (below right), each with a speed stat of 5; despite its name, Slowpoke has a speed of 15.

**Heaviest...** The Pokédex lists the weights of all Pokémon in kilos and pounds (to one decimal place); the extra-dimensional Celesteela (above) and Protostar Cosmoem (below) both weigh 999.9 kg (2,204.4 lb).

## ILLUSTRATOR
ポケモンイラストレーター

**Most expensive *Pokémon* trading cards**
**Auction**: A 1998 "Pikachu Illustrator" card (top) sold for ¥25,000,000 ($233,581; £183,666) at a ZenPlus auction in Japan on 23 Jul 2020.
**Retail**: In Oct 2016, a very limited-edition, solid-gold (24-karat) reissue of the first Pikachu card went on sale for ¥216,000 ($2,061; £1,690).

**Fastest time to gross $100 m by a mobile game**
Launched in Australia, New Zealand and the USA on 6 Jul 2016, Niantic's GPS-based *Pokémon GO* took just 20 days to make $100 m (£76.1 m) in revenue. This was doubly impressive given that the game didn't release in Japan – the spiritual home of *Pokémon* – until 22 Jul. It reached the milestone of $2 bn (£1.51 bn) 791 days later.

The **best-selling *Pokémon* games**, with 31.37 million sales by Aug 2013, are the paired Game Boy titles *Pokémon Red Version* and *Blue Version* (Game Freak, 1996). Originally published in Japan as *Pocket Monsters: Red & Green*, these were the first *Pokémon* titles available overseas.

In Nov 1999, *Pokémon* became the **first videogame on the cover of *TIME* magazine**. The article inside this prestigious weekly news title warned of the risks of "Pokémania", and the cover featured Poliwhirl and friends instead of the usual politicians and celebrities.

## Best-selling RPG videogame series
As of 28 Sep 2020, the *Pokémon* series had shifted 368.04 million units, according to VGChartz. The role-playing phenomenon was created in 1995 by Japanese videogame designer Satoshi Tajiri and has spawned an entire industry of games, movies, manga, trading cards and licensed merchandising. In this relatively short space of time, the brand has grossed over $100 bn (£75.8 bn) globally, making it one of the most – if not *the* most – lucrative media franchises of all time, ahead of the likes of Mickey Mouse and *Star Wars*.

Pikachu – the most recognizable Pokémon – has been a part of the famous Macy's Thanksgiving Day Parade in New York, USA, since 2001. Here, the 53-ft-tall (16-m) pop-culture icon floats down the streets of Manhattan guided by 90 Pokéfans.

## Highest-grossing film series at the global box office

The 12 *Star Wars* movies had earned a collective $10,320,189,178 (£7.41 bn) as of 16 Mar 2021, according to The-Numbers.com. This figure includes re-issues and special editions. Based around three core trilogies known as the "Skywalker Saga" (above), the *Star Wars* series tells the continuing story of the battle between the Jedi and the Sith in a galaxy far, far away.

### Largest *Star Wars* costuming group

The ranks of the 501st Legion (USA) had swelled to 14,141 members as of 18 Nov 2020. More than 30,000 costumes had received official Legion approval. The group, formed by Albin Johnson in 1997 as a "stormtrooper fan club", now welcomes allies of the Galactic Empire and bounty hunters alike.

### Largest personal fortune made from a film franchise

*Star Wars* creator George Lucas (USA) had a net worth of $6.4 bn (£4.8 bn) as of 11 Dec 2020, according to *Forbes*. He is pictured with Kathleen Kennedy (USA), the **highest-grossing film producer at the global box office (female)**. Kennedy-produced movies – which include five *Star Wars* titles – have earned a total of $12.8 bn (£9.6 bn).

In 2020, the lifetime revenue generated by *Star Wars* toys and other merchandise was estimated at $20 bn (£14.7 bn), making it the **most successful movie merchandising campaign**.

Steve Sansweet (USA) has amassed the ❯ **largest collection of *Star Wars* memorabilia**. Of his estimated 500,000 unique items at Rancho Obi-Wan in California, USA, "only" 93,260 items have been audited and catalogued.

Steve reckons his most expensive item to be a Darth Vader costume, parts of which appeared in the original 1977 *Star Wars* film.

### Largest personal insurance pay-out

Following Carrie Fisher's untimely passing on 27 Dec 2016, Lloyds of London had to pay out $50 m (£41.6 m) to Disney. The studio had taken out an insurance policy to protect it in the event that Fisher was unable to reprise her role as Princess Leia in any of the new *Star Wars* movies (Episodes VII, VIII or IX).

# MINECRAFT

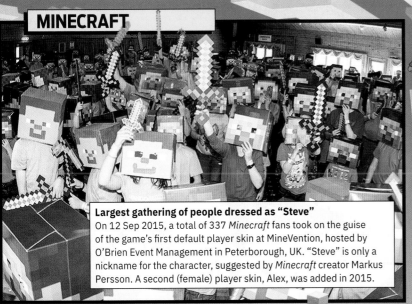

The "DanTDM" channel of *Minecraft*-mad Daniel Middleton (UK) has the ● **most views for a dedicated *Minecraft* YouTube channel** – 17,832,739,882, as of 16 Mar 2021.

### Largest gathering of people dressed as "Steve"

On 12 Sep 2015, a total of 337 *Minecraft* fans took on the guise of the game's first default player skin at MineVention, hosted by O'Brien Event Management in Peterborough, UK. "Steve" is only a nickname for the character, suggested by *Minecraft* creator Markus Persson. A second (female) player skin, Alex, was added in 2015.

### A very conventional game...

The *Minecraft* community love nothing more than getting together to share their passion at events such as MineCon 2015 (pictured). The **first official *Minecraft* convention** was MineCon 2011, held on 18 Nov 2011 in Las Vegas, Nevada, USA. Minefaire 2016 in Philadelphia, Pennsylvania, USA, sold 12,140 tickets – making it the **largest convention for a single videogame**.

### Fastest time to make 10 cakes in *Minecraft* with a mouse and keyboard (Survival Mode)

On 3 Apr 2018, Joseph Garrett (UK) – aka YouTuber "stampylonghead" – whipped up 10 cakes in 3 min 51 sec at GWR HQ in London, UK. Joseph's YouTube career exploded when he started uploading *Minecraft* videos as "Stampy Cat". His channel had 9.79 million subscribers as of 2 Jan 2021.

### ▶ Longest journey in *Minecraft*

Kurt J Mac (USA) has been documenting his passage to *Minecraft*'s Far Lands on YouTube since Mar 2011. On 31 Aug 2019, he pressed F3 to reveal that he had travelled 3,857,848 blocks (3,857 km; 2,396 mi) through the game. Amazingly, Kurt still has 70% of the way to go. He has uploaded more than 800 videos charting his trek, which is in aid of charity.

### Best-selling videogame

In May 2020, Microsoft announced that sales of *Minecraft* (Mojang/Microsoft, 2011) had topped 200 million. It may be a decade old but the block-building videogame shows no sign of waning in popularity, with 126 million active monthly users. According to YouTube, *Minecraft* videos received 201 billion views in 2020 – three times that of *Fortnite* videos!

The ● **largest LEGO®** *Minecraft* **diorama** is this fantasy cityscape measuring 17.13 m² (184 sq ft) in area. It was constructed at the Brick 2014 exhibition in London, UK, on 27–30 Nov 2014.

## ANPANMAN

Let's Go! Anpanman has aired in Japan since 1988 and is still one of the most popular anime children's cartoon series there. Anpanman himself was inspired by "anpan" bread rolls (shown right, a selection based on the series' characters). Written by Takashi Yanase (JPN), Let's Go! Anpanman had featured more than 2,300 parts as of Oct 2018, the **most characters in an animation series**. It began life as a manga picture book in 1973.

## SHŌNEN

**Best-selling Japanese magazine**
Based on the most recent figures from the Japanese Magazine Publishers Association, the most popular manga magazine is Shueisha's Weekly Shōnen Jump, with a circulation of 1.64 million copies for the period Jan–Dec 2019. Lifetime sales are estimated to have exceeded 7.5 billion copies. "Shōnen" manga is aimed at a broadly teenage, predominantly male readership.

Kenshiro (right) is the star of manga Fist of the North Star. The series first appeared in Weekly Shōnen Jump in 1983–88, but has grown into one of the most lucrative media franchises, earning more than $20 bn (£14.7 bn).

## DISNEY PRINCESS

**Cartoon royalty**
Walt Disney (USA) – who, between 1932 and 1969, won the **most Oscars** (26) – reintroduced the world to fairy-tale princesses in his much-loved animated movies. In 2000, Disney executives created a spin-off franchise called Disney Princess, now estimated to be worth c. $46 bn (£33.8 bn), the majority of which stems from lucrative merchandise sales (pictured).

**Fastest-selling Kingdom Hearts videogame**
Disney Princesses Rapunzel, Ariel, Elsa and Anna all appear in Kingdom Hearts III. According to Square Enix, the game shipped more than 5 million units, physically and digitally, in one week following its release on 29 Jan 2019. The action role-player is already nearing the lifetime sales of both 2002's Kingdom Hearts and its 2006 sequel.

**Most expensive animation**
A lengthy on/off pre-production period – and the development of cutting-edge CGI – ensured that Tangled (USA, 2010) remains the costliest animation ever made, at an estimated $260 m (£168 m). Taking inspiration from the fairy tale Rapunzel, it was the 50th movie released by the Disney studio. It went on to gross $585,727,091 (£439.2 m) at the worldwide box office.

# MARIO

Mario – then called Jumpman – debuted in the **first true platform videogame**: Nintendo's 1981 arcade game *Donkey Kong*. It was also the first game by designer Shigeru Miyamoto.

*Super Mario Bros.* (Nintendo, 1985) on NES is the **best-selling *Mario* game**. As confirmed by VGChartz, it had shipped a total of 40.24 million copies by 11 Jan 2019.

**Most ubiquitous videogame character**
Gaming's best-loved plumber – full name Mario Mario – appeared in 237 distinct videogame titles as of 24 Nov 2020, excluding remakes and re-releases. He's seen here as depicted in 2017's *Super Mario Odyssey*. His next outing will be *Super Mario 3D World + Bowser's Fury* – an expanded re-release for the Switch slated for Feb 2021.

**Best-selling videogame character**
In 2020, the Mario brothers celebrated their 35th anniversary. As of 30 Sep that year, the videogames that Mario graced had shipped 657.46 million copies according to VGChartz. This excludes titles in which he appears as a guest, such as *NBA Street V3* and *SSX on Tour*. *Mario Kart Live: Home Circuit* for the Switch (pictured) – the 15th instalment of the popular kart-racing series – launched in late 2020.

*Super Mario Kart* debuted on the SNES on 27 Aug 1992. As of the release of the Switch's *Mario Kart Live: Home Circuit* 28 years 50 days later on 16 Oct 2020 (see left), it was the **longest-running kart series**.

*Mario Kart 8 Deluxe* (2017) is the **best-selling Switch title**, having shipped 28.99 million copies by 30 Sep 2020, according to Nintendo.

### Longest-running videogame character

With the release of Traveller's Tales' *LEGO DC Super-Villains* (far right, top) on 16 Oct 2018, Superman had featured in videogames for 39 years 289 days. The Man of Steel made his videogame debut in Dec 1978 in *Superman* for the Atari 2600 (far right). He survived the critical Kryptonite of *Superman 64* in 1999 and rose again in 2017's acclaimed fighter *Injustice 2* (right).

### Most Emmys for a comic-book series

HBO's *Watchmen* (USA) picked up 11 trophies, including Best Limited Series, at the 72nd Annual Primetime Emmy Awards on 20 Sep 2020. The show was a continuation of Alan Moore and Dave Gibbons's 1986–87 DC Comics series, providing new storylines for their alternate world of masked vigilantes.

### Most Oscars won by a superhero franchise

Batman films have won five Academy Awards: Best Production Design for 1989's *Batman*; Best Sound Editing and Best Supporting Actor (Heath Ledger as Joker, left) for 2008's *The Dark Knight*; and Best Original Score and Best Actor (Joaquim Phoenix) for 2019's *Joker*. Robert Pattinson will hope to add to the list when his starring turn in *The Batman* (below) is released in 2022.

### Best-selling superhero videogame series

Warner Bros. Interactive Entertainment's *Batman: Arkham* series had shipped 24.81 million copies as of 10 Mar 2021, according to VGChartz. The "Arkhamverse" consists of four main titles and sees the Winged Knight pitted against a variety of archenemies. A *Suicide Squad* spin-off is planned for 2022.

### ▶ Largest mechanical cosplay wings

A cosplay costume of DC's Hawkman has a wingspan of 5.84 m (19 ft 2 in). It's the work of Andy Holt (USA), who first spread his wings on 24 Oct 2019 in Irvine, California, USA. The wings are operated by linear actuators linked to a handheld remote control.

### First superhero team

Evil-battling ensembles such as DC's Justice League (resurrected in a 2017 movie release, pictured) now dominate the cinema screen. They owe their origins to All-Star Comics, a forerunner of DC Comics. In *All-Star Comics 3* (winter 1940, inset), heroes such as Hawkman and the Flash assembled as the Justice Society of America.

**Fastest movie to gross $1 billion at the global box office**
*Avengers: Endgame* (USA, 2019) banked $1 bn within just five days of its worldwide release. The 22nd instalment of the Marvel Cinematic Universe became only the fifth film to earn $2 bn globally. From Jul 2019 to Mar 2021, it reigned as the **highest-grossing movie** of all time; this record reverted to *Avatar* (USA/UK, 2009) after a re-release in China in early 2021 saw it top $2.8 bn (£2.01 bn).

The **best-selling comic (single edition)** is *X-Men #1* (Marvel Comics, 1991), with sales of 8,186,500 copies. It was produced by Chris Claremont (UK) and artist Jim Lee (USA), who created five different interlocking cover designs.

According to figures provided by global comic-book wholesaler Diamond Comic Distributors, Marvel Comics is the **largest comic-book publisher**. It had the largest retail market share – 40.3% – of any comic publisher at the end of 2019. DC Comics came in second, with 29.23%.

**Highest-grossing female superhero movie**
*Captain Marvel* (USA, 2019), starring Brie Larson as Carol Danvers/Vers/Captain Marvel, had earned $1,129,727,388 (£814 m) at the global box office as of 10 Mar 2021.

The original Captain Marvel (now owned by DC and rebooted as *Shazam!*) started life in *Whiz Comics #2* (Feb 1940). In 1941, the character inspired the **first superhero movie**, starring Tom Tyler (left) as the titular hero.

*Adventures of Captain Marvel* (USA, 1941, above) was the first comic-book movie to feature a costumed hero with superhuman powers.

*Black Panther* is the **highest-grossing superhero origin movie**, with global box-office returns of $1.33 bn (£963 m).

**First superhero movie nominated for a Best Picture Oscar**
*Black Panther* (USA, 2018), starring the late Chadwick Boseman, was a critical and box-office smash. It lost out to *Green Book* (USA, 2018) at the 91st Academy Awards but won for Original Score, Costume Design and Production Design – the **most Oscars for a superhero movie**.

# WIZARDING WORLD

*Accio!* Victoria Maclean (UK) has summoned up the ● **largest collection of *Wizarding World* memorabilia**, consisting of 3,686 items as of 28 Feb 2019. She has spent 18 years acquiring objects related to the *Harry Potter* and *Fantastic Beasts* franchises. Among her most prized acquisitions is a 24-karat gold-plated Golden Snitch puzzle from Japan.

## Highest-grossing play on Broadway

*Harry Potter and the Cursed Child* had taken $174,056,581 (£133 m) on Broadway up to 10 Mar 2021 – more than any other non-musical. The two-part play was written by Jack Thorne, J. K. Rowling and John Tiffany (all UK). According to figures by Nielsen and NPD BookScan, the script book (inset) had sold 9,237,886 copies as of 7 Nov 2020 – making it the **best-selling playscript** since book sales have been tracked.

SPECIAL REHEARSAL EDITION SCRIPT

**HARRY POTTER AND THE CURSED CHILD**

PARTS ONE AND TWO

BASED ON AN ORIGINAL NEW STORY BY
**J.K. ROWLING**
JOHN TIFFANY & JACK THORNE
A NEW PLAY BY JACK THORNE

## Highest-grossing movies adapted from a book series

The eight *Harry Potter* films (2001–11) had earned a combined worldwide gross of $7,684,330,574 (£5.53 bn) as of 10 Mar 2021. This figure is based on the original seven-book series written by J. K. Rowling and does not include the two *Fantastic Beasts* spin-offs. If all "Wizarding World" titles are accounted for, the total reaches $9.2 bn (£6.82 bn).

On 22 Nov 2017, inspired by their favourite boy wizard, West Byford Primary School in Perth, Australia, organized the **largest gathering of people dressed as Harry Potter** – a spellbinding gathering of 997 wand-waving pupils.

## Best-selling children's book series

J. K. Rowling's *Harry Potter* books had sold more than 500 million copies as of Feb 2018, according to publisher Bloomsbury. This figure includes sales of the seven books in the original series (left) and three companion volumes. The tales of wizardry had been translated into more than 80 languages.

# GRAND THEFT AUTO

**Fastest entertainment property to gross $1 bn**
When *Grand Theft Auto V* was released for home consoles on 17 Sep 2013, the felonious action-adventure videogame took just three days to break the $1-bn barrier. Developers Rockstar claimed that the title made $800 m (£500 m) of that in 24 hr.

"Criminal Records" is the **most-played job in *Grand Theft Auto Online***, with 225.9 million plays as of 14 Oct 2020. The multiplayer race mission allows up to eight players to tear up the track around Bolingbroke Penitentiary in the Great Senora Desert.

# TRANSFORMERS

The first Optimus Prime toy was released in Japan in 1984 as "Battle Convoy", part of the Diaclone toy line. Rebranded as a Transformer, Prime embodied the "Robots in Disguise" conceit with features such as its iconic cab-front torso.

**Largest collection of *Transformers* memorabilia**
AJ Ard (USA) has assembled 3,626 items relating to the *Transformers* franchise, including not only toys but comic books, trading cards, clothes, kites and a lunchbox. His collection was verified on 9 Jan 2018 in Moreno Valley, California, USA. Among AJ's rarest objects is a die-cast metal Japanese edition of the Autobot Metalhawk.

**Highest-grossing robot movie**
*Transformers: Dark of the Moon* (USA, 2011) netted a worldwide gross of $1,123,794,079 (£727.1 m) – only the 10th film to earn more than $1 bn. The third instalment in the live-action robot series, it charted the continuing war between Autobots – such as Optimus Prime (pictured) – and their Decepticon enemies.

GUINNESS WORLD RECORDS

# FORTNITE

Ninja, aka Richard Tyler Blevins (USA), has the **most-followed Twitch channel**, with 16,632,966 fans as of 21 Jan 2021. The gamer, whose popularity soared when he began playing *Fortnite*, signed an exclusivity deal with the short-lived Mixer platform in 2019, but began streaming on Twitch again in 2020.

## Most concurrently played videogame

*Fortnite* is one of the few games to register simultaneous gamers into the tens of millions. The peak was reached on 1 Dec 2020, when the *Fortnite Galactus* event drew 15.3 million concurrent players. The special Marvel-themed mission allowed gamers to do battle against Galactus – the Devourer of Worlds – beside superheroes such as Iron Man and Wolverine.

Fuelling the ongoing success of *Fortnite* are prize battles such as the Winter Royales (pictured), which are open to players of any Arena rank.

According to Tracker Network's *Fortnite* stats, the **most eliminations in *Fortnite Battle Royale*** is 273,341, by BH nixxxay (CAN) as of 12 Feb 2021. He had a Kill/Death ratio of 9.39, placing him in the top 0.1%.

Twitch Ship (USA) had claimed the **most wins of *Fortnite Battle Royale*** – 22,764, as of 12 Feb 2021, according to Tracker Network. This is almost twice as many as any other player. Ship has a win ratio of 51.9% and is second only to BH nixxxay for eliminations (see left).

## First battle-royale videogame with 250 million registered players

On 20 Mar 2019, Epic Games confirmed that *Fortnite Battle Royale* had a quarter of a billion registered players. This figure had doubled in the space of just nine months. The all-conquering free-to-play shooter continues to defy predictions that its popularity will wane. On 6 May 2020, Epic announced that they had reached 350 million registered players.

Released on 26 Sep 2017, *Fortnite Battle Royale* had a simple premise: 100 online players fight it out to be the last person standing. From this, the game has grown into a global franchise worth more than $4.5 bn (£3.3 bn).

## TOY STORY

## GUNDAM

**Largest mobile humanoid robot**
In Sep 2020, a towering Gundam robot measuring 18 m (59 ft) in height took its first public steps in Yokohama, Japan. It has since been filmed walking, flexing its fingers and even kneeling. The 22-tonne (24-ton) humanoid's design is based on the RX-78-2 Gundam from the original 1979 anime Japanese TV series *Mobile Suit Gundam*. It was built by GUNDAM GLOBAL CHALLENGE (JPN), an incorporated association that was launched in 2014 with a view to celebrating the franchise's 40th anniversary.

*Toy Story 4* (USA, 2019) is the **highest-grossing G-rated movie**, with worldwide box-office takings of $1,073,394,813 (£822.1 m).

**First feature-length computer-animated movie**
*Toy Story* (USA, 1995) – the first film produced by the Pixar studio – was animated entirely on computer. The adventures of Woody and Buzz Lightyear (voiced by Tom Hanks and Tim Allen, respectively) was a smash hit with audiences, grossing more than $360 m (£232 m) and spawning three sequels. In Dec 2010, *Toy Story 3* (USA, 2010) became the **first animated film to make $1 billion**.

## DRAGON BALL

**Most money earned playing**
***Dragon Ball FighterZ***
As of Oct 2020, GO1, aka Goichi Kishida (JPN), had earned $62,882 (£48,457) playing Bandai Namco's 3D fighter. On 3 Aug 2019, he beat Dominique "SonicFox" McLean to secure his first EVO Championship Series victory.
Another *Dragon Ball* gaming achievement in 2020 was the **fastest completion of *Dragon Ball Z: Kakarot* (PC)**, by Ohh_Snap (USA) in 3 hr 55 min 43 sec on 11 Mar.

*Dragon Ball* was created by Akira Toriyama in 1984 as a *Shōnen Jump* manga series (see p.192), with a TV anime following a decade later. The franchise is now valued at *c.* $30 bn (£22 bn). Pictured is the series' main protagonist, Goku, a martial-arts warrior on a quest to seek out a series of orbs known as Dragon Balls, which contain wish-granting dragons.

# Movies

*all box-office figures from TheNumbers.com as of 20 Apr 2021, unless otherwise indicated.

## Highest-grossing film
*Avatar* (USA/UK, 2009) returned to cinemas in China in 2020, boosting its worldwide lifetime gross to $2.80 bn (£2.01 bn) as of 16 Mar 2021. The sci-fi epic reclaimed its crown as the all-time most successful movie from *Avengers: Endgame* (see p.195). As many as four sequels are planned; *Avatar 2* is due for release in 2022.

## Academy Awards 2021
The 93rd Oscars ceremony was delayed by two months because of COVID-19. It was finally held on 25 Apr 2021 as a red-carpet affair, and nominees were encouraged to attend in person. Among the records broken (see right and below) were:

**Oldest acting winner**: Sir Anthony Hopkins (UK, b. 31 Dec 1937) was aged 83 years 115 days when he won Best Actor for the title role in *The Father* (UK/FRA, 2020). The **oldest acting nominee** is Christopher Plummer (CAN, b. 13 Dec 1929), who was 88 when recognized in 2018 for playing J Paul Getty in *All the Money in the World* (USA, 2017); he died in Feb 2021 and was honoured in the "In Memoriam" segment.

**Most nominations for a Black actress**: Viola Davis (USA) received her fourth Oscar acknowledgement – for Best Actress – thanks to her performance in *Ma Rainey's Black Bottom* (USA, 2020). Davis had previously been nominated in the same category for *The Help* (USA, 2011); she also received Best Supporting Actress nominations for *Doubt* (USA, 2008) and *Fences* (USA/CAN, 2016) – the latter of which delivered Davis her first Academy Award win.

**First Black winners of Best Makeup and Hairstyling**: The biopic of blues singer Ma Rainey also resulted in an award for African-American hairstylists Mia Neal and Jamika Wilson (both USA), shared with make-up artist Sergio Lopez-Rivera. And the film's costume designer, Ann Roth (USA, b. 30 Oct 1931), became the **oldest woman to win a competitive Oscar**, claiming her prize at the age of 89 years 177 days.

## Most female Oscar nominees for Best Director in the same year
Two women received Best Director nominations at the 93rd Academy Awards in 2021. Chloé Zhao (CHN) was shortlisted for *Nomadland* (USA/DEU, 2020), starring Frances McDormand (above); and Emerald Fennell (UK) was acknowledged for *Promising Young Woman* (UK/USA, 2020), with Carey Mulligan (inset). It was Zhao who claimed the award, becoming the **first Asian woman to win Best Director**. The **first** (and only other) female to win this coveted prize is Kathryn Bigelow (USA) for *The Hurt Locker* (USA, 2009).

## Longest title for an Oscar-nominated film
Mockumentary *Borat Subsequent Moviefilm: Delivery of Prodigious Bribe to American Regime for Make Benefit Once Glorious Nation of Kazakhstan* (UK/USA, 2020) boasts 110 characters in its title and was nominated for Best Adapted Screenplay on 15 Mar 2021. Maria Bakalova was also nominated for Best Supporting Actress for her role as Borat's daughter, Tutar. Very nice!

## Highest annual earnings for a film actor
According to the latest estimates by Forbes, actor/producer Tyler Perry (USA) earned $97 m (£78.5 m) in the 12 months to 1 Jun 2020. The multi-talented Perry is best known for his *Madea* franchise, in which he plays the eponymous no-nonsense lady.

The **film actress** record is held by Angelina Jolie (USA, inset), with reported earnings of $35.5 m (£28.7 m) for the same period.

## Youngest BAFTA nominee
In Mar 2021, at the age of 8 years 320 days, Alan S Kim (USA, b. 23 Apr 2012) was shortlisted by members of the British Academy of Film and Television Arts for Best Supporting Actor. The Korean-American was just seven years old when he landed the role of David Yi in the Oscar-nominated *Minari* (USA, 2020).

The 2021 BAFTA ceremony, held on 11 Apr, saw *The Father* star Anthony Hopkins (see left) become the **oldest winner for Best Leading Actor**, claiming the prize aged 83 years 101 days.

## Most cinemas (country)
The movie industry may have been hit hard by the COVID pandemic, but the number of movie screens in China rose by nearly 6,000 in 2020 to a total of 75,581, at some 12,700 complexes. By comparison, the USA had 40,998 screens, according to the National Association of Theatre Owners.

### Highest box-office career gross by a living...

| Role | Name | Accumulated gross |
| --- | --- | --- |
| Leading actor | Robert Downey Jr (USA) | $14.39 bn (£10.3 bn) |
| Leading actress | Scarlett Johansson (USA) | $13.65 bn (£9.8 bn) |
| Supporting actor | Warwick Davis (UK) | $14.49 bn (£10.4 bn) |
| Supporting actress (screen) | Cate Blanchett (AUS) | $8.07 bn (£5.8 bn) |
| Supporting actress (voice) | Laraine Newman (USA) | $8.38 bn (£6.0 bn) |
| Director | Steven Spielberg (USA) | $10.54 bn (£7.5 bn) |
| Screenwriter | Christopher Markus & Stephen McFeely (both USA; partnership) | $9.36 bn (£6.7 bn) |
| Producer | Kevin Feige (USA) | $22.55 bn (£16.2 bn) |
| Executive producer* | Louis D'Esposito (USA) | $22.24 bn (£15.9 bn) |
| Cinematographer[†] | Dariusz Wolski (POL) | $7.51 bn (£5.4 bn) |
| Production designer | Rick Carter (USA) | $11.96 bn (£8.6 bn) |
| Editor | Michael Kahn (USA) | $11.96 bn (£8.6 bn) |
| Composer | Hans Zimmer (DEU) | $29.89 bn (£21.4 bn) |
| Costume designer | Judianna Makovsky (USA) | $11.33 bn (£8.1 bn) |
| Casting director | Sarah Halley Finn (USA) | $28.18 bn (£20.2 bn) |

*The movies of Stan Lee (USA, 1922–2018) grossed $32.04 bn (£23.2 bn)
[†]The movies of Andrew Lesnie (AUS, 1956–2015) grossed $7.89 bn (£5.6 bn)

ROBERT **DOWNEY JR**    SCARLETT **JOHANSSON**    CATE **BLANCHETT**    WARWICK **DAVIS**

Our made-up movie *Block Bu$ter!* stars the **highest-grossing actors** and **creatives** currently working in Hollywood, according to data sourced from TheNumbers.com (see table below left). Based on record-breaking box-office data for **production method, creative type, genre, source** and **rating**, it's a live-action, contemporary adventure with an original screenplay and a PG-13 rating. So, grab your popcorn, turn off your phone and enjoy what should be – on paper, at least – the most successful movie ever made!

# BLOCK BU$TER!

★★★★★
**"BOX-OFFICE GOLD"**
Guinness World Records

★★★★★
**"A GUARANTEED SMASH HIT"**
TheNumbers.com

GUINNESS WORLD RECORDS PICTURES PRESENTS A MOVIE THAT IS... OFFICIALLY AMAZING!

IN ASSOCIATION WITH TheNUMBERS.com A STEVEN SPIELBERG FILM

ROBERT DOWNEY JR "BLOCK BU$TER!" SCARLETT JOHANSSON WITH CATE BLANCHETT WARWICK DAVIS FEATURING THE VOICE OF LARAINE NEWMAN

COSTUME DESIGNER JUDIANNA MAKOVSKY MUSIC HANS ZIMMER EDITOR MICHAEL KAHN PRODUCTION DESIGNER RICK CARTER DIRECTOR OF PHOTOGRAPHY DARIUSZ WOLSKI ASC

CASTING SARAH HALLEY FINN EXECUTIVE PRODUCER LOUIS D'ESPOSITO PRODUCER KEVIN FEIGE SCREENPLAY BY CHRISTOPHER MARKUS & STEPHEN McFEELY DIRECTED BY STEVEN SPIELBERG

**THE NUMBERS**    COMING SOON?    OFFICIALLY  AMAZING

PARENTS STRONGLY CAUTIONED
**PG-13**

# Music

## Most streamed act on Spotify in one year

Tracks by Bad Bunny (b. Benito Ocasio, PRI) were streamed 8.3 billion times in 2020. The reggaeton star and WWE wrestler released three albums during the year, including *YHLQMDLG* (the **most streamed album** of 2020, with 3.3 billion plays). He edged out Drake's previous record of 8.2 billion plays in 2018.

## Biggest-selling digital single (current year)

"Blinding Lights" by The Weeknd (b. Abel Tesfaye, CAN) registered 2.72 billion "subscription stream equivalents" across all digital formats in 2020, as revealed by the International Federation of the Phonographic Industry on 9 Mar 2021. Released on 29 Nov 2019, "Blinding Lights" went to No.1 in more than 30 countries and was Spotify's **most streamed track** of 2020 (1.6 billion). In the US, it topped *Billboard*'s year-end Hot 100 Songs chart and set new records for the **most weeks in the Hot 100's Top 5** (43) and **Top 10** (57) as of 1 May 2021.

## Most streamed group on Spotify

As of 27 Apr 2021, the music of BTS (KOR) had been streamed 16.3 billion times on Spotify. "Dynamite" (829.7 million) and "Boy with Luv" (642.6 million) are the band's most popular tracks. For more on the K-pop icons, see pp.212–13.

## Most concerts performed in 12 hours (multiple cities/towns)

On 7 Dec 2019, Minhee Jones (UK, b. USA) played in eight English locations in half a day: Abingdon, Milton Keynes, Banbury, Aylesbury, Northampton, Coventry, Wolverhampton and Stoke. As per the guidelines, each gig was a minimum of 50 km (31 mi) apart, in places with a population of at least 15,000. The alt-pop artist attempted this record to support grassroots music venues and to spread some Christmas cheer.

## Fastest time for a music track to reach 100 million streams on Spotify

"Drivers License" by Olivia Rodrigo (USA) took 10 days to register 100 million streams on Spotify, between 8 and 17 Jan 2021. The debut single by the actress-turned-singer became a huge viral hit and topped charts around the world. It is the **most streamed track on Spotify in one week**, with 89,013,286 plays on 11–17 Jan.

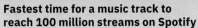

## Most followed group on Spotify

US rock band Imagine Dragons had amassed 33,795,204 followers on Spotify as of 27 Apr 2021. They were the first rock act to reach 1 billion streams for two songs – "Believer" and "Thunder" – while their 2013 smash hit "Radioactive" still holds the record for **most weeks on the *Billboard* Hot 100**, with 87 non-consecutive weeks between 18 Aug 2012 and 10 May 2014.

## Most Premio Lo Nuestro (PLN) nominations in one year (male)

Reggaeton singer J Balvin (COL) was nominated 14 times ahead of the 33rd PLN Awards on 18 Feb 2021. His nominations included Artist of the Year, Album of the Year (*Colores*) and Song of the Year ("Morado"). However, he won only one; the big winner on the night was Bad Bunny (left), who claimed seven gongs. The **female** (and overall) record is 15 nominations, earned by Natti Natasha (b. Natalia Batista, DOM) for the 31st PLN Awards in 2019.

## Most tracks to debut at No.1 on the *Billboard* Hot 100

On 7 Nov 2020, "Positions" by Ariana Grande (USA) became the pop superstar's fifth No.1 debut on the US Hot 100 singles chart. The others were "thank u, next", "7 rings", "Stuck with U" (feat. Justin Bieber) and "Rain on Me" with Lady Gaga.

As the world went into lockdown in 2020, Spotify recorded a 1,400% increase in "working-from-home" playlists.

## Most streamed acts on Spotify

**Male**: As of 27 Apr 2021, tracks by the Canadian singer/rapper Drake had been streamed 37.9 billion times on Spotify. His most popular song is "One Dance", with 2.01 billion streams registered.

**Female**: Ariana Grande's (USA) songs have been streamed 24.4 billion times; "7 rings" is her most in-demand track, with 1.43 billion streams. She is also currently the **highest-earning female musician**, with an estimated income of $72 m (£58.3 m) in the 12 months up to 1 Jun 2020, according to Forbes.

## Biggest-selling Christmas album of the 21st century (UK)

*Christmas* by Michael Bublé (CAN/ITA) had sold 3,030,043 copies in the UK as of 9 Jan 2020, according to the Official Charts Company. Since its release in 2011, *Christmas* has returned to the UK Top 10 every year bar 2015, spending a total of 44 weeks there. It features Bublé's take on classics such as "Jingle Bells" and "White Christmas".

POP CULTURE

## Most ARIA awards for Album of the Year

Tame Impala (b. Kevin Parker, AUS) won his third Album of the Year prize at the Australian Recording Industry Association (ARIA) awards on 25 Nov 2020, for *The Slow Rush*. This equals the rock band Powderfinger (AUS), who won in 1999, 2001 and 2003.

At the same awards, rock quartet 5 Seconds of Summer (AUS) secured the **most ARIA awards for Song of the Year** with "Teeth" – their third gong to date.

## Oldest UK singles chart entrant

Dame Vera Lynn (UK, b. 20 Mar 1917) was 103 years 62 days old when "We'll Meet Again" debuted at No.55 on the UK's Official Singles Chart on 21 May 2020, just a month before her death. The song featured in the 75th-anniversary celebrations of VE Day in 2020. Dame Vera became the **oldest UK albums chart entrant** on the same day, when *100* re-entered at No.30.

## Most consecutive decades with a No.1 on the UK albums chart (female)

Kylie Minogue (AUS/UK) has scored UK No.1s on the Official Albums Chart in five consecutive decades: 1980s (*Kylie*; *Enjoy Yourself*, inset), 1990s (*Greatest Hits*), 2000s (*Fever*), 2010s (*Aphrodite*; *Golden*; *Step Back in Time – The Definitive Collection*) and 2020s (*Disco*). Her 15th studio release, *Disco*, hit the top on 19 Nov 2020.

## Shortest gap between new No.1 albums on the US *Billboard* 200 (female)

Taylor Swift (USA) released two surprise albums in 2020 that hit the No.1 spot on the US *Billboard* 200 albums chart just 140 days apart. *folklore* did it on 8 Aug 2020, followed by "sister album" *evermore* on 26 Dec. The folk-pop collections, produced with Aaron Dessner, were created during the pandemic lockdown.

## Most tickets sold for a livestreamed concert by a solo female artist

Dua Lipa (UK) sold 284,000 tickets worldwide for her "Studio 2054" concert, which was livestreamed on 27 Nov 2020. The four-part gig cost a reported $1.5 m (£1.12 m) to produce and featured guest performers such as J Balvin and Elton John.

The **male** record is held by Louis Tomlinson (UK), who sold 160,000 tickets worldwide for his "Live from London" charity concert on 12 Dec 2020. The ex-One Direction star raised more than $1 m (£755,000) for charity.

## Most US singles chart entries before reaching No.1

On 16 May 2020, Nicki Minaj (TTO) made No.1 for the first time on the US *Billboard* Hot 100 with her 109th chart entry, "Say So". The rapper appeared as a featured artist on the hit by Doja Cat (USA, b. Amalaratna Dlamini); it meant the pair became the **first female rap duo to reach No.1 on the US singles chart**.

## Most Grammy nominations

With three nominations for the 63rd Annual Grammy Awards in 2021, Jay-Z (b. Shawn Carter, USA) took his career total to 80, matching the tally of producer Quincy Jones (USA) between 1961 and 2019. Jay-Z's wife, Beyoncé (see right), is only one behind on 79 – the **most Grammy nominations (female)**.

## Most Album of the Year Grammy awards won by a performer

On 14 Mar 2021, Taylor Swift became the first female vocalist to scoop an Album of the Year Grammy hat-trick, with *Fearless*, *1989* and *folklore* (see top right). She joins an exclusive group: Frank Sinatra, Stevie Wonder and Paul Simon (all USA).

Between them, Beyoncé and husband Jay-Z have won the **most Grammy Awards by a married couple** – 51.

## Longest-held vocal note in a UK hit single (female artist)

"Húsavík (My Hometown)", performed by actor Will Ferrell (USA) and Swedish vocalist Molly Sandén for the Netflix film *Eurovision Song Contest: The Story of Fire Saga* (USA, 2020), features an 18-sec vocal note at the climax of the ballad. It spent four weeks on the UK's Official Singles Chart, peaking at No.59 on 16 Jul 2020.

The **longest-held vocal note in a US hit single** is 19.3 sec, on the 1989 No.1 "When I'm with You" by Canadian rockers Sheriff.

## Most Grammy awards won by a female artist

Beyoncé (USA) won four trophies at the 63rd Grammy Awards on 14 Mar 2021 to take her total to 28, one more than bluegrass star Alison Krauss. Beyoncé claimed Best R&B Performance ("BLACK PARADE"), Best Rap Song and Best Rap Performance – as a featured artist on "Savage" by Megan Thee Stallion (below, right) – and Best Music Video ("BROWN SKIN GIRL"). The latter also starred Beyoncé's daughter Blue Ivy Carter (USA, b. 7 Jan 2012), who became the **youngest individually credited Grammy winner**, aged 9 years 66 days.

# Social Media

## Platform leaders: social media's most popular individuals

| | | | |
|---|---|---|---|
| Facebook | M | Cristiano Ronaldo (PRT) | 124,726,150 likes |
| | F | Shakira (b. Shakira Ripoll, COL) | 111,705,557 likes |
| YouTube | M | PewDiePie (b. Felix Kjellberg, SWE) | 109,000,000 subscribers |
| | F | Diana (USA, b. UKR) – *Kids Diana Show* | 77,400,000 subscribers |
| Instagram | M | Cristiano Ronaldo (PRT) | 277,859,815 followers |
| | F | Ariana Grande (USA) | 232,322,350 followers |
| Twitter | M | Barack Obama (USA) | 130,272,840 followers |
| | F | Katy Perry (b. Katheryn Hudson, USA) | 109,576,700 followers |
| Pinterest | F | Joy Cho (USA) – *Oh Joy* | 14,866,413 followers |
| | M | Trey Ratcliff (USA) | 6,419,152 followers |
| TikTok | F | Charli D'Amelio (USA, see opposite) | 113,600,000 followers |
| | M | Zach King (USA) | 58,800,000 followers |

### Fastest time to reach 1 million followers on Instagram

Rupert Grint (UK) accumulated 1 million fans just 4 hr 1 min after joining Instagram on 10 Nov 2020. The *Harry Potter* actor's first post showed him with his daughter, Wednesday. Grint's feat broke the record set by British TV naturalist David Attenborough (see pp.54–55), who gained 1 million followers in 4 hr 44 min just two months before.

### Highest-earning YouTuber

Ryan Kaji (USA) earned $29.5 m (£23.8 m) in the year to 1 Jun 2020, as reported by Forbes. Then aged just nine, his videos include unboxing and toy reviews, skits (sometimes including members of his family), science experiments and DIY tips.

He also has the **most views for an individual on YouTube (male)**. The videos on channel *Ryan's World* had been watched 46,636,891,195 times as of 22 Apr 2021.

### Most subscribers for a band on YouTube

BLACKPINK (KOR) currently have 60.3 million followers on YouTube, which they joined on 29 Jun 2016. The quartet scored more than 86 million views of their video premiere for the single "How You Like That" in just one day. Posted on 26 Jun 2020, it became the **most viewed video on YouTube in 24 hours**, before being overtaken by fellow K-pop mega-stars BTS (see right).

### Most viewed video on YouTube

"Baby Shark" by Pinkfong (KOR) has been watched 8,386,967,151 times. First uploaded on 18 Jun 2016, the earworm singalong is sung by Hope Segoine, a Korean-American who was 10 years old at the time. It features two Korean child actors (above; the girl is Elaine Johnston), who perform the accompanying dance moves. The song hit No.32 on the *Billboard* Hot 100 and No.6 in the UK.

### Most views for an individual on YouTube

Seven-year-old Anastasia Radzinskaya (RUS) has attracted 56,548,162,410 views for her children's channel *Like Nastya*.

Radzinskaya is also the **highest-earning YouTuber (female)**, having netted $18.5 m (£14.9 m) in the 12 months to 1 Jun 2020.

### Most viewed video on YouTube in 24 hours

On 22 Aug 2020, South Korean boy band BTS racked up 101.1 million views of the music video for their single "Dynamite". (For more on BTS, see pp.211–13.)

At one point on the previous day, the video was being watched by more than 3 million users, the **most concurrent viewers for a video premiere**.

### Most viewers for a live-streamed DJ set on Facebook

French DJ David Guetta drew a peak of 161,823 viewers for his online *United at Home* set, streamed on Facebook from Miami, Florida, USA, on 18 Apr 2020.

### Most followers for a rat on Instagram

Ice Cube the rescue rat currently has 25,745 fans on Instagram. The ailing rodent was rescued in Jan 2019 after losing his paws and tail to frostbite. He was saved from the streets of Montreal, Quebec, Canada, by Audrée-Rose Fallu Landry (CAN).

## Most downloaded apps (Jan–Nov 2020. *Source: App Annie Intelligence*)

| 1. TikTok | 2. Facebook | 3. WhatsApp | 4. Zoom | 5. Instagram | 6. Messenger | 7. Google Meet | 8. Snapchat | 9. Telegram | 10. Likee |

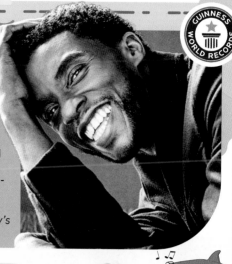

All records as of 22 Apr 2021 unless otherwise stated

## Most YouTube channels with 100,000 subscribers (individual)

As of 22 Jan 2021, Jack Welsh (UK) had created nine channels on YouTube boasting 100,000-plus subscribers each. Although his early posts were devoted to *Minecraft* content, today his output incorporates gaming, unboxing, commentary on Tesla cars and more. His main channel is *JackSucksAtLife*.

## Most liked tweet

By 1 Sep 2020, more than 7.5 million Twitter users had reacted to a message confirming the passing of US actor Chadwick Boseman. The tweet also revealed his four-year battle with cancer. Boseman is best known for award-winning turns in *Black Panther* (2018; see p.195), in which he played the lead, and *Ma Rainey's Black Bottom* (2020).

## Highest-earning TikToker

Addison Rae Easterling (USA) earned an estimated $5 m (£4 m) in the 12 months to 1 Jun 2020, as reported by Forbes. She shot to fame after her dance videos rapidly went viral, leading to lucrative deals with the likes of Reebok and teen clothing brand American Eagle.

Her nearest **male** rival is self-described "edgy teen" and latter-day media executive Josh Richards (USA, inset), with earnings of $1.5 m (£1.2 m) in the same period.

## First TikToker with 100 million followers

Having joined TikTok in summer 2019, Charli D'Amelio (USA) gained her 100-millionth follower on 22 Nov 2020. Her videos mostly focus on lip-synching and short dance routines. The influencer was crowned "Favorite Female Social Star" at the 34th Nickelodeon Kids' Choice Awards on 13 Mar 2021 – and got the customary slime treatment!

## Fastest time to reach 10 million followers on Douyin

Actor and film producer Andy Lau (CHN) gained his 10-millionth fan in 12 hr 22 min on this Chinese network on 28 Jan 2021. The platform enables users to create short videos, carry out in-video product searches and make reservations.

By the end of the day, Lau's account had also accrued the **most Douyin followers in 24 hours** – 19,569,754.

## Most disliked movie trailer on YouTube

The official trailer for *Sadak* 2 (IND, 2020; below) has had 13,478,901 thumbs-down, prompted by controversy and a negative online campaign.

The **most disliked video** on the platform overall is *YouTube Rewind 2018: Everyone Controls Rewind*, with 19,124,328 dislikes. It was pilloried for its outdated and off-the-mark content.

## Most expensive tweet sold at auction

On 21 Mar 2021, the **first tweet** – "just setting up my twttr", sent exactly 15 years earlier by Twitter co-founder Jack Dorsey – sold as a non-fungible token (NFT) for $2,915,835 (£2,101,470). The winning bidder was cryptocurrency entrepreneur Sina Estavi. An NFT is a virtual certificate, confirming that a particular asset/file is the "real" one. The ownership of this token is logged on a digital ledger, so it can't be duplicated or stolen. An NFT makes it possible for someone to own "original" tweets, memes, video clips or even the **most expensive digital artwork** (see p.173).

Easterling currently has 79.8 million-plus TikTok fans, putting her in second place on the platform behind Charli D'Amelio (left).

**Highest consumer spend on apps** (Jan–Nov 2020. *Source: App Annie Intelligence*)

1. Tinder   2. TikTok   3. YouTube   4. Disney+   5. Tencent Video   6. Netflix   7. iQIYI   8. Google One   9. BIGO LIVE   10. Pandora Music

# Gaming Tech

**100%**

**575**

### First console
Released in 1972, the Magnavox Odyssey was a simple device that worked through a television set and was powered by batteries. Despite poor sales, it is credited with starting the home computer and videogame revolution.

### Most expensive console (inflation-adjusted)
Were inflation to be taken into account, the ill-fated 3DO would be the most expensive gaming console ever. It launched on 4 Oct 1993, priced at $699.99 (£465). As of 31 Dec 2020, its retail value would have been $1,251 (£921). Given that hefty price tag, it is perhaps little wonder that it was discontinued in 1996.

### Most buttons on a controller
The Fender Mustang PRO-Guitar controller for Mad Catz's *Rock Band 3* (2010) has 113 buttons – representing every possible finger position on a 17-fret guitar. It features more individual inputs than any peripheral in console history, and even more than a standard PC keyboard.

### Smallest functioning controller
On 12 Feb 2018, console modder Madmorda (USA) unveiled a Nintendo GameCube controller just 63 mm wide, 45 mm high and 31 mm deep (2.4 x 1.7 x 1.2 in). It is fully functional, even down to the rumble feature. Using a GameCube controller keychain as the basis, Madmorda added 3D-printed parts for extra pieces such as the L, R and Z buttons.

### First ninth-generation console
Microsoft's Xbox Series X (and its lower-cost variant, the Series S) launched on 10 Nov 2020, beating rival Sony's PlayStation 5 to stores by two days. The Nintendo Switch, although the successor to the eighth-generation Wii U, is not seen as a ninth-generation console but as a handheld/home console hybrid (see opposite).

### Largest joystick
This scaled-up version of a classic Atari CX40 controller is 9 ft (2.74 m) tall – nearly 14 times the size of the original. Entitled "[giantJoystick]", it was created by artist Mary Flanagan (USA) in 2006. Her ambition was that it would "produce a childlike scale" and "generate discussion and group play". Crafted from wood, steel and rubber, the giant joystick is currently housed at the ZKM Center for Art and Media in Karlsruhe, Germany.

### Best-selling home-console brand
As of 18 Dec 2020, an estimated 465.31 million PlayStation units had been shipped, based on figures from VGChartz. (That tally includes only provisional figures for the PlayStation 5, however; see opposite.) Manufactured by Sony Interactive Entertainment (USA), the console was first released in Japan in 1994. The shipment figure for the PlayStation brand rises to 562.61 million if the handheld PlayStation Portable and PlayStation Vita are included. According to VGChartz, the **best-selling console** is Sony's PlayStation 2 (2000). More than 157.68 million systems were shipped worldwide over its 13-year lifespan.

Console generations update every six years or so, when manufacturers release new sets of competing hardware.

### First official adaptive controller
In the past, gamers with disabilities had to find ways of using existing controllers, but the Xbox Adaptive Controller (XAC) represents technology designed to fit the user. Microsoft began developing the device in 2015, releasing it on 4 Sep 2018. The rectangular box includes ports that correspond to the buttons on an Xbox One controller, allowing almost any combination of customized devices and controllers (insets) to be hooked up to an Xbox or PC.

## Largest playable Game & Watch device

Thomas Tilley (AUS) created a Game & Watch device measuring 1.93 m long, 1.16 m wide and 0.14 m deep (6 ft 4 in x 5 ft 2 in x 5 in), as verified in Port Elliot, Australia, on 21 Oct 2017. It runs the Nintendo game *Octopus*, aka *Mysteries of the Sea* and *Mysteries of the Deep*.

## Best-selling handheld console

According to the latest available figures, the Nintendo DS has shipped more than 154.88 million units. The console was launched on 21 Nov 2004 in North America and in Japan the following month.

## First rumble peripheral

The Rumble Pak was launched in Apr 1997 to coincide with the release of Nintendo's rail-shooter *Star Fox 64*. It slotted into the controller's expansion slot and gave feedback to the player. The first controller with a built-in rumble feature was the Sony DualShock, released in Nov 1997.

## First online-capable console

The Sega Dreamcast launched on 27 Nov 1998. Modem adaptors had been released as first- or third-party peripherals for some 1990s consoles, but the Dreamcast was the first to have this functionality built in as standard. Its phone-line port was actually a removable module that included a 56-kilobit modem, which gamers could use to connect to SegaNet.

## Largest screen on a handheld console

The Nintendo Switch home/handheld console hybrid has a 6.2-in (157-mm) screen. The Switch took this title on its release on 3 Mar 2017, beating the record held by the PlayStation Vita's 5-in (127-mm) screen, which was set on its Japanese release on 17 Dec 2011. The Switch weighs around 10.5 oz (297 g), excluding controller.

## First consoles with an SSD

The Xbox Series X and Series S (see opposite) both incorporate a solid-state drive (SSD). The Series X has a 1-TB drive, while the cheaper Series S has a 512-GB drive. Both consoles have a port for a 1-TB external expansion drive.

In Aug 2018, to celebrate the milestone of 500 million PlayStation systems shipped, Sony released the 500 Million Limited Edition PS4 Pro console. It came with a 2-TB hard drive – the **highest storage capacity in a console**.

## Best-selling consoles

• **First generation**: Magnavox Odyssey (1972–75), created by Ralph Baer (USA), 330,000 units (see opposite).
• **Second generation**: Atari 2600 (1977–92), 27.64 million units.
• **Third generation**: Nintendo Entertainment System (NES; 1983–2003), 61.91 million units.
• **Fourth generation**: Super Nintendo Entertainment System (SNES; 1990–2003), 49.1 million units.
• **Fifth generation**: Sony PlayStation (1994–2006), 102.5 million units.
• **Sixth generation**: Sony PlayStation 2 (2000–13), 157.68 million units.
• **Seventh generation**: Nintendo Wii (2006–13), 101.64 million units.

## Largest Game Boy

Ilhan Ünal (BEL) produced an upsized version of this classic console measuring 1.01 m tall, 0.62 m wide and 0.2 m deep (3 ft 4 in x 2 ft x 7.8 in). It was verified in Antwerp, Belgium, on 13 Nov 2016.

Created by Jeroen Domburg (NLD), the **smallest Game Boy** is 54 mm (2.1 in) long, as confirmed in Shanghai, China, on 15 Dec 2016.

The PS5's large size results from efforts to keep the console cool without incorporating noisy fans.

## Best-selling eighth-generation console

As of 30 Sep 2020, the PlayStation 4 (PS4, above) had sold 113.5 million units. Its primary rival, the Xbox One, had sold around 50 million units. The PS4 launched on 15 Nov 2013.

The PlayStation 5 (right), which launched on 12 Nov 2020, is the **largest console**. Its dimensions are approximately 390 x 260 x 104 mm (15.3 x 10.2 x 4 in), dwarfing other famously hefty hardware such as the original Xbox and the launch version of the PS3.

# eSports & Streaming

### First videogame tournament
The Intergalactic *Spacewar* Olympics took place on 19 Oct 1972 at Stanford University's Artificial Intelligence Laboratory in California, USA. Around 24 players were reported to have competed at the 1962 combat game *Spacewar*. Arguably the **first eSports event**, it was won by Stanford grad student Bruce Baumgart, who earned himself a year's subscription to *Rolling Stone* magazine – the competition's sponsors. See p.148 for more.

### Highest score on *Donkey Kong*
Arcade game high-score competitions were the eSports of the 1980s, and still draw gamers today. On 15 Jun 2020, Robbie Lakeman (USA) racked up 1,260,700 points playing Nintendo's 1981 classic platformer *Donkey Kong*. Lakeman live-streamed his world-record run across 4 hr on Twitch.

### Largest audience for an eSports tournament
The 2015 *League of Legends* World Championship attracted a total of 334 million unique viewers when it was broadcast live via online and TV channels for four weeks in Oct 2015. The tournament hosted 73 games in several European locations, including the UK, France and Germany. According to publisher Riot Games, each match drew an average of 4.2 million concurrent viewers.

### Most viewers for a debut stream on Twitch
On 19 Oct 2020, US politician Alexandria Ocasio-Cortez took to Twitch to play *Among Us* (Innersloth, 2018) as part of a voter outreach event, drawing 439,000 concurrent viewers at the stream's peak. She was joined by streamers HasanAbi and Pokimane (see left) and fellow congresswoman Ilhan Omar. Ocasio-Cortez is a keen gamer who reached the Silver III rank in *League of Legends* in Jul 2020.

### Most followed female gamer on Twitch
Pokimane, aka Imane Anys (CAN, b. MAR), had 7,230,762 followers on Twitch as of 8 Feb 2021, placing her in the Top 10 of all streamers on the platform. Having started her channel in 2013, she made her name playing *League of Legends* and *Fortnite*, and won the Shorty Award for Twitch Streamer of the Year in 2018.

### Most followed content creator on Steam
Luke Millanta (AUS) had 121,754 followers on Valve's digital distribution service, as verified on 23 Sep 2020. During his six years as a contributor, he has worked with brands such as Fnatic and Razer and created content for games including *Counter-Strike: Global Offensive*, *Team Fortress 2* and *Dota 2*. Luke is pictured with his GWR certificate, which he says "has found a very special place on my wall".

### Highest-earning eSports team
Team Liquid had earned $36,233,860 (£26.3 m) from 1,900 tournaments, as of 8 Feb 2021. The eSports organization was founded in the Netherlands in 2000. Its roster features more than 60 players from around the world, who compete in 14 of the most popular games. Liquid's biggest win came when its European *Dota 2* team claimed the jackpot at The International 2017, earning more than $10.8 m (£8.3 m). But it has also enjoyed notable success playing *Counter-Strike: Global Offensive* and *League of Legends*.

### Longest losing streak for an eSports team
The Shanghai Dragons (CHN) lost 42 matches in a row in the *Overwatch* League between 2018 and 2019. The Dragons finished the 2018 season with a winless 0–40 record before finally ending their unlucky run on 22 Feb 2019, when major changes to the team line-up resulted in a 3–1 victory over Boston Uprising.

### Largest eSports prize pool for a single tournament
A total of $40,018,195 (£30.9 m) in prize money was raised between 22 May and 9 Oct 2020 for The International 2020. The COVID-19 pandemic caused the event's cancellation, meaning that players have to wait for a shot at the mega prize pool. The prize pot was accumulated by in-game purchases in Valve's multiplayer strategy game *Dota 2*.

One player who knows all about *Dota 2* glory is N0tail, aka Johan Sundstein (DNK, inset). The **highest-earning eSports player**, he had accrued $6,944,322 (£5.2 m) as of 12 Nov 2020, according to eSportsearnings.com.

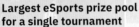

## Billy Mitchell

An appeal made to GWR by arcade gamer Billy Mitchell (USA) has seen the reinstatement of a number of records that had previously been disqualified. As reaffirmed in Jun 2020, Mitchell was the **first gamer to reach the kill screen on *Donkey Kong*** (Nintendo, 1981), hitting the glitched 117th level on 7 Nov 1982. This achievement was, at the time, the **highest score on *Donkey Kong***, a record that Mitchell went on to beat on 4 Jun 2005 by amassing 1,047,200 points – making him the **first player to reach one million points on *Donkey Kong***. He beat the high score record again on 14 Jul 2007 with 1,050,200 points and once more on 31 Jul 2010 with 1,062,800.

Mitchell is also the **first person to achieve a perfect score on *PAC-Man*** (Namco, 1980). On 3 Jul 1999, he accrued 3,333,360 points by eating every dot, energizer, ghost and fruit in all 256 levels, without losing a life. On the 256th screen, a glitch results in a kill screen that ends the game.

## Most concurrent viewers of a gaming livestreaming service

On 11 Jun 2020, Twitch hit a peak of 6,059,527 simultaneous viewers. Although daily viewership on the platform had risen sharply in the spring of 2020 on account of the COVID-19 pandemic, the record owed much to the reveal of the PlayStation 5, which drew in around 3.1 million viewers.

## Most money raised by a videogame livestream fundraiser

Z Event is a yearly online fundraiser in which popular French Twitch and YouTube streamers play videogames for charity. The 2020 event, staged from 16 to 19 Oct 2020 in Montpellier, raised €5.7 m ($6.6 m; £5.1 m) for Amnesty International.

## Longest marathon on a virtual-reality game

On 14–16 Apr 2020, Collin Cabral (USA) donned the Valve Index headset for 48 hr 8 min 31 sec in Bristol, Rhode Island, USA. He played VR titles such as *Boneworks* (Stress Level Zero) and *Half Life: Alyx* (Valve).

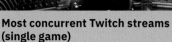

## Most concurrent Twitch streams (single game)

*Fortnite*'s "Device" event on 15 Jun 2020 attracted simultaneous Twitch streams from 117,582 channels. Around 20 million viewers tuned in as the Midas doomsday clock hit zero in the finale of Chapter 2, Season 2. Streamers and players watched as the Agency building exploded and the ever-present electrical storm turned into a wall of water.

## Most downloaded PS Plus game

PlayStation's online subscription service grants users access to free games every month. Within weeks of its release on 4 Aug 2020, the chaotic cartoon battle royale *Fall Guys: Ultimate Knockout* (Mediatonic/Devolver Digital) had hit the top of all-time PS Plus download charts. It overtook big-budget titles such as *Call of Duty: Black Ops III* and *Destiny 2*.

## Largest music concert in a videogame

On 24 Apr 2020, a total of 12.3 million concurrent viewers tuned in to the "Astronomical" concert by US rapper Travis Scott on a virtual stage inside *Fortnite*. During the 10-min show, Scott unveiled a new song with Kid Cudi entitled "The Scotts" – which debuted at No.1 on the *Billboard* Hot 100 on 9 May.

## Most current Formula One (F1) drivers in an eSports series

With the 2020 F1 season suspended owing to COVID-19, its drivers took to the circuits of Codemasters' *F1 2019*. A total of 11 F1 drivers took part in the Virtual Grand Prix series. Ferrari's Charles Leclerc (FRA) recorded the **first F1 eSport race win by an F1 driver** on 5 Apr, but it was Williams' George Russell (UK) who claimed the **most F1 eSport race wins by an F1 driver**, sweeping four of the eight races.

## Most liked YouTube videogame trailer

EA's "Battlefield 1 Official Reveal Trailer" – promoting the 14th title in the *Battlefield* military shooter series – has received 2.3 million likes since 6 May 2016.

The **most disliked YouTube videogame trailer** is the "Official Call of Duty®: Infinite Warfare Reveal Trailer", with 3.9 million thumbs-down since 2 May 2016. Fans appeared nonplussed by the new outer-space setting for the FPS franchise.

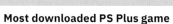

On 28 Aug 2020, *Fall Guys* attracted a peak of 708,865 viewers on Twitch.

# Round-Up

categories in a year, including Lead Actor (Eugene Levy), Lead Actress (Catherine O'Hara) and Support Actor and Actress, for Dan Levy and Annie Murphy.

### Oldest online gaming guild
Founded in Feb 1996, The Syndicate (USA) had been active for 24 years 337 days as of 2 Jan 2021. The community focuses on MMORPG titles such as *Ultima Online* (1997) and *EverQuest* (1999).

### Most BAFTA Award nominations for a videogame
*The Last of Us Part II* (Naughty Dog, 2020) continued the post-apocalyptic series' critical success with 13 nominations for the 17th British Academy Games Awards. It triumphed in three of the categories on 25 Mar 2021, including the fan-voted EE Game of the Year.

### Youngest recipient of a BAFTA Special Award
British YouTuber and campaigner Nikki Lilly (b. 22 Jul 2004) was 15 years 133 days old on receiving one of the British Academy's highest honours on 1 Dec 2019. Born with arteriovenous malformation – a condition that causes facial swelling, migraines and nose bleeds – Nikki has been vlogging about disability, bullying and the power of positivity since she was eight. "I'm just doing all that I can to help people feel a little less dark," she said.

### Most Emmy Award nominations for a network in a single year
In the lead-up to the 72nd Primetime Emmy Awards – a largely virtual event that took place on 20 Sep 2020 – Netflix netted 160 nominations for its smash-hit series, including *The Crown*, *Stranger Things* and *Ozark* (the latter was its top performer with 18 nods). It went on to convert "just" 21 of those into awards on the night.

### Most Emmy Awards won by a comedy series in a season
*Schitt's Creek* (Pop TV, CAN) was laughing it up at the 2020 Emmys, with the show's sixth season taking nine gongs. It is the first time a series has won all the major comedy

### Most kills in a *CoD: Warzone* match using a mouth-operated joystick
RockyNoHands, aka Rocky Stoutenburgh (USA), took out 17 players during a bout of *Call of Duty: Warzone* (Activision, 2020) on 18 Nov 2020. Since an accident in 2006 left him paralysed, Rocky has mastered a Quadstick mouth controller so that he can keep gaming. Using this device to devastating effect, he has also set two records playing *Fortnite*.

### Highest-altitude mass-attended music concert
During her *Ultimate* world tour, pop star Karen Mok (CHN) performed to more than 10,000 spectators in Lhasa, Tibet Autonomous Region, China, at 3,646 m (11,962 ft) above sea level on 12 Oct 2019. The show was staged by The Mok-a-Bye Baby Workshop, ChengDu ShowTime Culture Media, Sony Music Entertainment China Holdings and Utopian Entertainment.

The **deepest concert underground**, meanwhile, was played by the Shaft Bottom Boys (CAN) at 1,893 m (6,210 ft) below sea level in Vale's Creighton Mine in Greater Sudbury, Ontario, Canada, on 7 Mar 2020.

### Most searched-for TV show on the internet
Based on Google's annual trends report, no TV series in 2020 piqued more people's curiosity than *Tiger King: Murder, Mayhem and Madness* (Netflix). Released on 20 Mar – coinciding with the first wave of COVID lockdowns – it offered an eye-opening snapshot into the life of American zookeeper Joe Exotic, who (spoiler alert) has since been jailed.

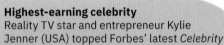

### Highest-earning celebrity
Reality TV star and entrepreneur Kylie Jenner (USA) topped Forbes' latest *Celebrity 100* list with estimated earnings of $590 m (£477.4 m) between 1 Jun 2019 and 1 Jun 2020. The lion's share came from the sale of her make-up company Kylie Cosmetics in 2019.
The **top-earning male** (in second place overall) was musician Kanye West (USA), bringing in $170 m (£137.5 m). The two were related by marriage until Jenner's half-sister Kim Kardashian filed for divorce from West in Feb 2021.

### Most concurrent viewers for a Twitch stream
An avid player of *Fortnite* (Epic Games, 2017), David Cánovas Martínez (ESP) – better known as TheGrefg – attracted the biggest audience in the history of the videogame live-streaming platform on 11 Jan 2021. A peak viewership of 2,468,668 watched as he revealed his new "skin" (right), an avatar of himself that he had created for others to download in *Fortnite*.

## Most Primetime Emmys for Outstanding Host for a Reality/Competition Program

RuPaul Charles (USA) – described by *TIME* magazine as the world's "most influential drag queen" – picked up his fifth consecutive Emmy for presenting *RuPaul's Drag Race* (Logo TV, VH1; USA) on 20 Sep 2020. The show has been nominated for 39 Emmy Awards in total and has won 19.

## Most times to see a movie at the cinema

Marvel mega-fan Ramiro Alanis (USA) saw *Avengers: Endgame* 191 times in Riverview, Florida, between 25 Apr and 29 Jul 2019. The personal trainer watched the 3-hr epic five times on its opening weekend alone! This almost doubled the previous record: Australia's Joanne Connor saw 108 screenings of *Bohemian Rhapsody* (UK/USA, 2018).

## Longest-running TV crime drama

*Tatort* ("Crime Scene") – first aired on Das Erste (DEU) – celebrated its 50th year on 29 Nov 2020. It is Germany's most enduring TV drama series in any genre.

## Largest comic book published

Kodansha (JPN) released a supersized version of its popular comic *Attack on Titan*, with each page measuring 1 x 0.7 m (3 ft 3 in x 2 ft 3 in), as verified on 13 Apr 2021. It is more than six times the size of a regular *tankōbon* (anthology of manga chapters). The comic has spawned a hit anime, which itself has been recognized as the **most in-demand animated TV series** (see right).

## Largest collection of playable gaming systems

Retro gamer Linda Guillory of Garland, Texas, USA, had amassed 2,430 gaming machines – including mini tabletop versions of arcade classics such as *PAC-Man* (Coleco, 1981), *King Kong* (Tigervision, 1982) and *Adventure Vision* (Entex, 1982) – as of 26 Oct 2019. Her vintage games archive also incorporates the **largest collection of LCD gaming systems**: 1,599 devices.

## Most expensive...

**Fancy-dress crown**: a $6 (£4) plastic crown worn by the late hip-hop artist The Notorious B.I.G. (b. Christopher Wallace) for his "King of New York" photoshoot sold for $594,750 (£461,856) at Sotheby's on 16 Sep 2020.

**Videogame**: a sealed copy of *Super Mario Bros.* for NES (Nintendo, 1985) realized $666,000 (£478,211) on 2 Apr 2021 when put up for sale online by Heritage Auctions.

## Most weeks at No.1 on *Billboard*'s Digital Song Sales chart

On 10 Apr 2021, "Dynamite" by BTS (KOR) spent an 18th cumulative week at the top of the *Billboard* Digital Song Sales chart. It thus eclipsed the 17-week chart-topper "Despacito", by Luis Fonsi, Daddy Yankee and Justin Bieber, in 2017.

"Dynamite" also enjoyed the **most weeks on the US Hot 100 by a K-pop track**: 32 weeks, as of the same date. For more records smashed by the Bangtan Boys, turn the page.

### Defining demand: Parrot Analytics

To rank the most popular TV series, GWR has joined forces with experts at Parrot Analytics. They use a metric known as "Demand Expressions" to rate the hottest shows in a given period. This measurement is based not only on streams, but also on other forms of engagement such as comments or likes on social media. The top shows are established by comparing their demand to a baseline – e.g., *The Mandalorian* (right) is 57.6 times more "in demand" than the average TV show.

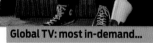

The first season of *The Mandalorian* reportedly cost around $100 m (£90 m) to make – $12.5 m (£10 m) per episode!

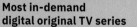

## Global TV: most in-demand...

| Genre | Demand | Show |
|---|---|---|
| Drama & overall | 74.1 | *Game of Thrones* (HBO, USA) |
| Comic adaptation | 62.0 | *The Walking Dead* (AMC, USA) |
| Sci-fi | 57.6 | *The Mandalorian* (Disney+, USA; right) |
| Animated | 52.7 | *Attack on Titan* (MBS, JPN) |
| Sitcom & comedy | 49.9 | *Brooklyn Nine-Nine* (FOX, USA) |
| Medical drama | 47.8 | *Grey's Anatomy* (ABC, USA) |
| Superhero | 45.4 | *The Boys* (Amazon Prime, USA; above) |
| Children's | 40.8 | *SpongeBob SquarePants* (Nickelodeon, USA) |
| Debut series | 28.8 | *Raised by Wolves* (HBO Max, USA) |
| Documentary | 27.0 | *The Last Dance* (ESPN, USA) |

*Parrot Analytics, 1 Mar 2020–28 Feb 2021*

## Most in-demand digital original TV series

Disney+'s *Star Wars* spin-off *The Mandalorian* (USA) was 57.6 times more popular than the typical TV show as of 28 Feb 2021. This also makes it the **most in-demand action & adventure** and **sci-fi series**. Set prior to the *Episode VII* movie, it follows bounty hunter Din Djarin ("Mando") – played by Pedro Pascal – and his alien charge, the Force-wielding Grogu ("Baby Yoda").

# BTS

**K** orean boy band BTS – a seven-strong collective featuring RM, Jin, Suga, J-Hope, Jimin, V and Jungkook – has led the K-pop charge from the Asian charts to global domination. And 2020 saw them underline their status as arguably the biggest band in the world today.

Formed between 2010 and 2012, BTS released their debut album, *2 Cool 4 Skool*, on 12 Jun 2013. Their combination of glossy pop and emotional authenticity struck a chord with listeners and the band acquired an "ARMY" – their legion of devoted fans. The ARMY are particularly active on social media, which has contributed to many of the group's records.

Having become the biggest sensation in Asian pop, BTS set their sights on the USA. On 2 Jun 2018, they became the **first K-pop act to reach No.1 on the US albums chart** – debuting at No.1 on the *Billboard 200* with *Love Yourself: Tear*.

In 2020, BTS went from strength to strength. They released two best-selling albums, won industry prizes at home and abroad, staged a series of record-breaking online concerts, and broke the internet with their video for "Dynamite" (see p.211). On 4 Mar 2021, in recognition of their achievements, BTS were named the International Federation of the Phonographic Industry's Global Recording Artist of the Year for 2020. The world was well and truly theirs.

**VITAL STATISTICS**
**Name:** BTS
**Nationality:** South Korean
**Debut:** 2013
**Members:** Kim Nam-joon, Kim Seok-jin, Min Yoon-gi, Jung Ho-seok, Park Ji-min, Kim Tae-hyung, Jeon Jung-kook
**Total album sales:** c. 20 million
**Music Awards:**
• *Billboard*: 5
• MTV Europe: 10
• Mnet Asian: 33

BTS stands for the Korean phrase Bangtan Sonyeondan – in English, "Bulletproof Boy Scouts".

J-Hope (Jung Ho-seok)

Jimin (Park Ji-min)

Jin (Kim Seok-jin)

RM (Kim Nam-joon)

Jungkook (Jeon Jung-kook)

Suga (Min Yoon-gi)

V (Kim Tae-hyung)

**1.** On 22 Aug 2020, the official video for "Dynamite" became the **most viewed YouTube music video in 24 hours,** earning 101,100,000 views on the day of its debut.

**2.** BTS devotees call themselves the ARMY – the "Adorable Representative MC for Youth". Their fervent support propelled the band to four consecutive wins in the fan-supported "Top Social Artist" category at the *Billboard* Music Awards in 2017–20.

**3.** On 24 Sep 2018, BTS addressed the United Nations General Assembly at the launch of Generation Unlimited, which aims to improve global education and training for young people.

**4.** BTS came up trumps again at a socially distanced Mnet Asian Music Awards in 2020, extending their record for the **most *daesang* ("grand prize") awards** to 13.

**5.** *BANG BANG CON: THE LIVE,* an online BTS concert performed during lockdown on 14 Jun 2020, drew 756,000 fans – the **most tickets sold for a livestreamed concert.**

**6.** BTS's seventh album, *Map of the Soul: 7,* had sold 4,440,818 copies in their home country as of Mar 2021 – making it the **best-selling album in South Korea.**

MAP OF THE SOUL 7

Find out more about BTS in the Hall of Fame section at www.guinnessworldrecords.com/2022

# Victoria and Albert Museum

**Location:** Cromwell Road, Kensington & Chelsea, London, UK

**Established:** 1852

**Grounds area:** 12 ha (29 acres)

**Collection:** 2.3 million objects

**Galleries:** 145

**Most popular exhibition:** *Christian Dior: Designer of Dreams* (2019) – 594,994 visitors

**Annual visitors:** 3.9 million (2019)

For almost 170 years, the oldest design museum in the world has sought to entertain and educate its visitors. Its collection, which numbers more than 2 million pieces, celebrates 5,000 years of human creativity – from ancient ceramics to 20th-century rock-star paraphernalia.

The idea for the museum grew out of a desire to teach the English public about art and design. Henry Cole, the founding director, declared that it should be a "schoolroom for everyone". Initially named the Museum of Manufactures, it opened at Marlborough House in London in May 1852. Five years later, it moved to its current location and was renamed the South Kensington Museum.

It was an innovative institution, the first of its kind to collect photographs as art, to offer its visitors refreshments and to use gas lighting – which enabled the museum to open in the evenings, with the hope of attracting more working people through its doors.

On 17 May 1899, the museum changed its name once more, becoming the Victoria and Albert Museum (the V&A). Queen Victoria herself was present to lay the foundation stone for the new Aston Webb building – her final public ceremony. Decades later, during World War II, some of the museum's collection was moved to the Aldwych Underground tunnel for safe-keeping.

Today, visitors to the V&A can wander through 7 mi (11 km) of galleries. The millions who pass through its doors each year speak to its enduring appeal, and the fulfilment of Henry Cole's great vision.

## Wedding suit of James II

The V&A's British Galleries contain the coat and breeches worn by the Duke of York (later King James II) at his wedding to Mary of Modena on 21 Nov 1673 in Dover, Kent, UK. One of the oldest-surviving wedding suits, it signalled a new style of English fashion inspired by a French military coat known as a *justacorps*.

## Henry Cole's Christmas card

In 1843, the V&A's founder asked artist John Callcott Horsley to create a festive message he could send to friends. The result was the **first printed Christmas card**, which depicted a family raising a toast. A thousand copies were produced, each of which could be personalized with a handwritten greeting. In 2001, an original was sold by UK auctioneers Henry Aldridge & Son for £22,000 ($36,120), making it the **most expensive greetings card sold at auction.**

## Ardabil Carpet

A floor covering on display in the Islamic Middle East room of the V&A bears an inscription dating it to 946 in the Muslim calendar (1539–40 CE) – the **oldest-dated carpet**. It was one of a pair commissioned by the ruler of Iran, Shah Tahmasp, for the shrine of his ancestor, Shaykh Safi al-Din, in the city of Ardabil.

*Central medallion design*

*360,000 knots per m² (232 per sq in)*

## Great Bed of Ware

At 2.67 m high, 3.26 m wide and 3.38 m deep (8 ft 9 in x 10 ft 8 in x 11 ft 1 in), the **largest four-poster bed** can reputedly accommodate four couples at a time. It was made c. 1590 for an inn at Ware in Hertfordshire, UK – likely as a tourist draw. Guests often carved their initials into the bedposts and headboard.

### The Three Graces

Antonio Canova's neoclassical marble masterpiece was carved for an English collector between 1815 and 1817. *The Three Graces* was jointly purchased by the V&A and the National Gallery of Scotland in 1994 for £7.5 m ($11.7 m). At that time, it was the **most expensive sculpture** – a record now held by *Pointing Man* by Alberto Giacometti, which sold in 2015 for $141.2 m (£91.4 m).

*Three daughters of Zeus: Euphrosyne, Aglaia and Thalia*

*Tomb of Cardinal Ascanio Sforza (1505–09; cast 1852–54)*

*Nymph of Fontainbleau by Benvenuto Cellini (1542; cast c. 1864)*

The V&A's Cast Courts contain reproductions of some of the world's most famous sculptures.

*Michelangelo's David (1501–04; cast 1856)*

*Monument to Carlo Marsuppini (1453–60; cast 1890)*

### Parliament Street photograph

An image of Parliament Street taken from Trafalgar Square is one of the earliest-surviving photographs of London. It was one of several taken by a Monsieur St Croix, who came to the English capital in Sep 1839 to demonstrate a new French invention: the daguerreotype, a unique image formed on a silvered copper plate.

*The Visitation by Luca della Robbia (c. 1445; cast c. 1883)*

*Pulpit from Pisa Cathedral (1260; cast c. 1864)*

*Socket for a flag pole (1505)*

### Elton John

A photography gallery in the V&A is named after record-breaking singer-songwriter Elton John and his husband David Furnish. John – whose "Something About the Way You Look Tonight"/"Candle in the Wind 1997" is the **best-selling single since charts began**, with worldwide sales of 33 million – also donated a number of his trademark glasses to the V&A (inset).

White diamanté studs

*Pulpit from Pisa Cathedral (1302–10; cast c. 1865)*

*Tomb of St Peter Martyr (1338; cast c. 1869)*

**Youngest World Athlete of the Year**
Armand Duplantis (SWE, b. USA,
10 Nov 1999) was crowned Male World
Athlete of the Year aged 21 years 25 days at
a virtual ceremony on 5 Dec 2020. One of the
rising stars of athletics, the young pole vaulter
won all 16 competitions he entered in 2020, and
became only the second athlete ever to make
10 clearances of 6 m (19 ft 8 in) in a season.
Duplantis recorded the **highest pole vault** –
6.18 m (20 ft 3 in) – indoors on 15 Feb (see
p.225). He also achieved the highest outdoor
pole vault of 6.15 m (20 ft 2 in) on 17 Sep
in Rome, Italy, although World
Athletics does not recognise this
as a world record as the
indoor mark is higher.

The son of a pole vaulter and a heptathlete, Duplantis has been pole vaulting since the age of three.

## CONTENTS

# American Football

## Fewest games to throw 100 touchdown passes
On 8 Nov 2020, Patrick Mahomes threw his 100th NFL TD pass in his 40th game for the Kansas City Chiefs, a 33–31 win over the Carolina Panthers. He beat Dan Marino's previous record by four games. Six weeks earlier, on 28 Sep, Mahomes had completed the **fewest games to reach 10,000 passing yards** – 34.

*All records are National Football League (NFL) and all record holders USA, unless otherwise indicated.*

## Most career passing yards
Quarterback Drew Brees retired in Mar 2021, having racked up 80,358 passing yards since his NFL debut in 2001, and the **most pass completions** – 7,142. Between 18 Oct 2009 and 25 Nov 2012, Brees completed the **most consecutive games throwing a touchdown pass** – 54.

## Oldest coach
Romeo Crennel (b. 18 Jun 1947) was aged 73 years 199 days when he oversaw the Houston Texans' 41–38 loss to the Tennessee Titans on 3 Jan 2021. Crennel had previously broken the record of George Halas, which had stood since 17 Dec 1967.

## Most consecutive games recording a sack
By the end of the 2020 NFL season, the Pittsburgh Steelers' defense had sacked the quarterback 73 games in a row. The streak began on 6 Nov 2016 against the Baltimore Ravens. At least 29 defensive players contributed, led by T J Watt. The Steelers broke the Tampa Bay Buccaneers' record of 69 between 1999 and 2003.

## Most career touchdowns
Wide receiver Jerry Rice reached the end zone 208 times in 303 games while playing for the San Francisco 49ers (right), Oakland Raiders and Seattle Seahawks from 1985 to 2004. His tally includes the **most Super Bowl touchdowns** – eight. Selected by the 49ers in the 1985 NFL Draft, Rice won three Super Bowls and played for 20 seasons, setting numerous receiving records.

### NFL career leaders

| Most... | Record | Name | Career span |
|---|---|---|---|
| Yards receiving | 22,895 | Jerry Rice (above) | 1985–2004 |
| Yards rushing | 18,355 | Emmitt Smith | 1990–2004 |
| Touchdown passes | 581 | Tom Brady | 2000– |
| Field goals | 599 | Adam Vinatieri | 1996–2019 |
| Sacks | 200 | Bruce Smith | 1985–2003 |
| Interceptions | 81 | Paul Krause | 1964–1979 |
| Games played | 382 | Morten Andersen (DNK) | 1982–2007 |

## Fewest games to reach 400 touchdown passes
On 6 Dec 2020, Aaron Rodgers threw career touchdown pass No.400 in his 193rd NFL game for the Green Bay Packers. He followed up on 19 Dec with his 40th touchdown pass of the season, during a 24–16 win against the Carolina Panthers. It was the third time Rodgers had hit this landmark (after 2011 and 2016) – the **most seasons with 40-plus touchdown passes**.

## Most pass receptions in first 100 games
Keenan Allen caught 624 passes in his first 100 NFL games from 2013 to 2020, playing for the San Diego/Los Angeles Chargers.

## Most kickoff returns for touchdowns
On 16 Nov 2020, Cordarrelle Patterson ran in his eighth career kickoff return for touchdown, a 104-yard effort for the Chicago Bears against the Minnesota Vikings. He tied the mark set by Joshua Cribbs and Leon Washington.

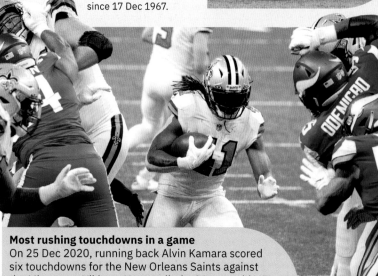

## Most rushing touchdowns in a game
On 25 Dec 2020, running back Alvin Kamara scored six touchdowns for the New Orleans Saints against the Minnesota Vikings. He equalled a 91-year-old NFL record set by the Chicago Cardinals' Ernie Nevers on 28 Nov 1929. This is also the overall record for **most touchdowns in a game**, shared with the Cleveland Browns' William "Dub" Jones (25 Nov 1951) and the Chicago Bears' Gale Sayers (12 Dec 1965).

## Most Super Bowl wins by a quarterback
In 2021, Tom Brady secured a fairytale seventh Super Bowl in his first season with the Tampa Bay Buccaneers. He had won six with the New England Patriots from 2002 to 2019. The 43-year-old also extended a host of his Super Bowl records, including **most appearances** (10), **most passes completed** (277), **most touchdown passes** (21) and **most MVP awards** (five).

# Baseball

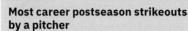

### Fewest innings for a pitcher to reach 100 strikeouts in a season
Shane Bieber of the Cleveland Indians reached a century of strikeouts during the 2020 season in 62 ⅓ innings. He passed Max Scherzer's record of 63 innings, which he set in 2018. Bieber went on to win the 2020 Cy Young Award for best American League pitcher.

### Most strikeouts by a team in a nine-innings postseason game
Tampa Bay Rays pitchers combined for 18 strikeouts against New York Yankees batters during Game 2 of the American League Division Series on 6 Oct 2020. Tyler Glasnow struck out 10 in five innings; Nick Anderson struck out four; Diego Castillo (DOM) and Pete Fairbanks struck out two.

### Most career postseason strikeouts by a pitcher
Clayton Kershaw has recorded 207 postseason strikeouts for the Los Angeles Dodgers since 2008. He passed Justin Verlander's mark of 205 during Game 5 of the 2020 World Series against the Tampa Bay Rays, his 37th postseason appearance. The Dodgers took the World Series 4–2, earning Kershaw his first championship.

### Henry "Hank" Aaron (1934–2021)
Baseball legend Henry Aaron died on 22 Jan 2021. Over 23 MLB seasons from 1954 to 1976 – 21 with the Milwaukee/Atlanta Braves – he set a host of records, including **most runs batted in** (2,297) and **most base hits** (6,856). Aaron broke Babe Ruth's record for **most home runs**, and his total of 755 remains second only to Barry Bonds (762).

*All records are Major League Baseball (MLB) and all record holders USA, unless otherwise indicated.*

Henderson was notable for batting right-handed, despite being a left-handed thrower.

### Most consecutive home runs in an inning (team)
The Chicago White Sox hit four dingers in a row against the St Louis Cardinals on 16 Aug 2020. Batters Yoan Moncada, Yasmani Grandal, José Abreu (all CUB) and Eloy Jiménez (DOM) each went deep in the fifth inning. They equalled a feat previously achieved on nine occasions.

The **most home runs in an inning (team)** is five, and has been accomplished seven times. The New York Yankees are the most recent team to achieve it, during the fourth inning of their 10–7 win over the Toronto Blue Jays on 17 Sep 2020. Batters Brett Gardner, DJ LeMahieu, Luke Voit, Giancarlo Stanton and Gleyber Torres (VEN) all hit homers off Blue Jays pitcher Chase Anderson.

### Longest-duration nine-innings game
The New York Yankees and the Cleveland Indians slugged it out for 4 hr 50 min during their Wild Card Series game on 30 Sep 2020. The Yankees won out, 10–9. They beat the previous longest nine-innings game – between the Yankees and Boston Red Sox on 18 Aug 2006 – by 5 min.

The **longest-duration game** outright took place between the Chicago White Sox and the Milwaukee Brewers on 8–9 May 1984. The White Sox eventually won 7–6 in the 25th inning, after 8 hr 6 min of play.

### Most career stolen bases
Rickey Henderson stole 1,406 bases between 1979 and 2003, earning himself the nickname "Man of Steal". No other player in MLB history has passed 1,000. Henderson stole 130 bases in 1982 alone, the **single-season** record. A two-time World Series champion, he played for nine MLB teams, amassing the **most runs** (2,295) and the **most lead-off home runs** (81).

### Most runs in a postseason inning
On 14 Oct 2020, the Los Angeles Dodgers racked up 11 runs during the first inning of their National League Championship Series Game 3 against the Atlanta Braves. They surpassed the 2019 St Louis Cardinals, 2002 Anaheim Angels, 1968 Detroit Tigers and 1929 Philadelphia Athletics, who all managed 10. The Dodgers went on to win the game 15–3.

### Most games hitting three home runs
Mookie Betts of the Los Angeles Dodgers notched his sixth career three-homer game on 13 Aug 2020, against the San Diego Padres. He matched the total of Johnny Mize and Sammy Sosa (DOM), but reached it in significantly fewer games (813, to 1,884 and 2,354 respectively). Betts is also a professional ten-pin bowler.

### Most home runs in a postseason
Randy Arozarena (CUB) hit 10 dingers for the Tampa Bay Rays in the 2020 postseason – two more than the previous best. He hit four against the Houston Astros in the American League Championship Series and was named MVP. Arozarena also recorded the **most hits in a postseason** – 29 – as the Rays made it to the World Series.

# Basketball

*All records are National Basketball Association (NBA) and all record holders are USA, unless otherwise indicated.*

## Most Championship titles
The Los Angeles Lakers claimed their 17th NBA title in 2020, equalling the feat of the Boston Celtics between 1957 and 2008. The Lakers also extended their record for **most Finals appearances** to 32.

## Most points scored in a playoffs debut
On 17 Aug 2020, Luka Dončić (SVN) scored 42 points for the Dallas Mavericks during their Western Conference First Round game against the Los Angeles Clippers. Dončić broke George Mikan's record of 37, which had stood for more than 70 years.

## Most three-point field goals in a game (team)
On 29 Dec 2020, the Milwaukee Bucks sank 29 shots from downtown during their 144–97 win against the Miami Heat. Twelve players converted, from a total of 51 attempts.

The **individual** record is 14, by Klay Thompson for the Golden State Warriors against the Chicago Bulls on 29 Oct 2018.

## Largest half-time lead
On 27 Dec 2020, the Dallas Mavericks closed out the second quarter 50 points up on the LA Clippers, leading 77–27. The Mavericks went on to win 124–73.

## Most career assists
Point guard John Stockton laid on 15,806 assists in 1,504 games for the Utah Jazz from 1984 to 2003. This includes the **season** record of 1,164, set in 1990/91. On defense, Stockton racked up the **most steals** – 3,265. He formed one of the great basketball partnerships with Karl Malone (above left) – who holds the record for **most free throws converted**: 9,787.

## Most Finals MVP awards won with different teams
LeBron James of the LA Lakers was named Finals MVP for the fourth time in 2020 (inset), having previously claimed the award while playing for the Miami Heat (2012 and 2013) and the Cleveland Cavaliers (2016). James continues to rewrite the basketball record books. The 17-time All-Star has now recorded the **most playoff appearances** (260), **minutes played** (10,811) and **points** (7,491).

## Most WNBA championship titles
The Seattle Storm secured their fourth WNBA championship in Oct 2020, sweeping the top-seeded Las Vegas Aces 3–0 in the Finals. Seattle joined an exclusive club of four-time winners, along with the Houston Comets and the Minnesota Lynx.

In beating the Aces 92–59 on 6 Oct, the Storm also achieved the **largest margin of victory in a WNBA Finals game** – 33.

## Most assists by a player in a WNBA game
Courtney Vandersloot laid on 18 assists during the Chicago Sky's 100–77 win over the Indiana Fever on 31 Aug 2020. She beat the single-game record of 16, set by Ticha Penicheiro (PRT) in 1998 and 2002.

## Youngest player to achieve a triple-double
LaMelo Ball (b. 22 Aug 2001) was aged 19 years 140 days when he put up 22 points, 12 rebounds and 11 assists for the Charlotte Hornets during their 113–105 victory over the Atlanta Hawks on 9 Jan 2021. LaMelo's older brother, Lonzo, had previously held the same record from Nov 2017 to Apr 2018.

Abdul-Jabbar also leads the NBA with the **most minutes played** (57,446) and the **most fouls** (4,657).

## Most career points scored
Kareem Abdul-Jabbar (b. Ferdinand Lewis Alcindor Jr) scored a total of 38,387 points for the Milwaukee Bucks and the LA Lakers between 1969 and 1989. The 2.18-m (7-ft 2-in) centre – famed for his trademark skyhook (right) – scored 6,712 free throws and the **most field goals**: 15,837. Only one of these was shot from three-point range.

## Most rebounds in a WNBA career
Sylvia Fowles has claimed 3,400 rebounds since 2008. The 1.98-m (6-ft 6-in) centre, who has played for Chicago Sky and the Minnesota Lynx, overtook Rebekkah Brunson's mark of 3,356 on 28 Jul 2020. In 2018, Fowles set the **season** record, with 404 rebounds. She is a three-time WNBA Defensive Player of the Year. For more all-time league leaders, see the table below.

### WNBA career leaders

| Most... | Record | Name | Career span |
|---|---|---|---|
| Points | 8,931 | Diana Taurasi | 2004– |
| 3-point field goals | 1,164 | Diana Taurasi | 2004– |
| Free throws | 2,125 | Diana Taurasi | 2004– |
| Assists | 2,888 | Sue Bird | 2002– |
| Steals | 1,074 | Tamika Catchings | 2002–16 |
| Blocks | 877 | Margo Dydek (POL) | 1998–2008 |
| Games played | 519 | Sue Bird | 2002– |

# Ice Hockey

## Most ice time in a playoff game

Columbus Blue Jackets defenseman Seth Jones (USA) was on ice for 65 min 6 sec during Game 1 of their first-round series against the Tampa Bay Lightning on 11 Aug 2020. The Blue Jackets lost the fourth-longest game in NHL history 3–2 in the fifth period of overtime. The marathon match also saw Blue Jackets goaltender Joonas Korpisalo (FIN, below) make the **most saves in a playoff game** – 85.

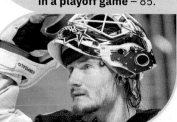

## Most matches played

On 19 Apr 2021, Patrick Marleau broke Gordie Howe's 41-year-old record by making his 1,768th career appearance in the NHL. It was Marleau's 23rd season in the league, with spells at the San Jose Sharks, the Toronto Maple Leafs and the Pittsburgh Penguins. Game No.1,768 was his 899th consecutive appearance – the second-longest active iron man streak in the NHL.

*All records are National Hockey League (NHL) and all record holders are CAN, unless otherwise indicated.*

## Most wins by a goaltender in a single postseason

Andrei Vasilevskiy (RUS) recorded 18 postseason wins as the Tampa Bay Lightning marched to Stanley Cup glory in 2020. He played in every game of the playoffs – including the extra qualifying round introduced for that year – clocking a total playing time of 1,708 min 12 sec.

## Most career hits

As of 12 Apr 2021, Dustin Brown (USA) had made 3,526 hits on opposition players while playing for the Los Angeles Kings. This is since 2005/06 – the earliest season for which the NHL has consistent data.

The **most hits in a game** is 15, by Nikita Zadorov (RUS) on 22 Mar 2018. He was playing for the Colorado Avalanche during their 7–1 loss to the Kings.

## Most shootout goals

On 29 Feb 2020, Jonathan Toews helped the Chicago Blackhawks to a win over the Florida Panthers with his 50th shootout goal. Shootouts were introduced to the NHL in the 2005/06 season as a way of deciding games tied after overtime.

The **most shootout winning goals** is 23, by Frans Nielsen (DNK) for the New York Islanders and the Detroit Red Wings.

## Most seasons to finish as top scorer

Alex Ovechkin (RUS) of the Washington Capitals ended the COVID-abbreviated 2019/20 season as the league's top scorer for the ninth time. He shared the honours with David Pastrňák (CZE) of the Boston Bruins, both players finishing on 48 goals.

On 30 Jan 2021, Ovechkin extended his record for **most regular-season overtime goals** with his 24th game-deciding strike. The Capitals defeated the Boston Bruins 4–3.

## Most matches won by a goaltender

Martin Brodeur won 691 games for the New Jersey Devils and St Louis Blues from 26 Mar 1992 to 2 Jan 2015. Over the course of 22 seasons in the NHL – 21 with the Devils – Brodeur won the Stanley Cup three times and compiled the **most goaltending appearances** (1,266) and **most shutouts** (125). He also scored three career league goals, more than any other goaltender.

## Most...

**Consecutive games played**: 964, by Doug Jarvis from 8 Oct 1975 to 10 Oct 1987.

**Teams played for**: 12, by Mike Sillinger between 1990 and 2009.

**Penalty minutes**: 3,971, by Dave "Tiger" Williams in 962 games between 1974 and 1988.

**Points scored in overtime**: 37, by Patrik Eliáš (CZE) for the New Jersey Devils from 1995 to 2016.

**Shots on goal**: 6,206, by Ray Bourque for the Boston Bruins from 1979 to 2001.

**Stanley Cup wins by an individual**: 11, by Henri Richard for the Montreal Canadiens between 1956 and 1973.

**Games coached**: 2,141, by Scotty Bowman from 1967 to 2002.

**Lady Byng trophies**: 7, by Frank Boucher from 1928 to 1935. The Lady Byng trophy is awarded each season to the player who exhibits the most sportsmanlike behaviour.

## Most goals

Wayne Gretzky scored 894 times between 1979 and 1999, playing for the Edmonton Oilers, Los Angeles Kings, St Louis Blues and New York Rangers. Few athletes can match Gretzky's statistical dominance of his sport. He also claimed the **most hat-tricks** (50), the **most assists** (1,963) and the **most points** (2,857). In 1985/86, "The Great One" racked up the **most points in a season** (215) playing for the Oilers. No other player has ever passed 200 points in an NHL season – Gretzky did it four times.

# Soccer

### Most FIFA World Cup goals as captain

Diego Maradona scored six times for Argentina at the World Cup between 1986 and 1994, a mark equalled by England's Harry Kane in 2018. At the 1986 tournament in Mexico, Maradona propelled his nation to glory, displaying the extraordinary skill, vision and leadership – and talent for courting controversy – that made him one of the sport's most electrifying players. He died on 25 Nov 2020.

### Most consecutive wins in the UEFA Champions League

Bayern Munich (DEU) won 15 Champions League games in a row between 18 Sep 2019 and 25 Nov 2020. They claimed the 2019/20 title to become the first side to win every match in a season of the competition. Their run finally ended with a 1–1 draw against Atlético Madrid on 1 Dec 2020. For more on Bayern, see right.

### Most consecutive seasons to score in the UEFA Champions League

Lionel Messi (ARG) scored in the Champions League for the 16th successive season on 20 Oct 2020, converting a penalty for Barcelona against Ferencváros. His feat was matched by Karim Benzema (FRA), who struck for Real Madrid against Borussia Mönchengladbach on 27 Oct 2020.

Benzema stands on 70 career goals in the competition; Messi has 120. The Argentine remains behind his great rival Cristiano Ronaldo (PRT), whose total of 134 in 176 games is the **most UEFA Champions League goals**. Ronaldo and Messi share the competition record for **most hat-tricks**, with eight.

### Youngest player in the UEFA Champions League

Youssoufa Moukoko (DEU, b. CAM, 20 Nov 2004) was aged 16 years 18 days when he took to the pitch for Borussia Dortmund against Zenit St Petersburg on 8 Dec 2020. Ten days later, Moukoko became the **youngest Bundesliga goalscorer**, firing home against Union Berlin aged 16 years 28 days.

### Most consecutive women's national top-flight league titles

SFK 2000 Sarajevo won the Bosnia and Herzegovina Women's Premier League 18 times in a row between 2002/03 and 2019/20. Their most recent title – declared on 1 Jun 2020, following a season abbreviated by COVID-19 – saw them surpass the mark set by Faroese side KÍ Klaksvík Kvinnur from 2000 to 2016.

The **men's** record is held by Tafea FC of Vanuatu, an island country in the South Pacific Ocean. They claimed the first 15 editions of the Port Vila Football League, staged in 1994–2007 and 2008/09.

### Most Serie A appearances

Gianluigi Buffon (ITA) played 656 times in the Italian top flight from 19 Nov 1995 to 21 Apr 2021. The World Cup-winning goalkeeper returned to Serie A in 2019 and surpassed Paolo Maldini with his 648th league appearance on 4 Jul 2020. Buffon also claimed his 10th Scudetto with Juventus – the **most Italian top-flight league titles by an individual**.

### Most wins of the CAF Champions League

On 27 Nov 2020, Egypt's Al Ahly claimed their ninth Confederation of African Football (CAF) Champions League title, defeating compatriots Zamalek 2–1 in a one-legged final thanks to an 86th-minute winner by Mohamed Magdy. Inaugurated in 1964 as the African Cup of Champions Clubs, the CAF Champions League is an annual continental tournament contested by the top club sides in Africa.

In Sep 2020, Al Ahly extended their record for **most Egyptian top-flight league titles** to 42 – still 13 behind the domestic record by Scottish side Rangers (below).

### Most AFC Champions League goals

Striker Lee Dong-gook (KOR) scored 37 times in the Asian Football Confederation Champions League between 2010 and 2019, while playing for Korean side Jeonbuk Hyundai Motors.

### Most national top-flight titles

Rangers secured their 55th Scottish top-division title on 7 Mar 2021 – their first Premiership title in a decade. This was the earliest point in the season that the Scottish league had ever been decided. Rangers moved one championship ahead of Linfield in Northern Ireland, who sat top of their league as of the same date.

32Red · WE ARE CHAMPIONS · 20|21

## Most international goals scored by a defender (male)

Sergio Ramos scored 23 times for Spain between 12 Oct 2005 and 6 Sep 2020. The centre-back notched twice against Ukraine during a 2020 UEFA Nations League tie to overtake Argentina's Daniel Passarella, who scored 22. In 2018–19, Ramos went on a streak of eight goals in nine international games.

## Most UEFA Women's Champions League titles

French side Olympique Lyonnais Féminin claimed their seventh Champions League crown on 30 Aug 2020, defeating VfL Wolfsburg 3–1 in the final. Lyon players Eugénie Le Sommer, Wendie Renard and Sarah Bouhaddi (all FRA; inset, left to right) played in all seven final victories – the outright **individual** record. They surpassed the **men's** record of six, by Real Madrid's Francisco Gento between 1956 and 1966.

## Youngest National Women's Soccer League (NWSL) goalscorer on debut

Trinity Rodman (USA, b. 20 May 2002) was 18 years 325 days old when she scored for the Washington Spirit on 10 Apr 2021. Rodman, the daughter of basketball legend Dennis, struck just 5 min after coming on.

The **youngest NWSL goalscorer** outright is Ellie Carpenter (AUS, b. 28 Apr 2000), aged 18 years 21 days on 19 May 2018.

## Youngest person to play in La Liga

Luka Romero (ARG, b. MEX, 18 Nov 2004) appeared for RCD Mallorca aged 15 years 219 days in their league tie against Real Madrid on 24 Jun 2020.

## Fastest Serie A goal

AC Milan's Rafael Leão (PRT) scored after just 6.76 sec against Sassuolo on 20 Dec 2020, at the Mapei Stadium in Reggio Emilia, Italy. This is the fastest goal across the so-called "big 5" European leagues:
• **English Premier League (EPL)**: 7.69 sec, by Shane Long (IRL) for Southampton against Watford on 23 Apr 2019.
• **La Liga**: 7.8 sec, by Joseba Llorente (ESP) for Real Valladolid against Espanyol on 20 Jan 2008.
• **Ligue 1**: 8 sec, by Michel Rio (FRA) for Caen against Cannes on 15 Feb 1992.
• **Bundesliga**: 9 sec, by Karim Bellarabi (DEU) for Bayer 04 Leverkusen against Borussia Dortmund on 23 Aug 2014; and Kevin Volland (DEU) for Hoffenheim against Bayern Munich on 22 Aug 2015.

## Oldest winner of the EPL Golden Boot

Leicester City striker Jamie Vardy (UK, b. 11 Jan 1987) finished as top scorer during the 2019/20 EPL season with 23 goals, securing the Golden Boot trophy on 26 Jul 2020 aged 33 years 197 days.

## Most Bundesliga titles won (individual)

On 8 May 2021, Bayern Munich's David Alaba (AUT) and Thomas Müller (DEU) sealed their 10th German top-flight league titles – one more than five current or former teammates. Since 2012/13, Bavarian powerhouse Bayern has racked up the **most consecutive Bundesliga title wins** – nine.

## Highest margin of victory in an Eredivisie game

Dutch giants AFC Ajax romped to a 0–13 away win in a league match against VVV-Venlo on 24 Oct 2020. Lassina Traoré scored five times.

## Most goals scored in the FA Women's Super League

Arsenal's Vivianne Miedema (NLD) has struck 59 times in the top flight of English women's football. She surpassed Nikita Parris's all-time record of 49 on 18 Oct 2020, with a hat-trick against local rivals Tottenham. Miedema's tally includes the **season** record of 22, set in 2018/19. On 1 Dec 2019, she set the **match** record of six during Arsenal's 11–1 demolition of Bristol City (pictured).

## Youngest player to score 100 goals in the French top flight

On 21 Mar 2021, Kylian Mbappé (FRA, b. 20 Dec 1998) scored twice for Paris Saint-Germain against Lyon to record a century of Ligue 1 goals aged 22 years 91 days. This is more than a year earlier than Saint-Étienne's Hervé Revelli in 1969. Mbappé struck 16 league goals for Monaco before moving to Paris in 2017.

Miedema made her league debut in Dutch women's football in 2011, at the age of just 15.

# Athletics

## Outdoor track events

| MEN | Time/Distance | Name | Location | Date |
|---|---|---|---|---|
| 100 m | 9.58 | Usain Bolt (JAM) | Berlin, Germany | 16 Aug 2009 |
| 200 m | 19.19 | Usain Bolt (JAM) | Berlin, Germany | 20 Aug 2009 |
| 400 m | 43.03 | Wayde van Niekerk (ZAF) | Rio de Janeiro, Brazil | 14 Aug 2016 |
| 800 m | 1:40.91 | David Rudisha (KEN) | London, UK | 9 Aug 2012 |
| 1,000 m | 2:11.96 | Noah Ngeny (KEN) | Rieti, Italy | 5 Sep 1999 |
| 1,500 m | 3:26.00 | Hicham El Guerrouj (MAR) | Rome, Italy | 14 Jul 1998 |
| 1 mile | 3:43.13 | Hicham El Guerrouj (MAR) | Rome, Italy | 7 Jul 1999 |
| 2,000 m | 4:44.79 | Hicham El Guerrouj (MAR) | Berlin, Germany | 7 Sep 1999 |
| 3,000 m | 7:20.67 | Daniel Komen (KEN) | Rieti, Italy | 1 Sep 1996 |
| 5,000 m | 12:35.36 | Joshua Cheptegei (UGA) | Fontvieille, Monaco | 14 Aug 2020 |
| 10,000 m | 26:11.00 | Joshua Cheptegei (UGA) | Valencia, Spain | 7 Oct 2020 |
| 20,000 m | 56:26.00 | Haile Gebrselassie (ETH) | Ostrava, Czech Republic | 27 Jun 2007 |
| 1 hour | 21,330 m | Mo Farah (UK) | Brussels, Belgium | 4 Sep 2020 |
| 25,000 m | 1:12:25.40 | Moses Cheruiyot Mosop (KEN) | Eugene, USA | 3 Jun 2011 |
| 30,000 m | 1:26:47.40 | Moses Cheruiyot Mosop (KEN) | Eugene, USA | 3 Jun 2011 |
| 3,000 m steeplechase | 7:53.63 | Saif Saaeed Shaheen (QAT) | Brussels, Belgium | 3 Sep 2004 |
| 110 m hurdles | 12.80 | Aries Merritt (USA) | Brussels, Belgium | 7 Sep 2012 |
| 400 m hurdles | 46.78 | Kevin Young (USA) | Barcelona, Spain | 6 Aug 1992 |
| 4 x 100 m relay | 36.84 | Jamaica (Nesta Carter, Michael Frater, Yohan Blake, Usain Bolt) | London, UK | 11 Aug 2012 |
| 4 x 200 m relay | 1:18.63 | Jamaica (Nickel Ashmeade, Warren Weir, Jermaine Brown, Yohan Blake) | Nassau, The Bahamas | 24 May 2014 |
| 4 x 400 m relay | 2:54.29 | USA (Andrew Valmon, Quincy Watts, Butch Reynolds, Michael Johnson) | Stuttgart, Germany | 22 Aug 1993 |
| 4 x 800 m relay | 7:02.43 | Kenya (Joseph Mutua, William Yiampoy, Ismael Kombich, Wilfred Bungei) | Brussels, Belgium | 25 Aug 2006 |
| 4 x 1,500 m relay | 14:22.22 | Kenya (Collins Cheboi, Silas Kiplagat, James Kiplagat Magut, Asbel Kiprop) | Nassau, The Bahamas | 25 May 2014 |

**Fastest 5,000 m (male)**
Joshua Cheptegei (UGA) ran 5,000 m in 12 min 35.36 sec on 14 Aug 2020 at Stade Louis II in Monaco. He averaged 4 min 3 sec a mile. It was the first of two long-standing track records set by Kenenisa Bekele that Cheptegei smashed in 2020: on 7 Oct, he completed the **fastest 10,000 m** in 26 min 11 sec, taking 6 sec off the previous best.

| WOMEN | Time/Distance | Name | Location | Date |
|---|---|---|---|---|
| 100 m | 10.49 | Florence Griffith-Joyner (USA) | Indianapolis, USA | 16 Jul 1988 |
| 200 m | 21.34 | Florence Griffith-Joyner (USA) | Seoul, South Korea | 29 Sep 1988 |
| 400 m | 47.60 | Marita Koch (GDR) | Canberra, Australia | 6 Oct 1985 |
| 800 m | 1:53.28 | Jarmila Kratochvílová (TCH) | Munich, Germany | 26 Jul 1983 |
| 1,000 m | 2:28.98 | Svetlana Masterkova (RUS) | Brussels, Belgium | 23 Aug 1996 |
| 1,500 m | 3:50.07 | Genzebe Dibaba (ETH) | Fontvieille, Monaco | 17 Jul 2015 |
| 1 mile | 4:12.33 | Sifan Hassan (NLD) | Fontvieille, Monaco | 12 Jul 2019 |
| 2,000 m | 5:23.75 (i) | Genzebe Dibaba (ETH) | Sabadell, Spain | 7 Feb 2017 |
| 3,000 m | 8:06.11 | Wang Junxia (CHN) | Beijing, China | 13 Sep 1993 |
| 5,000 m | 14:06.62 | Letesenbet Gidey (ETH) | Valencia, Spain | 7 Oct 2020 |
| 10,000 m | 29:17.45 | Almaz Ayana (ETH) | Rio de Janeiro, Brazil | 12 Aug 2016 |
| 20,000 m | 1:05:26.60 | Tegla Loroupe (KEN) | Borgholzhausen, Germany | 3 Sep 2000 |
| 1 hour | 18,930 m | Sifan Hassan (NLD) | Brussels, Belgium | 4 Sep 2020 |
| 25,000 m | 1:27:05.90 | Tegla Loroupe (KEN) | Mengerskirchen, Germany | 21 Sep 2002 |
| 30,000 m | 1:45:50.00 | Tegla Loroupe (KEN) | Warstein, Germany | 6 Jun 2003 |
| 3,000 m steeplechase | 8:44.32 | Beatrice Chepkoech (KEN) | Fontvieille, Monaco | 20 Jul 2018 |
| 100 m hurdles | 12.20 | Kendra Harrison (USA) | London, UK | 22 Jul 2016 |
| 400 m hurdles | 52.16 | Dalilah Muhammad (USA) | Doha, Qatar | 4 Oct 2019 |
| 4 x 100 m relay | 40.82 | USA (Tianna Madison, Allyson Felix, Bianca Knight, Carmelita Jeter) | London, UK | 10 Aug 2012 |
| 4 x 200 m relay | 1:27.46 | USA "Blue" (LaTasha Jenkins, LaTasha Colander-Richardson, Nanceen Perry, Marion Jones) | Philadelphia, USA | 29 Apr 2000 |
| 4 x 400 m relay | 3:15.17 | USSR (Tatyana Ledovskaya, Olga Nazarova, Mariya Pinigina, Olga Bryzgina) | Seoul, South Korea | 1 Oct 1988 |
| 4 x 800 m relay | 7:50.17 | USSR (Nadezhda Olizarenko, Lyubov Gurina, Lyudmila Borisova, Irina Podyalovskaya) | Moscow, Russia | 5 Aug 1984 |
| 4 x 1,500 m relay | 16:27.02 | Nike/Bowerman Track Club (Colleen Quigley, Elise Cranny, Karissa Schweizer, Shelby Houlihan, all USA) | Portland, USA | 31 Jul 2020 |

**Farthest run in one hour (male)**
Mo Farah (UK, b. SOM) set his first outdoor track world record on 4 Sep 2020 at the age of 37, covering 21,330 m – farther than a half marathon – in 60 min. The rarely run event was staged at a Diamond League meeting in Brussels, Belgium. Trackside LED lights helped the athletes gauge world-record pace.

**Farthest run in one hour (female)**
Sifan Hassan (NLD, b. ETH) ran 18,930 m in 60 min on 4 Sep 2020 in Brussels. With a minute left in the race, she broke clear from Brigid Kosgei (above left) – who was later disqualified for stepping off the track. Hassan, 2019 world champion at both 1,500 m and 10,000 m, has set world records in three different events.

*All nationalities listed as of the date of record performance.*

**(i) indoor performance**
Since 1998, World Athletics (formerly the IAAF) has ruled that world records can be set in a facility "with or without a roof" – meaning that times, heights and distances achieved indoors can also stand as outdoor records, providing they meet certain conditions, e.g., no banked running track.

## Road racing

| MEN | Time | Name | Location | Date |
|---|---|---|---|---|
| 5 km | 12:51 | Joshua Cheptegei (UGA) | Monaco | 16 Feb 2020 |
| 10 km | 26:24 | Rhonex Kipruto (KEN) | Valencia, Spain | 12 Jan 2020 |
| Half marathon | 57:32 | Kibiwott Kandie (KEN) | Valencia, Spain | 6 Dec 2020 |
| Marathon | 2:01:39 | Eliud Kipchoge (KEN) | Berlin, Germany | 16 Sep 2018 |
| 100 km | 6:09:14 | Nao Kazami (JPN) | Lake Saroma, Japan | 24 Jun 2018 |
| Road relay | 1:57:06 | Kenya (Josephat Ndambiri, Martin Mathathi, Daniel Muchunu Mwangi, Mekubo Mogusu, Onesmus Nyerere, John Kariuki) | Chiba, Japan | 23 Nov 2005 |

| WOMEN | Time | Name | Location | Date |
|---|---|---|---|---|
| 5 km | 14:44 (Wo) | Sifan Hassan (NLD) | Monaco | 17 Feb 2019 |
| | 14:43 (Mx) | Beatrice Chepkoech (KEN) | Monaco | 14 Feb 2021 |
| 10 km | 30:29 (Wo) | Asmae Leghzaoui (MAR) | New York City, USA | 8 Jun 2002 |
| | 29:43 (Mx) | Joyciline Jepkosgei (KEN) | Prague, Czech Republic | 9 Sep 2017 |
| Half marathon | 1:05:16 (Wo)* | Peres Jepchirchir (KEN) | Gdynia, Poland | 17 Oct 2020 |
| | 1:04:02 (Mx)* | Ruth Chepngetich (KEN) | Istanbul, Turkey | 4 Apr 2021 |
| Marathon | 2:17:01 (Wo) | Mary Keitany (KEN) | London, UK | 23 Apr 2017 |
| | 2:14:04 (Mx) | Brigid Kosgei (KEN) | Chicago, USA | 13 Oct 2019 |
| 100 km | 6:33:11 | Tomoe Abe (JPN) | Lake Saroma, Japan | 25 Jun 2000 |
| Road relay | 2:11:41 | China (Jiang Bo, Dong Yanmei, Zhao Fengting, Ma Zaijie, Lan Lixin, Li Na) | Beijing, China | 28 Feb 1998 |

**Fastest half marathon (female, mixed)***
On 4 Apr 2021, Ruth Chepngetich (KEN) won the N Kolay Istanbul Half Marathon in 1 hr 4 min 2 sec in Turkey. World Athletics divides women's road race world records into "women-only" (Wo) and "mixed" (Mx) categories, as the latter are deemed to gain an advantage by competing alongside male runners.

**Fastest 50 km road walk (female)**
On 9 Mar 2019, Liu Hong (CHN) became the first woman to break the 4-hr barrier for the 50 km race walk, finishing the Chinese Race Walk Grand Prix in 3 hr 59 min 15 sec. She held the **20 km** record for six years, before losing it to Yang Jiayu on 20 Mar 2021.

## Race walking

| MEN | Time | Name | Location | Date |
|---|---|---|---|---|
| 20,000 m | 1:17:25.6 | Bernardo Segura (MEX) | Bergen, Norway | 7 May 1994 |
| 20 km (road) | 1:16:36 | Yusuke Suzuki (JPN) | Nomi, Japan | 15 Mar 2015 |
| 30,000 m | 2:01:44.1 | Maurizio Damilano (ITA) | Cuneo, Italy | 3 Oct 1992 |
| 50,000 m | 3:35:27.2 | Yohann Diniz (FRA) | Reims, France | 12 Mar 2011 |
| 50 km (road) | 3:32:33 | Yohann Diniz (FRA) | Zurich, Switzerland | 15 Aug 2014 |

| WOMEN | Time | Name | Location | Date |
|---|---|---|---|---|
| 10,000 m | 41:56.23 | Nadezhda Ryashkina (USSR) | Seattle, USA | 24 Jul 1990 |
| 20,000 m | 1:26:52.3 | Olimpiada Ivanova (RUS) | Brisbane, Australia | 6 Sep 2001 |
| 20 km (road) | 1:23:49* | Yang Jiayu (CHN) | Huangshan, China | 20 Mar 2021 |
| 50 km (road) | 3:59:15 | Liu Hong (CHN) | Huangshan, China | 9 Mar 2019 |

*pending ratification by World Athletics.

## Outdoor field events

| MEN | Distance/Points | Name | Location | Date |
|---|---|---|---|---|
| High jump | 2.45 m (8 ft) | Javier Sotomayor (CUB) | Salamanca, Spain | 27 Jul 1993 |
| Pole vault | 6.18 m (20 ft 3 in) (i) | Armand Duplantis (SWE) | Glasgow, UK | 15 Feb 2020 |
| Long jump | 8.95 m (29 ft 4 in) | Mike Powell (USA) | Tokyo, Japan | 30 Aug 1991 |
| Triple jump | 18.29 m (60 ft) | Jonathan Edwards (UK) | Gothenburg, Sweden | 7 Aug 1995 |
| Shot | 23.12 m (75 ft 10 in) | Randy Barnes (USA) | Los Angeles, USA | 20 May 1990 |
| Discus | 74.08 m (243 ft) | Jürgen Schult (GDR) | Neubrandenburg, Germany | 6 Jun 1986 |
| Hammer | 86.74 m (284 ft 6 in) | Yuriy Sedykh (USSR) | Stuttgart, Germany | 30 Aug 1986 |
| Javelin | 98.48 m (323 ft 1 in) | Jan Železný (CZE) | Jena, Germany | 25 May 1996 |
| Decathlon† | 9,126 points | Kevin Mayer (FRA) | Talence, France | 15–16 Sep 2018 |

† 100 m, 10.55 sec; long jump, 7.80 m; shot, 16.00 m; high jump, 2.05 m; 400 m, 48.42 sec; 110 m hurdles, 13.75 sec; discus, 50.54 m; pole vault, 5.45 m; javelin, 71.90 m; 1,500 m, 4 min 36.11 sec

| WOMEN | Distance/Points | Name | Location | Date |
|---|---|---|---|---|
| High jump | 2.09 m (6 ft 10 in) | Stefka Kostadinova (BGR) | Rome, Italy | 30 Aug 1987 |
| Pole vault | 5.06 m (16 ft 7 in) | Yelena Isinbayeva (RUS) | Zurich, Switzerland | 28 Aug 2009 |
| Long jump | 7.52 m (24 ft 8 in) | Galina Chistyakova (USSR) | Leningrad, USSR | 11 Jun 1988 |
| Triple jump | 15.50 m (50 ft 10 in) | Inessa Kravets (UKR) | Gothenburg, Sweden | 10 Aug 1995 |
| Shot | 22.63 m (74 ft 2 in) | Natalya Lisovskaya (USSR) | Moscow, USSR | 7 Jun 1987 |
| Discus | 76.80 m (251 ft 11 in) | Gabriele Reinsch (GDR) | Neubrandenburg, Germany | 9 Jul 1988 |
| Hammer | 82.98 m (272 ft 2 in) | Anita Włodarczyk (POL) | Warsaw, Poland | 28 Aug 2016 |
| Javelin | 72.28 m (237 ft 1 in) | Barbora Špotáková (CZE) | Stuttgart, Germany | 13 Sep 2008 |
| Heptathlon†† | 7,291 points | Jacqueline Joyner-Kersee (USA) | Seoul, South Korea | 23–24 Sep 1988 |

†† 100 m hurdles, 12.69 sec; high jump, 1.86 m; shot, 15.80 m; 200 m, 22.56 sec; long jump, 7.27 m; javelin, 45.66 m; 800 m, 2 min 8.51 sec

| Decathlon††† | 8,358 points | Austra Skujytė (LTU) | Columbia, USA | 14–15 Apr 2005 |
|---|---|---|---|---|

††† 100 m, 12.49 sec; long jump, 6.12 m; shot, 16.42 m; high jump, 1.78 m; 400 m, 57.19 sec; 100 m hurdles, 14.22 sec; discus, 46.19 m; pole vault, 3.10 m; javelin, 48.78 m; 1,500 m, 5 min 15.86 sec

**Highest pole vault (male)**
On 15 Feb 2020, Armand Duplantis (SWE, b. USA) pole-vaulted over a bar set at 6.18 m (20 ft 3 in) at the Müller Indoor Grand Prix in Glasgow, UK. It was the second time in a week that the athlete known as "Mondo" had broken the world record for the event, which had previously stood for six years. Turn to pp.216–17 for more.

# Para Sport

### Fastest 2,000 m single sculls para row (PR1)

On 1 Sep 2019, Roman Polianskyi (UKR) won the final of the PR1 men's single sculls event in 9 min 12.99 sec at the World Rowing Championships in Linz-Ottensheim, Austria. Polianskyi (pictured in 2020) took four seconds off the previous world-best time. Originally a para canoeist, he switched to rowing in 2013.

In addition to his two Paralympic gold medals in the long jump, Rehm has another in the 4 x 100 m relay.

### Farthest long jump (T64, male)

"Blade Jumper" Markus Rehm (DEU) leapt 8.48 m (27 ft 9 in) on 25 Aug 2018 at the World Para Athletics European Championships in Berlin, Germany. This was farther than the winning jumps at the previous two Olympics. Rehm lost his lower right leg in a wakeboarding accident and competes using a carbon-fibre prosthesis.

### First World Marathon Majors Grand Slam

Wheelchair racer Manuela Schär (CHE) won every leg of Series XII of the World Marathon Majors from 16 Sep 2018 to 28 Apr 2019, triumphing in Berlin, Chicago, New York City, Tokyo, Boston and London (pictured). She also set the **fastest wheelchair marathon (T54, female)** – 1 hr 35 min 42 sec – on 17 Nov 2019 in Oita City, Japan.

### First para athlete to compete at an Olympic Games

Gymnast George Eyser (USA, b. DEU) competed with a prosthetic wooden left leg at the 1904 Olympic Games in St Louis, Missouri, USA. On 28 Oct, he won six medals in one day, including golds in the rope climbing, vault and parallel bars events.

The Paralympic movement was born on 29 Jul 1948, when a wheelchair archery event was organized to coincide with the opening of the London Olympics. The first Paralympic Games took place on 18–25 Sep 1960 in Rome, Italy. The **first Paralympian to compete at an Olympic Games** was Neroli Fairhall (NZ). She qualified for the women's individual archery event at the 1984 Olympics, having participated in two Summer Paralympics (1972 and 1980).

### First Olympic and Paralympic medallist

In 1991, fencing Olympic bronze winner Pál Szekeres (HUN) was injured in a bus accident. He switched to wheelchair fencing and represented Hungary at five Paralympic Games from 1992 to 2008, winning three gold and three bronze medals.

### Most Paralympic medals

Swimmer Trischa Zorn (USA) claimed 55 medals across seven Summer Paralympic Games between 1980 and 2004. Zorn, who was born visually impaired, won five bronze, nine silvers and 41 golds – the **most Paralympic golds**. In 2012, she was inducted into the International Paralympic Hall of Fame.

The **most Paralympic medals (male)** is 34, by Heinz Frei (CHE) between 1984 and 2016. His total included 15 golds. Frei competed at the Summer Paralympics in athletics and road cycling, and won a further eight medals in cross-country skiing at the Winter Paralympics.

### Fastest wheelchair marathon (T54, male)

Heinz Frei won the Oita International Wheelchair Marathon in 1 hr 20 min 14 sec on 31 Oct 1999 in Oita City, Japan. This is the fastest men's wheelchair marathon on a record-eligible course. Marcel Hug won the 2017 Boston Marathon – which is not record-eligible, on account of its net downhill elevation and the distance between start and finish points – in 1 hr 18 min 4 sec. On 22 Oct 2020, Daniel Romanchuk completed a virtual New York City marathon in just 1 hr 13 min 57 sec. He raced alone on a course through central Illinois in the USA.

### Fastest para cycling men's 200 m time trial (C1)

Ricardo Ten Argilés (ESP) cycled 200 m in 12.325 sec on 31 Jan 2020 at the Para Cycling Track World Championships in Milton, Ontario, Canada. A three-time Paralympic gold medallist in swimming, Ten Argilés only took up track cycling in 2017. He had both arms amputated, and one leg below the knee, following a childhood accident.

Ricardo Ten Argilés was awarded Spain's Gold Medal of the Royal Order of Sports Merit in 2019.

## Farthest distance para cycling in one hour (C5, female)

On 28 Feb 2015, Sarah Storey (UK) cycled 45.502 km (28.273 mi) in 60 min in London, UK. She fell short of the absolute UCI Women's Hour record by just 563 m (1,847 ft). As of 2020, Storey had won 38 world titles and 14 Paralympic golds in swimming and cycling (road and track).

## Most wins of the Women's Wheelchair Basketball World Championship

Canada are five-time world champions in women's wheelchair basketball. They won in 1994, 1998, 2002, 2006 and 2014.
The **men**'s record is six, by the USA.

## Most World Wheelchair Rugby Championships

Originally known as "murderball" on account of the high level of physical contact, wheelchair rugby is a mixed team sport for quadriplegic athletes. The USA has won the world championships four times, in 1995, 1998, 2006 and 2010.

## First flag-bearer at an Olympic and Paralympic Games

Swimmer Natalie du Toit (ZAF) lost her lower left leg aged 17 in a scooter accident in Feb 2001. Incredibly, she returned to the pool to qualify for the Commonwealth Games just 18 months later. Du Toit won five gold medals at the 2008 Paralympics in Beijing, China, and qualified for the 10 km open water swim at the 2008 Olympics. She carried the South African flag at both Games.

## Para powerlifting

| MEN | Weight Lifted | Name | Location | Date |
| --- | --- | --- | --- | --- |
| -49 kg | 183.5 kg | Lê Văn Công (VNM) | Mexico City, Mexico | 4 Dec 2017 |
| -54 kg | 205 kg | Sherif Osman (EGY) | Dubai, UAE | 6 Apr 2014 |
| -59 kg | 211 kg | Sherif Osman (EGY) | Rio de Janeiro, Brazil | 9 Sep 2016 |
| -65 kg | 221 kg | Paul Kehinde (NGA) | Dubai, UAE | 19 Feb 2018 |
| -72 kg | 229 kg | Roohallah Rostami (IRN) | Jakarta, Indonesia | 9 Oct 2018 |
| -80 kg | 240 kg | Majid Farzin (IRN) | Rio de Janeiro, Brazil | 12 Sep 2016 |
| -88 kg | 234 kg | Ye Jixiong (CHN) | Jakarta, Indonesia | 11 Oct 2018 |
| -97 kg | 243 kg | Mohamed Eldib (EGY) | Dubai, UAE | 18 Feb 2016 |
| -107 kg | 247 kg | Sodnompiljee Enkhbayar (MNG) | Nur-Sultan, Kazakhstan | 18 Jul 2019 |
| 107+ kg | 310 kg | Siamand Rahman (IRN) | Rio de Janeiro, Brazil | 14 Sep 2016 |

| WOMEN | Weight Lifted | Name | Location | Date |
| --- | --- | --- | --- | --- |
| -41 kg | 104.5 kg | Cui Zhe (CHN) | Nur-Sultan, Kazakhstan | 13 Jul 2019 |
| -45 kg | 118 kg | Guo Lingling (CHN) | Nur-Sultan, Kazakhstan | 13 Jul 2019 |
| -50 kg | 131 kg | Esther Oyema (NGA) | Gold Coast, Australia | 10 Apr 2018 |
| -55 kg | 132 kg | Mariana Shevchuk (UKR) | Manchester, UK | 25 Mar 2021 |
| -61 kg | 142 kg | Lucy Ejike (NGA) | Rio de Janeiro, Brazil | 11 Sep 2016 |
| -67 kg | 140.5 kg | Tan Yujiao (CHN) | Jakarta, Indonesia | 9 Oct 2018 |
| -73 kg | 150 kg | Souhad Ghazouani (FRA) | Aleksin, Russia | 25 May 2013 |
| -79 kg | 142.5 kg | Bose Omolayo (NGA) | Manchester, UK | 27 Mar 2021 |
| -86 kg | 150.5 kg | Folashade Oluwafemiayo (NGA) | Manchester, UK | 28 Mar 2021 |
| 86+ kg | 160 kg | Josephine Orji (NGA) | Rio de Janeiro, Brazil | 14 Sep 2016 |

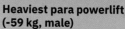

## Heaviest para powerlift (-59 kg, male)

On 9 Sep 2016, Sherif Osman (EGY) won gold in the 59 kg weight class with a lift of 211 kg (465 lb) at the Paralympic Games in Rio de Janeiro, Brazil. Osman, who contracted polio at nine months old, is currently the only para powerlifter to hold world records in more than one category on the Paralympic programme (54 kg and 59 kg).

## Most gold medals at the Winter Paralympics (country)

Norway won 136 golds at the Winter Paralympics from 1976 to 2018. The Scandinavian nation topped the medal table at four different Games: 1980, 1988, 1994 and 1998.

Norway's total is bolstered by the **most Winter Paralympic gold medals (individual)** – 22 – by Ragnhild Myklebust (far right) in cross-country skiing, ice sledge speed racing and biathlon from 1988 to 2002. She also won three silvers and two bronze, giving her the **most Winter Paralympic medals (individual)** – 27.

# Boxing

### Most world titles in different weight divisions
On 13 Nov 2010, Manny Pacquiao (PHL, right) defeated super welterweight Antonio Margarito for his eighth world title at a different weight. He won his first belt at flyweight, before moving up through the divisions to defeat lauded fighters such as featherweight Marco Antonio Barrera and welterweight Miguel Cotto.

### Most world titles at different traditional weight divisions held simultaneously
The eight traditional or "glamour" weight divisions of boxing were codified by the National Sporting Club of London around 1909–10. Only one boxer in history has held titles at three of these divisions at the same time: Henry "Homicide Hank" Armstrong (USA). In defeating Lou Ambers on 17 Aug 1938, he became the simultaneous world champion at welterweight, featherweight and lightweight. In 1940, Armstrong tried for a fourth world title, at middleweight, only to draw with champion Ceferino Garcia.

### Most world title recaptures
Sugar Ray Robinson (USA, b. Walker Smith Jr) held the middleweight title on five separate occasions. He reclaimed it for the fourth and final time on 25 Mar 1958, defeating Carmen Basilio at the Chicago Stadium in Illinois, USA. Robinson lost only one of his first 123 fights and has been ranked as the world's greatest-ever pound-for-pound boxer by both ESPN and *The Ring* magazine.

### First undisputed four-belt world champion at two weights
On 5 Mar 2021, Claressa Shields (USA) became the undisputed women's middleweight and light-middleweight champion in just her 11th professional fight. Victory over Marie-Eve Dicaire saw Shields add the IBF and vacant WBA light-middleweight belts to her WBC and WBO titles. She had previously united the middleweight belts by beating Christina Hammer on 13 Apr 2019.

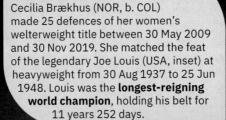

### Most consecutive world title defences
Cecilia Brækhus (NOR, b. COL) made 25 defences of her women's welterweight title between 30 May 2009 and 30 Nov 2019. She matched the feat of the legendary Joe Louis (USA, inset) at heavyweight from 30 Aug 1937 to 25 Jun 1948. Louis was the **longest-reigning world champion**, holding his belt for 11 years 252 days.

### Most participations in *The Ring*'s "Fight of the Year"
Muhammad Ali (USA, b. Cassius Clay) fought in six bouts named "Fight of the Year" by *The Ring* magazine from 1963 to 1978, winning four of them. These included his iconic victories over George Foreman in 1974 – the "Rumble in the Jungle" (above) – and over Joe Frazier in 1975 – the "Thrilla in Manila".

### Youngest world champion
Wilfred Benítez (PRI, b. USA, 12 Sep 1958) was 17 years 176 days old when he took the WBA light-welterweight title on 6 Mar 1976 in San Juan, Puerto Rico. He turned pro aged 15 and won his first 25 fights before earning a title shot.

### Fewest fights to win a world title
On 11 Oct 2008, Choi Hyun-mi (KOR, b. PKR) won the vacant WBA women's featherweight title in her first professional fight. Choi (b. 7 Nov 1990) also became the **youngest female world champion**, aged 17 years 339 days. She had defected from North to South Korea four years earlier.

### Youngest World Boxing Super Series winner
Naoya Inoue (JPN, b. 10 Apr 1993) won the bantamweight division of the World Boxing Super Series on 7 Nov 2019, aged 26 years 211 days. He beat Nonito Donaire in a bout named *The Ring*'s "Fight of the Year" (see above).

### Youngest undisputed four-belt world champion
On 17 Oct 2020, Teófimo López (USA, b. 30 Jul 1997) unified the WBO, WBA, WBC "Franchise" and IBF world lightweight titles aged 23 years 79 days. López – nicknamed "The Takeover" – upset Vasyl Lomachenko with a unanimous decision victory in their unification fight (pictured). He became the youngest of the nine four-belt undisputed world champions to be crowned since the WBO was formed in 1988.

# Artistic Sports

**Biles currently has four gymnastic skills named after her: two on the floor, one on the beam and one on the vault.**

### First Olympic winter sport
Sixteen years before the first Winter Olympics, figure skating was included at the 1908 Olympics in London, UK. The events were staged at a Knightsbridge ice rink in October, several months after the rest of the Games had ended.

### Most Olympic medals (female)
Gymnast Larisa Latynina (USSR) won 18 medals between 1956 and 1964: nine golds, five silvers and four bronze.

The **most Olympic medals at a single Games (female)** is seven, by Soviet gymnast Maria Gorokhovskaya in 1952. She claimed two golds and five silvers in Helsinki, Finland.

### Highest figure skating short program score (male)
On 7 Feb 2020, Yuzuru Hanyu (JPN) scored 111.82 for his short program at the Four Continents Championships in Seoul, South Korea. The double-Olympic champion reprised his routine from the 2018 Winter Olympics. It was the 10th time Hanyu had set a new best for the short program, which lasts around 2 min 40 sec and contains seven set elements.

### First perfect 10 awarded in Olympic gymnastics
On 18 Jul 1976, 14-year-old Nadia Comăneci (ROM) was given a perfect score for her uneven bars routine in the team competition in Montreal, Canada.

### Most World Championship and Olympic gold medals in gymnastics
Simone Biles (USA) won a combined total of 23 golds from 2013 to 2019. She secured four at her only Olympics to date, in 2016, and has also won the **most golds at the Artistic Gymnastics World Championships** – 19. She claimed a record-equalling five at one competition in 2019 in Stuttgart, Germany (above).

### Most gold medals at the Rhythmic Gymnastics World Championships
Rhythmic gymnast Yevgeniya Kanayeva (RUS) won 17 golds across four world championships between 2007 and 2011. In 2009, she won an unprecedented clean sweep of the five individual events – ball, hoop, ribbon, rope and all-around – together with the team event. She repeated the feat in 2011. Kanayeva also won Olympic gold in 2008 and 2012, in the rhythmic individual all-around event.

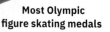

### Most consecutive Olympic appearances by a gymnast
Oksana Chusovitina (UZB, b. 19 Jun 1975) participated in seven Olympic Games between 1992 and 2016. She competed in the vault at Rio 2016, becoming the **oldest Olympic gymnast (female)** aged 41 years 56 days.

### Most Olympic figure skating medals
Tessa Virtue and Scott Moir (both CAN) claimed five medals between 2010 and 2018. The pair won two golds and a silver in the ice dance, and a further gold and silver in the team event. Moir equalled the **most Olympic figure skating gold medals (male)**, set by Gillis Grafström (SWE) between 1920 and 1928. Virtue is tied for the **female** record with Sonja Henie (NOR), who won three singles titles from 1928 to 1936, and Soviet skater Irina Rodnina, who claimed a trio of golds in the pairs event between 1972 and 1980.

### Most individual tumbling world championship titles
Jia Fangfang (CHN) won five individual tumbling world titles between 2011 and 2018. She claimed a further five in team events. Tumbling has been part of the Trampoline Gymnastics World Championships since 1976. The **most individual trampolining world championship titles** is five, by Judy Wills Cline (USA), Irina Karavaeva and Alexander Moskalenko (both RUS).

### Most Olympic artistic swimming gold medals
Russia has claimed 10 of the 17 possible golds in the sport formerly known as synchronized swimming since its Olympic debut in 1984. Remarkably, these came consecutively, as Russia won every event between 2000 and 2016. Team members Anastasia Davydova (2004–12), Svetlana Romashina and Natalia Ishchenko (both 2008–16) have amassed the **most Olympic artistic swimming gold medals (individual)**, with five apiece.

# Tennis

### First open-era Grand Slam
The 1968 French Open (27 May–9 Jun) heralded the dawn of the open era, when professionals were able to compete alongside amateurs at tennis's most prestigious tournaments. Ken Rosewall won the men's singles titles; women's champion Nancy Richey was an amateur and thus unable to keep her winnings of 5,000 francs ($1,005; £421).

### Highest annual earnings (female)
Naomi Osaka (JPN) made $37.4 m (£30.2 m) in the 12 months to 1 Jun 2020, according to Forbes. This is the **highest annual earnings for a female athlete ever**, eclipsing Maria Sharapova's $29.7 m (£19.4 m) in 2014–15. Osaka's money comprised $34 m (£27.5 m) in endorsements and $3.4 m (£2.7 m) in prize money. She won her fourth Grand Slam title at the Australian Open in Feb 2021.

### Most weeks ranked No.1 in men's singles
As of 5 Apr 2021, Novak Djokovic (SRB) had been top of the men's singles rankings for a total of 315 weeks, after surpassing Roger Federer's record of 310 on 8 Mar. On 21 Feb 2021, Djokovic extended his record for the **most Australian Open men's singles titles** to nine, beating Daniil Medvedev 7–5, 6–2, 6–2. It was his 18th Grand Slam title, leaving him just two behind his great rivals (see above). Djokovic has amassed the **highest career earnings**: $147,744,252 (£106 m) in prize money, as of 5 Apr 2021.

### Most Grand Slam men's singles titles
On 11 Oct 2020, Rafael Nadal (ESP, right) claimed his 20th Grand Slam crown, defeating Novak Djokovic (see left) in the final of the French Open. It was Nadal's 13th victory on the clay at Roland Garros – the **most wins of a Grand Slam singles title**. He also has four US Open wins, two at Wimbledon and one at the Australian Open.

Nadal's rival Roger Federer (CHE, below) has also won 20 Grand Slams, including the **most Wimbledon men's singles titles** – eight. He has six wins in Australia, five in the US and one in France.

### Most men's singles titles
Jimmy Connors (USA) won 109 men's singles titles between 1972 and 1996 – six more than his nearest rival, Roger Federer. Connors also recorded the **most men's singles matches won (open era)** – 1,274.

The **most men's titles** is 155, by John McEnroe (USA) – a total of 77 singles and 78 doubles titles, including 17 Grand Slams.

### Most Grand Slam wheelchair titles
On 13 Sep 2020, Shingo Kunieda (JPN) claimed his 45th Grand Slam title by beating Alfie Hewett in the wheelchair men's singles final at the US Open. Kunieda's win took him one clear of Esther Vergeer (see p.241).

### Most Grand Slam singles matches won
On 16 Feb 2021, Serena Williams (USA) beat Simona Halep in the quarter-finals of the Australian Open to draw level with Roger Federer's mark of 362 victories in Grand Slam singles competition. Williams remains one shy of equalling the **most Grand Slam women's singles titles** – 24, by Margaret Court (AUS). She has also won 16 Grand Slam doubles titles (14 with sister Venus) and four Olympic gold medals.

### Most WTA titles
Martina Navratilova (USA, b. CZE) won 167 singles and 177 doubles titles on the Women's Tennis Association (WTA) Tour from 1975 to 2006. Among her 344 tournament victories were 18 Grand Slam singles titles and the **most Grand Slam doubles titles** – 41 (31 in women's doubles and 10 in mixed). No tennis player can match Navratilova's 59 Grand Slams in the open era. The **most Grand Slam titles** outright is 64, by Margaret Court (AUS) between 1960 and 1975.

Williams is the only player to have won all four Grand Slams and Olympic titles in both singles and doubles.

# Test Cricket

### Most career runs
Sachin Tendulkar (IND) scored 15,921 runs in 329 innings between 1989 and 2013 – more than 2,500 runs ahead of his closest rival, Australia's Ricky Ponting. Tendulkar, the "Little Master", made his Test debut as a 16-year-old on 15 Nov 1989 and went on to play 200 matches, averaging 53.78. His tally includes six double-hundreds and the **most Test centuries** – 51.

### Highest team innings
On 4–6 Aug 1997, Sri Lanka scored 952 for 6 against visitors India at the R Premadasa Stadium in Colombo. Sanath Jayasuriya top-scored with 340, the seventh-highest individual innings of all time. The match was drawn.

### Highest individual innings
Brian Lara (TTO) scored 400 not out for the West Indies against England at the Antigua Recreation Ground on 10–12 Apr 2004. His innings included four sixes and 43 fours.

The **longest individual innings** is Hanif Mohammad's (PAK) epic 337 against the West Indies in Bridgetown, Barbados, on 20–23 Jan 1958. It lasted 16 hr 10 min.

### Highest fourth-innings score on debut
Kyle Mayers (BRB) scored 210 not out in his first match for the West Indies, against Bangladesh in Chattogram on 6–7 Feb 2021. Having scored 40 in the first innings, Mayers's double-century guided the visitors to a winning target of 395.

### Most runs in an innings (female)
On 15–16 Mar 2004, Kiran Baluch (PAK) scored 242 runs in her first innings against the West Indies at the National Stadium in Karachi, Pakistan. She faced 488 balls and hit 38 fours. Baluch put on an opening stand of 241 with Sajjida Shah, the **youngest Test cricketer**. Shah (b. 3 Feb 1988) made her debut against Ireland on 30 Jul 2000 aged just 12 years 178 days.

### Most wickets in an innings
Two bowlers have taken all 10 wickets in a Test match innings: England's Jim Laker, against Australia on 30–31 Jul 1956 at Old Trafford, UK; and Anil Kumble (IND), against Pakistan on 7 Feb 1999 in New Delhi, India.

The **female** record is eight, by left-arm spinner Neetu David (IND) against England in Jamshedpur, India, on 26–27 Nov 1995.

### Most wickets by a bowler against one team
Shane Warne (AUS) took 195 wickets in 36 matches against England between 1993 and 2007. He took a wicket with his first delivery in the Ashes, the so-called "Ball of the Century" to Mike Gatting on 4 Jun 1993.

### Youngest bowler to take a hat-trick
Pakistan pace bowler Naseem Shah (b. 15 Feb 2003) took three Bangladesh wickets with successive deliveries aged 16 years 359 days on 9 Feb 2020.

### Most career dismissals by a wicket-keeper
South Africa's Mark Boucher dismissed 555 batsmen in 147 Tests between 19 Oct 1997 and 27 Mar 2012. His 532 catches is 153 more than the next-best gloveman, Adam Gilchrist. Boucher also stumped 23 batsmen. Additionally, he took a single Test wicket bowling – that of the West Indies' Dwayne Bravo on 3 May 2005.

### Highest career batting average
Sir Don Bradman (AUS) averaged 99.94 in 52 Tests for Australia between 1928 and 1948. No cricketer has come close to matching this figure. Bradman hit 6,996 runs, including the **most double-hundreds** – 12. Famously, he was dismissed for a duck in his final innings, at the UK's Oval on 14 Aug 1948, when just four runs would have secured him an average of 100.

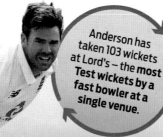

Anderson has taken 103 wickets at Lord's – the **most Test wickets by a fast bowler at a single venue.**

### Most wickets by a fast bowler
England's James Anderson had taken 614 Test wickets as of 6 Mar 2021. He opened his account with a five-wicket haul against Zimbabwe in May 2003. Eighteen years later, aged 38, he took his 600th scalp during England's Third Test against Pakistan at The Ageas Bowl in Hampshire, UK. Pace bowler Anderson stands fourth on the all-time wicket list, behind three spinners. The player with the **most Test wickets** is Sri Lanka's Muttiah Muralitharan (inset), with 800 in 133 matches from 1992 to 2010.

#raisethebat #raisethebat #raisethebat

# Golf

### Youngest No.1-ranked player
Lydia Ko (NZ, b. KOR, 24 Apr 1997) reached the top of the women's World Golf Rankings aged 17 years 284 days on 2 Feb 2015. Already the **youngest LPGA Tour winner** – aged 15 years 124 days, on 26 Aug 2012 – Ko went on to become the **youngest winner of a women's major**, aged 18 years 142 days, at the Evian Championship on 13 Sep 2015.

### Lowest single-round score on the PGA Tour
Jim Furyk (USA) went through 18 holes in 58 shots on 7 Aug 2016 at the Travelers Championship in Cromwell, Connecticut, USA. He holed 10 birdies (seven consecutively) and an eagle, taking just 24 putts. This is the lowest round of more than 600,000 shot on the Tour.

The **LPGA** record is 59, by Annika Sörenstam (SWE) on 16 Mar 2001 at the Standard Register PING. The **European Tour** record is also 59, by Oliver Fisher (UK) at the Portugal Masters on 21 Sep 2018.

### Most appearances on the PGA European Tour
As of 7 Feb 2021, Miguel Ángel Jiménez (ESP) had teed off at 712 European Tour events since 20 Oct 1983, earning around €24 m ($29 m; £21 m) in prize money. Jiménez had also hit the **most holes-in-one on the European Tour** – 10.

### Longest putt holed on the PGA Tour
On 27 Jan 2008, Craig Barlow (USA) sank a putt from 111 ft 5 in (33.9 m) at the Buick Open, held at Torrey Pines in San Diego, California, USA.

### Most match wins at the...
**Ryder Cup**: 23, by Nick Faldo (UK) from 1977 to 1997.
**Solheim Cup**: 22, by Annika Sörenstam (SWE) from 1994 to 2007; and Laura Davies (UK) from 1990 to 2011.
**Walker Cup**: 18, by Jay Sigel (USA) from 1977 to 1993.
**Curtis Cup**: 18, by Carol Semple Thompson (USA) from 1974 to 2002.

### Longest PGA Tour average drive (season)
Bryson DeChambeau (USA) recorded an average drive of 322.1 yards (294.5 m) over the 2019/20 PGA Tour season. He caused a stir by bulking up his physique through physical training and diet, increasing his power around the course. On 20 Sep 2020, DeChambeau claimed his first major, the US Open, by six shots, averaging 325 yards (297 m) off the tee.

### Lowest total score at the US Masters
On 15 Nov 2020, Dustin Johnson (USA) sealed victory at the Augusta National Golf Club with a 72-hole score of 268 (20 under par). The tournament had been delayed on account of COVID-19, and Johnson took full advantage of the softer autumn greens. The former world No.1 completed a wire-to-wire victory, leading after every round and becoming the first player to reach 20 under par at the Masters.

### Lowest score in a major championship round
On 11 Sep 2014, Kim Hyo-joo (KOR) shot 61 in the first round of the 2014 Evian Championship at Évian-les-Bains, France. Her 10-under-par round featured 10 birdies. She went on to win the tournament by one shot.

The **male** record is 62, by Branden Grace (ZAF) on 22 Jul 2017 at The Open Championship at Royal Birkdale in Merseyside, UK.

### Most major championships
Jack Nicklaus (USA) won 18 majors between 1962 and 1986. The "Golden Bear" won each of the four tournaments at least three times, amassing the **most wins of the US Masters** (6), the **PGA Championships** (5, with Walter Hagen [USA]) and the **US Open** (4, with Willie Anderson [UK], Bobby Jones and Ben Hogan [both USA]).

### Highest PGA Tour career earnings
Tiger Woods (USA) had earned $120,851,706 (£88 m) on the PGA Tour as of 25 Jan 2021. This was almost $30 m (£21 m) more than his nearest rival, Phil Mickelson. Woods is a 15-time major winner (behind only Jack Nicklaus, above left) and has equalled Sam Snead's 82 wins on the PGA Tour. He has also achieved the **most weeks ranked No.1** – 683, in 11 stints. This is twice that of the next-best golfer, Greg Norman (331 weeks).

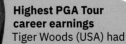

## Tour leaders

| | PGA Tour | PGA European Tour | LPGA Tour |
|---|---|---|---|
| Most wins (career) | 82 (Sam Snead, USA; Tiger Woods, USA) | 50 (Seve Ballesteros, ESP) | 88 (Kathy Whitworth, USA) |
| Most wins (year) | 18, in 1945 (Byron Nelson, USA) | 6, in 1986 (Seve Ballesteros, ESP) | 13, in 1963 (Mickey Wright, USA) |
| Lowest score (72 holes) | 253 (Justin Thomas, USA) | 257 (Andy Sullivan, UK) | 257 (Kim Sei-young, KOR) |
| Lowest score to par (72 holes) | -31 (Ernie Els, ZAF) | -29 (Ernie Els, ZAF) | -31 (Kim Sei-young, KOR) |
| Highest career earnings | $120,851,706 (Tiger Woods, USA) | €37,946,253 (Lee Westwood, UK) | $22,577,025 (Annika Sörenstam, SWE) |

# Backyard Sports

## Most Endurance Boomerang catches

Manuel Schütz (CHE) threw and caught a boomerang 81 times in 5 min on 2 Oct 2005 in Milan, Italy. Schütz (pictured in 2017) holds a number of world records in the sport, as recognized by the International Federation of Boomerang Associations. This includes the **farthest Long Distance Boomerang**: 238 m (780 ft 10 in) at its farthest point from the thrower, on 1 May 1999 in Kloten, Switzerland.

## Highest jump on a pogo stick

On 20 Nov 2018, high-flying Dmitry Arsenyev (RUS) bounced over a bar set at a height of 3.40 m (11 ft 1 in) in Rome, Italy. A former freestyle champion at Pogopalooza, Arsenyev is the proud holder of multiple GWR pogo titles, including **most consecutive stickflips** – 26, set on 5 Nov 2017 in Wilkinsburg, Pennsylvania, USA – and **most consecutive no-handed backflips** – 11, which he achieved on 8 Jun 2020 in Saint Petersburg, Russia.

## Farthest thrown flying disc

On 28 Mar 2016, David Wiggins Jr (USA) hurled a flying disc 338 m (1,108 ft 11 in) at the High Desert Distance Challenge in Primm, Nevada, USA. He took advantage of a 38-mph (61-km/h) tailwind to smash the existing record. Jennifer Allen (USA) had set the **female** record of 173.3 m (568 ft 6 in) at the same event two days earlier. Both throws were recognized by the World Flying Disc Federation.

## Most World Horseshoe Tournament titles

Alan Francis (USA) was crowned men's division champion 24 times at the National Horseshoe Pitchers Association World Tournament between 1989 and 2019. The 2020 event was called off due to COVID-19.

## Longest cornhole shot

Cornhole players try to toss bags of corn kernels into a hole in the far end of a raised board. On 28 Jul 2020, Joshua Biggers (USA) hit the target from 55 ft (16.764 m) in Clearwater, Florida, USA.

## Most consecutive jumps on a pogo stick

On 2 Jul 2015, Jack Sexty (UK) completed 88,047 pogo jumps in a row at Pogopalooza 2015, held at Paine's Park in Philadelphia, Pennsylvania, USA. Sexty's marathon effort lasted 10 hr 20 min – an average of two-and-a-half jumps a second.

The **longest jump on a pogo stick** is 5.52 m (18 ft 1 in), by Dalton Smith (USA) on 18 May 2019 in Tokyo, Japan.

## Most Croquet World Championships

On 23 Feb 2020, Reg Bamford (ZAF) won his fifth world championship in Melbourne, Australia. He equalled the feat of Robert Fulford (UK) between 1990 and 2002.

Also in Melbourne, Stephen Mulliner (UK) increased his record for **most Croquet World Championship appearances** to 16. He has missed only one tournament to date, and won the competition in 2016.

## Fastest 100 m egg-and-spoon race

Australian sprint hurdler Sally Pearson completed the school sports-day classic in 16.59 sec on 23 Sep 2013 in Sydney, New South Wales, Australia.

## Highest career earnings on the Professional Disc Golf Association Tour

Disc golf shares many similarities with golf, but instead of holing a ball players try to land a flying disc into an elevated metal basket. As of 8 Mar 2021, Paul McBeth (USA, above) topped the career money list with $511,880 (£369,802). He has triumphed at 130 events since 2006, including five world championships.

The **most wins of the PDGA World Championships (male)** is 12, by Ken Climo in 1990–98, 2000, 2002 and 2006. The **female** record is five, by Elaine King, Juliana Korver and Paige Pierce (all USA). Pierce is pictured left, on her way to her fifth title in 2019.

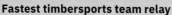

## Fastest timbersports team relay

Australia chopped and sawed their way to glory in 45.10 sec on 19 Oct 2018 at the Stihl Timbersports Team World Championship semi-final in Liverpool, UK. The team relay consists of four events: stock saw, underhand chop, single buck and standing block chop (right). The "Chopperoos" – Jamie Head, Brayden Meyer, Brad de Losa and Glen Gillam – defeated the USA in the final (below).

## Most points scored in an archery 1440 round (compound, male)

On 30 Aug 2020, Mike Schloesser (NLD) shot a score of 1,421 for his 1440 round in Boekel, Netherlands. The event consists of four sets of 36 arrows fired over increasing distances. Schloesser scored 360 out of 360 at 30 m, 353 at 50 m, 356 at 70 m and 352 at 90 m, breaking a record that had stood for 11 years.

# Formula One

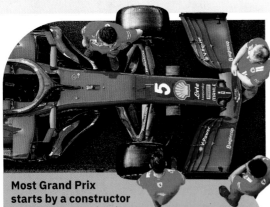

## Most Grand Prix starts (male)

As of 18 Apr 2021, Kimi Räikkönen (FIN) had competed in 331 F1 races since his debut at the 2001 Australian Grand Prix. He surpassed Rubens Barrichello's record of 322 starts at the 2020 Eifel Grand Prix. Räikkönen has raced for Sauber, McLaren, Ferrari (twice), Lotus and Alfa Romeo. He claimed the 2007 F1 Championship for Ferrari and has 21 race wins.

## Most Grand Prix starts (female)

Maria "Lella" Lombardi (ITA) lined up for 12 races between 1 Mar 1975 and 15 Aug 1976 – one of only two women to compete in an F1 Grand Prix. Driving for the March-Ford team, Lombardi scored half a point for finishing sixth in the abbreviated 1975 Spanish Grand Prix on 27 Apr 1975 – to date, the only championship points earned by a female driver.

## Most Grand Prix starts by a constructor

Scuderia Ferrari (ITA) competed in 1,010 Formula One races between 21 May 1950 and 18 Apr 2021. The famous marque celebrated race No.1,000 at the 2020 Tuscan Grand Prix. To mark the occasion, both cars sported the same burgundy livery (above) as the 125 S, the very first Ferrari, which was built in 1947. The "Prancing Horse" team holds the record for **most race wins** (238) and **most constructors' championship titles** (16).

## Highest average lap speed

On 1 Sep 2018, Ferrari's Kimi Räikkönen (FIN, see above) qualified on pole for the Italian Grand Prix at Monza after a flying lap with an average speed of 263.5 km/h (163.7 mph). He completed the 5.7-km (3.5-mi) course in 1 min 19.119 sec.

The **highest average Grand Prix speed** over a full race is 247.5 km/h (153.8 mph), by Ferrari's Michael Schumacher (DEU) on 14 Sep 2003 – also at Monza.

## Longest circuit

The 1957 Pescara Grand Prix took place on a 25.8-km (16-mi) road course winding through the hills around Pescara in Italy. The race, held on 18 Aug, was won by Stirling Moss. It also saw Jack Brabham filling up his Cooper-Climax at a roadside petrol station.

## Youngest race winner

Max Verstappen (NLD, b. BEL, 30 Sep 1997) triumphed at the 2016 Spanish Grand Prix in Montmeló aged 18 years 228 days. The Dutch ace is also the **youngest driver to earn a World Championship point**, aged 17 years 180 days, at the Malaysian Grand Prix on 29 Mar 2015.

## Most consecutive wins of the same Grand Prix

Ayrton Senna (BRA) claimed victory at Monaco five times in a row between 1989 and 1993 while driving for McLaren: a record matched by Lewis Hamilton (UK) at the Spanish Grand Prix from 2017 to 2021. Senna earned the nickname "King of Monaco" due to his legendary performances on the street circuit, winning there six times in total. He also recorded the **most consecutive pole positions** – eight – between the 1988 Spanish and the 1989 USA Grands Prix.

## Oldest world champion

Juan Manuel Fangio (ARG, b. 24 Jun 1911) claimed his fifth and final F1 championship on 4 Aug 1957, aged 46 years 41 days. One of the sport's greatest drivers, Fangio won 24 times from 51 starts and lifted the title for four different teams: Alfa Romeo, Ferrari, Mercedes-Benz and Maserati.

The **youngest world champion** is Sebastian Vettel (DEU, b. 3 Jul 1987), who claimed his first title on 14 Nov 2010, aged 23 years 134 days.

## Most races driven before a win

On 6 Dec 2020, Racing Point's Sergio Pérez (MEX) triumphed at the Sakhir Grand Prix in Bahrain on his 190th start in F1. A crash on lap 1 had left Pérez in last place, but he battled his way through the field to victory.

## Most Grand Prix wins

Lewis Hamilton (UK) had recorded 98 victories in F1 as of 9 May 2021. He overtook Michael Schumacher's mark of 91 at the 2020 Portuguese Grand Prix, and equalled the German's record for **most World Championships** by claiming his seventh title for Mercedes. Hamilton has also achieved the **most pole positions**: 100, as of 8 May 2021. However, his run of **most consecutive race starts** – 265 – ended when he missed the Sakhir Grand Prix on 6 Dec 2020.

# X Games

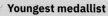

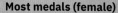

## Youngest medallist

Cocona Hiraki (JPN, b. 26 Aug 2008) won a silver medal in Women's Skateboard Park aged just 10 years 341 days on 2 Aug 2019. She was beaten by 13-year-old Misugu Okamoto, in what was the youngest field in X Games history. Hiraki is also the **youngest competitor (female)**. For more on the outright record holder, Gui Khury, turn to p.179.

### Youngest X Games gold medallists

| SUMMER GAMES | Age | Name | Event |
|---|---|---|---|
| Male | 12 years 229 days | Tom Schaar (USA, b. 14 Sep 1999) | Mini Mega (2012) |
| Female | 13 years 1 day | Brighton Zeuner (USA, b. 14 Jul 2004) | Skateboard Park (2017) |
| WINTER GAMES | Age | Name | Event |
| Male | 15 years 225 days | Tucker Hibbert (USA, b. 24 Jun 1984) | Snowmobile SnoCross (2000) |
| Female | 13 years 193 days | Kokomo Murase (JPN, b. 7 Nov 2004) | Snowboard Big Air (2018) |

## First gold medallist

On 25 Jun 1995, Justin Seers (AUS) triumphed in the Barefoot Jumping waterskiing event to become the first "Extreme Games" champion. Seers beat four-time world champion Ron Scarpa in a head-to-head final at Roger Williams Park in Providence, Rhode Island, USA.

## Most gold medals

Shaun White (USA) won 15 titles from 2003 to 2013. These include the **most winter discipline golds** – 13 in snowboarding – and two Skateboard Vert titles, at the 2007 and 2011 Summer Games.

## Most skiing medals

Henrik Harlaut (SWE) won the Ski Knuckle Huck at X Games Aspen 2021 to take his medal tally to 13 – eight golds and five silvers. He surpassed Tanner Hall's total of 11 skiing medals with a gold at X Games Aspen 2020.

## Oldest medallist

Chris Devlin-Young (USA, b. 26 Dec 1961) won the Mono Skier X event aged 53 years 27 days at X Games Aspen 2015 on 22 Jan. Paralysed in a plane crash while serving in the US Coast Guard, Devlin-Young went on to become a two-time Paralympic skiing gold medallist. He beat the previous record – by Angelika Casteneda in the 1996 X Venture Race – by just days.

The **oldest competitor** is John Buffum (USA, b. 4 Oct 1943), who was aged 63 years 305 days when he lined up for the Rally Car Racing event at X Games Los Angeles 2007.

## Most gold medals at a single Games

Three athletes have won three golds at one competition: Dave Mirra (USA) in 1998 in BMX Vert, Vert Doubles and Park; Rodil de Araujo (BRA) in 2002 in Skateboard Park, Street and Street Best Trick; and Travis Pastrana (USA) in 2006 in Rally Car Racing, Moto X Freestyle and Moto X Best Trick. In a performance that went down in X Games folklore, Pastrana claimed the Best Trick crown by completing the **first double backflip on a motorcycle**.

## Most medals (female)

At X Games Aspen 2021, Jamie Anderson (USA) triumphed in Snowboard Slopestyle and Big Air to take her career tally to 19 medals – eight golds, seven silvers and four bronze. Sixteen of these have come in Slopestyle. Anderson currently stands just one behind snowboarder Mark McMorris's (CAN) overall record for **most winter discipline medals**.

## Most medals (male)

Skateboarder Bob Burnquist (BRA) won 30 medals between 1997 and 2015: 14 golds, eight silvers and eight bronze. He competed at every Summer X Games from its inception in 1995 until 2017 – the **most appearances** (26). Among his career highlights was his jaw-dropping Skateboard Vert gold-medal run in 2001, which scored 98.00 and was described by Tony Hawk as the "best vert run we've ever seen".

## Most Moto X medals

Nate Adams (USA) claimed 19 medals at the X Games between 2003 and 2015. He overcame serious shoulder injuries to amass a career five golds (two in Freestyle, three in Speed & Style), six silvers and eight bronze.

The **most consecutive gold medals in a Moto X discipline** is four, by Jarryd McNeil (AUS) in Step Up from 2016 to 2019.

## Most gold medals on debut (female)

Freestyle skier Eileen Gu (CHN, b. USA, aka Gu Ailing) won two golds at X Games Aspen 2021 – her first appearance in the competition. The 17-year-old claimed victory in Ski Superpipe and Slopestyle, and won a bronze in Ski Big Air. Gu is also an accomplished pianist and cross-country runner; she has modelled for *Vogue China* and earned early acceptance from Stanford University.

# Swimming

# Swimming

*World swimming federation FINA recognizes records set in two types of pool: long course (50 m) and short course (25 m). On this page we focus on the short course world records – several of which were broken in 2020 during the International Swimming League (ISL) in Budapest, Hungary.*

### Fastest short course 4 x 50 m mixed freestyle relay

Mixed short course relay records were first recognized by FINA in 2014. The USA team of Caeleb Dressel, Ryan Held, Mallory Comerford and Kelsi Dahlia swam the 4 x 50 m freestyle relay in 1 min 27.89 sec on 12 Dec 2018 in Hangzhou, China.

The **mixed medley relay** record is 1 min 36.22 sec, by the Russian team of Kliment Kolesnikov (backstroke), Vladimir Morozov (breaststroke), Arina Surkova (butterfly) and Maria Kameneva (freestyle) on 5 Dec 2019 in Glasgow, UK.

### Fastest short course 100 m backstroke (male)

Kliment Kolesnikov (RUS) powered Energy Standard's 4 x 100 m medley relay team to victory at the ISL Grand Final, completing the lead-off backstroke leg in 48.58 sec. Kolesnikov reclaimed the world record from China's Xu Jiayu, having first broken it at the age of just 17 on 22 Dec 2017.

### Fastest short course 50 m backstroke (female)

On 14 Nov 2020, the London Roar's Kira Toussaint (NLD) won the women's 50 m backstroke in 25.60 sec at the first ISL semi-final. She went on to match this time on 18 Dec 2020. Toussaint's technique is notable for her underwater kicks, which she does while lying on her side.

*\*pending ratification by FINA*

### Fastest short course 100 m individual medley (male)

Caeleb Dressel (USA) swam the 100 m individual medley in 49.28 sec at the ISL Grand Final on 22 Nov 2020. This is almost a second faster than anyone else has managed in the event. Dressel helped his team, the Cali Condors, to the 2020 ISL title and was named MVP, having recorded four world-record swims in the competition.

## Short course swimming (25-m pool)

| MEN | Time | Name | Location | Date |
|---|---|---|---|---|
| 50 m freestyle | 20.16 | Caeleb Dressel (USA) | Budapest, Hungary | 21 Nov 2020 |
| 100 m freestyle | 44.94 | Amaury Leveaux (FRA) | Rijeka, Croatia | 13 Dec 2008 |
| 200 m freestyle | 1:39.37 | Paul Biedermann (DEU) | Berlin, Germany | 15 Nov 2009 |
| 400 m freestyle | 3:32.25 | Yannick Agnel (FRA) | Angers, France | 15 Nov 2012 |
| 800 m freestyle | 7:23.42 | Grant Hackett (AUS) | Melbourne, Australia | 20 Jul 2008 |
| 1,500 m freestyle | 14:08.06 | Gregorio Paltrinieri (ITA) | Netanya, Israel | 4 Dec 2015 |
| 4 x 100 m freestyle relay | 3:03.03 | USA (Caeleb Dressel, Blake Pieroni, Michael Chadwick, Ryan Held) | Hangzhou, China | 11 Dec 2018 |
| 4 x 200 m freestyle relay | 6:46.81 | Brazil (Luiz Altamir Melo, Fernando Scheffer, Leonardo Coelho Santos, Breno Correia) | Hangzhou, China | 14 Dec 2018 |
| 50 m butterfly | 21.75 | Nicholas Santos (BRA) | Budapest, Hungary | 6 Oct 2018 |
| 100 m butterfly | 47.78 | Caeleb Dressel (USA) | Budapest, Hungary | 21 Nov 2020 |
| 200 m butterfly | 1:48.24 | Daiya Seto (JPN) | Hangzhou, China | 11 Dec 2018 |
| 50 m backstroke | 22.22 | Florent Manaudou (FRA) | Doha, Qatar | 6 Dec 2014 |
| 100 m backstroke | 48.58 | Kliment Kolesnikov (RUS) | Budapest, Hungary | 21 Nov 2020 |
| 200 m backstroke | 1:45.63 | Mitch Larkin (AUS) | Sydney, Australia | 27 Nov 2015 |
| 50 m breaststroke | 25.25 | Cameron van der Burgh (ZAF) | Berlin, Germany | 14 Nov 2009 |
| 100 m breaststroke | 55.34 | Ilya Shymanovich (BLR) | Brest, Belarus | 19 Dec 2020 |
| 200 m breaststroke | 2:00.16 | Kirill Prigoda (RUS) | Hangzhou, China | 13 Dec 2018 |
| 100 m medley | 49.28 | Caeleb Dressel (USA) | Budapest, Hungary | 22 Nov 2020 |
| 200 m medley | 1:49.63 | Ryan Lochte (USA) | Istanbul, Turkey | 14 Dec 2012 |
| 400 m medley | 3:54.81 | Daiya Seto (JPN) | Las Vegas, USA | 20 Dec 2019 |
| 4 x 100 m medley relay | 3:19.16 | Russia (Stanislav Donets, Sergey Geybel, Evgeny Korotyshkin, Danila Izotov) | St Petersburg, Russia | 20 Dec 2009 |

| WOMEN | Time | Name | Location | Date |
|---|---|---|---|---|
| 50 m freestyle | 22.93 | Ranomi Kromowidjojo (NLD) | Berlin, Germany | 7 Aug 2017 |
| 100 m freestyle | 50.25 | Cate Campbell (AUS) | Adelaide, Australia | 26 Oct 2017 |
| 200 m freestyle | 1:50.43 | Sarah Sjöström (SWE) | Eindhoven, Netherlands | 12 Aug 2017 |
| 400 m freestyle | 3:53.92 | Ariarne Titmus (AUS) | Hangzhou, China | 14 Dec 2018 |
| 800 m freestyle | 7:59.34 | Mireia Belmonte (ESP) | Berlin, Germany | 10 Aug 2013 |
| 1,500 m freestyle | 15:18.01 | Sarah Köhler (DEU) | Berlin, Germany | 16 Nov 2019 |
| 4 x 100 m freestyle relay | 3:26.53 | Netherlands (Inge Dekker, Femke Heemskerk, Maud van der Meer, Ranomi Kromowidjojo) | Doha, Qatar | 5 Dec 2014 |
| 4 x 200 m freestyle relay | 7:32.85 | Netherlands (Inge Dekker, Femke Heemskerk, Ranomi Kromowidjojo, Sharon van Rouwendaal) | Doha, Qatar | 3 Dec 2014 |
| 50 m butterfly | 24.38 | Therese Alshammar (SWE) | Singapore | 22 Nov 2009 |
| 100 m butterfly | 54.61 | Sarah Sjöström (SWE) | Doha, Qatar | 7 Dec 2014 |
| 200 m butterfly | 1:59.61 | Mireia Belmonte (ESP) | Doha, Qatar | 3 Dec 2014 |
| 50 m backstroke | 25.60 | Kira Toussaint (NLD) | Budapest, Hungary | 14 Nov 2020 |
| | | | Amsterdam, Netherlands* | 18 Dec 2020 |
| 100 m backstroke | 54.89 | Minna Atherton (AUS) | Budapest, Hungary | 27 Oct 2019 |
| 200 m backstroke | 1:58.94 | Kaylee McKeown (AUS) | Brisbane, Australia | 28 Nov 2020 |
| 50 m breaststroke | 28.56 | Alia Atkinson (JAM) | Budapest, Hungary | 6 Oct 2018 |
| 100 m breaststroke | 1:02.36 | = Rūta Meilutytė (LTU) | Moscow, Russia | 12 Oct 2013 |
| | | = Alia Atkinson (JAM) | Doha, Qatar | 6 Dec 2014 |
| | | | Chartres, France | 26 Aug 2016 |
| 200 m breaststroke | 2:14.57 | Rebecca Soni (USA) | Manchester, UK | 18 Dec 2009 |
| 100 m medley | 56.51 | Katinka Hosszú (HUN) | Berlin, Germany | 7 Aug 2017 |
| 200 m medley | 2:01.86 | Katinka Hosszú (HUN) | Doha, Qatar | 6 Dec 2014 |
| 400 m medley | 4:18.94 | Mireia Belmonte (ESP) | Eindhoven, Netherlands | 12 Aug 2017 |
| 4 x 100 m medley relay | 3:44.52 | USA (Olivia Smoliga, Lilly King, Kelsi Dahlia, Erika Brown) | Budapest, Hungary | 21 Nov 2020 |

# Tour de France

## Most stage wins
Eddy Merckx (BEL) won 34 stages of the Tour from 1969 to 1975. "The Cannibal" dominated the race, and remains the only cyclist to win the general, points and mountain classifications in the same year (1969). He did not enter the race in 1973 and was hampered by injury in 1975. Merckx recorded the **most wins of the Tour de France** – five, in 1969–72 and 1974. He shares this record with Jacques Anquetil (FRA), between 1957 and 1964; Bernard Hinault (FRA), between 1978 and 1985; and Miguel Indurain (ESP) in 1991–95.

## Closest race
The 1989 Tour was won by Greg LeMond (USA, above left) in 87 hr 38 min 35 sec – just 8 sec ahead of Laurent Fignon (FRA, above right). LeMond went into the final stage with a 50-sec deficit but produced the then-fastest individual time trial in Tour history to edge past his great rival. The two riders were never separated by more than a minute throughout the race.

## Largest attendance at a sporting event
The Tour de France attracts an estimated 10–12 million spectators every year, according to sports newspaper *L'Équipe*.

## Youngest winner
Henri Cornet (FRA, b. 4 Aug 1884) won the 1904 Tour de France aged 19 years 355 days. Cornet finished the race in fifth position but was awarded the victory after the first four riders were all disqualified.

## Longest edition
The 1926 Tour traced a 5,745-km (3,569-mi) anticlockwise path along the French borders. Stage 10 – a mountainous 326 km (202 mi) from Bayonne to Luchon – has been dubbed one of the hardest in Tour history, and was won by eventual race winner Lucien Buysse in 17 hr 12 min 4 sec.

## Longest solo escape (post-war era)
On 11 Jul 1947, Albert Bourlon (FRA) burst clear from the peloton and cycled 253 km (157.2 mi) alone to win the stage between Carcassonne and Luchon. He finished in 8 hr 10 min 11 sec – more than 16 min ahead of the field – to record his only stage win on the Tour. During World War II, Bourlon had won the Bucharest-Ploiești-Bucharest classic while a fugitive from a German PoW camp.

## Fastest individual time trial
On 4 Jul 2015, Rohan Dennis (AUS) won the opening stage of the Tour de France with an average speed of 55.446 km/h (34.452 mph). He finished the 13.8-km (8.5-mi) leg in Utrecht, Netherlands, in 14 min 56 sec.

The **fastest team time trial** was by Orica GreenEDGE (AUS) on 2 Jul 2013 in Nice, France. They completed the 25-km (15-mi) stage at an average speed of 57.841 km/h (35.940 mph).

## Most...
**Wins of the mountain classification**: seven, by Richard Virenque (FRA) in 1994–97, 1999 and 2003–04.
**Wins of the young rider classification**: three, by Jan Ullrich (DEU) in 1996–98 and Andy Schleck (LUX) in 2008–10.
**Mass-finish stage wins**: 30, by Mark Cavendish (UK) from 2008 to 2016.
**Appearances**: 18, by Sylvain Chavanel (FRA) from 2001 to 2018.
**Races completed**: 16, by Sylvain Chavanel and Hendrik "Joop" Zoetemelk (NLD), in 1970–86.

## Most wins of the points classification
Since 1953, points have been awarded to riders on the Tour according to their final position on each stage, with extra points for intermediate sprints during certain stages. The rider heading the category traditionally wears the *maillot vert* (green jersey). Peter Sagan (SVK, centre) has won the points classification seven times, in 2012–16 and 2018–19. He has triumphed on 12 Tour stages.

# Extreme Earth Sports

## Largest no-grip wingsuit formation (FAI-approved)

On 17 Oct 2015, a team of 61 skydivers led by Taya Weiss (USA) formed a colourful diamond shape 5,500 ft (1,676 m) above Perris Valley in California, USA. Judges from the Fédération Aéronautique Internationale (FAI) were on hand to check that the team maintained their designated flying spaces, without holding on to one another.

## Fastest speed parachuting (female, FAI-approved)

On 6 Nov 2017, Amber Forte (NOR, b. UK) reached a speed of 283.7 km/h (176.2 mph) at the FAI World Cup of Wingsuit Flying in Overton, Nevada, USA. Wingsuits have fabric under the arms and between the legs to increase surface area. Once the parachute is deployed, pilots can unzip their arm wings to better control the descent.

## Fastest speed skiing (female)

On 26 Mar 2016, Valentina Greggio (ITA) skied at 247.083 km/h (153.530 mph) in Vars, France. This is faster than a high-speed *Acela* train. Speed skiing dates to the 19th century. Concerns about competitor safety have so far dashed hopes of its inclusion as an official event at the Winter Olympics.

## Most wins of the Red Bull Cliff Diving World Series

Gary Hunt (FRA, b. UK) won the Red Bull Cliff Diving World Series eight times between 2010 and 2019. His lowest finish in the overall standings to date is second. In Sep 2020, Hunt switched nationality in the hope of competing for France in the 10 m diving event at the 2024 Olympic Games in Paris.

## Most Marathon des Sables wins

First staged in 1986, the Marathon des Sables is a six-day, 250-km (155-mi) ultra-distance race through the Sahara Desert in Morocco. Lahcen Ahansal (MAR, right) triumphed 10 times, in 1997 and 1999–2007. Lahcen's brother Mohamad is a five-time winner who also holds the **fastest time** for the event: 16 hr 22 min 29 sec, in 1998.

## Fastest...
### Speed skiing

On 26 Mar 2016, Ivan Origone (ITA) was clocked at 254.958 km/h (158.423 mph) at the Speed Masters event in Vars, France. No human in a non-motorized vehicle has ever travelled faster on land. Ivan broke the mark set by his elder brother, Simone, skiing the 100-m timing stretch near the bottom of the course in 1.41 sec. The **female** record was broken on the same day at Vars (see above).

### Speed sand skiing

Henrik May (NAM, b. East Germany) hit 92.12 km/h (57.24 mph) while skiing down the dunes of Swakopmund in Namibia on 31 May 2010. As a child, May was a Nordic combined skier. After emigrating to Namibia in 1998, he swapped snow for the sand of the Namib Desert. "It's similar to deep-snow skiing," he said, "but you don't sink as much."

## Speed windsurfing

Antoine Albeau (FRA) achieved a speed of 53.27 knots (98.65 km/h; 61.3 mph) in Lüderitz, Namibia, on 2 Nov 2015. It is one of a host of speed-sailing records set on a purpose-built 800-m-long (2,625-ft) trench in Lüderitz, which offers a perfect combination of strong winds and flat water. Albeau's feat was verified by the World Sailing Speed Record Council (WSSRC).

The **female** record, also set at Lüderitz, is 46.49 knots (86.09 km/h; 53.49 mph), recorded by windsurfer Zara Davis (UK) on 22 Nov 2017.

## Speed sailing (500 m)

On 24 Nov 2012, Paul Larsen (AUS) piloted *Vestas SailRocket 2* at 65.45 knots (121.21 km/h; 75.31 mph) in Walvis Bay, Namibia. He covered 500 m (1,640 ft) in 14.85 sec. Larsen's long-standing record may come under threat in 2022, when a team of Swiss engineers are hoping that their *SP80* hydrofoil vessel – which is propelled by a giant kitesail – will break the 80-knot barrier.

## Deepest no-limit freedive
Herbert Nitsch (AUT, below right) plunged 214 m (702 ft 1 in) on a sled off the Greek island of Spetses on 14 Jun 2007. This is the deepest recorded freedive in history. On 6 Jun 2012, during an attempt to beat his own record, Nitsch lost consciousness and suffered severe decompression sickness. He was in a wheelchair for six months. The no-limit freedive – in which divers can use any means to propel themselves deeper – has since been closed as a category by diving federation AIDA.

## ▶ Largest wave surfed (female)
On 11 Feb 2020, Maya Gabeira (BRA) rode a 22.4-m-tall (73-ft 5-in) wave during the World Surf League's Nazaré Tow Surfing Challenge in Portugal. Nazaré's Praia do Norte has become a magnet for surfers ever since Garrett McNamara rode a then-record 23.77-m (78-ft) wave there in 2011. The monster waves are caused by a deep undersea canyon that squeezes and channels the swell as it heads for shore.

## Freediving

| MEN'S DEPTH DISCIPLINES | Depth | Name | Location | Date |
|---|---|---|---|---|
| Constant weight with fins | 130 m (426 ft 6 in) | Alexey Molchanov (RUS) | Long Island, The Bahamas | 18 Jul 2018 |
| Constant weight with bi-fins | 113 m (370 ft 8 in) | Alexey Molchanov (RUS) | Sharm el-Sheikh, Egypt | 26 Nov 2020 |
| Constant weight without fins | 102 m (334 ft 7 in) | William Trubridge (NZ) | Long Island, The Bahamas | 20 Jul 2016 |
| Variable weight | 150 m (492 ft 1 in) | Walid Boudhiaf (TUN) | Sharm el-Sheikh, Egypt | 17 Jan 2021 |
| No limit | 214 m (702 ft 1 in) | Herbert Nitsch (AUT) | Spetses, Greece | 14 Jun 2007 |
| Free immersion | 125 m (410 ft 1 in) | Alexey Molchanov (RUS) | Long Island, The Bahamas | 24 Jul 2018 |

| WOMEN'S DEPTH DISCIPLINES | Depth | Name | Location | Date |
|---|---|---|---|---|
| Constant weight with fins | 114 m (374 ft) | Alenka Artnik (SVN) | Sharm el-Sheikh, Egypt | 7 Nov 2020 |
| Constant weight with bi-fins | 92 m (301 ft 10 in) | Alenka Artnik (SVN) | Panglao, Philippines | 11 Jun 2019 |
| Constant weight without fins | 73 m (239 ft 6 in) | Alessia Zecchini (ITA) | Long Island, The Bahamas | 22 Jul 2018 |
| Variable weight | 130 m (426 ft 6 in) | Nanja van den Broek (NLD) | Sharm el-Sheikh, Egypt | 18 Oct 2015 |
| No limit | 160 m (524 ft 11 in) | Tanya Streeter (USA) | Turks and Caicos Islands | 17 Aug 2002 |
| Free immersion | 98 m (321 ft 6 in) | Alessia Zecchini (ITA, above) | Curaçao | 16 Oct 2019 |

## Speed parachuting (FAI-approved)
Travis Mickle (USA) flew at a speed of 325.4 km/h (202.1 mph) on 6 Nov 2017 at the FAI World Cup of Wingsuit Flying in Overton. See opposite for the **female** record, which was set on the same day.

## Speed parachuting canopy piloting (FAI-approved)
Mario Fattoruso (ITA) flew a 70-m (230-ft) course in 1.943 sec on 23 Nov 2019 at the 10th FAI World Cup of Canopy Piloting in Pretoria, South Africa.

## 1 km Ice Swim
On 16 Feb 2019, Sven Elfferich (NLD) swam a kilometre (0.6 mi) in 3.6°C-water (38.4°F) in 11 min 55.4 sec at the Austrian Ice Swimming Championships in Altenwörth. He was 19 at the time. The race was held under International Ice Swimming Association regulations.

The **female** record is 12 min 48.7 sec, by Alisa Fatum (DEU) on 6 Jan 2019 at the Ice Swimming German Open in Veitsbronn. The water temperature was 1.4°C (34.5°F).

## North Pole Marathon
Thomas Maguire (IRL) won the North Pole Marathon in 3 hr 36 min 10 sec on 15 Apr 2007, completing 10 laps of the course at a Russian ice base in the Arctic Ocean. Maguire ran in snowshoes, three layers of clothing, goggles and a balaclava. He described conditions as "extremely hard, like running in sand dunes".

Herbert Nitsch has set more than 30 freediving world records across eight different disciplines.

## Fastest Antarctic Ice Marathon
On 13 Dec 2019, William Hafferty (USA, right) battled wind-chill temperatures of -15°C (5°F) to win the Antarctic Ice Marathon in 3 hr 34 min 12 sec, beating the race record by 35 sec. The location was Union Glacier, in the shadow of the Ellsworth Mountains. The **fastest marathon on Antarctica** is 2 hr 54 min 54 sec, by Michael Wardian (USA, inset) on 23 Jan 2017. It was the first leg of the World Marathon Challenge, in which runners have a week to run a marathon on each of the seven continents.

# Ultra-Running

**Fastest Pennine Way ultra-run**
Damian Hall (UK) ran the length of Great Britain's oldest national trail in 61 hr 35 min 15 sec on 22–24 Jul 2020. The Pennine Way runs for 431 km (268 mi) between the Scottish Borders and Derbyshire and has a vertical gain of 11,836 m (38,832 ft). Hall slept for no more than 40 min across his entire run. A committed environmentalist, he litter-picked as he went (inset) and consumed only plant-based products such as tea and hummus and avocado sandwiches.

**Longest annual running race**
The Sri Chinmoy Self-Transcendence 3,100 Mile Race is held every summer around an extended block in New York City, USA. Competitors have 52 days to complete the distance – equivalent to around 60 mi (96 km) a day – and can face stifling humidity and downpours. The **fastest winning time** is 40 days 9 hr 6 min 21 sec, by Ashprihanal Aalto (FIN, above) on 14 Jun–24 Jul 2015.

**Fastest-run 50 km (female)**
On 1 Sep 2019, Alyson Dixon (UK) broke a 30-year-old record on her ultra-running debut, winning the IAU 50 km World Championship in 3 hr 7 min 20 sec in Braşov, Romania. Seven days later, Dixon donned a Wonder Woman outfit to run the **fastest half marathon in superhero costume (female)** – 1 hr 18 min 26 sec – at the Great North Run in Tyne and Wear, UK.

**Oldest ultra-marathon**
The Comrades Marathon was established on 24 May 1921 in honour of South African soldiers killed in World War I. The hilly course runs for c. 90 km (55 mi) between Durban and Pietermaritzburg in South Africa, with the direction of the race alternating between "Up" and "Down" each year. The **fastest winning time** is 5 hr 18 min 19 sec, by David Gatebe (ZAF) on the "Down" course on 29 May 2016.

**Fastest-run Spartathlon**
Yiannis Kouros (GRC) completed the iconic Greek ultra-marathon in 20 hr 25 min on 30 Sep 1984. First held in 1983, the Spartathlon is a 246-km (153-mi) race between Athens and Sparta. Runners seek to emulate the feat of the ancient Athenian messenger Pheidippides, who was said to have run to Sparta in 490 BCE to seek aid against the Persians for the Battle of Marathon.

The **female** record is 24 hr 48 min 18 sec, by Patrycja Bereznowska (POL, see below) on 30 Sep 2017.

**Fastest completion of The Barkley Marathons**
Brett Maune (USA) finished the idiosyncratic US ultra-race in 52 hr 3 min 8 sec on 2 Apr 2012. The brainchild of Gary "Lazarus Lake" Cantrell, The Barkley Marathons takes in five 32-km (20-mi) loops through the Tennessee hills, with a total elevation gain of 18,000 m (59,000 ft) – twice the height of Everest. Only 18 athletes have completed the full race inside the 60-hr time limit. Around 40 runners take part each year, including a "human sacrifice" who is considered least likely to finish. The start time is kept secret, with entrants given an hour's warning by the blowing of a conch shell.

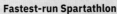

**Fastest-run Badwater 135 ultra-marathon (female)**
On 15–16 Jul 2019, Patrycja Bereznowska (POL) completed the gruelling Californian race in 24 hr 13 min 24 sec, finishing as the fastest woman and in overall second place. The Badwater course runs 217 km (135 mi) from Death Valley to Mount Whitney, the lowest and highest points in the contiguous USA. Temperatures can soar to 53°C (127°F).

## Ultra-distance running

| MEN | Time/Distance | Name | Location | Date |
|---|---|---|---|---|
| 50 km | 2:43:38 | Thompson Magawana (ZAF) | Cape Town, South Africa | 12 Apr 1988 |
| 100 km | 6:09:14 | Nao Kazami (JPN) | Lake Saroma, Japan | 24 Jun 2018 |
| 100 miles* | 11:19:13 | Zach Bitter (USA) | Milwaukee, USA | 24 Aug 2019 |
| 1,000 km | 5 days 16:17:00 | Yiannis Kouros (GRC) | Colac, Australia | 26 Nov–1 Dec 1984 |
| 1,000 miles | 10 days 10:30:36 | Yiannis Kouros (GRC) | New York City, USA | 20–30 May 1988 |
| 6 hours | 97.2 km (60.39 mi) | Donald Ritchie (UK) | London, UK | 28 Oct 1978 |
| 12 hours* | 168.79 km (104.88 mi) | Zach Bitter (USA) | Milwaukee, USA | 24 Aug 2019 |
| 24 hours | 303.50 km (188.59 mi) | Yiannis Kouros (GRC) | Adelaide, Australia | 4–5 Oct 1997 |
| 48 hours | 473.49 km (294.21 mi) | Yiannis Kouros (GRC) | Surgères, France | 3–5 May 1996 |
| 6 days | 1,036.8 km (644.23 mi) | Yiannis Kouros (GRC) | Colac, Australia | 20–26 Nov 2005 |

| WOMEN | Time/Distance | Name | Location | Date |
|---|---|---|---|---|
| 50 km | 3:07:20 | Alyson Dixon (UK) | Braşov, Romania | 1 Sep 2019 |
| 100 km | 6:33:11 | Tomoe Abe (JPN) | Lake Saroma, Japan | 25 Jun 2000 |
| 100 miles | 12:42:40 | Camille Herron (USA) | Vienna, USA | 11 Nov 2017 |
| 1,000 km | 7 days 16:08:37 | Paula Mairer (AUT) | New York City, USA | 29 Sep–6 Oct 2002 |
| 1,000 miles | 12 days 14:38:40 | Sandra Barwick (NZ) | New York City, USA | 16–28 Oct 1991 |
| 6 hours | 85.49 km (53.12 mi) | Nele Alder-Baerens (DEU) | Münster, Germany | 11 Mar 2017 |
| 12 hours | 149.13 km (92.66 mi) | Camille Herron (USA) | Phoenix, USA | 9–10 Dec 2017 |
| 24 hours | 270.11 km (167.84 mi) | Camille Herron (USA) | Albi, France | 26–27 Oct 2019 |
| 48 hours | 397.10 km (246.75 mi) | Sumie Inagaki (JPN) | Surgères, France | 21–23 May 2010 |
| 6 days | 883.63 km (549.06 mi) | Sandra Barwick (NZ) | Campbelltown, Australia | 18–24 Nov 1990 |

*pending ratification by the International Association of Ultrarunners*

# Dominant Champions

### Longest winning streak in track athletics
Edwin Moses (USA) won 122 consecutive 400 m hurdles races between 1977 and 1987. Aided by a huge 2.9-m (9-ft 9-in) stride, he went on an unbeaten run that lasted for nine years, nine months and nine days. "My slow is faster than most athletes' fast," he said. On 4 Jun 1987, Moses finally lost a race in Madrid, Spain, having hit the final hurdle.

The **longest winning streak in field athletics** is 150 competitions, achieved by Romanian high jumper Iolanda Balaş from 1957 to 1967. She set 14 world records in the event, and on 18 Oct 1958 became the first woman to clear 6 ft (1.8 m).

### Longest unbeaten run in squash
Heather McKay (AUS) went undefeated for 19 years between 1962 and her retirement in 1981. A prodigious athlete who was also selected for Australia at hockey, McKay's hard-hitting physicality and racket skills enabled her to dominate the squash court. She lost only two matches in her entire career and claimed the **most British Open Championships** – 16 in a row. She won the 1968 final against Bev Johnson 9–0, 9–0, 9–0 in just a quarter of an hour.

### Most World Championship and Olympic gold medals for Greco-Roman wrestling
Aleksandr Karelin (USSR/RUS) won three Olympic and nine world titles at super-heavyweight from 1988 to 1999. Famed for his incredible strength and ability to reverse body-lift his opponents, Karelin went unbeaten for 13 years. His PhD thesis was entitled *Methods of execution of suplex counter throws*.

### Most horse racing wins by a jockey
Jorge Ricardo (BRA) had ridden 13,069 winners as of 15 Mar 2021. He moved past the total of the previous record holder, Russell Baze, on 7 Feb 2018 and rode his 13,000th winner – aged 58 – on 25 Sep 2020 at his home track in Rio de Janeiro, Brazil. Based predominantly in South America, Ricardo has won 26 consecutive Brazilian jockey titles.

### Most world championship titles in windsurfing
Björn Dunkerbeck (CHE, b. DNK) claimed 42 windsurfing world titles between 1988 and 2016. His tally included 12 consecutive Professional Windsurfing Association overall championships, plus 10 slalom, nine racing, seven wave, three speed and one freestyle title.

### Most Biathlon World Championship medals
Ole Einar Bjørndalen (NOR) won 45 world championship medals between 1997 and 2017. The "King of Biathlon" also earned the **most Winter Olympic medals (male)** – 13.

### Most consecutive wheelchair tennis singles matches won
Esther Vergeer (NLD) won 470 wheelchair tennis singles matches in a row between 2003 and 2012. She was world champion for 12 straight years and claimed seven Paralympic titles – four in singles and three in women's doubles. According to the International Tennis Federation, Vergeer's winning streak is second in sport only to squash legend Jahangir Khan (PAK, inset), who recorded 555 victories in a row from Nov 1981 to Nov 1986 – the **longest unbeaten run in men's squash**.

### Most ASP/World Surf League World Championships (male)
Kelly Slater (USA) won 11 world titles between 1992 and 2011, and is both the **youngest** (20 years 299 days) and **oldest** (39 years 302 days) men's world surfing champion. He also has the **most ASP/ World Surf League Championship Tour event wins (male)** – 55. Credited with ushering in a new era in the sport with his fluid style and aerial tricks, Slater has also devoted years to developing artificial wave-pool technology.

### Most Trials World Championships
In 2020, trials rider Antoni Bou (ESP) claimed his 28th consecutive world championship since 2007. He has won 14 titles indoors – at the Fédération Internationale de Motocyclisme (FIM) X-Trials (right) – and 14 at the FIM Trial World Championship. Motorcycle trials are non-speed events in which riders navigate obstacles without touching the ground with their feet.

# Round-Up

### Most snooker ranking titles

Ronnie O'Sullivan (UK) claimed his 37th ranking title in style on 16 Aug 2020, lifting the World Snooker Championship trophy for the sixth time. "The Rocket" won his first ranking title – the UK Championship – on 28 Nov 1993 at the age of just 17. His trophy haul includes the **most UK Championships** – seven – and the **most Masters titles** – also seven.

### Fastest...
### 15 m speed climb (female)

On 21 Nov 2020, Iuliia Kaplina (RUS) scaled a 15-m (49-ft) standardized climbing wall in 6.964 sec at the International Federation of Sport Climbing European Championships in Moscow, Russia.

### 1,500 m indoor run (female)

Gudaf Tsegay (ETH) won a women's 1,500 m race in 3 min 53.09 sec at a World Athletics Indoor Tour Gold meeting on 9 Feb 2021 in Liévin, France. She smashed the previous record by more than two seconds.

### Rugby Super League try

Centre Ben Crooks (UK) touched down after just 7 sec for Hull Kingston Rovers against the Huddersfield Giants on 16 Apr 2021. Hull ran out 25–24 winners.

### Most...
### AFL Norm Smith Medals

First presented in 1979, the Norm Smith Medal is awarded to the player judged to have been the "best on ground" in the Australian Football League Grand Final. Dustin Martin (AUS) won it for the third time on 24 Oct 2020 as Richmond defeated Geelong by 31 points to claim their third premiership in four years. He recorded four goals and 21 disposals.

### FIS Freestyle Ski World Championships gold medals

Mikaël Kingsbury (CAN) claimed his fifth and sixth world championship golds in Mar 2021. The freestyle skier ended an injury-hit season on a bright note, winning the individual and dual moguls in Almaty, Kazakhstan, to move two clear of Kari Traa and Jennifer Heil's all-time record.

### Fastest speed skating 10,000 m

On 14 Feb 2021, Nils van der Poel (SWE) won gold in the men's 10,000 m at the ISU World Single Distances Speed Skating Championships in 12 min 32.95 sec. His time was notable for the fact that it was set at sea level, in Heerenveen, Netherlands. Every other current ISU world record was set at altitude, where the ice is faster and skaters face less air resistance.

### Most Dakar Rally wins

Stéphane Peterhansel (FRA) secured his 14th Dakar Rally title at the 2021 edition, staged in Saudi Arabia on 3–15 Jan. He won six titles in the motorcycle category between 1991 and 1998, and eight car titles – seven alongside navigator Jean-Paul Cottret. Peterhansel is the only driver to have won the Dakar Rally on three different continents: Africa, Asia and South America. He also boasts the **most stage wins** – 81, since 1988.

### Most FIS Alpine Ski World Cup race wins in one discipline (female)

Mikaela Shiffrin (USA) has won 45 slalom races at the FIS Alpine Ski World Cup. She surpassed Lindsey Vonn's mark of 43 in the downhill with victory in Flachau, Austria, on 12 Jan 2021. Shiffrin stands just one behind the **male** record, 46, by Ingemar Stenmark (SWE) in the giant slalom between 23 Feb 1975 and 19 Feb 1989.

### Gaelic Football All-Ireland Final consecutive wins

On 19 Dec 2020, Dublin collected their record sixth Sam Maguire Cup in a row, defeating Mayo 2–14 to 0–15 at Croke Park in Dublin, Ireland.

### ITTF World Tour Grand Finals men's singles titles

Ma Long (CHN) claimed his sixth singles title at the International Table Tennis Federation World Tour Grand Finals on 22 Nov 2020. On the same day, Chen Meng equalled Zhang Yining's (both CHN) **women's singles** record with her fourth win in a row.

### Professional Bowlers Association major championships

Jason Belmonte (AUS) wrapped up his 13th major championship by defeating Anthony Simonsen 213–190 on 15 Mar 2020 at the PBA World Championship. Belmonte is only the second ten-pin bowler after Mike Aulby to complete the "Super Slam" of all five PBA major tournaments.

### First female jockey to win the Grand National

On 10 Apr 2021, Rachael Blackmore (IRL) rode to glory on board Minella Times at Aintree Racecourse in Merseyside, UK. Blackmore gained a degree in equine science before becoming a professional jockey in 2015. She is one of only 19 women to ride in the Grand National since the steeplechase was first run in 1839.

## Most rugby union international appearances

Alun Wyn Jones has played 157 international Test matches: 148 for Wales, and nine for the British and Irish Lions. He made his debut against Argentina on 11 Jun 2006, and surpassed Richie McCaw's record of 148 caps on 31 Oct 2020. Wyn Jones has captained Wales for more than 10 years, and skippered the Lions to a decisive Third Test win over Australia in 2013.

## Rugby union internationals refereed

On 28 Nov 2020, Nigel Owens (UK) officiated his 100th international Test match – the Autumn Nations Cup clash between France and Italy at the Stade de France. Following the game, he announced his retirement from international rugby. The Welshman made his Test debut in 2003, officiating a match between Portugal and Georgia, and went on to oversee the 2015 Rugby World Cup final.

## Superbike World Championships

Kawasaki Racing Team's Jonathan Rea (UK) claimed his sixth consecutive Superbike title in 2020. He surpassed compatriot Joey Dunlop's five straight titles in TT Formula One (a World SBK forerunner) in 1982–86.

Rea also extended his record for **most Superbike race wins** to 99; he logged his first victory on 21 Jun 2009.

## Super Netball goals in a regular season

Jhaniele Fowler (JAM) scored 795 goals for West Coast Fever in the 2020 Super Netball regular season. Her total included 13 "Super Shots", worth two points. She increased her overall total to 965 goals in the play-offs, where the West Coast Fever reached the Grand Final, only to lose out 66–64 to the Melbourne Vixens.

Fowler's season tally included the **most goals scored in a Super Netball game** – 69 – which she achieved on 12 Sep 2020 against the New South Wales Swifts.

## UFC victories (female)

Amanda Nunes (BRA) won her 14th Ultimate Fighting Championship bout on 6 Mar 2021, defeating Megan Anderson via a first-round submission at UFC 259. Victory extended Nunes's record for **most consecutive victories (female)** to 12. She has recorded first-round wins over every women's bantamweight and featherweight champion in UFC history.

## UFC fights won by KO/TKO

On 20 Feb 2021, Derrick Lewis (USA) racked up his 12th UFC knockout at UFC Vegas 19, tying the mark of Vitor Belfort (BRA).

## People to complete a remote marathon in 24 hours

The first-ever virtual Virgin Money London Marathon was held on 4 Oct 2020 and saw 37,966 runners finish. Although the physical race was closed to all but elite runners on account of COVID-19, entrants from around the world could run the full distance on a course of their choosing.

## Women's Luge World Cups

Natalie Geisenberger (DEU) earned her eighth crystal globe at the FIL's Luge World Cup, winning the 2020/21 women's singles title only four months after returning to competition following the birth of her child.

## First person with Down syndrome to complete an IRONMAN® triathlon

On 7 Nov 2020, Chris Nikic (USA) made history by finishing the IRONMAN Florida triathlon in 16 hr 46 min 9 sec. The 21-year-old, who endured multiple childhood surgeries and couldn't walk until he was four, trained for up to 8 hr a day for the race: a 3.8-km (2.4-mi) swim, 180-km (112-mi) bike ride and 42.1-km (26.2-mi) marathon.

## Most medals in the Karate 1 Premier League

Sandra Sánchez (ESP) won 36 medals in the Karate 1 Premier League from 10 Jan 2014 to 12 Mar 2021: 18 gold, 10 silver and eight bronze. She competes in the women's kata discipline, in which karatekas present a choreographed pattern of karate moves and techniques. Competitors are judged on technical performance and athletic display.

# Eliud Kipchoge

C overing a distance of 26.2 mi (42.1 km), the marathon is one of the most iconic – and testing – events in sport. And one man has run it faster than it was ever thought possible.

Eliud Kipchoge started running at a young age, racing 2 mi (3.2 km) to school every day. Aged 18, he became a world champion over 5,000 m, and made his marathon debut in 2013. Eliud dominated the event, winning 11 of his first 12 races. At the 2018 Berlin Marathon, he completed the **fastest run marathon** in 2 hr 1 min 39 sec. But he had designs on running even faster.

For many years, the idea of breaking the 2-hr barrier for the marathon had been considered a physical impossibility. Eliud set out to prove that wrong. The INEOS 1:59 Challenge was a special marathon exhibition held on 12 Oct 2019 at Prater Park in Austria, Vienna – selected on account of its flat course and proximity to sea level. An electric car set the pace, while athletes such as the Ingebrigtsen brothers ran in formation around Eliud, who was wearing a bespoke version of Nike's hi-tech Vaporfly trainers. The arrangements meant that his time could not be an official marathon world record: Eliud was racing against history instead. In the final straight, he sprinted clear to cross the line in 1 hr 59 min 40 sec – the **first marathon distance run under two hours.**

**VITAL STATISTICS**
Name: Eliud Kipchoge
Born: 5 Nov 1984
Birthplace: Kapsisiywa, Kenya
World Marathon Majors....
 • race wins: 9
 • series titles: 4
Olympic marathon titles: 1 (2016)
Male World Athlete of the Year awards: 2 (2018 & 2019)

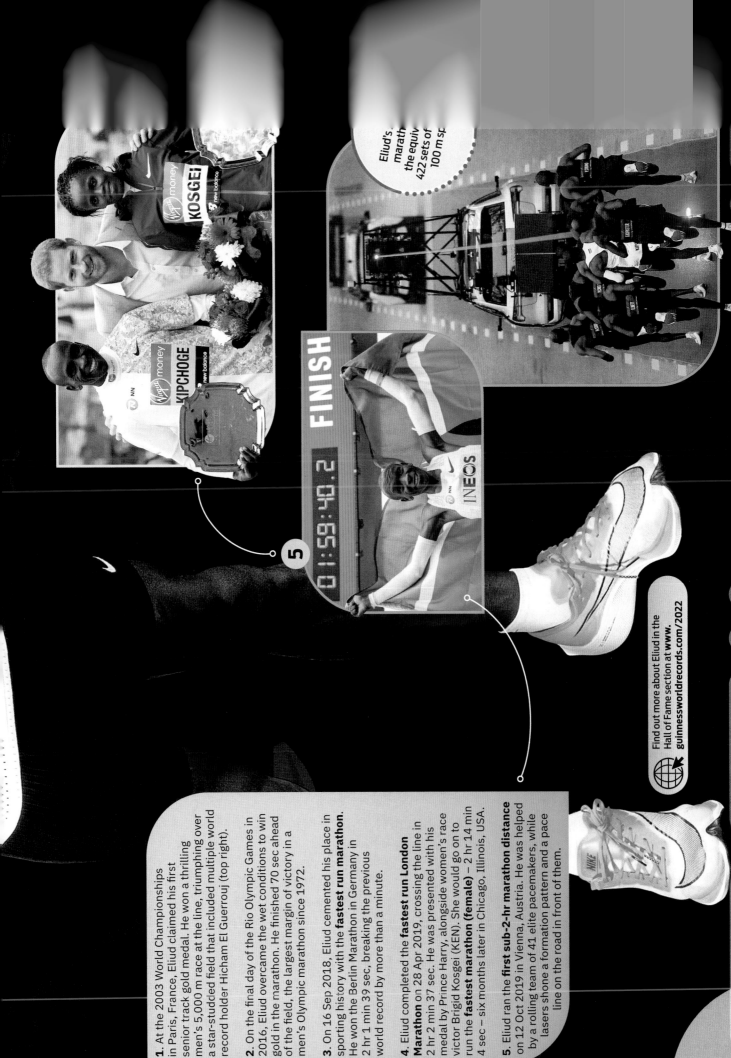

**1.** At the 2003 World Championships in Paris, France, Eliud claimed his first senior track gold medal. He won a thrilling men's 5,000 m race at the line, triumphing over a star-studded field that included multiple world record holder Hicham El Guerrouj (top right).

**2.** On the final day of the Rio Olympic Games in 2016, Eliud overcame the wet conditions to win gold in the marathon. He finished 70 sec ahead of the field, the largest margin of victory in a men's Olympic marathon since 1972.

**3.** On 16 Sep 2018, Eliud cemented his place in sporting history with the **fastest run marathon.** He won the Berlin Marathon in Germany in 2 hr 1 min 39 sec, breaking the previous world record by more than a minute.

**4.** Eliud completed the **fastest run London Marathon** on 28 Apr 2019, crossing the line in 2 hr 2 min 37 sec. He was presented with his medal by Prince Harry, alongside women's race victor Brigid Kosgei (KEN). She would go on to run the **fastest marathon (female)** – 2 hr 14 min 4 sec – six months later in Chicago, Illinois, USA.

**5.** Eliud ran the **first sub-2-hr marathon distance** on 12 Oct 2019 in Vienna, Austria. He was helped by a rolling team of 41 elite pacemakers, while lasers shone a formation pattern and a pace line on the road in front of them.

FINISH
01:59:40.2

KOSGEI
KIPCHOGE

Eliud's
marath
the equiv
422 sets of
100 m sp

**Find out more about Eliud in the Hall of Fame section at www. guinnessworldrecords.com/2022**

To help verify records, GWR collaborates with many institutions, federated bodies and specialist groups, a few of which are highlighted below. For a full list, visit www.guinnessworldrecords.com/about-us/partners.

## 8000ers.com
Eberhard Jurgalski has developed the system of "Elevation Equality", a method of classifying mountain ranges and peaks. His website has become the main source of altitude statistics for the Himalayas and Karakoram ranges.

## American Crossword Puzzle Tournament
Founded in 1978 by Will Shortz (now the crossword editor of *The New York Times*), the ACPT is the world's oldest and largest crossword event. It draws nearly 1,000 enthusiasts every year to its annual contest in Stamford, Connecticut.

## Botanic Gardens Conservation International
There are an estimated 3,000 botanic gardens and arboreta in the world, attracting 750 million visitors each year. BGCI is the pivotal centre of this network. Its mission is to mobilize botanic gardens and engage partners in securing plant diversity for the wellbeing of people and the planet.

## CANNA UK National Giant Vegetables Championship
Each year, Martyn Davis welcomes expert growers to the Malvern Autumn Show held in Worcestershire, UK, and ensures that all the vegetables comply with the strict criteria and are measured appropriately.

## Council on Tall Buildings and Urban Habitat
Based in Chicago, USA, the CTBUH is the world's leading resource for professionals focused on the design, construction and operation of tall buildings and future cities.

## ESPN X Games
Since 1995, ESPN's X Games has been the leading action-sports competition, spotlighting the world's best action-sports athletes in BMX, skateboard and Moto X in the summer as well as skiing, snowboarding and snowmobiling at its winter events.

## Gerontology Research Group
Established in 1990, the GRG's mission is to slow and ultimately reverse ageing via the application and sharing of scientific knowledge. It also keeps the largest database of supercentenarians (people aged 110+), managed by Robert Young.

## Great Pumpkin Commonwealth
The GPC cultivates the growing of giant pumpkins – among other prodigious produce – by establishing universal standards and regulations that ensure quality of fruit and fairness of competition.

## International Ice Swimming Association
Founded by Ram Barkai, the IISA was formed in 2009 with a vision to formalize swimming in icy water. It has put in place a set of rules to allow for maximum safety measures and to regulate swim integrity in terms of distance, time and conditions.

## International Ornithologists' Union
The IOU is a member-supported global organization dedicated to research in avian biology from ecosystems to molecules, linking basic and applied research, and nurturing education and outreach. Its current president, tenured between 2018 and 2022, is Dr Dominique Homberger.

## Major League Eating
While GWR ratifies certain eating records of its own, MLE is the body that oversees professional eating contests globally. The organization developed the sport of competitive eating and coordinates the International Federation of Competitive Eating. It holds some 70 events annually.

## The Marine Biological Association
Based in Plymouth, UK, the MBA is one of the world's longest-running societies dedicated to promoting research into our oceans and the life they support. Since 1884, they have provided a unified, independent voice on behalf of the marine biological community.

## Monster Jam
Established in 1992, Monster Jam is the world's premier competition for monster-truck drivers. Global tour events pit trucks and their drivers against each other in races, two-wheel skill challenges and freestyle trick contests.

## The National Museum of Computing
Located at Bletchley Park in Oxfordshire, UK, The National Museum of Computing is an independent charity housing a vast collection of functional historic computers such as *Colossus*, the **first code-breaking computer**, and the **oldest working digital computer**, the *WITCH*.

## Natural History Museum Vienna
Dr Ludovic Ferrière is a geologist and expert on meteorites and impact craters. He is chief curator of the prestigious meteorite and impactite collections at the Natural History Museum in Vienna, Austria.

## Ocean Rowing Society International
The ORSI was established in 1983 by Kenneth F Crutchlow and Peter Bird, later joined by Tom Lynch and Tatiana Rezvaya-Crutchlow. The organization documents all attempts to row the oceans and major bodies of water, and classifies, verifies and adjudicates ocean-rowing achievements.

## Parrot Analytics
Parrot Analytics is the leading global content demand analytics company for the modern multi-platform TV business. It tracks more than 1.5 billion daily expressions of demand in over 100 languages.

## Polar Expeditions Classification Scheme
PECS is a grading and labelling system for extended, unmotorized polar journeys that is overseen by a committee of polar-expedition specialists, managed by Eric Philips. Polar regions, modes of travel, routes and forms of aid are defined under the scheme and give expeditioners guidance on how to classify, promote and immortalize their journeys.

## Royal Botanic Gardens, Kew
Kew Gardens (pp.110–11) in London, UK, is a world-famous organization, globally respected for its outstanding collections as well as its scientific expertise in plant diversity, conservation and sustainable development. It was accredited as a UNESCO World Heritage Site in 2003.

## Scripps National Spelling Bee
Administered on a not-for-profit basis by The E W Scripps Company, the SNSB is the USA's longest-running educational programme. Its remit is to help students improve spelling, increase vocabularies, learn concepts and develop correct English usage that will help them all their lives.

## Speedrun.com
This gaming website provides leaderboards, resources, forums and more for speedrunning – the act of playing a videogame with the intent of completing it as quickly as possible. The site has amassed 2 million runs across almost 23,000 games.

## The Numbers
TheNumbers.com is the web's biggest database of cinema box-office information, with figures on 50,000 movies and 200,000 people in the film industry. It was founded in 1997 by Bruce Nash and is visited by more than 8 million people every year.

## UK and International Timing Adjudication
The UK&ITA was established (as UKTA) in 2013 when Straightliners Ltd and SPEE3D Ltd united to enhance and promote land-speed record-breaking in Britain and Europe. It ensures that land-speed contenders can compete under all governances.

## University College London: The Bartlett School of Architecture
Iain Borden is Professor of Architecture & Urban Culture at The Bartlett School at UCL in London, UK. He has authored more than 100 books and articles, including numerous titles on architects, buildings and cities.

## VGChartz
Established in 2005 by Brett Walton, VGChartz is a business intelligence and research firm. It publishes over 7,000 unique weekly estimates relating to videogaming hardware and software sales/shipments, and hosts an ever-expanding games database.

## World Beard & Moustache Championships
Advocating for facial hair since 2003, Beard Team USA® represents facial hair in the USA and at international beard and moustache competitions, all while promoting positive facial-hair awareness and the charitable community nationwide. BTUSA also hosts and organizes the National Beard and Moustache Championships®.

## World Cube Association
The WCA governs competitions for mechanical puzzles that are operated by twisting groups of pieces, such as the Rubik's Cube. Its mission is to have more competitions in more countries, all participating under fair and equal conditions.

## World Freestyle Football Association
The WFFA is the global governing body for freestyle football – the art and sport of juggling a soccer ball using all parts of the body to entertain audiences and outperform opponents in competition. Spanning 114 countries, the WFFA manages the World Freestyle Football Championships.

## World Memory Sports Council
The mind sport of memory was founded in 1991 by Tony Buzan and Raymond Keene OBE. The 10 disciplines that formed the basis of the first competition have since been adopted worldwide for all competitive memory contests.

## World Meteorological Organization
Dr Randall Cerveny is a President's Professor in Geographical Sciences who specializes in weather and climate. He has held the position of Rapporteur of Weather and Climate Extremes for the WMO since 2007.

## World Sailing Speed Record Council
The WSSRC was recognized by the International Yacht Racing Union (now World Sailing) in 1972. The council of experts draws members from Australia, France, Great Britain and the USA.

## World Ultracycling Association
WUCA is a non-profit organization dedicated to supporting ultracycling across the world. It holds the largest repository of cycling records for all bike types, and certifies successful rides for its members.

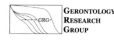

We also work with hundreds of individuals who know their subjects inside out. Newcomers to GWR's roster of experts this year brought insight into food history, pandemics, recycling, anthropology and carnivorous plants, to name just a few topics. For a full list, visit www.guinnessworldrecords.com/about-us/partners.

**Evan Ackerman** has been writing about robots for over 10 years. After co-founding his own robotics blog in 2007, he began contributing to *IEEE Spectrum* magazine, and has now written thousands of articles on robotics and emerging technology. Evan lives in Washington, DC, USA, with a steadily growing collection of robot vacuums.

**Mark Aston** has served as a Science & Technology consultant for GWR since 2010. He brings nearly 30 years of experience of high-technology science and engineering to ensure GWR's sci-tech records are accurate and informative. Mark's involvement in both academia and commercial companies has led to a lively career in optics development.

**Tom Beckerlegge** is an award-winning writer whose books have been translated around the world. He is also GWR's lead sports consultant, researching and updating hundreds of new records every year across all athletic disciplines. This year has introduced him to timbersports, tower running and the wartime feats of cyclist Albert Bourlon.

**Darra Goldstein** is a food historian and founding editor of the *Gastronomica* journal. She is the author of six award-winning cookbooks and series editor of *California Studies in Food and Culture*. She has consulted for the Council of Europe as part of a group exploring ways in which food can be used to promote tolerance and diversity.

**David Grierson** is Deputy Head of Architecture at the University of Strathclyde, UK, where he has delivered numerous postgraduate courses on eco cities and sustainable architecture. He has carried out research all over the world and currently is the editor of the book series *Architecture and Urbanism in the Global South*.

**Thomas Haigh** has degrees in both computer science and the history of science. He's a professor of history at the University of Wisconsin–Milwaukee and a visiting professor at Siegen University. Find out more at **www.tomandmaria.com/tom**, including details on his latest book, *A New History of Modern Computing* (2021).

**Carolyn Harris**, who advises GWR on regal matters, is a historian, author, royal commentator and instructor in history at the University of Toronto School of Continuing Studies. She is an expert in the history of European monarchy, and her writing has appeared in numerous publications. Dr Harris is also a prolific guest lecturer.

**Clive Jones** is an Emeritus Senior Scientist at the Cary Institute of Ecosystem Studies in New York, USA. A research ecologist, he has studied how species affect the physical environment – i.e., "ecosystem engineering". Recognized as the founder of this rapidly growing field, he has authored more than 200 publications, including six books.

**Jonas Livet** is founder of the website Les Zoos dans le Monde, which offers insights from his visits to more than 1,500 zoological parks; the project has also earned him the GWR title for **most zoos visited**. He has a Master's degree in Conservation Biology from the Durrell Institute of Conservation and Ecology in Kent, UK.

**Hannah Mawdsley** is a Property Curator for the National Trust in London, UK. Her PhD thesis – which was co-supervised by a curator at Imperial War Museums and academics at Queen Mary, University of London – focused on the politics of commemoration behind the global 1918–19 influenza pandemic, aka the "Spanish Flu".

**Leanne Melbourne** is a lecturer in Marine Palaeontology at the University of Bristol, UK, where she gained her PhD. Her research focuses on how climate change impacts on marine calcifiers over time – more specifically, how it affects the structural integrity of ecosystems such as coral reefs. She is also a Fellow of The Linnean Society.

**Patrick O'Hare** is a UKRI Future Leaders Fellow at the University of St Andrews in the UK. He received his Master's and doctorate in social anthropology at the University of Cambridge, and specializes in the anthropology of waste, recycling and labour. He principally conducts research around recycling enterprises in Latin America.

**Clare Ostle** coordinates the Pacific Continuous Plankton Recorder (CPR) Survey at The Marine Biological Association based in Plymouth, UK. Her research focuses on the use of CPR data for investigating plankton as indicators of the marine environment, linkages with ocean acidification and the marine carbon cycle, and oceanic plastics.

**Barry Rice** is an astrobiologist and college professor in astronomy. As a botanist, he worked for 10 years at The Nature Conservancy and has engaged in fieldwork, focusing on carnivorous plants, for more than 25 years. He has served as an editor for the journal of the International Carnivorous Plant Society for more than two decades.

**Nancy Segal** is Professor of Psychology and Director of the Twin Studies Center at California State University. She has authored more than 200 publications and several books on twins. She also received the James Shields Award for Lifetime Contributions to Twin Research from the International Society for Twin Studies in 2005.

**Karl P N Shuker** has a PhD in Zoology and Comparative Physiology from the University of Birmingham, UK, and is a Scientific Fellow of the Zoological Society of London, a Fellow of the Royal Entomological Society and a Member of the Society of Authors. He has penned 25 books and hundreds of articles covering many aspects of natural history.

**Chris Stringer** is a Research Leader in Human Origins at London's Natural History Museum, and holds honorary professorships at University College London and Royal Holloway. He has authored numerous papers and books on human evolution, including *The Origin of Our Species* (2011) and *Our Human Story* (2018, with Louise Humphrey).

**Robert Van Pelt** is an Affiliate Professor at the University of Washington, USA, and an authority on giant trees. He has extensively studied North America's old-growth forests, particularly in California and the Pacific Northwest. He is the Washington coordinator of the National Big Tree Program and penned *Forest Giants of the Pacific Coast* (2001).

**Paul Walker-Emig** is a lifelong gamer and has been writing about videogames professionally for eight years, both online and in print. He has written for a host of renowned publications and websites, including *The Guardian*, *PC Gamer*, *Retro Gamer*, *Wireframe* and Kotaku. Paul also hosts the podcast *Utopian Horizons*.

**Lindy Weilgart** has specialized in underwater noise pollution and its effects on marine life since 1994. Before that, her degrees and post-doctoral studies focused on free-ranging whale acoustic communication. She is currently an Adjunct Research Associate at Canada's Dalhousie University, and serves as Scientific Advisor for the International Ocean Noise Coalition and Ocean Policy Consultant for OceanCare.

## THANKS ALSO TO...

David Agle, Andrew Good (NASA JPL); Jane Allan (World Quizzing Championships); Daniel Antoine (British Museum); Anne Austin; Tarryn Barrowman, Andre Schuiteman (Kew Gardens); Edward Bell (Tiniest Babies Registry); Marion Benaiteau (Louvre); Heather Bingham (UNEP-WCMC); Dane Cave; Prosanta Chakrabarty; Leon Claessens; Catriona Clark (Wave Energy Scotland); Lauren Clement (WCA); Gerald Leonard Cohen; Patrick Collins (National Motor Museum, Beaulieu); Philip J Currie; Nims Dai; Love Dalén; Chris Day (WMSC); Amy Dickin (PDSA); Terri Edillon (NSF Office of Polar Programs); Mischa Egolf (Cool Roof Rating Council); Peter Fankhauser (ANYbotics); David Fischer; Mike Fromm; GCHQ (David A, Fiona S, Matt L); Christian Gelzer (NASA Armstrong Flight Research Center); Marshall Gerometta (CTBUH); Manuel Gnida; Danny Groves (Whale and Dolphin Conservation); Becky Gunn; Thaneswar Guragai; Lauri Harris (USA Cheer); Robert Headland (Scott Polar Research Institute); Maximiliano Herrera; Mark Honigsbaum; Radley Horton; Marco Hutter (ETH Zürich); Alan Jamieson; Alexandra Jones; Gareth Jones' Lab; Steve Jones; Łukasz Kaczmarek; Matthew Kamlet; Jian Kang; Todd Kline; Kraig Kraft; Anna Kralova (The Kennel Club); Dante Lauretta; Michael Levy, Francis Sanzaro (*Climbing* magazine); Jordan Lewis, Shannon Nash (V&A); Michael Lindqvist (Onsala Space Observatory); Matt Lodder; Erik Loomis; Jonathan McDowell (Harvard-Smithsonian Center for Astrophysics); Lisa MacKenzie (European Marine Energy Centre); João Pedro De Magalhães (AnAge); Pádraig Mallon (Irish Long Distance Swimming Association); Tom Matthews; Fanny Mietlicki; Jannicke Mikkelsen; Scott Miller; Alison Mitchell (Smithsonian); Andrew Mitchell; Erin Morton; Steven Munatones (World Open Water Swimming Association); Mark O'Shea; Corina Oertli (Cybathlon); Larry Oslund (WUCA); Boaz Paldi, Christina Pascual (UN/The Lion's Share); Fiann Paul (ORSI); Khulu Phasiwe (Square Kilometre Array); Alistair Pike; Beth Pike (Marine Conservation Institute); Barry Popik; Bastien Queste; Lindsay Renick Mayer (Re:Wild); Alan Robock; Leafy Rous; Xiulin Ruan; Florian Schimikowski (Deutsches Espionage Museum); Brian Schroeder (Institute for Forensic Art); Paul Smith (BGCI); Brett Smitheram (The Association of British Scrabble Players); Christopher Smout; Samuel Stadler (Parrot Analytics); Carrie Stengel; Chris Stokes; Brian Toon; Linda Veress (Yellowstone National Park); Mark Weeden (School of Oriental and African Studies); Mikaela Weisse (World Resources Institute); Matthew White; Carys Williams; Mark Williams (Royal United Services Institute for Defence and Security Studies); Paul Williams; Anatoly Zak (Russian Space Web); Ben Zimmer

## ACKNOWLEDGEMENTS

**SVP Global Publishing**
Nadine Causey

**Editor-in-Chief**
Craig Glenday

**Managing Editor**
Adam Millward

**Editor**
Ben Hollingum

**Layout Editors**
Tom Beckerlegge,
Rob Dimery

**Proofreading
& fact-checking**
Matthew White

**Head of Publishing
& Book Production**
Jane Boatfield

**Head of Pictures & Design**
Fran Morales

**Picture Researcher**
Abby Taylor

**Design**
Paul Wylie-Deacon and
Rob Wilson at 55design.co.uk

**Cover Design**
Rod Hunt

**Talent Researchers**
Charlie Anderson,
Hannah Prestidge

**Production Director**
Patricia Magill

**Production Coordinator**
Thomas McCurdy

**Production Consultants**
Roger Hawkins, Tina Marke

**Head of Visual Content**
Michael Whitty

**Original Photography**
Ricardo Cellere,
Jeroen de Beer, Erol Gurian,
Paul Michael Hughes,
J-F Rioux, Cameron Spooner,
Brian Storey, Ceara Swogger

**Indexer**
Marie Lorimer

**Director of Publishing Sales**
Joel Smith

**Head of International Sales**
Helene Navarre

**Key Account Manager**
Mavis Sarfo

**Supply Chain &
Distribution Manager**
Isabel Sinagola

**Head of Marketing**
Nicholas Brookes

**Senior PR Manager**
Amber-Georgina Gill

**Senior Publicist**
Jessica Dawes

**Marketing Manager**
Lauren Johns

**PR Executive**
Jessica Spillane

**Reprographics**
Resmiye Kahraman and
Louise Pinnock at Born Group

**Printing & Binding**
MOHN Media Mohndruck
GmbH, Gütersloh, Germany

**Augmented Reality**
*Augmentifylt®* (Peapodicity)

**British Library** Cataloguing-in-
publication data: a catalogue record for this
book is available from the British Library

UK: 978-1-913484-11-8
US: 978-1-913484-10-1
Middle East: 978-1-913484-13-2
Australia: 978-1-913484-14-9

Records are made to be broken – indeed, it is one of the
key criteria for a record category – so if you find a record
that you think you can beat, tell us about it by making
a record claim. Always contact us before making a
record attempt.

Check **www.guinnessworldrecords.com** regularly
for record-breaking news, plus video footage of record
attempts. You can also join and interact with the
Guinness World Records online community.

**Sustainability**
The trees that are harvested to print *Guinness World
Records 2022* are carefully selected from managed
forests to avoid the devastation of the landscape.

The paper contained within this edition is manufactured
by Stora Enso Veitsiluoto, Finland. The production site
is PEFC Chain-of-Custody certified and
operates within environmental systems
certificated to ISO 14001 to ensure
sustainable production.

PEFC04-31-1033

Thanks to innovative use of combined heat
and power technology, up to 52% less
$CO_2$ was emitted in printing this product when compared
with conventional energy use.

minus 52% $CO_2$

OFFICIALLY AMAZING

**Global President**
Alistair Richards

**Governance**
Alison Ozanne
**Finance:** Elizabeth Bishop,
Jess Blake, Lisa Gibbs, Lucy
Hyland, Kimberley Jones, Okan
Keser, Maryana Lovell, Sutha
Ramachandran, Jamie Sheppard,
Scott Shore, Andrew Wood
**Legal:** Matthew Knight, Raymond
Marshall, Mehreen Moghul
**People & Culture:** Jackie Angus,
Isabelle Fanshawe, Stephanie
Lunn, Monika Tilani

**IT & Operations**
Rob Howe
**IT:** Céline Bacon, John
Cvitanovic, Diogo Gomes,
Benjamin McLean
**Digital Technology:** Veronica
Irons, Alex Waldu
**Central Record Services:**
Lewis Blakeman, Adam Brown,
Megan Bruce, Betsy Cunnett,
Tara El Kashef, Mark McKinley,
Will Munford, Emma Salt, Will
Sinden, Mariana Sinotti Alves de
Lima, Sheila Mella Suárez, Luke
Wakeham, Dave Wilson

**Content & Product**
Katie Forde
**Brand Communications:**
Doug Male
**Brand & Product Management:**
Lucy Acfield, Juliet Dawson,
Emily Osborn, Louise Toms
**Demand Generation:**
James Alexander-Dann
**Design:** Momoko Cunneen,
Fran Morales, Alisa Zaytseva
**TV & Digital Content:** Karen
Gilchrist, Jesse Hargrave,
Matthew Musson, Joseph O'Neil,
Alan Pixsley, Dominic Punt,
Connie Suggitt, Dan Thorne,
Michael Whitty
**Content Licensing:** Kathryn
Hubbard, Catherine Pearce
**Creative:** Paul O'Neill

**Global Consultancies**
Marco Frigatti

**Beijing Consultancy**
Charles Wharton
**Brand & Content Marketing:**
Chloe Liu, Angela Wu
**Client Account Services:**
Catherine Gao, Xiaona Liu,
Congwei Ma, Tina Ran,
Amelia Wang, Elaine Wang
**Commercial Marketing:**
Theresa Gao, Lorraine Lin,
Karen Pan
**Event Production:** Fay Jiang
**Legal:** Mathew Alderson,
Jiayi Teng
**People & Culture:** Crystal Xu,
Nina Zhou
**PR:** Echo Zhan, Yvonne Zhang
**Records Management:**
Ted Li, Vanessa Tao,
Alicia Zhao, Xinying Zou

**Dubai Consultancy**
Talal Omar
**Brand & Content Marketing:**
Mohamad Kaddoura
**Client Account Services:**
Sara Abu-Saad, Naser
Batat, Mohammad Kiswani,
Kamel Yassin
**Commercial Marketing:**
Shaddy Gaad
**Event Production:** Daniel Hickson
**People & Culture:** Monisha Bimal
**PR:** Hassan Alibrahim
**Records Management:** Reem
Al Ghussain, Sarah Alkholb,
Karen Hamzeh

**London Consultancy**
Neil Foster
**Client Account Services:**
Nick Adams, Fay Edwards,
Sirali Gandhi, Irina Nohailic,
Sam Prosser, Nikhil Shukla
**Commercial Marketing:**
Iliyan Stoychev, Amanda Tang
**Event Production:**
Fiona Gruchy-Craven
**Records Management:**
Andrew Fanning, Paul Hillman,
Christopher Lynch,
Francesca Raggi

**Americas Consultancy**
Carlos Martinez
**Brand & Content Marketing:**
Luisa Fernanda Sanchez,
Kristen Stephenson
**Client Account Services:**
Mackenzie Berry, Brittany
Carpenter, Carolina Guanabara,
Ralph Hannah, Nicole Pando,
Kim Partrick, Michelle Santucci
**Commercial Marketing:**
Rachel Silver
**People & Culture:** Rachel Gluck,
Jennifer Olson
**PR:** Amanda Marcus, Elizabeth
Montoya, Alice Pagan
**Records Management:**
Raquel Assis, Spencer
Cammarano, Christine
Fernandez, Hannah Ortman,
Callie Smith

**Tokyo Consultancy**
Kaoru Ishikawa
**Brand & Content Marketing:**
Masakazu Senda
**Client Account Services:**
Minami Ito, Wei Liang, Takuro
Maruyama, Yumiko Nakagawa,
Masamichi Yazaki
**Commercial Marketing:**
Hiroyuki Tanaka, Eri Yuhira
**Event Production:** Yuki Uebo
**Legal:** Mika Yamada
**People & Culture:**
Emiko Yamamoto
**PR:** Kazami Kamioka
**Records Management:**
Aki Ichikawa, Momoko Omori,
Naomi-Emily Sakai, Lala Teranishi

THE JIM PATTISON GROUP

## Picture credits

**1** Jason deCaires Taylor; **2–3** Shutterstock, Rod Hunt; **4 (AUS/NZ)** Getty, Shutterstock, Tones and I/ YouTube; **5** Joerg Mitter/Red Bull Content Pool; **6** Australia Zoo; **7** PECS, Earthwatch, Shutterstock; **4 (MENA)** Sacha Jafri/Pyong Sumaria; **5** Global Village; **6** Mahmoud Gaballah/GWR; **7** Anasala Family, Ashghal, Earthwatch, Shutterstock; **4 (US)** Marsai Martin, Alamy, NBC *Today Show*; **5 (US)** VICE Media, NASA, Nickelodeon, Getty; **4 (UK)** ITV Studios, BBC, Capital FM; **5 (UK)** BT Sport, BBC, Fun Kids Radio, Orchard TV; **6 (UK/US)** Shutterstock; **7 (UK/US)** WWT, Earthwatch, Shutterstock; **8–9** Shutterstock; **10** GWR; **12** Shutterstock, Rod Hunt, Smithsonian Institution, NASA, Alamy; **13** Smithsonian Institution, Alamy; **14–15** Alamy, Getty, ESA; **16** Getty, Alamy, NASA; **17** NASA, Shutterstock, Alamy, Getty; **18** Lina Östling, Alamy, Getty; **19** Alamy; **20** Newcastle University, Shutterstock; **21** Getty; **22** Alamy, Getty, Science Photo Library, Joseph Diamond/SKA; **23** Shutterstock, Mairie de Villeneuve-le-Roi, Thames Water, PA, Getty; **24** Science Photo Library, Alamy, Ichijo Co, Orstead; **25** Alamy, Orbital Marine, GE Renewable Energy, Tim Fox/GE Renewable Energy, CIF, ESA; **26** Alamy, Shutterstock; **27** AeroFarms, Getty, Reef Arabia, Alamy; **28** Dirk Collins/National Geographic, Mark Fisher/National Geographic, René Robert/International Polar Foundation, Benjamin Eberhardt; **29** Von Wong, Alamy, Greta Thunberg, Shutterstock; **30** Daniella Zalcman/Greenpeace, Philippa Walker/University of Bristol; **31** Alamy, Getty; **32** Rod Hunt, Australia Zoo, Alamy, Shutterstock; **33** Australia Zoo, Ben Beaden/Australia Zoo, Shutterstock; **34–35** Shutterstock; **36** Alamy, Nature PL; **37** Shutterstock, Alex Maisey, Alamy; **38** Andrew Cannizzaro, Shutterstock, NOAA, Alamy; **39** Shutterstock, Marcial Quiroga-Carmona; **40** Shutterstock, *AugmentifyIt®*; **41** Shutterstock; **42** Shutterstock, Getty, Kip Evans Photography, Ben Jones, The Ocean Agency/Ocean Image Bank; **43** thevortexswim, Alamy, Noe Sardet/Emmanuel Reynaud, Jason deCaires Taylor; **44** Alamy, Tony Camacho/Science Photo Library, Shutterstock; **45** CC Curtis/California State Library, Alamy, Dr Robert Van Pelt; **46** Science Photo Library, Sadowski *et al*, Noah Elhardt, Alamy, Shutterstock; **47** Alamy, Jeremiah Harris; **48** Alamy, Shutterstock, Wildlife Reserves Singapore, Royal Burgers' Zoo; **49** Royal Burgers' Zoo, Shutterstock, SEA LIFE Brighton, Thomas Eckhoff, Alamy; **50** Adriana Dinu/UN/The Lion's Share, Shutterstock, Alamy; **51** Re:Wild, Re:Wild/Carlos Vasquez Almazan, Re:Wild/Frank Glaw, Re:Wild/ Southern Institute of Ecology/Leibniz Institute for Zoo and Wildlife Research/NCNP, Re:Wild/Clay Bolt, Alamy, Shutterstock; **52** Frank Glaw, Michael Brown/ Giraffe Conservation Foundation, Alamy, Getty; **53** Alamy, Shutterstock; **54** BBC, Nobu Tamura, Martin Whiting, Alamy; **55** Alamy, Shutterstock, Nature PL; **56** Shutterstock, Rod Hunt, Miniatur Wunderland Hamburg; **57** Richard Bradbury/GWR, Miniatur Wunderland Hamburg; **58–59** Paul Michael Hughes/GWR; **60** Shutterstock, Science Photo Library; **61** Science Photo Library, Alamy; **62** NHM Vienna/OREA OAW, Shutterstock, Getty; **63** Getty, Craig Glenday/GWR; **64** Judi Dench, Time Inc., ZUMA Press, Alamy; **65** Alamy, Shutterstock; **66** Owee Salva/GWR, Sanjib Ghosh/GWR, Paul Michael Hughes/ GWR, Riccardo Cellere/GWR, Erol Gurian/GWR; **67** Alamy, J-F Rioux/GWR, Ronald Mackechnie/GWR; **68** British Museum, Javier Pierini/GWR, Alamy; **69** Olivier Ramonteu/GWR, Abraham Joffe; **70** Ronald Mackechnie/GWR; **71** Shutterstock, Alamy, USAF; **72** Alamy, Smithsonian Institution, Ronald Mackechnie/GWR, John Wright/GWR, Richard Bradbury/GWR; **73** Ceara D Swogger/GWR, NBMC, Shutterstock; **74** Paul Sturgess, Mahmoud Gaballah/ GWR, Jeroen de Beer/GWR; **75** Cameron Spooner/ GWR, Manoj Patel/Create Studio/GWR, Laetitia Ky; **76** Paul Michael Hughes/GWR, Wessels Schuhe, Richard Bradbury/GWR; **77** Tim Anderson/GWR, Richard Bradbury/GWR; **78** Rod Hunt, Shutterstock, NPS/Jacob W Frank; **79** Alamy, NPS, Shutterstock; **80–81** Paul Michael Hughes/GWR; **82** Paul Michael Hughes/GWR, WFFA; **83** John Farnworth, WFFA, Olaf Pignataro/Red Bull Content Pool, Dean Treml/Red Bull Content Pool; **84** Chris Allan/GWR, Jeff Binns, Dean Kyritsis; **85** Harald Riise, SWNS; **86** Alamy, Shutterstock; **87** Alamy, Ryan Schude/GWR, Don Christensen/ACPT; **88** Deanna Dent/ASU; **89** Paul Michael Hughes/GWR; **90** Getty, MGM, Shutterstock; **91** Getty, Alamy; **92** Paul Michael Hughes/GWR; **93** Paul Michael Hughes/GWR; **94** Shutterstock, Alamy; **95** Shutterstock, Getty, Monique Wiendels; **96** Jason Parnell Photography, Shutterstock, MLE; **97** Paul Michael Hughes/GWR; **98** Alamy; **99** Marc Martí; **100** Star Wars/LEGO; **101** LEGO Systems, LEGO; **102** Richard Bradbury/GWR, James Ellerker/ GWR; **103** Feld Entertainment; **104** Alamy; **105** Karen Maxfield/SWNS; **106** Hadley Hadlen; **107** Carnival Magic Park, Rui da Cruz; **108** Paul Michael Hughes/ GWR; **109** Marawa, Marawa/Lincoln Children's Books, Shutterstock; **110** Shutterstock, Rod Hunt, Alamy, Adam Millward/GWR, Board of Trustees, RBG Kew, Getty; **111** RBG Kew, Alamy, Shutterstock; **112–13** Maxim Ivanov; **114** Team Joe Barr, Greg Macvean Photography; **116** Getty, Shutterstock, Alamy, Ira Block/National Geographic, Etienne Claret; **117** Alamy; **118** Børge Ousland, Shutterstock, Alamy, Per Breiehagen, Getty; **119** Per Breiehagen; **120** Karlis Bardelis, Shutterstock, Shilpika Gautam; **121** Alamy, Jacqueline McClelland (ILDSA), Getty; **122** Shutterstock, Getty, Nimsdai/Red Bull Content Pool; **123** Ternua, Paul Michael Hughes/GWR, Alamy, Mingma Gyalje; **124** Getty; **125** Bojan Haron Markičević, Shutterstock, Alamy; **126** Ben Uttley/ Stamp Productions Ltd, Donnie Campbell; **127** Peter Wilson, Mike Hamill; **128** Ray Demski, Karina Oliani, Marcelo Rabelo; **129** Alastair Lee/Posing Productions, Enrique Alvarez; **130** Josue Husai; **132** Shutterstock, Rod Hunt, Alamy, Getty; **133** Alamy, Getty, Shutterstock; **136** NASA, Alamy, Instituto de Astrofísica de Canarias; **137** Jacqueline Orrell/SLAC National Accelerator Laboratory, SLAC National Accelerator Laboratory, ESO, NASA, Shutterstock; **138** Shutterstock, SpaceX, NASA/JPL-Caltech/MSSS, NASA/JPL-Caltech; **139** NASA; **140** Alamy, Petra Appelhof, Brooks Kraft/APPLE/EPA-EFE/ Shutterstock; **141** Apple, Shutterstock; **142** ETH Zürich/Alessandro Della Bella, Shivraj Gohil/ Spacesuit Media, Right Light Media, Marc Urbano/ Porsche; **143** BBC, eMining; **144** USAF, NASA; **145** USAF, Solar Impulse/Stefatou/Rezo.ch, Siemens AG, Mark Mauno, Alamy; **146** NASA, University of Southern California, Genesis Motor Sales, ETH/ Alessandro Della Bella, ETH Zürich/CYBATHLON; **147** ETH Zürich/CYBATHLON, University of Pennsylvania, Gil Weinberg, JSK Lab/University of Tokyo; **148** Alamy, Shutterstock, General Precision Inc/USAF, NASA/JPL-Caltech; **149** NASA, Getty, Alamy, Terry Harris; **150** DeepMind, NASA, Shutterstock, Alamy, University of Glasgow; **151** Alamy, Jasper de Winkel, Open Bionics; **152** NASA/Goddard/University of Arizona, Shutterstock, JAXA, Command Sight; **153** YouTube, NASA, Animal Avengers, IMECHE; **154** NASA; **155** GWR/YouTube, NASA, Shutterstock; **156** Shutterstock, Rod Hunt, Royal Tyrrell Museum of Palaeontology; **157** Royal Tyrrell Museum of Palaeontology, Shutterstock; **158–59** Shutterstock; **160** Getty, Alamy, Shutterstock; **161** Matthew Minard - USA TODAY NETWORK, Shutterstock, Getty, Alamy; **162** Paige Olsen; **163** Paul Michael Hughes/GWR, Sherry Lemcke Photography, Alamy; **164** Shutterstock, Alamy; **165** Shutterstock, Netflix/ Sony Pictures/Alamy, Alamy; **166** Shutterstock, Craig Glenday/GWR; **167** Shutterstock; **168** Alamy, Getty; **169** Alamy, Shutterstock; **170** Richard Bradbury/ GWR, Ronald Mackechnie/GWR, Shutterstock; **171** Shutterstock, Historic Royal Palaces, Paul Michael Hughes/GWR, Alamy, Château La Tulipe, Getty; **172** Maxime Aubert/Griffith University, Alamy, Marta Osypińska, Anika Moritz; **173** Shutterstock, Eat Just, Beeple/Christie's, Alamy; **174** Hannah Orenstein, Shutterstock; **175** Alamy, Shutterstock; **176** *It GiRL* Magazine; **177** RSPB; **180** Porsche, Kennedy Grace Photography, Cody Schindel/ CanadianKartingNews.com; **181** Getty, Adam Millward/GWR, Shutterstock; **182** Eyevine, Time Inc., Simon & Schuster, Getty; **184** Shutterstock, Rod Hunt, Alamy, Guangdong Science Center; **185** Guangdong Science Center, Shutterstock; **186–87** Andreas Jones/Razorien; **188** Paul Michael Hughes/GWR, Ronald Mackechnie/GWR; **189** Getty, Time Inc., Nintendo, Shutterstock; **190** Alamy, Getty, Paul Michael Hughes/GWR; **191** Paul Michael Hughes/ GWR, Alamy, Shutterstock, Paul Michael Hughes/ GWR, James Ellerker/GWR, Mojang/Games Press; **192** TMS Entertainment, Shutterstock, Shueisha, Games Press, Walt Disney/Alamy, Alamy, Square Enix/Games Press; **193** Nintendo/ Alamy, Nintendo/Games Press, Nintendo/MOBY, Nintendo, Shutterstock; **194** Games Press, LEGO/DC, MOBI, DC/HBO/Alamy, Warner Bros./Alamy, Shutterstock; **195** Walt Disney/Alamy, Alamy, Marvel Studios/Alamy, Marvel Studios/Walt Disney/Alamy, Shutterstock; **196** Johan Persson, Alamy, Warner Bros./Alamy, Bloomsbury; **197** Games Press, Rockstar Games, Alamy, Shutterstock; **198** Getty, Epic/Games Press; **199** Walt Disney/Shutterstock, Shutterstock, Games Press; **200** Alamy, Shutterstock, Searchlight Pictures/Alamy, Merie Weismiller Wallace/Focus Features/Alamy, Amazon Prime/Alamy; **201** Shutterstock; **202** Getty, Geffen Records/YouTube, Shutterstock; **203** Shutterstock, Alamy, Beth Garrabrant, Getty; **204** Shutterstock, Pinkfong/YouTube, BLACKPINK/YouTube, Audrée-Rose Fallu Landry; **205** Chadwick Boseman/ Twitter, Getty, Alamy, Vishesh Films/YouTube; **206** ZKM Center for Art and Media, Microsoft/Games Press, Altitude Arts/Games Press; **207** Ben MacMahon/GWR, Ronald Mackechnie/GWR, Shutterstock, Sony/Games Press; **208** AOC/Twitch, Alamy, Shutterstock; **209** Brian Storey/GWR, Epic Games, PlayStation/Games Press; **210** Thomas Alexander/BAFTA/Shutterstock, Shutterstock, The Gregf, Epic Games; **211** RuPaul/World of Wonder Productions, Lucas Films/Walt Disney Studios/Alamy, Amazon/Alamy; **212** Shutterstock, BTS/YouTube, PA Images; **213** Big Hit Entertainment; **214** Shutterstock, Rod Hunt, Alamy, Victoria and Albert Museum; **215** Getty, Victoria and Albert Museum, Alamy, Shutterstock; **216–17** Shutterstock; **218** Shutterstock, Getty; **219** Getty, Shutterstock; **220** Alamy, Getty; **221** Getty, Shutterstock; **222** Shutterstock, Getty; **223** Shutterstock; **224** Shutterstock; **225** Getty, Shutterstock, Alamy; **226** Getty, Casey B Gibson; **227** Alamy, Getty, Reuters, Shutterstock; **228** Alamy, Shutterstock, Getty; **229** Shutterstock, Getty; **230** Shutterstock; **231** Shutterstock, Alamy, Getty; **232** Shutterstock, Getty; **233** Adam McLaughlin, Paul Michael Hughes/ GWR, PDGA, Alyssa Van Lanen/PDGA, Getty, Andreas Langreiter/Limex Images, Joerg Mitter/Limex Images; **234** Shutterstock, Alamy; **235** ESPN, Getty; **236** Mike Lewis, Shutterstock; **237** Getty, Alamy, Shutterstock; **238** Norman Kent, Amber Forte, Dean Treml/Red Bull Content Pool, Rémi Morel, Getty; **239** WSL, Laura Babahekian, Herbert Nitsch, Mark Conlon/World Marathon Challenge, Mark Conlon/Antarctic Ice Marathon; **240** Dave McFarlane/inov-8.com, Sri Chinmoy Ultra Photos, Ana-Maria Oancia, Aneta Mikulska; **241** Getty, Shutterstock, Reuters, Alamy; **242** Benjamin Mole/WST/Shutterstock, Getty, Shutterstock, Alamy, Julien Delfosse/DPPI/Red Bull Content Pool; **243** Shutterstock, Getty, IRONMAN®; **244** Shutterstock, Alamy; **245** Shutterstock; **256** Rod Hunt

Every effort has been made to trace copyright holders and gain permission for use of the images in this publication. We welcome notifications from copyright holders who may have been omitted.

### Official adjudicators

Camila Borenstain, Joanne Brent, Jack Brockbank, Ahmed Bucheeri, Sarah Casson, Dong Cheng, Swapnil Dangarikar, Casey DeSantis, Brittany Dunn, Kanzy El Defrawy, Michael Empric, Pete Fairbairn, Victor Fenes, Christina Flounders Conlon, Fumika Fujibuchi, John Garland, Andrew Glass, Sofia Greenacre, Iris Hou, Rei Iwashita, Louis Jelinek, Kazuyoshi Kirimura, Lena Kuhlmann, Maggie Luo, Mai McMillan, Solvej Malouf, Mike Marcotte, Ma Mengjia, Shaifali Mishra, Rishi Nath, Kellie Parise, Pravin Patel, Justin Patterson, Glenn Pollard, Natalia Ramirez, Stephanie Randall, Cassie Ren, Susana Reyes, Philip Robertson, Paulina Sapinska, Tomomi Sekioka, Hiroaki Shino, Lucia Sinigagliesi, Tyler Smith, Brian Sobel, Richard Stenning, Şeyda Subaşı Gemici, Carlos Tapia Rosas, Lorenzo Veltri, Xiong Wen, Peter Yang

### Acknowledgements

55 Design Ltd (Hayley Wylie-Deacon, Tobias Wylie-Deacon, Rueben Wylie-Deacon, Linda Wylie, Vidette Burniston, Lewis Burniston, Paul Geldeart, Sue Geldeart), Adrian Jones, After Party Studios (Richard Mansell, Joshua Barrett), Alex Laszlo, Alex Rodrigues, Alun Jones, Andy Keplinger, Ann Thomas, ATN Event Staffing (US), Banijay (Joris Gijsbertse, Maria Kultina, Carlotta Rossi Spencer), Becky Robinson, Beverley Williams, Brenda Bisner, Buzzfeed's Pero Like, Casper Wrede, Chris Jones, Codex Solutions Ltd, Craig Hunter, Daniel Chalk, Dave Brighouse, David Rush, Denmaur Paper (Julian Townsend), Devonte Roper, DJ Willrich, Emily Taylor, EXPOZONE, Finlay Coulter, FJT Logistics Ltd (Ray Harper), Gianluca Schappei, Global Village (Jaki Ellenby, Aiham Zidan, Asma Al Saify), Gracie Lewis, Hackney Literacy Pirates, Ian Henderson, Integrated Colour Editions Europe Ltd (Roger Hawkins, Susie Hawkins), Ivy Barker, Jack Lewis, Jackie Ginger, Jacqui Saunders, James Clampin, Jane Street, Joanne McIver, John Zaller, Jon Coventry, Jon Weston, Jordan Hughes, Jordan Warkol, Kevin Batchelor, Kevin Fast, Kidoodle (Brenda Bisner), *Live with Kelly and Ryan*, Maria Kultina, Marsai Martin, Mohn Media (Tina Marke, Astrid Renders, Jeanette Sio), NBC *Today Show*, Nickelodeon Kids' Choice Awards, Penny LeVesconte, Polina Butenko, Quest Marine (Uday Moorthi, Karun Sharma), Rashad Al Ghadban, Rhidian Evans, Rhodri ap Dyfrig, Ripley Entertainment (William Anthony, John Corcoran, Christie Coyle, Brian Relic, Rick Richmond), Rob Partis, Robert Light, Ross Brandon, RuPaul/World of Wonder Productions, Safiyyah Abdulla, Samer Al Ammar, Science North (Kirsti Kivinen, Guy Labine, Emily Macdonald, Bryen McGuire, Julie Moskalyk, Katie Runions, Darla Stoddart, Michel Tremblay, Amy Wilson), Sian Jones, SLB Enterprises (Susan Bender, Sally Treibel), Stonewall, Stora Enso Veitsiluoto, Suman Manning, Taku Kaskela, VICE Media, Victoria Grimsell, YouGov

### Abbreviations

| | |
|---|---|
| **ABW** | Aruba |
| **AFG** | Afghanistan |
| **AGO** | Angola |
| **AIA** | Anguilla |
| **ALB** | Albania |
| **AND** | Andorra |
| **ANT** | Netherlands Antilles |
| **ARG** | Argentina |
| **ARM** | Armenia |
| **ASM** | American Samoa |
| **ATG** | Antigua and Barbuda |
| **AUS** | Australia |
| **AUT** | Austria |
| **AZE** | Azerbaijan |
| **BDI** | Burundi |
| **BEL** | Belgium |
| **BEN** | Benin |
| **BFA** | Burkina Faso |
| **BGD** | Bangladesh |
| **BGR** | Bulgaria |
| **BHR** | Bahrain |
| **BHS** | The Bahamas |
| **BIH** | Bosnia and Herzegovina |
| **BLR** | Belarus |
| **BLZ** | Belize |
| **BMU** | Bermuda |
| **BOL** | Bolivia |
| **BRA** | Brazil |
| **BRB** | Barbados |
| **BRN** | Brunei Darussalam |
| **BTN** | Bhutan |
| **BVT** | Bouvet Island |
| **BWA** | Botswana |
| **CAF** | Central African Republic |
| **CAN** | Canada |
| **CCK** | Cocos (Keeling) Islands |
| **CHE** | Switzerland |
| **CHL** | Chile |
| **CHN** | China |
| **CIV** | Côte d'Ivoire |
| **CMR** | Cameroon |
| **COD** | Congo, DR of the |
| **COG** | Congo |
| **COK** | Cook Islands |
| **COL** | Colombia |
| **COM** | Comoros |
| **CPV** | Cape Verde |
| **CRI** | Costa Rica |
| **CUB** | Cuba |
| **CXR** | Christmas Island |
| **CYM** | Cayman Islands |
| **CYP** | Cyprus |
| **CZE** | Czech Republic |
| **DEU** | Germany |
| **DJI** | Djibouti |
| **DMA** | Dominica |
| **DNK** | Denmark |
| **DOM** | Dominican Republic |
| **DZA** | Algeria |
| **ECU** | Ecuador |
| **EGY** | Egypt |
| **ERI** | Eritrea |
| **ESH** | Western Sahara |
| **ESP** | Spain |
| **EST** | Estonia |
| **ETH** | Ethiopia |
| **FIN** | Finland |
| **FJI** | Fiji |
| **FLK** | Falkland Islands (Malvinas) |
| **FRA** | France |
| **FRO** | Faroe Islands |
| **FSM** | Micronesia, Federated States of |
| **GAB** | Gabon |
| **GEO** | Georgia |
| **GHA** | Ghana |
| **GIB** | Gibraltar |
| **GIN** | Guinea |
| **GMB** | Gambia |
| **GNB** | Guinea-Bissau |
| **GNQ** | Equatorial Guinea |
| **GRC** | Greece |
| **GRD** | Grenada |
| **GRL** | Greenland |
| **GTM** | Guatemala |
| **GUM** | Guam |
| **GUY** | Guyana |
| **HMD** | Heard and McDonald Islands |
| **HND** | Honduras |
| **HRV** | Croatia (Hrvatska) |
| **HTI** | Haiti |
| **HUN** | Hungary |
| **IDN** | Indonesia |
| **IND** | India |
| **IRL** | Ireland |
| **IRN** | Iran |
| **IRQ** | Iraq |
| **ISL** | Iceland |
| **ISR** | Israel |
| **ITA** | Italy |
| **JAM** | Jamaica |
| **JOR** | Jordan |
| **JPN** | Japan |
| **KAZ** | Kazakhstan |
| **KEN** | Kenya |
| **KGZ** | Kyrgyzstan |
| **KHM** | Cambodia |
| **KIR** | Kiribati |
| **KNA** | Saint Kitts and Nevis |
| **KOR** | Korea, Republic of |
| **KWT** | Kuwait |
| **LAO** | Laos |
| **LBN** | Lebanon |
| **LBR** | Liberia |
| **LBY** | Libya |
| **LCA** | Saint Lucia |
| **LIE** | Liechtenstein |
| **LKA** | Sri Lanka |
| **LSO** | Lesotho |
| **LTU** | Lithuania |
| **LUX** | Luxembourg |
| **LVA** | Latvia |
| **MAR** | Morocco |
| **MCO** | Monaco |
| **MDA** | Moldova |
| **MDG** | Madagascar |
| **MDV** | Maldives |
| **MEX** | Mexico |
| **MHL** | Marshall Islands |
| **MKD** | North Macedonia |
| **MLI** | Mali |
| **MLT** | Malta |
| **MMR** | Myanmar |
| **MNE** | Montenegro |
| **MNG** | Mongolia |
| **MNP** | Northern Mariana Islands |
| **MOZ** | Mozambique |
| **MRT** | Mauritania |
| **MSR** | Montserrat |
| **MUS** | Mauritius |
| **MWI** | Malawi |
| **MYS** | Malaysia |
| **NAM** | Namibia |
| **NER** | Niger |
| **NFK** | Norfolk Island |
| **NGA** | Nigeria |
| **NIC** | Nicaragua |
| **NIU** | Niue |
| **NLD** | Netherlands |
| **NOR** | Norway |
| **NPL** | Nepal |
| **NRU** | Nauru |
| **NZ** | New Zealand |
| **OMN** | Oman |
| **PAK** | Pakistan |
| **PAN** | Panama |
| **PCN** | Pitcairn Islands |
| **PER** | Peru |
| **PHL** | Philippines |
| **PLW** | Palau |
| **PNG** | Papua New Guinea |
| **POL** | Poland |
| **PRI** | Puerto Rico |
| **PRK** | Korea, DPRO |
| **PRT** | Portugal |
| **PRY** | Paraguay |
| **QAT** | Qatar |
| **REU** | Réunion |
| **ROM** | Romania |
| **RUS** | Russian Federation |
| **RWA** | Rwanda |
| **SAU** | Saudi Arabia |
| **SDN** | Sudan |
| **SEN** | Senegal |
| **SGP** | Singapore |
| **SHN** | Saint Helena |
| **SJM** | Svalbard and Jan Mayen Islands |
| **SLB** | Solomon Islands |
| **SLE** | Sierra Leone |
| **SLV** | El Salvador |
| **SMR** | San Marino |
| **SOM** | Somalia |
| **SRB** | Serbia |
| **SSD** | South Sudan |
| **STP** | São Tomé and Príncipe |
| **SUR** | Suriname |
| **SVK** | Slovakia |
| **SVN** | Slovenia |
| **SWE** | Sweden |
| **SWZ** | Eswatini |
| **SYC** | Seychelles |
| **SYR** | Syrian Arab Republic |
| **TCA** | Turks and Caicos Islands |
| **TCD** | Chad |
| **TGO** | Togo |
| **THA** | Thailand |
| **TJK** | Tajikistan |
| **TKL** | Tokelau |
| **TKM** | Turkmenistan |
| **TMP** | East Timor |
| **TON** | Tonga |
| **TTO** | Trinidad and Tobago |
| **TUN** | Tunisia |
| **TUR** | Turkey |
| **TUV** | Tuvalu |
| **TZA** | Tanzania |
| **UAE** | United Arab Emirates |
| **UGA** | Uganda |
| **UK** | United Kingdom |
| **UKR** | Ukraine |
| **UMI** | US Minor Islands |
| **URY** | Uruguay |
| **USA** | United States of America |
| **UZB** | Uzbekistan |
| **VAT** | Vatican City |
| **VCT** | Saint Vincent and the Grenadines |
| **VEN** | Venezuela |
| **VGB** | Virgin Islands (British) |
| **VIR** | Virgin Islands (US) |
| **VNM** | Vietnam |
| **VUT** | Vanuatu |
| **WSM** | Samoa |
| **YEM** | Yemen |
| **ZAF** | South Africa |
| **ZMB** | Zambia |
| **ZWE** | Zimbabwe |

# Stop Press

*The following entries were approved and added to our database after the official closing date for this year's submissions.*

## Largest horn spread on a goat
A Sempione (*Capra sempione*) named Albino had a span of 1.44 m (4 ft 8 in) between the tips of his horns, as measured on 23 Jun 2020. The billy goat lives in Naters, Switzerland, and is owned by Roland Fercher (CHE).

## Most consecutive Japanese No.1 singles from debut
KinKi Kids (JPN) celebrated their 42nd Japanese chart-topper in a row on 29 Jun 2020 with "KANZAI BOYA". The duo first hit No.1 on 28 Jul 1997 and have recorded the **most consecutive years with a Japanese No.1 single**: 24.

## Largest single-location professional soccer tournament
A total of 24 Major League Soccer clubs participated in the "MLS is Back Tournament", staged from 8 Jul 2020 at ESPN Wide World of Sports Complex in Orlando, Florida, USA. The World Cup-style competition was won by the Portland Timbers on 11 Aug.

## Heaviest chilli pepper
Paul Davies (UK) grew a red poblano (*Capsicum annuum*) weighing 460 g (16.22 oz) in Halesowen, West Midlands, UK. It was measured on 7 Sep 2020.

## Most handball passes by a team in one hour
On 12 Sep 2020, handball clubs from across Germany competed for a new world record in an event initiated by the Schleswig-Holstein Handball Association. TSV Sieverstedt emerged triumphant, completing 5,392 passes over a distance of 5 m (16 ft) in 60 min.

## Most viewers for a cardiovascular health awareness livestream on YouTube
On 29 Sep 2020 – World Heart Day – a livestream by the Transcatheter Aortic Valve Replacement World Tour drew 2,502 viewers at its peak. Twenty experts from across the world all performed procedures at the same time. It was part of an initiative led by The Heart Valve Centre India.

## Largest collection of socks
Ashan Fernando (USA) has amassed 660 pairs of unworn socks, as verified on 30 Sep 2020 in Berkley, Massachusetts, USA. His collection boasts a variety of bold and striking designs, including a pair of blue ankle socks depicting the late Supreme Court Justice Ruth Bader Ginsburg.

## First high-frequency stopwatch
The Compteur de Tierces ("Thirds Timer") is a chronograph designed by Louis Moinet (FRA) in 1816. It beats at 216,000 vibrations an hour. The stopwatch is now owned by Les Ateliers Louis Moinet (CHE) and was verified on 1 Oct 2020 in Saint-Blaise, Switzerland.

## Largest attendance at a virtual marketing conference in one week
On 2 Oct 2020, the Internet Marketing Association's (USA) "IMPACT 20" summit drew an online attendance of 11,151 people.

## Tallest branch shelter
Snack company Barni Mondelēz (RUS) constructed a 10.21-m-tall (33-ft 6-in) tent structure from responsibly sourced branches. It was completed on 4 Oct 2020 at Nikola-Lenivets Art Park in Kaluga, Russia.

## Most users to take an online AI lesson in 24 hours
On 14 Oct 2020, to spread awareness to children about artificial intelligence, Intel India and the Indian Ministry of Education hosted a virtual lesson for 12,701 participants.

## ▶ Largest collection of Funko Pop! figurines
As of 15 Nov 2020, David Mebane (USA) of Knoxville, Tennessee, USA, owned 7,095 Funko Pop! models. He purchases around 20–30 figurines a week and, since 2014, he estimates he has spent around $150,000 (£114,000) on the collection.

## Most diamonds set in one ring
Renani Jewels (IND) spent three years creating a ring set with 12,638 conflict-free diamonds, as verified on 30 Nov 2020 in Meerut, Uttar Pradesh, India.

## ▶ Fastest time to solve three rotating puzzle cubes simultaneously using the hands and feet
On 9 Dec 2020, Atharva R Bhat (IND) cracked a trio of rotating puzzle cubes in 1 min 29.97 sec in Bangalore, Karnataka, India. He completed one with each hand and one with his feet.

## Most people making heart-shaped hand gestures online simultaneously
A total of 137 people shared the love online during the Digicon Conference organized by BT Group (UK) on 10 Dec 2020.

## Longest table-tennis rally
On 12 Dec 2020, brothers Chris and Will Darnell (both AUS) played a marathon ping-pong rally lasting 11 hr 50 min 36 sec in Dubai, UAE.

## Oldest sloth in captivity
A male Linne's two-toed sloth (*Choloepus didactylus*) named Jan was at least 50 years 225 days old as of 12 Dec 2020. Born in the wild in South America, he was found on 1 May 1970, conservatively aged around six months. Jan has been a resident at Krefeld Zoo in Germany since 30 Apr 1986 – the date that has now been adopted as his birthday.

## Most martial-arts kicks by a mixed pair in one minute
On 13 Dec 2020, Pushpa P and Prabhakar Reddy P (both IND) combined forces to perform 200 alternating kicks in 60 sec in Nellore, Andhra Pradesh, India.

## Fastest time to throw and catch five flower leis (team of two)
On 23 Dec 2020, David Rush took 3.18 sec to throw five flower garlands around the neck of Jonathan Hannon (both USA) from a distance of 1.5 m (4 ft 11 in) in Boise, Idaho, USA.

## Smallest modified Nintendo 64 console
Modder Gunnar Turnquist (USA) built a portable N64 console measuring 11.8 cm (4.6 in) in width – only slightly larger than the original game cartridges. Gunnar premiered his "Holy Grail of mods" on his YouTube channel on 24 Dec 2020.

## Most flame projections launched simultaneously at a music concert
On 31 Dec 2020, US rock legends KISS teamed up with Landmarks Live (USA) and ffp (DEU) to light up the sky with 73 columns of fire during their "KISS 2020 Goodbye" New Year's Eve online concert at Atlantis: The Palm in Dubai, UAE. The **highest flame projection at a music concert** – 38.53 m (126 ft 4 in) – was also recorded at the same event.

## Largest collection of *Power Rangers* memorabilia
As of 2 Jan 2021, Michael Nilsen (USA) had accumulated 9,364 items related to the live-action superhero franchise in Gilbert, Arizona, USA.

## Most hammer flips in one minute
Tier Miles (USA) flipped and caught a hammer 89 times in 60 sec on 4 Jan 2021 in Wichita, Kansas, USA.

## Greatest distance cross-country skiing indoors in 12 hours (individual)
On 5 Jan 2021, Princess Märtha Louise of Norway joined TV personality Harald Rønneberg (both NOR) to ski 52.428 km (32.577 mi) at the SNØ indoor ski arena in Lørenskog, Norway.

## Largest jute bag
On 7 Jan 2021, Chaitali Das and Rakshak Foundation (both IND) presented a jute bag measuring 30.68 m wide and 24.87 m high (100 ft 8 in x 81 ft 7 in) in Kolkata, West Bengal, India. They sought to underline the necessity of ecological conservation and embracing eco-friendly material such as jute.

## Smallest magazine advertisement
To celebrate the premiere of the final season of Netflix Original Series *Busted!*, Netflix Korea ran an advert in the 14 Jan 2021 issue of *Variety* measuring just 1.71 x 2.52 cm (0.67 x 1 in).

## Fastest time to stack seven cups by a dog
A five-year-old Jack Russell terrier named Rebel stacked seven nesting cups inside one another in 12.08 sec in Polegate, East Sussex, UK, on 16 Jan 2021. Rebel is trained by Kathleen Tepperies (DEU).

## Heaviest pomelo
Kazuki Maeda (JPN) grew a specimen of the Asian citrus fruit *Citrus maxima* (or *C. grandis*) weighing 5.386 kg (11 lb 13.9 oz) in Yatsushiro, Kumamoto, Japan. The prodigious pomelo was verified on 20 Jan 2021.

## Most unboxing videos uploaded to a bespoke platform in one hour
Austrian cosmetics firm RINGANA organized an unboxing event on Stackla with 2,798 participants on 23 Jan 2021.

## Largest national flag created in *Minecraft*
On 24 Jan 2021, Daniel Ibáñez Padial (ESP) unveiled an Italian flag consisting of 2,001,615 blocks inside sandbox videogame *Minecraft*. He chose to honour Italy in the wake of the COVID-19 pandemic.

## Most people dipping food into vinegar online simultaneously
A total of 167 people took part in a virtual VIP meal experience organized by Filipino dipping-sauce brand NutriAsia (Datu Puti) on 24 Jan 2021. Celebrities such as Eric "Eruption" Tai and singer Maymay Entrata dipped in to join the fun.

## Most magic tricks performed in one minute
On 28 Jan 2021, magician Raman Sharma (CAN) reclaimed his former record by demonstrating 35 tricks in 60 sec in Mississauga, Ontario, Canada.

## Oldest orangutan in captivity
Bella the Sumatran orangutan (*Pongo abelii*) – a resident at Tierpark Hagenbeck in Hamburg, Germany – saw in her 60th birthday in 2021. She has lived there

since 15 Apr 1964 (now her nominated birthday) and was alive and well as of 29 Jan 2021. The zookeepers describe Bella as honest, prudent, curious, intelligent and loving.

## Most mugs held in one hand
On 30 Jan 2021, serial record breaker Rocco Mercurio (ITA) grasped 25 empty mugs in Villa San Giovanni, Italy.

## Largest cloth face mask
As a public reminder about the need to wear face masks, the Longhushan National Park Administration Committee of Yingtan (CHN) created a giant version with an area of 121.181 m² (1,304.381 sq ft) on 30 Jan 2021. The mask was draped over Xiangbishan ("Elephant Trunk Hill"), which is a local landmark in Jiangxi Province, China.

## Tallest stack of M&Ms®
On 31 Jan 2021, Will Cutbill (UK) balanced five button-shaped chocolates on top of one another in Solihull, West Midlands, UK.

## Oldest wild bird
A Laysan albatross, or mōlī (*Phoebastria immutabilis*), named Wisdom was at least 70 years old as of 2021. Wisdom was first ringed in 1956 – when she was estimated at five years old – at the Midway Atoll National Wildlife Refuge in the Pacific Ocean. She was observed there again on 29 Nov 2020, brooding a clutch of eggs. Her latest chick hatched on 1 Feb 2021 – also making her the **oldest breeding sea bird**. Wisdom is believed to have raised more than 35 chicks over her lifetime.

## Highest margin of victory in an EPL soccer match
Manchester United demolished Southampton 9–0 at Old Trafford in Manchester, UK, on 2 Feb 2021. They equalled their own English Premier League record, set on 4 Mar 1995 against Ipswich Town, and matched by Leicester City on 25 Oct 2019 – also against Southampton.

## Most hula-hoop rotations around the head in one minute
On 4 Feb 2021, film actor K Gokulnath (IND) completed 141 hula spins in Chennai, Tamil Nadu, India.

## Most sweaters worn at once
Twelve-year-old Theodore Kinsella (USA) wrapped up warm by donning 30 sweaters in Los Angeles, California, USA, on 15 Feb 2021.

## Largest mental arithmetic multiplication
On 17 Feb 2021, Sanaa Hiremath (USA) correctly calculated the 12-digit product of 617,286 x 315,969 in her head in Hernando, Florida, USA. The 11-year-old, who is on the autistic spectrum and cannot speak or write, typed out the answer on a keypad in less than two minutes.

## Farthest swim while wearing handcuffs
Benjamin Katzman (USA) swam 8.61 km (5.35 mi) in handcuffs on 20 Feb 2021 in Virginia, USA. His manacled marathon lasted 3 hr 58 min.

## Most No.1s on the US Digital Song Sales chart
"Love Story (Taylor's Version)" provided Taylor Swift (USA) with her 22nd chart-topper on the US Digital Song Sales chart on 27 Feb 2021. Her first – "Today was a Fairytale" – reached No.1 on 6 Feb 2010.

## Farthest distance thrown by a trebuchet (20-kg-plus projectile)
On 2 Mar 2021, Sierra Nevada Brewing Company (USA) launched their new beer brand by flinging a keg with a home-made trebuchet a distance of 133.75 m (438 ft 9 in) in Chico, California, USA.

## Most sixes in an over in international cricket
On 3 Mar 2021, West Indies skipper Kieron Pollard (TTO) hit six sixes in six balls off Sri Lankan spinner Akila Dananjaya during a Twenty20 match in Antigua. Pollard became only the third player to do so in an international, along with Herschelle Gibbs (ZAF) and Yuvraj Singh (IND).

## ▶ Fastest time to eat a banana (no hands)
On 6 Mar 2021, Mike Jack (CAN, see pp.94–95) gobbled up a banana in 37.782 sec without using his hands in London, Ontario, Canada.
On the same day, Mike also achieved the **fastest time to eat a head of lettuce**, taking 1 min 31.053 sec.

## Most soccer touches with the feet while skipping in 30 seconds
Freestyle football world champion Liv Cooke (UK) completed 62 keepy-uppies in half a minute while jumping a rope on 7 Mar 2021. The attempt took place live on TikTok from Wembley Stadium in London, UK.

## Most expensive comic book
A mint-condition copy of *Action Comics #1* – the first comic to introduce Superman, released in 1938 – sold for $3,250,000 (£2,328,380) in a private sale brokered by ComicConnect on 12 Mar 2021.

## Oldest igneous rock found on Earth
A stony meteorite found in south-west Algeria in May 2020 has been dated to c. 4.565 billion years old – making it older than Earth itself. Scientists believe that "Erg Chech 002" may have originated in the crust of a protoplanet – a celestial body born just a few million years after the Solar System itself coalesced. A paper detailing the dating process was published in *Proceedings of the National Academy of Sciences* on 16 Mar 2021.

## Most parallel bar dips in one minute with a 60-lb pack
On 19 Mar 2021, Alejandro Soler Tarí (ESP) completed 57 parallel bar dips in 60 sec while wearing a 60-lb (27-kg) pack on his back in La Marina, Alicante, Spain.

## Highest occupiable skybridge floor
The Address Beach Residences at Dubai Marina in the UAE consist of two towers linked by a skybridge at levels 63–77. The highest habitable floor on the skybridge is at 294.36 m (965 ft 8 in), as verified on 24 Mar 2021.

## Most desk call bells rung with the chin in one minute
Mr Cherry, aka Cherry Yoshitake (JPN), used his chin to ring 149 desk call bells on 24 Mar 2021 for TV show *Non Stop!* in Tokyo, Japan.

## Farthest ice swim
Krzysztof Kubiak (POL) swam 3.75 km (2.33 mi) at Lake Bystrzyckie in Poland on 28 Mar 2021. He spent 1 hr 4 min 30 sec in water with an average temperature of 4.48°C (40.06°F). His chilling achievement was ratified by the International Ice Swimming Association.

## Largest collection of wind-up toys
As of 30 Mar 2021, Marla Mogul (USA) had amassed 1,258 clockwork toys over 30 years in Los Angeles, California, USA. Marla shows off her collection on her YouTube channel *The Windup Project*.

## Most flavours of ice-cream identified in one minute (blindfolded)
On 31 Mar 2021, Nancy Moussa (EGY) battled brain freeze to correctly identify 16 varieties of ice-cream at Dolato Gelateria in Cairo, Egypt. It was part of the "Dolato Dare Challenge", to see who could name as many of the store's 24 flavours as possible against the clock.

## Largest collection of *Wizarding World* memorabilia
Tracey Nicol-Lewis (UK) had her "wand-rous" collection of all things *Wizarding World* verified at 5,434 items on 3 Apr 2021 in Bargoed, Mid Glamorgan, UK.

## Most DC characters identified in one minute
On 4 Apr 2021, S Mohammed Harsath (IND) recognized 53 DC Comics characters from their images in 60 sec in Tamil Nadu, India.

## Greatest distance travelled by train in 24 hours
High-speed-rail enthusiast Yang Yongdan (CHN) travelled from Guizhou North Station to Guangzhou South Station on 9–10 Apr 2021 – covering a total distance of 5,412.76 km (3,363.33 mi).

## Youngest ten-pin bowler to achieve a televised 7–10 split
Anthony Neuer (USA, b. 26 Apr 2002) knocked down a 7–10 split – toppling the left- and right-most pins, #7 and #10 – aged 18 years 350 days on 11 Apr 2021. Neuer was competing in the semi-final of the Professional Bowlers Association US Open. He became only the fourth person in history to achieve the notorious spare during a televised match.

## Most connected actor
As of 15 Apr 2021, the lowest-scoring living actor on The Oracle of Bacon was Harvey Keitel (USA), with a score of 2.90805. The Oracle, created by computer scientist Brett Tjaden in 1996, determines the interconnectedness of movie stars listed in Wikipedia, with a low score equating to more connections – making Keitel the "Center of the Hollywood Universe".

## Oldest pig ever
Baby Jane (b. 1 Feb 1998) was 23 years 77 days old, as verified on 19 Apr 2021. She was raised by owners Patrick Cunningham and Stanley Coffman (both USA) in Mundelein, Illinois, USA.

## Longest-running science-fiction audio play series
*Doctor Who – The Monthly Adventures* had racked up 275 instalments by 20 Apr 2021. The series, which began in Jul 1999 with "The Sirens of Time", is the work of Big Finish Productions (UK).

## Heaviest weightlifting +87 kg total (female)
On 25 Apr 2021, Li Wenwen (CHN) won the women's super heavyweight title at the Asian Weightlifting Championships with a total of 335 kg (738 lb 8 oz). The 21-year-old recorded the **heaviest snatch** – 148 kg (326 lb 4 oz) – and the **heaviest clean & jerk** – 187 kg (412 lb 4 oz) – in Tashkent, Uzbekistan.

## Most capital cities named on a rollercoaster in one minute
On 6 May 2021, James "Diags" Bennewith (UK) identified 38 capitals while riding on the *Colossus* coaster at Thorpe Park in Surrey, UK. The attempt was filmed for reality-TV show *The Only Way Is Essex*.

## Most NBA triple-doubles
On 10 May 2021, the Washington Wizards' Russell Westbrook (USA) completed his 182nd triple-double in the NBA, recording at least 10 points, 10 assists and 10 rebounds in a game. He surpassed the mark set by Oscar Robertson, which had stood for 47 years.

# Where's Wadlow?

Following the popularity of last year's book cover, we decided to extend our "Discover Your World" theme, and with it our partnership with illustrator Rod Hunt. And as for the subject matter... well, after a year cooped up indoors, we wanted to leave the city and head for the beach!

From his vantage point above the sandy shores of GWR Island, Rod has been able to squeeze in hundreds of record-breaking people, animals and objects for this year's front and back covers. Almost every detail of this intricate illustration has a record associated with it. On this page, Rod has selected 20 of his favourite superlative superstars that feature on the cover (see the inside covers for a version of his artwork without any text). As a fun test of your powers of observation, see how quickly you can find them! Also, can you locate all 14 members of the Eight-Foot Club?

Slide your shiny new copy of *Guinness World Records 2022* up to your old, well-loved edition from last year and you'll see that the covers align!

**Most hair skips in 30 seconds**
Laetitia Ky (CIV): 60 skips. *See p.75*

**Most soccer touches while balancing a ball on the head**
Chinonso Eche (NGA): 111 touches. *See p.178*

**Largest afro (female)**
Aevin Dugas (USA): 24 cm (9.4 in) tall. *See p.58*

**First person with Down syndrome to complete an IRONMAN® triathlon**
Chris Nikic (USA): 7 Nov 2020. *See p.243*

**Fastest electric mobility vehicle**
Jason Liversidge (UK): 107.546 km/h (66.826 mph). *See p.80*

**Appear on the cover of *Guinness World Records 2023***
We're excited to announce that next year, Rod Hunt will be jetting into space to complete his trilogy of *Guinness World Records* covers. To celebrate, we're giving YOU the chance to feature on the final cover, joining a galaxy of record-holding astronauts, rockets, spacecraft and robots. To find out how you can win this special prize, visit **guinnessworldrecords.com/2022**

**First female contestant in a "full beard" category at the World Beard and Moustache Championships**
Rose Geil (USA). *See p.73*

**Fastest 50 m by a robotic fish**
BREED (CHN): 22.92 sec. *See p.147*

**Tallest teenager**
Olivier Rioux (CAN): 226.9 cm (7 ft 5.33 in). *See p.67*

**Longest ears on a dog**
Lou (USA): 34 cm (1 ft 1.3 in). *See p.162*

**Farthest lache (bar-to-bar swing)**
Najee Richardson (USA): 5.56 m (18 ft 3 in). *See p.85*

**Longest career as a flatulist**
"Mr Methane" (UK): 30 years. *See p.170*

**Fastest 5 m on a scooter by a dog and cat**
Lollipop and Sashimi (both CAN): 4.73 sec. *See p.163*

**Shortest twins (female)**
Elisabeth and Katharina Lindinger (both DEU): 128 cm (4 ft 2 in). *See p.66*

**Most bounce juggles in one minute (four basketballs)**
Zaila Avant-garde (USA): 255 bounces. *See p.183*

**Oldest tandem parachute jump (male)**
Alfred "Al" Blaschke (USA): 103 years 181 days. *See p.65*

**Tallest professional bodybuilder**
Olivier Richters (NLD): 218.3 cm (7 ft 1.9 in). *See p.74*

**Heaviest sleigh pulled**
Kevin Fast (CAN): 16.5 tonnes (18.1 tons). *See p.84*

**Largest planetary rover**
*Perseverance* (USA): 1,026 kg (2,262 lb). *See p.138*

**Largest camera-trap wildlife survey**
National Tiger Conservation Authority (IND): 2,461 tigers. *See p.51*

**Fastest wheelbarrow**
Kevin Nicks (UK): 74.335 km/h (46.190 mph). *See p.92*

The 18th-century dandy is Ireland's Patrick Cotter O'Brien (b. 1760), the first person confirmed to have stood more than 8 ft tall.

**About the illustrator**
Not surprisingly, Rod Hunt was passionate about comics as a child. They inspired him to start drawing, and by the time he was a teenager he had begun to consider a career as an illustrator. Over the years, Rod has honed his artistic technique. Firstly, he mulls over the project and doodles simple pencil sketches; then he creates a more complete drawing. Next, he scans this into his computer and builds it up, layer by layer, using digital-illustration software.

Find out more about Rod and other amazing illustrations that he has created at **www.rodhunt.com**

**Tall order: finding the Eight-Foot Club**
On p.76, you'll be introduced to the Eight-Foot Club – the exclusive gang of 13 men and one woman accepted by GWR as having grown to a height of more than 2.43 m. They've gone walkabout on Rod's record-packed cover and, despite their titanic tallness, are surprisingly difficult to spot! Before you start your search, here's a clue: Robert Wadlow, the tallest of them all, is in his bathing suit...